Jane Crow

Jane Crow

The Life of Pauli Murray

ROSALIND ROSENBERG

OXFORD
UNIVERSITY PRESS

OXFORD
UNIVERSITY PRESS

Oxford University Press is a department of the University of Oxford. It furthers
the University's objective of excellence in research, scholarship, and education
by publishing worldwide. Oxford is a registered trade mark of Oxford University
Press in the UK and certain other countries.

Published in the United States of America by Oxford University Press
198 Madison Avenue, New York, NY 10016, United States of America.

Library of Congress Cataloging-in-Publication Data
Names: Rosenberg, Rosalind, 1946– author.
Title: Jane Crow : the life of Pauli Murray / Rosalind Rosenberg.
Description: New York, NY : Oxford University Press, 2017. |
Includes bibliographical references and index.
Identifiers: LCCN 2017000717 (print) | LCCN 2017000857 (ebook) |
ISBN 9780190656454 (hardback) | ISBN 9780190656461 (Updf) |
ISBN 9780190656478 (Epub)
Subjects: LCSH: Murray, Pauli, 1910–1985. | African American
intellectuals—Biography. | African American poets—Biography. | African
American lawyers—Biography. | African American civil rights
workers—Biography. | African American feminists—Biography. | Episcopal
Church—Clergy—Biography. | Social reformers—United States—Biography. |
Civil rights movements—United States—History—20th century | BISAC:
BIOGRAPHY & AUTOBIOGRAPHY / Women. | BIOGRAPHY & AUTOBIOGRAPHY /
Cultural Heritage.
Classification: LCC E185.97.M95 R67 2017 (print) | LCC E185.97.M95 (ebook) |
DDC 305.42092 [B]—dc23
LC record available at https://lccn.loc.gov/2017000717

1 3 5 7 9 8 6 4 2

Printed by Sheridan Books, Inc., United States of America

For Gerald Alan Rosenberg (in memoriam)
and
Jeffrey John Parish

CONTENTS

perspective for me. Nick, a psychotherapist, provided insightful psychological commentary all along the way.

My grandson, Henry Noah Rosenberg, and my granddaughter, Jasmine Sooyeung Park Rosenberg, have not read any part of this book, but each has brightened my life beyond measure. Somehow the writing always went better, after spending time with them.

ABBREVIATIONS

AAUW   American Association of University Women
ACLA   Amalgamated Clothing Workers of American
ACLU   American Civil Liberties Union
AFL   American Federation of Labor
AJC   American Jewish Congress
BFOQ   Bona Fide Occupational Qualification
CCPR   Committee on Civil and Political Rights [of the PCSW]
CIO   Congress of Industrial organizations
CLSA   Commission on Law and Social Action of the AJC
CORE   Congress of Racial Equality
CPO   Communist Party Opposition
CPP   Convention People's Party [of Ghana]
EEOC   Equal Employment Opportunity Commission
ERA   Equal Rights Amendment
ESCRU   Episcopal Society for Cultural and Racial Unity
ETS   Episcopal Theological Seminary (Cambridge, MA)
FEPC   Fair Employment Practices Committee
FLSA   Fair Labor Standards Act
FOR   Fellowship of Reconciliation
FTM   Female to Male Transsexual
GTS   General Theological Seminary
HEW   Department of Housing Education and Welfare
HUAC   House Un-American Activities Committee
ILGWU   International Ladies Garment Workers Union
LWU   Laundry Workers Union
LWJB   Laundry Workers Joint Board
MOWM   March on Washington Movement

NAACP	National Association for the Advancement of Colored People
NALC	Negro American Labor Council
NCC	National Council of Churches
NCCN	North Carolina College for Negroes
NCNW	National Council of Negro Women
NCW	National Council of Women
NLRB	National Labor Relations Board
NOW	National Organization for Women
NPC	Negro People's Committee to Aid Spanish Refugees
NUL	National Urban League
NWP	National Woman's Party
PCSW	President's Commission on the Status of Women
OPA	Office of Price Administration
PM	Pauli Murray
SCLC	Southern Christian Leadership Conference
SFSC	San Francisco State College
SNCC	Student Nonviolent Coordinating Committee
STFU	Southern Tenant Farmers Union
TYP	Transitional Year Program [at Brandeis University]
UNC	University of North Carolina
VTS	Virginia Theological Seminary
WDL	Workers Defense League
WPA	Works Progress Administration
WTUL	Women's Trade Union League

A NOTE ON PRONOUNS AND OTHER
WORD CHOICES

In early drafts, I experimented with the use of male pronouns in writing about Murray in her twenties and thirties, the years in which her sense of self as male was strongest. I then experimented with gender-neutral pronouns such as "ze/hir/hirs" for her forties on. But my efforts ultimately struck me as ahistorical. Murray lived in a gender-binary culture. To use male pronouns for someone assigned female at birth in a time when that was not culturally possible, or gender neutral pronouns when, even to this day, no consensus exists on what those pronouns should be, I concluded, would undercut the immensity of the struggle in which Murray was engaged and the significance of her contributions.

Where references to race, sex, and gender are concerned, I have found squaring modern use with historical practice easier, because there is a greater consensus on usage. Murray viewed "Negro," in its capitalized form, as a badge of honor, and she used "Negro" and later "Euro-African-American" in her speeches and writings long after the broader culture had embraced "black" and "African American." I honor Murray's preference by quoting the words she used, but in writing about her and others of African descent, I generally use "black" and "African American."

"Gender" and "sex" are a little trickier. Murray, in common with others of her generation, used sex to refer to sexuality, as well as to both the biological and cultural differences associated with being categorized as male or female. I have followed modern practice in limiting "sex" to the discussion of sexuality. Whereas Murray spoke of sex differences, I write about gender differences, and whereas Murray referred to transsexuals, I say transgender persons.[1]

Introduction

On a trip to Baltimore in 1919 when Pauli Murray was eight, her aunt, namesake, and foster mother, Pauline Fitzgerald Dame, took advantage of being in a big city to buy her a winter outfit. Aunt Pauline headed for the girls' department of a clothing store, but Pauli insisted on shopping in the boys' section instead. There she found a chinchilla coat with red lining and a Tyrolean hat. A firm believer that children should be allowed to make their own decisions, Pauline bought the outfit and allowed Pauli to wear it, despite the laughter it elicited from neighbors and schoolmates back home in Durham, North Carolina. She also allowed Pauli to wear the broad-brimmed soldier's hat someone gave her at the end of World War I wherever she liked. Except to church. According to Pauli, "That was the one place Aunt Pauline drew the line." Church aside, Pauline Dame cared more about fostering independence than she did about upholding conventional norms of middle-class black respectability. Thus encouraged, Pauli Murray grew up to be an activist, lawyer, poet, professor, and priest, who challenged other well-settled conventions, mostly in obscurity, but with transformative effect.[1]

In the 1950s, Murray's legal scholarship on race discrimination encouraged Thurgood Marshall to shift course and attack segregation directly as a violation of equal protection in *Brown v. Board of Education* (1954). In the 1960s, her attacks on the federal government for failing to protect women against gender discrimination persuaded Betty Friedan to join her in founding a National Association for the Advancement of Colored People (NAACP) for women, which Friedan named NOW (National Organization for Women). In the early 1970s, Murray's concept of Jane Crow—the depiction of gender discrimination as analogous to race discrimination—propelled Ruth Bader Ginsburg to her first Supreme Court victory, establishing a woman's constitutional right to equal protection in *Reed v. Reed* (1971). And in the late 1970s, Murray became the first black female Episcopal priest, in the process extending her critical thinking on race and gender to the realm of theology.[2]

Murray accomplished all this while struggling with what we would today call a transgender identity. Since at least her childhood choice to wear boys' clothes,

Murray had felt "queer," "in between," outwardly female but inwardly male—a "boy-girl" in Aunt Pauline's words. In some ways, her gender-nonconforming persona made it difficult to win the recognition she might otherwise have achieved, but it also made possible her most important insight: that gender was not, any more than race, a fixed category.[3]

Fortunately for her biographer, Murray was a pack rat. At her death, she left to the Schlesinger Library at Radcliffe College at Harvard University more than 135 boxes of diaries, interviews, scrapbooks, organizational minutes, papers, speeches, articles, poems, sermons, medical records, pictures, audiotapes, books, and letters (those received, as well as copies of those sent). These papers are remarkable not only for their breadth but also their depth. Murray kept detailed notes, for instance, on her conversations with doctors during her repeated hospitalizations for acute emotional distress. Murray also left early drafts of a family history, *Proud Shoes* (1956), and drafts of an autobiography, initially entitled "Jane Crow." This title conveyed economically the external threat Murray faced from race and gender discrimination, as well as the internal conflict she experienced from these intersecting oppressions.[4]

Orphaned at three, Murray viewed her pack-rat impulses, family history, and autobiography as a way to connect with her absent parents, as well as to understand what she enigmatically called "my confused world of uncertain boundaries." In the process she developed a keen sense of her place in a civil rights movement that stretched back to the early nineteenth century. She belonged to people who mattered; people who stood for education, equality, and freedom; people who had made sacrifices to secure those rights for themselves and others. Their example inspired her to do the same and to detail the effort.[5]

Murray's personal papers reveal that her uncertainty over boundaries was rooted in more than her parents' early deaths. She suspected from early childhood that she was really a boy. From at least the age of eight, she favored boys' clothes, boys' games, boys' chores. In college, she cropped her hair. Then, days after her twentieth birthday, in an attempt to be a "normal woman," she married on an impulse. The marriage lasted a weekend. Trying to understand why something in her fought against sexual relations with a man, Murray read every scientific book and article she could find on the science of sex. She concluded that she was a "pseudo-hermaphrodite." Had she been born several generations later, she might have embraced a transgender identity. But in the 1930s, she had no such language, nor a social movement that would have supported her use of it. Instead, finding herself sexually attracted to feminine, heterosexual women, she suffered recurring nervous breakdowns when the objects of her affection could not accept her as the heterosexual male she felt herself to be. She begged doctors for hormones to give her a more masculine voice and appearance. They refused. About to undergo an appendectomy, she asked a surgeon to search for "secreted male genitals." He found none. She worried about her mental health. So did the doctors. One pronounced her schizophrenic. Her gender troubles sometimes immobilized her; they often put off those who might have helped her. Ultimately, they inspired insights that were to change her life and the lives of others.[6]

In the 1950s, around the age of forty-five, Murray ceased her medical campaign, even as hormones and sex-change surgery began to be available. She had come to see her trouble with "boundaries," her sense of herself as "queer," as strengths, qualities that allowed her to understand gender and race not as fixed categories, but rather as unreasonable classifications. A series of experiences facilitated this change: an operation for a hyperthyroid condition, which had long amplified her emotional turmoil; the psychotherapy she undertook to help her write her family history; the beginning of professional success, first as a writer, then as a lawyer; a deepening of her Episcopal faith, which convinced her that God had placed her in the middle to be useful to others; and, most important, the love and acceptance of a woman, Irene Barlow. No longer did Murray believe that one had to be either female or male; one could be both, a person in between, more male than female perhaps, but with qualities of both. The two decades that followed proved to be her most productive.[7]

Murray's experience of race and class reinforced her skepticism about the boundaries most people took for granted. She once wrote of her "inability to be fragmented into Negro at one time, woman at another, or worker at another." She experienced her gender, race, and class as so interconnected that her feeling of in-betweenness in one reinforced that feeling about the others. Born into a mixed-race southern family, and raised by a grandmother and aunts who could have passed for white, she attended school with children darker than she. Her grandmother admonished her to comb her hair and stay out of the sun so as not to look "niggerish." Her black classmates taunted her as "You half-white bastard! You dirty-faced Jew baby! Black is honest! Yaller is dishonest!" Throughout her childhood and into the first couple of years of college, race preoccupied Murray more than class, but with the onset of the Great Depression class came to the fore.[8]

Class had always been there in the background, intertwined with her mixed racial heritage. Murray descended from what she called a "Euro-African-American" mix of white, anti-slavery Quakers; Episcopalian slave owners; mixed-race slaves; freedmen farmers; and Cherokee Indians. Her family, though poor, taught her that she belonged to a proud, respectable, educated elite. Growing up within an ever more restrictive system of Jim Crow, in North Carolina, Murray learned that she also belonged to society's lowest caste. At fifteen, she fled to New York.

Murray worked her way through Hunter College, embraced radical politics, and joined the labor movement. Class led back to race, as her radical training and identification with beleaguered workers during the Depression inspired her to join the civil rights movement twenty years before most whites recognized that the struggle existed. In 1938 she applied to graduate school in sociology at the University of North Carolina, where one of her white great-great-grandfathers had been a trustee. The university denied her application on account of race. Two years later she challenged, without success, race discrimination in public transportation in Virginia. That same year, with the help of Eleanor Roosevelt, she entered a two-year campaign to save the life of a Virginia sharecropper, Odell Waller, who was on death row. He was executed despite their efforts. In 1941, these defeats drove Murray to Howard Law School, where she hoped to accomplish as a civil rights lawyer what she had failed to achieve as an activist. Not that she abandoned her organizing efforts altogether. In her second year of law school, she led the first successful restaurant sit-in in Washington, DC, two decades before sit-ins would spread across the South.

Murray graduated from Howard Law School in 1944, first in her class and the only woman. Her senior seminar paper, "Should the *Civil Rights Cases* and *Plessy v. Ferguson* Be Overturned?" laid out a strategy to strike down segregation as a violation of the Thirteenth and Fourteenth Amendments. Her classmates laughed when she first advanced her argument. At a time when litigators believed that the most they could achieve was to make segregated facilities more equal, her proposal seemed radical, even reckless. And yet, just a few years later, Thurgood Marshall's team used her paper as they prepared to argue *Brown v. Board of Education* (1954).[9]

Race led back to gender. Belittled from her first day at Howard, Murray coined the term Jane Crow to stand for the double discrimination she faced as a black female. Two decades would pass before she put this concept to practical use, for it took that long to win the professional recognition she needed to take the next step. She did so in 1962, when Eleanor Roosevelt asked her to serve on John F. Kennedy's Presidential Commission on the Status of Women (PCSW). Roosevelt hoped that Murray's background in civil rights and labor, as well as law, would enable her to break a deadlock in the women's movement, between those who supported an Equal Rights Amendment (ERA) and others who feared that the ERA would invalidate protective labor laws for women workers. Murray persuaded the commissioners that a tailored litigation strategy under the Fourteenth Amendment offered a more realistic path to equal rights for women than could the ERA. She added that such a strategy need not jeopardize protective labor laws. Arguing that sex was analogous to race, Murray proposed that lawyers follow the same approach that had been used in *Brown* to overturn laws that discriminated against women. She recommended an attack on discrimination against women on juries, for example, and maintaining maximum-hour, minimum-wage, and other laws for women that she believed to help even out the playing field between male and female workers.[10]

The commissioners agreed. So did American Civil Liberties Union (ACLU) attorneys, who asked Murray to work with them on the Alabama juror-selection case, *White v. Crook*, which they won in federal court in 1966. That same year Murray persuaded Betty Friedan to help her found NOW. Building on these legal and organizational achievements, Ruth Bader Ginsburg persuaded the Supreme Court in 1971, in the estate-executor case *Reed v. Reed*, that sex discrimination violated the Fourteenth Amendment. Acknowledging her debt to Pauli Murray, Ginsburg put her name on the brief.

As Murray challenged the supposedly fixed boundaries of race and gender, she continued to worry about class, specifically the impact of her proposed reforms on working-class women, the poorest of whom were black. In addition to her work on the PCSW, Murray played a key role in adding "sex" to Title VII in 1964. She argued that women could attain equality in hiring and promotions without losing the laws that shielded them for exploitation from employers. In the case of conflict, she predicted, courts would require that protections in place for women be extended to cover men. In this she proved naïve. Within a decade, protective labor laws would vanish in the United States, just as black women were finally breaking into the service industries the laws had covered. To Murray's dismay, victory against Jane Crow succeeded for professional but not for working-class women, especially women of color.

In 1970, Murray wrote, "If anyone should ask a Negro woman in America what has been her greatest achievement, her honest answer would be, 'I survived!'" In many ways her own survival was her most remarkable achievement, and it bound her in her final years to assist poor black women. In 1973, following the death of Irene Barlow, Murray abruptly left a chaired, tenured professorship at Brandeis University—a position she had fought hard to achieve and had held for only two years—to enter divinity school. In her writings and sermons, she reinterpreted biblical writings to show, through the stories of Eve, Hagar, and Mary, an alternative to the traditionally patriarchal readings of those texts. In the process, she laid the foundation for what would become known as Womanist Theology, a theology attentive not only to the struggles of women of color but also to the poorest among them.[11]

Becoming one of the first female Episcopal priests, and the first black female priest, in 1977, Murray achieved some celebrity but no regular employment. She worked as a supply priest, filling in for others from time to time. She volunteered at a nursing home for black women. She preached widely, broadening her mission as she did so to include a search for racial reconciliation and the celebration of diversity in all its forms. She used her identity as someone in between, someone who had trouble with "boundaries," to serve as a bridge between white and black, male and female, rich and poor, believer and materialist, and to fight for the acceptance of all people society denigrated as different.

Many LGBTQ (lesbian, gay, bisexual, transgender, and queer/questioning) activists have claimed Murray as an icon, but Murray was extremely guarded in her public—and for the most part her private—comments about her gender identity and sexual orientation. Some of those closest to her were astonished to learn, long after her death, that some believed she was a butch lesbian or a trans man. Although a pioneering leader in both the civil rights and feminist move-ments, Murray insisted to the end of her life that nontraditional gender identity and sexual orientation were private matters that should be protected as part of the campaign for human rights, not used for the purposes of separate organizing efforts. She never joined the Daughters of Bilitis, worried with Betty Friedan that radical lesbians within NOW might destroy the nascent organization, and kept identification of what she called her "boy-girl," "pixie," "imp" self from all but a very few intimates.[12]

The closest she came to a public announcement of her gender identity was through her dress and the name she adopted in college. Rejecting "Anna Pauline Murray," the name on her birth certificate that identified her as female, she chose instead the gender-ambiguous Pauli Murray. Under that name she challenged all of the boundaries that shackled her from birth, as a poor, black, female person—labels that had long deemed her and those like her unworthy of human rights.

PART I

COMING OF AGE, 1910–1937

1

A Southern Childhood

"Small, Afraid, and Silent"

Born at home in Baltimore, on November 20, 1910, Pauli Murray was the fourth child to arrive in the Murray household in five years. By the time she was three, her mother, Agnes, had borne two more. Agnes was, by all accounts, a loving, skilled, and efficient mother. Trained as a nurse, she could handle challenging medical crises as well as multiple domestic chores. But her closely spaced pregnancies left too little time for her body to recover and insufficient energy for Pauli, a child in constant motion. Murray later remembered standing in the family's kitchen in Baltimore, when she was three, "entangled in my mother's billowing white skirts to which I clung as she went about her work."[1]

In the early years of her marriage, Agnes Murray had been able to look to her husband, William (Will) Murray, a teacher, and later principal, for support. But as her maternal and domestic cares mounted, his mental health deteriorated. For several years he had experienced spells of immobilizing depression. Worse, he displayed unpredictable, violent outbursts. She began to worry for her safety and that of her children. That worry ended on March 26, 1914, not many weeks after Pauli's only memory of her, when Agnes suddenly died and Pauli was taken away.[2]

No one would have predicted this outcome when Agnes Fitzgerald and William Murray married in 1903. A mixture of European, African, and Native American ancestors had bestowed on them both striking good looks, set off by wavy black hair and light brown skin. Well educated, healthy, and hard-working, they seemed destined for middle-class success.[3]

The Fitzgeralds and the Murrays

Agnes Fitzgerald Murray was born on Christmas Eve, 1878, near Durham, North Carolina, the fourth of five daughters and one son of Robert and

Cornelia Fitzgerald. Hers was an educated but poor family, whose roots sank
deep into the northern soil of Quaker freed people on her father's side and the
southern soil of Episcopalian planters and slaves on her mother's. Her father
had left Ashram Institute (later Lincoln University) in Pennsylvania to fight for
the Union in the Civil War. In an early battle, he suffered a bullet wound to his
temple and temporary blindness. At the war's end, inspired by the Freedmen's
Bureau, he moved to North Carolina to teach former slaves. There he met and
married Cornelia Smith, the spirited daughter of a white lawyer, Sidney Smith,
and a slave, Harriet, whom Sidney brutally and repeatedly raped. Harriet's
owner, Sidney's unmarried sister, Mary Ruffin Smith, refused to send Cornelia
to the slave quarters of the plantation where they all lived but instead raised
her in the house, taught her needlework, and baptized her in the Episcopal
Church.[4]

Robert and Cornelia had high hopes for their six children. They educated
them all, despite terrifying raids from the Ku Klux Klan, which tried to drive
Robert from the school he built, and despite the return of blindness from

Figure 1.1 The Fitzgerald Family, circa 1895. First row, left to right: Cornelia Smith
Fitzgerald, Robert George Fitzgerald, and Roberta Annette Fitzgerald. Back row, left to
right: Mary Pauline Fitzgerald, Agnes Georgia Fitzgerald, and Sallie Fitzgerald. Estate of
Pauli Murray, Schlesinger Library, Radcliffe Institute, Harvard University.

Robert's war wound, which eventually forced him to give up teaching. With his children's help, Robert made bricks and farmed, but enjoyed little success. To support the family, Cornelia took in sewing and sold whatever she could, including at one point the family's cow. The eldest daughter, Pauline, left school at fourteen and became a teacher. Marie, the second daughter, took her cue from their mother and became a skilled seamstress. Sallie, the third daughter, followed Pauline into teaching.[5]

Agnes wanted to be a nurse, but Robert and Cornelia objected. The physical demands, indignities, and health risks of the work made nursing an unsuitable career for the daughter of a respectable black family. Agnes had her mother's fiery personality, however, and persisted. During a visit to her sister Pauline, who had married and was teaching black children in Hampton, Virginia, she learned of the newly opened Hampton Training School for Nurses, which promised an up-to-date medical education. She wore down her parents' resistance and enrolled. While a student there, she met William Murray in 1901.[6]

Pauli Murray's father, William Henry Murray, was born in 1872 in Reistertown, Baltimore County, the eldest of four children—three boys, followed by a sister—to parents of mixed race. His father, Nelson Goucher, was the child of a black slave and her white owner; his mother, Annie Price, was the child of a mulatto slave and her white master. At some point, perhaps with Emancipation in 1865, Nelson completed his liberation from slavery by changing his surname to Murray, the name of one of the most prominent African American families in Baltimore and Washington, DC.[7]

Nelson became a waiter and later a church sexton. Annie washed the fine linen of wealthy whites. William waited tables with his father and carried laundry back and forth for his mother, but whenever his parents could spare him, he worked with a private teacher to learn to read and write. When the family moved to Baltimore, he attended one of the few black public schools then available. Completing the equivalent of the eighth grade at the age of sixteen, he became a teacher. William's brother Lewis, the family's third child, followed William into teaching. The second son, Joseph, remained a waiter. The family's one daughter, Rosetta (Rose), after a failed early marriage, lived with her parents.[8]

Like many other teachers, William taught in the winter and returned to school in the summer, to earn the credits that would qualify him for a better placement. To continue his education, he entered the federally funded preparatory school at Howard University in Washington, from which he graduated in 1899, at the age of twenty-seven. At that time, only 6 percent of all Americans earned a secondary school degree; only half of 1 percent of all blacks did so. In 1897, while still at Howard, William married a classmate, Florence Gray, whom he credited with inspiring him to "follow a systematic line of work." But he lost her and their new baby in childbirth, three years later.[9]

suicide. The family refused to believe that, but they did conclude that Will was too ill to care for six children on his own. The three older children remained with him. Will's younger sister Rose and brother Lewis, who lived nearby, claimed the two babies, although Agnes had never trusted them to care for her children. What to do with Pauli remained an open question. Agnes had written to Pauline, shortly before her death, that she wanted her older sister to take Pauli, should anything ever happen to her, but there was at least some discussion of keeping the three-year-old with the other children. When Pauli was given the choice of where to go: with her father and the older children or with Aunt Pauline, she chose her aunt, the one adult who had made her feel "secure" in her young life. She then burst into tears. No choice was a good one. Long after, Pauli committed to poetry her sense of helplessness over the "unhappy circumstances" that culminated in her mother's death. She felt "small, afraid, and silent among the eternal spheres."[24]

Pauli remembered nothing of her father from this time. Only later did her sister Mildred, four years her senior, reveal what happened next. Increasingly depressed, Will stopped going to work and stopped paying the mortgage on their home. The bank foreclosed on both houses he owned. There remained a little money, on which Will relied to feed his children and pay the rent. He shopped for groceries and hunted game to eat, but his relatives worried about him. Finally, an uncle, Joe Spriggs, intervened and called the police. Will attacked the officers with a razor as they removed the children. Rose and Lewis added them to their household. With the help of Dr. Wright, Joe Spriggs committed Will to the local mental hospital, Bay View, in 1917, and a year later to Crownsville State Hospital for the Negro Insane.[25]

Murray later told an interviewer that the "most significant fact of my childhood was that I was an orphan." Except for one visit to her father when she was eight, she did not interact with her parents after the age of three. And yet, the period before her mother's death shaped her life. Pauli was an unusually bright and sensitive child, who witnessed, and perhaps experienced, domestic violence during the period when children begin to form their gender identity. She was an early talker and had things to say even in the midst of tragedy. "You just wait till my Aunt Pauline comes. She'll straighten everything out," she declared when told of her mother's death. Murray later wrote extensively about her family, but one topic she never broached was the possible significance of her father's violence for her emerging sense of self. Instead, she painted an idealized image of her father, the immaculately dressed teacher, school principal, scholar, poet, pianist, intense chain smoker, and coffee drinker; and of her mother, the beautiful, sweet-tempered but occasionally fiery woman who gave her life to the physical well-being of others. The most revealing thing Murray said about these unchanging figures was that they had left her with a profound uncertainty about what she called "boundaries." Most of the world accepted as self-evident the difference between male and female. Pauli never did. Her inability to take that, or any other conventional boundary, for granted provided the source of her deepest anguish, but also of her most significant insights throughout her life.[26]

The Homestead

In March 1914, Pauli returned to Durham to live in the house that her Fitzgerald grandfather had built in the 1890s, just above an area known as the Bottoms. When Grandfather purchased the one-acre plot, it lay on the outskirts of town and offered attractive possibilities for expansion. He had taken out an option to farm the uphill field behind the property line and to exploit the clay deposits on the property for a brickyard. The forested area on the other side of the plot offered yet further opportunities, should his brickmaking business develop.[27]

Over the next two decades, however, the city encroached from both directions. Shacks to shelter poor blacks in Durham's flourishing tobacco industry replaced the forested Bottoms, and the city cancelled Robert's hillside farming and clay-digging option to give Maplewood Cemetery, for whites, the space to expand. As graves inched ever closer to the house at the bottom of the hill, the run off from decomposing bodies drained over the family's property, and the house began to sink. There was not much that Grandfather could do about the situation. He had lost whatever political leverage he had in the years around 1900, when conservative white Democrats passed a series of amendments that disenfranchised virtually all black men.[28]

The house was a simple one, "a story and a jump," as he described it. It had six rooms, two bedrooms upstairs under the sloping roof, with half windows and sloping ceilings. The ground floor had a parlor and another bedroom divided by a narrow hallway, which ran from the front door to the dining room and kitchen at the back of the house. Each room had a fireplace, which fed into one of two chimneys at either end of the dwelling. The house had simple furnishings and cold running water, but no bathroom or electricity. The parlor, the room Pauli loved best, provided the house's one touch of elegance, with its three-piece set, upholstered in red brocade, and the artifacts of family pride: the bookcase, overflowing with books and magazines, portraits of her mulatto great-grandfather Thomas Fitzgerald, with his twinkling eyes, and of her white great-grandmother Sarah Fitzgerald, with her prim, sad look. On the mantelpiece sat grandfather Robert Fitzgerald's three-masted model schooner—a symbol of Yankee bravery from his days in the navy. Above it hung great-aunt Mary Ruffin Smith's painting of a mother-of-pearl fountain, cascading from a silver basin—a mark of genteel refinement. Outside, wisteria flowed over the front porch. Old elms and young

Figure 1.3 Durham House, 906 Carroll Street, 1910–1918. Estate of Pauli Murray, Schlesinger Library, Radcliffe Institute, Harvard University.

fruit trees populated the garden. Honeysuckle and morning glory vines covered the sagging fences. This homestead represented the family's heritage and achievements, but also the ever-present risk that they might slide into the Bottoms.[29]

In this household, Pauli was the center of attention of her elders, who imparted her earliest lessons in the meaning of race. Those lessons quickly turned into training in class and gender, for the three were so intertwined that instruction in one inevitably entailed cautions about the others. The Fitzgeralds, she learned, were members of the "respectable poor," a family that, despite its obvious poverty, was of a higher class than the blacks in the Bottoms, by virtue of their lighter skin color, educational achievements, home-owner status, and cultural values. They were people of refinement, courage, and unflinching devotion to duty. Beyond these shared values, significant differences in personality separated the adults in the household. Navigating among them proved to be the key challenge of Pauli's young life and provided her first lessons in the complexities inherent in the concept of race.[30]

First Lessons

Grandfather Robert held the position of honored family patriarch. A military man, he had treated his children like soldiers and insisted that they march, not walk, as they carried out his orders. At the same time, his blindness had created "a basis for interdependence and reciprocal relationships" in the family. The women of the family learned to be sensitive to his needs without making him feel inadequate.[31]

Rocking with his little granddaughter on the front-porch swing, Grandfather told her of the Quaker schools he had attended in Delaware and Pennsylvania, the anti-slavery meetings he had gone to with Harriet Tubman and Frederick Douglass, and the time he had sat on a platform with Susan B. Anthony. He recounted his battles in the Civil War and his struggles in his second war against ignorance. He taught her, as he had taught others before her, with a stern emphasis on correct speech—a good in itself but also, implicitly, a weapon against race prejudice and a defense of class standing. By his example, Grandfather also countered the prevailing concepts of men's and women's work. He was proud to have entered a profession 90 percent of whose members were women. Devotion to his principles had come at a cost, to be sure. In the Civil War, he had risked his life to defy racial prejudice, battle slavery, and secure his own citizenship. Afterward, he had sacrificed his future economic prospects to teach others. For years, the Union he had loyally served had resisted awarding him the pension that was his due. The southern state he had adopted repeatedly denied him his basic civil and political rights. The employees he hired to help him in his blindness proved to be thieves. In many ways, life had defeated him, but he remained unbowed. He was a proud man of color, an intellectual, and a man of standing in the community, albeit a man without much in the way of worldly goods.[32]

As a child, Pauli "resented" her grandfather's strictness, as well as his privilege in the household. When she was five or six, she uttered her first passionate protest against inequality the morning Aunt Pauline served her one "tiny" pancake for breakfast, after giving her grandfather three good-sized ones. And yet, she admired his dedication, courage, and ideals, and would one day write a book that celebrated his life.[33]

Aunt Pauline, who claimed primary responsibility for Pauli, most resembled her white great-aunt, Mary Ruffin Smith, in coloring and physical appearance. But in values and bearing she was her father's daughter. Stern, erect, unflappable in a crisis, she was effectively the head of the household by the time Pauli arrived. She taught her godchild to face down danger, meet unpleasant challenges, and obey orders. She was "a doer," Pauli later recalled, "a woman of few words, who was intensely practical and who seldom smiled." She was also "strict" and "never allowed me to dawdle over my chores or to evade responsibility for misdeeds." Once when Pauli was about five Aunt Pauline took her to dinner at the home of friends. Pauli asked for a second helping of meat. Aunt Pauline said no. The hostess assured her friend that there was plenty. Emboldened, Pauli repeated her request. Pauline firmly reminded her that no meant *no*. Stubbornly, Pauli asked once more, at which point, her aunt led her to another room and "whipped" her.

Pauli recalled only two other whippings, one for lying and the second for disobeying an order that she must never stop to play on the way home from school.[34]

Despite her strict discipline, Aunt Pauline was unusually sensitive to children's needs. She encouraged Pauli to express herself and allowed her to make her own choices, even when those choices seemed odd, for a girl. Pauli played with dolls, lining them up as pupils in her pretend schoolroom when she was sick, but she preferred to play with her male Fitzgerald cousins, from whom she learned "skills normally associated with boys." Pauli was a regular "tomboy," an athletic girl who liked to be outdoors. As time went on, however, Pauline began to see that Pauli's sense of boyness went deeper. Pauli hated to wear dresses, so her aunt allowed her to wear pants. When Pauli declared her dislike of sewing and cooking, Aunt Pauline allowed her to cut and stack wood and to take on a newspaper route. So accepting was Pauline of her young niece's eccentricity that she called her " 'my little boy-girl,' quite innocently and openly to other people."[35]

Aunt Sallie, who, like Pauline, taught at the local grade school for black children, competed for Pauli's affection. No less understanding of Pauli's "boy-girl" self, she had the added attraction of being more artistic, imaginative, and entertaining than Pauline. In contrast to her sister's plain fare, Aunt Sallie's meals were works of art and well worth eating, if one could endure the wait for them. Sallie was the aunt in whom Pauli confided as she grew older, but she lacked Pauline's organization, as well as her consistency.[36]

For many years, Sallie showed no sign of wanting to marry. She valued her independence, her teaching, and her work in the church. But two years after Pauli's arrival, when Sallie was almost forty, the Reverend John Ethophilus Grattin Small, an Episcopal priest from Barbados, persuaded her that she could make a greater contribution to the church as his wife. Her parents and sister were horrified. Each suitor for a Fitzgerald daughter's hand had to pass both a professional and a color test. The Reverend Small was very dark. Sallie married him anyway and bore two sons, James and then Joshua, who became Pauli's godson. Pauli spent a good bit of time at the Smalls' rectory, a more fun-loving place than her grandparents' home, and a place where the burden of color weighed a little lighter.[37]

Though the aunts had very different personalities and feelings about color, they tried to convey a consistent message of racial pride. Their salaries were half those of their white peers, but they were respected as leaders in the black community and guardians of the next generation. They were "race women," who, though they could have passed for white, cast their lot with "the colored race" and worked all their lives for its betterment. They subscribed to the NAACP's journal, the *Crisis,* and followed closely the news it reported. To them, race was a matter of commitment and character, a view Pauli adopted.[38]

Figure 1.4 Left to Right: The Reverend John Ethophilus Grattin Small, James Fitzgerald Small, and Sallie Fitzgerald Small, circa 1920. Estate of Pauli Murray, Schlesinger Library, Radcliffe Institute, Harvard University.

Of all her caregivers, Pauli loved "Granma" Cornelia best. Cornelia was affectionate and demonstrative, the "heart" of the family. She rocked Pauli in her arms, called her "Baby," "petted" her, and slipped her treats when Aunt Pauline was not looking. Cornelia was also volatile, as her favorite child, Agnes, had been, and as Pauli was in her turn. "Grandmother and I were . . . nervous and excitable, easily stampeded, as vulnerable to imaginary terrors as we were to real dangers," Pauli later recalled. "We were the sensitive exposed ones who can't stand pressures, took everything to heart, were torn by conflicts and cried out in protest when we were wronged or hurt, whether anyone heeded or even heard us."[39]

Though born a slave, Cornelia never thought of herself as one. Nor did she feel any less a Smith when Mary Ruffin Smith left her a mere 100-acre life estate in unimproved land when she died, while leaving the bulk of the family fortune to the whites-only University of North Carolina, where her father had been a trustee. Neither the fact of slavery nor Aunt Mary's injustice ever stopped Cornelia from taking pride in her pedigree: "You got good blood in you," she told Pauli, "folks that counted for something—doctors, lawyers, judges, legislators. Aristocrats, that's what they were, going back seven generations right in this state."[40]

Grandfather Robert hated this kind of talk and stormed out of the room whenever Cornelia broached the subjects of the University of North Carolina or the Smith aristocrats. But to Cornelia these ancestors lived on in herself and in her descendants. One could see it in their features and hear it in their voices. Her lawyer father may have been a rapist, but he also "had a voice that could hold you spell bound for hours," Cornelia declared. Pauli believed her, especially when she heard her lambaste a black neighbor who had the temerity to set foot on her front lawn.[41]

Many people regarded Cornelia as "flighty and contentious," but Pauli admired her as a strong figure who had sacrificed to feed and educate her children. When Pauli was six, her grandmother fell victim to pellagra, a disease that induced vomiting, debility, dementia, and terrible body sores. Aunt Pauline called in Dr. Caldwell, a revered black doctor from Chapel Hill, who had made a study of pellagra. Through his clinical experience and wide reading, he had come to discount the prevailing view that the disease was contagious or the product of poverty per se. The problem was a combination of Cornelia's diet and the water at the Homestead. Early in motherhood, Cornelia had assumed the habit of giving whatever meat, milk, and vegetables she could produce to her family, while she subsisted on cornmeal and molasses. As Italian researchers had recently discovered, people who consumed mainly corn, as peasants in much of Italy did, suffered from pellagra if the corn they ate had been prepared in soft water from clay soil. The very soil that had inspired Grandfather to buy the Homestead property for his brickyard had helped make Grandma sick. Dr. Caldwell recommended that the family feed her a diet rich in meat, milk, and vegetables. He also ordered that they find a limestone well and give her water from it three times a day. Pauli, little as she was, volunteered for the task and thereby helped save her beloved grandmother's life.[42]

For all her love and coddling, Cornelia also gave Pauli her most unsettling first lessons in race. Sensitive to the privilege that her own white skin conferred and determined, in her way, to protect her "Baby" from the consequences of being darker, Cornelia, more than any other member of the family, must have been the one to speak the words Pauli later remembered as the most wounding in her young life: "Brush your hair, child, don't let it get kinky! Cold cream your face, child, don't let it get sunburned! Don't suck your lips, child, you'll make them look niggerish!"[43]

Pauli gained a more positive understanding of race when she accompanied her grandparents and aunts to gatherings at "The Maples," a nearby grand, eighteen-room mansion that belonged to her great-uncle Richard Fitzgerald. While Grandfather had fought in the Civil War and pioneered public school education in North Carolina, Uncle Richard had built his own brick-making business and amassed considerable wealth. Though Pauli was poor, her great-uncle's wealth, together with her grandfather's heroism in the Civil War and her aunts' honored position as teachers, combined to reassure her about her racial and class status: "All about me among my own kin was evidence that a Fitzgerald was *somebody*."[44]

West End School

Pauli embarked on life beyond her Fitzgerald clan when she began to accompany Aunt Pauline to school. Durham's West End School stood on Ferrell Street, across the road from Liggett & Myers' tobacco warehouses, near the Southern Railroad tracks. A graded public school for colored children, it was a major improvement over the ungraded schools that persisted in rural areas, but it lagged far behind the neighboring white school. Weather-beaten, with peeling paint, the two-story wood building was so dilapidated that the wind howled through it on windy days. To reach the privies in the basement, the children had to wade through standing, fetid water. In contrast, the white children had a new brick building, surrounded by a lawn and a fence.[45]

Technically, schools did not allow children to enter before the age of six. Fearful of complaints from parents, Aunt Pauline insisted that Pauli sit at the back of the room and not participate in any lessons. Pauli learned anyway and could read by the end of the year. Pauline also took her niece along with her to night school, where she taught adults who had not had the chance to learn to read or write as children. Falling cotton prices, the scourge of the boll weevil, and the brutality of white-dominated southern agriculture drove many blacks into towns, where they hoped to find jobs. In Durham, many went to work in the tobacco sheds and attended school afterward. Little Pauli was put to work cleaning erasers and helping older students with their lessons.[46]

Newly at ease with words, Pauli proceeded to read the Bible to her grandmother and the news from the *Durham Morning Herald* to her grandfather. On her own, she plowed through the family library, reading *Dying Testimonies of the Saved and Unsaved; Up from Slavery; Chambers's Encyclopedia; Works of Paul*

Laurence Dunbar; and *The Remarkable Advancement of the Afro-American Negro from the Bondage of Slavery, Ignorance, and Poverty to the Freedom of Citizenship, Intelligence, Affluence, Honor and Trust*. Having exhausted the resources at home, she moved on to the Durham Colored Library. The librarian led her to the children's books, where she was delighted to find *The Boy Allies* series, about boys in World War I, and a set of nature books about a boy named Frank: *Frank the Young Naturalist, Frank in the Woods,* and *Frank on the Prairie*. One year she won the prize for the most books read.[47]

When finally allowed to enter regular classes, Pauli delighted her teachers with her quick mind and won steady A's. Deportment was another matter. She was never deliberately disobedient; she just had more energy than her teachers thought any child, particularly a girl child, should have. She bobbed up and down in her seat, waving her hand to recite. She talked behind her teacher's back, passed notes, and stirred up her classmates. Her third-grade teacher had to take Pauli with her whenever she left the classroom on some errand, as she dared not leave Pauli behind for fear the child would have the entire class in an uproar by the time she returned.[48]

Pauli differed from her classmates in other ways. She was left-handed at a time left-handed children were forced to use their right hand. "You're doing it all wrong," family members told her. Even the usually sensitive Aunt Pauline proved inflexible on this point. Pauli dutifully learned to write an awkward script with her right hand, but on her own, she developed a beautiful, clear script with her left. And then there was sewing and cooking. "I would have enjoyed working with a hammer and tools, but cooking and sewing seemed beyond me," she later complained. One year she had to make a dress. The lopsided result, which she had to wear in a public ceremony "was so humiliating it put an end to my efforts on the sewing machine." Finally, Pauli faced the problem of color. "Too dark at home," she was "too light at school." Whenever conflict at school ended in taunting, her classmates yelled, "You half-white bastard, You dirty-faced Jew baby! Black is honest! Yaller is dishonest." Pauli's inability fit in, in either gender or racial terms made her resentful of familial and state efforts to make her conform to standards that made no sense to her.[49]

Encountering Jim Crow

Initially confined either to the family's front porch or Aunt Pauline's classroom, Pauli began to explore the wider neighborhood and the city beyond as she grew older. Durham was known as the capital of the black middle class in the early twentieth century, and yet, black people never knew when whites would turn on them with a shotgun or a lynching rope.[50]

Pauli first encountered that danger in the summer of 1917, in the midst of fetching fresh limestone water from a neighbor's well. Suddenly, she heard screaming and noticed everyone running toward something. Under strict orders from Aunt Pauline to return immediately with the water, she nonetheless went to look. Down the hill and through a forested area she found the body of John Henry Corrigan, a boy not much older than she, dead of a bullet wound. He must have strayed too close to the land of a white man, who suspected that neighborhood black boys were stealing his watermelons. John Henry's little brother had witnessed the shooting, but a white male jury would not believe anything he said. After a while no one spoke of the matter anymore.[51]

Pauli never saw anyone lynched, but whispered reports went out from time to time, and she lived in fear of violence. The rate of lynching actually declined from its peak in the 1890s through the years of Pauli's childhood, in part because of the exodus of blacks from rural areas to towns, but by World War I a subtler form of social control tightened its grip: legally imposed Jim Crow laws. In the wake of the Supreme Court's ruling in *Plessy v. Ferguson* (1896) that states could require separate public accommodations for whites and blacks, so long as they were equal, the conservative, white-dominated state legislature in North Carolina passed a series of segregation statutes. In 1899, it segregated railroad cars and in 1907 streetcars. In 1908 it prohibited black and white children from attending the same schools. In 1921, it declared miscegenation a felony, and in 1925, it passed a law requiring that seats on all buses be segregated by race.[52]

By the time Pauli was old enough to lead her grandfather to town to cash his pension check of $25 a month, she saw "things which Grandfather could not see—in fact had never seen—the signs that literally screamed at me from every side—on streetcars, over drinking fountains, on doorways: FOR WHITE ONLY, FOR COLORED ONLY, WHITE LADIES, COLORED WOMEN, WHITE, COLORED." The incongruity of cashing a check that represented the government's recognition of her grandfather's service amid state-imposed segregation struck her forcibly.[53]

As Pauli grew older, she mounted her own private protest, supported by Aunt Pauline. She walked or rode her bicycle rather than take a Jim Crow streetcar, and she gave up movies rather than climb the back stairs to the segregated "peanut gallery." Once when a fair-skinned cousin came to visit and took Pauli into town for company, the cousin asked Pauli to wait outside while she went into the stores on Main Street on the theory that she would get better service if the clerks thought she was white. When Aunt Pauline heard the story, she exploded and told Pauli she was never to accompany that cousin again.[54]

For a child who loved school as much as Pauli did, the worst part of segregation was the separate and unequal schools. "Each morning I passed white children as poor as I going in the opposite direction on their way to school. We never had fights; I don't recall their calling me a single insulting name. It was worse than that. They passed me as if I weren't there." For Pauli, the hardships she endured were not nearly as bad as the contrast between what she and her classmates had and what the white children had, together with the clear message from the white that blacks were nobodies.[55]

Not all whites looked through her. She later remembered the friendliness of their long-time postman. Mr. Pritchard, of Pritchard and Jones Shoe Store, praised her intelligence and urged Aunt Pauline to allow her to express herself freely. And there were the Greenbergs, who kept a grocery store near Aunt Sallie and her new husband. The Smalls shopped there and found the Greenbergs friendly, even more so after the Jewish family learned that Reverend Small could read Hebrew. For the most part, however, Pauli learned to be wary of whites.[56]

The End of an Era

The summer Pauli was eight, Aunt Pauline took her to Baltimore for a long promised visit to see her siblings. The visit did not go well. Aunt Rose had told the younger children that she was their mother and the older children that they must never indicate otherwise. When Pauli spilled the beans, her younger sister and brother cried out in protest. Rose started to punish her, but Aunt Pauline intervened. She would not allow Pauli to be penalized for telling the truth. Matters deteriorated further when Pauline told Rose that she intended to take Pauli to visit her father at Crownsville Mental Hospital for the Negro Insane. No one in William Murray's family had visited him since his commitment two years earlier. Pauli's older sister Mildred, who had been especially close to her father, saw Aunt Pauline's plan as her one chance to see him, but Aunt Rose refused to let her go, so Pauline and Pauli set off, on their own, carrying a basket of cigarettes and muffins.[57]

Pauli had imagined a joyful reunion with the parent whom her aunt said she resembled in many ways—especially in her intelligence and restless energy. They arrived. They waited. Then, almost at the end of visiting time, a guard brought her father out. Though forty-seven, William Murray looked old. Affectless and unkempt, he did not recognize Pauli and said nothing to her. She could not bring herself to say anything to him. He talked only to Aunt Pauline and only of himself. By way of explaining his lateness and disheveled appearance, he made reference to his temper. There had been an outburst, for which he was being punished. Pauli's one memory of her father, as of her mother, was of a silent exchange, tinged with fear. After the trip to Baltimore, Pauline adopted Pauli so that there could be no question about her custody. Pauli asked if she could call her Mother, and Pauline agreed.[58]

The trip to Baltimore ended abruptly with a telegram from Durham. Grandfather was gravely ill. Pauline and Pauli rushed home, reaching Durham two days before he died in August 1919. Although Robert Fitzgerald had been blind and dependent, he had provided a sense of stability and security. After his death, Grandmother Cornelia lost her moorings and began to relive the terrors of the Ku Klux Klan. It did not help that the KKK was once again on the rise. Provoked as much by the massive immigration of Catholics from southern and eastern Europe as by the black migration into southern and northern cities, the second Klan staged a last ditch defense of the white, Protestant way of life.[59]

At night, Cornelia barricaded the doors and windows, put her husband's guns under her bed, and waited. Sometime in the middle of the night, she would start to scream, convinced that the KKK was outside, preparing to burn down the house. These ravings so bothered Aunt Pauline that she could not complete her class preparations. She finally moved out of the house for a time to live with Sallie. Pauli, alone with her beloved, deranged grandmother, huddled under her bedcovers each night, waited until Cornelia fell into one of her brief periods of sleep, and then escaped to a friend's house. In time, the terrors subsided, but not before they had reinforced Pauli's fears that violence might erupt at any moment.[60]

In 1921, when she was ten, Pauli began spending summers with her Aunt Sallie and her family in a rural area of Maryland to which the Episcopal Church had sent Reverend Small. Pauli helped care for James and Joshua. In a letter to Aunt Pauline, she mentioned that Sallie would not allow her to go to the store. "Mother as you say there are lots of little girls raped between Washington and N. Y., so Aunt Sallie doesn't let me go to the store as there is a thick woods between here and there." That level-headed Pauline put such fears into her adopted child's head seems out of character, but she may have been worried by Pauli's newest scheme: to go to school in New York. All around, families were picking up and moving north—friends, even cousins. If she lived in New York, Pauli believed, she could go to an integrated school and sit wherever she liked on the bus or at the movies. Pauli made clear that she was still thinking about this possibility, because the next sentence in her letter home read, "I'd like the NY Education but Mother I am afraid of being raped or assaulted."[61]

Actual violence disrupted Pauli's life when she was twelve. A white guard murdered her father at Crownsville in 1923. Only years later did she learn the full story. William Murray had been doing well; indeed, he was about to be released, when a Polish guard began to bait him, sticking a piece of flypaper on his nose. William tore it off and lunged at the guard. The guard said he would get him later. And he did. That afternoon, he dragged William to the basement and in front of others clubbed him to death with a baseball bat. The hospital sent William's body home to Baltimore. Pauline and Pauli returned for the funeral.

Pauli grew up in the shadow of her father's mental illness. Her earliest experience of his violence, reinforced by the knowledge of his violent death, led her to worry throughout her life that she would one day "go berserk and do harm to people around me."[62]

The summer following William Murray's death, Grandmother Cornelia died, while Pauli was with Aunt Sallie. When Pauli learned that Cornelia was failing, she volunteered to stay with the boys, so that Aunt Sallie could return to Durham. Thirteen-year-old Pauli's offer to care for her nephews on her own, together with her grandmother's death represented the beginning of the end of her childhood. She still had her aunts, but the one person who had coddled and petted her was gone.[63]

Hillside High School

Pauli completed the sixth grade at West End School in 1921, when she was only ten. Students who continued past grade school entered the seventh grade at Whitted High School, which burned down mysteriously that year and had to be replaced. Pauli had the good fortune of entering the eighth grade at Hillside, a brand new brick building, with an auditorium, which doubled as a gym, and a cafeteria.[64]

Pauli was lucky to go to high school at all. In 1899, the Supreme Court had sanctioned racial discrimination in school funding in *Cumming v. School Board of Richmond County Georgia*. Two years before, Georgia had closed its only black high school and redirected the school's budget to hire more teachers for lower grades. Justice John Marshall Harlan, the Court's most reliable supporter of civil rights, ruled for the majority that the plaintiffs had failed to prove that the closing of the high school was racially motivated, even though half the school-age population was black and the remaining two high schools admitted whites only. Legally, white school boards could do as they pleased. As a result, most of the South still had no high schools for blacks when Pauli entered Hillside.[65]

Even the privileged few like Pauli who made it to high school lost out in educational funding to their white peers. As Pauli reported in the school newspaper, *Hillside SKI HI*, some students wanted to study French. The local white schools had French books, but the school board refused to provide them to Hillside. Undaunted, she and her friends decided to raise their own funds by selling Christmas cards. In doing so, they were following a black tradition, pioneered by Grandfather Fitzgerald and others of his generation, of raising private funds for the basic school supplies that their white peers took for granted.[66]

For Pauli's high school class, job opportunities remained so limited that many classmates, seeing no advantage in further schooling, simply dropped out. Boys in particular grew discouraged. Of the forty students who graduated, only three were male. Girls could look forward to jobs as teachers or clerical workers in the black community. Boys would find little opportunity outside of agriculture or the tobacco plants, even with a high school degree.[67]

Those students who remained were the first to spend four years in the combined middle and high school. Most black high schools ended with the tenth grade, but Hillside added an additional, eleventh grade, as well as chemistry and commercial courses. The principal recruited college-trained teachers from prominent black schools, including Wilberforce and Howard. They introduced a host of innovations: art exhibits, a glee club, boys' and girls' basketball, a school newspaper, and a yearbook. They also founded a debating team, which competed with schools across the state. The school provided so many activities that for the first time in her life, Pauli's grades in conduct improved. Apart from one unfortunate episode in the spring of eleventh grade, when a teacher caught her in the midst of an eraser fight, she made it through high school with only minor lapses. An all-round athlete, she played forward on the girls' basketball team and served as its manager. She especially liked the fact that the star boy basketball player, who coached the girls, allowed them to play by boys' rules, which meant using the entire court. A member of the debating team all four years, editor-in-chief of the newspaper, president of the literary society, and secretary of her class, she had plenty to do.[68]

Pauli never asked for money from her Aunt Pauline but earned her own from the time she was eight: cleaning for her Aunt Sallie, selling newspaper subscriptions, and delivering papers. In high school she typed insurance forms at the black-owned North Carolina Mutual Life Insurance Company and worked as "an office boy" for the black newspaper, the *Carolina Times.* At the *Times,* she performed any jobs that needed doing: "custodian, sweeper, cleaner, editor." To her great delight, the editor published her first literary effort, "The Angel in the Desert," as a serial. Pauli later remembered this first publication with some embarrassment as a "lurid little novel" created from the very stereotypes that had bedeviled her childhood. Her heroine was a blond girl with blue eyes, the villain a sister with dark hair.[69]

In 1926, aged fifteen, Pauli graduated first in her class. Her yearbook picture showed a confident young person, hair bobbed, nicknamed "Paul." For a "boy-girl," the 1920s was a good time to come of age. Young women all over the country were embracing the greater freedoms they associated with masculinity: cutting their hair, shortening their skirts, adopting male nicknames. Pauli's friend Violet Louise Perry went by "Jack." For most young women, these male affectations represented a youthful protest against what they viewed as the exaggerated femininity of their mothers' generation. But Pauli's choices represented a still deeper sense of male identification. Whereas her friends planned to be stenographers, social workers, teachers, and occasionally doctors—all helping professions, she announced that she would "study law," her great grandfather Sidney's career. Her friends shortened their skirts; she mostly wore pants. Her female classmates continued the self-abnegating tradition of their mothers' generation in the yearbook mottos they offered: "Give to the world and the world will give back to you"; "Let your character be your staff"; and "Think twice before you speak." Pauli, by contrast, announced, "The best I can do to help others is to be the best I can myself."[70]

To be the best that she could be, Pauli resolved to go to college. Aunt Pauline encouraged Pauli to enroll at the North Carolina College for Negroes, founded in Durham in 1910 by her good friend Dr. James E. Shepherd. But Pauli wanted to leave the South. Her teachers thought she should attend black Wilberforce College in Ohio and voted to award her a small scholarship to get her through her first semester. Pauli turned it down. She wanted to go to New York City.

Pauli had been talking about going to school in New York for at least the past five years. Aunt Pauline had taken her on a trip there the summer before Pauli entered eleventh grade to visit Cousin Maude Womack, who lived with her family in Queens. Pauli loved the excitement and freedom of New York: the skyscrapers, Coney Island, the Statue of Liberty. Most of all she loved being able to sit anywhere she liked on the subways, streetcars, and buses, as well as in the theaters. Inspired by a teacher, Miss Nash, who came back to Hillside from summer classes in New York wearing a letter "C," for Columbia, on her stylish sweater coat, Pauli planned her escape.[71]

Escape to New York

The Wages of Jim Crow

When Pauli reached Columbia with her Aunt Pauline in the summer of 1926, she discovered not one college but many, spread across a large urban campus. Most of Columbia's graduate schools, including Teachers College, where Miss Nash had attended summer classes, accepted women as well as men. Not so Columbia College. If Pauli wanted a bachelor of arts degree, she would have to attend the university's undergraduate college for women, Barnard. Pauli objected. To her, attending a college for women would just be exchanging segregation by race for segregation by gender. Her objections were soon rendered moot. A few words with the Barnard registrar revealed that Aunt Pauline could not afford the college's tuition. The fee of $300, plus a comparable amount to cover living expenses, would come to two-thirds her annual salary, at a time when few colleges, even elite ones, provided much financial aid. Worse, Pauli could not meet Barnard's entrance requirements. One of the consequences of having been educated in the Jim Crow school system was that she had completed only eleven grades. Barnard required twelve years of preparation, including a number of classes that Hillside had not offered. Sympathizing with the dejected aunt and niece, the registrar suggested they try Hunter College, the city's public college for women, and wrote down instructions on how to get across town to 68th Street and Park Avenue.[1]

Pauli had never heard of Hunter, not to mention its reputation as the "poor girls' Radcliffe." As a tuition-free college, Hunter did not pose the economic hurdle that Barnard did, but the same academic requirements blocked her there. She faced an additional year and a half to two years of study before she could hope to qualify. The Hunter officials suggested that she complete the necessary work at a high school in the city. With a degree from a New York public school, she would win automatic acceptance. But to be eligible to enroll in a city high school one had to be a resident.[2]

Aunt Pauline appealed to Cousin Maude, who talked the matter over with Cousin James. They offered to let Pauli live with them and attend Richmond Hill High School. They even took out adoption papers for her so that she could meet the residency requirement. Aunt Pauline agreed to pay a small sum for her room and board. Overcoming her initial reservations, Pauli set her sights on Hunter and resolved to complete all the work required for admission in one year.[3]

New York City high schools were far more rigorous than anything Pauli had ever encountered. She struggled, both mentally and emotionally. The only "colored person" in a school of 4,000 students, she watched in horror as her grades dropped to a "mortifying" 65 in Latin, 77 in French, and only fair numbers in other subjects. Even achieving these grades meant devoting every waking hour to study. Under the stress of the unaccustomed academic pressure, she stopped menstruating, but her efforts paid off. By taking the maximum number of credits allowed and auditing the additional classes needed to pass the mandatory Regents exams, Pauli fulfilled all the requirements for admission to Hunter by the end of the year. According to her yearbook entry, she began using the name Agnes (rather than Anna) Pauline Murray for official purposes, in tribute to her two mothers, but she continued to use the nickname "Paul."[4]

Ready to enroll at Hunter, Pauli learned to her distress that Aunt Pauline could no longer afford to help her financially. When Grandmother Cornelia died in 1924, Grandfather's pension ended. The farm Cornelia had inherited passed to her children, but with southern agriculture already sunk in a depression that would spread to the rest of the country in a few years, there was no market for what was mostly unimproved land. Better to let a tenant work the property in the hope of generating at least enough income to pay the taxes and to wait for values to rise. That left the house Grandfather Robert had built. Pauline and her surviving siblings decided to sell it and divide the proceeds. Not able to bear the thought of the house passing into the hands of strangers, and having nowhere else to live, Pauline resolved to buy it back. Her bid of $2,200 secured the property when it was put up for auction, but she had to assume a mortgage. Despite her forty-two years of teaching experience, she made only $970 a year, and, as a black teacher, she could not expect a pension. Paying a mortgage and supporting Pauli in New York was more than she could manage. So Pauli returned home to Durham to work and save for college.[5]

After spending the summer of 1927 as a janitor, typist, and reporter back at *Carolina Times*, Pauli landed a job as a junior stenographer at the black-owned and -run Bankers Fire Insurance Company. As the youngest person on a staff of ten, all working in one room, Pauli had to submit to close supervision. But the skills she learned that year were valuable for the rest of her life. When all else failed, she could almost always find work as a typist.[6]

Figure 2.1 Pauli "Lenie" Murray, 1927, inscribed to Aunt and Uncle, probably her cousins Maude and James Womack, at the time of her graduation from Richmond Hill High School in Queens, New York. Photographer: Herring. Estate of Pauli Murray, Schlesinger Library, Radcliffe Institute, Harvard University.

That year Aunt Pauline received word that the Right Reverend Henry B. Delany, the family's long-time pastor and priest, had fallen gravely ill. The first black bishop of the racially segregated Episcopal Church, Reverend Delany had confirmed Pauli when she was nine. Worried that he was near death, Aunt Pauline took Pauli to see him in Raleigh. Pauli would always remember his final words to her, that she was a "child of destiny." Whatever obstacles she encountered, the fact that a bishop on his deathbed had blessed her reinforced her religious faith and her determination to persevere.[7]

At the Y, Pauli enjoyed the residential experience she had hoped to find in college. She formed warm friendships with young women who had come to New York to work; others, like her, who attended college; and a few who had already graduated. They encouraged each other and served as models to younger women. Anna Arnold Hedgeman, from Minnesota, was the Y's membership secretary. Dorothy Height, from Pennsylvania, served on the director's staff. Ella Baker, a fellow North Carolinian, who worked a couple of blocks away at the 135th Library, visited the YWCA frequently, taking meals at the cafeteria and attending special events.[16]

The Harlem YWCA also offered entrée to the rich political, social, and cultural life of Black Manhattan. Every important politician, civil rights leader, minister, and writer made an appearance. Langston Hughes and Countee Cullen read their poetry, served as judges of an essay contest, and encouraged Pauli's early writing efforts. The Fitzgerald family idol, W. E. B. DuBois, addressed her. Paul Robeson filled the YWCA's auditorium with his splendid basso voice. A. Philip Randolph, founder of the Brotherhood of Sleeping Car Porters, instructed her about the need for a trade union movement. The venerable clubwomen Mary Church Terrell and Mary McLeod Bethune inspired her with their lectures on the contributions of black women in America.[17]

During the summer of 1929, Pauli left her work at the YWCA for a better-paying job as a waitress at the Alice Foote MacDougall restaurant on West 46th Street. She worked five-hour shifts, six nights a week for a base salary of $4.00, plus tips. Though grateful to find employment, Pauli resented the restaurant's color line. Alice Foote MacDougall hired colored waitresses (as long as they were not too dark), but it served only whites. Once, when a black couple was denied service, the entire kitchen crew and waitresses walked out in spontaneous protest, but they failed to change the restaurant's policy. As a further indignity, the black staff could not order from the menu; instead, they had to eat leftovers in the basement.[18]

At least the tips were good. Pauli invested any surplus in the city's cornucopia of cultural events: *The Merchant of Venice* at the Shubert Theater; *Richelieu* at Hampden's Theater; *Tristan und Isolde* at the Metropolitan Opera; the Fisk University Choir at Carnegie Hall; and the Hall Johnson Negro Choir at Town Hall.[19]

Not even the stock market crash in the fall of 1929 put an end to these outings, but the economic downturn made it increasingly difficult for her to cover her expenses. Anxious to hold onto her room at the YWCA, she deposited her salary each week at the residence hall and tried to make up the balance with tips the following week. She cut back on food, subsisting on coffee and tea sandwiches, saved by an afternoon waitress, and the occasional purloined chicken dinner. She and her friends would order one more dish than diners requested and take it off the tray before serving their customers, hoping not to be caught. Pauli started to smoke. By the end of her sophomore year, she had lost fifteen pounds.[20]

By June 1930, business at Alice Foote MacDougall was so bad that Pauli lost her job. She went back to work at the YWCA part-time while she looked for full-time work. Prospects were grim. She found a part-time job as a typist at the headquarters of the Congregational and Christian Church for 50 cents an hour for two months. She responded to an ad for a housekeeper cook to a professional woman but, never having learned to cook, was fired after serving her first meal. Unable to cover her expenses, she decided to drop out of school and concentrate on her job hunt. Then she got a break. In October 1930, she learned through the YWCA employment office about a full-time job at Open Road, a travel agency at 20 West 43rd Street.[21]

Open Road wanted an "intelligent colored girl" to work as a switchboard operator and stenographer for $20 a week, "five dollars more than I had ever earned," Pauli marveled. Everyone knew that downtown offices hired only white applicants, but Open Road was different. The agency organized tours to the Soviet Union. Convinced that the success of their revolution had rested on the support of ethnic minorities within the Russian Empire, Soviet leaders had ordered the abolition of "white chauvinism" within the Communist Party. A business that arranged tours to the Soviet Union needed to demonstrate its rejection of racial prejudice. Ironically, class prejudice seems to have received less scrutiny; Pauli had to pass a voice test on the telephone to win an interview. Thanks to Grandfather Fitzgerald's stern training in middle-class speech, she got the job.[22]

"A Terrible Mistake"

Around this time, Pauli met William ("Billy") Roy Wynn. He worked in "a women's residence," likely Emma Ransom, and slept in the basement. Both were on their own, without family support. Pauli did not even have Cousin Susie anymore, for Elliott had left in the summer after Pauli's arrival to head the Home Economics Department of Tuskegee Institute. "When matters began to get serious," Pauli later wrote, she and Billy decided to get married. In those days, a significant minority of young women Pauli's age (roughly 20 percent) did not feel the need to marry just to engage in sexual intercourse, but she was apparently not one of them. Premarital sex violated her training at home and church, her respectable middle-class black status, and her faith.[23]

Pauli married Billy the day after Thanksgiving, November 30, 1930. They could easily have married a few blocks away at St. Phillips, but Pauli feared that word of the wedding might get back to the Y and that she would lose her room there. They therefore took the hour and a half train ride out to All Saints Episcopal Church in Richmond Hill and married in secret. The marriage certificate gave her new name as Anna Pauline Wynn. "It was a dreadful mistake," Pauli quickly concluded. Their honeymoon weekend, spent in a "cheap West Side Hotel" was a disaster, an experience that she later attributed to their youth and poverty. The truth was more complicated. As Pauli explained in notes to herself a few years later, she had felt repelled by the act of sexual intercourse. Part of her had wanted to be a "normal" woman, but another part resisted. "Why is it when men try to make love to me, something in me fights?" she wondered.[24]

A few weeks after her wedding, as Pauli wrestled over what to do, she met Ted Poston, a young journalist, with whom she felt instantly at ease. Unlike Billy, Ted, who knew nothing of her marriage, treated her like a pal, patting her on the back, joking with her. This was what she wanted from a man: comradely encouragement, not sex. Theodore Roosevelt Augustus Major Poston came from a family of educators with high ambitions, as his name suggested. When Pauli met him, he had just talked the *Pittsburgh Courier* into letting him write a column called "Harlem Shadows." She was his first subject. "I, who am aged, met youth tonite," Poston began,

> Youth—in a stripling girl;
> Youth—with Ambition, Hope, and Fight —
> Youth—with Illusions unfurled. . . .
>
> When she told me her dreams, I thought of my own
> Which were shattered in ages long past;
> When she spoke of her hopes, I stifled a groan—
> To think I'd lost mine so fast. . . .
>
> But now I'm old . . . and she is so young—
> She's hardly twenty—no more. . .
> While I, from Hope and Ambition are flung,
> Am decrepit and old . . . twenty four.

From that first meeting, they developed a "lunch counter friendship," as Pauli called it. Rushing to meet deadlines, Ted would call to ask her to meet him at the Monterey Luncheonette, at 137th and Seventh Avenue, down the street from the YWCA. Pauli remembered him, whizzing in "for a cup of coffee between assignments." They would "twirl on our stools, chatting a few minutes, before he rushed away." Pauli idolized Ted and yearned to be like him, not a wife.[25]

Shortly thereafter, Billy left town. So did Pauli; in fact, she may have left first. Having registered at Hunter for the spring term in February 1931, she dropped out only four weeks later, the second time that academic year. In her autobiography, she claimed that she was forced out of her job at Open Road when it merged with World Travel Agency. In later notes to herself, Pauli admitted she had simply been "running away."[26]

As a woman, Pauli could not get a job as a porter and travel the rails for a living, but she could hitchhike. With a friend, Dorothy Hayden, she set off. Dressed as Boy Scouts, with close-cropped hair, the two young women made a credible pair of male traveling companions, according to a newspaper story out of Bridgeport, Connecticut, which Pauli later pasted into a scrapbook she labeled "Vagabondia." Shortly after arriving in Bridgeport, however, the two were picked up by a representative of the Traveler's Aid Society at the Bridgeport railway station. The Society was a venerable institution, dating back to the Progressive era, dedicated not only to helping travelers but also to policing the moral conduct of young people, especially young women.[27]

The representative knew something was wrong when she saw a Boy Scout (Dorothy) head for the women's room. When she discovered that the Boy Scout was a woman, she relaxed, and the matter would have ended there had not Pauli exited the men's room at that very moment. The representative "questioned the pair about the propriety of a boy and girl hiking around the country together and then called the police." Pauli concluded that the only way out of the predicament was to confess to the police that she was really a woman and that the two friends had been engaged in a prank. Back pedaling furiously, Pauli explained, "We weren't trying to fool you, but it was good fun while it lasted. It'll make great material for the book we are going to write." Satisfied, the police released them to the Travelers Aid Society representative. She arranged for them to spend the night in the Bridgeport Protective Home, gave them a good breakfast, and sent them on their way. So long as they were just pretending to be boys, no harm had been done.[28]

Neither woman ever wrote a book about their adventure, but Pauli dreamed of being a writer, and if possible, a poet. She filled a scrapbook with fragments of poems she found inspiring, together with her own, as she found publishers for them. At first she submitted to student literary magazines, but within a couple of years, with the help of Langston Hughes, she joined the greats of the Harlem Renaissance in an anthology of poetry, edited by Nancy Cunard, called *Negro*. Pauli's early poetry revealed that she was experimenting with names for herself, including "Pete" (short for Peter Pan), "Dude," and "Paul," according to the captions in her yearbooks and scrapbooks. In the end, she settled on "Pauli" for public use. This was the name she believed most likely to meet with acceptance in the larger world, while still capturing her inner sense of herself as more male than female. Never again would she call herself Pauline, even in official documents. Certainly not Anna Pauline Wynn. She would be, simply, Pauli Murray.[29]

support the idea of human evolution. Hired as the museum's curator in 1896, Boas rejected these arrangements and insisted that everything be shown in its cultural setting. When Pauli arrived, she found not hierarchically arranged artifacts but models of villages from around the world that displayed the rich variety of human experience within specific cultural contexts. The portrayal of village life and art of African and American Indian peoples affected her especially. Here were the two streams of her ancestry about which she felt somewhat embarrassed displayed in the same positive light as Western European villagers.[40]

That same spring, Pauli wrestled with whether to accept what seemed the "opportunity of a lifetime," to accompany twenty-two other young blacks on a trip to the Soviet Union to make a film about the exploitation of blacks in the American South. Many friends from Harlem were going, including Langston Hughes and Ted Poston. These friends had been radicalized by the deepening Depression, together with events in Scottsboro, Alabama. Just before Pauli embarked on her trip to California, a brief story had appeared in the *New York Times* about nine black teenage boys, pulled from a freight train, jailed in Scottsboro, Alabama, and charged with raping two young white women. When Pauli returned from her own harrowing freight-train ride, twenty-four days later, she discovered that the nine teenagers had been summarily tried, convicted, and sentenced to death. Thousands of protestors had filled the streets of Harlem, demanding that the convictions be appealed.[41]

The Communist Party, having made racial justice a priority, had recently sent organizers into the South. When the NAACP hesitated to get involved in a rape case that could sully its reputation, Communist lawyers took over. Many of the writers Pauli most admired, particularly Hughes, had come to think that only the Communists had the courage and determination to save defenseless blacks from economic exploitation and racial violence. Terrified of rape since at least the age of ten, Pauli had initially identified with the white girls, but as she learned more, she came to believe they had been pressured into lying. Sympathetic to the Scottsboro Boys' plight and drawn by the promise of a more just society in the Soviet Union, Pauli was sorely tempted to travel there. But having dropped out of college twice already, she was afraid to do so again. It was just as well. The film project collapsed. Poston, who developed doubts about the Soviet experiment in the course of the trip, returned to America immediately, while a more hopeful Hughes and others stayed for a time. Pauli regretted having missed the trip. She kept a scrapbook of the newspaper articles that covered it and became increasingly interested in communism.[42]

More convinced than ever that she wanted to be a writer, Pauli joined the Journalism Club, signed on as a stringer for the black newspaper *New York Age,* and won admission to Hunter's coveted English major, despite some out only four weeks later, the second time that academic year. In her autobiography, she claimed that she was forced out of her job at Open Road when it merged with World Travel Agency. In later notes to herself, Pauli admitted she had simply been "running away."[26]

As a woman, Pauli could not get a job as a porter and travel the rails for a living, but she could hitchhike. With a friend, Dorothy Hayden, she set off. Dressed as Boy Scouts, with close-cropped hair, the two young women made a credible pair of male traveling companions, according to a newspaper story out of Bridgeport, Connecticut, which Pauli later pasted into a scrapbook she labeled "Vagabondia." Shortly after arriving in Bridgeport, however, the two were picked up by a representative of the Traveler's Aid Society at the Bridgeport railway station. The Society was a venerable institution, dating back to the Progressive era, dedicated not only to helping travelers but also to policing the moral conduct of young people, especially young women.[27]

The representative knew something was wrong when she saw a Boy Scout (Dorothy) head for the women's room. When she discovered that the Boy Scout was a woman, she relaxed, and the matter would have ended there had not Pauli exited the men's room at that very moment. The representative "questioned the pair about the propriety of a boy and girl hiking around the country together and then called the police." Pauli concluded that the only way out of the predicament was to confess to the police that she was really a woman and that the two friends had been engaged in a prank. Back pedaling furiously, Pauli explained, "We weren't trying to fool you, but it was good fun while it lasted. It'll make great material for the book we are going to write." Satisfied, the police released them to the Travelers Aid Society representative. She arranged for them to spend the night in the Bridgeport Protective Home, gave them a good breakfast, and sent them on their way. So long as they were just pretending to be boys, no harm had been done.[28]

Neither woman ever wrote a book about their adventure, but Pauli dreamed of being a writer, and if possible, a poet. She filled a scrapbook with fragments of poems she found inspiring, together with her own, as she found publishers for them. At first she submitted to student literary magazines, but within a couple of years, with the help of Langston Hughes, she joined the greats of the Harlem Renaissance in an anthology of poetry, edited by Nancy Cunard, called *Negro*. Pauli's early poetry revealed that she was experimenting with names for herself, including "Pete" (short for Peter Pan), "Dude," and "Paul," according to the captions in her yearbooks and scrapbooks. In the end, she settled on "Pauli" for public use. This was the name she believed most likely to meet with acceptance in the larger world, while still capturing her inner sense of herself as more male than female. Never again would she call herself Pauline, even in official documents. Certainly not Anna Pauline Wynn. She would be, simply, Pauli Murray.[29]

Figure 2.2 Pauli Murray, dressed in her Boy Scout uniform, on her hitchhiking trip with Dorothy Hayden in 1931, Bridgeport, CT. Murray saved this photo, captioned "The Vagabond" in a scrapbook. Estate of Pauli Murray, Schlesinger Library, Radcliffe Institute, Harvard University.

Pauli and Dorothy's hiking adventure through Connecticut did not satisfy Pauli's newfound wanderlust. Having heard rumors of job opportunities in California, in early April 1931 she decided to hitchhike across the country. Before she set off, however, a friend of Dorothy's, who had driven to New York, offered to take Pauli with her on the return trip to Northern California, in exchange for help with the driving. They followed US Route 30, which Pauli memorialized in her poem "The Song of the Highway." She marveled over the "rustling fields of rye, of wheat, of tassled corn" on the Great Plains; "the breathtaking

Figure 2.3 Pauli Murray as "The Dude," dressed in a sailor suit on her hitchhiking trip with Dorothy Hayden in 1931, Bridgeport, CT. Estate of Pauli Murray, Schlesinger Library, Radcliffe Institute, Harvard University.

mountain passes in the Rockies"; and the "sands—white hot" of the Great Salt Lake Desert." Arriving in Vallejo, California, across the bay from San Francisco, Pauli looked forward to a new beginning, far from Billy and past mistakes.[30]

The possibility of a new beginning dissolved, however, when her friend's parents handed her a letter from Aunt Pauline, intercepted by Dorothy in New York and forwarded to California. Aunt Pauline was ill and wanted Pauli to return home immediately. Knowing that her aunt would never have allowed her to drive across the country, Pauli had taken the precaution of not telling her about her plan. She had to return, but she had no cash. Her hosts suggested that she could cross the country in two weeks by "jumping" rides on freight trains. According to a study under way at the Children's Bureau, some 200,000 homeless transients, Pauli's age or younger, were riding the rails in search of work. Having just arrived in California, Pauli decided to join them for a return trip to the East.[31]

Terrified of the dangers she was about to face, she donned her Scout uniform, and headed for the freight yard in Oakland. Running a gauntlet of armed railroad guards, who threatened to shoot when she tried to board a train, she felt her legs fly out from under her as she grabbed a boxcar handle and "then realized I was dangling in air." She fortunately was able to pull herself onto a car. Riding the rails was a constant learning experience, and Pauli had to learn fast. If she settled into a car too far from the engine, she froze. If she got too close, she suffered burns from flying cinders. She caught "cattle trains," "fruit-butter-and-egg trains," "hot shots," and, fastest of all, the "manifestos." Banged up and filthy, but otherwise unharmed, Pauli arrived back at Dorothy Hayden's apartment a few days later.[32]

Later, she filled a scrapbook with stories of death and dismemberment on the rails, including one story of a "girl who had lost her legs under the wheels of a freight." She also wrote a story, "Three Thousand Miles on a Dime in Ten Days," a companion piece to her poem "The Song of the Highway," which Nancy Cunard published in Negro. The story, a thinly fictionalized account of her trip, told of traveling with a boy named "Pete" who "jumped the rails" to get back to his "desperately ill" mother. Pete was Pauli's fearless twin, her daredevil foil.[33]

When Pauli reached Durham, she found Aunt Pauline in better health than she had feared. Later letters suggest that she told her adoptive mother why she had been so uncommunicative in recent months. Aunt Pauline no doubt tried, once again, to persuade Pauli to stay in Durham, but, unable to deter her, she acquiesced in her return to New York, reassured, at least, that the whole experience had provided a kind of "shock therapy" that might help her finish college.[34]

Returning to College

Returning to Hunter in the fall of 1931 as a junior, Pauli graduated to the main campus at 68th Street and Park Avenue. She had lost a year and now resolved to complete her work as quickly as possible, in three semesters if she could. As always, she faced financial problems. To stay in school she had to find cheaper accommodations and another job. Helped once again by the YWCA, she found a young art student, Louise E. Jefferson, willing to share the room she rented above a funeral parlor on Seventh Avenue. Pauli's share of the rent was $3 a week, half the cost of her room at the Y. The women were not alone. In an arrangement that was common at a time when 40 percent of all households in Harlem had to take in boarders to make ends meet, three young men shared the apartment with them. That crowding put a lot of pressure on the bathroom and kitchen. Lou proved to be an important stabilizing force in Pauli's life. She had survived polio as a child, and though the disease had left her legs crippled, she had become a champion swimmer. Her "passion for order, her precision in her work, and deliberateness," Pauli later remembered, "were steadying influences on one inclined to be harum-scarum and impulsive."[35]

To meet expenses, Pauli found a job at another Alice Foote McDougall restaurant, but, increasingly unwilling to submit to the indignities of racial subordination, she soon lost it. With $2.50 left in savings, she went to the Hunter employment office, where her secretarial experience proved her salvation. She landed a part-time clerical job in the journalism office that paid $6 a week, enough to cover her half of the rent with Lou, but leaving only $3 for everything else. Fortunately, the assistant dean helped further, with clothes contributed by faculty for needy students.[36]

Beginning her junior year at Hunter required her to commit to a major. Although history was her tentative choice, Pauli hated the yearlong course in American history she took in her junior year. Her grandfather and her teachers at Hillside had made her love history and appreciate the role that African Americans had played in fostering public education and other democratic institutions in the war-torn South. At Hunter, by contrast, her teacher gave the standard account, still being taught at Columbia graduate school in the 1930s, that blacks, because they were less evolved than whites, had held the South back. Losing all interest, Pauli earned two Cs in the class.[37]

The one social science course Pauli liked was the college's introduction to anthropology, an elective in the spring term, 1932. Pauli loved its teacher, Dorothy L. Keur, a summa cum laude graduate of Hunter with an M.A. in anthropology from Columbia, who was only five years her senior. The course proved to be the most important academic experience of her college career. For the first time, a white teacher gave her a positive perspective on her multiracial background.[38]

Keur, a student of Franz Boas and Ruth Benedict, imparted the still radical notion that race was an idea, not a fixed biological condition; indeed, race was not even a particularly good idea, for it obscured individual differences rather than illuminating them. According to Boas, cultures change, not through biological evolution but as ideas and practices from one group spread to another. If some people seemed more advanced than others, it was not because of anything inherent in them; they had simply had the good fortune to find themselves at the crossroads of cultural exchange.[39]

Keur, who was writing her doctoral dissertation on the Navajo Indians, required that her students visit the Hall of Man at the American Museum of Natural History each week. The museum had once organized its specimens to support the idea of human evolution. Hired as the museum's curator in 1896, Boas rejected these arrangements and insisted that everything be shown in its cultural setting. When Pauli arrived, she found not hierarchically arranged artifacts but models of villages from around the world that displayed the rich variety of human experience within specific cultural contexts. The portrayal of village life and art of African and American Indian peoples affected her especially. Here were the two streams of her ancestry about which she felt somewhat embarrassed displayed in the same positive light as Western European villagers.[40]

That same spring, Pauli wrestled with whether to accept what seemed the "opportunity of a lifetime," to accompany twenty-two other young blacks on a trip to the Soviet Union to make a film about the exploitation of blacks in the American South. Many friends from Harlem were going, including Langston Hughes and Ted Poston. These friends had been radicalized by the deepening Depression, together with events in Scottsboro, Alabama. Just before Pauli embarked on her trip to California, a brief story had appeared in the *New York Times* about nine black teenage boys, pulled from a freight train, jailed in Scottsboro, Alabama, and charged with raping two young white women. When Pauli returned from her own harrowing freight-train ride, twenty-four days later, she discovered that the nine teenagers had been summarily tried, convicted, and sentenced to death. Thousands of protestors had filled the streets of Harlem, demanding that the convictions be appealed.[41]

The Communist Party, having made racial justice a priority, had recently sent organizers into the South. When the NAACP hesitated to get involved in a rape case that could sully its reputation, Communist lawyers took over. Many of the writers Pauli most admired, particularly Hughes, had come to think that only the Communists had the courage and determination to save defenseless blacks from economic exploitation and racial violence. Terrified of rape since at least the age of ten, Pauli had initially identified with the white girls, but as she learned more, she came to believe they had been pressured into lying. Sympathetic to the Scottsboro Boys' plight and drawn by the promise of a more just society in the Soviet Union, Pauli was sorely tempted to travel there. But having dropped out of college twice already, she was afraid to do so again. It was just as well. The film project collapsed. Poston, who developed doubts about the Soviet experiment in the course of the trip, returned to America immediately, while a more hopeful Hughes and others stayed for a time. Pauli regretted having missed the trip. She kept a scrapbook of the newspaper articles that covered it and became increasingly interested in communism.[42]

More convinced than ever that she wanted to be a writer, Pauli joined the Journalism Club, signed on as a stringer for the black newspaper *New York Age*, and won admission to Hunter's coveted English major, despite some embarrassing Cs in a few classes that had bored her. She even won election to the national English honorary society, Sigma Tau Delta.[43]

As an English major, Pauli worked with some of the most talented students at Hunter. One in particular inspired her: Ruth Goldstein, who published Pauli's first article, "A Working Student," in the student magazine, *Echo*. In a slightly fictionalized account of her own experience at Hunter, Pauli wrote of the struggle to combine academics with self-support in a collapsing economy. In her class of 900 students, about a third worked outside of school, mostly at part-time jobs. A smaller number worked full-time, at a tremendous cost to their academic life. Pauli had pursued both part-time and full-time jobs. She knew what it was like to be unable to complete one's assignments, to come to class unprepared, and to face "the mild contempt of instructors and colleagues." Many such students flunked out or their health failed. Those young women who survived, however, learned a valuable lesson: the power of simple perseverance.[44]

Hard Times

In January 1933, Pauli graduated from Hunter College, one of four blacks in a mid-year class of 232 women. Even before the stock market crash of 1929, black college graduates had faced grave difficulty finding jobs commensurate with their learning. But the winter of 1933 marked the nadir of the Great Depression. Unemployment, which stood at 25 percent in the country, topped 50 percent in Harlem. Having a bachelor's degree helped little if one was black, less if one was also female.[45]

A few weeks after Pauli's graduation, Franklin Roosevelt entered the White House with the promise of a New Deal for a desperate country. Most Hunter students had been wildly enthusiastic about the candidacy of the former New York governor. Not Pauli. To her, the Democratic Party stood for the Solid South and Jim Crow. As long as members of her family had been able to vote, they had cast their ballots for the Party of Lincoln. True, that party's latest standard-bearer, Herbert Hoover, had brought only misery. She therefore refused to vote for either major party. And yet, the privilege of casting a ballot meant too much to her to sit out her first election. The Communists seemed genuinely committed to fighting racism, but the Soviet's recent torpedoing of her Harlem friends' film *Black and White* gave her pause. In the end, she voted for the Socialist candidate, Norman Thomas.[46]

Pauli briefly considered a career in social work and even submitted an application to the New York School of Social Work in the hope that a job would open up by the time she earned her degree. She failed to win the needed fellowship.

Macy's had a few openings for salesclerks but was known to hire only white grad-uates. Temporary work existed for teachers, but Pauli had taken no education courses beyond the minimum required for graduation at Hunter. She naively believed she could support herself as an author, but newspapers, the only source of regular employment for writers, were firing reporters. Ellen Tarry, a friend of Ted Poston's who had come to New York with the hope of finding work on one of the black newspapers, felt lucky to land a job as an elevator operator. Thinking that she might like to be a college professor, Pauli signed up for a graduate English course in philology at Columbia, with the vague idea of qualifying for a graduate fellowship there. She lasted a day.[47]

Fortunately, a friend recommended Pauli as her replacement to run the Hunter College switchboard in the evenings. Pauli was the first black ever to hold the job, which paid $11 a week, twice what she had earned in the Journalism Office. Allowed to stay on after graduation, she weathered the worst months of the Depression, while taking advantage of the time when the switchboard was quiet to write poetry, and in writing poetry begin to come to terms with who she was.[48]

At the Hunter switchboard, she penned "Youth, 1933" and "The Newer Cry," poems that conveyed her deeply conflicted feelings about her place in the world. In "Youth" she celebrated the young Communists from Harlem to Berlin—friends and strangers, "Armed with red banners, placards, and worthless diplomas . . . perched on soapboxes, platforms and ladders," preaching to anywho would listen, distributing "hand-bills, pamphlets and tickets," exhorting all who stopped to "Read it, Comrade, and join the Movement!" She read, but she did not join, for she was suspicious of a group, "certain of its individuality," yet daring not to "walk alone, stand alone, think alone."[49]

"The Newer Cry" was more personal, an expression of "racial identity." Above all, she worried that white youths did not appreciate the danger of violence as fully as their black counterparts, nor the power of individual strength in standing up to oppression. "Man is slave only to himself," she wrote, not convinced that a larger social structure was fully to blame for her condition. She had learned to endure and even turn to positive ends the pain of martyrdom, as a "door to deeper Understanding." The pain that the young Communists threatened to cre-ate through revolution, by contrast, would lead only to chaos. "Let us fight—but only when we must fight! . . . Let us never cease to laugh, to live, to love and to grow. " Pauli was too steeped in Christian teachings and too bitterly experienced in the effects of violence to be a proper revolutionary. She was also spending too much time with witty, skeptical Ted Poston, and a new friend, Maysie Stone, in Greenwich Village.[50]

Before Poston had left New York for the Soviet film misadventure in 1932, he had taken a crash course in Russian with Stone, the Russian-speaking daughter of Jewish immigrants. A sculptor, Stone worked in a studio on the top floor of a commercial building on West 15th Street. There she drilled Poston in Russian vocabulary and persuaded him to let her sculpt his head. Pauli often came along to watch and marveled at Stone's skill. By the time Maysie had finished Ted's bust, she had persuaded Pauli to sit for one of herself. To distract this fidgety subject, whom she came to call the "girl of a thousand faces," Maysie answered Pauli's myriad questions about the Soviet Union and the differences among various left-wing groups. Maysie also drew Pauli out about her past, and over the months that they shared in the studio, Pauli came to see the possibility of a book on the history of the Fitzgeralds; indeed, she started that summer, drafting stories in her journal whenever she could. Like Maysie, she considered herself an "artist." The "function of an artist," she asserted, was "to picture whatever <u>he</u> sees, <u>as</u> he sees it," even though that picture might appear "too bold, or ugly and distorted or inaccurate" to others. Slavery and racism had done terrible things to her family members, and she did not intend to flinch from telling the truth as she saw it.[51]

Finally, in the fall of 1933, a full-time job came through. The National Urban League, a civil rights group, hired Pauli at $15 a week as a field representative to build the subscription base for its journal, *Opportunity*. Pauli approved the journal's motto, "Not alms but opportunity," which captured the Urban League's goal: to persuade white business leaders to open jobs to blacks. She bought a used Chevrolet sports roadster to drive to social work conferences to promote *Opportunity*. Driving at night, when traffic was lighter, she avoided Jim Crow hotels and pulled over to sleep when tired. *Opportunity*'s editor, Elmer A. Carter, had already launched the careers of a number of the members of the Harlem Renaissance, including her friends Langston Hughes and Lou Jefferson. When he published some of Pauli's early poetry, she felt that she had arrived. In gratitude, she threw herself into her job with increased passion, crisscrossing the country with little attention to food or sleep.[52]

Within a year, Pauli had wrecked her health. She developed a hacking cough, which worsened with the onset of cold weather. Unlike most of her Harlem neighbors, Pauli had access to excellent medical care. Her physician, Dr. May E. Chinn, was the first black woman to graduate from Bellevue Hospital Medical College, as well as the first to intern at Harlem Hospital. Dr. Chinn had been caring for Pauli since her arrival at the Harlem YWCA and had seen her through repeated bouts of illness, brought on by too much smoking, too little food, and inadequate sleep. This time, Dr. Chinn diagnosed pleurisy and warned Pauli that she was in danger of developing tuberculosis. She should stop smoking, eat better, learn to moderate her activity, and rest—in a warm place like Florida or California, if possible, or in an upstate sanitarium, if necessary. Pauli objected that she could not afford to travel and would not go to a sanitarium, so Chinn searched for an alternative. She found it at Camp Tera, a racially integrated camp for women, not far from the city.[53]

Camp Tera

Soon after Franklin Roosevelt took office, he approved one of the New Deal's most popular programs: the Civilian Conservation Corps (CCC) for unemployed young men. But "what about the women?" Eleanor Roosevelt had asked. No program existed to help them. The first lady knew of an abandoned camp at Bear Mountain near the Roosevelt home in Hyde Park. Through her determined efforts, Camp Tera—and ninety sites like it around the country—came into being.[54]

Some new campers who had never been outside New York City took one look at Camp Tera and climbed back on the bus for the return trip. Pauli, who had grown up without indoor plumbing and who loved the outdoors, was delighted by what she found, when she arrived in December 1934. Campers lived in winterized barracks, two to a cubicle, and took their meals and participated in indoor activities in the main building. A well-trained staff planned a variety of activities: hiking and rowing in the warm weather; sledding, skiing, and ice skating once winter arrived; and theater and arts and crafts throughout the year. With vigorous outdoor exercise and regular meals Pauli gained weight and lost her cough.[55]

One of the first people to greet Pauli at the camp was Pee Wee Inness, a good friend and hiking companion from the Harlem YWCA who had been assigned to be her roommate. Inness had a fierce determination to combat social injustice and did so by writing letters to the editor and to important people she hoped to mobilize. As Pauli helped Pee Wee untangle her syntax and correct her misspellings, she drew inspiration for what would become her favorite form of protest: "confrontation by typewriter."[56]

Pauli loved the outdoors and the camaraderie of the camp. She especially loved one of the staff members, a pretty blond woman, a year older than she, Peggie Holmes, the staff member in charge of hiking and other outdoor activities. "Peggie seemed utterly without racial or class prejudice," Pauli marveled. Although she was the daughter of a banker and had grown up in conservative Putnam County, New York, she was steeped in the history of abolitionism and civil rights and had been radicalized by the Depression. Shyly, Pauli showed Peggie her poems, to which Peggie responded positively, though with some surprise. Reacting perhaps to "The Newer Cry," with its insistence that, no matter the pain and humiliation of slavery, blacks should "never cease to laugh, to live, to love and to grow," Peggie declared: "I would be bitter if I were a Negro."[57]

Pauli loved everything about Camp Tera except its director, Miss Mills. An ambulance driver during World War I, Mills ran the camp along military lines. Pauli found Mills patronizing. Mills found Pauli cocky. The camp director also disapproved of Pauli's friendship with Peggie, since fraternizing with a staff member violated camp rules. Pauli upset Miss Mills in another way. One day, Eleanor Roosevelt visited, driving up with her secretary and a bodyguard. Pauli knew that the First Lady had been the moving force behind the creation of Camp Tera, and she was grateful. She had also come to believe, however, that the New Deal was temporizing in the face of an economic catastrophe, while depending for its political power on the Jim Crow South. Feeling torn, she responded accordingly. She washed up and put on a fresh shirt in Mrs. Roosevelt's honor, then sat, reading a newspaper, when the First Lady walked through the social hall.[58]

Mrs. Roosevelt took the incident in stride. Miss Mills did not. The director later called Pauli into her office and rebuked her for failing to stand. Pauli's defense, that she had shown respect by cleaning up for the occasion, did not pass muster. It was bad enough that misogynists denigrated Camp Tera as a She-She-She camp. Worse, rumors had begun to spread that it was a hotbed of Communist activity. Neighbors had heard about camp women singing the "Internationale," reading controversial material, and giving speeches. From that point forward, Pauli was under surveillance. Only a few weeks later, Miss Mills called her into her office again. She had discovered a copy of *Das Kapital* among the books in Pauli's cubicle, thereby confirming her suspicion that Pauli was a Communist organizer. Pauli professed shock. She was not a Communist, much less an organizer. She had bought the offending book for a course in political philosophy in her last semester at Hunter, but, as with so many other assigned works, had not had the time to read it. She hoped she could at Camp Tera. Miss Mills was not persuaded, and Pauli had to leave, after only a three-month stay, by now deeply curious about what *Das Kapital* actually said.[59]

Learning about "Sex"

Back in New York City with nowhere to live, Pauli appealed to Maysie Stone, who let her stay in her studio in Greenwich Village. Unable to find work, Pauli sold her car and hoped that the proceeds could sustain her until a job turned up. Not that she actively looked for one. She had other matters on her mind. Whenever Maysie needed her studio to sculpt, Pauli repaired to the New York Public Library, where she spent her days in the American History Room, a quiet antechamber to the much larger central Reading Room. The library, with its vast holdings, well-organized card catalogue, and helpful reference librarians, was an ideal place to expand her knowledge—on communism and something else. She wanted to know more about her "boy-girl" self.[60]

From works by Gregorio Marañón, Otto Weininger, Ruth Benedict, Magnus Hirschfeld, and Havelock Ellis, she learned that many modern scientists rejected the idea that there were two sexes, distinct and opposite from each other, with a third "intermediate" category into which hermaphrodites and sometimes homosexuals were placed. Instead, they believed that everyone was "bisexual," partly male, partly female. Marañón wrote that all females retained vestiges of male sexual anatomy, and that they were not "dead vestiges," but "latent dispositions." Weininger envisioned sex as a continuous spectrum "in which the different degrees grade into each other without breaks in the series."[61]

Just as anthropologists, such as Franz Boas, were showing that the category of race masked wide variations within so-called racial groups, psychologists and statisticians were demonstrating that men and women did not fall into neat categories; indeed, women differed from one another more than they did from men. Those differences could be mapped across every human characteristic, including gender. The year before, Columbia anthropologist Ruth Benedict had published *Patterns of Culture,* which included a discussion of the variability in gender patterns, with particular reference to the *Berdache,* or she-men of the Plains Indian tribes: men, honored by their tribes, who dressed and lived as women.[62]

As she read, Pauli learned that the human embryo, in its earliest stages of development, did not manifest its sex. Even in later stages, sexual differentiation was partial. Testes resembled ovaries, and the penis resembled the clitoris. Even when fully formed, males and females retained vestiges of the other sex. Hirshfeld, who had championed the rights of homosexuals, hermaphrodites, transvestites, and other "intermediates" in an increasingly hostile German climate of the late 1920s, believed, "The human is not a man *or* woman, but rather man *and* woman."[63]

The new field of endocrinology helped explain how the apparent distinction between males and females masked this underlying bisexual condition. Scientists discovered hormones in the late nineteenth century and identified them as either male or female. They saw chromosomes as the initial determinants of sex but identified hormones as the fluid carriers that shaped the development of each embryo and the many variations they saw. The British sexologist Havelock Ellis, the most widely read expert on "Sexual Inversion," believed that anatomical predisposition and hormonal influences explained the existence of what he called "sexo-aesthetic inversion," by which he meant transvestites, as well as "pseudo-hermaphrodites," people who appeared anatomically to be male or female, but identified as members of the opposite gender. Ellis distinguished the "sex-aesthetic" inverts, whose condition he regarded as physiologically fixed, from homosexuals, whose condition he believed to be acquired in the course of growing up and whom he thought might be changed with psychological help. Of all the authors she read, Pauli found Havelock Ellis the most helpful. His writing on "pseudo-hermaphrodites" suggested that such people might appear to be female and yet possess testes secreted within their bodies. Combining his theory with her reading on hormones, she wondered why someone who believed she was internally male could not become more so by taking male hormones.[64]

Better read but lonely, Pauli brightened when Peggie Holmes followed her to New York a month later. Peggie stayed with Pauli in Maysie's studio, and their love for one another deepened in their late-night "bull sessions" about radical politics, social justice, race, and gender identity. Here was a meeting of mind, soul, and body like nothing Pauli had ever experienced. Together, they set off in late April on a five-week hitchhiking trip to Nebraska and back. Pauli was "scared about the trip. Wondering if we're doing the right thing." She knew well the hazards of hitchhiking and riding the rails. They could be arrested, raped, even killed. Just as troubling as these physical risks to Pauli was her worry that the trip might tear them apart. "Have no way of knowing yet," she confessed to her diary. Could she persuade Peggie that she was the one? Peggie was so white and feminine and heterosexual. Color did not seem to be a problem, but could Peggie accept her as the male Pauli believed herself to be? "At least we are trying to solve our problems in the best way possible," Pauli reasoned.[65]

Pauli dressed in her Boy Scout uniform, Peggie in white pants or a skirt. They carried light packs and made their way through a combination of walking, riding freight trains, and hitchhiking. Sometimes they traveled in cars, sometimes in farmers' wagons, once sharing space with a load of manure. They never accepted a ride that would leave them on the road at night. They avoided big cities and at the end of most days stopped in a village or town and found their way to the Salvation Army or the police station for shelter. When that did not work, they camped in the woods, washed in streams, and subsisted on "raw franks."[66]

They sought odd jobs—mowing a lawn, stacking wood—in return for a meal. Often, they went hungry. From time to time, the police pulled them off trains or questioned their traveling together. Their association posed multiple challenges to social and sometimes legal norms: a male traveling with a female, a mixed-race couple, or just a couple breaking a law against hitchhiking. Despite being repeatedly hassled, they suffered nothing worse than a night in jail and a lousy breakfast the next morning before being sent on their way. They were, by turns "wet," "cramped and cold," "sunburned and dirty." By May 18, their "net capital" had dwindled to "80 cents." But they reveled in each other's company. Pauli's last entry for the trip, Friday, May 24, 1935, read simply, "1 leg of a warm pajama." A week later, they were back in New York, staying at Maysie Stone's studio, with no money and no prospects.[67]

The Making of a Radical

Congress had just created the Works Progress Administration (WPA), which promised jobs for those who qualified for relief. Desperate for work, Pauli applied. Waiting to be interviewed in the dress she felt obliged to wear for the occasion, she began a short story, in which a male WPA interviewer surveyed a room of applicants. Noticing a person of uncertain gender, obviously Pauli, the interviewer paused. Something was not right, something made obvious "in the walk when its owner approached the desk—neither fast nor slow, but deliberate and a bit defiant he thought." The problem was the dress the interviewee was wearing; it "did not enhance that particular form," the interviewer concluded.[68]

Most of Pauli's friends also applied for relief, and together they became part of an astonishing statistic: 45 percent of the nonwhite population in New York City depended on government assistance by 1935. They were grateful for the help, but angered at the discrimination that limited their opportunities for work and thus forced them into this state of dependency. Rage over this social injustice, together with what residents viewed as police mistreatment, had led to a riot in Harlem while Peggie and Pauli were away. The violence had died down before their return, but the seething resentment remained palpable as Pauli scrambled to find odd jobs.[69]

At least she could type. Most black women could hope for nothing better than work in domestic service, and even those jobs were scarce. An article that Ella Baker coauthored in 1935 with black journalist Marvel Cooke vividly described black women's plight. In what they called "The Bronx Slave Market" black women gathered each morning on certain street corners in the Bronx to wait for white middle-class housewives to look them over and hire a lucky one for the day.[70]

Cooke placed "The Bronx Slave Market" in *The Crisis*, probably because the owners of the *Amsterdam News* had just fired her, along with the entire editorial staff, including Ted Poston, for trying to unionize. Pauli read a story in the *New York Times* about the firing and immediately called Ted to see what she could do. As a former waitress and office worker, Pauli had no experience with unions, which had traditionally targeted higher-paid, blue-collar, mostly white men. But the Depression had energized workers throughout the country, skilled and unskilled alike. Even journalists had begun to organize. In 1933, famed writer Heywood Broun of the *New York Post* had formed the Newspaper Guild, in which Ted Poston and Marvel Cooke hoped now to include black journalists. To Pauli's query about how she might help, Poston told her that she could join the picket line. Without even thinking, she headed uptown.[71]

Federal law seemed to be on the writers' side. On July 5, 1935, President Roosevelt had signed the National Labor Relations Act, which put the federal government behind workers' efforts to engage in collective bargaining and protected them from being fired. Poston, Cooke, and their colleagues also had some influential public support. Mayor LaGuardia lambasted the paper's owners for refusing to negotiate, and Heywood Broun joined the locked-out writers on the picket line. Zora Neale Hurston showed up, and Ella Baker was likely there as well. Pauli would be in good company, but for all her bravado her "deeply engrained notions of respectability" gave her pause as she approached the picket line. "It was one thing to ride freights anonymously or sleep in jails in strange towns where I was unknown," she later reflected. "It was quite another to carry a picket sign in the heart of Harlem, where many people knew me." She began to relax as she marched with the other picketers and joined in their labor songs, but she tensed up again when a squad of policemen arrived. Herded into a police wagon, she "worried about having an arrest record" as she headed off to jail. Fortunately, a sympathetic judge dismissed the charges the next day, but the experience radicalized her. As soon as she was released, she rejoined the picket line.[72]

Pauli would have loved to to have won a job with the Federal Writers' Project, but inexperienced, black, female beggars could not be choosers. The WPA assigned her instead to a job as a remedial reading teacher at Public School 8, just south of Greenwich Village. At a salary of $23.86 per week, the most she had ever earned, she was able to rent a room in the Village so that she could walk to work. Little else about the job pleased her. She hated her isolation from the regular teachers, who looked down on both remedial education and WPA workers. They tended to send her their discipline problems, when they deigned to send anyone at all. Chafing under this indifference to her efforts, Pauli looked for something more fulfilling.[73]

Inspired by Ted Poston's picket line and conversations with Peggie Holmes, Pauli returned to the New York Public Library to read more on labor unions, socialism, and communism. She quickly concluded, however, that she needed more than books to understand such difficult ideas. She had to go back to school. Ella Baker talked up the New Workers School at 131 W. 33rd Street, as the place to get the best introduction to the doctrinal distinctions among the myriad factions on the Left. Baker urged her to take classes with the school's founder, Jay Lovestone.[74]

Brought to the United States from Lithuania as a child, Lovestone embraced socialism as a teenager in New York City, joined the left wing of the party as a student at City College, became a Communist in 1919, and rose to the position of national secretary, effectively the head of the American Communist Party, when he was only twenty-nine in 1926. He also exhibited an independent mindedness that raised hackles among the Soviet leadership in Moscow. As a corollary to their belief that minorities had been the key to the Communist Party's triumph in the Russian Revolution, Joseph Stalin and his supporters argued for the right of self-determination of blacks in the Black Belt of the American South. In their view, separate states should be carved out of those areas where blacks outnumbered whites, so that blacks could become the vanguard of a Communist revolution in America.[75]

Jay Lovestone rejected that view. American capitalism was stronger and rural blacks less open to revolution, he argued, than Soviet leaders supposed. He saw promise, however, in the black migration to northern industrial jobs, which was bringing blacks into a shared class-consciousness with whites. Communists should be working in unions to raise workers' consciousness, not tilting at windmills in the South. When Stalin expelled Lovestone from the Communist Party in 1929, he formed what he called the Communist Party Opposition (CPO), moved into the mainstream labor movement, and created the New Workers School as a vehicle to spread his ideas and recruit members to his party. Beginning in the spring of 1936 and continuing through the summer, Pauli took night classes with Lovestone and others at his school including Marxist Philosophy, Historical Materialism, Marxian Economics, and Problems of Communist Organization.[76]

At the end of the 1935–1936 school year, Pauli's political education intensified when she won a transfer from her job as a remedial reading teacher to the Workers' Education Project of the WPA in Greenwich Village. There, she worked under the direction of Isabel Taylor, whose background included teaching coal mining families in Pennsylvania. Pauli was one of eighty on a staff that represented every party and tendency on the left. Pauli's friend and fellow Lovestone-follower, Ella Baker, was there; so too were Conrad Lynn, a lawyer for the Young Communist League, and Agnes Martocci, a friend from Hunter and a member of the Socialist Party. Whatever their particular affiliation, these teachers all wanted to instruct workers about their new rights under the National Labor Relations Act and to train them in practical skills: how to organize, bargain collectively, and file grievances. Pauli encountered considerable resistance, however, from union officials doubtful that anyone without union experience could teach anything of value.[77]

Pauli worried they were right. She had never worked in a factory or belonged to a union. Her classes at the New Workers School had given her only a theoretical foundation in Marxism; she wanted more practical training. Ella Baker had spent a semester at Brookwood Labor College in 1931 and encouraged Pauli to do the same. The college reserved two scholarships each year for members of the Communist Party Opposition, an opportunity that almost certainly explains Pauli's decision to join the CPO at that time.[78]

A residential labor college in Katonah, New York, established in 1921 by socialist and pacifist labor leaders and philanthropists, Brookwood groomed workers for union leadership. At Brookwood, Pauli joined thirty-five to forty other students, mostly trade unionists; she was one of three women and two blacks, the other a teacher from Mississippi who had worked with sharecroppers. Together they undertook a crash course in the history of the labor movement, principles of unionism, labor economics, and labor journalism. Pauli later remembered it as an "intensive experience," which produced in its students an "almost religious fervor," unlike anything she had ever experienced. She sang labor songs, volunteered as an organizer of a nearby Tarrytown automotive plant, put out a strike newspaper, and watched some of the men at Brookwood leave to fight in the Spanish Civil War.[79]

For all the excitement of the college's engagement with the most important political struggles of the day, Pauli missed New York City and Peggie Holmes. In February, she applied to the Rosenwald Fund, which awarded research grants to black scholars, for a $1,500 fellowship that would allow her to join Peggie, who was studying at Columbia. Unfortunately, her proposed topic, "A Study of the Negro in Industry and Labor since 1930," failed to impress the fellowship committee. Without outside funding, she had to give up the idea of further education, at least for the time being, but she was determined to be with Peggie. In March 1937, she returned to the Workers Education Project, where she began to teach a variety of classes on labor and economics, mostly in Harlem. That summer Pauli took the month of August to hitchhike with Peggie to Newport, Rhode Island.[80]

In the months that followed, Pauli grew increasingly disillusioned with the CPO. She had been drawn to it as it seemed to be a radical critic of other left-wing organizations, but even its independent form of communism began to seem doctrinaire to her. She disliked the party's rejection of religion; she found party discipline irksome; she objected to being told that she had to vote for the Communist candidate, Earl Browder, in the 1936 presidential elections; she found the news from Moscow of trials and summary executions of party dissidents appalling. Moreover, she could not help but note that Communists were better about addressing their white chauvinism than they were about confronting their male chauvinism. As a few brave souls were beginning to point out, only about 25 percent of the party membership was female, black women were a tiny handful, and there appeared to be no room for women in positions of leadership. By the fall of 1937, Pauli resigned.[81]

Collapse

Disillusionment over communism bothered Pauli. But a strain that had developed in her relationship with Peggie Holmes troubled her more deeply. Peggie

Figure 2.4 Peggie Holmes, in a picture taken by Pauli Murray on a backpacking trip to Newport, Rhode Island, in the summer of 1937. Estate of Pauli Murray, Schlesinger Library, Radcliffe Institute, Harvard University.

loved Pauli, but she could not accept her as a man. In December 1937, Pauli suffered an emotional collapse. It was not her first. Ever since she was nineteen, she had endured terrible breakdowns, as often as once a year. The problem would start when she became romantically involved with someone—at least once, in the case of Billy, with a man, but more typically with a woman. The relationship would flounder. Pauli would lose weight, be unable to sleep, fall ill, and eventually dissolve into inconsolable sobbing. She would go to see Dr. Chinn, who would counsel her to give up smoking, stop pushing herself so hard, eat sensibly, and get some sleep. Dr. Chinn would then do what she could to help her work toward these goals. In August 1935, in the early months of Peggie and Pauli's romantic involvement, Pauli had confided her emotional turmoil to Dr. Chinn. Concluding that Pauli needed psychiatric attention, Chinn referred her to Bellevue Hospital. But the psychiatrists there failed to give Pauli any relief.[82]

By December 1937, Pauli was so distraught by the conflict she experienced over her gender identity that she found her life intolerable. Perhaps through Dr. Chinn, Pauli found her way to Dr. Ruth Fox, an endocrinologist, who after examining her concluded that what she most needed was a good rest, open air, nutritious food, and a thorough psychiatric workup. Dr. Fox sent her to the Long Island Rest Home in Amityville. Founded in 1882 as the Long Island Hotel for Nervous Invalids, the home did not take black patients. To get Pauli admitted, Dr. Fox, or someone on the staff, identified her as Cuban.[83]

Notes that Pauli kept during her stay reveal a great deal about her under-standing of her condition at the time. Based on how she felt, reinforced by her reading in the New York Public Library, Pauli was convinced that her emotional problem stemmed from somatic, not psychological sources. She liked the Long Island Rest Home and was grateful for the kind care and good food, but she believed that the medical staff did not understand her condition. Reporting that she had suffered from "nervous" excitability her entire life, she stressed that her condition had worsened in recent years. She was subject to mood swings, "periods of extreme energy when I must be doing something, then periods of extreme weariness." She also recalled that her menses had stopped for five months when she was sixteen, and that she had gained fifteen pounds, a condition she associated with being incompletely female but which almost certainly related to the extreme stress she experienced at Richmond High School that year. She had trouble living with other people. The one thing that brought her peace from her internal conflict was "being alone" and "out of doors."[84]

Pauli anticipated the suggestion of the psychiatrist to whom she first spoke that her emotional problems might be related in some way to race. She did not think so. "I am proud of my Negro blood," she insisted. Neither did she accept the psychiatrist's suggestion that she might have problems with authority. "I do submit to authority as far as I am able, until I am proven wrong, or my point of view is accepted." In later years, Pauli would come to a deeper understanding of herself. She *was* proud of being black, but she was also deeply ashamed, and that shame created perpetual conflict for her. As for authority, in truth she had always had problems with authority; indeed, she had been encouraged by her family from an early age to challenge it. Her belief that she was a male who had to put up with male authority figures who did not take her seriously made her life all the harder. But race and authority were topics for another day. Her chief problem, she believed, was the conflict she felt over her gender identity.[85]

Her "terrific breakdowns," she explained, came "after each love affair that has become unsuccessful." In the past she had "run away," as she had in the wake of her failed marriage to Billy, and she had found peace in the outdoors. But in this instance, with a woman involved, she was experiencing "a willingness to fight." Pauli had never had a satisfactory sexual experience with a man. She had tried, but, as she had discovered with Billy, "something in me fights." Did this experience not provide evidence that she might have internal male sex organs? "What are the possibilities that one of the 'genitalia' is male in composition?" she wanted to know. The psychiatrist thought this was not possible but ordered a gynecological exam.[86]

The physical exam produced no evidence to support her theory, but she continued to argue her case that she must be a pseudo-hermaphrodite. Conflating gender identity and gender norms, as the literature she had read typically did, she asked rhetorically, "Why the inverted sex instinct—wearing pants, wanting to be one of the men, doing things that fellows do, hating to be dominated by women unless I like them?" The doctor did not think it possible that she was a pseudo-hermaphrodite but conceded that her problem could be, at least in part, "glandular." Encouraged, Pauli pressed on. She had experienced "the very natural falling in love with the female sex," but she did not believe, as the doctor appeared to, that this feeling meant that she was a homosexual. She felt the "greatest attraction" toward "extremely feminine and heterosexual women." If she were homosexual, she thought, she would have fallen in love with another homosexual woman rather than the very "feminine and heterosexual" Peggie. Moreover, if she were a lesbian, then "Why do many other Homosexuals irritate me instead of causing a bond of sympathy"? Immediately following her questions on homosexuality she asked again about the possibility that one of her genitalia might be male. The doctor responded, "Impossibility." But she pressed on. "Why cannot I accept the homosexual method of sex expression but insist on the normal [heterosexual] first?"[87]

She offered a three-part answer. In the first place, she did not believe that she was a woman. Yes, to all outward appearances she was a female, but if she had undescended testes, she would be a "pseudo-hermaphrodit[e] with secreted male genitals." Given how strongly she felt that she was male, there must be something inside her to confirm this feeling, perhaps an internal "organism (this one human) fighting for survival." Another reason the "homosexual method of expression" did not appeal to her was that she did not like to go to bars. Although she had on occasion visited them with her friends and had once been teased into taking a drink, she had felt so sick the next day she had never ventured to drink again. Finally, she did not think she could be a lesbian, because she wanted very much to have a monogamous relationship. She wanted to be married, as a normal man to a feminine, heterosexual woman: "Why do I desire monogamous married life as a completion" if I am a lesbian, she asked? Casual sex, which she associated with homosexuality, had no appeal. In short, none of her feelings squared with being homosexual, as she understood the term.[88]

She rejected the offer of psychiatric treatment. Although she had considered the possibility that her problems might stem from a "mother fixation," she believed that the emotional conflict she experienced was rooted in her body, not her mind. "I believe that psychiatry does not have the answer to true homosexuality but that experimental science does," she told the obviously doubtful doctor. Pauli's confusing statement is difficult to interpret. Here, she seems to be admitting that she is a true homosexual, but, in context, she was saying something else. She believed with Hirshfeld and Ellis that psychiatrists made the mistake of conflating homosexuals, on the one hand, and pseudo-hermaphrodites and transvestites like herself, on the other. One might be predisposed toward homosexuality, but one became a homosexual only in the course of social experience, mental development, and moral choice. Pseudo-hermaphrodites and transvestites, by contrast, were biologically intermediate between male and female and had no control over that fact; they were the products of nature's experiments on their bodies. Psychiatry might be able to help homosexuals, but only experimental science, through hormones or surgery, could help the pseudo-hermaphrodite.[89]

Pauli noted the tension between her faith in science and her "deep religious nature," by which she seemed to be saying that under normal conditions, her religious upbringing would have made her suspicious of science, but in this case, her visceral sense of herself as male was so strong that she could not help but appeal to it. Pauli did not broach the obvious point that homosexuality was highly stigmatized, especially in her church, as a moral failing. It is difficult to gauge how important this stigma was to Pauli's sense of herself. Clearly she thought that she was better off being "one of nature's experiments." If she was, then God had made her so and would give her the wisdom to see the meaning in his plan. But whether this religious justification caused her, unconsciously, to reject the label of homosexual is not clear.[90]

What was clear was that she felt herself to be in the middle, essentially intersexed, and she felt much more strongly her male than her female side. She was looking to science for an answer to her felt need to be more fully male. She knew that scientists had learned to manufacture hormones and she wanted some. She stated her position in the form of questions, but the questions were always rhetorical; she already knew the answer. "Why do I prefer experimentation on the male side, instead of attempted adjustment as a normal woman?" Because, she wanted her doctors to understand, she was already more male than female. She theorized that her true self could emerge more clearly if only she could be given male hormones. "Is [Dr. Fox] willing to experiment with male hormones?" The answer was no.[91]

In the end, Pauli was released from the Long Island Rest Home no closer to resolving her conflicts but more than ever convinced that endocrinology, not psychiatry, held the solution to her deepest conflicts. In January 1938, she visit Dr. Fox to have endocrine tests done in the hope of demonstrating, once and for all, that she was more male than female and deserved medical help to become fully male. To her dismay, the tests revealed that her levels of "female" hormones were "normal," and that her "male" hormones were "deficient, even for a normal female." Dr. Fox may well have thought that these findings would persuade Pauli that she was not biologically male, but they did not. Pauli felt divided and the tests did not change that feeling, which she believed to be, somehow, biologically rooted. She would not give up her search for a medical solution to this problem; indeed, she would devote much of the next two decades to it. But she was through with running away. She was ready to fight for what she wanted, not just the gender that felt true to her, but also the end of arbitrary restrictions on her freedom, whatever they might be. At twenty-seven, she had come of age.[92]

PART II

CONFRONTING JIM CROW, 1938–1941

3

"Members of Your Race
Are Not Admitted"

The Family Claim

Following her release from the Long Island Rest Home, Murray returned to the Workers Education Project, where she taught black workers in Harlem and on the Lower East Side. Monday and Wednesday evenings she lectured on "Social Security" and "Wages and Hours Legislation" at the YWCA on West 137th Street. Thursday evenings she explored "Labor Problems" at St. James Presbyterian Church at West 141st Street. Fridays she examined the challenges faced by "Women" and "Workers" in the Great Depression at the Brotherhood of Sleeping Car Porters on West 125th Street. From time to time, she jumped on the subway to lower Manhattan, where she worked on projects at Henry Street Settlement and the Education Project's headquarters. Her goal, she told her supervisors, was to help students overcome feelings of "inferiority and timidity," so that they could "see the world as theirs," a place from which they could "take what rightfully belongs to them."[1]

Grateful though Murray remained for the work, she worried about the future. On her salary of $23.86 a week, she could afford only a single room in Harlem, with walls so thin that she suffered periodic evictions when the neighbors complained of the noise of her typing. Even those low wages were at risk, for, rumor had it, the WPA would soon end. Looming unemployment made her consider her long-term goals. Her immediate supervisor and friend Agnes Martocci urged her to get a master's degree in adult education as a first step toward promotion and greater job security. Murray contemplated this step, but she had bigger dreams. She had learned at Brookwood that the plight of workers was part of a larger struggle for freedom—one in which blacks had long played a central role—and one in which forces beyond class seemed increasingly important. Events in Europe yielded an important insight, that Nazi treatment of Jews in Germany paralleled the repression of blacks in the American South. Gradually, she came to see Jim Crow not merely as the ultimate form of class oppression but also as a form of domestic fascism that threatened human rights more broadly. She added a lecture on "Fascism and Racial Prejudice" to her class list. As she talked, she began to think that the best way to fight fascism in America was not in Harlem but on its home turf in the South.[2]

Aunt Pauline had been asking Pauli to return home for years. Having given up her own dreams of higher education at the age of fourteen to go into teaching, she had been supporting the Fitzgerald clan ever since. Adding to her burden, Aunt Sallie and her two sons had moved in with her, after the Reverend Small died of a stroke. At sixty-seven years old, Pauline yearned to retire, but she could not afford to lose her salary. The Social Security Act of 1935 might have helped, but it excluded large classes of workers, including teachers. North Carolina provided pensions for teachers, but only white ones. With scant savings and no retirement income, Aunt Pauline wanted Pauli to acknowledge what reformer Jane Addams had once called the "family claim," the responsibility of the unmarried daughter to care for parents and other relatives unable to care for themselves. Murray found it difficult enough to endure the indignities of the segregated public transportation to which her periodic visits to Durham exposed her. The prospect of returning home to live the same Jim Crow circumscribed life she had worked so hard to escape filled her with dread. And yet, she could not ignore what she considered her adoptive mother's legitimate request.[3]

Repeatedly, over the course of the next three years, the family claim would draw Murray south, and each time, almost despite herself, she found herself in a confrontation with Jim Crow. She was not alone. Across the South, other blacks were defying the laws and customs that stunted their lives—applying to the whites-only state universities, protesting poor treatment on buses, criticizing the concentration of political power in the hands of a white elite through such devices as the poll tax. But few of these southern protesters enjoyed Murray's elite ancestry, her educational advantages, her experience of living in the North, or her talent as a journalist. Even fewer, in these years, conceived of their seemingly isolated protests as part of a larger national, even international movement for human emancipation, a movement for legal but also cultural change. What set Murray apart, even in this small group, was her sense of being what she called "a minority of minorities"—in her race, her class, *and* her gender. Her mixed-status caused her great pain but also enabled her to see herself as an instrument of change. Murray capitalized on these advantages, this vision, and this pain, between 1938 and 1941, to conceive of a blueprint for a civil rights movement that would coordinate legal reform with mass action.[4]

The University of North Carolina

In the fall of 1938, pressure from Aunt Pauline to come home turned Pauli's attention to possible opportunities in Durham. She might teach, if there were any openings, but she was by no means sure she would qualify. Moreover, she did not wish to reprise her aunt's life in the city's segregated school system. After more than fifty years of hard work, Aunt Pauline made only $62 a month, almost 20 percent less than she had made before the Depression; that was 40 percent less than Pauli earned at the WPA. Even with her college degree, Murray would not earn much more than her aunt as a teacher.[5]

She had a better idea. Ever since her time at Brookwood, she had been think-ing about graduate work in the social sciences. Why not apply to the University of North Carolina (UNC), where she could work with two of the country's leading specialists in race relations, Howard W. Odum and Guy B. Johnson? Although UNC had never admitted a black student and was barred by the state constitution from doing so, it had a reputation as a liberal institution, Odum and Johnson taught classes on blacks, so why wouldn't they welcome one as a student?[6]

Howard W. Odum, a descendent of slave owners, gave no evidence in his early career that he might be sympathetic to the aspirations of people of color. In his 1910 Columbia dissertation, *Social and Mental Traits of the Negro*, he announced that blacks were "bright enough" as children but attained "little in the intellectual way beyond childhood" and grew up to be "shiftless, untidy, and indolent." By the time Murray began to think of applying to UNC, how-ever, Odum had come to rethink his earlier views, in large part due to the gradu-ate students he recruited to the research institute he founded at Chapel Hill. Chief among the newcomers was Guy Johnson, born in Texas and educated at the University of Chicago, who arrived in 1925 with his wife, Guion. In an era when academic wives almost always had to give up any scholarly aspirations in the face of anti-nepotism rules and domestic pressures, Guion Johnson earned a Ph.D. from UNC's history department and worked as a research associate in Odum's institute. Guy Johnson encouraged his wife while introducing his men-tor to the Harlem Renaissance—even inviting Langston Hughes to campus.[7]

Graduate students who arrived in the midst of the Great Depression pressed harder for change. They challenged both Odum and Johnson to see the personal and economic damage done by racial discrimination. Lee Coleman reported that a recent race riot, assumed by whites to have been instigated by blacks, had in fact been provoked by white policemen's "mistreatment" of black residents. The very month that Murray considered applying to UNC, graduate student Janet Seville called for an end to segregation in an article in the university's *Carolina*

Magazine. Jim Crow, Seville argued, not only injured black people; it failed all southerners by suppressing the region's productivity.[8]

Aware of the liberal currents shaping sociology at UNC, from her reading and visits home, Murray saw reason to hope. She knew that graduate work would be expensive, more than $500 a year. But she also knew that fellowships were available, at least one of which had been funded by her great-great aunt Mary Ruffin Smith.[9]

Murray later explained that her decision to apply had stemmed from "a convergence of factors," including a growing concern about domestic fascism and optimism about UNC's progressive stance. But the "key fact," she stressed, was a "personal problem that I was trying to work out." This personal problem was actually twofold, one voiced, the other not. She frankly admitted her feeling of obligation to her adoptive mother to come home, but she also felt the need to find some solution to her inner turmoil. Perhaps a fresh start in Durham was the answer.[10]

Those Who Paved the Way

Murray was not the first to try to break the color line at UNC. A childhood friend, Thomas Raymond Hocutt, had already attempted to do so. A year behind Murray in school, he had been one of the few boys of their generation to graduate from Hillside High. Continuing on to the North Carolina College for Negroes (NCCN) in Durham, he had settled on a career as a pharmacist, but NCCN offered no course work in that field. Only the University of North Carolina did. Hocutt applied to UNC in 1933, with the help of a couple of young black lawyers in Durham, Conrad Pearson and Cecil McCoy. As expected, the registrar turned Hocutt away. Convinced that they had a good case against the university, the lawyers decided to sue, but they soon encountered difficulties. Even if the registrar had turned Hocutt away because of his race, the university could argue that it had rejected him for either of two other reasons. First, Hocutt, having attended the academically inferior NCCN (a grade "B" institution), did not qualify on academic grounds for admission to UNC (a grade "A" institution). Second, and more immediately damaging, NCCN President James E. Shepard, fearful that success for Hocutt would jeopardize state funding for NCCN, refused to release Hocutt's transcript. Convinced that she could make a stronger case for admission than Raymond Hocutt had done, Murray resolved to try again. As she later told an interviewer, glossing over the missing transcript problem, "They turned him down because of the inferior segregated Negro school which they had. Let's see what they do about a Hunter College degree."[11]

New energy at the NAACP fueled Murray's bravado. By the mid-1930s, divisions at the civil rights organization over how to deploy its resources had been resolved in favor of a challenge to segregation in higher education. According to an article by NAACP litigation director Charles Houston in the January 1938 issue of the *Crisis*, the legal campaign was proceeding on multiple fronts. The most promising battle of the year was in Missouri, where Lloyd Gaines was seeking admission to the all-white law school. Murray later denied advance knowledge of *Gaines*, and if by that she meant that she decided to apply to UNC before the Supreme Court handed down its decision, that is true. But she almost certainly saw Houston's article and was therefore aware of his litigation plans. The *Crisis* had been her favorite magazine since childhood.[12]

In early November 1938, just after the Supreme Court heard oral arguments in *Gaines*, Murray decided to act. She wrote UNC to request a graduate catalogue and an application form. To her consternation, the application form arrived with two typed additions to the blanks to be filled in by the applicant. Obviously added recently, they were "Religion" and "Race," fueled by fears of applications by African Americans and Jews.[13]

Murray sat on the application for almost a month. Submitting it would put Aunt Pauline in a potentially awkward position, because NCCN President James E. Shepard was among her closest friends. Murray's attempt to desegregate the University of North Carolina threatened not only his funding-raising efforts but also the livelihood of every teacher at the school. Then, two nationally reported events stiffened Murray's resolve. A few days before Thanksgiving 1938, UNC President Frank Graham gave a stirring address in favor of human rights at the founding meeting of the Southern Conference on Human Welfare in Birmingham, Alabama. Two weeks later President Franklin D. Roosevelt gave a speech at UNC praising the university's liberalism. Covered on the front pages of newspapers across the country, these speeches convinced Murray the time had arrived to hold liberalism to account.

The New Deal and the South

President Roosevelt faced a major problem in the South. For years, conservative Democrats there had threatened his New Deal programs. He wanted these foes replaced by liberals, and he looked to the Southern Conference on Human Welfare as a last ditch effort to build support for his programs. The opening conference for the organization, scheduled for November 1938 and presided over by UNC President Frank Graham, promised to do that.[14]

Frank Graham had made his university a haven for liberals in the South. He encouraged research on race and often protected left-wing faculty members from those who wanted them fired. In Birmingham, just a week after a vicious Nazi assault on Jews throughout Germany—the infamous Kristallnacht—Graham linked fascism abroad and Jim Crow at home. Addressing the 1,300 delegates, a quarter of them black, he declared that the South's treatment of "the black man" provided "the primary test of democracy and Christianity," and that they had all come to Birmingham to take their stand "for the simple thing of human freedom."[15]

Birmingham's Commissioner of Public Safety, Theophilus Eugene (known as "Bull") Connor, had no interest in passing such a test. Alerted that members of the audience were not observing the city's segregation ordinance, he sent in officers to separate the attendees into "white" and "colored" sections.[16]

Eleanor Roosevelt, one of the conference's featured speakers, arrived the following day for a session on youth problems. Mary McLeod Bethune, her closest friend in the black community and the woman she had successfully lobbied FDR to name as head of Negro Affairs at the National Youth Administration, had organized the session. Late and out of breath, Mrs. Roosevelt took a convenient seat, only to be told by Bull Connor's deputies that she was on the "colored" side of the aisle and would have to move. Unwilling to break the law, but not wanting to give in, the first lady asked that her chair be placed with the speakers facing the whole group. When asked her opinion about Birmingham's segregation ordinance that evening, she diplomatically responded, "I would not presume to tell the people of Alabama what to do." But she had made her point, and young people like Murray knew they had a friend. As the weekly *Baltimore Afro American* later editorialized, "Sometimes actions speak louder than words." As Murray read a report on the conference in the *New York Times* on Thanksgiving Day, she took heart that she might stand a chance at UNC.[17]

Two weeks later, Graham bestowed the university's highest honor on the nation's president. Addressing himself to the undergraduates who crowded the school gymnasium, FDR announced that it was time to take "definite action" to bring about "the improvement of social and economic conditions." "That is why," he continued, "I . . . associate myself so greatly with the younger generation." They are the ones most able to take "affirmative action" to correct social problems and not to wait for "evolutionary processes" to solve them.[18]

Murray read excerpts of the speech the next day with mounting indignation. How could the president of the United States praise democratic liberalism at a southern university without acknowledging that the university denied large numbers of its local citizens their basic civil rights? How could he proffer his identification with the "younger generation" before him without noting that his audience was exclusively white? What kind of liberal democratic example did the United States set a world threatened by fascism, when an entire region engaged in racial discrimination and worse, thereby driving large numbers, herself included, into exile?

Murray immediately pounded out a letter of protest on behalf of all blacks then living in the North. "We are as much political refugees from the South as any of the Jews of Germany," she declared, in one of her first attempts to deploy a compelling analogy for rhetorical advantage. She and others had "come to Northern cities to escape the mental and physical cruelties of the land in which we were born and the land we love." The president, she noted, had associated himself with young people, had pointed to the University of North Carolina as a liberal institution, and had called for changes in the law to achieve a more democratic society. Did the president feel, as she did, "that the ultimate test of democracy in the United States will be the way in which it solves its Negro problem?" Did he mean, further, to say that the University of North Carolina should now "open its doors to Negro students" so that they could sit down with white students to study problems of mutual concern? Or, did his speech have "no meaning for us as Negroes"? Did Roosevelt mean to say, in sum, "that again we are to be set aside and passed over for more important problems?"[19]

Guessing that the president would likely never see her letter, she sent a copy to Eleanor Roosevelt, with a cover letter as a reminder of their first sighting at Camp Tera. "You do not remember me," Murray began, "but I was the girl who did not stand up when you passed through the Social Hall of Camp Tera during one of your visits in the winter of 1934–35. Miss Mills criticized me afterward, but I thought and still feel that you are the sort of person who prefers to be accepted as a human being and not as a paragon." Within a few days, Eleanor Roosevelt responded, saying, "I understand perfectly, but great changes come slowly. I think they are coming, however, and sometimes it is better to fight hard with conciliatory methods."[20]

Murray treasured Eleanor Roosevelt's response, the first of what was to be a decades-long correspondence and deepening friendship. But she was not mollified. The president had urged "affirmative action" and yet was unprepared to take any. She, however, was ready to act and to do so in as public and noisy a manner as she could.

The best way to get the word out to the black community, Murray knew, was to alert Dr. Shepard. From her small room in Harlem, she reminded the college president of her place in the community: the granddaughter of Robert Fitzgerald and the adopted daughter of Pauline Dame. She then proceeded to make her case for integrating UNC. "Please do not misunderstand me," she reassured him, "I am not opposed to the establishment of Negro universities per se." She well knew that he sought state funding to add graduate departments to NCCN. But, she continued, that effort must not stand in the way of desegregating the state's flagship university. Then she went for the jugular, calling him a collaborationist in the suffering of his people for resisting the integration of UNC. "Each day the newspapers report further and more brutal injustices against our brothers and sisters in Germany, the Jews. . . . [C]an we then, as Americans and members of a minority group collaborate on any policy which will stop short of equality?" Murray did not expect to change Shepard's views; she was preparing for a wider attack.[21]

But first, she needed to do something about the application form still sitting on her desk. She filled it in, identified her race as "Negro," and mailed it.[22]

Four days later, December 12, 1938, the Supreme Court handed down a decision in *Missouri ex rel. Gaines* v. *Canada* that confirmed Murray's belief that the time to push, and to push hard, had arrived. There had been no question of Gaines's qualifications. The valedictorian of his high school class, he had graduated with honors in history from all-black, fully accredited, "A" class ranked, Lincoln University. He applied to the University of Missouri Law School, which turned him down because of his race and offered him a scholarship to study out of state. Gaines refused the money and, represented by Charles Houston and Thurgood Marshall, he sued, lost, and appealed all the way to the Supreme Court. Only two years before, a positive ruling from the famously conservative Court would have been out of the question, but much had changed. Justice Owen Roberts had started to vote with the liberals, shifting the balance on the Court from four liberals to five. The appointment of Hugo Black provided another liberal vote; and there was a vacant seat that might soon be filled with still another. In fact, the decision came with a seat still empty: 6–2 in favor of Gaines. Ruling unconstitutional Missouri's scheme of paying out-of-state tuition for black graduate students, the Court declared that—in the absence of a law school open to blacks in Missouri—the state must admit Gaines to the University of Missouri Law School. Murray rejoiced. North Carolina had no separate graduate or professional schools for Negroes. According to the Court's ruling, she reasoned, UNC would have to admit her.[23]

"Members of Your Race Are Not Admitted"

But two days later, on December 14, 1938, she received a letter of rejection: "Under the resolutions of the Board of Trustees of the University of North Carolina, members of your race are not admitted to the University," Dean W. W. Pierson informed her. He went on to say that the state legislature was expected "to make provision for graduate instruction for Negroes," although he could not say "the precise form which this provision will take."[24]

Murray was not surprised. The letter had likely been written before the dean knew of the Supreme Court's action. Eager to put the university on notice that its rejection of her application was illegal in light of the *Gaines* decision, she wrote directly to President Graham. She did not want to go to court, she informed him, but was prepared to do so if necessary. That same day she wrote a friend from high school, Felicia Miller, "Lisha," asking her to contact the lawyers who had represented Raymond Hocutt "pronto," and also to let Aunt Pauline know what she was doing. This story was going to create a storm; Murray wanted to "keep Mother posted, so as not to shock her."[25]

The next day, she wrote to Gaines, offering her "congratulations" and urging him to "accept your admission" no matter how "uncomfortable" whites might try to make him. As a *New York Times* editorial had opined that morning, "some Negro leaders" would likely use his achievement to pressure state legislatures "to provide adequate facilities" to avoid a "showdown." Murray hoped that Gaines would ignore pressure to await creation of a separate law school in Missouri, follow through on his victory, and register for classes immediately at the University of Missouri Law School.[26]

Murray's next step was to send a copy of her application to Walter White at NAACP headquarters downtown. She included a copy of an "Open Letter to President Roosevelt" to be passed on to Roy Wilkins for possible publication in the *Crisis*. The letter was an abridged version of the one she had sent to the president. Having heard nothing from FDR, she opted for a public presentation of her views. White referred the open letter to Wilkins and the application materials to Thurgood Marshall, who instructed her to have her transcript from Hunter sent to the NAACP and to charge the $1 cost to them. Wilkins was worried. He knew Murray and thought her too radical, too difficult to control. But Wilkins was not part of the legal department. Marshall would decide.[27]

Within a few days, the story of Murray's application to UNC was all over the news. On January 5, 1939, Aunt Sallie heard on the radio that "a Negro woman from N.Y. has applied to the U. of N.C. to enter school. We don't know what the outcome will be." In a letter to Murray the next day, Aunt Pauline assured her that she had said nothing, but "I suppose everyone who knows you . . . may think it's you. Please be careful what you do about all of this for you can make it very uncomfortable for me . . . . Don't do anything rash please. You know it will take time to change the South. They have a Negro in jail here accused of raping a girl of Chapel Hill."[28]

The alleged rape had roiled Chapel Hill for several weeks. A telephone call from one of Guy Johnson's male graduate students in mid-December had alerted Guion Johnson to the trouble. Explaining that her husband was in New York, talking to Gunnar Myrdal about his study of race relations in America, she asked what was wrong. The student responded that a mob of white farmers was forming to "get" a black farmer who had raped a white high school girl during the noon recess. Students with shotguns and bloodhounds were roaming the town. The caller wanted to organize a group of graduate students and faculty to head off a possible lynching. Who was the girl? Johnson asked. The graduate student told her. "That can't possibly be true," Johnson responded.[29]

The president of the high school PTA, Johnson knew the girl, in fact had seen her at midday at a local store giggling with a girlfriend and had reprimanded her for being out of school. Johnson sought the help of Howard Odum, but Odum refused to get involved; he did not want to alienate the white farmers whom he considered his friends. Johnson then called the school superintendent and pieced together what had likely happened. The girl had been slipping out of school to meet her white boyfriend for some time. She was probably pregnant by him and wanted an abortion. Knowing that she could not get one if the truth were known, she had accused a black neighbor of rape. Johnson promptly called the mayor, from whom she learned that the farmer had been arrested and was in a small jail near Chapel Hill. She urged that the accused man be removed to Durham for safety. The mayor did so, and that is where matters stood when Aunt Pauline wrote to Murray on January 6. The man was safe and would eventually be released, thanks to Guion Johnson's intervention. But for Aunt Pauline, the danger had not passed. A state in which lynching remained a present danger was not a state that would accept the integration of UNC.[30]

The *Daily Tar Heel*, UNC's student newspaper, said as much: the campus had taken on "an antebellum air." One student speculated menacingly about the possibility of "murder"; others "vowed that they would tar and feather any 'nigger' that tried to come to class with them." An editorial in the *Durham Morning Herald* declared, "No one in his right mind" wanted to end segregation. Another editorial in the *Daily Tar Heel* estimated that a majority of undergraduates would resist any effort to force integration on them. North Carolinians, the editors stressed, quoting North Carolina Governor Clyde R. Hoey, did not believe in "social equality."[31]

Confrontation by Typewriter

With growing outrage, Murray read the headlines and accompanying stories about her application from complimentary copies of the *Daily Tar Heel*, provided to her by friends at the Columbia University *Spectator*, and North Carolina news stories, sent by friends from home: "New York Woman Seeks to Enter Grad School," "Negress Applies to Enter Carolina," "Administration Is Confronted with 'Liberalism' Issue." Deeply "hurt" by the slur of "Negress" and the suggestion that she was no more than an outside agitator, Murray readily understood that Frank Graham was also under attack. According to the headline writers, he had brought this calamity on the university through his ill-considered support of liberal ideas. Murray fired off a letter to the editors of the *Daily Tar Heel*. In doing so, she took her friend Pee Wee Inness's strategy of "confrontation by typewriter" to a whole new level.[32]

Murray wanted the students at UNC to think hard about what they meant by the term "social equality" and why they feared it so much. Many of them had spent their formative years cared for by a black nanny. Why, now, did they object to sitting next to a black classmate? Why was social intimacy acceptable in the first instance and not in the second? Why, when someone who merely sought the same educational opportunities that they took for granted, did they "go into tantrums, organize 'lynching' parties and raise the old cry of Klu Klux Klan"?[33]

For some time Murray had been sending letters to public officials whose work fell short of her expectations, but in applying to the University of North Carolina she went further. She created open letters, by forwarding her correspondence— with Franklin and Eleanor Roosevelt, James Shepard, Frank Graham, and the editors of the *Daily Tar Heel*—to the editors of every black periodical she could think of. With luck, she would turn what had been private exchanges between a handful of aspiring black students and university administrators in the South into a national forum on civil rights.[34]

A vocal minority came immediately to Murray's support. Ten graduate students, out of a student body of 405, insisted to the *Daily Tar Heel* that they had "no objection to the admission of blacks to the graduate and professional schools of this University." Indeed, they vastly preferred integration to the idea of setting up separate graduate and professional schools for black students. "It has taken over a hundred years to make this university what it is. The Negroes should not have to wait that long. The only solution then, consistent with the constitution of the United States, is to allow the authorities to admit Negroes here." In a straw poll, graduate students voted 82 to 38 in support.[35]

Support came also from the monthly student journal, *Carolina Magazine*. Editor John Creedy, a British-born senior in economics, decided to devote the February issue to the broader debate over integration spurred by the *Gaines* decision and Murray's application. He sent a telegram to Murray to ask if she was the author of "Song of the Highway," and if so whether he could reprint it. He believed it would show the community what they were missing in denying Murray admission. Creedy had also hoped to print an article on student views of integration. Sociology graduate student Janet Bragdon had attempted a systematic study of freshman opinion with the help of friends in the English department: an analysis of 581 first-year themes on the topic, "Would you favor a Negro's entering the university?" The head of the English department put an end to the study, however, when he learned that Creedy intended to feature it in the February issue of *Carolina Magazine*. The suddenly streamlined issue instead offered essays from different points of view on the debate. The NCCN dean of men, James T. Taylor, urged that graduate instruction be offered at existing black institutions, such as NCCN. Howard Odum agreed, adding that faculty from UNC and Duke might offer some graduate classes at NCCN and a few NCCN students might take the occasional graduate class at the white universities for credit at their home institution.[36]

Sociology graduate student Glenn Hutchinson agreed with Odum that black students should be admitted to graduate classes at UNC, but he went further. He wanted to admit Murray directly and end segregation. Born, like Odum, in rural Georgia, Hutchinson spoke for a new generation of sociologists. "In admitting Negroes to our graduate and professional schools, their gain would also be our gain," Hutchinson declared. "We are impoverishing ourselves as well as the Negro by sitting behind a caste wall. . . . I would be really proud if the University of North Carolina would be the first in the South to crack open that iron gate which we have closed in the face of the Negro."[37]

A few faculty also spoke out in favor of Murray's admission, most decisively Howard K. Beale, a thirty-eighty-year-old American political and economic historian trained at the University of Chicago. Beale declared that there were many faculty and students "who feel that it would be of value to our white students as well as to the Negro to admit Negroes at the graduate level." To deny a qualified black applicant admission, he insisted, would be to act contrary to the university's liberal values. The university's discriminatory treatment, moreover, flew in the face of the findings of its foremost scholars, especially in the sociology department, that blacks were fully capable of work as good as that of white students. "Wisdom as well as expediency often necessitates progress in low gear," he concluded, "but let's not allow our emotions to put us into reverse."[38]

Support for Murray came from beyond Chapel Hill, as well. Jonathan Daniels, a 1921 graduate of UNC and the influential editor of the *Raleigh News and Observer,* told an audience at a campus tea-time talk, "I don't see how anyone can object to taking a graduate course at the University with a Negro." Elbert Russell, dean of the Divinity School at Duke University, also lent his support. In the midst of the controversy he gave a powerful sermon one Sunday morning that was carried into black homes via the local radio. Comparing the treatment of blacks in North Carolina to the treatment of Jews in Germany, he noted, "Negroes know what it is to have school doors slammed in their faces." Black listeners were astonished. Lewis Austin proclaimed, "Long Live Dean Russell" in the *Carolina Times.*[39]

A month into the debate over Murray's application, the campus YMCA and members of the American Student Union organized an interracial panel at which warring factions of students, faculty, and other interested parties from both black and white colleges, and across the political spectrum, faced off over the wisdom of ending segregation in graduate education. YMCA Director Harry F. Comer and Government Professor E. J. Woodhouse opposed integration. English Professor E. E. Ericson, who had caused a furor three years earlier when he had gone out to dinner with James Ford, the vice presidential candidate for the Communist Party, supported it. So too did Pulitzer-winning playwright Paul Green, a graduate of UNC widely respected by black actors for the serious parts he created for them. After a passionate debate that lasted past midnight, the group passed a resolution urging "the legislature to consider a policy whereby qualified and carefully chosen Negro students could be educated in graduate and professional levels by the means and forces already existing in the state."[40]

Murray won strong support at UNC but not where it mattered most. President Frank Graham and the sociology faculty could not see a way to help. Finally answering Murray's letters in early February 1939, Graham noted that he was fully aware "of the iniquities" that she had pointed out, but that he must defer to the state legislature, which was striving to satisfy both the state constitution's mandate of separate education and the Supreme Court's ruling that the state "must make substantially equal provision for graduate and professional work." Unless the Supreme Court were to overrule the state constitution, nothing more could be done, short of a popular referendum—and that he feared very much. He worried that any attempt to end segregation would provoke a ferocious back-lash, one that would undo the progress of the past forty years and return the South to the lynching and race riots of the 1890s. His promise of full coopera-tion to bring about greater equality in black schools, he conceded, "might seem to you to be an inadequate and minimum program, but it is going to take the cooperation and the struggle of us all to bring it to pass." He closed by saying, "As you may know I am under very bitter attack in some parts of North Carolina and the lower South for what little I have tried to do in behalf of Negro people, organized and unorganized workers and other underprivileged groups. I realize I am also subject to attack because I understand the limitations under which we must work in order to make the next possible advance."[41]

Gradually, Murray faced the fact that neither Frank Graham, on whom she had pinned high hopes, nor the sociology faculty, in whose department she had hoped to study, could be persuaded to support her. Howard Odum continued to say that "it is asking too much of a region to change over night the powerful folkways of long generations." Guy and Guion Johnson also thought that the wis-est course at that moment was to do everything in their power to equalize black schools. In the midst of the debate over whether Murray should be admitted to UNC, Guion Johnson spoke at the Baptist Student Forum. She began by lay-ing out statistics on the inequality in funding between white and black schools in North Carolina. The state spent more than twice as much educating each white child as it did educating each black child. Despite this inequality, how-ever, she perceived little support among black students for integration. Reading from freshman essays by black students on whether they favored integration, she pointed to one male student who worried that black students would be treated unjustly if they were to enter white schools. As a consequence he thought it better to build up black schools instead. Johnson did not offer her own opinion. She did not have to.[42]

Meeting with Thurgood Marshall

Unable to generate enough support at UNC to advance her case there, Murray visited Thurgood Marshall at the NAACP legal offices on Fifth Avenue and 15th Street to discuss the possibility of suing the university. As she later recalled the conversation, the biggest strike against her was that she was no longer a resident of North Carolina. When she protested that there were many students at UNC from other states, Marshall responded that under the Supreme Court's decision in *Gaines,* states had a responsibility only to their own residents.[43]

Beyond the legal considerations, Marshall pointed to "personal circumstances" and "background" that counted against her. Murray bore all the markings of the outside agitator: she lived in New York, had been arrested as a picketer, had been a member of the Communist Party Opposition, and had attended Brookwood College. She was everything a conservative judge would not like. Legally, these personal matters were irrelevant to Murray's proposed challenge to racial segregation in graduate education, but the NAACP wanted plaintiffs free of any personal characteristics that might distract a judge from the claim being advanced. Hers were not good facts for mounting a legal challenge in the South.[44]

Marshall almost certainly did not know the most distracting fact about Murray: her ongoing search of hormones. Even as she battled UNC, she tried to persuade a new set of physicians at New York Hospital to give her a masculine appearance by giving her testosterone. To her disappointment, Dr. Charles Richardson and his associates came to the same conclusion that Dr. Ruth Fox had arrived at a year before. Murray's hormone levels were normal for a female. Her body structure was "boyish, but not particularly virile." Dr. Richardson suggested psychiatric treatment, a recommendation that Murray dismissed, as she had before, on the grounds that she could "solve non-physical problems myself." Murray would not have mentioned these medical consultations to Marshall, for knowledge of them would have closed off any possibility of Marshall's taking her case. Yet, their timing and the frustration they produced helps explain why Murray, having suffered a setback in the medical battle, fought as hard as she did in the seemingly more winnable battle for admission to UNC.[45]

Murray's effort to break the color line at UNC brought some benefits, even in defeat. In early April, she returned to Durham to celebrate Easter. Visiting the University of North Carolina to satisfy herself that she "was not afraid to appear on the campus," she was "surprised at the cordial reception [she] got from a number of students and faculty members." It was a good week for racial progress. Eleanor Roosevelt and Harold Ickes had just arranged for Marian Anderson to sing at the Lincoln Memorial that Easter Sunday, after the Daughters of the American Revolution had turned her away from their Constitution Hall on account of her race. As Anderson sang "My Country 'tis of Thee, Sweet Land of Liberty" to an audience of 75,000, equal rights seemed a little nearer.[46]

Taking the Long View

Murray did not give up, at least not immediately. She applied to UNC law school but again was turned away. By this time, the North Carolina legislature had voted to allow NCCN to teach graduate classes, including classes in law. It had also cut the college's budget by a third, however, making any real change impossible. For a time, Murray thought she had found a North Carolina resident who might succeed where she had failed on residency grounds: Carl DeVane, a graduate of Shaw College in Raleigh. But when she learned that Shaw ranked as a Class "B" institution and that Thurgood Marshall would risk representing only applicants with degrees from Class "A" schools, her hopes plummeted. NCCN was out, even though it had been reclassified a Class "A" school, because of President Shepard's refusal to send transcripts of students who wished to apply to UNC. Among private institutions, North Carolina had only two Class A black colleges, Smith and Bennett; neither produced a willing candidate. As word began to spread that Lloyd Gaines had disappeared— possibly murdered for his effort to win admission to a white law school—a disappearance that has never been solved, the chance of finding a plaintiff diminished still further.[47]

The only southern states to integrate their graduate or professional schools before the 1950s were the border states of Maryland and West Virginia. Elsewhere, the result of Gaines and Murray's efforts was the mobilization of southern state legislatures to create further segregation. Perversely, other southern states began to adopt the very out-of-state scholarship laws that the Court had invalidated in *Gaines*. Only five states had such laws in 1938, but by 1943 eleven did, and by 1948, seventeen. Not until 1951, under a federal appeals court order, would UNC admit its first black student.[48]

In the end, Murray took the long view. Thomas Raymond Hocutt had tried and failed to win admission to UNC in 1933 but had inspired her to try in 1938. Others would surely follow. In the meantime, the NAACP focused its attention on equalizing teachers' salaries and benefits in the South, a strategy that Aunt Pauline fervently supported.[49]

|| 4 ||

Bus Trouble

"Quite the Self-Confident Fellow"

Her hopes of winning admission and a fellowship to UNC dashed, Murray continued work at the WPA in New York, until federal funding ran out in July 1939. For the next two years, she supported herself in a series of short-lived, fundraising jobs for labor and civil rights organizations, among them the Southern Tenant Farmers Union (STFU) and the Workers Defense League (WDL). To satisfy Aunt Pauline's demand that she assume greater responsibility for her family, Murray offered a new proposal. She would ease the burden on her aunts by taking charge of her nephews, James, now twenty, and Joshua, seventeen. Like most of their male friends, the boys had dropped out of high school. Unable to find a job at home in Durham, Jimmy had come to New York, where he worked as a busboy at Macy's. Joshua was still in Durham, coming under the influence of "underworld people," as his mother put it. Murray proposed to assume the role of the father her nephews had lost. Taking advantage of New York's better schools and job opportunities, she would guide them to high school degrees and regular employment. In the meantime, they would all maintain family ties through trips home to Durham.[1]

Murray wished she had a car for those trips, but her meager earnings did not permit such an extravagance. The only other way to get home was by train or bus, and both segregated their passengers once they reached Virginia. Economy dictated taking the bus, but she especially hated that form of transportation. It was bad enough to be directed to a different car on the train. The public embarrassment of separation within the bus bothered her more. Beyond the fact of segregated seating, Murray loathed the typical white bus driver's swaggering manner and contemptuous treatment of black passengers. Once, she watched a black mother, holding a baby, stand for miles in a bus with a number of vacant seats, simply because the driver refused to ask white passengers to move forward so that she could take a seat in the rear. Another time, she faced the humiliation that accompanied an urgent need to use a rest room at a bus stop in southern

Virginia. A line prevented her from using the room for "Colored" before the bus was scheduled to leave, and the driver would not permit her to use the empty one for whites. She had two choices: she could follow the bus driver's dismissive direction that she relieve herself in a nearby field, or she could ride in agony for the remaining two hours of the journey home. In protest over one of these degrading incidents, she fired off a letter to the Trailways Bus Lines and sent a copy to Walter White at the NAACP. Her dread of these southern trips notwithstanding, the obligation she felt toward Aunt Pauline made her promise that she would return regularly with her nephews.[2]

Murray had already found a place in Harlem that would accommodate James and Joshua. With a new friend from the WPA, Adelene (Mac) McBean, she had sublet rooms in an eight-room apartment in Harlem, at 35 Mt. Morris West, a few blocks south of 125th Street. If she had any doubts about her ability to shoulder the role she was about to assume, she had total faith in Mac, whom she characterized in letters home as her "girlfriend." Born in Harlem to West Indian immigrant parents, Mac had all the domestic skills Murray lacked. She would cook and care for the boys; Murray would direct family life. "I think I'm quite a self-confident fellow to take moral responsibility for two boys in New York City," Murray crowed to Aunts Pauline and Sallie.[3]

Murray enrolled Joshua in a good high school in Chelsea and helped him find a part-time job. She hunted down night classes for Jimmy that would allow him to complete the credits he needed for his high school degree, as he continued to work full-time. She counseled Jimmy on everything from budgeting to his health, while running interference for Joshua at his new school. When a teacher informed her that, according to tests, Joshua's IQ was only 84, Murray insisted that he had simply never been challenged to use his mind. She had recently read that southern blacks who attended New York City schools for more than four years scored 12.3 percent higher in IQ than did newcomers. On the basis of that evidence, Murray insisted that the school give Joshua remedial education, while she worked to enforce steady work habits. As hard as she tried to help, however, her nephews resisted her efforts. After five months, she diagnosed the problem for her aunts: "Joshua and Jimmy need a strong man's hand for guidance."[4]

"A Minority of Minorities"

Feeling acutely the disadvantage of her gender as she struggled for economic security, romantic attachment, and parental authority, Murray informed Aunt Pauline of her latest medical foray. She had "been doing some conferring at the Post Graduate Hospital with some of the physicians in the endocrine department." In a bit of wishful thinking she added, "They may do some experimentation with hormones to help balance my emotional self." Murray had just read a story in the *World Telegram* that gave her hope: "Pill 'Planted' in Body Turns Weak, Effeminate Youths into Strong, Virile Men; 200 Doctors View Results of New Hormones." According to the article, tablets of synthetic testosterone implanted under the skin had transformed the lives of young men, suffering from high voices and lack of facial hair. "This one wanted to kill himself," the lead researcher, Dr. Joseph Eidelsberg, told the doctors gathered at Post Graduate Hospital. "He indicated a husky, solid young man, who grinned." Murray was jubilant. Here was research that confirmed that her problems could be solved by testosterone.[5]

Further encouragement came a few days later, when the *New York Amsterdam News* published a front-page story on the breakthrough in hormone research. Seeing Murray's excitement, Mac sent a letter praising the newspaper's liberality. "Our own racial group, perhaps more than any others," she lamented, "is guilty of great ignorance on this subject." As a consequence, blacks who suffered from any "sexual maladjustments" became a "minority of minorities, misunderstood by their family and friends, condemned without trial by social custom, isolated, excluded and made to endure a 'living death.' "[6]

Mac was not the only friend to stand by Murray. Peg Holmes continued to offer comfort and support, even though the love of Murray's young life had moved to a job at the YWCA in New Bedford, Massachusetts. They visited back and forth, talked by phone, and corresponded about everything from their worries over political events in Eastern Europe to Murray's difficulties in assuming parental responsibilities for her nephews. Murray would have loved a closer relationship. No one else shared so completely her political and personal concerns, but all hope of that ended in February 1940, when Peg decided to move to California.[7]

Desperate to change Peg's mind, Murray hitchhiked to New Bedford in the male attire she favored whenever she was not at work. Somewhere in Rhode Island, either on her way to Bedford or back, the state police picked her up and turned her over to the custody of female corrections officer Marion Barry in Providence. Officer Barry turned out to be a sympathetic soul. Twenty-five years later, she still vividly recalled the distraught young black woman who had told her she was a "homosexual and was taking hormone [*sic*]." Although Murray always denied being a lesbian, she occasionally admitted to "homosexual tendencies" as the only available descriptor that people would accept. As for the report that she was taking hormones, nothing in her correspondence with doctors supports that claim. She wanted testosterone badly enough, however, that she may well have told the corrections officer that doctors had agreed to give it to her. Barry did not arrest Murray for hitchhiking but rather escorted her to the New York City Police Department, where officers decided to take her to

Bellevue Hospital. There, Murray poured out her story to a psychiatrist, who gave her a diagnosis of "schizophrenia." In the doctor's view, she suffered from a delusion: she believed that she was a man.[8]

Permitted to call a family member, Murray contacted her "cousin" Mac. The next day, Mac checked her out of Bellevue and, probably on the recommendation of Dr. Chinn, took her to a private psychiatric facility, Dr. Rogers's Hospital, at 345 Edgecombe Avenue, on the corner of 150th Street. Murray was lucky. If Mac had not come to her rescue, Bellevue psychiatrists were prepared to seek her commitment to one of the vast, overcrowded state hospitals for the mentally ill.[9]

On the typewriter Mac brought to her, Murray itemized the causes of her "nervous collapse": overwork; lack of desire to either eat or sleep; anxiety over parental responsibilities; and the "temporary disappearance of a friend." All of these factors played a part; however, Murray believed that the principal source of her emotional crisis was the same problem with which she had wrestled for a decade: the fact that she repeatedly fell in love with women without having any "opportunity to express such an attraction in normal ways," that is, as a heterosexual male in love with a heterosexual female. The only people who seemed to accept her for who she was were "the unsophisticated people in the environment" [people like her aunts and the ever-loyal Mac] who "accept me pretty much as one of nature's experiments; a girl who should have been a boy, and react to me as if I were a boy." Doctors at the Rogers hospital proved no more willing to cooperate in Murray's efforts to become the man she knew herself to be than those elsewhere. When they released her in mid-March, she had nothing to show for her stay beyond a medical bill for $80, which she could not pay. On top of everything else, Aunt Pauline insisted she come home for Easter.[10]

Bus Trouble

Short on funds at Christmas, Murray had sent Jimmy and Joshua home alone. She could not fail to visit at Easter. She warned her aunt, however, that this time she would travel with Mac rather than her nephews, whom she had given up trying to parent. Murray confessed that she had some "misgivings" about taking along her "peppery, self-assertive" roommate, who found American blacks altogether too timid in the defense of their rights. Aunt Pauline strongly advised against bringing her friend, but Murray was grateful for Mac's loyal support through her most recent crisis and believed that, with a little planning, she could forestall any problems. She arranged to travel with Mac by Greyhound Bus as far as Washington, where they would visit briefly with her older sister, Mildred. Having followed their mother into nursing, Mildred had risen to the position of head nurse at Freedman's Hospital and had been able to purchase a car. Murray hoped to borrow it for the final leg of the trip into Jim Crow Virginia and North Carolina. Unfortunately, Mildred's car was being repaired, and Murray found herself stranded and out of money. Frantically, she wired home, "MAC AND I WITH MILDRED. NO MONEY TO CONTINUE TRIP." Determined that Pauli should make it home for Easter, Aunt Pauline sent a money order the next morning. Left with no alternative, Murray and Mac boarded a Greyhound Bus on March 23, Easter Eve, and headed south.[11]

According to the bus schedule, the trip to Durham would take eight hours, with a stopover and change of bus in Richmond. The initial Greyhound coach was large and comfortable, but the bus to which they were scheduled to transfer in Richmond proved too small to accommodate all the passengers that busy holiday weekend. Murray and Mac found themselves among those forced to transfer to an "old-style, relief" bus. Their suitcase remained on the regular motor coach leaving them with only their carry-on items. Murray lugged her black typewriter, briefcase, and books (tied with a luggage strap) onto the relief bus. Mac carried her gray cardboard hatbox. The bus driver promised that they would be able to change back to the regular bus later in the trip, as soon as space freed up.[12]

Well aware of the rigidly enforced southern rule that colored passengers board buses from the back to the front, Murray led Mac to the only free seats, a bench uncomfortably positioned over the right-rear wheel. In addition to the half-dozen or so blacks seated near them, there were about a dozen white passengers scattered throughout the front, including two children seated just ahead of them, their mother, and several college-aged students, apparently on their way back to school from their spring vacation.[13]

When the relief bus was finally loaded, at about 5:30 PM, the driver, whose nameplate identified him as Frank W. Morris, took off at top speed, hoping to catch up with the regular bus. As he careened around curves, Mac developed a sharp, stabbing pain in her side. Seeing two free seats at the front of the bus, she suggested moving to them. Murray said no, citing the segregation law. Mac persisted. Determined to avoid arrest, Murray tried a safer solution. Making her way to the driver's side, she asked that he move the white children, seated just ahead of them, forward to the empty seats behind him, so that she and Mac could take the seats they vacated. The driver, Murray later noted, "refused curtly, and taking his arm, he pushed [her] backward." Returning to her seat, Murray told Mac that she would have "to endure the discomfort until they reached Petersburg."[14]

When they arrived at the Petersburg bus terminal, several white people got off, and all the white passengers moved forward to fill the empty seats, leaving seats ahead of Murray and Mac free. More than a dozen black passengers pressed against the front door, ready to board, and Murray calculated that they would easily fill the back of the bus. While Morris busied himself with their luggage and tickets, she and Mac moved forward, first to the next seat, but finding that seat broken, to the one ahead of that, a position that was still behind the white passengers.[15]

Looking up, the driver saw them and yelled loudly, "YOU'LL HAVE TO MOVE BACK." They explained that the seat behind them was broken, but Morris threatened "arrest under the segregation laws," if they failed to follow his order. Mindful that they were in Petersburg, Virginia, where her Grandfather Fitzgerald had fought, defending the Union, Murray stiffened. She replied that she knew the law and that they were "entirely within their rights" under the Fourteenth Amendment of the United States Constitution. They had boarded from the back of the bus, as required, and had moved forward only as dictated by the minimally accepted standards of health and comfort that were owed by the bus to all passengers. Most important, they had not breached the line separating whites and blacks. To Murray's legal argument, Mac added a bitter condemnation of Morris for treating her inhumanely simply because she happened to have brown skin. Furious, Morris stormed off the bus.[16]

Satyagraha

While Murray and Mac waited for Morris to return, they considered their options. Since the early 1920s, American civil rights advocates had been discussing the possible use of Mahatma Gandhi's technique of Satyagraha, nonviolent resistance to injustice, combined with goodwill in all communication. Some leaders feared that American blacks could not achieve the level of discipline of the Indians, whose cultural traditions and long training enabled them to endure the punishing and sometimes lethal blows of police clubs without striking back, but Murray thought otherwise. Having recently read *War without Violence: A Study of Gandhi's Method and Its Accomplishments,* by Columbia graduate student Krishnalal Shridharani, she believed that the technique, inspired in part by Henry David Thoreau's principle of civil disobedience, deserved a try.[17]

Satyagraha offered a strategy that could inspire blacks to stand up for their right at least to equal treatment under the hated segregation statutes, while shaming whites into recognizing the injustice of Jim Crow itself. For all its appeal, it was not something Murray wanted to try on Easter Eve, not with Aunt Pauline expecting her, not without further discussion and planning. Unfortunately, it was beginning to look as though she would have no choice. At least Mac seemed to understand the nonviolent resistance part. If only she could be trusted with the good-will-in-communication dimension of the Indian technique.[18]

Gone for about forty-five minutes, Morris found two police officers, Andrews and McGhee, and demanded that they arrest Murray and McBean. The officers responded that they could not do so without a warrant from Greyhound. Morris

called his superiors in Raleigh, who debated what to do. As soon as he had authorization, Morris swore out warrants and returned to the bus with the policemen.
Seeing the armed officers, Mac exploded. They could not scare her with their
"shiny bullets," she cried. She was ill and would not ride over a wheel or in a broken seat. Officer Andrews, acknowledging the problem, asked Morris to fix the
broken seat, which, after examining it for the first time and finding that it needed
only a simple adjustment, he did. Hoping to avoid an arrest, Andrews asked
Murray and McBean to compromise, not to return to the seat over the wheel,
but to take the now repaired seat behind them. They agreed. But Mac was not
finished. According to Murray, she "suggested to the driver that he apologize to
her for the discourteous way in which he had handled the entire situation." Such
a demand, from a black woman to a white man in 1940 in Virginia was astonishing, but Murray recorded that Morris's only response was "something about, 'he
wanted everybody to have a square deal.' " Relieved, Murray concluded that the
incident was behind them.[19]

Before starting up the bus to leave, however, Morris passed out traffic accident " 'report' cards" to all the white passengers. Indignant that Morris was so
flagrantly "discriminating against the Negro passengers," Murray asked that
the cards be distributed to everyone. Outraged, Morris left the bus again and
returned with the police officers, who arrested them on charges of "disorderly
conduct and creating a disturbance."[20]

Murray collected her things and left the bus, but Mac, now hysterical over the
confrontation, fainted into the arms of a couple seated to the left. The police carried her out and loaded her into the police wagon, leaving her belongings scattered
over the floor of the bus. A black passenger, Lee McLofton, who was on his way to
Durham, gathered them up and carried them out to the patrol wagon. He agreed
to let Aunt Pauline know what had happened. Before Murray joined Mac in the
police wagon, another man touched her arm. He introduced himself as Mr. E. C.
Davis of the Petersburg NAACP, took their names, and promised to get help. The
police took Murray and Mac to a nearby hospital, where, Murray later reported,
they received sympathetic treatment before being released to the city jail.[21]

As upset as she was, Murray recognized that their experience could have
been much worse. Virginia continued to strictly enforce its segregation code,
but a rise in negative publicity over police brutality in interracial incidents had
prompted the state to improve its police training. The Petersburg officers had
been polite throughout their encounter; moreover, they had prompted Morris
to call his supervisor before allowing him to fill out warrants for their arrest. In
the time opened by this restraint, Murray and Mac had ventured their first, awkward attempt at Satyagraha, and their efforts had enjoyed some success. After an
initial reluctance to get involved, white passengers had begun to debate the pros
and cons of the conflict. Some had voiced concern over Mac's illness. The black

riders had supported them. Murray and Mac had kept an interracial dialogue about equal rights going for well over an hour.[22]

Jail, No Bail

For all Murray and Mac's brave talk about defending their rights, they were in no way prepared for the reality of the segregated, southern jail to which they were taken from the hospital. Since they had little money, they refused to post bail, which, though not their preference, at least allowed them to be consistent with the Satyagraha principle that protestors should accept jail once arrested. For Murray and Mac the experience was deeply humiliating. The night jailor took Murray's typewriter, briefcase, and books, and Mac's hatbox. Fortunately, Murray had had the presence of mind to tuck a flashlight, pencils, and paper in her raincoat, which she was allowed to keep. Murray's request to contact family was denied, and when she protested the deputy shouted, "Don't you come in here trying to boss me. We're the boss now, an' if you don't shet up I'll set your ass in the dungeon. Time them rats down there get through with you, you'll wish you'd keep your mouf shet!"[23]

Led down a corridor lined with black male prisoners "lying on pallets" due to overcrowding, they were shut into a filthy, narrow cell, fifteen feet wide and thirty feet long, behind a heavy door. Four bunk beds, with bug-eaten straw mattresses, were pushed against its walls. There were no sheets or pillows, only one "grease-caked blanket" for each prisoner. One foul-smelling toilet stood at the end of the room, next to a rust-covered sink. Three other black women were already there, two charged with soliciting, the third with breaking a bottle over her boyfriend's head. They took little notice of the newcomers, busy as they were building a small fire from saved scraps of paper to ward off the water bugs that had invaded through the cracks in the walls. Hungry and tired, Murray and Mac would have loved to sleep, but the other prisoners warned them of bed bugs, so they did not dare. Breakfast arrived Easter morning: cold pancakes and molasses, accompanied by coffee served from a pail into tin cups. Dinner came at 3:00 PM, "tough hunks of half-cooked rooster, cold mashed potatoes, stewed apples and dumplings." Murray asked "for a towel, a pillow and a pillowcase," only to learn that "towels are given out only at a Federal prison." She inquired rhetorically about "the accommodations for white prisoners" and, confirming her expectations, learned that "these prisoners have cleaner quarters and more comforts."[24]

Spying a list of "Rules for Prisoners," which included the order that "Each prisoner shall keep his person, clothing and cell equipment clean," Murray had an idea. They would use Satyagraha to improve their conditions. She wrote a letter indicating their desire to follow the rules and respectfully requesting the materials necessary to do so: a sheet and towel for each of them, and a bar of soap to share.[25]

Both the female and the male prisoners viewed the two interlopers with hostility tinged with amusement. Bantering back and forth among themselves in an openly sexual way, they left Mac and Murray feeling increasingly ill at ease. But as the two protestors tried to explain why they were there and the importance they attached to fighting against racial discrimination on behalf of everyone, the other women began to talk to them in a friendlier way, and the men slipped notes under the door. One read, "Thanks for your advise [sic]" and another from a man who had been on his way from New York to Florida when he was arrested for something he said he had not done: "Dear friend, Wish it is some way you can help me. . . . Maybe some day I can return the favor." And a male prisoner wrote that he was from Durham and believed he knew Pauline Dame. "I am very sorry that you got in here and hope that you get out."[26]

Unlike the other prisoners, Murray and Mac had powerful friends to contact in their hour of need. By Easter Sunday, the telegraph wires were humming and the phones ringing up and down the East Coast. Murray managed to get a telegram to Aunt Pauline the day after their arrest: "EASTER GREETINGS. ARRESTED PETERSBURG, WARRANT GREYHOUND BUS. DON'T WORRY. CONTACT WALTER WHITE." She also sent telegrams to Agnes Martocci and to her landlords at 35 Mt. Morris Park, Mr. and Mrs. Rufus Kirkpatrick, with the same request to notify the New York office of the NAACP.[27]

The first to respond was a local NAACP attorney, Robert H. Cooley Jr. of the Petersburg firm of Valentine and Cooley. After securing Murray and Mac's names at the patrol wagon, E. C. Davis had contacted the head of the NAACP in Petersburg, who had alerted Cooley. Davis had also found Mildred's phone number in Washington and had informed her of Murray and Mac's plight. Mildred, in turn, had contacted Charles Houston, who had also spoken with Cooley. The Petersburg attorney met with Murray and Mac in the jail on Easter Sunday and offered to represent them. They gratefully agreed after Cooley explained that if they won their case they could bring a claim against Greyhound and if they recovered any money Cooley could be paid from that. On the basis of his interview, Cooley sent a letter to Houston detailing the basic facts and the charge of "disorderly conduct and creating a disturbance." The "Ladies DO NOT want bail," he emphasized. The trial was scheduled for Tuesday morning, 9:00AM.[28]

Sometime on Monday, lawyers for Greyhound telephoned Cooley to discuss the case. As Cooley later told Murray, they frankly admitted that they were "embarrassed" to have to litigate the matter. For them, the timing could not have been worse. The heads of the Greyhound Bus Corporation and its subsidiaries across the country were all in Washington, DC, that day to celebrate the opening of Greyhound's newest terminal. The last thing they needed was a dispute between one of their bus drivers and two female passengers, represented by an NAACP attorney. [29]

For years Greyhound had sought to persuade the NAACP to charter its buses for their annual conventions, but the civil rights group had steadily refused on the ground that the company discriminated against black riders. Since the early 1930s conditions for black riders had improved in the North, but the company still faced bitter complaints of mistreatment in the South. Greyhound's insistence that its hands were tied where state laws dictated policies did nothing to quell complaints. Being forced to ride over a rear wheel was a particular sore point for passengers, according to the newspaper stories. New buses had helped to overcome that problem, but as the bus to Petersburg demonstrated, there were not enough new buses on busy weekends to accommodate all passengers.[30]

Cooley told the Greyhound attorneys that his clients had not intended to violate the Virginia segregation laws, although they thought the laws unjust. They had merely objected to the bus driver's order to move to the back of a bus where the only available seats were either broken or over the wheel. Cooley wanted to clarify what the law required, but he could not do so as long as Virginia persisted in its longtime policy of simply charging protesters with creating a disturbance. Given the wide latitude that courts accorded states in the exercise of their police power, the state almost always won. Cooley asked Greyhound to amend the warrants to include a charge that the defendants had violated Virginia's segregation laws in refusing an order to fill all seats from the rear of the bus. Hopeful of improving relations with the NAACP, the Greyhound lawyers consented.[31]

By Monday, further encouragement arrived for Murray and Mac. Aunt Pauline wired, "HOPE YOU OK DID AS REQUESTED WIRE ME YOUR NEEDS." Dave Clendenin, for whom Murray had recently worked at the Workers Defense League (WDL) telegraphed that he had asked R. A. Thompson in Petersburg to help and that Roy Wilkins was following up with the national NAACP. Mildred telegraphed Eleanor Roosevelt, who urged the governor of Virginia to investigate. Mac and Murray were two prisoners who would not have to face a judge alone.[32]

Police Court

Tuesday morning, Murray scribbled in her notes, "13 prisoners, black and white, ride together in the station wagon to the city court house." The irony that her trip to court to challenge Jim Crow took place in an integrated car did not escape her. Apparently, if one fell far enough down the social ladder to end up in a southern city jail, economy took precedence over the segregation laws. As they entered the courtroom, Murray could see that the WDL and the NAACP had spread the word. More than 200 spectators, half white and half black, packed the room. Hearing the charges read, Murray noticed with satisfaction that a complaint that she and Mac had violated the state's segregation laws had been added to the original "disorderly conduct and disturbing the peace" charges.[33]

It had been agreed that Murray would testify; Mac would not. Murray told Judge Clemens what had happened and then, under cross-examination, refused to accept the prosecutor's charge that she and Mac had disturbed the peace. Instead, as she later wrote of her use of Satyagraha in the courtroom, "I constantly laid stress on the real crux of the dispute—our refusal to stand by and see open discrimination of Negro passengers without protesting."[34]

For his part, Cooley demonstrated that the Virginia Motor Vehicles Codes relating to "Segregation of Races on Motor Vehicles," included no language stating that black passengers must fill up buses from the rear. Bus companies may have adopted this policy for their own convenience in southern states, but at least in Virginia that policy did not have the sanction of law. Even if the court were to find that the bus driver had acted properly, Cooley insisted, the implementation of the segregation law in this instance did not live up to the constitutional requirement, well settled since *Plessy v. Ferguson* (1896), that any business engaged in public transportation provide "equal facilities for both races." The most uncomfortable seats must not be reserved for blacks.[35]

Cooley persuaded Judge Clemens that the Virginia statutes did not require that blacks board buses from the rear, but to Murray's dismay, the judge dismissed the charge rather than finding the defendants not guilty of it. Her one hope of advancing civil rights on the legal front that day thereby vanished. Worse, Judge Clemens found the defendants guilty of the original charge of disorderly conduct and creating a disturbance. He fined them each $5.00 and costs. Cooley made a motion for a retrial.[36]

That afternoon Murray and Mac caught the 2:00 PM bus from Petersburg to Durham only to find that their bus driver was, once again, Frank Morris. This time, however, Morris was "the epitome of courtesy." The arrival of two Greyhound guards, who observed Morris closely for the entire trip, guaranteed his good behavior. Although Murray noted that the guards were also watching them, she regarded the guards' presence as "the first step in a change of policy on the part of the Greyhound Lines toward Negro patrons."[37]

At home in Durham, the weary travelers could finally rest. "Spring is at its best here—thank God for it," Murray wrote Candace (Pan) Stone, a friend from the WDL and the great niece of the nineteenth-century women's rights leader Lucy Stone. "Nature has outdone herself to help us back to health and resiliency." They soon realized that rest was all that they felt emotionally ready for. Murray, worried about the debt still owed to the Rogers hospital, the fines and court fees that would be due if they lost their second trial, and the ongoing cost of food and shelter, tried to find ways to make money. As she wrote to Dave Clendenin of the WDL, she did not feel able to work more than part-time, but she and Mac had to each earn at least $8 a week to survive. "Let me know if you or Morris [Milgram, Dave Clendenin's assistant] can think of any . . . kind of small income for which we could render value received," she pleaded. Milgram suggested that she try to find a job with the Socialist Party, which needed workers for the Norman Thomas presidential campaign. Murray felt an affinity with the Socialists but she had grown weary of the sectarian battles on the Left. She would rather devote her energies to a Gandhi-type movement on behalf of civil rights. But when her old friend and mentor Lewis Austin of the *Carolina Times* encouraged her to move home to Durham to lead such a campaign, she concluded that she did not have the psychic strength to live permanently in the South and lead a movement. Her first experience of arrest and jail had proved too disturbing for her to become a professional organizer.[38]

When Murray felt troubled, she often found solace in writing, and to writing she now turned. She sent off a piece on prison conditions in the Petersburg City Jail to the *Nation,* which declined to publish it. Further efforts stalled when she found that she just didn't have the energy to finish any of the articles she started. The one form of writing she managed was correspondence, which alone produced income in the form of gifts from concerned friends.[39]

The only published articles to come out of Durham while Murray was home were written by others. Lewis Austin wrote a long account of the bus episode in the *Carolina Times* in which he stressed the protest as part of broader problem of unequal accommodations for blacks in America. Austin saw Murray and Mac as pioneers in a new movement, one in which leaders were willing to go to jail. "Perhaps Miss Murray and Miss McBean are the beginning of a new type of leadership for the race—a leadership that will not cringe and crawl on its belly merely because it happens to be faced with prison bars in its fight for the right," Austin wrote hopefully. Ted Poston happened to be in town to cover a labor dispute in the tobacco industry, and he wrote a sympathetic article for the *Pittsburgh Courier.* His was the only account to publicize the critical fact that "the state of Virginia's segregation law does not provide that Negroes must fill up buses from the rear."[40]

Murray began to recover her equilibrium with the help of her friends. Attorney Cooley assured her that her case had generated wide support among both blacks and whites and that the national office of the NAACP was taking an interest. Murray felt let down by only one letter, which Mildred forwarded to her from Eleanor Roosevelt's secretary, Malvina Thompson. The governor of Virginia had indeed looked into Murray's arrest, but according to Thompson, he had replied, "Miss Murray was unwise not to comply with the law." To this

Thompson added Eleanor Roosevelt's advice, "As long as these laws exist, it does no one much good to violate them." Murray felt thoroughly deflated. She had broken no law and she found the first lady's reliance on the word of the governor of Virginia infuriating. Eleanor Roosevelt seemed not to understand what blacks were up against.[41]

Appeal in Hustings Court

On Monday, April 29, Murray and Mac were tried once again, this time in Petersburg's Hustings Court. To their dismay, Judge R. T. Wilson upheld Judge Clemens's dismissal of the charge of violation of segregation statutes and like Clemens found the defendants guilty of "creating a disturbance." In further punishment, he raised the fine to $10 each, plus the accumulated costs. Lincoln "Link" Johnson of the NAACP National Legal Counsel rushed from Washington to help the local lawyers. Arriving too late for the brief trial, he asked Judge Wilson to hold a special hearing to reconsider his verdict. The judge did so that afternoon and granted each side until May 8 to file briefs on the interpretation of "disorderly conduct" as it relates to the common law. A rehearing was scheduled for Friday, May 10. Following the ruling, the lawyers invited Murray and Mac to come to Washington to confer with the NAACP legal team on their brief.[42]

In Washington, Murray and Mac had the thrill of meeting with Thurgood Marshall, Link Johnson, Judge William H. Hastie, and Dr. Leon A. Ransom, the foremost civil rights attorneys of the time. Listening to them debate how best to challenge the state of Virginia, Murray felt part of a larger war to overthrow all segregation law. Since the judge in this case had dismissed the segregation charge, they could not challenge segregation directly. Johnson therefore proposed to argue, and the rest agreed, that raising one's voice in defense of one's civil rights does not constitute "disorderly conduct."[43]

On Friday, May 10, Murray and Mac returned to Petersburg Hustings Court for Judge Wilson's decision. The judge rushed into his courtroom a minute late, stepped up to his bench and, without looking at either Murray or McBean, declared, "About these two girls—there's nothing in this brief to make me change my mind. I still fine them $10.00 and costs." That added up to $21.70 each. The following Tuesday, Judge Hastie, speaking for the NAACP defense team, declined to take an appeal. He explained that the chance of success was too slight to justify the $300 the appeal would cost. Unable to pay the fine of $43.40, Murray and Mac returned to jail until friends at the WDL were able to borrow the sum and wire it to them.[44]

Freed once more, Murray wrote despondently to Aunt Pauline that the trial had been a "complete loss for us." Aunt Pauline was none too sympathetic. "Keep out of these radical things," she admonished Pauli. "Had you come home alone, I do not believe you would have had that trouble but you would not take my advice. You have placed yourself in the limelight all over the country. It is passed for the present and cannot now be remedied, but you can be careful as you go on." Getting that grievance off her chest, Aunt Pauline softened a little. "I'm very sorry you've had to suffer so much, but such is life. . . . I do hope you can find something to your liking soon and not work too hard."[45]

Although the case was over, Murray continued to wonder why Hastie, apparently ready to take the case all the way to the US Supreme Court, had in the end changed his mind. Yes, $300 was a stiff price to pay for an uncertain outcome on a question of whether speaking loudly in defense of civil rights constituted creating a disturbance, but attorneys Cooley and Stone had been eager to press forward, even after Judge Wilson's ruling. She worried that there might be more to Hastie's decision than fear of eventual defeat.[46]

An Eyewitness Account

There was, in fact, another problem. An eyewitness account of the bus incident in Petersburg had just appeared in the May issue of *Opportunity,* and it differed sharply from the report Murray had given. Seeing the article, "Color Trouble," in the magazine that Murray had sold and in which she would have loved to publish her own story, was a deeply upsetting experience. Although she had not realized it at the time, one of the young whites on the bus in Petersburg was a first-year graduate student in sociology at UNC, Harold Garfinkel. An alumnus of the State College of New Jersey (later Rutgers), Garfinkel, a Jew, had spent a year at a Quaker-led community project in Georgia before enrolling in the sociology program at UNC.[47]

Garfinkel framed his account as a conflict of cultural perspectives. He presented the confrontation from the southern, white, male, working-class point of view of the bus driver. But he added a telling introductory epigram: "It Can't Happen Here," the title of Sinclair Lewis's 1937 novel about a fascist-populist take over of the US government. With that choice, he tipped his hand as a northerner on the lookout for manifestations of fascism, which he found in Petersburg, in the form of a man, for whom "common sense" dictated a set of presuppositions that Mac and Murray had challenged.[48]

Garfinkel's and Murray's accounts shared some basic facts, but the two versions diverged in style, perspective, and much of their content. Murray's notes and letters provided a bare bones report, with only a few, brief direct quotations. Garfinkel's story was an elaborately constructed tale with extended and, Murray later charged, largely fabricated dialogue. Evidence that the story was closer to fiction than to fact-checked reportage came from Garfinkel's decision the following year to publish it again as a short story in Edward J. O'Brien's *The Best American Short Stories of 1941*.[49]

In Garfinkel's telling, Murray barely figured. The main actor was Mac, a "slender, light colored, but not very good looking" young woman, who was "about 24 years old, high spirited, loud and infectious in her laughter." Garfinkel's next observation must have startled Murray. "The young man with her," Garfinkel noted "was lighter than she, of slight build, thin shoulders, flat chest, sensitive, self-conscious in voice and manner. He carried with him a pile of books which were stacked laterally in high school fashion."[50]

It had happened again. Murray, dressed in her preferred pants, her short hair slicked back with pomade, had been taken for an adolescent male, a reaction that always produced conflicting emotions. She felt pleased to be seen for what she felt deep down she really was, but uncomfortable, even fearful, to be identified so publicly as someone society had never allowed her to be. Murray also must have felt angry, because, apart from Garfinkel's description of her appearance and apparent gender, he ignored almost completely her role in the drama. In his telling, Murray did not open her mouth until the arrival of the police, an hour into the standoff.[51]

When Officer Andrews arrived, in Garfinkel's telling, he asked what the problem was, to which the "young man" responded, "Nothing's wrong officer. Nothing at all is wrong. We are simply sitting in these seats we paid to ride in. My friend here is ill. She can't ride over the wheel, and besides the seat back there is broken.'" Garfinkel found Murray's voice "just a bit too loud and too clear." The young sociologist sensed that something about this fellow was off. Given his age, his race, and the circumstances, he should have assumed a quiet, obsequious demeanor, but, instead, he spoke loudly, clearly, in a carefully worded way. Garfinkel did not see Murray as she saw herself: a mature "fellow," speaking with authority, trying to protect a distraught female companion; rather, Garfinkel observed "an arrogant adolescent repeating by rote." Trying, tentatively, to put Satyagraha into practice, Murray might have succeeded better had she dressed and performed the role of a middle-class professional woman. As a teenage male, she failed, not only with Garfinkel but also, by his report, with others on the bus. "The whites were not attracted to him," Garfinkel noted, "because he was neither white nor black, spoke like neither, and threatened to upset a good fight." Perhaps Murray made the whites feel uncomfortable not so much because of her indeterminate race and speech, but rather because her masculine performance was not entirely convincing. "Why doesn't that guy shut up and let her do the talking?" Garfinkel had one of the white passengers say. And then, from Officer Andrews: "Aw be quiet." To this affront, the "arrogant adolescent," according to Garfinkel, responded by "gaping up insolently, conspicuously, into the officer's face," a tactic which the "older man rendered . . . ineffective by choosing to ignore it." Murray could only have felt humiliated and frightened by such an account.[52]

In Garfinkel's telling, Mac was the more compelling, the more recognizable figure of protest: "You can't scare us," he recorded her as shouting. "We're not animals. We're not dirt. Just because we're colored you think you can push us around like sacks of meal! I'm not afraid of you, do you hear me? You don't frighten me one bit, not one tiny bit, with your gold-plated badge and your shiny bullets. . . . Coming in here to bulldoze me with your bullets!'" Deference toward middle-class women was a common-sense presupposition of Mac's West Indian, predominantly black culture.[53]

"Here was a situation far more complicated than the cop had figured on," and Garfinkel suspected that "the bus driver was due to catch hell for this." Put on the defensive, the driver had defaulted to the outmoded idea that he could treat all blacks the same way—as inferiors. Officer Andrews had a more up-to-date understanding, one that he thought should have guided Morris: "This girl was educated and you had to handle them different," Garfinkel guessed Andrews was telling himself. "'Why didn't you tell me?' he complained to the driver as he swung out of the doorway."[54]

To his seatmate, a Pennsylvania high school senior on his way to Duke to inquire about a football scholarship, Garfinkel explained, "He can't touch her because she's right and he knows it. According to plain common sense she's right, and don't think he wouldn't be glad to get out of the whole damn thing. What he's trying to figure out is how he can get through with her and still be able to say to his boss or her lawyers if she brings it to court, that he was acting in the name of common sense and the public trust." Garfinkel believed that the two cultures had converged enough in relevant presuppositions for the main actors to come to an agreement. Bus drivers could enforce segregation, but they must provide equal accommodations to all riders. If he could do that, the confrontation would end. As in Murray's account, so too in Garfinkel's, the driver sought accommodation by following the police officer's advice to fix the broken seat. No longer demanding that the protesters move back to their original seat over the wheel, he would be satisfied if they could compromise on their moving back just one row, to the now-repaired seat. Equal accommodations provided, crisis resolved.[55]

But there was a further problem, one not of rights but of custom. Mac "was saying things too bluntly," Garfinkel judged. "Who ever speaks these things out? Mention them to your priest; argue about them in class; a joke or two perhaps; but never, *never* shout. There are still some common decencies which white persons expect the educated Negro to observe."[56]

Shouting was the least of it. No sooner had Morris repaired the broken seat than the "colored girl" did what to Garfinkel was unthinkable. She announced to Morris, "I think that as a gentleman you owe me an apology." " 'Apologize, apologize for what?' " Morris sputtered. Garfinkel reported that his "words were thick with effort." "For the way you spoke to me," Garfinkel recorded Mac as saying. Garfinkel described a shocked reaction throughout the bus. The driver "blind with rage . . . was out of the bus in three clattering leaps." Calling Mac a "black fool," he returned moments later with the police officers, who arrested both protestors. Garfinkel had trouble hearing the names and addresses that Murray and Mac gave for the arrest warrants. He heard "Alice," not Adeline, but he got "McBean," which Mac slowly spelled out. Murray's name was another matter. Somehow he heard "Oliver Fleming." He wrote that they lived at different addresses, neither of them 35 Mt. Morris West. It is possible that, in a moment of panic the two women gave false names and addresses, but there is no other evidence that they did. It seems more likely that Garfinkel misheard part of the information and made up the rest.[57]

With the arrests made, Morris prepared to leave Petersburg, but first he collected the accident cards he had distributed earlier from the white passengers. One brought a startled reaction. Obviously submitted by Garfinkel, it read, "Nonsense . . . Bone-head playing all around." In the graduate student's view, everyone had behaved badly. The driver should have listened to the young black woman's complaints about the seats and made the necessary repairs in the first place. He should not have issued accident forms, for there had been no accident. The police should not have issued warrants, for no laws had been broken. The young black woman should not have demanded an apology from the driver, thereby inflaming an already tense situation. Her companion should have remained silent, for he added nothing. All the actors violated basic rules of common sense, based in part on class differences, something that many of Garfinkel's professors outside the sociology department at UNC denied existed in the South but for which he had, here, irrefutable evidence.[58]

Garfinkel concluded his story by quoting himself, in conversation with some pretty girls seated behind him on the bus, "Well, there you have it," he pontificated. "The next time someone speaks to you about our 'classless society,' you tell them about what you saw and ask them for an interpretation." They had all witnessed two tales of common sense, one of a middle-class person who refused to be ordered around by a working-class person, and another of a white person, who refused to be defied by a colored person. A shared common sense required an understanding of and eventual resolution of both class and racial differences in America. Garfinkel said nothing about the role that gender had played in the drama.[59]

Nor did Murray say anything of gender. She always claimed that she and Mac were arrested as a direct result of Murray's legal charge of discrimination, based on the driver's distribution of witness cards to whites only. Garfinkel did not even mention Murray's complaint in his account. He may not have heard it, preoccupied as he was by completing his own card; or, having heard the complaint, he may have dismissed it as unimportant. Largely barred from the voter rolls, blacks rarely served on juries or testified in court in the South when a white person was charged. What possible good could come of black passengers completing the cards?

In Murray's view, however, the Fourteenth Amendment's protection meant, at the most fundamental level, procedural due process. How could justice be guaranteed if blacks were not represented in the judicial process, at the very least as witnesses to events that concerned civil rights? She also wanted the record to reflect that she and Mac were challenging clear racial discrimination, not just bad manners, and doing so in a way that could not possibly be construed as creating a disturbance.

If William Hastie had been willing to gamble on taking a "disorderly conduct" case to the Supreme Court, reading Garfinkel's article could well have changed his mind. Winning a landmark case was never easy. Why risk taking on a case with the complicating factors described by Garfinkel: one defendant who was a cross dresser and another whose defiance of official authority was so far outside the accepted norms as to be reasonably characterized as "disturbing the peace."

Aftermath

In the end, William Hastie, Thurgood Marshall, and their colleagues at the NAACP decided to wait for a case in which they could attack segregation directly. Another four years would pass before they got their chance, in a case involving, once again, transit through Virginia on a Greyhound bus. Irene Morgan, recovering from a miscarriage and going home to see her doctor, boarded a Greyhound bus in Gloucester, Virginia, bound for Baltimore, Maryland, in July 1944. She took a seat in the black section. Asked by the bus driver to surrender her seat to a white person, she refused. When a police officer tried to arrest her, she tore up the warrant, kicked him in the groin, and struggled against his attempts to remove her from the bus. Charged with resisting arrest and violating Virginia segregation law, she pled guilty to the first but fought the second. Convicted, she appealed. William Hastie and Thurgood Marshall took the case, *Morgan v. Virginia*, to the Supreme Court with the argument not used since Reconstruction: that Virginia state law imposed an "undue burden" on interstate commerce. In 1946 they won.[60]

Despite this historic victory, years would pass before the NAACP lawyers' success had much practical consequence. Following the decision in *Morgan v. Virginia*, Murray, together with other young civil rights activists, including

Bayard Rustin, planned a Journey of Reconciliation, modeled on Gandhi's principles, in which equal numbers of blacks and whites would travel together on
interstate buses. Some blacks would sit in front; some whites would sit in the
back; and other blacks and whites would sit side by side. Murray wanted women
to participate alongside men, but Rustin and the other male organizers vetoed
the idea as too dangerous. Challenging race taboos was one thing. Challenging
cross-race sex taboos could get them all killed. The protesters embarked on journeys in the Upper South, where they anticipated less violence than they would
encounter deeper in the Old Confederacy. Like Murray and Mac, they suffered
abuse and arrest, without changing anything. State officials simply refused to
enforce the Court's decision, and segregation, mandated by state statute and
supported through custom, persisted. As with her effort to win admission to
UNC, so too with her experimental use of Satyagraha in Petersburg, Virginia,
Murray failed. She served as a model to others, however, as her vision of civil
disobedience, supported by legal action, gained widespread acceptance within
the American civil rights movement.[61]

5

A Death Sentence Leads
to Law School

The Poll Tax Jury

Unemployed once again, Murray received an invitation to serve on the Executive Board of the Workers Defense League in June 1940. The position carried no salary, but she accepted out of gratitude to all the friends in the organization who had stood by her during her bus ordeal. To her surprise and relief, this position quickly led to paying work. The WDL, founded in 1936 by A. Philip Randolph and Norman Thomas, provided legal assistance for workers in need, including sharecroppers. One of the cases to come before the executive board in August 1940 was that of a black sharecropper, Virginia-born Odell Waller. On July 15, 1940, Waller had shot his white employer, Oscar Davis, when Davis refused to give him his quarter share of their wheat crop. Waller had fled the state but had been picked up in Columbus, Ohio, on July 24. He was extradited to Virginia to stand trial on a charge of premeditated murder, for Davis had subsequently died. If convicted, Waller would face death in the electric chair.[1]

To defend a black sharecropper accused of murdering his white employer was about as difficult a challenge as the WDL could take on. Waller claimed to have shot in self-defense, but on the basis of early reports, the director of the WDL, Dave Clendenin, feared that he was probably guilty as charged. Murray, new to the executive committee, said nothing when Clendenin presented the case for discussion, but her Petersburg experience made her sympathetic to any black person caught in the grip of the southern judicial system. She approved the committee's decision to finance Waller's defense. By intervening in this case, the WDL might not only save a man's life, but it could also expose the nation to the ways in which southern politics had come to distort both southern justice and American democracy.[2]

The South's white Democratic male elite had regained power in the aftermath of Reconstruction. That elite maintained its dominance through a system of laws that severely restricted voting. One of the most effective laws imposed a poll tax that only a small portion of the adult population managed to pay. According to the state constitution of Virginia, only those who had paid the $1.50 annual poll tax for three consecutive years could register to vote; moreover, they had to have done so in February, months before any election. If a payment was ever missed, past taxes, plus the current tax must be paid, up to a total of $4.50. For poor white men, most black men, and virtually all women, the tax and rules governing its payment proved an insuperable barrier to voting. As a result, only 26 percent of the adult population in Virginia could vote, compared to 92 percent in neighboring West Virginia, which imposed no poll tax. In rural Pittsylvania County, where Waller was tried, only 10 percent of the adult population qualified.[3]

This narrowing of the field of potential voters gave a small group of southern Democrats extraordinary power not only in states like Virginia, but over the rest of the country. Because the South was a one-party region, congressmen and senators, once victorious in all-white, privately organized primaries, faced no more than token opposition in general elections. As a result, they could expect to hold onto their seats indefinitely. Because Congress ran on a seniority system, southern senators and congressman had come to chair most important committees. If southern committee chairmen did not like a proposed piece of legislation they either bottled it up in committee or rewrote it to suit their views.

One piece of legislation that survived southern Democratic scrutiny, the Agricultural Adjustment Act, could have helped sharecroppers like Odell Waller weather the economic storm of the Depression years, by granting him cash benefits in return for his agreement to limit the land he planted. But Oscar Davis, himself in debt and desperate for any economic advantage he could find, removed from production land that Odell Waller had been farming. Rather than share the government payment with Waller, he kept it all for himself. All that Waller had left was a little bit of land that could be planted in wheat. When the wheat harvest was over in 1940, Waller had the right to fifty-two bags, which constituted one-quarter share of the wheat harvest, but Davis denied him even that.[4]

Not only did the Solid South distort national politics and deny poor whites and blacks the same economic benefits being made available to other workers, but it also denied poor whites and especially blacks the right to a jury of their peers should they be charged with a crime. By custom, juries in Virginia, as in much of the South, were drawn from the voter registration rolls. Since the poll tax kept most blacks and poor whites from registering to vote, juries in the South were effectively poll tax juries, filled with white male landowners and businessmen.

The only local attorney available to represent Waller before such a jury was Thomas H. Stone, an attorney affiliated with the Revolutionary Workers League. The last thing the WDL wanted was an alliance with self-professed revolutionaries, who were likely to turn the case into a political football and destroy any chance Waller might have of a sympathetic hearing in Virginia. But there was no one else. Stone began by seeking to quash the indictment on the grounds that the grand jury had been selected exclusively from a list of poll tax payers. Unfortunately, Stone, though probably correct, offered no evidence to support his claim, and the judge denied his motion. Stone then challenged the inclusion on the trial jury of anyone who employed sharecroppers on the grounds that such a person could not be impartial in this case. The judge once again denied Stone's motion, and the final jury of twelve comprised eleven white farmers, six of whom employed sharecroppers, and a carpenter-contractor.[5]

Waller did not deny that he had shot Davis, but he consistently claimed that he had acted in self-defense. As he testified at trial, he had fired only after Davis, having refused to give him the wheat that was his due, reached into his pocket for what Waller thought was a gun. Unconvinced, the jury deliberated for only fifty-two minutes before returning a verdict of murder in the first degree, punishable by death in the electric chair. The WDL, hoping to challenge the poll tax in Virginia, resolved to finance an appeal to the state supreme court, but the appeal was made difficult by the fact that Stone had never asked the prospective jurors, or Waller for that matter, whether they had paid their poll tax.[6]

Special Field Secretary

To raise the $350 needed to pay for the appeal, the WDL executive committee asked Murray to go to Richmond, Virginia, to seek contributions from local organizations sympathetic to the plight of sharecroppers. Unwilling to return to the state that had incarcerated her, Murray initially declined, but every other possible candidate was tied up with other responsibilities. Faced with the fact that Waller would be electrocuted in a few weeks if nothing was done, she reluctantly agreed, with the understanding that she would not travel by bus.[7]

Two WDL friends, Candace (Pan) Stone and Gene Phillips, offered Stone's car, with Phillips as driving companion. The 1931 convertible coupe was not in peak condition. But the bigger problem was that Phillips (like Stone) was white. An interracial couple driving through Virginia would be taken for Communists. Murray decided to assume that risk.[8]

Arriving in Richmond, Murray realized that her best hope to raise the needed funds was at a noon meeting of black Baptist ministers. As Murray slipped into the room where the ministers were meeting to consider contributions to worthy causes, she felt ill with anxiety. Representatives of various groups appealed to the ministers for contributions. Chief among them was Howard Law School professor Leon Ransom, in town to help the NAACP prepare for trial in the case of a group of young black men accused of raping a white waitress. As Murray listened to the eloquent Ransom and watched ministers contribute their parishioners' funds to his cause, her additional appeal seemed hopeless. She moved to leave, but the Reverend Joseph T. Hill, who had offered her the chance to speak, called her to the platform and introduced her. Too terrified to talk, she asked Reverend Hill to read her prepared statement. By the time Hill had finished, she had collected herself and stood to face the audience. Her words poured out as she related her struggle to raise the $350 needed to appeal Waller's conviction. In almost a week of effort she had not been able to find anyone in the community who would "take responsibility" for helping this unknown, friendless sharecropper who faced death in the electric chair in a few weeks. When she finished, she dissolved in tears. As she struggled to regain control of herself, a minister who had been sitting to the side stood and said that he was Waller's spiritual adviser at the local prison. Saying that Waller was a good man, he laid down a dollar of his own money. The other ministers did the same.[9]

That day, Murray also had a chance conversation with Leon Ransom that was to change her life. She ran into him when Gene Phillips joined her for dinner in the black hotel where Murray was staying. Ransom, who was sitting with Thurgood Marshall at a nearby table, gave her a big smile and praised her for the appeal she had made before the ministers. To cover her embarrassment, Murray declared that she might as well become a lawyer, given her repeated brushes with the law in the past two years. Ransom did not laugh but instead urged her to come to Howard Law School. She said she could not afford to. He replied that he would find a work scholarship for her if she applied.[10]

The rest of the week was less encouraging. Turned away by one group after another, Murray and Phillips barely raised enough money to cover their trip. To top it off, they had to head back to New York in an icy rainstorm and heavy fog. The weather matched their mood. With the exception of the Baptist ministers and Leon Ransom, they had met only discouragement from both blacks and whites. As members of the WDL, they were committed to legal reform, but legal action would be doomed if it could not be funded. The country needed a civil rights movement, the kind that Murray, Phillips, and Stone had been discussing over the past year, one built on the principles of Satyagraha.[11]

They were not alone. J. Holmes Smith, a Methodist missionary to the Lal Bagh Ashram in Lucknow, India, from 1930 to 1940, had just decided to open an ashram in Harlem. The Methodist Board of Foreign Missions had recently recalled Smith from India for signing a manifesto critical of the British government—a violation of the pledge required of all missionaries since 1919 to uphold the duly elected government of the country to which they were assigned.[12]

Smith intended his new ashram to continue his and other missionaries' efforts to blend Christianity and Satyagraha in what they called Kristagraha.

Regarding racial injustice as America's most important social problem, Smith opened his ashram in Harlem to be in close contact with black leaders, as well as the staff of the Fellowship of Reconciliation (FOR), a Christian pacifist group, on whose national council he sat. Murray, who had known of the FOR at least since her time at the Brookwood Labor College, became a charter member of the Harlem Ashram, as well as a contributing member of the FOR, soon after her return from Virginia. Having left her nephews to their own devices, Murray moved with Mac into the cooperative's building at 2013 Fifth Avenue, just south of 125th Street.[13]

Smith organized the Harlem Ashram as a commune, with each person contributing what he or she could, a policy that greatly eased Murray and Mac's ongoing financial worries. Mostly white at first, the group also included two Indians—Haridas Muzumdar, who for many years had been introducing Americans to Gandhi through articles and speeches, and Krishnalal Shridharani, the author of *War without Violence,* the book that had inspired Murray and Mac's civil disobedience in Petersburg. Later recruits included black FOR members James Farmer, who lived there for varying times, and Bayard Rustin, who visited often.[14]

Murray's residence at the Ashram ended after only a few months. On January 4, 1941, she was waiting with other residents for the arrival of A. J. Muste, a founding member of the FOR and for many years the head of the faculty at the Brookwood Labor College. Murray lit a cigarette as she waited. Haridas Muzumdar touched her on the shoulder and said, "No Smoking." Enraged, but mindful of her Satyagraha-inspired vow to control her temper and not show resentment, Murray retreated to the upstairs bedroom she shared with Mac. There she smoked while denying herself the chance to see Muste. As she explained her actions in her diary the next day, "I agree with Haridas that we must have discipline, but it must be self-inspired, not dictated from without." She concluded by noting, "If the ashram is to become a convent or a monastery, then I have no place here." A decision at the WDL provided an excuse for a graceful exit.[15]

An American Joan of Arc

The national board of the WDL, far from viewing Murray and Phillips's Virginia trip as a failure, voted to send Murray on a national tour to raise money for Odell Waller's defense. Murray's first action was to invite Odell's foster mother Annie Waller to New York to tell her story to church and labor groups. Short, stooped, and uneducated, Mother Waller, as she came to be known, spoke with a dignity that captivated audiences and attracted the attention of the press. Murray leveraged that attention into a publicity campaign that produced a steady increase in contributions, enough to cover the costs of an appeal. Thomas Stone persuaded Governor Price to grant Odell a reprieve until March 14, 1941, and Murray arranged to meet the man she was fighting so hard to save. Visiting him with Mother Waller in prison, she let him know that he had many friends and that there was reason to hope that he would not die in the electric chair. The next step was a Midwest tour. In January 1941 Annie Waller and Murray found themselves on a Zephyr train to Minnesota. Both women marveled over the courteous treatment and clean accommodations on the train, so different from Jim Crow travel in the South.[16]

To her surprise, Murray found a letter waiting for her at their first stop in Minneapolis. It was from Vivian Odems, a young black woman, who ran the WDL office in New York. As she had in past jobs, Murray had been spending long hours in the office, stuffing envelopes late into the night. Vivian, like Murray a Hunter College graduate, stayed late to help and the two grew close. Murray began to confide in her. Like other friends before her, Vivian was put off by the idea that Murray believed herself to be a man and was seeking hormones so that her body would conform more closely to her self-image. The letter waiting for Murray in Minneapolis urged her to accept herself as a lesbian and not try to be something she was not. "Although few people are willing to accept this fact," Odems wrote, "there definitely are three classes of human beings, the true man, the true woman, and the homosexual. If you have tendencies to swerve toward the third class, then that is where you belong. Why try to change yourself? . . . I can only say that I would not have you if you feel this way." Odems married soon thereafter but remained a good friend.[17]

No doubt distraught by her inability, once again, to persuade a friend to accept her as a man, Murray threw herself into the tour. She spoke with Annie Waller to local branches of the NAACP, WDL, local churches, student groups, YWCA, teachers, and social workers, making eleven appearances in ten days and clearing $286. The success of the midwestern tour led to a more ambitious, six-week trip in April and May. Traveling together, once again, Murray and Mother Waller began in New York and then moved on to Boston, Pittsburgh, Cleveland, Detroit, Chicago, Milwaukee, Denver, and out to the West Coast. There they spent their final week in Los Angeles. Mother Waller appealed for her son. Murray appealed for all people, providing the broader context of the plight of sharecroppers in the South and the anti-democratic effect of the poll tax system. They spoke to small groups organized by the local branches of the WDL, NAACP, the Brotherhood of Sleeping Car Porters, and the International Ladies Garment Workers Union.[18]

They made a striking pair, these two daughters of the South, the sharecropper who appeared older than her years and the college-educated companion who looked younger than hers, both so obviously sincere. They captivated

Figure 5.1 Pauli Murray, circa 1940, when she toured the country, raising money for the legal defense of Odell Waller. Estate of Pauli Murray, Schlesinger Library, Radcliffe Institute, Harvard University.

Ted LeBerthon, a white columnist for the Los Angeles labor publication the *Daily News*. Like many other writers, LeBerthon was struck by Annie Waller's dignity, but he devoted most of his column to Murray, whom he described as "a slim, lissome and almost exquisitely pretty colored girl," who wore "a simple cotton dress which must have cost about $1 but was in excellent taste." LeBerthon judged Murray's speech "one of the best addresses I had heard anywhere in recent years." Her "marshaling of the facts, her obviously fair interpretation of them, her sense of historic sequence, her choice of the right word and the most honestly expressive phrase would have won the respect and alert attention of any body of churchmen or educators."[19]

The young woman who had dissolved in tears before a group of ministers in Richmond six months earlier had become a polished speaker. More, she had become a charismatic figure. "Frankly," LeBerthon declared, "I thought of Joan of Arc, and wondered if at some more fortuitous time she might not become something of a deliverer of her people from bondage, from long suffered ghastly indignities." Murray struck him as not just the spokesman for other blacks but "their emissary to the rest of us." She belonged in a huge auditorium, speaking over a national radio hookup, not where she was "talking to a shabby little crowd in the shallow, cheerless little hall."[20]

LeBerthon attributed the poor attendance to the widespread belief that only Communists were supposed to be interested in the lot of the black. Undaunted, the "brave and lovely colored girl, a graduate of Hunter College, spoke as if she addressed thoughtful thousands. She spoke of plain, painful facts clearly, without heat, without malice. There was not anger in her, only perhaps a quiet and humble sorrow before a mountainous task." For his white readership, LeBerthon stressed that "Slim Pauli Murray spoke, not as the champion of the Negro, but of all the oppressed. She spoke equally for the poor whites of the south." She spoke of the poll tax, the "worn out soil, the frightful diet, the vile housing, the diseases that make for lassitude and decay."[21]

In her most powerful image of the distorting effect of the poll tax, Murray drew her listeners' attention to the fact that their state of California cast 400,000 *more* votes in the 1940 presidential election than did the eight southern poll tax states combined. And yet, those California votes elected only two senators and twenty congressmen whereas the eight southern states elected sixteen senators and seventy-eight congressmen, whose accumulated seniority placed them at the head of all the powerful congressional committees. In those positions, they rejected or tabled any legislation to better the lot of sharecroppers who made on average 10 cents a day.[22]

Repeatedly, LeBerthon referred to Murray as "pretty" and "lovely," a description meant to be positive, and a striking contrast to Garfinkel's negative description of her masculine performance a year before. Murray disdained those terms as applied to herself, but these were the qualities that attracted positive press. How hard for Murray that must have been. And yet, it was the Joan of Arc image, not the youth in pants, that made the Waller case a national story and raised enough money to delay execution again and again.

The Decision to Go to Law School

By the end of her national tour with Annie Waller, in the spring of 1941, Murray concluded that she could not tolerate life on the road. She needed time for quiet reflection, time to write, the opportunity to take classes. Still not sure what she wanted to do, she applied to Howard Law School but also considered the Master's in Writing program at the University of Iowa. She was not sure whether speaking, writing, or law would allow her to fight Jim Crow most effectively, but she concluded somewhat ruefully that only a law degree would give her a marketable skill. At the time less than 1 percent of all law students were women. That fact did not faze Murray. She knew, deep down, that she was not what she appeared to be. But June arrived and she had yet to hear from Leon Ransom. [23]

Over the summer of 1941 Murray gave speeches to Socialist camps in return for a cabin in the Catskills. Mac accompanied her, working briefly at a nearby sanitarium. Murray focused on her writing, making good progress on what would ultimately be her family history, *Proud Shoes,* but she sold nothing that summer. Aunt Pauline asked once more that she return home to work and help care for her, but Murray could not bear to move back to Durham. Morris Milgram at the WDL offered a job, but one that did not pay enough to live on. She was about to go to Iowa, when, in August, Ransom came through with an offer of admission to Howard and a work-study scholarship.[24]

Murray commented in her memoir that two racist incidents, in addition to her work on behalf of Odell Waller, made her decide on law school. The first occurred when Milgram offered his apartment to Murray, while he and his wife were on a summer vacation. The building's superintendent, not knowing who she was, but observing that she was black, told her to "Go back to Harlem." The second incident followed the tragic death of WDL director David Clendenin in an automobile accident in August 1941. Murray and Vivian Odems sought to pay a condolence call on Clendenin's sister, who lived in an apartment building on the East Side of Manhattan, but were stopped by the doorman, who ordered them to take the service elevator. It took a call to the building superintendent and, in Murray's words, "a little of Dave's militance," to win them access to the front elevator with everyone else. Faced with such blatant discrimination, and with all other appealing work insufficient to provide even minimal support, legal training exerted a powerful attraction for Murray. In September 1941, she entered Howard Law School in Washington, DC.[25]

The Odell Waller story was not over. Murray returned to the WDL in New York and the Waller campaign for the summer of 1942, following her first year at Howard. By then, the WDL had raised $30,000, but it spent over $32,000, even though the lawyers all donated their services. There were the salaries of the staff, including Murray's, the cost of the mailings and publications, the travel expenses, and the basic, reimbursable costs of legal defense and publicity. As a result of this spending, the Waller case drew large, national attention and by the end of the campaign the public had gained a clearer understanding of the poll tax's distortion of the political and judicial system. Tragically, that attention and broader understanding was not enough to save Odell Waller. The Supreme Court denied certiorari on the ground that an inadequate foundation had been laid at trial. President Roosevelt asked the governor to consider commuting Waller's sentence to life in prison, but when the governor refused, the president did not press the matter, believing that he lacked the power to overrule a state official in what he viewed as a state matter.[26]

Murray would not accept defeat. Neither, as it turned out, would Eleanor Roosevelt. Both worked up until the last moment to forestall the inevitable. The evening before Waller's scheduled execution, the first lady tried to persuade the president to intervene one last time—to no avail. At the Washington office of the NAACP, Murray listened in on party lines with Anna Arnold Hedgeman, Mary McCleod Bethune, A. Philip Randolph, and six others, as the first lady reported in a trembling voice that she had done all she could to save the young sharecropper. The next day, July 2, 1942, the state of Virginia electrocuted him. [27]

The Silent March

A. Philip Randolph, determined to protest Waller's execution, proposed to organize a march in New York City. This was not Randolph's first threatened demonstration. For several years, he had been pressuring President Roosevelt to integrate the armed services. Failing to make any progress, in January 1941 he proposed a March on Washington to force the issue, and by the late spring the predicted number for the occasion, scheduled for July, had reached 100,000. A week before it was to take place, an alarmed President Roosevelt formed the Fair Employment Practices Committee (FEPC). He did not integrate the armed services, but he promised to require industries that did business with the United States to hire African Americans. In response, Randolph called off the protest, but the March on Washington Movement (MOWM) continued.[28]

Needing an organizer for his new march in 1942, Randolph persuaded the WDL to lend him Murray. Seeing a perfect opportunity to follow in the foot-steps of Gandhi's Salt March to the Sea (undertaken in defiance of British law that forbade Indians from collecting their own salt), Murray promptly agreed to organize a "Silent Protest March." To her distress Randolph flew off to an NAACP convention in Los Angeles without having secured any organizational or financial support. With limited funds and time, Murray turned to her black female friends for help. Anna Arnold Hedgeman responded immediately, as did Dollie Lowther, a longtime friend from the Laundry Workers Union.[29]

A fellow North Carolinian, Lowther had moved to Brooklyn in 1930, when she was sixteen, with her mother, a hairdresser and cook. Following high school, the only work Dollie could find was at Colonial Laundry, which employed 300 mostly black women. Laundry workers remained largely unorganized until 1937, when a series of strikes led to the unionizing of about 30,000 of them. Dollie helped lead the strike at Colonial where she and others sweated seventy-two hours a week for a wage of only $6.00. By 1942, she had risen through the ranks to become an assistant to Bessie Hillman, director of education for the majority-black Laundry Workers division of the Amalgamated Clothing Workers of America (ACWA), part of the Congress of Industrial Organizations (CIO).[30]

Active in the Women's Trade Union League (WTUL), Lowther recruited other leaders for the march, including most importantly Maida Stewart Springer, of the Garment Workers Union (of the rival AFL). Born in 1910 in Panama, Maida Stewart immigrated to the United States at the age of seven with her Panamanian mother and Barbadian father. Her parents soon divorced, and her mother, who worked as a laundress, caterer, and hairdresser, raised her in Harlem. Unhappy over the discrimination Maida met in the local schools, her mother sent her to Bordentown, a New Jersey boarding school, modeled on Tuskegee, where Maida learned dressmaking. She also got a foundation in the liberal arts from a brilliant black faculty. Dartmouth graduate Lester Granger served as the school's "Commandant" and football coach before he left to head

Figure 5.2 Dollie Lowther, education director of the Amalgamated Clothing Workers Joint Board, with laundry workers. Kheel Center, Cornell University.

the National Urban League. Amherst graduate William Hastie taught Maida science. Radcliffe and Harvard graduates taught her Latin, black history, and English.[31]

Married at seventeen and a mother at nineteen, Maida did not work until the onset of the Depression, when her husband suffered a drastic cut in his wages. She tried to get a job as a waitress at the Alice Foote MacDougall Restaurant, where Pauli worked while at Hunter, but she was rejected for being too dark. Her dressmaking skills saved her, giving her entrée to the garment trade. In 1933, she joined Local 22 of the International Ladies' Garment Workers' Union (ILGWU), and in the years that followed she rose to chair the union's educational committee. Springer, who, with Dollie Lowther, would become one of Murray's closest friends and biggest boosters, later remembered her first sighting: "I walked into this meeting with Dollie and other trade union people, and we heard this small person with cropped hair, wearing these white sailor pants and standing on the table. She was on *fire*, talking about social injustice and Jim Crow."[32]

Thanks to the frantic efforts of these three women, the March on Washington Movement conducted its first actual march on July 25, 1942. Wearing black

Figure 5.3 Maida Springer, the first black business agent for the International Ladies Garment Workers' Union (ILGWU), with white garment workers and businessmen, 1949. Kheel Center, Cornell University.

armbands and walking to the sorrowful beat of muffled drums, the mostly black participants made their way from 56th Street and Eighth Avenue to Union Square at 14th Street and the memorial service for Waller and other victims of racial injustice. As they marched they lifted banners that denounced lynching, Jim Crow, and the poll tax. Murray, Springer, and Lowther carried one that read, "Jim Crow Has to Go!" with the tall and powerfully built Lowther holding up the middle, and the short and slightly built duo of Murray and Springer carrying the ends. Newspapers gave the "Silent Protest March" a respectful coverage, but for all Murray's work, the parade drew not the tens of thousands she had hoped for but fewer than 500 people.[33]

The Steadying Hand of Eleanor Roosevelt

The terrible experience of Odell Waller's execution brought Murray closer to Eleanor Roosevelt. The first lady regularly invited Murray to tea, both because she admired the determined young woman and because she hoped through Murray to rein in the more radical elements among younger civil rights advocates. While Murray worked steadily to push the first lady toward a more active embrace of civil rights, Roosevelt sought to instruct Murray in the practical politics of reform.[34]

Despite their obvious differences, Roosevelt and Murray shared other experiences that drew them together. Both had been orphaned at a young age, raised by female kin, and nurtured throughout their lives by female friendships. Both belonged to the Episcopal Church. Both felt a deep responsibility for the oppressed, especially oppressed women, black as well as white. Despite Murray's initial hostility to her at Camp Tera, Pauli had come to see the First Lady in a more positive light as she followed Roosevelt's developing relationship with older black leaders, most particularly Mary McLeod Bethune. Murray had been deeply impressed by the first lady's refusal to be segregated at the 1938 Southern Conference on Human Welfare in Birmingham and by her kind response a few weeks later to Pauli's furious letter of protest to FDR after his speech at UNC. In 1940, Murray had asked Roosevelt to speak at the concluding celebration of National Sharecroppers Week, an event sponsored by the Southern Tenant Farmers Union (STFU) and the Workers Defense League (WDL), and the first lady had agreed to do so. When Murray, hospitalized for her nervous collapse in March 1940, was not able to attend the celebration, Roosevelt sent her flowers. That gesture sparked a friendship that deepened when Roosevelt responded positively to Murray's plea to help Odell Waller.[35]

The friendship was often rocky. Murray, frustrated after the Silent March that she had not produced a more dramatic event, lashed out at President Roosevelt.

Reading reports that Japanese Americans were being removed from their homes in the West, reportedly for their own protection, she fired off what she later admitted was "an ill-conceived letter" to FDR. Not considering the possibility that the stories were wrong, that the Japanese were being removed for other reasons entirely, including exaggerated fear of Japanese sabotage, Murray attacked. If the president had the power to remove Japanese Americans to protect them from violence, she began, then surely he had the power to remove blacks from the South to protect them from injustice and violence. She went on to compare the president unfavorably to Wendell Wilkie, whom he had defeated in 1940, but who was already campaigning for 1944 and speaking out in favor of civil rights.[36]

Having sent Eleanor Roosevelt a copy of the letter to make sure that FDR would receive it, Murray was stunned to receive a blistering response from the first lady. "How many of our colored people in the South would like to be evacuated and treated as though they were not as rightfully here as any other people?" Mrs. Roosevelt demanded. The first lady did not tell Murray that she opposed the removal of the Japanese, writing only, "I am deeply concerned that we have had to do that to the Japanese who are American citizens, but we are at war with Japan." As for FDR's Republican challenger, "I wonder if it ever occurred to you that Mr. Wilkie has no responsibility whatsoever?" The first lady could not understand how Murray could fail to appreciate how much the president was doing for blacks, such as establishing the Fair Employment Practices Committee (FEPC) to protect them against discrimination in war industries. For a law student "who must really have a knowledge of the workings of our kind of government," Eleanor Roosevelt declared, "your letter seems to me one of the most thoughtless I have ever read." Shocked at the first lady's rebuke but unbowed, Murray fired back. She conceded that her letter might seem "thoughtless," but it had been written from a deep "desperation" to make clear how untenable it was "to fight in democracy's name" when blacks were "victims of a racial theory as vicious as Hitler's." She wrote also from a feeling of "disgust" that the president was not doing more to protect black citizens from discrimination and violence. Even the creation of the FEPC had hardly been the president's idea. He had offered it only in reaction to A. Philip Randolph's threat of a March on Washington.[37]

Murray's blunt letters made the First Lady think of her as a "firebrand," but they also earned her "respect." As Murray grew to know her better, she came to believe that the measure of Mrs. Roosevelt's "greatness was her capacity for growth, her ruthless honesty with herself, and the generosity with which she responded to criticism." The First Lady might have responded to Murray's outburst with a polite acknowledgment. Instead, she invited her to tea. Stronger in front of her typewriter than in person, Murray quailed at the prospect of a meeting in which she might lose her ability to speak frankly. She asked Anna Hedgeman to accompany her and secured Mrs. Roosevelt's permission to bring her along. The First Lady met them at the door and gave Pauli a hug. Speaking of Odell Waller's execution a few weeks before she said, "Oh, that was a terrible night, wasn't it?" Although Hedgeman characterized the meeting as one in which "Pauli . . . threw the dynamite while I threw the sand!" Murray left the tea feeling "unreserved affection" for the First Lady.[38]

The next confrontation came barely two weeks later over an international issue. The International Student Assembly met in Washington in early September 1942, and Murray attended as a delegate. She and some other members of the American delegation wanted to pass a resolution condemning the British for imprisoning Gandhi and denouncing the Soviets for occupying Lithuania. At a picnic for the assembly on the White House lawn, a "stern" First Lady cornered Murray and tried to persuade her to drop the resolutions out of concern that the British and Soviet delegations would walk out. Murray listened in silence, not wanting to refuse Mrs. Roosevelt, but not willing to abandon her principles. Her group lost the vote on the Soviet resolution but succeeded in getting a compromise on the British measure, one that urged England to reopen negotiations on the question of Indian political freedom. No one walked out. Murray's friends also won support for a statement in favor of "the abolition of all discriminations based solely on race, color, creed, or national origin." There was no mention of discrimination based on "sex." That addition would have to wait until 1948 when it would be incorporated into the Universal Declaration of Human Rights, under the leadership of Eleanor Roosevelt at the United Nations.[39]

Eleanor Roosevelt never allowed disagreements, no matter how heated, to stand in the way of friendship. She quickly followed arguments with invitations to tea, either at her New York City home on Washington Square or the White House. As Murray later recalled, Eleanor Roosevelt "gave me a sense of personal worth"; moreover, "she warmed me with a maternal quality which made me want to strive to walk in her footsteps." That maternal quality steadied Murray as she trained to be a lawyer.[40]

PART III

NAMING JANE CROW, 1941–1946

"I Would Gladly Change My Sex"

Howard Law School

Pauli Murray came to Howard Law School to fight Jim Crow, prejudice based on race. To her dismay, she encountered what she came to call "Jane Crow," prejudice based on gender. Nothing in her prior experience had prepared her for this indignity. Her maternal grandfather, "patriarch though he was," thought that his daughters should be "self-sufficient" and placed no limitations on what they could do. Her maternal grandmother, her aunts, and her mostly female teachers taught her to be confident in her abilities. The women of the Harlem YWCA and Hunter College mentored her. First Lady Eleanor Roosevelt and the director of the Worker's Education Project of the WPA, Hilda Smith, provided examples of female leadership at the national level. The organizations for which she had subsequently worked included large numbers of women, and although the leaders were male, they treated her as a valued member in a common cause.[1]

Howard Law School was different. It was the first virtually all-male environment in which she had ever found herself and the first in which she was made to feel unwelcome. Entering with a class of thirty students, including one female classmate, who dropped out before the end of the first term, Murray experienced the lonely distinction of being the sole woman, apart from the registrar (herself a Howard Law School graduate) in the entire school. In her memoir, Murray professed never before to have noticed the kind of marginalization she experienced at Howard, so preoccupied had she been with race and, in the 1930s, class discrimination. Privately, of course, she admitted that she had been discriminated against for other reasons, as well. One could be a "minority of minorities," as Mac had put it in her letter to the *Amsterdam News* the year before. Up until Murray's entry into Howard, however, the minority-of-minorities status that most troubled her was the "sexual maladjustment" she suffered from being a black man trapped in a black woman's body. Howard forced her to acknowledge another, much broader status: that of being a woman in a man's world. As Murray put it, "The racial factor was removed in the intimate environment of a Negro law school dominated by men, and the factor of gender was fully exposed." She found it shocking that men who had come to Howard, at least in part because of its reputation as a center of civil rights litigation, could so thoughtlessly discriminate against her, just because she appeared to be a woman.[2]

Murray's experience of feeling unwelcome would prove pivotal for her. From that moment, she began to think about the battle for civil rights more broadly, as a movement that should encompass attacks not only against race discrimination but also against gender discrimination. She thought initially in personal terms, of the injustice done to her individually by the men she considered her mentors and peers and of personal strategies to overcome it. By the time she graduated from law school, however, she had sketched out a legal argument that anticipated the Supreme Court's 1954 decision on behalf of race equality in *Brown v. Board of Education*, as well as its 1971 decision on behalf of gender equality in *Reed v. Reed*.[3]

"The men were not openly hostile; in fact, they were friendly," Murray recalled of her first days at Howard Law School. She quickly learned, however,

Figure 6.1 Pauli Murray, in a portrait taken in 1941 and inscribed to "Mother" (Aunt Pauline), as she began law school at Howard University. Estate of Pauli Murray, Schlesinger Library, Radcliffe Institute, Harvard University.

"that women were often the objects of ridicule disguised as a joke." One professor said that he did not know why women came to law school, but that since they were there the men would have to put up of with them, a comment that brought forth loud laughter from the male students. Shocked and humiliated, Murray did not respond, but the professor "had just guaranteed," she grimly remembered, "that I would become the top student in his class."[4]

Murray believed that her voice compounded her marginal status. No matter how well prepared she might be or how often she raised her hand, the professors rarely called on her. Murray did not think that the professors ignored her deliberately. Her lighter voice, she believed was the culprit. In the back and forth of the classroom, "the men's deeper voices" obliterated "my lighter voice, and my classmates seemed to take it for granted that I had nothing to contribute." So many female law students later complained of being ignored by their professors, it seems at least possible that gender discrimination was at work here also. Moreover, the gendered norms that governed classroom debate likely made matters worse. By her own admission, Murray "raised [her] hand" and waited to be called on, rather than forcing her way into the debates as the men were doing. But Murray attached no importance either to professorial prejudice or peer privilege. She attributed her exclusion entirely to not having a deeper male voice, a judgment that underscores how thoroughly she focused on vocal register as a source of power and how committed she was to escaping discrimination by becoming more male. Judging from tapes made in her fifties, Murray was a contralto, a low register for a woman, but one much higher than she thought hers should or could be. If testosterone could deepen the voices of effeminate men, it could do the same for her. She continued to ask for the hormone, but throughout her years at Howard, the doctors she consulted refused her entreaties.[5]

Most humiliating of all that first year of law school was the matter of the legal fraternity. Murray had taken great pride in her election at Hunter College to Sigma Tau Delta, a national English honorary society. She was therefore dismayed when, several months into the school year, she saw an announcement on the school bulletin board for a smoker, sponsored by the national legal society Phi Alpha Delta, which specifically limited the invitees to "male students of the First Year Class." Noting that the smoker was to be held at the residence of Professor Leon Ransom, Murray demanded an explanation from the man who had recruited her. Ransom told her that the national society, a "fraternity," had just established a chapter at Howard and that the smoker was to "look over First Year Men for likely prospects." "What about us women?" she protested. Her mentor suggested forming a legal sorority. Murray felt betrayed: "The discovery that Ransom and other men I deeply admired because of their dedication to civil rights, men who themselves had suffered racial indignities, could countenance exclusion of women from their professional association, aroused an incipient feminism in me long before I knew the meaning of the term 'feminism.' "[6]

Excluded by the faculty and her fellow students from full participation in class and extra-curricular activities, Murray threw herself into her course work. By the end of her first year, she ranked first in her class. On the basis of that success, she won election as one of two class representatives to the Howard Law School Court of Peers. At the end of the second year, she again led the class. By tradition, Howard students elevated the top-ranking second-year student to the position of Chief Justice of the Court of Peers, but not this time. Unwilling to be led by a woman, they left the position vacant.[7]

And then the men underwent a conversion experience. In the fall of 1943, with student ranks decimated by the military draft, a decision was made to combine the second and third year classes for a class called "Bills and Notes." This famously difficult course covered the rules governing checks, promissory notes, bills of lading, and other commercial documents in different jurisdictions. The previous year, Professor Spottswood Robinson had failed nine of the fifteen students in the class. Desperate to master the voluminous material, students began to meet in study groups. Murray had tried such an approach before, only to discover that she fared better on her own, but partway into the term she found herself drawn into a two-person group arrangement. Billy Jones, a classmate who had been doing well, had dropped out due to a disease that caused temporary blindness and had returned to repeat the second year. Unfortunately, he had fallen sick again and had missed a large number of classes. No one else would work with him, but Murray, thinking of her blind grandfather, could not refuse Jones's plea. She taught herself the material and then taught it to him. When the grades were posted, she saw that she had earned a 95 and Billy Jones an 85. The rest of the class scored 70 or below. Shamed by Murray's humanity and success, the Law Students Guild promptly elected her Chief Justice of the Court of Peers. Her classmates elected her president of the senior class.[8]

Murray achieved this academic glory in the face of constant financial pressure. In deciding whether she could afford law school in September 1941, she had calculated that she would need $650 a year to cover tuition, fees, an off-campus room, food, books, clothes, and incidentals. She had hoped to win a full scholarship, so that she could focus exclusively on her studies, but Ransom had been able to offer only a work scholarship, which meant the right to a part-time position in the law school library. That job would generate only $350 for the year, leaving a deficit of $300. In despair, Murray wrote Jessie Overholt, a WDL supporter she had met in southern California while speaking on behalf of Odell Waller. Informing Overholt that she would have to find a second job to afford law school, Murray hinted at her fear of another breakdown should she have to work two jobs in addition to carrying a full course load, adding, "Law may be too strenuous for someone of my temperament." Overholt responded immediately. "I am enclosing a check for one hundred dollars." That check and the many that followed from her made law school possible.[9]

The Continuing Torment of Gender

Although successful academically and afloat financially, Murray continued to suffer from extreme emotional distress. She could not dispel her feelings of gender dysphoria. That conflict seems to have manifested itself in a recurring pattern in her years at Howard. Each fall, she channeled her energies into her academic work and civil rights activities, but as the months passed she found that effort increasingly difficult to sustain. By the spring she experienced acute distress. In the summer of 1942, following her first year at Howard, the death of Odell Waller, and the Silent Protest March in his memory, she renewed her search for a doctor willing to be "experimental." She began with a letter to Dr. Joseph Eidelsberg, the researcher whose testosterone treatments of effeminate males two years earlier had given her hope that he would give her the same hormone. He had declined, but Murray tried once more. "Anything you can do to help me will be gratefully appreciated, because my life is somewhat unbearable in its present phase, and though a person of ability, this aspect continually blocks my efforts to do the things of which I am capable." A week later, apparently having received no response, she re-sent her letter, with a new postscript: "What I mean is that though I do an effective job over a short period of time, my conflicts interfere with permanent long-time work and keep me constantly afraid to accept new responsibilities."[10]

In an accompanying detailed memorandum, she offered her assessment of her condition. She provided such basic information as her "age: 31; weight; 105 pounds; and height: 5 ft. 2.5 in." She mentioned her "Appearance: boyish characteristics . . . physically strong and active." She also noted her contralto, "low voice . . . high and thin under excitement," as well as her "Mental characteristics: Above average intelligence . . . top of [law school] class . . ."; her "Emotional characteristics: Alternates between extreme self-consciousness and bold aggressiveness . . ."; and her 'Character: Honest; influenced by deep religious convictions." She concluded with a statement of her "Present problem: No crucial emotional crisis; motivated to seek help on a long standing emotional and mental conflict, popularly known as homosexuality."

Murray then proceeded to list three possible diagnoses for her condition. The first was that her "mental conflict" was "solely psychological." Every doctor she had seen had given her this diagnosis, but she had "always resisted psychiatric treatment" and was willing to discuss this possibility "only after other theories have been exhausted." The second possible diagnosis was that she suffered from a "glandular disturbance" or "fibroid tumor or growth" that resulted in a "lack of sufficient female hormones, causing apparent virility and resultant conflicts." No such lack had yet been found, but she was open to further testing. Finally, and "most acceptable" to her, was the possible "Presence of male organ (a) secreted in [her] abdominal cavity; (b) possible division between one ovary and one testes." Murray admitted that this was the "most radical theory," but she insisted that she would not consider any other diagnoses until this topic was "thoroughly exhausted."

As evidence that her problems were rooted in a pseudo-hermaphrodite condition, Murray reported feeling "terrific mental conflict on the point of wearing dresses or pants," because in "pants, it is difficult to make persons believe she [Murray] is not a boy; in dresses her awkwardness is the object of hilarious comment on the part of her closest friends." Regarding her sexual orientation, she reported a "consistent emotional attraction toward the female sex," which was met by the "consistent attraction of apparently bi-sexual women." Murray sharply distinguished her sexual longings for women from her workplace preferences. In business and in intellectual discussions, she experienced a "preference for male company."[11]

Although Murray cast her memorandum in the third person as a scientific case history with all possible diagnoses, it was, in fact, a brief in favor of distinguishing her condition from the one "popularly known as homosexuality." Unlike lesbians, as she understood the term, she was not attracted to other lesbians but only to females who were themselves bisexual, which, in her understanding, meant that they were heterosexual women attracted to her inner maleness, but who—as in the case of Peg Holmes two years before—invariably abandoned her as insufficiently male. Moreover, unlike the lesbians she knew or had read about, she did not dislike men; indeed, for the most part, she preferred their company professionally. Murray's conflict over dress underscored, in her mind, her in-between state. She felt ridiculous in dresses. As for male attire, she professed discomfort in this memorandum to medical experts, but her language gave her away. When she wrote that in pants "it is difficult to make persons believe she is not a boy," she was really saying, why should she have to make others believe she was not a boy, when, in fact she was one, struggling to become a man.[12]

A few days later, Dr. Eidelsberg responded, "I am sorry but medical science is not entirely in keeping with your conclusions. We would gladly do what we can with you and your problem, make an exhaustive study to determine whether there is a glandular disorder, and treat such if it can be found." Any help, however, would have to wait until September, when the clinic would reopen after summer vacation.[13]

Undaunted, Murray tracked down Dr. Ruth Fox, the endocrinologist who had sent her to the Long Island Rest Home and who, Murray discovered, was vacationing on Martha's Vineyard in July 1942. When Dr. Fox had first interviewed Murray five years earlier, she apparently cautioned her not to engage in self-diagnosis based on her reading of medical literature in the New York Public Library. Murray sought to assure Fox that her symptoms were not the product of an overwrought imagination, fueled by reading. On the same day that she led the Silent Protest March down to Union Square, she wrote to Dr. Fox, "After five years of thought, work and no reading, I'm still faced with the same personal problem I had then. It transcends any personal relationship and makes impossible a satisfactory relationship with anyone." She enclosed her memorandum and letters to Dr. Eidelsberg and implored her "to think over this matter carefully and let me know your reaction." Murray was desperate, willing to go anywhere—to Martha's Vineyard or even to the Mayo Clinic in Rochester, Minnesota, to find help. "I hope you are in an experimental mood," Murray concluded.[14]

Obviously concerned, Dr. Fox responded within a few days. She urged Murray to return to Dr. Eidelsberg's clinic when it reopened in the fall. "You know that I believe it is a psychological matter, but any of us would be glad to find a physical basis for your trouble and I am heartily in favor of your having the tests."[15]

Murray was in no mood to wait. Probably through Dr. Chinn, she arranged for her reproductive organs to be x-rayed. The report was disappointing. The x-ray showed that her fallopian tubes were normal, the uterus "small" and "malpositioned" (probably retroverted, a normal condition), and the endometrium "hyperplastic" (likely caused by an excess of one kind of female hormone, estrogen). In other words, Murray's reproductive organs were grossly normal. There was no sign of masculine hormones or secondary sex characteristics. She might well have a hormonal imbalance, though not one that she had anticipated. Murray must have felt deeply disappointed by the failure of this test to support her strong belief that she was physiologically at least partially male. But there was nothing more to do on the medical front.[16]

The Women of Howard

Returning to Howard in September 1942, Murray felt thoroughly rung out by the summer's battles—and lonely. Mac had moved with her to Washington to take undergraduate classes at Howard, but they no longer lived together, and their relationship, always fraught, grew more distant. Murray thought she would fare better if she could live on campus. Although Howard made no provision for female graduate housing, she knew someone who might help. Cousin Susie Elliott was now the dean of women at Howard and offered to let her live in the "powder room," tucked away beyond the stairs, on the first floor of Sojourner Truth Hall, the freshman women's dormitory. Shoe-horned into this tiny space, Murray studied in relative quiet until the women students learned of her presence and "began to make shy visits, bombarding me with questions on law and particularly on civil rights." These students provided Murray with much-needed companionship.[17]

A new hire in the Howard history department, Caroline (Lina) Ware, a white woman, offered not only companionship but also scholarly validation and critical guidance in the evolution of Murray's thinking about Jane Crow. Murray's prior exposure to the history profession in college had not been positive. Reading W. E. B. DuBois's *Black Reconstruction* after college had restored her faith in what history could teach, but she remained suspicious of white scholars, until she met Ware.[18]

Despite a privileged background, which included descent from a long line of Harvard graduates, Ware connected immediately with Murray. During the Civil War, her grandfather had journeyed to the South to teach the newly freed slaves of Port Royal, South Carolina, just as Grandfather Robert Fitzgerald had in neighboring North Carolina. After graduating from Vassar College, Ware pursued a Ph.D. in economic history at Harvard. She planned to write a history of black workers, but her thesis adviser, fearing a paucity of sources, directed her instead to a manuscript collection on early textile manufacturing. From this archive Ware made a pioneering and award-winning contribution to business and women's history. While at Harvard, Ware met a fellow graduate student, Gardiner Means, an economist three years her senior, whom she married in 1927, keeping her own name. After teaching for several years at Vassar, she moved with her husband to Washington in 1933, Means to work as an adviser to Henry Wallace in the Department of Agriculture, and Ware to serve on the Consumer Advisory Board of the National Recovery Administration. Later Ware joined the Consumer Division of the Office of Price Administration (OPA), where she fought for the racial integration of the staff and against efforts to cut consumer protection, as the nation prepared for war. Her work attracted the disapproving attention of Texas Representative Martin Dies and his House Un-American Activities Committee (HUAC), as well as the FBI, which concluded that she was a subversive. When HUAC forced her to resign in 1942, Howard promptly hired her.[19]

Word of Ware's arrival quickly spread, and Murray decided to audit her course on the history of the Constitution. In Ware, Murray found an important mentor and friend. Through her, Murray came to see that race discrimination hurt whites as well as blacks. "*My* constitutional rights are being violated," Ware insisted "when I am prohibited by segregation laws from associating with my friend and am compelled to sit in a separate car!"[20]

Figure 6.2 Caroline F. Ware, when she served at the Consumer Division, Office of Price Administration (OPA), 1941. Library of Congress LC-USE6-D-000395.

Ware also spurred Murray to think about the ways in which racism paralleled sexism. They began by discussing what constituted a reasonable classification under the Constitution. The courts had long held that laws could treat people differently, so long as there was a good reason for doing so. States barred ten-year-olds from driving, for example, but no state barred people from driving on account of their race or gender. To classify a group in that way for the purpose of granting a driver's license was clearly arbitrary—an obvious violation of the Equal Protection Clause of the Fourteenth Amendment. How then, could a state justify as "reasonable" a law that barred black and white people from sitting next to one another on a bus or in a restaurant or in a classroom? How, for that matter, could a state justify barring women from serving next to men on a jury? Moreover, should not the standard for discrimination on the grounds of race or gender be even more stringent than that for barring children from driving? One could outgrow childhood. One could not change one's race or, as Murray was constantly told by her doctors, one's gender. Was not race, and perhaps also gender, an "arbitrary classification"? Discussion around these questions played out in Ware's classroom and continued at Ware and Means's residence, the Farm.[21]

In 1935, Ware and Means had decided to buy a seventy-acre farm in Virginia, twelve miles from Washington, where they raised sheep, dogs, and a few cattle. Murray happily pitched in as a FIBUL, Ware's acronym for "Free Intelligent But Unskilled Labor." She painted the barn, chopped and stacked wood, weeded the garden, and raked weeds. She also took long walks with one of the Ware-Means's Shetland sheep dogs. Ware called them her "staff of psychiatric dogs," meant to divert visitors from weighty matters. In this setting, Murray found common ground with Ware, whom she nicknamed "Skipper" because of the way she "whizzed around blind corners and up and down narrow roller-coaster roads" in her convertible.[22]

Satyagraha in a Time of War

Murray's discussions with Ware played out against the backdrop of World War II. Three months after her enrollment at Howard, the United States declared war on the Axis Powers. Three days after her graduation, the Allies invaded Normandy. America's entry into the war sparked anxious discussion among the men at Howard about the draft. Why should they enlist in a fight against fascism abroad when the country sanctioned fascism at home? "All I can give is a listening ear," Murray confessed in her diary, as each man struggled to decide whether he was willing "to die for a cause he cannot believe has a meaning for him." When one classmate declined to be inducted, forty others sent an open letter to the liberal New York newspaper *PM* in his support. In the end, most ended up fighting. The alternative was jail. Over the course of the next two and a half years, Murray's class shrank from thirty students to seven. As she watched her classmates march off to war, her own immunity from conscription, because she was a woman, made her feel an extra responsibility to "battle for democracy at home."[23]

Howard offered a rich pool of potential recruits for her battle. Some 4,000 students from forty-five states and twenty-four foreign countries attended the university at that time. Over half of the mostly middle-class student body came from outside the South. Many had never been exposed to segregated public facilities and were shocked to encounter racial insults when they left campus to see a movie or stopped at a soda fountain while shopping.[24]

The faculty shared their indignation. President Mordecai Johnson had recruited a highly talented group of scholars. Most were black, including philosopher Alain Locke, political scientist Ralph Bunche, sociologist E. Franklin Frazier, medical researcher Charles Drew, and poet and literary critic Sterling Brown. There was also a smattering of whites. John Herz, a political scientist and a Jew, who had fled the Nazis in 1938 and taught briefly at Princeton, found refuge at Howard in 1941. Caroline Ware joined the faculty the following year. All were dedicated not only to their specialized fields but also to the cause of civil rights. Together with graduate students like Pauli Murray, they provided a lively intellectual environment and urged students to challenge the status quo.[25]

Attacks on Jim Crow in other parts of the country provided further encouragement. By December 1942, A. Philip Randolph, outraged that the federal government, despite the creation of the FEPC, was doing little to combat discrimination and violence against blacks, threatened a campaign of civil disobedience and noncooperation. Two of Murray's friends from the Harlem Ashram and the Fellowship of Reconciliation (FOR), Bayard Rustin and James Farmer, supported him. Rustin, who toured the country as a field secretary for FOR, reported in September 1942 that "only a spark is needed to create a terrible explosion." As someone who would serve two years in prison for refusing to join the army, Rustin ruefully reported that pacifism was going nowhere in a country gripped by war but that racial and religious reconciliation were popular everywhere. He pressed for disciplined, well-organized, nonviolent direct action on behalf of racial justice.[26]

The FOR's other black field secretary, James Farmer, agreed. A nationally acclaimed debater from Texas with a Ph.D. in religion from Howard, Farmer agreed with Murray that the FOR needed to focus on racial injustice by following Gandhi's model of nonviolent resistance to racial wrongs. Assigned by FOR to Chicago, Farmer helped found the Congress of Racial Equality (CORE) in the spring of 1942 and began to challenge restrictive covenants in housing and discrimination at restaurants. In May, a group of twenty-eight whites and blacks entered Chicago's Jack Spratt restaurant in parties of two, three, and four and refused to leave until the blacks were served. Their effort failed, but it was a start.[27]

At Howard, Murray's small room in Sojourner Truth Hall became an informal meeting place for women students interested in civil rights. No better place existed to demand freedom than in Washington, DC, the symbolic center of the war against fascism. Washington also had the benefit of being more open to blacks than cities farther south. The District of Columbia had no segregation ordinance, blacks could sit where they wished on streetcars and buses, and they could eat where they liked at a few establishments in the black neighborhood. With those exceptions, however, segregation prevailed. Blacks were barred, by custom not law, from most of the city's hotels, restaurants, theaters, movie houses, and other places of public accommodation. When Murray read about Rustin and Farmer's efforts to pursue nonviolent direct action against Jim Crow, she gained greater confidence that it might be possible to do the same in Washington, perhaps with a little "American showmanship" added in the form of pickets and clever signs.[28]

The spark that united the campus was the arrest of three female undergraduates at the United Cigar Store on Pennsylvania Avenue in January 1943. Ruth Powell from Massachusetts, together with Marianne Musgrave and Juanita Murrow from Ohio, sat down at the store's lunch counter and ordered three hot chocolates. The waitress refused to serve them and instead called the police. When the police arrived, they questioned the students and, finding that they were violating no law, ordered the waitress to serve them. She complied but then overcharged the students: 35 cents for each cup instead of the menu price of 10 cents. Students put down only 35 cents for the three drinks, plus a tip, and began to leave, at which point they were arrested, carted off to jail, searched, and thrown into a cell with other criminal suspects.[29]

Howard administrators were upset as much by their fear of parental reaction as by the jailing itself. Howard was supposed to be acting in loco parentis toward a student body that, with the departure of growing numbers of male students to the military, was increasingly female. The police quickly released the students into the custody of Dean Elliott. No charges were filed, for they had done nothing wrong, but Elliott urged them to work through established organizations. That advice inspired the students to join the campus chapter of the NAACP. Throughout the spring of 1943, Murray's room served as a center of planning for the sit-in campaign, with Murray as legal adviser, to assure that the students acted within the law.[30]

The Sit-In at Little Palace Cafeteria

The students began with a survey of student opinion. They were relieved to discover that 97 percent of those questioned believed that blacks should not suspend the battle for equal rights until the end of the war. Emboldened by this support, the students formed a Civil Rights Committee under the sponsorship of the Howard NAACP and chose a nearby restaurant—the Little Palace Cafeteria—as a target for their first organized sit-in. Owned by two Greek men, the restaurant was one of the few "White Trade Only" establishments to operate in the mostly black community surrounding the university. Local blacks particularly resented it.[31]

Under Murray's guidance, the students planned meticulously. They held pep rallies; raised money for paper, postage, and picket signs; and invited experienced political leaders to speak to them at town hall meetings. Murray assured the students that there was no law in Washington that required restaurants to be segregated. To be sure that the students would not be arrested on a charge of disorderly conduct, she stressed the importance of dignified dress and comportment, and she made everyone who wanted to participate pledge nonviolent conduct, no matter how great the provocation. Finally, on Saturday, April 17, they were ready. Groups of four students left the campus, five minutes apart, and walked the ten minutes to the Little Palace Cafeteria. Three entered, while one remained outside as an observer. Inside, the volunteers took trays to the steam table, and when they were refused service, carried their empty trays to vacant tables, where they pulled out books and "assumed an air of concentrated study." They spoke not a word. As subsequent groups arrived, the outside observers formed a picket line with colorful signs that read: "Our Boys, our Bonds, our Brothers are Fighting for You! Why Can't We Eat Here?" "We Die Together—Why Can't We Eat Together?" "There's No Segregation Law in D.C. What's Your Story Little Palace?"[32]

The owners called the police department, which dispatched the city's only African American lieutenant and several patrolmen to the scene. Sizing up the situation, the lieutenant ordered his men to stand aside and merely be alert to any disorder. In frustration, the owners closed the restaurant eight hours early. Those inside joined the picketers, who continued to circle. Within forty-eight hours the owners capitulated and began to serve black customers. A few weeks later, CORE members in Chicago enjoyed a victory at Spratt Restaurant.[33]

With so many men away in the armed services, 60 percent of the protestors were women. Murray credited the protests not only with winning a battle against Jim Crow but also with inspiring young black women to believe that through joint effort they could bring about significant change.[34]

"This Little 'Boy-Girl Personality'"

Hard on the heels of this civil rights triumph, another emotional storm threatened to upend Murray's law school career. As she confided to Jessie Overholt, "the crack up was serious, I lost the last three weeks out of school, including my final examinations. The faculty gave me permission to take them the second week in September before registration for my third year."[35]

It began when "a young sophomore sort of walked into my life without my realizing what was happening to me." Murray had confessed her feelings. The student had apparently been taken aback. "Some gossip had started around campus." Murray assured Aunt Pauline that she had "done nothing of which to be ashamed," but she acknowledged that her "little 'boy-girl' personality," as her adoptive mother had long "jokingly" called it, "sometimes gets me into trouble." Murray tried to live by "society's standards," but the effort "causes me such inner conflict that at times it's almost unbearable. . . . This conflict rises up to knock me down at every apex I reach in my career and because the laws of society do not protect me, I'm exposed to any enemy or person who may or may not want to hurt me."[36]

Concluding that she could no longer remain at Howard, she had applied to the University of Michigan; then, deeply depressed, she had taken refuge in the university infirmary. The doctor who examined her wanted to send her to Gallagher Hospital for psychiatric observation, but Cousin Susie Elliott, Caroline Ware, and Leon Ransom rallied around her. They reassured her that she was "brilliant," a "legal genius," too valued a member of the community to let go. Suffering rapid weight loss, Murray believed she needed to get herself "straightened out sort of once and for all." She considered Freedman's Hospital, but her sister Mildred, still a nurse there, worried that anyone who examined Pauli would find evidence of the "mad Murrays."[37]

Released from the infirmary after six days, on May 19, Murray recovered enough on her own to accept an invitation to tea at the White House on June 1. Following the sit-in at the Little Palace Cafeteria, an angry white man had written the student protesters a letter condemning what they had done: "Who wants to sit down to a table to eat with a dirty, greasy, stinking nigger; no matter how many times he bathes, he still 'stinks'?" he asked. "Instead of wasting your time by picketing, start at the beginning and educate the NEGRO—not to steal, lie, rape and assault women." The students reprinted the letter, with the comment: "THIS IS YOU!!" What are you doing about it?" Murray sent the letter to Eleanor Roosevelt, together with her own detailed account of the sit-in campaign. The first lady, appalled, invited Murray and a friend, Pauline Redmond of the National Youth Administration (NYA), to tea. If most restaurants in Washington remained closed to them, at least they could eat at the White House. "Dear Mother," Murray excitedly wrote Aunt Pauline, "The tea with Mrs. Roosevelt was exquisite." Scheduled for thirty minutes, the occasion lasted an hour and a half, and "you would have thought I was talking to either you or Aunt Sallie, the way she talked to me." The next day, Murray accepted Ware's invitation to go to the Farm to rest, eat, and build up her strength.[38]

A week later, Murray went home to Durham, bringing with her the newest of Ware's "psychiatric dogs," a Shetland sheep puppy she named Toni. Having heard that Duke had a good endocrinology clinic, she secured a referral from the family physician, Dr. John Cordice, to see Dr. Julian Ruffin there. On arrival, she checked in with the Duke clinic's receptionist and was sent to an examining room. "When Dr. Ruffin came in and began to ask me questions I noticed he seemed increasingly ill at ease," Murray noted. "Suddenly, he announced that he was not going to examine me and told me to put on my clothes and leave. Flabbergasted, I asked him why. 'I'm not going to have anything to do with Eleanor Roosevelt movements!' Dr. Ruffin shouted as he stormed out of the examining room." Ruffin was responding to the inaccurate stories that had spread throughout the South that black women were forming Eleanor Clubs to demand higher wages, shorter hours, and unheard of privileges from their white employers.[39]

Murray never said whether the doctor had given her a chance to mention the real reason for her visit: to seek help for her "boy-girl" condition. If he had, that information would simply have confirmed his hostile reaction. Murray, having failed to secure the help she wanted at New York hospitals and unwilling to upset Mildred by going to Freedman's Hospital in Washington, had gambled that she might find a sympathetic ear, or at least a fresh perspective, at Duke. All she had succeeded in doing, however, was to convince yet another doctor that there was something wrong with her, something he had no intention of exploring further.

The Race Riots of 1943

Eleanor Clubs were a figment of the white imagination, but growing black anger against Jim Crow was real and the white response to it increasingly violent. Even before Murray reached Durham in early June, a girl was arrested there for not surrendering her seat to a white passenger, and a fight had broken out. Mother Pauline and Aunt Sally were terrified and begged Pauli not to do anything. As black and white workers poured into cities with rapidly expanding war industries, whites rebelled at having to live and work alongside blacks. No reaction was stronger than in Detroit, where white police converted a fight between a group of blacks and whites in a local park into a full-blown riot, in which a disproportionate number of blacks were killed and injured. When Thurgood Marshall investigated for the NAACP, he found the reason for the disparity. The Detroit police used "persuasion" with whites, but "night sticks, revolvers, riot guns, sub-machine guns, and deer guns," against blacks, many of them innocent bystanders. After thirty hours of rioting, the death of thirty-four, the injury of 600, and the loss of property in excess of $2,000,000, President Roosevelt finally declared a state of emergency and sent in 6,000 soldiers to patrol the city. Roosevelt said nothing publicly about the violence until New York Congressman Vito Marcantonio asked him about the impact of the riots on national unity and America's reputation abroad. Only then, did the president say mildly, "I am sure that every true American regrets this." So outraged was Murray over this belated and "mealy-mouthed" response that she punched out a poem, "Mr. Roosevelt Regrets":

> What'd you get, black boy,
> When they knocked you down in the gutter,
> And they kicked your teeth out,
> And they broke your skull with clubs
> And they bashed your stomach in?
> . . .
> What'd the Top Man say, Black Boy?
> "Mr. Roosevelt regrets . . ."

Murray sent her poem to Eleanor Roosevelt. "I am sorry, but I understand," the First Lady responded. Murray, who had avoided all political affiliations since resigning from the Communist Party Opposition in 1937, joined the Socialist Party. In her view, FDR had joined forces with the party of "white supremacy."[40]

By then, Murray was back in New York, having left Toni to be housebroken by the ever-supportive (but none-too-happy) Aunt Pauline. Still distraught over her personal situation and trying once again without success to find medical treatment in New York, Murray gave thought to taking a break from law school to focus on her writing. She rented a room in the Bronx apartment of her friend from the WDL office, Vivian Odems Lemon. Murray worked part-time as a waitress, tried unsuccessfully to find a job at a newspaper or magazine, and wrote. In an article entitled, "Negroes Are Fed Up," published in *Common Sense,* she correctly predicted further riots. In August, Harlem erupted in violence when a false rumor spread that a white police officer had killed a black soldier in an altercation over the arrest of a black woman. Six people were killed, hundreds injured, and much of Harlem gutted by fire. Murray admitted that the riots got the attention of the white media to a degree that her own carefully organized protests had not, but as a believer in nonviolent direct action, she found the riot appalling.[41]

In the final weeks of summer she poured all of the "pain and bitterness" the summer had unleashed into her poetry. Four years before, Murray had written to Stephen Vincent Benét. "He wrote me back a lovely letter, calling me Mr. Murray," Pauli had excitedly informed Aunt Pauline, and invited her to "send him some of my poetry immediately." After reading her work, Benét met with her and told her that he would rank her "in the top 30 poets under 30," she proudly reported; "though not in the top 10," she ruefully added. Inspired by her meeting, she returned to "Dark Anger," which became "Dark Testament." In the wake of the riots of 1943, Murray turned once more to this poem. When she completed it, she felt "as if a demon had been exorcised and a terrible fever inside me had been broken."[42]

Becoming a Feminist

When Murray confronted sex discrimination in her first year of law school, she treated it as an individual problem. Returning to Howard Law School for her third year, she met someone who insisted her distress was part of something larger. Betsy Graves Reyneau, a painter and member of the National Woman's Party (NWP) who arrived at Howard in the fall of 1943, introduced Murray to the history of women's rights and its relation to the abolitionists.[43]

Caroline Ware had always been interested in the welfare of women workers, but women's rights had not particularly concerned her. Growing up, she observed a neighborhood suffragist whose boys were bullies, and she concluded that if the woman could not control her own children she was not likely to accomplish much good in politics. Ware's feelings softened when she arrived at Vassar in 1916 and found the campus aflame with suffragist spirit, but she never identified with the militants in the NWP.[44]

Reyneau made Murray see herself as an heir to that militant movement for women's rights. Reassuring Pauli that she "was not especially excessive in the way [she] went about working for change," the older woman boasted that she, too, had gone to jail for her beliefs. It helped that Rayneau shared with both Ware and Murray a distinguished civil rights lineage. Her paternal grandmother, Ann Lapham Graves, had been a friend of Sojourner Truth and had operated a station of the Underground Railroad in the Graves's home in Michigan. Under the unhappy nose of her husband, Judge Benjamin F. Graves, Grandmother Graves helped slaves escape to Canada.[45]

Betsy Graves found her own way to defy male authority. Determined to be a painter, she ran away from home, first to Cincinnati and later to Boston, after her father, Attorney Henry B. Graves, forbade her from pursuing work he deemed inappropriate for a woman. While studying art at the Boston Museum School, Betsy became a social activist, picketing on behalf of dockworkers and women garment workers. Married in 1915 to Paul O. Reyneau, a French-born, Cornell-trained engineer, she continued her painting and activism. In 1917, she traveled with members of the National Woman's Party to Washington to join pickets in front of the White House, where she and others were arrested for "Block[ing] Washington Sidewalks." The protestors, sentenced to an unprecedented sixty days in the Occoquan Workhouse, found worms in their food, refused to eat, and were subsequently force fed. Later that year, Alice Paul gave brooches, modeled on a jail door with a lock and chain attached, to Reyneau and others. When Murray first saw the pin, she felt an immediate connection. It "had the same effect on me as my Grandfather Fitzgerald's Civil War saber and pistol that Grandmother always kept under her bed during my early childhood."[46]

When Murray met her in 1943, Reyneau had embarked on a project to capture on canvas the country's black leaders. She had come to Howard to paint Mordecai Johnson, the university's first black president. Reyneau, as Murray learned, delighted in the richly varied colors of black subjects, from "blond, blue-eyed Walter White of the NAACP to mahogany-hued Mary McCleod Bethune." Within a few years, working with black painter Laura Wheeling Ware, she had painted two dozen of the most important black leaders in the country. In 1944, their exhibition opened at the Smithsonian, with Eleanor Roosevelt in attendance.

Together the bi-racial team then toured the country. Wherever they went, their paintings stimulated protests against racial discrimination. Whereas Eleanor Roosevelt encouraged Murray's political engagement and Caroline Ware her scholarly ambitions, Betsy Graves Reyneau nurtured her incipient feminism.[47]

"How Do I Go about Killing Jane Crow?"

Murray's friendship with Reyneau, together with her ongoing efforts to desegregate public accommodations in Washington, made her increasingly impatient with the incremental strategy for civil rights litigation championed at Howard Law School. Why continue the battle to make separate facilities equal, she kept asking, rather than attack segregation directly? At the same time, her emerging feminism made her see an attack on race discrimination alone as inadequate. How much good would come to her personally, if she "killed Jim Crow" but could not at the same time kill "Jane Crow." Would it be possible, she wondered, to use the Thirteenth and Fourteenth Amendments to do both? Her classmates hooted derisively whenever she mentioned either topic. Yes, they had finally elected her Chief Justice of the Court of Peers, but that did not mean that they had come to see women's rights as part of civil rights. Even where the latter was concerned they continued to adhere to the gradualist approach as the only safe one. The faculty felt the same way. Spottswood Robinson accepted her wager of $10 when she bet him that *Plessy* would be overturned within the next twenty-five years. Convinced she was right, she persuaded Leon Ransom to let her write her senior seminar paper on whether a direct attack on racial segregation could be made using the Civil War Amendments.[48]

Murray's ambition to expand the power of the Fourteenth Amendment showed a certain audacity, but her desire to extend the reach of the Thirteenth Amendment exceeded what even the most far-sighted attorneys then contemplated. As of 1944, the boldest claim civil rights lawyers had risked making under the Thirteenth Amendment was that the peonage to which many share-croppers were subject constituted a new form of slavery and that the federal government therefore had the right to bypass the states and act directly on private individuals engaged in this form of economic exploitation. Murray wanted to go further. As someone preoccupied with private discrimination—not just that of lunch counter clerks and bus drivers against those deemed the wrong color, but also of employers and school officials against those deemed the wrong gender—Murray looked to the Thirteenth Amendment for redress. In doing so, she threatened to transform the American political system: to accord to the federal government power over private affairs—the transfer of personal property, the private management of public accommodations, the admissions policies of universities, even the governance of family relations—long regulated, if regulated at all, by the states.[49]

Precedent, of course, was against her. The Supreme Court had refused to revisit its decision in the Civil Rights Cases of 1883 that neither the Thirteenth nor the Fourteenth Amendment protected African Americans against discrimination in privately owned public accommodations. Moreover, the high court had consistently declined to reconsider its decision in *Plessy v. Ferguson* (1896) that, under the Fourteenth Amendment, states could force African Americans into separate institutions or facilities so long as these were equal to the ones provided to whites. But the more Murray considered the problem of Jim Crow, the more certain she was that a frontal attack would work. She found less and less time to work on her paper, however, or any of her other courses for that matter, as the civil rights campaign at Howard heated up in the spring of 1944.[50]

Sit-Ins Renewed

Inspired by the success of the prior year's effort to desegregate the Little Palace Cafeteria near the campus, Murray and the undergraduate members of the Civil Rights Committee intended to resume their sit-in campaign as soon as they returned to campus in the fall of 1943. A. Philip Randolph wanted to sponsor a nationwide protest against all forms of segregation that fall, and the Howard students could be part of that effort. But the race riots of the summer of 1943 gave them pause. James Farmer, for one, worried that mass protests by blacks not trained in principles of Satyagraha could lead to disaster. In the end, Randolph counseled his followers to allow a cooling off period. Murray agreed.[51]

As the fall term opened, Murray and the Howard undergraduates focused instead on legislative reform, particularly a civil rights bill then bottled up in congressional committees. By the spring, frustrated by the failure of the bill to make it through Congress, Ruth Powell proposed to move ahead with their "non-violent-direct action" campaign against Jim Crow, this time downtown in the white section of the city. With so many men in the armed services, the campaign drew more than ever on the energies of Howard's women and demonstrated their effectiveness in the emerging civil rights movement. Five out of nine members of the executive committee of the Howard NAACP's Civil Rights Committee were women. Ruth Powell headed the Direct Action Campaign. Once again, Murray signed on as an adviser, instructing the students on the principles of nonviolent direct action and acting as a recorder of their efforts.[52]

Cleverly, the students decided to target a national chain, John R. Thompson, which had three restaurants in Washington. One, located three blocks from the White House, seemed like the best place to start. The restaurant offered a convenient location, moderate prices, and twenty-four-hour service. Opening the restaurant to blacks would be a boon to government workers when their cafeterias were shut down at night. The Thompson chain, headquartered in Chicago, provided the added attraction of being a business against which court challenges to discrimination had already yielded results in Chicago.[53]

Murray insisted on careful planning, especially since they would be courting danger by moving into "foreign territory," outside the black neighborhood. She reminded the students that Washington had no segregation law nor did it ban picketing. Discrimination against blacks relied solely on custom. Inspired by her own experience in labor protests in the 1930s, Reyneau's stories of suffrage tactics, the principles of Satyagraha, and the successful campaign of the previous spring, Murray called for a campaign of "intelligent showmanship and an attitude of good will on the part of the demonstrators." This strategy was "calculated to minimize antagonism and to 'swing the crowd to our side.'" Murray instructed the students in picketing and public decorum, and she required each participant to sign a pledge to avoid all provocative behavior and not to respond to any provocation.[54]

The demonstration began at 4:00PM on Saturday afternoon, April 22, 1944. Walking in twos and threes, at ten-minute intervals, the Howard protestors headed for Thompson's restaurant. Following the same strategy that had worked the year before at Little Palace Cafeteria, some of them remained outside, picketing with signs that declared, "We Die Together, Why Can't We Eat Together?" Other demonstrators entered the restaurant, requested service and when refused, took vacant seats, pulled out newspapers and books, and began to read. By prearrangement, white sympathizers joined the demonstrators, chatted and shared food with them, or interviewed other white customers to determine their opinions. Murray and the undergraduate leaders spoke to the manager, emphasizing that the demonstrators did not want to provoke any trouble. When the manager worried that serving blacks would deter white customers, interviewers were able to establish that seven out of the ten white customers polled said they had no objection to eating with blacks.[55]

The pickets soon attracted a large audience, including soldiers and sailors in uniform. Most of the onlookers were white. There were catcalls, and one woman spat on the picketers. But others, "including some Wacs and Waves, cheered and called out words of sympathy." Some policemen stood by, watchful but not openly hostile. The highlight of the afternoon was the arrival of six black soldiers, who requested service and when refused sat at empty tables, pulled out the *PM* newspaper, and began to read. At adjacent tables a dozen white soldiers and sailors were eating. By this time, fifty-six demonstrators, including the black soldiers, occupied tables. A few minutes later, white military police arrived and asked the black soldiers to leave. The soldiers replied that they were waiting for service. The police left but soon returned with a white lieutenant, who asked the black soldiers to leave as "personal favor" so as not to embarrass the military "in case of an incident." Murray approached the lieutenant and suggested that if the army was afraid of being embarrassed it should ask all the soldiers to leave. The lieutenant agreed and cleared the restaurant of all uniformed personnel.[56]

Unable to persuade the remaining protestors to leave, the manager called headquarters in Chicago. Told to serve blacks as well as whites, the manager capitulated at 8:30PM. The entire episode lasted four and a half hours. The students proved correct in their decision to target a national chain with headquarters in the North. But Thompson's Chicago authorities were not the only figures with influence. No sooner had the students won than Howard President Mordecai Johnson asked them to desist. Shocked, they demanded to know why.[57]

Johnson told the students that the Senate District of Columbia Committee, chaired by Mississippi Senator Theodore Bilbo, was then reviewing Howard's appropriations for the next year. The leader of any institution of higher education, especially one that relied on federal funding for 55 percent of his budget, had reason to fear Bilbo. The senator's extreme racist views were legendary, and his position on the District Committee gave him the power to destroy Howard University.[58]

As the first black president of Howard, Johnson was under close scrutiny by the board of trustees. Civil rights demonstrations on his watch could be taken as proof that their experiment in hiring him had proved a failure. The students acceded to Johnson's order, for "there were only a few days left to the end of school and there wasn't very much we would have been able to do," Murray reported. But they did not give up entirely. "What we did do was to turn around and fight our own administration," Murray later told an interviewer. The Howard students denounced Johnson's order, insisted on their right to protest, and demanded greater power at the university through student and faculty representation in decision making.[59]

As this intramural war played out at the end of the school year, the Howard Law School librarian, A. Mercer (known as "Pop") Daniel, unearthed an astonishing document: an equal accommodations ordinance from 1872 that could have made all the difference to the fight against segregation in Washington if only the students had known about it the year before. The ordinance made it "a misdemeanor, punishable by a fine of $100, and forfeiture of license for a period of a year, for proprietors of restaurants, ice cream saloons, soda fountains, hotels, barbershops and bathing houses to refuse to serve any respectable, well-behaved person without regard to race, color or previous condition of servitude." Murray researched the subsequent history of the law and found that it had never been repealed. The law that civil rights advocates had been trying unsuccessfully to get through Congress was unnecessary in Washington, DC, for an anti-segregation ordinance had been on the books all along. But without a continuing civil rights campaign to enforce it, the ordinance remained a dead letter.[60]

"You Are Not of the Sex Entitled to Be Admitted"

As important as Ruth Powell and other female students were to Murray's growing belief in the power of black women to bring about change, no experience in her time at Howard did more to turn her into a self-conscious feminist than the bruising battle she confronted when she decided that she wanted to pursue graduate work in law. Late in the fall of 1943, Dean Hastie called her into his office to discuss her future. He proposed to recommend her for a Rosenwald fellowship, which would allow her to take a year of graduate study as preparation for returning to Howard to teach. Murray had tried unsuccessfully once before to win the coveted award, when in 1937 she had explored ways to fund graduate study in labor economics at Columbia. But in 1943, she was about to graduate first in her law school class. With that honor, together with a more clearly defined project (on changes in labor law) and a decline in the number of male applicants due to the war, she stood a much better chance.[61]

To Murray, graduate work meant study at Harvard. W. E. B. DuBois and Caroline Ware had earned their Ph.D.s at Harvard, half the Howard faculty had studied there, and her immediate predecessor as Chief Justice of the Howard Court of Peers was currently taking a post-graduate year at the Harvard law school. As she quickly discovered, however, Harvard had a woman problem. Ware, despite having studied exclusively with Harvard professors and having won a prestigious prize for her thesis, had been denied a Harvard Ph.D. She, in common with all women who studied there, received her degree from Radcliffe College. The law school went one step further; long after every other major law school in the country had agreed to accept women, Harvard held out. With applicants from men plummeting due to the draft, however, a rumor began to circulate that the law school, as well as the medical school, might finally open up to women. As a result, when Murray filled out her application to the Rosenwald Fund, she wrote in the space for choice of law school, "I should like to obtain my Master's degree at Harvard University [Law School], in the event they have removed their bar against women students. If not, then I should like to work at Yale University or at any other University which has advanced study in the field of labor law." She then inquired of the secretary at Harvard Law School whether the school would, in fact, accept a female applicant. On January 5, 1944, the reply came: "Harvard Law School . . . is not open to women for registration."[62]

For Murray this "verdict was disappointing, of course," but facing first-term law exams and plans for the Thompson sit-ins under way, she set the matter aside. What was the point of wasting time on next year when she did not yet know whether she would have the money to devote to further study. Then, on April 20 the Rosenwald Foundation informed her that she had been selected; they simply needed to know whether she would accept before they announced the results. Murray must have said yes, because a month later, the Rosenwald Fund announced its awards. Most newspapers, including the *New York Times*, mentioned merely that the foundation had granted thirty-seven fellowships, but several prominent African American newspapers, including the *Chicago Defender,* the *Philadelphia Tribune,* and the *Pittsburgh Courier,* listed the names and plans of the recipients. The entry for Murray read that she had been given a grant "for graduate work at Harvard." Murray was mortified. She must have accepted the fellowship without indicating that Harvard had turned out not to be an option for her. Whoever drafted the Rosenwald Fund's press release had simply copied her intention to attend Harvard from her application.[63]

As friends, either unaware that Harvard Law School barred women or assuming that Murray had broken the barrier, began to congratulate her on her success, Murray felt increasingly embarrassed. Setting everything else aside, she finally wrote a letter of application to Harvard, hoping against hope that the announcement of her award would move the graduate committee to accept her, despite its declared policy. Her application was "duly processed," and she received a written request for her Hunter College transcript, along with a photograph. While waiting to hear from Harvard, Murray inquired about other options. To her dismay, she discovered that the war had depleted the country's law school faculties. Many professors had taken extended leaves to work for the government. Yale continued to teach law students but had suspended graduate training. The same was true at the University Wisconsin. Boalt Hall, at the University of California at Berkeley, could accept her but planned no courses in labor law until the spring of 1945, a plan repeated for Columbia. Only Harvard offered what she needed. But the news from Harvard was not good. As she later recalled, Professor T. R. Powell, chair of the Harvard Law School's Committee on Graduate Studies (and a leading advocate of minimum wage laws for women), responded "in due course" that "Your picture and the salutation on your college transcript indicate that you are not of the sex entitled to be admitted to Harvard Law School."[64]

Murray had not felt such indignation since 1938, when the dean of graduate studies at the University of North Carolina had written, "members of your race are not admitted to the University." In her mind, to be rejected because of her "sex" was no different from being rejected because of her "race." "Both were equally unjust, stigmatizing me for a biological characteristic over which I had no control." But there was an important difference. A strong and growing civil rights movement, in which she was centrally involved, cushioned her when she encountered race discrimination. As a woman facing gender discrimination, she felt much more alone. Eleanor Roosevelt supported her, as did Caroline Ware and Betsy Graves Reyneau. Ruth Powell and other undergraduate women looked up to her. But to most of the men at Howard, all of them "ardent civil rights advocates," Harvard's rejection of her "was a source of mild amusement rather than outrage." There were some exceptions, and they were noteworthy. Leon Ransom and William Hastie encouraged her to fight. So too, did Franklin Roosevelt, who, prompted by his wife, wrote directly to Harvard President James B. Conant on Murray's behalf.[65]

One other prominent man defended her: Lloyd K. Garrison, the great-grandson of the radical abolitionist William Lloyd Garrison, who had declared that all human beings possess basic rights "whatever may be the sex or complexion." Though more self-effacing than his ancestor, Lloyd K. Garrison possessed the same commitment to social justice. As chair of the National War Labor Board during World War II, he issued a report supporting "equal pay for equal work, regardless of race, color, creed, or sex."[66]

In addition to his government service, Garrison had extensive experience in the academic world. He was the former dean of the University of Wisconsin Law School, a Howard University Trustee, and a member of the Harvard Board of Overseers. Murray met Garrison in the spring of 1944 at a Court of Peers dinner at Howard. When she told him of her rejection by the Harvard Law School Admissions Committee and her desire to petition the Overseers for a review of her application, he warned her that her prospects were not good, given the group's conservatism. He promised, however, to defend her before his colleagues. Encouraged, Murray carried through on her appeal. The Overseers, perhaps in deference to Garrison, did not rule against her, but instead referred the matter for consideration to the Law School Faculty.[67]

"I Would Gladly Change My Sex . . ."

Murray had once told Caroline Ware that she believed "One person plus a typewriter constitutes a movement." Despite being given the runaround at Harvard, she sat down once more to hammer out an appeal, this time to the Faculty of Harvard Law School. Summarizing the correspondence thus far, she requested a meeting of the faculty "to reconsider my application and to decide whether it will recommend a change of the policy now in practice." In closing she came as close as she ever did to a public announcement of her gender identity: "Gentlemen,

I would gladly change my sex to meet your requirements but since the way to such change has not been revealed to me, I have no recourse but to appeal to you to change your minds on this subject. Are you to tell me that one is as difficult as the other?"[68]

At Ware's suggestion, Murray also wrote to Judge Sarah T. Hughes of the United States District Court of Texas, who chaired the Committee on Economic and Legal Status of Women of the American Association of University Women (AAUW). Hughes promised to take the matter up in the fall. In the meantime, the Harvard faculty debated what to do. The final vote, as Murray later learned, was seven for admitting women, seven against, and a final resolution to defer action until after the war.[69]

Murray's activism kept her from preparing for final exams. At the end of her first year, she had racked up straight As. After she took her deferred exams for the second year in the fall of 1943, a few Bs accompanied further As. At the end of the third year, after walking into her exams without having studied, half her grades were Cs, and she had yet to write her seminar paper for Leon Ransom. She must have wondered whether her activism had been worth her academic sacrifice. None of her efforts over the previous six years had succeeded: neither her application to UNC, nor her protest against discrimination in interstate transportation, nor her effort to end segregation in Washington, DC.[70]

For all the disappointments endured during her final semester at Howard, Murray approached graduation in high spirits. Even with her final string of Cs, she ranked first in her class. Having made good on her pledge to become a civil rights lawyer, she fired off a letter to Virginia Governor Darden, warning him that a live lawyer was more dangerous to Jim Crow than a dead sharecropper. She sent invitations to the ceremonies to family and friends, including Eleanor Roosevelt. The First Lady responded that she could not attend but sent a huge bouquet of flowers and invited Murray and her family to tea at the White House. Whereas the sit-in at Thompson's had garnered no newspaper coverage, Murray's graduation won wide attention in the black press. No one reading the *Pittsburgh Courier* article headlined "Pauli Murray, Brilliant Law School Graduate, Honored" would have suspected any of the bumps along the way to graduation. A friend of Eleanor Roosevelt, the star of her law school class, and the "spearhead" of a campaign that had ended Jim Crow in "a number of Washington restaurants," Murray had also mounted a powerful, if still implicit, attack on Jane Crow.[71]

California Promise, 1944–1946

"Go West, Young Man"

With commencement behind her, Murray faced the question of where to pursue graduate study. Although she continued to hold out the faint hope that over the summer Harvard would reconsider its rule against admitting women, Boalt Hall seemed like her best option. First, Boalt would accept her. Second, the faculty member to whom she would be assigned would be Professor Barbara Nachtrieb Armstrong, a leading expert on labor law, who in 1919 had been the first woman appointed to a major law school faculty. But moving to California would mean living 3,000 miles from Aunt Pauline and Aunt Sallie, now in their seventies and increasingly dependent on her. Part of her believed that she owed it to them to stay nearby.[1]

Mordecai Johnson spoke to that feeling of obligation and placed it in a larger context when he told Howard graduates in his 1944 Baccalaureate address to "Go South." Rather than taking the easy course of seeking their fortune in less prejudiced parts of the country, students ought to put their knowledge and skills at the service of southern blacks. Sensitive to student attacks that he had failed them in their moment of victory at Thompson's, he focused the graduates' attention on the political problem that he faced as Howard University president. Until blacks could vote in the South, states like Mississippi would continue to send men like Bilbo to Congress. Johnson therefore urged the graduates to emulate the actions of the university's founders, to launch a second Reconstruction of the South, one that would overthrow the southern white power structure that held blacks back, not only in the South but—because of the conservative white South's entrenched power in Congress—throughout the rest of the country.[2]

Angry though she remained at the president for thwarting student efforts to end segregation in Washington, DC, Murray took Johnson's challenge seriously. Grandfather Robert Fitzgerald had been among those northerners who had moved to the South after the Civil War in the hope of ensuring democratic freedom there. Why could not she summon the "physical and moral stamina" to do the same? What if all seven members of the graduating law school class at Howard moved to Mississippi? "In ten years we might come back to Congress," she declared in an open letter to the *Afro-American*. In the end, however, she concluded that the South was still too dangerous, certainly for her. She knew that her "pattern of living" would, at a minimum, get her into trouble. It could get her lynched. The editors of the *Afro-American* agreed on the danger to anyone determined to challenge Jim Crow in the South. A week after publishing her open letter, they ran an editorial: "Go South, Commit Suicide."[3]

Better, Murray concluded, to rejoin the exodus from the South. That migration had greatly accelerated during the war, as southern blacks moved to urban areas with booming war industries. African Americans were already in a position in some northern cities to constitute a balance of power within the Democratic Party. Murray briefly considered going to Columbia Law School with her Rosenwald Fellowship but in the end decided against it. "I'm sick of New York," she confided to Eleanor Roosevelt. Indeed, she was sick of the whole East Coast, having repeatedly failed to find the medical attention she sought in hospitals from New York to Durham.[4]

When Mildred announced her intention to take a better-paying job at a veterans' hospital in Los Angeles, Pauli decided to join her. They would take Mildred's Chevrolet and share the driving. Once on the West Coast, they would find an apartment and Pauli would cover her share of the expenses as a reporter until she began graduate study in the fall. The editor of the liberal newspaper *PM* offered to pay her to report on conditions there, and she could search out other reporting opportunities after she arrived. San Francisco, which would host the chartering conference for the new United Nations in the spring of 1945, promised further reporting (and income generating) possibilities, should she enroll at Boalt Hall. Had not the great newspaper editor Horace Greeley once said, "Go west, young man"? Perhaps her future lay not in Mississippi but in the Golden State. There she might more easily launch a Second Reconstruction, one that would destroy what her grandfather's generation called "the badges and incidents of slavery," the private discrimination that continued to cripple black lives. Moreover, working with Professor Armstrong, she might escape the double discrimination of race and gender she had experienced in the East.[5]

Together, the sisters set off on June 28 in Mildred's car on a two-week, un-air-conditioned, dust-choked drive over mostly gravel roads. Arriving in Los Angeles, they lived, until Mildred got her initial paycheck, on money Pauli earned writing stories for *PM* while she looked for a regular newspaper position. Their main problem was finding housing. Lured by job openings in wartime shipbuilding and aircraft industries, the African American population in Los Angeles had tripled between 1940 and 1944, from 49,000 to 150,000. During the same period about 450,000 whites had moved into the region. Housing became a battleground, as blacks moved in and whites resisted. A few blacks were able to buy or rent homes vacated by Japanese-American families forced into relocation camps, but most of the newcomers had to take whatever they could find.[6]

Fortunately, a black real estate agent friend came to their rescue. In a deal with a bank, he had just bought an old wooden house "for a song," as Murray excitedly informed William Hastie. The place was an eyesore in an otherwise neat neighborhood, but people still lived in it and one unit was vacant—a cold-water railroad flat on the ground floor. The flat had no phone or stove, but it did have a single bed and table. The friend told them that if they were willing to live in such a place, he would wait for the first month's rent. They took it. Pauli slept on the mattress on the floor. Mildred took the frame and box spring. They ate out of cans and turned their upended suitcases into stools. Although a little worried to be "the first Negroes to move into the block," as Pauli nervously informed Hastie, "nobody has thrown bricks through the window yet, and the neighbors on both sides have been kind and cooperative."[7]

Difficult though living conditions were in the summer of 1944, Murray enjoyed the most productive period she had ever known. While the Allies marched across Europe, liberating the continent, she wrote a series of essays on the meaning of freedom in America. The words just poured from her typewriter, as she summed up the lessons she had learned about fighting against race and gender discrimination.[8]

Reporting from Los Angeles

In "An American Credo," published in *Common Ground,* she attacked the idea of "race" through a meditation on the meaning of "blood." Soon after their arrival in Los Angeles, Mildred and Pauli had been approached outside a theater by someone seeking blood donations for wounded soldiers. The sisters readily agreed but only on condition that their blood not be segregated. The recruiter assured them they need have no such concern in Los Angeles. Further investigation revealed, quite the contrary, that in Los Angeles, as elsewhere, blood was in fact segregated, because white soldiers objected to receiving blood from blacks. This medically groundless objection infuriated Pauli as few other forms of discrimination did. Medical officials knew that there was no difference between blood from whites and blood from blacks, and yet they bowed to the irrational beliefs of a segment of the population. She could not change the policy, but she could attack the idea of this bogus "blood theory," which divided people into races. In "An American Credo," she referred to herself "as a representative of blended humanity, carrying in my blood stream the three great races of man—Caucasian, Negroid, and Mongolian." She therefore planned to "resist every attempt to categorize me, to place me in some caste, or to assign me to some segregated pigeonhole." She saw herself as part of an endless march toward freedom. The nineteenth-century abolitionists, black and white, had fought to destroy slavery, but "they left for me and my contemporaries of the twentieth century the task of destroying the incidents of slavery—segregation, discrimination, and prejudice." They would succeed, she promised, not through bloodshed but rather nonviolent direct action. Some would resist in the South, even if such resistance led to jail. Others would choose "regional exile" where it would be possible to "attack again and again such laws and customs." Together, they would "fulfill the prophecy that all men are created equal."[9]

Having laid out the broad principles of her campaign to end discrimination, Murray provided a more specific "code" for day-to-day living. This code, she stressed, would not take the place of organized action or protective legislation, but it could serve as a guide toward a better life. She urged her fellow blacks to see themselves as Americans and thereby make others see them as individuals. She advised them to keep up with current events, especially Court rulings on civil rights. She recommended that, wherever possible, they should build bridges of goodwill to whites while maintaining "self-control, dignity, poise." Most of all, she urged blacks to aim high: believe "that you can be president of the United States and take steps to prepare yourself for this opportunity."[10]

Murray's greatest excitement came with acceptance of her poem "Dark Testament" for publication in *South Today,* a journal devoted to southern politics and culture that included works by African Americans and women. "Dark Testament," like Murray's essays, spoke of freedom:

> Freedom is a dream
> Haunting as amber wine
> Or words remembered out of time.
> Not Eden's gate, but freedom
> Lures us down a trail of skulls
> Where men forever crush the dreamers—
> Never the dream.

The journal's publisher, white southern-born Lillian Smith, was a vocal opponent of segregation. She had just published her first novel, *Strange Fruit,* the story of an interracial love affair in a small Georgia town that ended in a lynching. An instant best seller, *Strange Fruit* was suppressed in Boston as obscene and barred from the US mails until Eleanor Roosevelt appealed to FDR to lift the ban. To be published in Smith's journal was to achieve widespread recognition in the literary arm of the civil rights movement.[11]

Murray found that she loved writing in exile from the South, but it did not take her long to discover that Jim Crow had pursued her to California. She covered hearings before a visiting FEPC board that revealed blatant race discrimination in the hiring of conductors for streetcars. She interviewed bank managers who frankly admitted that it had never occurred to them to hire blacks as tellers. The stories were disturbing, but they sold, and by August 5 she had secured regular employment at the *Sentinel*, the largest African American newspaper on the West Coast.[12]

The Experiment

While enjoying the greatest success she had ever known as a writer, Murray continued to agonize over her gender identity. Before leaving Washington, she had gone to Freedman's Hospital, even though Mildred had made it clear that she did not want Pauli treated where she worked. Murray felt vindicated in defying her sister when she found a sympathetic internist there, Dr. Edward C. Mazique, a recent Howard medical school graduate, who seemed willing to prescribe testosterone and, most important, to persuade Mildred to administer the hormone by injection.[13]

Expecting a positive response, Pauli had broached the topic of testosterone with Mildred on their drive west but was disappointed. "I was under the apprehension that you and Mildred were going to cooperate and she would give me the male hormone injections along the way," Pauli wrote Dr. Mazique a month after she arrived in Los Angeles and had had a chance to calm down, but "I discovered after leaving Washington that you had said nothing to her." Murray continued to be upset by Mildred's refusal to help her, but she decided not to blame Dr. Mazique. "I was disappointed and somewhat resentful," she admitted, but quickly added, "Well, it's water under the bridge now." She continued to believe he was on her side and that Mildred was the one who had scotched the testosterone idea. Besides, she was now onto another matter, and she needed his help.[14]

She had a pain in her side, which doctors she consulted in Los Angeles thought might require abdominal surgery. Rather than being alarmed, Murray viewed the prospect of surgery as a great opportunity. "What do you think?" she asked Dr. Mazique. "Would such an operation help or hinder our experiment? Is there anything they can look for while digging around in my insides, if I decide to have an operation?" "Please give me your honest opinion on this," Murray implored. "You and Dave were the only two people who really played ball with me, and I respect you for it. If I am to continue our experiment, it will have to be away from my family, because Mildred knows just enough medicine to be scared stiff and opposed to such things, and not enough to be experimental." Pauli did not, in fact, have an operation that summer, but she kept thinking about the possibility. Even as she attacked the arbitrariness of racial classification in public, she dwelled on the arbitrariness of gender divisions in private. The classification of males and females, which seemed so natural, indeed unquestionable, to most people, seemed anything but natural to her.[15]

An American Dilemma

In between reporting and plotting further medical experiments, Murray turned to her unfinished work from Howard. The sit-in campaign of the spring had taken so much time that she had been unable, among other things, to write her final paper for Leon Ransom. He had given her an extension to finish it over the summer, and she spent every spare minute in the Los Angeles County Law Library, determined to complete it.[16]

Ever since Murray had been rejected by UNC and imprisoned, she had had a particular interest in the Fourteenth Amendment's Equal Protection Clause, with its guarantee that "no state shall deny to any person the equal protection of the laws." But Murray's experience with restaurant sit-ins in Washington had led her to consider an additional problem. What about discrimination based not on state law but on custom, carried out not by state officials but by private persons? There was no law in Washington, DC, that required restaurants to deny service to blacks. Murray therefore began to focus on the use of the Thirteenth Amendment as providing a possible legal remedy for private discrimination. The Thirteenth Amendment not only abolished slavery and involuntary servitude, but it also authorized Congress to pass all laws necessary to enforce it. Even as the Supreme Court ruled in the *Civil Rights Cases* of 1883 that privately owned public accommodations could discriminate, it conceded that the Thirteenth Amendment had empowered Congress to legislate against "the badges and incidents of slavery." The Court's majority concluded, however, that to deny a black person admission to a hotel, theater, or trolley did not impose such a badge nor qualify as an incident of slavery. Murray decided to challenge that view.

Murray's belief that direct attacks on both state and private discrimination could succeed found support from two sources: the teaching of Caroline Ware and the publication in 1944 of Gunnar Myrdal's *An American Dilemma*. It would be difficult to exaggerate the importance of Ware's social historical approach to civil rights on Murray's thinking. At a time when courts paid little attention to historical context or even legislative history, Ware insisted on the importance of both. She also consistently pushed the idea that classification by race was inherently "arbitrary" and that laws that categorized groups on the basis of race—such as segregation laws—violated the clear intention of the framers of the Thirteenth and Fourteenth Amendments to protect newly freed slaves from the abusive power so easily and pervasively wielded by the dominant white population.

Justice John Marshall Harlan made this point in his dissents in both the *Civil Rights Cases* and *Plessy*. The problem in 1944 was to provide new evidence that would persuade a modern court that Harlan was right and the majority of justices in the late nineteenth century were wrong. Murray believed that Gunnar Myrdal's two-volume *American Dilemma* provided the evidence lawyers needed, and she decided to use it as a basis for her civil rights paper.[17]

Myrdal's magnum opus had been six years in the making. In 1938, Frederick Keppel, president of the Carnegie Corporation, commissioned a research project on race in America. Given the passions that the topic provoked in America, Keppel asked an outsider, the Swedish economist Gunnar Myrdal, to move to New York to direct the investigation.[18]

Understanding the limits of his own knowledge, Myrdal recruited the leading race specialists to advise him. African American scholars who had long failed to win foundation support because white scholars doubted their objectivity, suddenly had a sponsor, one willing to give them maximum freedom to pursue their own research and to publish it separately. As they tutored Myrdal on the realities of race in America, and as his travels, interviews, and observations confirmed their evidence, Myrdal began to write a book that mirrored their findings.[19]

The timing of the project proved just as important to the argument Myrdal came to make as the evidence his associates provided. He had long viewed economics as the driving force in the creation of social problems. But by the time he commenced writing *An American Dilemma*, World War II had altered his thinking. Under threat of invasion by Nazi Germany, Sweden had dramatically curtailed free speech. In Myrdal's mind America stood as a beacon of freedom to the world, but a beacon that was seriously compromised by the country's treatment of its black population. Myrdal came to the conclusion that America's "Negro problem" was really a "white man's problem," a problem that threatened not only the welfare of 13 million blacks but also the white man's soul and America's standing in the world.[20]

Murray had followed Myrdal's progress through two people: George Stoney, a white friend from the Henry Street Settlement, whom Myrdal hired to do field work among southern sharecroppers, and Doxey Wilkerson, a black scholar Myrdal hired to work full-time in New York on his specialty, black education. In 1939, Wilkerson had asked Murray to share the correspondence surrounding her failed effort to win admission to the graduate program at the University of North Carolina. She did. Murray's interest in the Myrdal project intensified in her years at Howard, because Myrdal tapped so many of the school's faculty to contribute monographs in their areas of expertise: Ralph Bunche in political science, E. Franklin Frazier in sociology, and Sterling Brown in literature. Myrdal also hired Howard graduate Kenneth Clark, who was completing his doctorate in psychology at Columbia, to investigate the psychological consequences of racism. When *An America Dilemma* appeared, she had a good idea what it would contain and was delighted to find that it fit so well the argument she wanted to make.[21]

Challenging the *Civil Rights Cases* and *Plessy*

Murray latched onto Myrdal's findings to answer the question she posed in her law school seminar paper: "Should the *Civil Rights Cases* and *Plessy v. Ferguson* Be Overruled?" Hardly anyone, including law students, she pointed out, ever read these two cases in their entirety. As a result, few had encountered the lonely dissents of Justice John Marshall Harlan. Moreover, only historians ever considered the context in which the Civil War Amendments had been passed and the Supreme Court rulings on them delivered. She therefore devoted her paper to a brief review of the history of the Thirteenth and Fourteenth Amendments, the dissents of Justice Harlan, and a discussion of how modern social science, gathered by Gunnar Myrdal in *An American Dilemma,* supported a direct challenge to the premises underlying the majority opinions in the *Civil Rights Cases* and *Plessy.*

Murray began by revisiting the original intent of the Thirteenth and Fourteenth Amendments, with Myrdal's idea of the conflict at the heart of white America in mind. Abraham Lincoln, she pointed out, had understood the inherent contradiction between the Founding Fathers' declaration that "all men are created equal" and the claim made by white southerners on the eve of the Civil War that "to enslave others is a 'sacred right of self-government.'" It was this contradiction, she believed, that the Civil War Amendments were designed to eliminate. The Thirteenth and Fourteenth Amendments, she insisted, established universal freedom, the first by requiring individuals to honor the freedom of all, the second requiring the states to do so. This freedom entailed "freedom of movement," the "right of association," "the right to enjoy all public privileges," the right "to live in peace," and to "work productively." To be denied any of these rights was to be marked with a "badge of inferiority." But the amendments, she believed, could not succeed on their own. Only through "the complete abolition of all laws and customs designed to enslave the black, to force him into an inferior category, to restrict his movements and his privileges as a human being endowed with inalienable rights," she contended, "could the institution of slavery be destroyed." That understanding had led to the inclusion of enabling clauses in the Thirteenth and Fourteenth Amendments, clauses that empowered Congress to act directly against any attempt to deny those of African descent their basic rights as citizens of the United States.[22]

Murray anticipated the likely objection that her reading of the Civil War Amendments was too broad. She believed, however, that the continuing power of slavery in American society—a power that majorities on the Supreme Court had conveniently ignored—justified her interpretation. Myrdal agreed, and Murray praised him for tracing the current inferior status of the black to the social relationships inherent in slavery. "What we are studying," Murray—quoting Myrdal—concluded, "is in reality the survivals in modern American society of the slavery institution."[23]

No Supreme Court justice had ever understood this point better than former Kentucky slave owner John Marshall Harlan. Born in 1833, raised a Whig, and trained as a lawyer, Harlan initially defended slavery, but a number of factors in his background softened his racial views. He had a slave half brother, who was treated to some degree as a member of the family and who, later freed, became a business success. He married a woman from a northern, anti-slavery family. When the Civil War broke out, Harlan joined the Union Party and fought on the Union side, in the hope that the union and slavery could both be preserved. But when slavery ended, the Union Party collapsed, and white terrorists took over both Kentucky and the Democratic Party, Harlan faced a difficult choice. He could support the arson, beatings, and murders inflicted on African Americans by the Ku Klux Klan and other groups, or he could become a Republican. Benjamin Bristow, the Republican US Attorney for Kentucky, helped him make up his mind. In August 1868, Bristow successfully prosecuted two white men in federal court, under the authority granted by the Thirteenth Amendment and the Civil Rights Act of 1866, for using an ax to hack to death members of a black family. Outraged by the wanton violence of the defendants, Harlan joined the Republican Party and embraced the Civil War Amendments. In 1877, Republican president Rutherford B. Hayes appointed him to the Supreme Court. As his colleagues on the Court adopted an ever-narrower interpretation of the Thirteenth and Fourteenth Amendments' power, Harlan insisted on what he believed to be the broad intent of the framers, to protect the civil rights of people of color against both state and private discrimination.[24]

Harlan dissented vigorously from the majority opinions in the *Civil Rights Cases* (1883) and *Plessy v. Ferguson* (1896). In the first, the Court ruled that Congress did not have the right under either the Thirteenth or Fourteenth Amendments to pass the Civil Rights Act of 1875, which barred privately owned public accommodations—such as trains, theaters, or hotels—from discriminating on the basis of race. In the second, the Court ruled that neither amendment barred a state from segregating its citizens by race, so long as the accommodations provided each group were equal.

Harlan, the lone dissenter in each case, "took a broader view," Murray noted approvingly. He argued that the Civil Rights Act of 1875 could be enforced under the Thirteenth Amendment, since the purpose of the Thirteenth Amendment was, in her paraphrase of his argument, "to abolish not only slavery but also the burdens, incidents and disabilities of slavery—those relations which placed the former slave in a position of inferiority attached to and associated with slavery." That included, she emphasized, "the denial of equal accommodations in public places and the inferior status such denial implied."[25]

Murray devoted so much of her essay to the *Civil Rights Cases* that she barely touched *Plessy v. Ferguson*; indeed, she never developed that part of her paper beyond a two-page, single-spaced outline. But her plan was clear: "the same arguments used to overturn the decision in the *Civil Rights Cases*" could be used to attack the majority opinion in *Plessy*. The "arbitrary separation of citizens, on the basis of race," as Justice Harlan wrote in his dissent in *Plessy*, "is a badge of servitude wholly inconsistent with the civil freedom and the equality before the law established by the Constitution. It cannot be justified upon any legal grounds." The act of discrimination in public accommodations was illegal under the Thirteenth Amendment insofar as it perpetuated a "badge and incident of slavery." That discrimination was also illegal under the Fourteenth Amendment, inasmuch as state law required it, for, as Harlan declared, "our Constitution is color-blind, and neither knows nor tolerates classes among citizens."[26]

Murray agreed with Harlan, but she faced a serious problem in determining how his views might be moved from the position of lonely dissent to majority opinion. For that to happen, she believed, lawyers would have to challenge the racial assumptions on which courts had based their opinions. Here, Myrdal was particularly helpful. He highlighted the arbitrariness of race as a category. In much of the United States the "Negro race" was defined by white people to include anyone with "a known trace of Negro blood in his veins"; in the rest of the Americas, the reverse was true: a person who was not entirely black was considered to be white. Race should therefore be considered, "a social and conventional, not a biological concept," Myrdal argued.[27]

The biological concept nonetheless exercised considerable power, as Murray was well aware, and to the extent that the courts relied on it to justify segregation, any challenge to segregation must confront it. Fortunately, modern social science offered an important corrective. Over the past generation, study after study had refuted beliefs in the biological inferiority of blacks. Moreover, as Murray noted in her paper, Myrdal went even further. As she summarized his findings in the outline she appended to her essay, "Not only is the doctrine of 'separate but equal' facilities a legal delusion, but positively its effect is to do violence to the personality of the individual affected, whether he is white or black. See recent psychological and sociological data supporting this assertion—*American Dilemma*." Not that scientific evidence had yet changed popular opinion. As Myrdal conceded, "Hardly anywhere else or in any other issue is there . . . such a wide gap between scientific thought and popular belief." But once the courts understood that segregation laws were rooted in discriminatory prejudice and not biology, Murray insisted, those laws could not survive, however strong popular opinion might be.[28]

Soon after completing her paper, Murray decided on a whim to try out her ideas on a current Supreme Court justice. In her capacity as a reporter for the *Sentinel*, she telephoned Supreme Court Justice Frank Murphy to ask what he thought about the possibility of a direct attack on *Plessy*. To her delight, he told her the time had come for a review of segregation cases. Moreover, he advised her, "Justice is the thing you want to hammer at—don't mind the precedents." Emboldened, she asked "what he thought of the idea that 'an arbitrary classification by color' was unconstitutional and not within the police power of the state." To further clarify her point, she added "that with other classifications, by change of status or circumstances one could remove himself from the classification affected, but that color was fixed and thus arbitrary." Murphy responded, "You're perfectly right." Murray reported the interview to Ware, crediting her mentor for helping her to develop the idea: "I'd never had the courage to advance it, if you hadn't held my hand all down the line."[29]

"A Parallel to the Negro Problem"

Murray believed that the approach she advocated for killing Jim Crow in America could work for killing Jane Crow, but she did not elaborate this point, even in outline form. The judicial precedents were solidly against her. So too was most social science of her day. But here, too, Gunnar Myrdal suggested a way forward. Myrdal drafted a chapter in which he described the "striking similarities" between the history, status, and problems of blacks and those of women and children. Male children outgrew their subordinate status, but blacks and women never did; both were "suppressed" in America. The most "important disabilities still affecting" women's "status," Myrdal argued, in words that Murray well understood, were "those barring her attempt to earn a living and to attain promotion in her work." Employers and labor unions conspired to segregate the job market not only by race but also by gender. As a result, women found themselves confined to those jobs that "are regularly in the low salary bracket and do not offer much of a career." Myrdal condemned this segregation as a central mechanism for keeping both black men and all women down. "A Parallel to the Negro Problem" went on to point out that women's subordination stemmed not only from economic forces but also from psychological factors. Men felt "a distaste for the very idea of having women on an equal plane as co-workers and competitor," and they found it "even more 'unnatural' to work under women." Worse, women played a role in their own subordination: "It is said about women that they prefer men as bosses and do not want to work under another woman,"

Myrdal reported. "Negroes often feel the same way about working under other Negroes."[30]

Gunnar Myrdal undoubtedly discussed this chapter with his wife Alva, and in a sense it is coauthored, because it relies so heavily on Alva Myrdal's previously published essay, "One Sex a Social Problem." One passage, however, went beyond what Alva had previously argued. She had always maintained that women's subordination was rooted in the industrial revolution. Gunnar's study of blacks in the United States persuaded him that sex and race discrimination had a common root in the traditional paternalistic order. This striking insight allowed him to explain how white males had managed to subjugate both the men and women of another race and the women of their own. By positing that all blacks and white women were their natural inferiors, closer to animals than to themselves, these patriarchs could argue that the rules of fairness did not apply to them. In just a few pages, Myrdal identified the ways in which a white patriarchal society constructed black men and all women as biologically inferior and caused them to internalize the negative views of the dominant society.[31]

Although Gunnar Myrdal originally intended "A Parallel to the Race Problem" to be a chapter in *An American Dilemma*, when Frederick Keppel read the manuscript he objected that both black men and [white] women would be startled by the comparison Myrdal was drawing. He was relieved when Myrdal agreed to turn the chapter into an appendix and bury it at the end of the two-volume work.[32]

Buried or not, "A Parallel to the Race Problem" spoke more directly to Murray than anything that preceded it in *An American Dilemma*. When she finished her paper for Ransom, she sent it to him with a cover note, which began, "This is the first installment of 'Who Killed Jim Crow?'" She then asked him, "What shall I do about killing 'Jane Crow?'" Though posed as a question, Murray already had the outline of an answer. Her immediate goal was to strike down Jim Crow, but from 1944 onward, she believed, supported by Appendix 5, that the same legal and social scientific reasoning could be used to undermine what she called "prejudice against sex."[33]

Murray made an explicit reference to the parallel between the dangers posed by "Jim Crow" and those inflicted by "Jane Crow" in a satirical piece published in the *Sentinel*: "[Jim Crow's] got a mate—Jane Crow. She doesn't bother the 'culud folks' unless they happen to be women. Women's her specialty. When she bites a woman, that woman is supposed to be inferior to the men." And in "An American Credo," Murray linked race and gender discrimination, when she swore never to tolerate "any practice of discrimination, segregation, or prejudice against any human being because of an accident of birth which has determined race, color, sex, or nationality." Twenty years before Congress added "sex" to title VII and the ACLU began its fight to expand the meaning of the Equal Protection

Clause to cover discrimination on the basis of gender, Pauli Murray had developed the outline of the ultimately successful argument against "Jane Crow."[34]

Discrimination in Housing

Just as she was about to send off her paper to Leon Ransom, Murray encountered a new and especially upsetting form of discrimination. A harassing, unsigned, typewritten letter with no return address arrived in the mail on August 23. Purporting to be from the South Crocker Street Property Owner's Association and addressed to Mrs. Mildred Fearing and Pauli Murray, the letter stated, "We the property owners of Crocker Street wish to inform you the flat you now occupy . . . is restricted to the white or Caucasian race only." The letter went on to demand that they vacate the premises within seven days.[35]

The memory of Granma Cornelia's nighttime terrors of the Ku Klux Klan came flooding back, as Pauli contemplated how vulnerable she was—a stranger in a ground-floor apartment in an isolated building—to a racist attack. Her landlord was in Mexico for three weeks. Mildred worked the evening shift at the VA hospital and would not be back before midnight. Having no one to talk to, Pauli rushed to the *Sentinel*, where she sought the advice of Loren Miller, one of the owners of the paper and an experienced lawyer. He told her that she was not alone. The courts in California teamed with cases involving associations of white private property owners who had signed "restrictive covenants" not to sell or rent property to African Americans and others. As it happened, he was handling "the overwhelming majority" of them.[36]

Miller secured police protection for the sisters and asked the FBI to investigate. Whether the federal government intervened is not clear, but soon local squad cars began patrolling the neighborhood at night. Believing that public exposure was the black community's best defense, Miller encouraged Murray to write a story for the *Sentinel*. Murray discovered, among other things, that the Southside Property Owners Protective League had organized 1,000 white property owners to keep blacks out of "white areas." At their first meeting, attended by 200 people, they resolved to enforce restrictions against " 'two non-caucasian families' living in the allegedly restricted area." Mildred and Pauli were one of the two families targeted for eviction.[37]

A few days later, Murray appeared on the *Sentinel*'s regularly sponsored radio show. Interviewed by *Sentinel* founder Leon Washington, she gave a brief history of restrictive covenants. She began with the Supreme Court case of *Buchanan v. Warley* (1917), which struck down a Louisville, Kentucky, ordinance restricting the sale of property on racial grounds. The question remained whether private restrictive covenants (as contrasted with local ordinances or state laws) were also unconstitutional. The Supreme Court had never addressed this, but interestingly, in 1892 a federal court in California had done so. In *Gandolfo v. Hartman*, a federal judge had overruled a restrictive covenant against leasing to a Chinese person. Unfortunately, later courts had ignored the case, a situation that Murray believed needed correction.[38]

The police protected the sisters until the end of September, when Mildred returned to Washington and Pauli moved to Berkeley. Murray found a reprieve from the suffering she had experienced in the restrictive-covenant wars in Los Angeles by securing admission to Berkeley's International House. Berkeley had leased the regular International House to the navy during the war; Murray therefore found herself housed in one of four large fraternity residences nearby. Forty-four women shared her house, three or four to each room. They studied and dressed there but slept in double-decker bunks on communal, unlighted porches open to wind, stars, and Berkeley fog.[39]

Among these new friends, Murray found a multiracial, multicultural enclave of acceptance in an idyllic setting. Climbing the Berkeley hills in the late

Figure 7.1 The women of International House, Berkeley, California, 1945. Pauli Murray, third from left. Estate of Pauli Murray, Schlesinger Library, Radcliffe Institute, Harvard University.

afternoon, she could look across the great bay to the coastal mountain range, down on San Francisco, and beyond to the setting sun behind the Golden Gate Bridge. Although she missed the seasons, she appreciated the Bay Area's mild climate; on the coldest day the temperature stayed above freezing. She did not need a winter coat. Talking to people from varied social and ethnic backgrounds gave Murray new perspective on her own racial problems. One roommate, Mijeko Takita, had just returned from three years in a Japanese relocation center in Topaz, Arizona. Uprooted almost overnight, she carried herself with a "quiet dignity" and "no sign of bitterness." A year later, at the news that a second atomic bomb had been dropped on Japan, she said quietly, "My grandparents live in Nagasaki," and turned her face away. A second roommate, Eva Schiff, came from Cologne. Her memories of early childhood rivaled Pauli's own: children stoned, human beings branded. Eva embraced America but felt deeply wounded when she was denied admission to a sorority at UCLA when someone learned she was a Jew. Jane Garcia's family had emigrated from Mexico five generations before, but she still did not feel accepted because of her "swarthy complexion." Lillian Li, born in China, had spent more than half her life in the United States but was still treated as foreigner. One day a lurching trolley car had thrown her against a white American, who shot back angrily, "Why don't you look where you're going you drunken Chink?" Another friend, the white daughter of missionaries in China, remembered being surrounded by Chinese children who taunted her as a "white devil." International House formed a microcosm of a western state that, drawing its population in ever increasing numbers from Asia and Mexico, as well as the rest of the United States, was moving beyond Gunnar Myrdal's biracial American society of black and white. The experience of living there greatly expanded Murray's understanding of civil rights and reinforced her commitment to housing free of discrimination.[40]

Boalt Hall

When Murray began classes at Berkeley's Boalt Hall School of Jurisprudence, she discovered she was the only graduate student. Even in peacetime, law school graduates at the country's top law schools hardly ever stayed on for graduate work. If they planned eventually to teach, they typically clerked for a federal judge, preferably a Supreme Court justice, to gain the advanced training thought best to produce an effective law school professor. The few students who enrolled for graduate work typically came from foreign countries. They sought a year's exposure to the common law tradition before returning home. The rare US student was almost always an African American who hoped that graduate training at an elite school would give him an edge at a teaching position at a black law school.[41]

Murray had planned to spend the year studying labor law with Barbara Armstrong, but Armstrong was on leave in Washington, DC, working for the Office of Price Administration. The author of *Insuring the Essentials* (1932), Armstrong had first won a position in the New Deal as chief of staff of the Committee on Economic Security and had helped draft the Social Security Act. Though difficult to please, she took a special interest in women law students and served as a symbol to women lawyers.[42]

Berkeley was not initially willing to admit Murray until Armstrong returned to campus in the spring and could supervise her research, but the administration finally agreed that she could enroll at the beginning of the academic year in October and take other classes, pending Armstrong's return. Among those classes, she signed up for a directed research with Dudley McGovney, Berkeley's distinguished professor of jurisprudence, a man known for his liberal interpretations of civil rights who was then working on the problem of discrimination in housing.[43]

Murray quickly learned that McGovney agreed with her that *Plessy* was unconstitutional and that separation on the basis of race was an unreasonable classification; however, he declined her challenge that he should say so in writing. As Murray reported his position to William Hastie, "He believes his effectiveness will be lost, if he did." Recently in touch with Justice Wiley B. Rutledge, McGovney thought that an attack on segregation should be postponed while lawyers focused on overturning restrictive covenants. In fact, he was then working on an article for the *California Law Review* on that subject, which became the basis of Murray's conversations with him for the rest of the term.[44]

McGovney saw nothing unconstitutional in a private person's discriminating on racial grounds in the sale of property, but he believed that court enforcement of a restrictive covenant constituted "state action" and thereby violated the Equal Protection Clause of the Fourteenth Amendment. His article built carefully on precedent, showing the Court's willingness to strike down as "state action," for instance, Alabama's denial of effective counsel to the Scottsboro Boys. At the time, McGovney doubted that the Court was ready to extend such reasoning to restrictive covenants; in fact, the Court did so less than four years later in *Shelley v. Kraemer* (1948), following his language.[45]

Murray agreed with McGovney that court enforcement of private discrimination constituted state action under the Fourteenth Amendment, but she believed that private discrimination could also be attacked under the Thirteenth Amendment's grant of power to the federal government to enforce not only the abolition of slavery but also its "badges and incidents." McGovney strongly disagreed; indeed, he thought the argument bordered on the "frivolous," so often had the courts rejected the idea that the Thirteenth Amendment banned any individual act other than enslavement or involuntary servitude.[46]

But Murray would not give up, so McGovney challenged her to prove her argument in her research project for him. A few weeks into the fall term, she gave him a draft of the essay she had sent to Ransom to show the approach she wanted to take. McGovney strongly disapproved. He cautioned her, in particular, against relying on Harlan's dissents in the *Civil Rights Cases* and *Plessy*. Constitutional scholars had long regarded Harlan as an eccentric, and in any event a solitary dissent or two provided shaky ground for overturning settled precedent.[47]

Moreover, McGovney identified a number of important topics that she had "not touched" in her Howard essay, including most particularly the legislative history of the Thirteenth Amendment. How could she be so sure that the framers of the amendment meant to protect individuals from private discrimination, without having investigated the "debates leading up to the proposal of the XIII" so as to determine "the intended scope of it?" Why, for that matter, had she not examined the legislative history of the Civil Rights Act of 1866 for evidence of Congress's intent?[48]

If Murray was to persuade McGovney that the Thirteenth Amendment protected blacks from discrimination by individuals, she would have to do a much more thorough job. He did not make her job easy. In a letter to Hastie, Murray reported that McGovney gave her "holy hell," as they "fought it out" over the fall term of 1945.[49]

Murray did not find much to help her cause in the congressional debates over the passage of the Thirteenth Amendment, but she hit pay dirt when she examined the Civil Rights Act of 1866 and statements leading up to its passage. Although her treatment was cursory, amounting to nothing more than quoting its language, she must have taken heart in the words of Senator Lyman Trumbull, head of the judiciary committee and the person most responsible for ushering the Thirteenth Amendment through the Senate. In support of the Civil Rights Act of 1866, he declared that if the Thirteenth Amendment meant only the end of forced labor, then the "promised freedom is a delusion. . . . With the destruction of slavery necessarily follows the destruction of the incidents of slavery." The enforcement clause, he continued, gave Congress the authority to pass laws prohibiting any infringement of civil rights associated with the institution and its "badges." Exactly what these "incidents" and "badges" were, Trumbull did not make clear. But the act provided, in the clearest language Murray was able to find of congressional intent, that "citizens of every race and color shall have the same right throughout the United States and its Territories to . . . purchase, lease, sell, hold, and convey real and personal property . . . as is enjoyed by white citizens." The "same" right to "lease" property, surely meant that two African American sisters had the same right as any white persons to rent a cold-water flat in Los Angeles. To deny the sisters this basic right of property solely because they were descended from slaves was to humiliate and stigmatize them with a "badge" of racial inferiority. To limit their economic opportunity in this way was to echo one of the worst "incidents of slavery," the denial to slaves of the right to own or lease land. McGovney was not persuaded. He gave Murray an A for her work but sent her off with the wry comment, "Fisherman go out to fish, but catch few fish."[50]

With the return of Barbara Armstrong to the Berkeley campus in the spring of 1945, Murray set aside her work for McGovney and embarked on research on employment discrimination. Not only was this the research for which she had won the Rosenwald Fellowship, but Murray also needed a publishable article to earn her master's degree, and an article on equal opportunity in employment seemed to offer a surer route to that goal than did her preliminary work on the Thirteenth Amendment.[51]

On Discrimination in Employment

Murray therefore commenced research on the ways in which the federal government had succeeded in using its power, albeit in provisional, limited, and tentative ways, to protect minorities and women from discrimination in employment. If she could not make the case that the Thirteenth Amendment protected individuals from private discrimination, perhaps she could show that the federal government was already taking steps to do so in limited circumstances and might build on that foundation to extend protections more broadly through legislation, most especially by making the Fair Employment Practices Committee permanent and giving it jurisdiction over not only race but also sex discrimination in employment. The federal government had already extended its authority in the area of race and sex discrimination through its position as the country's largest contractor and under its constitutional power over interstate commerce.[52]

Whereas McGovney fought Murray every step of the way over the relevance of the Thirteenth Amendment to the struggle against private discrimination based on race, Barbara Armstrong supported her attempt to chart the federal government's efforts to guarantee equal opportunity for minorities and women in the private sphere. Murray's resulting article, published in the fall 1945 issue of the *California Law Review,* highlighted the ways in which the federal government was already acting to guarantee race equality, and sometimes sex equality, in private employment through its power under the War Powers and Commerce Clauses. It had exercised oversight of railroad unions since 1920, supervised union activity through the National Labor Relations Board (NLRB) since 1935, and regulated employment in government and in the defense industries through the Fair Employment Practices Committee since 1941 and the National War Labor Board since 1942. In each of these venues, the federal government had used its power to end discrimination based on race, creed, color, or national origin, and in some instances sex, in hiring, promotion, and work conditions. Although Murray emphasized federal efforts to ban discrimination in employment, she also drew attention to those states that were acting as laboratories of progressive reform. In a footnote, she suggested the possibility that those states that were failing to prevent private discrimination might arguably be in violation of the Equal Protection Clause of the Fourteenth Amendment.[53]

Murray found that the courts, though reluctant to interfere with private employers, had proven ready to ban race discrimination in labor unions in certain circumstances. When labor unions controlled the labor market, the courts reasoned, they became quasi-public entities, affected by public interest, and therefore subject to regulation at common law. Murray left open the question of whether continuing discrimination in employment could better be defeated through legislative or judicial action, but she was clearly anticipating Title VII and subsequent court decisions upholding it in the face of conflicting state laws.[54]

Writing to Ware in the midst of her research, Murray reported, "With Mrs. Armstrong I've galloped through all the Labor Relations Reporters since 1936, and am getting a bird's eye view on the evolution of the right to employment without discrimination—collecting cases on Chinese, Filipinos, Negroes, Jews, Mexicans, and women." Murray believed that the government had taken "giant strides" in the last decade to bring about greater equality. "Already, however, I'm beginning to believe strongly the FEPC bill should be amended to include 'sex' along with its other 'race, color, creed or national origin' factors." That did not happened, for in 1946 Congress terminated the FEPC.[55]

Although Murray believed that she was finally on the right track, working for Armstrong proved even more difficult than working for McGovney. Armstrong approved Murray's topic, but she was so harshly critical of initial drafts that Murray despaired. Having no law review experience, she had little understanding of how to go about writing an article destined for publication in a legal journal. To add to her burden, Murray not only enrolled in an especially tough course in federal tax, "the hardest course in the law school," she reported to Ware, but also a class on "International Law and Relations" in the Political Science Department. None of this work stopped her from piling on extra-curricular work at International House in preparation for the United Nations chartering conference in San Francisco at the end of April. Among other activities she chaired the Wednesday evening discussion table on such topics as Dumbarton Oaks and Bretton Woods—a course in itself. At the same time, she organized half a dozen of her friends at International House into a panel on diversity. Performing at community centers around the Bay Area, she celebrated the group discussions as a contribution toward "Breaking Down Barriers." She was having the time of her life, but, as so often in the past, she was seriously overextended.[56]

In the midst of this frenzied activity, Murray learned of the death of President Roosevelt, who suffered a fatal stroke at his retreat in Warm Springs, Georgia, on April 12, 1945. Though her relationship with the president had long been fraught, she set aside her law books to write a poem in his honor. "A lone man stood on the glory road," she began, and a few lines later continued,

> He stumbled a pace, Groped about in the April twilight
> As one who feels his legs beneath him
> For the first time,
> Tests them on solid earth
> And finds them worthy of a good sprint.

Sustaining the image of a man—race unspecified—who has finally found the freedom that eluded him in life, she concluded,

> For a lone man walks on the glory road
> Waits for the final gun,
> The last exploding cannon,
> When a man can walk in Georgia twilight,
> Shouting as all free things do Finding themselves free.

When Murray showed her poem to Armstrong, the older woman delivered a backhanded compliment: "We may be trying to make a second-rate lawyer out of a first-rate writer."[57]

Despite her packed schedule, Murray still planned to cover the United Nations chartering conference in San Francisco for the black press. To her dismay, Dean Edwin D. Dickenson denied her permission to miss classes, telling her, "You've got to get tough with yourself." Murray tried to buckle down, but emotional turmoil, quite apart from her desire to be at the conference, made it hard for her to concentrate on her work. She was experiencing tremendous distress—the kind she had suffered repeatedly through the years, but worse. Agonizing over her inability to resolve her gender identity in the midst of the greatest academic pressure she had ever known, she began to unravel. Grades that should have been As turned into Bs. The tax course she found a challenge, ended up a C+. Worse, she failed to complete her master's essay by the end of the academic year.[58]

Armstrong insisted that Murray would have to continue working on her employment article through the summer and, if necessary, into the fall to meet her standards. Murray panicked. Her Rosenwald Fellowship had run out. She was desperate to study for the California Bar Exam so that she could get a job and to that end signed up for a review course. When Armstrong found out, she told Murray that she must drop the course and focus on her article. Murray reluctantly agreed, somehow pulled herself through her emotional collapse, and—as World War II finally ended on September 2, 1945—completed her work to Armstrong's satisfaction. She then studied for the bar on her own and, to Armstrong's amazement, passed the famously difficult exam.[59]

The publication of Murray's "The Right to Equal Opportunity in Employment" in the fall 1945 issue of the *California Law Review* marked the culmination of a seven-year odyssey, during which Murray addressed—through nonviolent direct action, newspaper columns, and scholarly research—every major civil rights issue of her time: state segregation laws that restricted access to education and public accommodations (1938–1940); political discrimination through the poll tax (1940–1942); segregation by custom at lunch rooms (1943–1944); and private discrimination in housing and employment (1944–1945). In the process, she came to identify Jane Crow as a form of bias that mimicked race discrimination and was best attacked using the same legal theories. Although she had failed to complete what she thought of as her most important project— a rethinking of the meaning of the Thirteenth Amendment—she was able to enjoy the satisfaction of seeing her law review article on employment discrimination published in the *California Law Review,* two issues after the one in which McGovney published his article on restrictive covenants.

With her work for Armstrong finally approved for publication, Murray earned her master's in law. And by passing the bar exam, she could apply for admission to practice in California. What to do remained a question. Having exhausted the funds from her Rosenwald Fellowship, Murray was once again broke, with no resources to support her through the writing of the doctoral thesis she wanted to write on the Thirteenth Amendment. She assumed that Boalt Hall would accept her for more advanced work. Having worked extraordinarily hard and having shown remarkable independence of mind over a twelve-month period, she had succeeded against fierce headwinds from her mentors. As she recalled a couple of years later in a letter to a friend: "Do you recollect the continual struggle I had with Barbara Armstrong and D. O. McGovney who refused to let me develop my own material and who literally wore me out battling against their more conservative points of view?" But the faculty had the last word. Though Murray did not learn this until much later, they quietly decided in November that the LL.M. would be Murray's terminal degree with them. McGovney was about to retire and no one else wanted to shepherd a headstrong, academically erratic student through a doctoral thesis with a losing argument.[60]

William Hastie urged her to get a couple of years of experience in general practice and offered to help her find a job: "I believe we could find a place for you here in Washington. . . . [W]herever you might go, I think the experience and practice which you would gain would be of tremendous value whether you should eventually go into teaching or government service, or with such an organization as the N.A.A.C.P. Incidentally, Dean Garrison says that if there is still a war and a War Labor Board this summer they can use you there." Murray wrote Hastie that her plan was to get a job with a firm in San Francisco that specialized in labor law. To her amazement, Armstrong (eager to help launch her student out of the world of academe) wrote her a strong recommendation. "I regard Miss Murray as a young woman of exceptional competence," she began. "She has, in addition to a very keen and quick mind, the capacity for hard work and an exceptionally pleasing personality. . . . I may add that Miss Murray had exactly three weeks in which to prepare for our recent bar examinations and that she passed these examinations when some of the graduates of our School who studied all summer failed to do so."[61]

Deputy Attorney General Murray

Nothing had materialized by the time Murray attended the swearing-in ceremony for those newly admitted to the California Bar on December 8, 1945. But her fortunes changed that day, when she was introduced to the man who presided: Attorney General Robert W. Kenny, the only Democrat to hold statewide office in a state that had recently elected Republican Earl Warren governor. An outspoken liberal, Kenny was also the president of the Los Angeles Chapter of the National Lawyers Guild, established in 1937, partly in protest against the American Bar Association's refusal to admit blacks to membership. Kenny was also the honorary chairman of a California committee working to pass state fair employment practice legislation, and he spoke out often in favor of fair treatment for minorities and women. When Kenny learned that Murray was the author of the *California Law Review* article on employment discrimination, he promptly offered her a temporary position as a lawyer in the Attorney General's Office and the hope of a permanent place in the future. Starting on January 2, 1946, she held the distinction of being the first black to hold the position of Deputy Attorney General in California.[62]

Murray had landed a dream job, one in which she was encouraged to work on problems on which she was now an expert: fair housing and employment discrimination. Unfortunately, she was sick from before the day she started with what doctors suspected was sub-acute appendicitis. Ideally, she would have had her appendix removed before she started work, but she had no health insurance. She went to work anyway, hoping to prove herself to her superiors and to make enough money before her appendix burst, to have the necessary operation.[63]

Murray's most important contribution at her new job was to bring stories in the black press to the attention of her white colleagues. Newspapers were almost completely segregated at that time. With a handful of exceptions, white papers hired only white reporters who covered only stories of interest to whites. Only the black press covered the routine stories of race discrimination and violence. The biggest story that the white public knew nothing about in January 1946 came out of Fontana, a town about fifty miles to the east of Los Angeles in San Bernardino County. Twenty years before, O'Day Short, a fair-skinned man of mixed European, African, and Indian heritage had moved to Los Angeles from Mississippi. Trained in refrigeration and electrical work, he had initially suc-ceeded. He married, fathered two children, and became a committed advocate of civil rights. Late in 1945 he accepted a job at a refrigeration firm in Fontana, where Kaiser had built a large steel mill. Hoping to make a better life for his family, he bought land and began to build a home. When neighborhood whites learned that he was black, they warned him to leave. He refused, complained to the FBI, and notified the *Sentinel* that he was being harassed. On December 16, a suspicious kerosene lamp explosion killed him and his family. The coroner ruled the deaths accidental, but black leaders refused to believe that and called for the district attorney to investigate. When he failed to do so, Murray presented clip-pings of stories from black newspapers, including the *Sentinel*, to Kenny, who launched an investigation, among the first of its kind in the state.[64]

For all the problems faced by people of color in California, Murray believed it was a far better place to live than the South. She said so in a series of four articles for the Baltimore *Afro American*. Beginning with a somewhat self-con-scious report on what it felt like to be on the other side of the desk and to receive the kinds of angry missives she had so long excelled at writing, she admitted to "stalling for time" as she thought through how to respond. She continued, nonetheless, to believe that she was the same person as before, a person who wanted to make the world a better place for her own people and everyone else. It pained her that she had been forced to swear to uphold state laws, some of which she abhorred, especially one that banned miscegenation, but this distressing fact made her want to prove that such laws were unconstitutional. In her next col-umn, a week later, she revisited Mordecai Johnson's exhortation to "Go South." Although she felt some guilt in having ignored his entreaties, she believed that the only reasonable solution to Jim Crow was for the blacks in the South all to move West and North. That was what she recommended in her final two col-umns. If civil rights leaders could not overturn segregation laws, southern blacks should simply pack up and leave en masse. Blacks, she believed, had a better chance of defeating segregation in exile than from within the South. In the pro-cess, they would be able to drive home the important point that America's race problem was a national, not a regional, problem.[65]

Murray's published writings and especially her appointment got her noticed. In early March she learned that the National Council of Negro Women had named her one of twelve "Women of the Year." The Awards Committee included some of Pauli's most ardent supporters: Caroline Ware, Anna Hedgeman, and Lillian Smith; so the award could not have been a total surprise. But Murray relished the honor and delighted in finding herself in the company of such other honorees as Virginia Durr, the Alabama-born white leader in the campaign against the poll tax; Helen Gahagan Douglas, a white actor, newly elected member of the House of Representatives from California, and an outspoken advocate of women's rights and civil liberties; and Maida Springer, Murray's black friend from the ILGWU. The awards were to be given in Washington by Mary McLeod Bethune on March 15, 1946, at the Bethune Council House at 1318 Vermont Avenue.[66]

Male Veterans and the Family Claim

When Murray began to urge southern blacks to leave the South, she included her aunts, but Aunt Pauline protested that she was too weak to travel; in fact, she was so weak that Aunt Sally implored Pauli to come home as soon as possible. Concerned, Murray sought a leave of absence from the Attorney General's Office, only to learn that a person in a temporary position had no right to a leave, even an unpaid leave. She felt that she had no choice. She had to go home. She took advantage of the crisis to travel by way of Washington to attend Mary McLeod Bethune's awards ceremony.[67]

She then continued on to Durham, where she discovered the situation so dire that she transferred Aunt Pauline immediately to Freedman's Hospital. Somehow the local doctors had failed to identify Pauline's illness: diabetes. Slowly, the seventy-five-year-old improved, and Pauli had the satisfaction of knowing that she had saved her life. But at a cost. In leaving her temporary position, she sacrificed any standing she had to be considered for a permanent position. New civil services exams, required of those who sought permanent appointments, were given while she was in Washington. Even if she had been able to take the exams, it was not at all clear that she could have won a permanent post. Her immediate supervisor wrote that he was not able to offer an appointment at that time because several former attorneys—all men—had just returned from military service. They had priority. Gradually, Murray came to realize that she had lost her best chance to battle Jim and Jane Crow.[68]

PART IV

SURVIVING THE COLD WAR, 1946–1961

8

"Apostles of Fear"

Searching for Work in a Time of Fear

With no prospect of returning to her position in the California Attorney General's Office, Murray began to look for other work. For a brief time, she thought she might be able to return to Howard as a professor. President Harry Truman had just appointed William Hastie to be governor of the Virgin Islands, and Murray's mentor, Leon Ransom, was expected to succeed him as dean, thereby opening a spot on the faculty. In the end, however, the Board of Trustees chose another candidate as dean, prompting Ransom and a second professor to resign. "The bitterness surrounding these resignations . . . created an untenable situation for me," Murray later recalled. One other possibility remained. Dean Hastie had mentioned the chance of a job with the federal government. A couple of her classmates already worked there, but she could find no openings, even though she ranked first in their graduating class. The return of veterans (nearly all men), to whom the GI Bill gave preference in hiring, posed a high hurdle for her.[1]

The return of male veterans was not the only obstacle she faced. A conservative backlash against the liberalism of the New Deal, which had been building in Congress since the late 1930s, hit flood tide just as she returned to Washington in the spring of 1946. For the next decade the capital would weather a Red Scare more sweeping than the one that had followed World War I. The inquisitors' putative goal was to ferret out Communist spies in government, but Communists proved scarce and Communist spies scarcer still. The real targets turned out to be those New Dealers who championed economic regulation, labor reform, and civil rights.[2]

As northern Democrats lost seats to Republicans, beginning in 1938, white southerners extended their control over the Democratic Party. Murray called them the "Apostles of Fear," powerful men from poll tax states, which had disenfranchised virtually all black and other minority men, the majority of poor white men, and women of all races. Returned to Congress time and again by as little as 5 percent of the electorate, these men were able to fight off any threat to their political, economic, or racial power. The conservative attacks cut a wide swath through the ranks of those on the left side of the political spectrum, but it hit women harder than men, those with suspected homosexual tendencies harder than heterosexuals, and blacks harder than whites. Murray sensed immediately the danger she faced. The ghosts of her past, some obvious, some hidden, threatened at every turn. To make matters worse, those most eager to help her—William Hastie and Caroline Ware—were themselves under assault.[3]

When President Truman nominated Hastie governor of the US Virgin Islands in 1946, southern Democrats emitted a howl of outrage. Senator Allen Ellender of Louisiana declared that the appointment of a "colored man" would "retard the development of the Virgin Islands as a tourist place." Senator James Eastland of Mississippi charged that Hastie was a Communist. Hastie's supporters rallied to his defense. Murray, having arrived in Washington just as confirmation hearings got under way, testified that the Howard dean had the broad support of the Law School alumni. In the end, support for Hastie offset the attacks. The Senate confirmed his nomination. Although Murray was proud to play a supporting role in Hastie's confirmation, and relished in particular being introduced as Mr. Pauli Murray from the Attorney General's Office in California, the experience also scared her. If a man with Hastie's distinguished record could run into trouble, then how was she ever going to find a job in Washington?[4]

Watching the political problems faced by Caroline Ware only heightened Murray's anxiety. In 1943, the director of the Office of Price Administration (OPA), Chester Bowles, asked Ware to chair the executive committee of his Consumer Advisory Committee—an unpaid position from which Representative Martin Dies's House Un-American Activities Committee could not fire her. Her committee explained price controls to consumers and generated grassroots support for the OPA. In April 1946, Ware testified before a Senate Committee in favor of continued price controls on behalf of twenty-three consumer organizations, most of whose members were wives and mothers. Conservatives were outraged. Seeking to undercut Ware's authority, the right-wing radio journalist Fulton Lewis Jr. asked how "*Miss* Ware," who had no children, could possibly speak for the Parent Teachers Association and other such groups. Dismayed, Murray decided to give New York City another chance.[5]

By May 1946 Murray had found a room in Greenwich Village from which she embarked on a new job hunt. Any new lawyer faced stiff competition in the spring of 1946, from attorneys laid off from jobs in Washington once the war ended and from veterans to whom employers routinely gave preference. Female lawyers confronted the added obstacle of the deeply entrenched bias against women in the legal profession. The lucky ones tended to work in support positions in back offices, where clients would not see them. Murray's race made her situation almost impossible, but on top of that she had not yet gained admission to the New York State Bar. Under the circumstances, she was qualified only to type, run errands, and provide assistance in legal research.[6]

Murray's best hope for a job with a large office was through Lloyd K. Garrison, who had just joined the firm of Paul, Weiss in New York. But when she approached him, Garrison ruefully informed her that the only young lawyers his new partners would consider were graduates of Harvard, Yale, or Columbia who had served on their law reviews and clerked for a federal judge. Murray would have loved to work for Thurgood Marshall at the NAACP, but Marshall, having just hired Constance Baker from Columbia Law School, had no vacancies. When Murray floated the idea of opening a regional office in San Francisco or Los Angeles, Marshall responded that he did not have the funds.[7]

Renewing the Fight against *Plessy*

Finally, in July, Murray learned of an opening at the Commission on Law and Social Action (CLSA), the legal arm of the American Jewish Congress (AJC). Securing an appointment with the Congress's director, Will Maslow, who knew of her through her *California Law Review* article and an earlier meeting at Howard, she won a follow-up interview with the chief consultant to the CLSA, Alexander Pekelis. A brilliant Russian-Jewish émigré, Pekelis had studied law in Germany, Austria, and Italy before assuming a professorship in jurisprudence at the University of Rome in 1935. Three years later, the rise of fascism had driven him to Paris, where he practiced law until the Nazi occupation of France forced him to flee with his wife and children, first to Lisbon and then, in 1941, to New York. For several years he taught sociology at the New School, while earning a law degree and serving as editor-in-chief of the *Columbia Law Review*.[8]

Pekelis needed a research assistant at the CLSA. Murray's expertise in the post–Civil War amendments won him over. Best of all, the pay, about $70 a week, was a good salary for a lawyer not yet admitted to the bar.[9]

The case on which Pekelis needed help most immediately concerned a group of Mexican American parents, led by Gonzalo and Felicitas Mendez, who had filed a lawsuit in federal court in southern California. The case, *Mendez v. Westminster* (1947), challenged the practice of segregating children in separate schools on the basis of their Spanish surnames. The parents won at the district court level, but the school district appealed. Pekelis wanted to file an amicus curiae brief on behalf of the parents to the Ninth Circuit Court of Appeals.[10]

For Murray, the case had special importance because the plaintiffs' lawyer had introduced social science testimony at trial that the segregation of Mexican American students from other children their age not only impeded learning but also fostered feelings of inferiority. The case also had the virtue of bringing together old friends. California Attorney General Kenny intervened on behalf of the parents. So too did Loren Miller, from the *Sentinel,* along with Thurgood Marshall and Robert Carter of the NAACP. The arguments differed. Kenny stressed the school district's violation of the California Constitution's guarantee of unfettered access to public education to all groups (except Indians and Asians, the only groups that could be segregated under state law). The NAACP simply recycled its standard argument, supported by evidence from southern black and white schools, that segregated institutions were never equal.[11]

In contrast, Pekelis and Murray saw in *Mendez* an opportunity to attack *Plessy v. Ferguson* directly. In a bold move, they argued that the circuit court should strike down segregation not only on behalf of blacks but also on behalf of other groups, including ethnic and religious minorities as well as women. Segregation by the state violated the Fourteenth Amendment they argued in their amicus brief, whether carried out in trains (as in *Plessy*) or in schools (as in *Mendez*). Moreover, segregation violated the Constitution, "whether or not 'equal' physical facilities are being furnished to both groups." The reason: segregation is a "humiliating and discriminatory denial of equality to the group considered 'inferior.'" More boldly still, they argued that not just segregation but the classification on which that segregation relied was unconstitutional.[12]

Here, Pekelis and Murray appealed to principles newly enunciated in the United Nations Charter and ratified by the United States. That charter required all signatory countries to ensure "fundamental freedoms for all without distinction as to race, sex, language, and religion." The inclusion of "sex" in the list constituted a major and, to many, a surprising addition. As it happened, a friend of Eleanor Roosevelt, Barnard College Dean Virginia Gildersleeve, the only woman on the United States delegation to the chartering conference, had been responsible for it. Murray brought the language of the United Nations Charter to Pekelis's attention, and he agreed to include mention of it in their brief.[13]

The AJC lawyers, who, taken together, had themselves been the victims of religious, ethnic, racial, and gender discrimination, closed their brief with the simple statement: "All discrimination is bad." But none is so "vicious" as that which leads to "the humiliation of innocent, trusting children, American children full of faith in life. Their humiliation strikes at the very roots of the American Commonwealth. Their humiliation threatens the more perfect union which the Constitution seeks to achieve."[14]

The repeated use of the word "humiliation" throughout the brief came from both Pekelis and Murray—Pekelis, mindful that the Nazis had compelled Jews to wear a yellow star on their outer garments, and Murray, mindful that social custom dictated that women wear skirts. In each case, articles of clothing stigmatized their wearers as different from and inferior to another. Most readers would have understood the humiliating signification of the yellow Star of David but not of the skirts custom dictated for women. Murray, so far ahead of the society in which she lived on that matter, did not bother, or even dare, to spell out her full meaning anywhere other than in her private papers, where she once referred to her wardrobe as made up of two kinds of clothes "completely opposed to each other": "slacks, belts, pants, sweaters, socks, boots, and the other kind!"[15]

In the end, Pekelis and Murray failed to persuade the Ninth Circuit Court of Appeals to overturn *Plessy,* much less to declare that discrimination on the basis of gender was illegal. In a unanimous opinion, the appellate court ruled, more narrowly, that the state constitution allowed for the segregation of students into separate schools only if they were "Indians under certain conditions," or if they were "children of Chinese, Japanese or Mongolian parentage." By segregating any other children, including those of Mexican descent, the state violated the state constitution, and in so doing violated the Due Process and Equal Protection Clauses of the Fourteenth Amendment.[16]

The Orange County school districts declined to take the case to the Supreme Court, and as a result, *Mendez* attracted little attention from the mainstream press. And yet, the case and the amicus briefs had a major impact because of the attention they drew from the NAACP. Thurgood Marshall was not yet persuaded that the time had come for a frontal attack on *Plessy,* but his associate on the *Mendez* case, Robert Carter, was. Carter reminded Marshall of the amici briefs in *Mendez* as well as the kind of social scientific evidence presented at trial, in preparing the NAACP case in *Brown v. Board of Education.* At the same time, Spottswood Robinson, another member of the *Brown* team, took a second look at Murray's 1944 paper, "Should the *Civil Rights Cases* and *Plessy* Be Overturned?" and decided that she had been right. Together, Carter and Robinson persuaded Marshall to make a frontal attack.[17]

With the *Mendez* brief filed, and nothing more to do on the case until the Ninth Circuit rendered a decision, Murray devoted her time to drafting memos about other pressing legal reforms. She wanted, for instance, to write model Fair Employment Practice legislation for state enactment, since southern Democrats in Congress had just killed the federal FEPC. In the meantime, she helped draft bills against defamation of minority groups, appeared before the New York State Commission against Discrimination in cases involving alleged discrimination in employment, prepared studies on the legal action taken by California and various other states' attorney generals against the Ku Klux Klan, and prepared news releases on the commission's achievements.[18]

But before any of these initiatives could get under way, tragedy struck. A plane carrying Alexander Pekelis, who was returning from a trip to a meeting of the World Zionist Congress in Switzerland, crashed in Ireland on December 28, 1946. The crash killed Pekelis and all but a few passengers. Suddenly, the

Commission on Law and Social Action lost its guiding spirit, the person with whom Murray worked most closely.[19]

On top of that trauma, rumors began to circulate that Communists and fellow travelers had begun to infiltrate the American Jewish Congress. The rumors lacked substance, but donations fell sharply. Such was the effect of the spreading Red Scare. "The organization is undergoing a tremendous cut in budget and has had to cut drastically its entire staff," Pauli informed Aunt Pauline. Deeply depressed and fearful that she, too, would soon be fired, Murray resigned on March 17.[20]

To add to her woes, two weeks later Murray was suddenly racked by severe abdominal pain. She had experienced this kind of pain, off and on, for a year and a half, but this time she had health insurance, albeit insurance that was about to run out. So she checked into Sydenham Hospital in Harlem, where a surgeon conducted exploratory surgery. Eager to find confirmation of a "pseudo-hermaphrodite" condition, Murray asked the doctor to look for "secreted male genitals" while he was at it. He found an infected appendix and two infected fallopian tubes, all of which he removed. He also found and removed a left cystic ovary. But to Murray's disappointment, he did not find the undescended testes, she had long hoped might be there.[21]

On top of her employment and medical problems, Murray faced a family crisis. Her nephew Joshua Small was arrested on a felony charge of tampering with the United States mail and had no one to represent him. Murray could not do so officially because she had not yet won admission to the New York Bar, but in May 1947, she secured "special permission" from the US Attorney for the Southern District of New York to act as counsel in *U.S. v. Joshua Small*, No. C-125-409. Stressing that Joshua was a first-time offender, Murray won him a reduced sentence of a year and a day at the federal prison in Danbury, making him eligible to apply for parole after three months. Having done what she could for Joshua, Murray returned to the search for work.[22]

The Single Female Professional

Liberal organizations such as the AJC had until recently offered attractive prospects, but they were all having funding problems in the midst of the Red Scare. Someone urged her to contact former Municipal Court Judge Dorothy Kenyon, then in private practice and a member of the board of directors of the American Civil Liberties Union. Meeting her for the first time, Murray learned how difficult it was for even a privileged white woman to succeed as a lawyer in the late 1940s.[23]

The daughter of a patent attorney in New York, Kenyon had grown up on the Upper West Side of Manhattan, attended Smith College, and graduated from New York University Law School in 1917. She had divided her time since among government jobs, private practice, and social activism. Although she had romantic relationships with a number of men, she made a conscious decision not to saddle herself with a husband. Kenyon never made much money as a lawyer, but she built a career in not-for-profit work and government positions. In 1930 she joined the board of the American Civil Liberties Union, and in 1939 New York Mayor Fiorello LaGuardia appointed her to fill a vacancy on the municipal court bench. Though she served only a year, she delighted in being called "Judge Kenyon" for the rest of her life. In addition to her legal practice and governmental positions, Kenyon campaigned to advance human rights across a broad field. She fought on behalf of birth control, consumer cooperatives, labor rights, civil rights, and women's rights. A close friend of Eleanor Roosevelt, who no doubt played a role in her being named, she became the US representative to the newly constituted United Nations Commission on the Status of Women in 1946.[24]

When Murray showed up for her interview in Kenyon's cramped office at 50 Broadway in Lower Manhattan, she quickly discovered that Kenyon had too little work of her own to be able to take on another lawyer. The older woman nonetheless showed an interest in Murray's struggle and did what she could to boost her spirits. "The legal profession is a long, hard battle for a woman," Kenyon conceded. "We are still only barely tolerated, . . . [but] if a woman has the guts to stick it out she somehow survives."[25]

Sticking it out proved especially difficult for a single woman in postwar America. Technically, Murray was married, but in practice she was not. In the 1930s being without a husband could be explained by economic exigencies. In the early 1940s, wartime conditions rendered the single state normal. But in postwar America, a woman's lack of a husband raised concerns that were difficult to allay without, at the very least, presenting oneself in a conventionally feminine, heterosexually available manner. Dorothy Kenyon adopted this approach, becoming famous for her flowery dresses and striking hats. Murray had long resisted any feminine adornment, but she adapted to the times. In a photo taken on her historic appointment to the California Attorney General's Office in February 1946, for release to news agencies, she appears with "the first—and last—upsweep hair do!" as she noted in her scrapbook. Such self-presentation stemmed from a felt need to compromise with increasingly conservative social expectations in the face of a tough job market.[26]

In another compromise, Murray wrote an article for *Negro Digest* entitled "Why Negro Girls Stay Single." By 1946, Murray was thirty-five years old, an age by which women were supposed to be married mothers. Under the circumstances, Murray felt compelled to explain herself. Dresses and lipstick were not enough. The reasons that so many highly educated Negro women remained

Figure 8.1 Portrait of Pauli Murray, February 1946, when she was the first African American to hold the position of deputy attorney general in California. Estate of Pauli Murray, Schlesinger Library, Radcliffe Institute, Harvard University.

single, Murray explained in her article, fell into three groups. First, there were too few educated black men to meet the demand for husbands of educated black women. Women stayed in school longer because there was greater economic reward to them from further schooling. In the racially segregated world in which they lived, they could be teachers and clerical workers in the communities in which they had been raised. Higher education provided useful training, but it also diminished their value on the marriage market. Black men, denied opportunities open to white men, did not want to marry black women whose educational attainments challenged their confidence. Miscegenation laws trapped everyone in racial stockades, making the lack of choice even worse.[27]

The second problem Murray called "sex [gender] mis-education." The black men and women who did marry had been socialized to play the same masculine and feminine roles celebrated in white society, whether or not they were temperamentally suited to them, or able, economically, to execute them. The result was often "frustration" and "broken homes." This frustration and domestic disharmony could occur in any family, but it was more common among blacks than whites, because black men were expected to act "as if they were lords of creation, bread winners and warriors," and yet were denied the economic opportunity that might allow them to fulfill this role. Black women felt forced, as a result, to support themselves and their families, a partial "emancipation" that defied social expectations and infuriated black men, who regularly vented their anger on hapless black women in true "Jane Crow" fashion.[28]

Gender "mis-education" led to a third problem: an "intensifie[d] homosexuality." Murray was tiptoeing into the dangerous territory of self-revelation. She had certainly been "mis-educated," and as a result had felt compelled to marry, a step she instantly regretted. She had occasionally referred to herself as a homosexual in letters to doctors, but she did not think the label fit. She tended to use that term for want of a more accurate description of what she believed she was: a man in a woman's body, or, alternatively, someone in between, tending toward the masculine. This unusual gender identity gave her a critical perspective on social norms, allowing her, for example, to conceive of the problem of "Jane Crow." But she had to be careful. No "perversion" was safe during the Red Scare. More government employees were dismissed in those years under suspicion of homosexuality than from charges of Communist subversion. By referring to homosexuality in this forthright (and negative) way, she may have tried, consciously or not, to inoculate herself from the suspicion that she might be one.[29]

A Job, at Last, and an Apartment, Too

Finally, in September 1947, Murray found a job as a law clerk for Charles L. Kellar, a black solo practitioner, at 1660 Fulton Street in Brooklyn. He offered her $25 a week, less than half of what she had made at the American Jewish Congress. She was grateful for the work, but her salary barely covered food and shelter. Not yet admitted to the bar, Murray served Kellar as a clerical assistant, tasked with filing papers, typing forms, and answering calendar calls in court. The one advantage of the job was that it led to an apartment of her own.[30]

Kellar supplemented his law income with speculation in the Bedford-Stuyvesant real estate market in a period of white flight. In the 1930s, the completion of the "A" train, which greatly facilitated transportation between Harlem and Brooklyn, accelerated migration to the outer borough. In 1940, 75 percent of Brooklyn residents were still white. By 1950 only 50 percent would be. By 1960, a mere 25 percent remained. Kellar bought row houses from whites fearful that the influx of blacks would destroy the value of their homes. Like other realtors, Kellar snapped up these properties for bargain prices, divided them into apartments, and resold them at a profit.[31]

Having started in 1933, at the bottom of the Depression, Kellar owned about a dozen properties. He had just purchased a modest, three-story, brick row house at 388 Chauncey Street, a few blocks from his office. To induce Murray to move to Brooklyn, he offered to let her rent the top floor for $45 per month, about the cost of her single room at International House up by Columbia University, an hour's subway ride away. Kellar further offered the opportunity to furnish the apartment for $60, the cost of the furniture from another house he had just bought. Like row-house apartments throughout Bedford-Stuyvesant, the apartment had a railroad-flat layout, with three box-like rooms (one behind the other) from the street to the back of the building. Doorways, without doors, connected one to the other, a less than ideal arrangement, but the apartment had its own kitchen and a bathroom, a luxury for someone accustomed to sharing with others. Finally, Murray would have a home of her own, big enough for Joshua to live with her when he was released from jail. Having a home he could come to, she believed, would make it more likely that he would be granted an early parole.[32]

Once Joshua found a job and his own place, she could invite Aunt Pauline to join her. At long last she would be able to care for her seventy-six-year-old, increasingly frail, adoptive mother. Under pressure from the NAACP, North Carolina had recently extended its teacher pension plan to include blacks, but those pensions, based on the low salaries paid to black teachers, were tiny. After sixty-two years of teaching, Aunt Pauline was struggling to live on a pension of $25 a month in a house without hot water or reliable heat and infested with termites to the point that she feared it might collapse, she needed Pauli more than ever.[33]

Aunt Pauline came for Christmas 1947 and stayed a month, delighting in Pauli's steam heat and hot water. Joshua joined Pauli in March 1948, after returning from jail and before shipping out as a merchant seaman. He was not able to contribute much financially because his asthma prevented him from working a good part of the year, but he helped with minor repairs until he tired of Pauli's day-to-day supervision and found a room in Manhattan. In the fall of 1948, Aunt Pauline rented the house in Durham and took Joshua's place. Not wanting to be left behind, Aunt Sallie decided to come along. Pauline had saved $600, most of it from her portion of the sale of Grandma Cornelia's farm. Aunt Sallie had about the same. These savings gave them a small financial cushion on which to embark on their retirement. Three women under one roof, with no doors to separate the cramped rooms, proved even more difficult than Pauli had anticipated, but she accepted what she saw as her duty to the women who had raised her: to care for them in their old age.[34]

Aunt Pauline, whose arthritis made the climb up and down two steep flights of stairs painful, spent her days sitting in the front room, writing poetry and watching the children at play under the supervision of their teachers in the schoolyard across the street. Aunt Sallie cooked and made tailored clothes. They all attended St. Philips Episcopal Church on Sunday and visited with other relatives. Pauli's younger brother Raymond, who lived nearby, brought his wife and children to visit. Cousin Maude Clegg Womack came from Richmond Hill, Queens. Pauli made regular trips to see her increasingly infirm Aunt Marie Fitzgerald Jeffers up on 125th Street and Second Avenue in East Harlem. Marie's son, Gerald Jeffers, visited from Long Island. As was true in many other extended black families, the center of family gravity had shifted from the South to the North by the late 1940s.[35]

Aunt Pauline saw the arrangement at 388 Chauncey Street as temporary. She planned to buy her own home near Pauli as soon as she sold her house in Durham and the other nearby lots she had inherited. In 1948, she received an offer of $6,000 for the house and lots, a sum she considered to be less than half their value. She therefore continued to rent the house and hold onto the lots in the hope that prices would improve. They failed to do so. Without a sale, Aunt Pauline had no hope of buying a house in Bedford-Stuyvesant. Those houses were going for upward of $8,500 (the price Kellar got for the house at 388 Chauncey Street). If only she had the funds to buy one, Aunt Pauline and Sallie could have lived on the main floor, Pauli above them, and they might have rented out the top floor, thereby covering all their expenses. Eventually, Pauli would have inherited the house. But it was not to be.[36]

And so they made do. To this apartment, Pauli added a dog. Smokey, a Shetland sheep dog, was the most recent in a long line of canines, acquired by Pauli, but cared for by Aunt Pauline. Like his predecessors, Smokey promptly set about destroying everything he could get his teeth into. Pauline refused to speak to Pauli for some days, but eventually she conceded that Smokey gave her "some pleasure" despite being "a great deal of trouble."[37]

Maida and Dollie

Smokey gave Pauli much more pleasure, because his need to be walked gave her a reason to escape her crowded apartment. Dog and owner roamed the neighborhood, often ending up at 730-A Macon Street, a spacious, four-story brownstone where Maida Springer lived with her husband, Owen, their college-age son, Eric, and Maida's mother, Adina (Moms) Stewart. Pauli and Maida had been friends since working together on the Silent Protest March, and Maida had risen through the leadership ranks at Local 22 of the International Ladies Garment Workers Union (ILGWU), an affiliate of the American Federation of Labor (AFL). Although the AFL was, for the most part, less interested than the Congress of Industrial Organizations (CIO) in organizing unskilled workers and fighting segregation, Local 22 was different. Manager Charles "Sasha" Zimmerman (a former Lovestonite) and ILGWU president David Dubinsky were committed to civil rights and determined to draw blacks into leadership positions. First Zimmerman and then Dubinsky recognized Maida Springer's strengths—her intelligence, graciousness, and unparalleled organizing skills—and they elevated her to ever more important positions. In 1948, Zimmerman promoted Springer to the position of business agent in Local 22. The first black person to hold this position, she represented the union in sixty shops, which employed 2,000 workers, only 5 percent of them black. Although representatives of the clothing manufacturers initially objected, Zimmerman held firm, and Springer soon demonstrated her skill at settling disputes between screaming adversaries.[38]

By the end of World War II, Maida and Owen Springer had joined the exodus from Harlem to Bedford Stuyvesant where they bought their brownstone and Owen set about renovating it. He put in modern plumbing and tiled bathrooms. This was the home that Pauli would have loved to buy for her own family, but her low salary and the absence of a male wage earner in the household made that impossible. Owen worked in a token booth for the Transit Authority, a job only recently opened to blacks. Though a disappointment to someone with Owen's intelligence and skills, this job, at about $1,800 a year, paid more than Pauli cleared even after she won admission to the bar. Maida and Owen together made at least twice what Pauli and her aunts did.[39]

The second person to whom Murray was close in Brooklyn was Dollie Lowther, who lived with her mother a few blocks away at 3 Agate Court. Dollie had introduced Pauli to Maida back in 1942, but they had not been particularly close until Pauli and Maida's move to Bedford Stuyvesant. Murray and Springer admired the way that Lowther could take command of a room. Whereas Pauli and Maida were both short and slightly built, Dollie was tall and strong. Maida later described her as a "physical and mental giant. . . . Fierce about workers' dignity. Fierce!"[40]

The three women were in some ways unlikely allies. Pauli had become a professional whereas Springer and Lowther made their careers in the working class. If a subtle class distinction might have divided the professional from the working-class members, a fierce rivalry within labor's ranks might just as easily have undermined Maida and Dollie's friendship. Bessie and Sydney Hillman of the Amalgamated Clothing Workers of the CIO had embraced Dollie's Laundry

Workers, whereas Sasha Zimmerman and David Dubinsky, chief promoters of Maida at the ILGWU at the AFL had declined to organize laborers they regarded as unskilled, in an industry with huge turnover. For Pauli, Maida, and Dollie, however, race and gender provided strong bonds that led them to distance themselves from these inter-union battles and potential class conflicts.[41]

Over the years to come, Pauli, Maida, and Dollie each proved to be an important source of support to the others. Maida and Dollie turned to Pauli for help in legal matters, as she turned to them for much needed business referrals. Pauli and Dollie found comfort in the spacious Springer household, where they met labor leaders from around the world and ate copious helpings of food prepared by Moms. Maida and Dollie found refuge at Pauli's when they needed the relative quiet of a home, albeit cramped, free of raucous union meetings. That mutual refuge proved all the more important to Maida when her marriage began to unravel. As Maida assumed ever-greater responsibilities within the AFL and achieved ever-greater success, tensions in the Springer household mounted. By 1955, Maida and Owen were divorced.[42]

Close friendships in Brooklyn brought Murray satisfaction. Her job did not. Charles Kellar relied on her legal skills but treated her as nothing more than an "errand girl." When a memorandum she drafted saved a client from a $10,000 lawsuit, Kellar got the praise and the fee. When he ran late for a calendar call, she got yelled at. "I'm so tired of being a whipping boy for other people's doings and not be able to answer back," Murray complained to Ware.[43]

When Murray passed the bar exam around Christmas 1947, she decided that six months with Kellar had been enough and began to look for a better job. She finally landed one, in March 1948, as a slightly better paid managing clerk in the office of Richard L. Baltimore, a black lawyer, with offices on Lower Broadway, near City Hall in Manhattan. "I have my own office, a lovely little place with beautiful furniture, my own phone, . . . Baltimore is tops—in brains, personnel relations and ethics." Pauli jubilantly informed Aunt Pauline. "YES YES YES!!," she continued, "My boss is married, has a wife and two children—a little girl around five or six and a baby boy."[44]

Despite Aunt Pauline's acceptance of what she called Pauli's "boy-girl" personality, she held out hope that her adoptive daughter would one day find a new husband. Maida Springer took a more active interest in Murray's marital prospects. Murray tried to dissuade Springer by mentioning her struggles with gender identity, but Springer dismissed her friend's confession by saying, "That's ridiculous!" Springer thought that Murray simply needed help in finding the right man. Richard Baltimore's sister, Harriet, apparently joined Springer's campaign. Harriet had known Murray at Hunter; indeed, she had been one of the three other black women who graduated mid-year with Pauli in 1933. She was probably the person behind Richard Baltimore's setting Pauli up with a date for a formal dance at his club. Springer lent Murray earrings and other "accoutre-ments." Moms Stewart styled her hair. Murray went along, because she wanted to please her new boss, but, as her "YES YES YES!!" to Aunt Pauline conveyed, she was not happy about being forced into what for her was an uncomfortable situation.[45]

Although Murray moved back to Manhattan to work, she continued to live at 388 Chauncey Street with her aunts. Much as Murray enjoyed living in Brooklyn, there was a downside to living there she had not anticipated. Manhattan and Brooklyn were in separate judicial departments, and the move from one to the other meant she had to wait an additional six months, the residency requirement in the new judicial department, before her application for admission to the bar could be processed. That delay proved to be the least of her problems.[46]

Applying for Admission to the New York State Bar

Nothing demonstrated more dramatically the shift in political climate from 1945 to 1948 than the difference Murray experienced between applying for admission to the bar in California and doing so three years later in New York. In 1945, she had won admission in California on the strength of passing the bar exam and submitting an affidavit. The mounting Red Scare made admission to the bar in New York much more difficult.

There were two problems. First, heightened concern over loyalty greatly increased the scrutiny given to each candidate. In addition to the usual ques-tions about name, marital status, current address, and any prior arrests or con-victions, applicants were required to list every address at which they had lived, every school they had attended, every employer for whom they had worked, and every organization to which they had belonged. They then had to secure letters confirming each residence, school, job, and organization membership. The let-ters were also expected to attest—in each instance—to the applicants' continu-ing good character and loyalty to the United States.[47]

Completing the application posed a challenge even for a heterosexual white male applicant born in New York who had grown up at a single address, com-muted to local schools, belonged to a local club, attended a nearby house of worship, and held a job or two to help pay school expenses. For Pauli—a poor, black, civil rights activist from the South, who had long suffered serious emo-tional conflicts over her gender identity—the task was almost overwhelming.[48]

Where the New York form requested the applicant to list all residential addresses, Murray identified thirty-eight, an astonishing number, but she wor-ried that she might not have remembered every one. She had sometimes moved several times a year in search of a room she could afford where the sound of

her typing would not get her evicted. Having worked for twenty-three different employers, she encountered a similar problem. Had she recalled them all?
Could she get a letter from each one? She had no problem with the student jobs
she had worked at Hunter, Howard, and Boalt Hall, but many other places of
employment had gone out of business. And then there were the organizations
she had joined, several of which raised red flags, especially the Communist Party
Opposition.[49]

There was more. The Bar Committee challenged a number of entries on her
application that they considered highly irregular, beginning with her marital status. Pauli had never lived with the man she married in 1930, and realizing that
this might raise questions when she sought admission to practice law, Pauli had
sought to find Billy Wynn while she was in law school at Howard, without success. In the spring of 1947 she had sought legal advice on the possibility of an
annulment: "I have not heard from the guy in 13 years and do not know where
he is," she explained to the lawyer she consulted in New York. She finally found
Billy in April 1948. He was in the army, stationed at Fort Belvoir in Virginia, and
after visiting Mildred, at Pauli's request, he agreed to a divorce.[50]

Pauli's relief at the prospect of putting that part of her life behind her was
undercut by a letter from Mildred, who, having met Billy could not understand
why Pauli would not consider patching things up with him. "How did you ever
let a fine guy like that loose. Pauli don't be an ASS, keep the guy and try him
again. . . . So how . . . could you find out what the two of you had for each other
in a few short days. He's someone you [would] not have your friends ashamed
of. He's also evidently made good too in the army and he's planning to go to
Germany soon." As further evidence that he was a catch, Mildred added that he
had driven up in "a beautiful grey convertible [Oldsmobile] coupe (1948)."[51]

Murray's marital status was only the first of a number of concerns that the
bar committee considered potentially disqualifying. Their notes added the following irregularities: her aliases, 1930–1931 job at Open Road, 1935 arrest for
picketing, 1936–1937 membership in the CPO, 1940 admission to Bellevue
Hospital, 1940 arrest in Petersburg, 1947 possible unauthorized legal practice
(on behalf of Joshua), titles of her published articles, inability to provide letters
from employers in every instance, and suspicious reasons for leaving jobs. Of
the first thirty-five items on the application, the committee had questions about
statements given in seventeen. The case dragged on for months. Distressed but
determined, Murray sent letter after letter to former friends, landlords, and
employers seeking support. In the end she submitted thirty-two letters of recommendation, including ones from Lloyd K. Garrison, William Hastie, and
Thurgood Marshall. Because the application form could not accommodate all
the information it required, she wrote out a staggering number of "Riders" and
prepared yet more affidavits. To explain the arrests, the name changes, and the

suspicious-sounding organizations, she composed still more riders and affida-vits. At long last, she submitted a record-breaking 230-page application in May 1948.[52]

An interview followed. One member of the seven-member committee, still not persuaded that she should be a member of the bar, voted against her admis-sion. The others, either satisfied or stunned by the blizzard of documentation she had supplied in response to each question, voted to admit her. On June 23, 1948, she celebrated having "just experienced the earthly version of the Final Judgment" by going out to lunch with Maida Springer.[53]

Solo Practitioner

Admitted to practice, Murray hoped to win a promotion, but Richard Baltimore dismissed that idea. He had no need for another lawyer in his firm. Discouraged, indignant, and by that time more than $1,400 in debt to ten different people, she set out to find work as an attorney. Three weeks later, she found a position with Carson DeWitt Baker, a prominent figure in the Democratic Political Club in Harlem and a man on his way to becoming the city's most successful black attorney. Baker had a law firm at 225 Broadway in Lower Manhattan and needed someone to help handle the cases that came to him from his political work. He offered the legal version of a sharecropping arrangement: Murray would keep one-third of any fees earned, whether on cases he assigned or cases she brought to the firm. Some weeks she made as much as $100, other weeks she made noth-ing, a pattern that kept her in a constant state of anxiety over whether she would be able to pay the rent and put food on the table.[54]

For all of the challenges she faced, Murray had just catapulted into a tiny sorority, one of only twelve to fifteen black women lawyers in New York at the time, fewer than 150 in the whole country, a mere 100 of whom actually prac-ticed law. Since the only work these private practitioners could typically get was from clients who were also black, female, and, as a consequence, mostly poor and frequently unemployed, they had a difficult time making a living. On top of these disadvantages, as Murray was the first to admit, a certain "fastidiousness" held her back when it came to business production; she simply could not bring herself to "hustle up" clients.[55]

She was not, however, without resources. Baker assigned criminal cases to her that he did not want to handle. Maida Springer, to whom Murray spoke by phone every day, passed along the legal problems of workers at Local 22, as well as some of her own. Dollie Lowther did the same at the laundry workers union. Most helpful of all was another woman lawyer, Ruth Whitehead Whaley. A fel-low North Carolinian, who in 1925 became the first African American woman to be admitted to practice in New York, Whaley had recently been named secretary of the New York City Board of Estimate. Winding up her private practice, she offered to refer her clients to Murray.[56]

The caseload could hardly have been more varied. Murray filed workers' compensation claims, represented clients in divorce proceedings, and drafted annulment petitions. She wrote contracts, took cases to small claims court, filed claims on behalf of tenants against landlords for their violation of rent control, and handled clients' immigration and naturalization problems. She represented a man charged with possession of numbers' slips and a woman threatened with eviction from her business. She wrote wills and administered estates. She completed and filed tax returns. She handled a matter for the ILGWU. She incorporated a church.[57]

Three cases had particular meaning for her. Each drove home the message that women, especially black women, had little power in American society. In one of her first cases, she represented two black women charged with prostitution. When the prosecuting attorney asked a witness in court to identify one of the prostitutes, the witness pointed to Pauli, provoking laughter throughout the courtroom. Apart from the humiliation of being fingered as a woman of the street, Murray was outraged that her clients were convicted and jailed, while the men who had availed themselves of their services were not even arrested.[58]

A second representation troubled her even more. Urith Josiah, three years her senior, was a former English instructor at black Virginia Union University. Married in Virginia, Josiah had moved to New York in the early 1930s, evidently without her husband. She shared an apartment with an aunt, taught in the WPA Adult Education Project, attended law school, and won admission to the New York Bar in 1943. Since then, she had struggled to make a living as a solo practitioner. Josiah had been brought before the Bar Committee, on charges of having defrauded a client, and faced possible disbarment. In fact, the person who brought the charge was a neighbor, whom Josiah had represented for free on a number of occasions when she faced eviction. Once Josiah had borrowed some money from her, promising to repay it as soon as an expected fee arrived. Rather than give a promissory note, Josiah, as a good faith gesture, had written a check for the full amount of the loan, asking only that the neighbor not deposit it until Josiah could verify that the funds were good. The neighbor ignored the request and deposited the check. The check bounced. Murray's job was to persuade the bar committee that her client had, at most, acted unwisely. The case could not have cut closer to home. Josiah's life history paralleled her own to a painful extent. The biggest difference between them was that Murray was much deeper in debt than her client. In the end, Murray persuaded the bar committee that Josiah had not committed fraud; indeed, the committee called her back to express gratitude for opening their eyes to the difficult circumstances of the black, female solo practitioner.[59]

A third representation disturbed Murray most of all. Her client was Charlotte Adelmond, the tall, strongly built laundry labor leader who had mentored Dollie Lowther back in the 1930s. Born in 1904 in Trinidad, Adelmond had emigrated to New York at the age of twenty in 1924. She went to work in a commercial laundry, where temperatures sometimes topped 126 degrees, and the heavy wet sheets brought on arthritis and other debilitating ailments. Her fellow workers admired Adelmond, in Lowther's words, as a "fierce" pioneer, a woman of "sheer guts and grit," a woman who defended them against abusive supervisors. At least one boss suddenly found himself on the floor, knocked senseless by one of Adelmond's famous head butts, in reaction to his bullying treatment of a laundress. After Adelmond's successful campaign to create the United Laundry Workers, within the Amalgamated Clothing Workers of the CIO in 1938, the union appointed her business agent for her local. For many years, she was the only black female business agent in the ULW.[60]

In addition to her fierceness and grit what struck people about Adelmond was that she dressed like a man. Dollie Lowther thought that Charlotte favored men's clothes—shirts, ties, and her signature felt hat, pulled down over short-cropped hair—to enhance her image of great strength, but Pauli saw that something more was at work. Charlotte lived with another woman, who was helping her raise a daughter, whom Adelmond had adopted from Trinidad as an infant a decade before. Pauli saw a kindred spirit.[61]

For all her imposing size and apparent strength, Adelmond suffered from the inevitable physical wear and tear of work in a laundry, including at least one burn, on her left arm, and chronic pain. On top of these problems, she injured her back from slipping on a "wet cigarette butt" in her apartment house in 1945 and fractured an ankle in stepping off a bus in 1949. She had already been through at least one other lawyer in her effort to win monetary damages for her injuries. All she had achieved by the time she approached Murray was a ruling from the State Insurance Board of partial disability, a reduction in her work schedule by the Workmen's Compensation Board to three days a week, and advice by a Workman's Compensation doctor that she lose forty-five of her 195 pounds. Pauli tried to win compensation for Charlotte's most recent accident, the fractured ankle, but the doctor who examined her opined that she suffered nothing more serious than a "partial minor disability" and needed at most some physical therapy and an elastic bandage, "for support" and "as psychotherapy."[62]

Not able to recover anything for Adelmond's injuries, Murray received only $40 as a retainer from her new client for "all matters pertaining to her employment by the Laundry Workers Joint Board." Not one to back down from a fight, Adelmond had already generated a number of LWJB "matters" for Murray to handle. A white male supervisor had suspended her on at least one occasion because "he didn't like her attitude." She was suspended again during a disagreement in which she took the lead in demanding more black representation in the laundry workers union. Unfortunately, for Murray, these matters and many others she handled for Baker, required a great deal of her time while generating very little income.[63]

Baker exacerbated Murray's financial woes by falling further and further behind on payments of her share of the fees on cases she had handled for him. By April 1949, eight months into her work at his firm, he was $400 in arrears. Moreover, she had yet to see him place her name on the door, as he had promised he would. Years later, Baker boasted that he had trained many young lawyers, "white and Negro, men and women." He kept them for only a year, he explained, because after that time he thought they were ready to go out on their own. If their experience paralleled Murray's, however, they may have left, as she finally did, not in gratitude for the training received but in indignation at the fees they had not been paid. Although Baker seems to have treated all subordinates badly, Murray's experience confirmed her growing conviction that gender compounded her professional problems: "Clearly my sex made me an easy target for that kind of exploitation."[64]

States' Laws

For all her anger at Baker, Murray might have remained in his employ but for an unexpected stroke of good fortune. In the fall of 1948, Thelma Stevens, executive secretary of the Women's Division of the Board of Missions of the Methodist Church, called to ask Murray's help on advising her organization's members on what they could do to integrate their multifarious southern operations and facilities without breaking local laws. She had asked the NAACP and the ACLU to direct her to a comprehensive reference on segregation laws, only to be told that none existed. ACLU staff counsel Clifford Forster, who knew of Murray's article on job discrimination, suggested that Stevens seek Pauli's assistance in drafting one.[65]

In a meeting with Murray on November 9, 1948, Stevens laid out her idea for a study of state laws that could guide her organization in determining which segregation practices were a matter of custom (and could safely be abandoned) and which were required by state law. As an example of the kind of problem the Methodist women confronted, Stevens mentioned that they operated Scarritt College in Tennessee, which admitted all races except blacks. She wanted to know whether they were required by law to discriminate in this way. Confirming her request in a letter, which enclosed a check for $100 for twenty hours of work, Stevens asked Murray to compile a list of the segregation laws of southern states.[66]

By December 1948, Murray had persuaded Stevens to fund research not only on segregation laws but also on anti-discrimination laws. Since the Methodists operated throughout the country, Murray reasoned, they should be aware of recent anti-discrimination laws in northern and western states that could provide models elsewhere. Stevens, who defied Murray's stereotype of a white Mississippi woman, agreed. Herself a graduate of Scarritt College, she had devoted her entire career to church work, much of it in the South. Now working in the Women's Division's New York office, she immediately accepted Murray's argument that there would be "tremendous educational value of exposing churchwomen of conscience to the actual texts of segregation statutes and allowing them to compare this legislation with civil rights laws." In December, Stevens sent an additional check for $500, enough to allow Murray to leave Baker's law firm. On April 1, 1949, Murray opened her own office at 6 Maiden Lane, near Wall Street. She was on her own.[67]

When Murray had graduated from law school in 1944, she had looked forward either to arguing civil rights cases before the Supreme Court or teaching law. Instead, she found herself spending every spare moment, including evenings, weekends, and holidays, at the New York County Law Library, copying out lengthy statutes by hand and then typing them up back in her office. The fact that she had little other income kept her going.[68]

Figure 8.2 Thelma Stevens, on the left, with Pauli Murray, reviewing a draft of the manuscript for *States' Laws*, 1949. Estate of Pauli Murray, Schlesinger Library, Radcliffe Institute, Harvard University.

Stevens envisioned a mimeographed pamphlet that could be copied at a low cost and distributed around the country. Instead, on January 12, 1950, Murray delivered a one-foot thick manuscript. To convey her findings in as striking and succinct a fashion as possible, she had drawn three charts, one of segregation laws and two others of civil rights statutes. Across the top of each chart, she listed every state. Along the left side, she identified every category—including, for instance, amusements, education, employment, hospitals, and transportation. At a glance, a reader could see the legal regulation of race in America.[69]

By then, the Women's Division had spent about $1,200 on this project. To publish Murray's tome would require significant additional funding. Stevens briefly considered publishing only Murray's charts, but in the end, she returned to her committee, which voted to pay for the publication of 2,000 copies. Murray was thrilled. "Aside from my three aunts being ill at the same time and my clients losing their jobs and having no money, things have been going along wonderfully!" Pauli informed Caroline Ware.[70]

On April 28, 1951, the Methodist Women released *States' Laws on Race and Color* in a public ceremony at their New York headquarters. Mrs. Frank G. Brooks, head of the Women's Committee, presented "first copies" to notable figures, including Paul North Rice of the New York Public Library, Ben Frederick Carruthers of the United Nation Commission on Human Rights, and Dorothy Kenyon on behalf of the American Civil Liberties Union. Pauli could not make the ceremony, having landed in the hospital—this time back at Freedman's in Washington. Once again, she suffered from an unexplained nervousness. In her place, Maida escorted a very proud Aunt Pauline and Aunt Sallie to represent her.[71]

As a reference work, *States' Laws* was inevitably difficult to sell or even get reviewed. But Stevens found funds to distribute it to libraries and legal organizations around the country. Murray was especially pleased when she later learned that Thurgood Marshall, calling it the "Bible" of civil rights litigators, acquired it for everyone on his staff. Murray publicized it with "Know Your Civil Rights," a four-part series, published in *Courier Magazine*, September–October 1951, that summarized her findings.[72]

A Life in Politics

With few clients knocking at her door, Murray decided to do something that new lawyers often did to get their name before the public. She ran for office. Until 1948, she had felt disaffected politically, despite her friendship with Eleanor Roosevelt. Maida got her interested in politics and persuaded her to register as a member of the Liberal Party, the party of the ILGWU. Together,

Figure 8.3 Dorothy Kenyon, on the right, accepting a copy of Pauli Murray's *States' Laws on Race and Color,* from Mrs. Frank G. Brooks, on behalf of the American Civil Liberties Union in 1951. Estate of Pauli Murray, Schlesinger Library, Radcliffe Institute, Harvard University.

they campaigned for Harry Truman on the Liberal Party line in response to his support for civil rights. Murray and Springer were among the few who believed that Truman would beat Thomas E. Dewey in the 1948 election.

The following year, leaders of the Liberal Party asked Murray to be their candidate for the City Council seat in New York's Tenth Senatorial District in Brooklyn. Murray initially rejected the idea. She had virtually no chance of winning on the Liberal Party ticket; New York City was a Democratic town. But Springer talked her into accepting the nomination. How else were women going to gain political power if they never ran for office? When Maida promised to be Pauli's campaign manager, Pauli persuaded herself that she had a chance. Caroline Ware contributed to her campaign, as did Eleanor Roosevelt. The Citizens Union endorsed her. So did the black press. Murray felt mixed emotions over the boost offered by the *Pittsburgh Courier*, with its banner headline, "Pauli Murray Would Add Glamour, Brains to Council." She accepted the "Brains," but winced at the suggestion of "Glamour."[73]

Former Howard students, now working in New York, among them Ruth Powell and Pat Roberts, campaigned for her. With insufficient funds for much in the way of radio time or posters, they focused on busy intersections. "Night after night we stood on street ladders, shivering in the brisk October air, shouting ourselves hoarse and passing out little blue-and-white fliers containing my photograph, qualifications and platform." For the last couple of days, Maida got them a sound truck, which they used to travel around the district. Trumpeting her slogan, "Good government is good housekeeping," Murray promised the same things that women political leaders had been calling for ever since the Progressive Era: better garbage collection, street lights, schools, libraries, and hospitals. In the end, she lost, but she racked up more votes than anyone else thought she could—virtually tying the count of the Republican candidate and coming in well ahead of the white woman who ran on the American Labor ticket.[74]

The campaign for City Council took away time from her law practice without generating new clients. So long as money kept coming in from the Methodist Women, Murray could cover her expenses, but when that source of income dried up, she would be in deep trouble. She therefore embarked on a search for a full-time job with any agency that would hire her. The possibility of a staff position with the American Civil Liberties Union in April 1950 raised her hopes, but in June she reported to Ware that "the ACLU job fell through. My price tag was too high." Moreover, she reported, she was too old and too experienced for a staff job. "They decided to take somebody with less experience who would be eager to earn what they offered." For years, she had faced race and sex discrimination. Now she encountered age discrimination.[75]

The Red Scare at Flood Tide

Then came a wonderful opportunity, one that built on her work on *States' Laws* and gave her a chance to go to Liberia for the "Liberian Codification Project." As part of a Cold War initiative mounted by the Truman administration to provide technical assistance to "third world" countries at risk of falling under Soviet influence, the US State Department had entered into an agreement with the Republic of Liberia to codify its laws. Expected to take three years, the project was to be carried out under the auspices of the New York School of Industrial Relations at Cornell University. Professor Milton Konvitz, a specialist in constitutional and labor law, would direct the project. Murray, with her law degrees and her work on *States' Laws*, felt uniquely qualified. Her race, usually a handicap, appeared, in the context of a study on Africa, to be an asset. Surely, she believed, Cornell would see the advantage of appointing a black person to a visible position in international affairs, if only to refute the frequent Soviet charge of American racism. Professor Konvitz strongly favored her candidacy.[76]

Murray might have secured the appointment as recently as 1948, when she won her case for admission to the bar, but since then, the Red Scare had intensified. In September 1949, Russia detonated an atom bomb; in October, China fell to the Communists. In January 1950, Alger Hiss, having denied that he had engaged in espionage, was convicted of perjury. Five months later, North Korea invaded South Korea. In September 1950, Congress passed the Internal Security Act over Truman's veto. The following May 1951, the House published a "Guide to Subversive Organizations." Murray, who took notes on the list in the New York County Law Library, found that she was or had been active in seven of the enumerated organizations. Shortly before she applied for the job on the Liberian Codification Project, Joseph McCarthy delivered his famous speech in Wheeling, West Virginia, in which he charged that the State Department harbored 205 Communists. These government workers, he implied, were responsible for American reverses in the Cold War. By this time, almost everyone with whom Murray had ever worked seemed to be in political trouble. Many had worked with Communists at one time or another, a few had belonged to the Communist Party Opposition. One had belonged to the Communist Party.[77]

Murray had lost touch with Peg Holmes after 1940, but in 1945 someone had forwarded a clipping about her. Margaret Holmes Gilbert, married and a mother, had been living in California but had moved to Cambridge, Massachusetts, during the war. At some point, she had joined the Communist Party and in 1944 had helped found the Samuel Adams School of Social Studies, where she taught and served as secretary. Pauli visited Peg once in the house where the Gilberts lived in Cambridge, probably in the summer of 1947. They never met again, but Pauli "worried" about her. Peg's house had become the principal meeting place for a Communist Cell. Later that year US Attorney General Tom Clark listed the Sam Adams School as a "subversive institution," and in 1951 Peg and several others were indicted under a 1919 Massachusetts sedition law.[78]

None of Pauli's other friends faced indictment, but several had been swept up in the intensifying witch-hunt. Dorothy Kenyon had attracted the attention of Senator McCarthy, who charged her with belonging to numerous Communist-front organizations. In February 1951, Murray expressed her dismay over the chilling effect of the Red Scare on free expression to Caroline Ware. "What disturbs me is that we are in such a state of uncertainty, we hesitate to take unpopular cases, to espouse unpopular causes," she lamented. Caroline Ware understood all too well, for she continued to face conservative attacks. At the same time that Murray applied for the job in Liberia, Ware applied to travel to Chile to work on community development, but the review board for the Pan-American Union of the Organization of American States, which screened Americans working for international organizations, denied authorization over concerns about her loyalty.[79]

By the spring of 1952, the Red Scare had spread to include even Ivy League institutions, state universities, and small private colleges. At Cornell, the scare provoked bitter debates over the limits of academic freedom. As late as 1949 the Cornell faculty had affirmed its policy to encourage free and open discussion of controversial issues. Everyone, Communists included, was welcome to speak on campus to give students all points of view. By 1951, however, the climate had turned frigid. Three hundred faculty members voted to ban any teacher who advocated the overthrow of the government. Such was the political situation at Cornell when Murray applied to work on the "Liberian Codification Project."[80]

Murray hoped that those who read her application would be able to distinguish between her frequent dissents from official policies, especially in southern states, and disloyalty to the American government. Konvitz seemed positively disposed, even enthusiastic, toward her, when she interviewed at Cornell on April 14. But his superior, M. P. Catherwood, dean of the School of Industrial and Labor Relations, harbored doubts. Catherwood found it worrying that Murray's references all came from liberals. Her case would be strengthened, he instructed Konvitz to inform her, if she could produce letters from conservatives. Murray responded that she did not know any conservatives well enough for them to write knowledgeably about her. Indeed, she declared, a black woman of her means could not be expected to have known any conservatives well, except as a servant. Unmoved, Catherwood concluded that Murray's "past associations" posed too great a risk for Cornell and turned her down.[81]

A Person In-Between

"Epitaph for a Law Practice"

Murray had faced rejection before: by UNC because of her race, Harvard because of her gender, and the ACLU because of her age. But the Cornell defeat hurt most of all. The university's explicit justification for declining to hire her did not come down to some arbitrary category she could dismiss as intellectually bankrupt. Instead, Dean Catherwood had voiced a suspicion about her "past associations." What did that mean? Did Cornell reject her because of the organizations she had joined, or, worse, because of her private life? "One thinks of all the personal errors, the deep secrets of one's life unrelated to political activities," she worried. More than anything else, she feared her "queerness" would be exposed. The rejection from Cornell tipped her into a particularly deep depression. Seeking relief, she turned to prayer and a religious pamphlet by Dora Willson, *The Self to the Self* (1946), which urged readers to learn how to love themselves if they hoped to love others and God. She tried.[1]

Murray's legal diary had almost no entries after June 1952, suggesting that her law worked dried up. By September, she was so desperate that she applied for a job as a social investigator at the Department of Welfare and was relieved when she was hired. By year's end, she had cleared $295. She earned another $271 for four week's work on Adlai Stevenson's failed presidential campaign. Offsetting that income, she experienced a $135 loss on her law practice, for a net income for the year of $431. Mother Pauline's pension raised that figure by $300. The combined income of $731, plus whatever Aunt Pauline received in rent from the Durham homestead (likely not more than $200), barely kept them going. According to the Bureau of the Census, the average family income in 1952 was $3,900; a family with an income below $999 ranked in the bottom 9 percent. By any measure, the Murray-Dame-Small household was impoverished.[2]

Murray's new job had clear benefits, apart from the regular, if meager, salary. After years of isolation, she appreciated working with colleagues, several of whom were lawyers like herself who had failed to support themselves as solo practitioners. She soon had a caseload of seventy-eight, and her days were filled with trips around the city to visit people, most of them Puerto Rican or black, whose life circumstances proved even worse than her own: the new mother, abandoned by her husband, who had no clothes for her newborn; a seventy-six-year-old woman, who had herself once worked as a social investigator, then as a domestic and hotel worker, and who had now run through her savings. These clients bestowed on Murray a feeling of accomplishment. Yet she could not escape a sense of defeat.[3]

On January 16, 1953, she closed her law office. Talking her aunts into letting her discard the old sofa in their apartment, she moved her desk and filing cabinet to 388 Chauncey Street. "Epitaph to a law practice," she wrote in her diary. She had been at 6 Maiden Lane for almost four years, her longest period in any job. "There were many triumphs and a few shattering defeats," but as she looked at her nineteen cartons of books and papers, her "worldly goods," she could not honestly say she was sorry to leave. She could not continue "the day-to-day waiting for clients that did not come, the growing panic of failure, the facing of blank walls, the feeling that I was trapped in a hopeless situation from which I could not escape."[4]

Murray's feeling of failure was only partially mitigated by mention of her in two national publications, published early in 1953. One, entitled "Lady Lawyers: Sex No Handicap to Careers," appeared in *Jet: The Weekly Negro Magazine*. Proud though she was to see herself included in a list of the country's five leading black female attorneys, Murray felt ashamed that her circumstances belied the article's central message. In a second article, in *Ebony*, Eleanor Roosevelt predicted a bright future for her protégé. "One of my finest young friends," wrote Roosevelt, "is a charming woman lawyer—Pauli Murray, who has been quite a firebrand at times but of whom I am very fond. She is a lovely person who has struggled and come through very well. I think there were times when she might have done foolish things. But now I think she is well ready to be of real use." Murray wrote immediately to tell Roosevelt that she was "deeply moved that you counted me among your close friends." She did not confess that she was beginning to doubt she could ever be useful. Crippled by her sense of living a life in-between as a mixed-race, mixed-class, and mixed-gendered person, she felt doomed to failure. But in the years that followed, she found a way to turn that feeling to her advantage.[5]

Back to the Typewriter

Long ago, Grandfather Robert Fitzgerald had advised his daughters to pursue at least two trades. Given life's uncertainties, especially for women of color, he wanted them to have insurance. Seek an education, he urged; train to be a teacher but develop other skills as well. All of Pauli's aunts could support themselves by sewing as well as teaching. Pauli followed her grandfather's counsel, and then some. Over the course of her life so far she had earned her keep as a typist, teacher, poet, civil rights organizer, journalist, lawyer, and social worker. In 1952, as her law practice ended, she thought of ways to augment her salary from the Department of Welfare. Having made money in Los Angeles as a writer in the summer of 1944, she resolved to do so again.[6]

Murray found a literary agent, Marie F. Rodell, who believed that white audiences were ready, indeed eager, to read works by African American authors. Black poet Gwendolyn Brooks had won the Pulitzer Prize for poetry in 1950. Random House had just published Ralph Ellison's *Invisible Man*, and Knopf had contracted to publish James Baldwin's *Go Tell It on the Mountain*. Although she failed to find a publisher for Murray's poems, Rodell remained convinced that she could succeed with Murray's proposed family history.[7]

Pauli had been working on a history of the Fitzgeralds ever since her first year at Hunter College, when she submitted a story about Grandfather Robert Fitzgerald to her first-year English teacher. Returning to the project after graduation, she wrote sketches of family members at the Hunter switchboard in her spare time. Stephen Vincent Benét, to whom she appealed for help on her poetry in 1939, had encouraged her to write about the black experience "from the inside." He even suggested a title: *Proud Shoes*. In 1946, she embarked on a letter-writing campaign with state officials to document family births and deaths. She continued her research in local archives on a trip south in March 1952.[8]

The Cornell defeat propelled her project forward. Outraged by the charge that her "past associations" marked her as unacceptable for a government-financed job, she ruminated over her earliest associates, her forebears. If "associations" mattered, then an account of their lives, especially that of Grandfather Robert Fitzgerald, would prove that she had been raised in the most unimpeachably American of families. Echoing her essay "American Credo" (1945), she pointed to her grandfather's contribution to the Civil War, commitment to education, unwavering defense of civil rights, and loyalty to America.[9]

To ease Murray's financial worries, Rodell encouraged her to apply for a grant from the Eugene F. Saxton Memorial Trust. Established by the publishing house Harper & Brothers to provide money to promising writers, the trust gave Murray a $2,500 grant in the fall of 1952. Though thrilled by the award, Murray asked that it be deferred until she could earn enough as a social investigator for the Welfare Department to pay off her most pressing debts. With the further help of a gift from Caroline Ware, in June 1953, she was ready to turn full-time to her family history. By the fall she had produced an outline and several chapters.

Rodell submitted them to Elizabeth Lawrence, a senior editor at Harper & Brothers, who offered a contract with a $900 advance.[10]

Buoyed by the recognition and the infusion of cash, Murray threw herself into the research and writing of *Proud Shoes*. Fortunately, Aunt Pauline had preserved the diary Grandfather had kept during the Civil War and the early years of Reconstruction. Pauline and Sallie recalled stories from their childhood. Murray traveled to Pennsylvania, Delaware, and North Carolina to check family lore against manumission records, property deeds, court records, and birth certificates.[11]

The research energized her. So did the Supreme Court's decision in *Brown v. Board of Education of Topeka Kansas,* which at long last overturned *Plessy v. Ferguson* on the grounds she had long advocated. Newly appointed Chief Justice Earl Warren, writing for a unanimous Court, stressed the psychological damage done to children by a system of state-sanctioned segregation. In "the field of public education," Warren concluded, "the doctrine of 'separate but equal' has no place. Separate educational facilities are inherently unequal." In the wake of this victory, Murray had the satisfaction of collecting on her bet with Spottswood Robinson, made in 1944, that *Plessy* would be overturned within twenty-five years. More satisfying still, Robinson admitted that her law school essay on the *Civil Rights Cases* (1883) and *Plessy* (1896), with its emphasis on Justice John Marshall Harlan's ringing dissents, had helped the NAACP lawyers formulate their argument in *Brown*.[12]

Writer's Block

Writing usually came easily to Murray, but the task of getting her family down on paper turned out to be much more difficult than she had anticipated. Her problem centered on Grandmother Cornelia. As Murray explained to Caroline Ware, "She was my favorite Fitzgerald, and quite contrary to what I supposed, I find her hardest to paint with words." With her livelihood on the line, she suddenly found herself unable to write. Despite Murray's long-standing resistance to psychotherapy, Rodell persuaded her to see Dr. Edmund Ziman, a psychiatrist and psychoanalyst at the William Alanson White Institute, for help in addressing her problem.[13]

A man three years Murray's senior, Ziman proved a sympathetic and engaged listener. As an undergraduate at George Washington University, he had composed and directed a musical comedy, "Take It Easy," an experience that drew him to creative patients. As a member of the White Institute, directed by feminist analyst Clara Thompson, he held professional women in high esteem. Moreover, as part of a psychiatric institute that featured regular lectures by anthropologists, he showed a sensitivity to cultural and racial context rare in analysts of his generation.[14]

Ziman helped by encouraging Murray "to pull out the hidden fears in my own life and look at them. I've been so anxiety ridden because of the terrors I live with all the time." They were many: the terror of violent storms, new situations, physical attack, mental illness, and—most frightening of all—the risk that her most personal secrets, especially her queerness, might come to light. To help Murray conquer these fears, Ziman apparently inspired her to write openly and honestly about her place in a family marked by color and class prejudice, poverty, disability, and mental illness. Whatever he said, Ziman must have succeeded, for Murray credited him with helping her to write again. He was one of those to whom—along with Caroline Ware, Marie Rodell, and Aunt Pauline—she dedicated *Proud Shoes*.[15]

There is not enough evidence to be sure of Ziman's position on the matter of Murray's gender identity. He would have been aware of the fierce debates then playing out in the journals of psychotherapy. One school of thought held that patients who felt trapped in the wrong bodies were mentally ill and needed to be led to the correct gender identification through intensive psychotherapy. Another held that gender identity, whatever its source, was established so early in life and was from that point so resistant to change that it was easier to change the body to comport with the sense of self than to do the reverse. This latter view achieved its most famous result in the early 1950s in the case of Christine Jorgensen, an American GI who transitioned to a woman through hormone treatments and surgery in Denmark. Ziman likely found himself between these two positions, believing that Murray's identity was rooted in early emotional conflicts, but that it had been so deeply established that she was not likely to be able to change how she felt. Since American medical practice did not yet sanction the hormone therapy Murray wanted, there was not much Ziman could do other than to offer some theories about why she felt the way she did.[16]

Ziman specialized in child development and had recently published *Jealousy in Children: A Guide for Parents*. His book included a discussion of a three-year-old girl who believed she was a boy. Ziman suspected that the little girl, jealous of an older brother, identified as male to compete more effectively for her mother's attention. Ziman may have suggested to Pauli that her birth a mere year after that of her brother William had fostered similar feelings. Ziman may also have suggested that her father's violence toward her mother, when Pauli was developing her gender identity, around the age of three, could have pushed her to identify as male as a means of protecting her mother and herself. Whatever his views on Murray's gender identity, Ziman probably focused first on the relatively easier problems of race conflict and fears about mental illness. And yet, Murray regarded her gender identity as her most troubling problem, the one for which she needed the most help, and the one that she still believed was, at root, glandular. A new health crisis encouraged her in this view.[17]

Hyperthyroidism

In the midst of her psychotherapy with Ziman, Murray once again fell ill. Always thin, she had lost fifteen pounds in the past two years. She was suffering from anemia, a dry cough, a rapid heartbeat, and growing nervousness. In early June 1954 she collapsed. Her long-time physician, Dr. May Chinn, diagnosed a thyroid adenoma, an overgrowth of normal thyroid tissue, which produces too much of the thyroid hormone thyroxine, which in turn leads to the symptoms Murray was experiencing. Dr. Chinn recommended immediate surgery, if a newly available diagnostic tool—a radioactive iodine test—confirmed her diagnosis. It did.[18]

The thyroid regulates the body's metabolism through the production of thyroid hormones, which affect every cell and organ in the body. If production falls, a person may suffer fatigue, weight gain, and depression; if it rises, as it did in Murray's case, the person may suffer anxiety, weight loss, and insomnia. Thyroid abnormalities were difficult to diagnose, especially in their early stages, because the symptoms they produced overlapped with so many other, more common afflictions, such as anxiety. Generally, only a skilled endocrinologist could make the diagnosis, but even those specialists often failed to spot the disease. Dr. Chinn had been sending Murray to endocrinologists since at least 1937, to no avail. Murray's insistence that she was a man seems to have led everyone, including the endocrinologists, to focus on what seemed to them a clear case of mental illness. They simply stopped thinking any further about what else might be troubling her.[19]

Surgeons at Freedman's Hospital in Washington operated on Murray on June 24, 1954. Almost immediately, Murray felt calmer. To her delight, Eleanor Roosevelt paid a call. "There was not a single living soul in Freedman's who did not know of your visit within almost minutes after you arrived," Murray wrote in thanks. Roosevelt should not think, Murray noted, that mere patients always had so many doctors, nurses, and attendants coming into and out of their rooms. They had arrived not to see the patient but rather to stare at the great woman. As one of the attendants later told Murray, "She ought to go back to the White House where she belongs!"[20]

Murray believed that her thyroid operation had finally put an end to the mood swings and associated miseries that had plagued her for as long as she could remember. She explained the importance she attached to the procedure to a number of people, most fully to her friend Joseph Lash. From early childhood, she explained, she had "suffered from great swings of the pendulum—tremendous overactivity, productivity, followed by physical and emotional collapse, like the shutting down of a factory system." Then, "in 1954," she continued, "it was finally discovered that a nodule on the right thyroid gland was irritating the thyroid and producing the pendulum swings. The operation . . . removed the nodule, most of the right thyroid, a considerable amount of cartilige (sp.?) from the Adam's Apple which made me look embarrassingly 'masculine' before it was removed." The operation changed her life. "I finally settled down to the first stability I had known during the first 44 years of my life. All that has followed since then has been trying to 'catch up' to the person I might have been had medical science been far enough advanced to have helped me when I was a teen-ager and the trouble first manifested itself."[21]

This medical intervention apparently freed Murray to be a calmer, more productive person, but it did not entirely relieve her anxieties about her mental health, much less her gender identity. In a letter to Dr. J. B. Johnson following surgery she wrote, "Will you be kind enough to make a complete surgical and medical summary, together with a summary of our four-way conference and your, Dr. Henry's and Dr. Burton's reaction to my second memo of July 4th." Murray concluded by saying, "At the moment, I shall concentrate on getting the medical odd bits and pieces taken care of—eyes, nasal drip, fibroid etc.— but as soon as *Proud Shoes* is completed, I shall be right back on the beam with this problem. I would like to keep things moving on it because I intend to see it through to the end, God willing." In separate letters to Eleanor Roosevelt on July 4 and to Edmund Ziman on July 7, she suggested that the "problem" was, at least in part, her mental health and that of her siblings.[22]

There had been so much mental illness in the Murray and Fitzgerald family that she wondered whether there might be a genetic basis for it, and if so whether others in the family suffered from some form of thyroid dysfunction that could be the source of their mental problems. After medical school, Ziman had served as the senior medical officer at St. Elizabeth's in Washington, where Pauli's brother Bill had been institutionalized. Ziman had observed lobotomies and may have been present at the one that William had undergone. As a member of the White Institute, however, he had moved away from such extreme medical intervention. He helped Murray face her fears about mental illness, to see them as possibly linked to a familial history of thyroid disease—possibly precipitated or aggravated by the larger social, economic, and racial context in which they lived.[23]

Ziman encouraged Murray to write to the superintendent at Crownsville State Hospital for the Negro Insane in Maryland to find out what might exist in the records of her father, who was there from 1918 to his murder in 1923, and her older sister Grace, who was there from 1941 to 1945. Murray did so on July 4, a week following her thyroid operation. In response, Superintendent Dr. Ralph H. Meng informed her that her father had been diagnosed on admission in 1918 as suffering from "Anxiety Neurosis," a diagnosis that could have been applied to a broad swath of the population. The next report in William's file, from 1921, was more revealing. William complained of headaches, poor eyesight, moodiness, and constant hunger—all symptoms of hyperthyroidism. The psychiatrist who examined him in 1921 gave him a diagnosis of "Manic Depressive," with a prognosis of "fair" and a recommendation for parole. Pauli's sister Grace was diagnosed as "Schizophrenia, paranoid type." At some point Mildred had a goiter (thyroid) operation. Rosetta suffered from mood swings.[24]

Murray came to conclude that the mental illness in her family was likely linked to two things: a family tendency toward thyroid disease, aggravated in the case of her father by the encephalitis experienced during his 1905 typhoid illness, and in the case of her brother William and sisters Grace and Rosetta by situational conditions of racism and poverty. If more had been known about thyroid disease when they were all younger, and if lithium had been more widely available, Murray believed that many of the members of her family could have led more productive lives.[25]

There remained the matter of Murray's gender identity. The diagnoses of hyperthyroidism explained many of the symptoms from which she had suffered for years. But those symptoms did not explain the meaning that she had attached to them.[26]

Murray apparently did not pursue one further option, treatment from a then little-known endocrinologist, the German-born Dr. Harry Benjamin. In 1949, Alfred Kinsey had introduced Benjamin to an unusual young man, one of the thousands of men Kinsey had interviewed for his 1948 study, *Sexual Behavior in the Human Male.* The young man believed he was a woman. Starting with this patient, and moving on in the next several years to a handful of others (including one female-to-male subject), Benjamin came to believe that these individuals must have experienced a biological accident before birth, possibly a hormone surge, which made them feel like the opposite sex. Also inspired by Kinsey, who believed that sexuality existed on a continuum from unvarying heterosexuality to unvarying homosexuality, Benjamin developed a scale of what he called "transsexual" identity along a spectrum from transvestites who liked to wear the clothes of the opposite gender but who were content with their gender identity, to transsexuals who could not be happy short of hormone therapy and sex reassignment surgery. If Murray had found her way to Benjamin's office in Manhattan, he would likely have placed her somewhere in the middle of his scale, someone who often dressed as a man and who sought hormone therapy, but not surgery. Benjamin would likely have given her the hormones that she wanted, since, in contrast to accepted medical practice, he offered them to those who asked. But Murray left no record of such treatment, indeed no evidence that she even knew of Benjamin's existence at that time. It seems likely that she worked solely with Ziman, and that he helped her see her queerness, in gender as in race and class, as a strength.[27]

The doctors at Freedman Hospital appear to have left Murray's psychological concerns to Ziman and to have focused instead on her post-surgical health. In their view, she needed to rest for a good six weeks to recover fully from her operation. Only one week into her recovery, however, Aunt Marie Fitzgerald Jeffers died at Riverhead on Long Island. Pauli and Mildred drove from Washington for the funeral on July 4. This death, sad though it was, created an opportunity. Aunt Sallie could move into the house vacated by Aunt Marie and ease the crowding at 388 Chauncey Street.[28]

"Where Our 'Queerness' Is Normal"

Harper editor Elizabeth Lawrence had a further thought to help Murray's recovery and focus. On her recommendation, Murray spent August and September 1954 at the MacDowell Colony in Peterborough, New Hampshire. Founded in 1907, MacDowell had evolved into one of the country's premier retreats for artists, composers, and writers. Located on 450 acres, the colony dedicated itself to the idea that "creativity requires time, space, and privacy," three things in short supply in Murray's life. The colony included twenty-five studios, scattered through the woods. A candidate could apply for a stay of up to two months to work in one of these studios, which provided simple amenities of electricity and heat, but no phones. A picnic basket with lunch appeared on the studio doorsteps each day. The artists typically gathered for breakfast and dinner at a common dining room and for group activities in the evening.[29]

At MacDowell, Murray found acceptance and the peaceful atmosphere she needed in order to write, as well as the daily intellectual stimulation of extraordinary artists. James Baldwin, then thirty, worked in the studio next to hers. Murray found him to be "intense," "sensitive," "soft spoken," and "delicately put together"—basically a copy of Pauli, except for the "soft spoken" part. He became so engrossed in his work that he ignored the dinner bell and Murray had to call out to him as she strode by his studio to be sure he got fed. Murray entertained Baldwin at her cabin and ventured into town with him. To Caroline Ware she wrote, "Jimmy Baldwin and I have gone to the movies, had beer in the local community 'pub' and the natives are polite, courteous, and do not lift eyebrows—which I thought would be the case."[30]

Murray guessed that Baldwin had come to MacDowell through the efforts of another resident, Sol Stein, who, in addition to working on a play of his own, served as Baldwin's editor. Close friends dating back to high school in the Bronx, Stein and Baldwin formed an odd pair. As Joseph Berger once characterized the two, "Stein was white, Jewish, and attracted to women. Baldwin was black, the stepson of a Pentecostal minister and attracted to men." But they were devoted to each other. While at MacDowell, Stein persuaded Baldwin to publish a book of his essays, *Notes of a Native Son* (1955), and encouraged him through an early draft of *Giovanni's Room* (1956), an explicitly bi-sexual, bi-racial novel. The two men never discussed Baldwin's homosexuality, but, Stein later reported, "he knew that I knew."[31]

Murray said nothing in her letters about whether her talks with Baldwin included any discussion of their respective struggles over gender identity and sexual orientation, apart from one remark. She wrote her friends that, like her, Baldwin suffered from "inner conflicts and terrors," her code for sexual or gender conflicts and the fear of being discovered—conflicts and fears that only writing could assuage. Given the length of time they spent in daily contact, it seems likely that each at least intuited the most private struggles of the other and felt a little less alone as a result.[32]

Other residents at MacDowell may not have guessed how much Murray and Baldwin shared, apart from their race, for they expressed themselves so differently. By her own admission, Murray "bluster[ed]" at the McDowell breakfast and dinner table, as she hammered away at the "race problem." Baldwin remained "silent . . . sweet . . . popular." To complicate matters, they switched places in their prose. Seeking feedback, Murray passed around "A Legacy of the South," a biographical essay on Lillian Smith she had just completed. Baldwin offered "A Stranger in the Village," his reflections of the meaning of race in Europe and America, following his stay in a remote Swiss hamlet. Conciliatory in her writing, the normally combative Murray emphasized the common humanity that underlay racial conflict in the South. By contrast, "sweet" Baldwin indicted European-American civilization for its crimes against blacks. White readers at MacDowell found Baldwin's essay "disturbing." To Murray's dismay, they found hers only "interesting."[33]

Two other residents, who arrived at MacDowell in September, after Baldwin had left, offered Murray greater encouragement. Henrietta Buckmaster, the author of *Let My People Go* (1941), a history of the Underground Railroad, was one of the first white writers to portray blacks as leaders in their own emancipation. She did so while combining historical research with a novelist's ear for dialogue. Sharing both Murray's publisher, Harper & Brothers, and her editor, Elizabeth Lawrence, Buckmaster came to MacDowell to work on a new historical novel on the life of the Apostle Paul and voiced immediate interest in Murray's family memoir.[34]

Another new arrival, the white scriptwriter Helene Hanff, offered interest and more. An aspiring playwright, Hanff got her first big break with the arrival of

Figure 9.1 Residents of MacDowell Colony, Peterborough, New Hampshire, August 1954. Pauli Murray, front row, seated eighth, left to right. Sol Stein and James Baldwin, back row, first and second, left to right. Photographer: Bernice B. Perry. Library of Congress, LC-DIG-ppmsca-13440.

television in the 1950s. Her scripts for the "Adventures of Ellery Queen" and the "Hallmark Hall of Fame" won her a month-long spot at MacDowell. "Then along you come," Hanff later recalled of her first meeting with Murray. In response, Murray tried to capture what MacDowell meant to them both: "For so long we have been homeless, wandering, square-pegs-in-round holes, unable to hold steady jobs and be solid citizens, and carrying a load of guilt that we don't function like other people—get married, have children, go to Europe, give big parties, etc., etc." Disappointments at MacDowell aside, Murray remained thankful, as she knew Hanff to be, "to find a place where our 'queerness' is normal, where our bodies and our souls are considered precious."[35]

Murray addressed Hanff playfully as "Butch"; Hanff responded by calling Murray "Love," "Sugar," and "Cookie." Both felt marginalized, led the hand-to-mouth existence of the undiscovered writer, lived alone when they possibly could, and adored the Brooklyn Dodgers. Unheralded and vulnerable, they supported each other emotionally through a difficult period for them both. Had Murray stayed in California, she might have been drawn to a new group, the Daughters of Bilitis, founded in San Francisco that very fall of 1955, by a few women who, like Murray, disliked going to bars but yearned for friendship with other women who shared their sense of being "queer." But the Daughters of Bilitis started to call themselves lesbians, a step that Murray would not have endorsed, had she known of the group's existence. She relied, instead, on Hanff, who similarly never identified as lesbian, and a few other close friends for support. Maida Springer sent regular letters, as did Caroline Ware, but Murray looked on Maida as her "side-kick" and Skipper as her mentor. Helene showed promise as a soulmate. After MacDowell, they continued to encourage each other. Hanff launched into a play about the Colony. Murray sent her manuscript to Elizabeth Lawrence.[36]

Proud Shoes

The manuscript for *Proud Shoes* had changed through successive drafts. Initially, Murray began with a prologue, one that rebutted Cornell's charges of disloyalty by showing her lineage of patriotic "past associations." Caroline Ware and Helen Lockwood, a professor of English at Vassar and Ware's close friend, to whom Murray also sent a draft, persuaded her to cut it. Starting defensively left them both "cold." They urged that she begin instead with the passage, buried in her manuscript, that would set the stage for a story of struggle and triumph: "If Grandfather Robert George Fitzgerald had not volunteered for the Union in 1863 and come south three years later as a missionary among the Negro freedmen, our family might not have walked in such proud shoes."[37]

Following their advice, Murray produced a strikingly original, multiracial family history that challenged the ethnocentrism of the 1950s. Long before historians accepted family history as a legitimate pursuit, Murray revealed how the story of one clan could illuminate the larger history of the country through its struggles. In the telling, Murray revealed female ancestors who did the work of men and male ancestors who did the work of women long before the modern women's movement legitimized doing so. In response to the well-worn claim that blacks were not ready for equal rights, she recounted the history of a long civil rights movement to which members of her family had contributed for over a century, overcoming hurdles along the way that most whites had never encountered and could barely imagine.[38]

In the fall of 1954, Murray waited hopefully for Elizabeth Lawrence's response. To her dismay, Lawrence demanded major changes. The manuscript revealed too much evidence of Murray's hard archival labors. That evidence should be compressed and pushed into the background. The key figures must to be pulled out and their stories enlivened. As Murray reported Lawrence's verdict to Ware, "I have let facts chain me and have not used my imagination in building scenes or improvising dialogue." Murray needed to write more like Harper's other historian of the black experience, Henrietta Buckmaster.[39]

Out of money, Murray worried that she was not up to the challenge. Before she could do anything else, she needed some income. Once again Marie Rodell came to her rescue. For the next year, as she struggled to rewrite *Proud Shoes,* Murray paid her rent by typing manuscripts for Marie Rodell's other authors. One was Betty Friedan. Murray and Friedan would later make common cause in the women's movement, but Murray must have had mixed emotions about the articles she typed in the mid-1950s. She was no doubt drawn to Freidan's upbeat articles (rarely published because editors deemed them too controversial) about racially integrated communities and women who battled against conformity. By contrast, she probably felt nonplused by the essays about unhappy suburban housewives (the ones that did get into print). What did they have to complain about?[40]

Added to her financial worries, Murray felt paralyzed once again by "writer's block." Wondering how she could possibly give Lawrence the book she wanted, Murray turned again to Dr. Ziman. He was likely the person who encouraged her to start over with a new first chapter, one in which she placed herself at the center. She moved the tale of Grandfather's military service and southern missionary endeavor to chapter two and started instead with a scene set at the Fitzgerald Homestead in 1916, narrated by her five-year-old self.

In this opening chapter, Pauli reads haltingly to her grandfather from the local newspaper about the war in Europe and then tries to calm her grandmother, who has begun to shriek at a neighborhood woman. For a few moments Granma Cornelia amuses the neighbors with empty threats about what she will do to them if they trespass on her property. But when the neighbors shout, "You half-white bastard," and she answers, "Humph! You think I'm insulted? I'll tell anybody I'm a white man's child," Cornelia raises the lid on class and color conflict in black communities. Conceived in the rape of a slave by an eminent North Carolina lawyer, Cornelia is proud of her paternity and her upbringing in the genteel traditions of needlepoint, literature, and high Episcopal service. By focusing on Granma Cornelia's battle with the neighbors, Murray establishes a darker, more troubled sense of pride than the one she initially envisioned when she began her story with Grandfather Robert's war service.[41]

The contrast between Robert Fitzgerald and Cornelia Smith's sources of pride underscores the tension in the household and reveals the complex results that miscegenation had in the Fitzgerald family. In Murray's telling, both grandparents instill in her a sense of class superiority, Grandfather through his stern correction of her pronunciation and insistence on high academic achievement, Grandmother through her repeatedly expressed pride in her elite white ancestry. As Cornelia excoriates the darker-skinned neighbor for crossing the invisible boundary that divides the Fitzgerald's middle-class home from the surrounding lower-class neighborhood, however, she delivers a lesson on the link between color and class that unsettles her darker-skinned granddaughter. That lesson instills in Pauli a sense of in-betweenness and makes her feel perpetually insecure, but it also fires Pauli's imagination.[42]

Ziman's influence reinforced what Murray had taken from her time with Baldwin, Buckmaster, and Hanff. *Proud Shoes,* which had started in 1953 as an argument against the Red Scare and had evolved in 1954 into a meticulously documented piece of upbeat historical nonfiction, had by 1955 taken on Baldwin's exhortation to dig more deeply into the meaning of race, as well as Buckmaster and Hanff's insistence on the importance of setting a scene and creating dialogue. As Murray rewrote the book once more, she turned it into a blend of the genres of biography and fiction to satisfy Lawrence's demands. The final manuscript also spoke in a much more sophisticated way to the fears of the postwar era. Wounded at MacDowell by her fellow artists' assessment of her work as "interesting," she tried to make it as "disturbing" as Baldwin's.

In the process, Murray took risks she had not previously had the courage to do. She told a frank story of miscegenation long before DNA evidence connected President Thomas Jefferson to the son of his slave Sally Hemmings. She wrote about rape but also of voluntary interracial sex; of race pride, but also of passing—all in the same family. Movingly, she told the story of a little girl praised for her high intelligence but constantly criticized by her own grandmother for skin that was too "dark," lips that were too "niggerish," and hair that was "too kinky." As she summed up what she was trying to accomplish in her final draft, Murray said that she had come to realize "that true emancipation lies in the acceptance of the whole past in deriving strength from all my roots, in facing up to the degradation as well as the dignity of my ancestors."[43]

In the final pages, Murray came close to addressing her gender identity, as someone more male than female. She did so by declaring that her family and the larger society had made her aware that she was a "minority within a minority"— the phrase Mac had used back in 1940, when she wrote on Murray's behalf to the *Amsterdam News* in gratitude for its support of the use of hormones to help people change their bodies to better accord with their sense of their gender. Coming when it does, the phrase "minority within a minority" at first seems off. Murray's message throughout *Proud Shoes* is that people like herself—people who defy strict racial and class categorization—represent large numbers, if not most Americans. But Murray is using "minority" in this instance to refer not to numerical minorities but rather to status minorities, those without power. Referring to herself as a "minority within a minority" hints at a deeper lesson: that the boundary between men and women is just as arbitrary as any of the other boundaries society draws. At the end of a book about the pain of being "neither very dark nor very fair," of being "nobody without identity," Murray turned her sense of being a person perpetually "between" into a positive condition, one that allowed her not only to show that her mixed race, mixed-class family was a representative of all American families, but also that she, in her in-betweenness, stood for virtually everyone.[44]

The final months of writing proved difficult. As Murray struggled to finish her revisions, the last members of the older generation died. Soon after Aunt Marie, Uncle Lewis Murray died. As of August 1955, Aunt Pauline was in good health, but she began to decline in September and on November 8 was dead of a heart attack. Aunt Sally lasted only two months more. When Murray submitted the final manuscript to Harper & Brothers, none of the older members of her family were alive to read it.[45]

At long last, Proud Shoes appeared in print on October 17, 1956. Given its bold themes, it inspired a mixed response. Many reviewers gave it high praise. Henrietta Buckmaster lauded Murray in the New York Times as a "writer of uncommon gifts." Ted Poston called her story "magnificent" in the New York Post. Bryon R. Bryant of the San Francisco Chronicle rated Proud Shoes "superior to most non-fictional works about the South." Margot Jackson of the Akron Beacon Journal noted the "uncanny newness" of a "Negro writing about slavery and the Civil War." In her daily column, Eleanor Roosevelt called it "American history which all Americans should read."[46]

Murray's treatment of miscegenation received the most comment. As black writer Roi Ottley noted in his appreciative review in the Chicago Daily Tribune: "Not so many years ago a distinguished white family, descendants of a Revolutionary war hero known to every schoolboy, paid a Negro family who bore his name a reported $50,000 to change its name. . . . There are thousands of such intertwined Negro and white families, particularly in the South." Murray had taken an important part of American history and current events, heretofore "shrouded in mystery" and prejudice, and had placed it at the center of her story.[47]

Not everyone celebrated her for doing so. To present miscegenation in positive terms marked one as dangerous at a time when twenty-eight states continued to outlaw interracial marriage. Patricia Speights of the Mississippi newspaper Clarion-Ledger & Jackson Daily News emphasized that danger in her review of Proud Shoes. She warned her readers that the "cause of miscegenation is herewith presented by a writer who has been actively associated with the cause of civil rights. . . . In these days of racial tension . . . a book such as this can serve no useful purpose." Speights was unusual in discussing Proud Shoes at all in a southern newspaper. For the most part, the southern press ignored the memoir, and bookstores in the region refused to stock it.[48]

In the end, Proud Shoes sold only 5,000 copies. Murray did not begin to receive royalties until 1963; it took that long for royalty payments to exceed the advances that Lawrence had made to her in the course of writing. When the royalties started coming in, they generated an infinitesimal profit over the advances long spent: $41.14 in 1963; $21.00 in 1964. Once again, Murray had been ahead of her time. Once again, she needed a job.[49]

Murray later reflected on the fact that Adlai Stevenson's two failed presidential campaigns, the first in 1952, the second in 1956, had "book ended the writing of *Proud Shoes.*" In both campaigns, Lloyd K. Garrison hired her to help get out the black vote for Stevenson. Having disdained Democratic Party politics her whole life, Murray had come to see the northern wing of the Democratic Party as blacks' best hope for winning civil rights protections. Moreover, work for Garrison provided critically needed income. In 1952, blacks voted overwhelmingly for the senator from Illinois. In Harlem, 83 percent of the ballots went to the Democrat. In 1956, blacks were again enthusiastic. Eleanor Roosevelt supported him and Murray enthusiastically accepted an offer to serve on the Stevenson for President Committee. But Murray's enthusiasm soon waned, as Stevenson—fearful of losing white votes in the South—declined to take a strong stand on behalf of federal support for the expanding civil rights movement. Mindful of mounting white resistance in the South to the Supreme Court's decision in *Brown*, Stevenson refused to support legislation drafted by Adam Clayton Powell Jr., which would have denied federal funds to schools that refused to desegregate. He also refused to support the use of federal troops to enforce court orders, out of concern that sending in soldiers would incite a second Civil War.[50]

Dismayed, Murray tried to persuade Eleanor Roosevelt that Stevenson was losing the black vote by his timidity. She could not understand why the presidential candidate criticized black supporters for pushing too hard while failing to criticize white southerners for their failure to accept federal law. As she predicted, Stevenson experienced a sharp drop in support among black voters as a result of his inaction. Murray's disappointment over Stevenson's campaign was offset, however, by the arrival of a professional opportunity that had long eluded her. Lloyd K. Garrison, who persuaded the failed presidential candidate to join his law firm in its Chicago office, told Murray that he might be able to hire her in New York. Murray's hopes for a real job soared. Perhaps someone queer could succeed after all.[51]

Paul, Weiss, Rifkind, Wharton & Garrison

The law firm Murray hoped to join dated back to the years after the Civil War. In 1875, two Jewish lawyers, Julius Frank and Samuel Weiss, shunned by established firms, formed their own to serve an elite client group of German Jewish merchants and bankers. In 1923, Samuel's son Louis Weiss formed a partnership with John P. Wharton, a Protestant classmate at Columbia Law School. Weiss & Wharton dedicated themselves to the proposition that Jews and Gentiles could work together as partners and employees. This iconoclastic mission oriented the firm toward the representation of a more diverse set of clients, which included the estate of Cole Porter and one of the Scottsboro boys. When Lloyd Garrison joined the firm in 1946, together with finance expert Randolph E. Paul, the firm became Paul, Weiss, Wharton & Garrison. Garrison furthered the firm's liberal, artistic, civil-rights mission by defending, among others, poet Langston Hughes, playwright Arthur Miller, and physicist J. Robert Oppenheimer from right-wing attack. In 1949, Garrison advocated hiring the firm's first black lawyer, William I. Coleman, a native of Philadelphia, who could find work neither there nor in New York, despite having graduated at the top of his class at Harvard Law School and having served as a law clerk to Supreme Court Justice Felix Frankfurter.[52]

The firm made one further bold move. In 1949 it made Carolyn Agger a partner in its Washington office. Agger, a Yale Law School graduate, accomplished tax attorney, and wife of Abe Fortas (the future Supreme Court Justice), had attracted public notice as a lawyer for the National Labor Relations Board in the late 1930s. Conservative politicians had denigrated the cigar-smoking feminist as one of the "short-haired women married to long-haired men" who had come to populate New Deal agencies. As part of his war on union organizing, Virginia Congressman Howard Smith went so far as to investigate her and two other female colleagues for their allegedly pro-union decisions at the NLRB. Liberals, however, admired Agger's politics, intelligence, and confidence.[53]

In 1950, having outgrown its offices, Paul, Weiss became the first Wall Street firm to move to midtown. Taking up several floors in a sparkling new office building at 575 Madison, between 56th and 57th Streets, the firm cemented its avant-garde reputation. Garrison, who had become the firm's managing partner and was beginning to feel overwhelmed by the job, persuaded his partners that they needed a professional to manage the non-legal staff. Asking around, he learned that the person he wanted was Irene Barlow, then office manager at Elizabeth Arden. Though women rarely occupied so significant a managerial position in those days, Garrison quickly concluded that Barlow, "the first and only person" he interviewed, would be perfect in the job. A thirty-eight-year-old who could manage 3,000 people at Elizabeth Arden could handle 100 at Paul, Weiss. But what really sold Garrison on Barlow was her ambition to build a support staff without regard to race, gender, religion, or ethnic background.[54]

Paul, Weiss expanded still further with the arrival of former federal judge Simon Rifkind, and the firm became Paul, Weiss, Rifkind, Wharton & Garrison. At the time, the firm had a dozen partners, only one of whom did trial work. Rifkind changed that. Widely recognized as the foremost advocate of his generation, he built litigation into the firm's largest department. Though a former

New Dealer and still politically connected, Rifkind exercised great caution in the cases he took. Unlike Garrison, he never represented anyone charged with being a security risk; moreover, he made known his aversion to hiring women. In 1956, the New York office of Paul, Weiss employed only two women among its forty associates. Neither was assigned to litigation.[55]

Murray's gender posed a problem at Paul, Weiss, but she faced other obstacles as well. Lawyers at the firm had typically graduated from Harvard, Yale, or Columbia Law School. Many had served on law reviews and clerked for federal judges or Supreme Court Justices. Murray had done none of these things, but Garrison was determined to hire her. He scored a minor victory when he persuaded his partners to offer her a job as a part-time librarian for a salary of $5,000 a year. Vastly more money than Murray had ever earned, the proposal tempted her, but she worried she would never be able to work as a lawyer again if she allowed herself to be sidelined into a support-staff position. She sought advice from Ware, who urged her to take the job. With a part-time schedule, she could write, Ware reasoned, and there might be the possibility of the occasional brief.[56]

Before Murray could accept this offer, however, Garrison noticed that the litigation department needed help and proposed instead that she join the firm as an associate attorney. He must not have cleared this idea with Judge Rifkind, because three months elapsed between the time Murray arrived at the firm in November 1956 and the day Garrison finally secured her a slot in Rifkind's department.[57]

By 1956, litigation had about a dozen attorneys. They worked on cases in two-person teams, a partner or senior associate, assisted by a younger associate. A very big case might have two associates, and on a rare occasion three, never more. One of the lawyers for whom Murray worked was Jay Topkis, a senior associate committed to liberal causes. Growing up in New York, he had attended Townsend Harris High School and Columbia College, where Lionel Trilling among others inspired in him a passion for social justice. He entered Yale Law School after the war and clerked for Judge Jerome Frank on the US Court of Appeals. These credentials qualified him for any law firm in New York, but he was a Jew, and employment opportunities following his clerkship proved severely limited. He was lucky to land a job at Paul, Weiss.[58]

Topkis, who greatly admired Garrison, was prepared, even eager, to work with the firm's newest associate, but his first sight of her took him aback. "She certainly looked strange," he later recalled, "a middle-aged woman." Paul, Weiss had taken on a small number of newly minted female law school graduates, but none, other than Agger in Washington, had lasted more than a few years. The only middle-aged women at the firm were secretaries and other office staff. Murray's attire contributed to her "strange" appearance. For all the effort Murray had put into dressing in an acceptably feminine fashion, she came across to others as a woman in the ill-fitting clothes and sensible, low-heeled shoes of an old-fashioned school-teacher, not the stylishly tailored suits, fitted dresses, and high heels of the mid-town professional woman. Topkis soon got over his shock, but he still faced the challenge of working with a woman fourteen years his senior, whose legal work for poor, black clients in no way prepared her for this firm's work.[59]

Murray was only too well aware of her deficiencies. Having spent her legal career either writing about civil rights or representing poor clients, mostly in small claims court, she found herself at sea. Partners asked her to research and submit memoranda on questions foreign to her experience on business problems—corporate mergers, bankruptcies, mechanics' liens, and copyright—she had not encountered since law school. In her first weeks at the firm a partner returned a memorandum with the criticism that her arguments wavered and that her conclusions were timid and uncertain. She tried again, but once more the partner deemed her work product unsatisfactory.[60]

Seeing Murray struggle, Garrison invited her to lunch. He listened as she reported on the criticism she had received and confessed her feelings of inadequacy. He responded that he too had felt overwhelmed when he started at the firm in 1946. After a decade teaching law and four years on the War Labor Board, he found that his announced area expertise—tax—had been transformed. It had taken him five or six years of hard work to begin to feel confident in his specialty. Reassured, she returned to work and began to treat the criticisms of her memos as opportunities for improvement. Gradually, she demonstrated that she could do competent work, and in later years, she reported that this feeling of competence in the face of the most exacting standards had done more to boost her sense of self-confidence than any other experience she had ever had.[61]

Murray even assisted Judge Rifkind, who accepted her help on a large bankruptcy case. Their initial meeting, in the elevator landing of the firm, was comically awkward. Recognizing the judge's superior status, Murray stood aside, as the elevator doors opened, and waited for Rifkind to enter. Rifkind, prejudiced against women lawyers but the soul of courtesy in the presence of a "lady," waited for Murray to go ahead. As each deferred to the other, the elevator doors closed. Murray ultimately lost the battle of the elevator, but she enjoyed another victory. One day, in court with Rifkind on the bankruptcy matter, she won a compliment from him on the sixty-four-page brief she had written in support of the firm's motion for $100,000 in attorneys' fees. "To think I'd come to this!" she lamented to Bill Hastie, in describing her discomfort at arguing for gargantuan legal fees when her dream had been to pursue civil rights litigation for the NAACP. But she had gained Rifkind's respect.[62]

Not all her cases concerned commercial disputes. Paul, Weiss prided itself on the number of matters on which its attorneys worked pro bono—without pay, for the public good. These cases provided an opportunity for the firm to support liberal causes, while also giving associates a chance to hone their legal skills. One pro bono matter that she handled was an appeal in a drug case. Researching and writing the brief dragged on, in part because she had reluctantly come to the conclusion that her client was guilty, and in part because she could find no legal authority to support an appeal. But then she stumbled onto the case she needed. In *Chambers v. Florida* (1940) a unanimous Supreme Court had declared that a coerced confession violated a defendant's right to due process under the Fourteenth Amendment. Whether or not her client had done what he was accused of doing, the record made clear that his confession had been coerced. When Murray discovered that the lawyers on the *Chambers* case were Thurgood Marshall and Leon Ransom, she remembered why she had gone to law school and polished off her brief in a day.[63]

"Neither 'My Girl' nor 'One of the Boys'"

Murray's biggest problem in adjusting to Paul, Weiss turned out to be loneliness. Even more than her age and race, her gender barred her from the camaraderie that the young men enjoyed with one another. Male attorneys simply did not view women as professional peers. Girlfriends, yes; secretaries, of course; colleagues, no. One female graduate of Harvard Law School later told an interviewer that she had sat down next to a male classmate on the first day of class and had said hello. "I'm married," he had replied. As Murray later put it, a woman lawyer was neither "my girl" (the condescending term reserved for a secretary, no matter how old she was) nor "one of the boys" (as the male associates—always young—were called). Once again, she found herself in-between.[64]

Murray did not want entirely for companionship. Two other female lawyers were already there when she arrived. Thacher Clarke, a twenty-nine-year-old Yale Law School graduate, had worked at another large firm and then at the office of a female solo practitioner before coming to Paul, Weiss. One of only five women in her class, she and two of the others won coveted spots on the editorial board of the *Yale Law Journal*. Despite this academic accomplishment, she found the transition to legal practice a struggle. Assigned at Paul, Weiss to trusts and estates, in which she had taken no classes, she floundered. She wrote well, her supervisors conceded, but she was not "sufficiently thorough." Being thorough meant, in part, mastering a highly technical, logic-tree style of writing, opaque to anyone but a specialist. For the first time in her life, Clarke did not exceed expectations. Not sure why, she found that no one was particularly interested in helping her recover from her early mistakes.[65]

The second female lawyer to precede Murray at Paul, Weiss was Julia Lovett Ashbey. A graduate of Barnard College and Columbia Law School, Julia Lovett found that a personal decision she had just made to marry a young banker compounded the disadvantage she suffered as a female attorney at Paul, Weiss. Barnard President Millicent McIntosh often told her students that they should strive to have it all—career, husbands, and children—but she was not particularly helpful in specifying how they were to do so in a professional culture dominated by men, who, though they typically married and had children, defined their lives by success in their careers and left family responsibilities almost entirely to their wives. Ashbey went on to have three daughters and a legal career, which culminated in her becoming a judge on the appellate division of the Superior Court of New Jersey, but she had to leave Paul, Weiss to find her way.[66]

Clarke and Ashbey soon left Paul, Weiss, but another young woman briefly took their place. Ruth Bader Ginsburg, who had just completed her second year at Harvard Law School, spent the summer of 1958 at the firm. Ginsburg later recalled thinking it strange that Lloyd K. Garrison offered her a summer internship after only three questions, but that's all it took to recognize her talent. Born to a Jewish family in Brooklyn in 1933 and a product of Brooklyn's public schools, Ginsburg had graduated from Cornell, where she met Martin (Marty) Ginsburg and persuaded him to go to law school. They married in 1954 and Marty supported his wife's desire to work.[67]

In 1956, with a new baby, Jane, in tow, Ginsburg entered Harvard Law School, to which her husband had returned from a stint in the army to take his place in the second-year class. After two years, during which time she served on the Law Review and helped her husband survive both an automobile accident and testicular cancer, Ruth followed Marty to New York when he, having graduated, was hired by the New York law firm of Weil, Gotshal & Manges. Wanting to keep her family together, Ruth transferred to Columbia Law School and applied for a summer job at Paul, Weiss. Garrison hired her on the spot.[68]

The initial friendship between Murray and Ginsburg was short-lived. Although most summer associates who performed well at Paul, Weiss won offers of full-time positions following completion of law school, Ginsburg did not. She possessed obvious talent, but she was also a wife and mother, roles that in Judge Rifkind's view disqualified her for permanent employment. The young lawyer suspected that the firm had another justification: "they had captured a two-fer in Pauli." Whatever the reason, Ginsburg later made light of her rejection, but it hurt.[69]

Murray helped her younger colleagues by confirming their suspicion that the difficulties they encountered at Paul, Weiss stemmed more from their gender than from any deficiency in talent. As Clarke remembered the intuition that Murray confirmed: "Some men were not comfortable with women in the room." The discomfort worked both ways. As women in a male environment, female associates often lacked the confidence and sense of entitlement that men brought first to law school and later to law firm practice. Murray harbored her own insecurities, but she provided her younger female colleagues an example of a mature woman who had figured out how to make it in a man's world. She was much "better adjusted to the work world," Clarke recalled. For Clarke and Ashbey, Murray provided an added benefit: she was "comfortable to be with, agreeable, nice, and not competitive [as the young men were]."[70]

Arriving at Paul, Weiss after the publication of *Proud Shoes,* Murray also impressed the younger women with her literary accomplishment and political engagement. Clarke, whose mother had been a suffragist in England and whose grandmother had been a Fabian Socialist, had read Caroline Ware's *Greenwich Village,* Virginia Wolfe's *Three Guineas* and *A Room of One's Own,* and Simone de Beauvoir's *The Second Sex.* Male lawyers did not read such books, but women did, and they valued talking about these works with a woman who had lived so many of the ideas expressed in them.[71]

Each of these young women considered Murray a friend, but "not in a let your hair down way," as Clarke put it. Murray did say that she had married and divorced, but she made no other mention of her private life, and the younger women did not press the point. They appreciated Murray for what she represented: a precise, lively, energetic, and—more than anything else— "stimulating" model of professional commitment and public engagement. Though they overlapped with Murray only briefly, she influenced them all in the years to come.[72]

The Partnership

The one female friend who stayed throughout Murray's tenure was Paul, Weiss's office manager, Irene Barlow, known to all as Renee, a woman three years Murray's junior. In her four years at the firm, Barlow had demonstrated a "genius for organization and efficiency." Just as important, she was even-tempered and witty, an able administrator who could handle "a volatile mix of personalities" with skill. Never waiting for problems to come to her, she moved "unobtrusively through the corridors," according to Murray, "untangling snafus which interrupted the flow of paperwork, hustling messengers on their rounds, putting out brushfires of revolt in the stenographers' pool, mediating between lawyers and secretaries, solving problems of space." She taught the new associates office procedures, assigned them a secretary, whom they shared with another associate, and boosted their spirits after bruising encounters with an irate partner.[73]

Tall, sophisticated, and white, Barlow appeared to have little in common with Murray. She "carried herself with an air of quiet self assurance," recalled Murray, who had to take "extra steps to keep up with her lope." Sharpening the contrast,

Barlow was "traditional in her dress—a lady!" Murray observed; "I was a vagabond, a Pixie!"—an androgynous figure in her attire and bearing.[74]

Despite her apparent privilege, Barlow understood how it felt to be an outsider. Born in Yorkshire, England, the youngest of five sisters, she had grown
up poor. Her father deserted the family when she was six and her mother immigrated with her girls to the United States in search of a better life. Renee felt like
an outcast at school, where other children made fun of her threadbare clothes
and strange accent. Working at menial jobs through high school and two years of
college, she broke into personnel at the Walsh-Kaiser shipyards in Rhode Island
during World War II. With that experience she landed her job at Elizabeth Arden
following the war, and after coming to Paul, Weiss, she completed college at

Figure 9.2 Irene Barlow, when she managed the staff at Paul, Weiss, circa 1960. Estate of
Pauli Murray, Schlesinger Library, Radcliffe Institute, Harvard University.

night. Renee Barlow knew what it was like to feel "shut out" and strongly identified with those who felt the same way.[75]

Encouraged by Garrison, Barlow established an affirmative action program at
Paul, Weiss two decades before other firms began to do so. She placed a standing
order with a friend at the Urban League to send promising African American
applicants for interviews, even if she had no openings, so that she would have
their names on file when an opening occurred. Through the Urban League and
other sources, she assembled a staff remarkable in the 1950s for its diversity. As
lonely and ill at ease as Murray initially felt at Paul, Weiss, she soon found comfort
in the midst of this cosmopolitan staff, which consisted of African Americans,
Hispanics, Asian Americans, and members of other ethnic groups and different
religious affiliations. She felt almost as though she were back in International
House at Berkeley. Barlow must have taken pleasure in arranging for Murray
to share a particular secretary, Rosemary Iwami, with a particular associate,
Stephen Wise Tulin. Iwami, a Japanese American, who had been interned with
her family during World War II, was one of the firm's best assistants. Tulin, the
grandson of Rabbi Stephen Wise (one of the founders of the American Jewish
Congress and the NAACP) and the son of Judge Justine Wise Polier (the first
woman judge in New York), was—in Murray's view— "a top-notch young lawyer." Barlow had arranged a working relationship among three highly intelligent
people: a German American Jew, an Afro-Euro-Native American Episcopalian,
and an Asian American Evangelical Protestant.[76]

Determined that Garrison's protégé succeed, Barlow asked Murray out to
lunch to get to know her better. Murray quickly discovered that they shared
not only a hardscrabble youth but also the same Episcopal faith. As Lent
approached, they attended services together at St. Bartholomew's Church a
few blocks from the office. Murray came to love Barlow for her "steadfastness,
her loyalty, her quiet support and the many things she did (without my ever
knowing it) to save me heartache." Barlow heard the criticisms of Murray from
others at the firm, and although she could not tell her what people were saying,
she urged her to be "more diplomatic, more graceful in her dress and speech,
less the rough diamond and more the sophisticate." Barlow was calm and
unflappable; Murray was impulsive and volatile. Barlow was "steady" and "thorough." Murray confessed that she "leapt like a deer from thought to thought,
was single-minded, overshot my mark, made mistakes and lost time picking up
behind myself." Barlow "could juggle several projects at a time"; Murray could
see "only the object in front of my nose, or the speck on the horizon." Renee
became "the closest person" in Pauli's life, closer even than Maida Springer,
Helene Hanff, or Caroline Ware. She took the place of Peg Holmes and Aunt
Pauline—"those loved ones I had lost either to life or death." At long last, Pauli
had found a life partner.[77]

Not that Murray lived with Barlow. Nearly a decade of caring for Aunt Pauline, Aunt Sallie, and Smokey in her three-room railroad flat in Bedford-Stuyvesant had demonstrated conclusively that she could not live comfortably with others in a small apartment. Barlow, who lived with her aging mother in a walk-up on Second Avenue in midtown Manhattan, was in no better position to add a live-in partner to her household. Murray and Barlow joined the parish church of St. Mark's-in-the-Bowery and regularly attended services there. Their Episcopal faith bound them to one another more than anything else they shared. Murray often visited the Barlow flat and indulged Renee's mother's desire to give her a more stylish appearance by tailoring her clothes. But Murray and Barlow maintained their separate households. They formed what they called a Damon-Pythias bond, after the Greek heroes whose devotion was so great that one offered to die for the other. Theirs was a "partnership," not like the legal one that governed Paul, Weiss, but both closer and more flexible. In Barlow's words, their partnership "'meshed' when necessary and 'disengaged' when it was no longer necessary to act as a unit." This union provided Murray the "guiding hand" and "spiritual embrace" she so longed for, as well as the freedom she needed to find her own way and make her own mark.[78]

Small Claims and Civil Rights

In October 1958, two years into Murray's time at Paul, Weiss, the firm offered her a permanent position, in charge of small claims. The partners and senior associates on track for partnership had found her work to be competent but not of a quality expected for promotion to higher rank. Normally, an associate whose annual reviews did not mark him or her as partnership material was encouraged to leave, but Murray was a special case. Garrison no doubt lobbied to find a position in which she could be kept on permanently, and small claims seemed like a good fit. As a solo practitioner, Murray had handled many such cases. She had hoped for more, but as Caroline Ware counseled her, this was a stable job, with a steady income, that she could do well and still have time for her writing.[79]

By February 1959 Murray reported taking satisfaction in having made a success of her new assignment, and she seemed as happy as she had ever been. Overall, her years at Paul, Weiss had given her greater confidence in herself. She had proven her competence at the most demanding level of a legal profession dominated by brilliant, hard-driving, white men. The discipline of big firm legal practice, together with her relationship with Renee Barlow, had curbed her impetuousness. She had learned to work steadily on major problems that could take years to resolve, as well as efficiently on small matters, important to the firm's clients. She still wrestled with feelings of insecurity and inadequacy, but she was better at quelling those demons and moving forward. She had achieved financial security for the first time in her life. Nonetheless, she felt restless. She had gone to law school to contribute to the civil rights movement, but at Paul, Weiss, aside from the occasional pro bono case, she spent her time collecting small debts for the firm's big clients. Inevitably, she felt disappointment in the course her life had taken.[80]

Her one effort to contribute to the civil rights movement at the end of the 1950s added to that disappointment. The spring of 1959 saw unprovoked, violent attacks on blacks throughout the South. In Mississippi, whites lynched a twenty-three-year-old black man, Mack Charles Parker, accused of raping a white woman in Poplarville. Although federal agents identified the killers, the state declined to press charges. Horrified by a lynching as terrible as any in her childhood, Murray poured out her anguish in two poems. The first, "Collect from Poplarville," she adapted from the *Book of Common Prayer*. "*Lighten our darkness, we beseech thee, O Lord,*" she began; "Teach us no longer to dread hounds yelping in the distance." In the second poem, "For Mack C. Parker," she cried out, "The cornered and trapped, The bludgeoned and crushed, . . . Each vainly rubbing the 'cursed spot,' Which brands him Cain."[81]

A second act of racial terrorism took place at about the same time in Florida, where four white men with guns and knives accosted two black couples after a college dance. Kidnapping one of the women, they brutally raped her multiple times. The assailants came to trial—an encouraging development—but the attorney for the four accused white men horrified blacks everywhere when he badgered the badly injured woman and tried to get her to admit that she had enjoyed the attack. Furious at this injustice and the failure of white juries to convict whites who lynched and raped, Robert F. Williams, president of a North Carolina branch of the NAACP, told reporters, "We must be willing to kill if necessary. We cannot take these people who do us injustice to the court and it becomes necessary to punish them ourselves."[82]

Brought to account before the national board of the NAACP in New York for his incendiary language, Williams sought Murray's help. Notwithstanding her own opposition to violence, Murray agreed to represent the North Carolina activist. She urged the NAACP to consider the context in which Williams had urged taking up arms. Williams's statement on May 5 had been made in anger, "and there was provocation—the same day that Mack Parker's body was found, and the same day the co-ed in Florida was raped, the same day the President of the United States of America said he would not call for stronger civil rights legislations. Violence was the order of the day." Addressing the Board, Williams backpedaled, insisting that he did not support retaliatory violence, but only self-defense. Nonetheless, the board suspended him from his position as chapter president.[83]

Discouraged both by how little she seemed to be accomplishing in her small claims and pro bono civil rights cases, Murray began to look for other work. She had won a modest success as an author and a lawyer. She had come to value her life in-between, to be quietly queer. She wanted more.

10

"What Is Africa to Me?"

Pan-African Promise

In early 1959, Maida Springer urged Murray to try something new. Just back from the All-Africa People's Conference in Ghana, she passed on a clipping from the *London Times,* which advertised a faculty position at the newly created Ghana School of Law. This opportunity could take Murray to the center of the Pan-African Liberation movement and allow her to make a contribution that really mattered: helping to train every new lawyer in the Republic of Ghana.[1]

Springer was among the earliest leaders in the American labor movement to foresee the importance of Africa to American workers in general and black workers in particular. The hard-won improvements in US wages would never last if those of colonial workers continued to undercut them. And colonial wages would never rise, Springer believed, unless colonized workers could organize as American workers had and could free themselves from the exploitation of European powers.

Beginning in 1955, Springer crisscrossed Africa, forming alliances with labor leaders in half a dozen places soon to be nation-states. Two years later, she felt vindicated, as she watched forty-seven-year-old Kwame Nkrumah, the chief advocate of pan-African union, take power as the new leader of Ghana. Within the next four years, another eighteen African colonies and territories would emerge as independent nations. "Freedom at last! Freedom at Last!" Nkrumah cried out to the celebrating crowd. Freedom for labor, however, proved short-lived. Nkrumah absorbed its trade unions into his own political party, the Convention People's Party (CPP), and labor disappeared as an independent political force. Discouraged but still sure that American labor had a role to play, Springer pressed ahead. Nkrumah needed economic investment, infrastructure, teachers, skilled workers, and civil servants. If Americans, and especially African Americans, could be part of Nkrumah's nation building, progress would be assured. To that end, Springer pressed Murray to apply for the faculty position at the Ghana School of Law.[2]

Murray did not share Springer's passion for Africa. She thought of herself as an American of mixed ancestry, not as an Afro-American, as Springer did. Through painstaking research for *Proud Shoes*, she had uncovered the origins of her European as well as her Native American ancestors. But she never discovered the origins of her African ancestors; nor, in the end, did she feel motivated to continue the quest, given the embarrassing link between those ancestors and slavery. As independence movements swept Africa, however, and as massive resistance to civil tights took hold in the American South, Murray began to sympathize with Springer's view that Ghana and other emerging nations constituted a new frontier, one where people of African descent were both the majority and the leaders—shapers of their own destiny. She understood when Springer, writing in the *Pittsburgh Courier* following Ghana's liberation from Britain, expressed envy of Africans who had a country of their own, where they belonged.[3]

Moreover, Murray had come to share at least a measure of Springer's enthusiasm for Pan Africanism when she spent time at Maida's Brooklyn home in the company of Africa's future leaders. Murray's "challenging conversations" with the young nationalists Tom Mboya of Kenya and Julius Nyerere of Tanzania reminded her of her childhood talks with Grandfather Robert Fitzgerald. He had exchanged the relative comfort of his life in Pennsylvania for the war-torn land of North Carolina. Perhaps moving to Ghana would allow her to shape a new society, as he had done. Murray talked to Caroline Ware and Marie Rodell about the possibility of going to Africa for three to five years, and they both urged her to do so. Here was her chance to be a law professor, her dream since law school, and to train the founding fathers of this new republic. In February 1959, she applied to the director of legal education in Ghana, John Lang.[4]

Determined to see Murray succeed, Springer wrote immediately to Prime Minister Kwame Nkrumah and Foreign Minister Ako Adjei (then serving as Ghana's ambassador to the United Nations) in support. Springer described her friend as "a lawyer with superior qualifications who is also dedicated, has a sense of history, the love of teaching and the ability to challenge searching young minds." For good measure, she sent Nkrumah copies of Murray's poem "Dark Testament" and *States' Laws on Race and Color.*[5]

Despite Springer's support, Murray received no response. Then, in June, Lang sent a discouraging reply. Whereas he would "welcome" her "to Ghana for a visit," he could not possibly extend an offer without meeting her; moreover, he currently had "no funds available," and he anticipated that any salary he could offer in the event that funds did become available "would not be adequate." Undaunted and now determined to make her mark in Africa, Murray embarked on a campaign to fund a trip of some kind. She approached the Ford Foundation, which was in the early stages of planning a program to send Americans to Africa to teach and conduct research. She consulted with Arthur Sutherland at Harvard, then serving on a commission to study the best way to set up legal education in Ghana, and secured his support. She recruited Adlai Stevenson to write a letter of recommendation. She persuaded the ever-generous Lloyd Garrison to go over Lang's head to the attorney general of Ghana, Geoffrey Bing, on her behalf and to give her a paid leave of absence from Paul, Weiss so that she could take courses at Columbia Law School to bring her knowledge of relevant fields up to date. Whenever an official from Ghana came to town, she wrangled an interview, as she did in the fall of 1959, when she met separately with Foreign Minister Ako Adjei and Attorney General Bing to plead her case. Within days of meeting her, Bing extended her an offer to be senior lecturer at the Ghana School of Law.[6]

Lang, bowing to Bing's decision, in a letter the following week, formalized the offer, with restrictions. He proposed that she come for eighteen months, the first nine to be spent preparing her courses, creating a law review, and providing legal counsel to Parliament as new laws and a revised constitution were drafted. With the start of classes at the end of September 1960, she would begin to train lawyers to fill Ghana's political and economic needs. If she proved herself, further contracts might be offered. He could not match her salary at Paul, Weiss—then over $8,000—but he could offer 2,000 British Pounds Sterling (roughly $5,900), first-class passage on any freighter coming to Ghana, and furnished housing, for which she would be charged 150 pounds a year. Given the lower cost of living in Accra and her eagerness to go to Africa, Murray accepted, although she believed she was being underpaid, relative to men in the same position.[7]

Aboard the S.S. Tatra

Murray needed another month to secure a passport, get the necessary immunizations, and pack all she would need for an extended stay. At long last, on February 3, 1960, she stood on the deck of the S. S. Tatra, a 450-foot-long Norwegian cargo ship, as it steamed down the East River. Watching the lights of the Brooklyn piers and the Manhattan skyline slowly recede into the distance, she steadied her nerves by taking detailed notes on the ship and its contents. Bound for Africa by way of Nova Scotia, the Tatra carried 6,000 tons of potatoes, rice, packaged goods, flour, automobiles, tractors, and other machinery; a crew of forty; eight passengers, including herself, and her dog, Smokey. Five of the passengers, three missionaries and two workers for Firestone Rubber Company in Liberia, had lived in Africa for extended periods of time. The sixth was a newly trained nurse headed for her first job at a hospital in Liberia, and the seventh was a wild animal trader on his way to Africa for the twenty-seventh time to find animals for American zoos. Over the course of the twenty-day Atlantic crossing, she quizzed them all about their experiences and current plans.[8]

Before Murray left, she discussed the year ahead with Harold Isaacs, a white political scientist at the Massachusetts Institute of Technology, then working on a study of race relations in the context of decolonization. Isaacs urged her to question her assumption that going to Africa would allow her "to remove the social restrictions of being a Negro" in a place where blackness was the norm. Might not new restrictions supplant the old, he asked? He urged her to reflect, instead, on the difference between what she expected and what she discovered once she arrived, and then to write about it. Just a few days out, Murray, desperately lonely, took a stab at this assignment. Thinking about Countee Cullen's famous 1924 query "What is Africa to me?" she jotted the obverse question in her diary: "What is America to me?" She gave a simple answer: America meant her friends—Renee most of all. She already missed them so much that she wept. She had never before set foot on a boat or traveled outside the United States; and here she was, suffering from nausea in the rough seas off New England, on her way to an undeveloped country on the other side of the Equator. What had made her think she could manage a three-week ocean voyage, much less a three-to five-year sojourn in Africa? As Isaacs had perceptively warned her, "We carry ourselves around with us wherever we go."[9]

If she had known that students in North Carolina had just started a sit-in campaign at a local lunch counter that would spark similar protests throughout the South and dramatically accelerate civil rights progress in America, she might have questioned her decision to move to Ghana even more seriously. But by the time she learned that one of her "lost causes" had been "found," she was already in Africa. In the meantime, she made the best of the course she had chosen.[10]

On February 23, twenty days after its departure from Brooklyn, and following an intermediate stop in Monrovia, Liberia, the ship finally reached the port of Takoradi, in Ghana. Murray watched nervously as stevedores lowered her possessions onto the dock. It was all there: more than twenty packages of clothes, linens, dishware and cutlery, books, papers, her typewriter, Smokey, his dog crate, two baskets of fruit, and a case of vacuum-packed American coffee (a gift from the workers in the mail room at Paul, Weiss). Whatever her new life held in store for her, she would be well equipped.[11]

Adjusting to Life in Africa

Jean Lang, the wife of law school director John Lang, met Murray at customs and drove her the 170 miles to Accra. Grateful for this gesture, Murray was nonetheless dismayed to discover that the house she had expected to occupy was still under construction. She found herself moving, instead, into a "dirty, run down" former government rest house on the edge of the Accra airfield.[12]

Disappointed by the prospect of having to live for some indefinite period out of her suitcase, and terrified by the sound of airplanes apparently coming through her windows, Murray found her misery compounded by the intolerable heat, noxious smells, and ubiquitous insects. When she arrived in Accra, the daily highs hovered around 88 degrees, but the humidity made the temperature seem higher. When one of the twice yearly rainy seasons began a couple of months later, the heat grew more oppressive, the smells more sickening, and the bugs more numerous. The mosquitos, in particular, tormented her. Broken screens in the windows of her temporary quarters offered scant protection and within a few weeks she fell ill with malaria. Recurring bouts of the malady would afflict her for the rest of her stay. Debilitated by the climate and disease, she needed three days to accomplish what at home would take three hours.[13]

In addition to the heat, smells, insects, and malaria, Murray felt overwhelmed by the challenges of day-to-day living. Although she delighted in the markets, where the "mammy traders," wearing their brightly colored kente dress, sold their wares, she bemoaned the absence of the many things she took for granted at home: paper bags, wrapping paper, counters, newspaper stands, stools, chairs, price tags, clerks. Problems of communication complicated life further. Ghana had 100 tribes and as many tongues. "One lives on an island of English surrounded by an ocean of indigenous languages," she informed friends at home. Although English was the official language, widespread illiteracy meant that it was used only at the higher levels of business and government. Most natives communicated with foreigners in a pidgin English that allowed for the exchange of only the simplest ideas. Under the circumstances, Murray felt unable "to know what people really think and feel."[14]

Jean Lang tried to persuade her to hire a steward to shield her from at least some of the problems of daily living. Never having employed a servant, Murray resisted Lang's advice, until a steady line of applicants made her understand that domestic service constituted an essential source of employment for the local population. She hired Yaro, the least obsequious of the job seekers and, against Lang's stern warnings, gave him complete authority over the household. Murray was relieved to surrender the shopping, cooking, and care of her quarters, simple as they were. She bought Yaro clothes, sent him to school, lent him funds for a bicycle, and promised to raise his wages if he learned English, which he proudly did. But she hated the hierarchy of the relationship and the fact that she could not order her own life.[15]

In her private letters and more public "Newsletters" home, Murray typed out lighthearted tales of characters encountered and challenges overcome. Her diary told another story. Not wanting to disturb her neighbors at night with the sound of her typewriter, she shifted to pen and ink in the evening hours and poured out her feelings of "loneliness" and "homesickness" in her journal.[16]

Most of all, she hated the atmosphere of fear, which she first encountered a few days after her arrival, when her next-door neighbor, Michael Scott, invited her to dinner. A white Anglican cleric and anti-apartheid pacifist, Scott had worn out his welcome in South Africa and come to live in Ghana, where he surrounded himself with fellow pacifists. One of them was Bill Sutherland, an African American member of the Fellowship of Reconciliation (FOR) from New Jersey, whom Murray knew through Maida Springer. Chief of staff to Nkrumah's finance minister K. A. Gbedemah, Sutherland was the person most responsible for getting US aid to Ghana for its massive Volta Dam Project, but he had fallen out of favor with the president. When in 1958 Nkrumah pressed for a Preventive Detention Act, which would empower the government to imprison without benefit of a trial anyone thought to be a threat, Sutherland had protested. Had he been anyone else, he soon learned, he would have been deported immediately—the implication being that any further dissent would lead to his ejection from the country. Adding the fear of deportation to the misery of the heat, disease, poverty, and difficulty of day-to-day life, Murray found it hard to believe that she would ever like living in Ghana.[17]

Concerned that she might be overreacting, Murray wondered in her journal whether her problem might be that she had "no friends of the heart" in Accra. Most Americans came as couples and had each other to help them through the hardship of adjustment as an outsider. She sorely missed Renee and could not hope to see her again before Christmas. They exchanged frequent letters, but, feeling that she had to destroy those she received from Renee as soon as she read them (so as not to reveal the nature of their relationship), Pauli could not ease her loneliness by rereading them. She felt thoroughly sorry for herself, but how could she complain when the book she was reading by Michael Scott described the brutal beatings to which South African prisoners were subject?[18]

She felt better by June, when workers completed her new house, with its securely screened bedrooms and study, fenced yard for Smokey, and separate cottage for Yaro. Discovering on closer inspection that the work was shoddy, she felt another wave of disappointment, but the contractor agreed to redo his work to her American standards and eventually she felt satisfied. In the meantime, she had purchased a little blue-gray Volkswagen Karmann Ghia, in which she toured the countryside. Making life still better, the newly completed law school was beautiful, her office air-conditioned, and the work of preparing for classes and reviewing draft legislation for the new republic absorbing. She hoped, in time, to fit in.[19]

Lessons from the Kwahu and Elmina Castle

Murray spent most of her time in Accra, principally in her law office, but she made occasional forays outside the capital. Over a four-day Easter weekend in April 1960, she visited the Kwahu village of Obo, 110 miles into the interior, at the invitation of Professor Frank Untermeyer, the son and grandson of prominent Jewish lawyers from New York. On loan from Roosevelt University, he was teaching government at University College at Logon, near Accra. One of Untermeyer's former students at Roosevelt University, a young man by the name of Mprensem of the Kwahu tribe, was back in Ghana working in the government. Mprensem invited Untermeyer to visit his native village for Easter, and Untermeyer invited Murray and an American couple, George Carroll, an African American lawyer, and his wife, who were visiting Ghana from Richmond, California. After a perilous drive over the twisting, narrow roads of the Kwahu escarpment, complete with a mechanical breakdown, they arrived in the prosperous region of cocoa farmers and traders several hours late.[20]

The visitors had brought a gift of beer for Mprensem's father, only to realize that, since the Kwahu were a matrilineal tribe, the gift should go to his maternal uncle, to whom Mprensem escorted them instead. Seeing the uncle and his family dressed in brilliantly colored kente cloth, the visitors asked permission to dress likewise and take pictures. The uncle then shepherded them to an audience with the Nifahene, one of the four sub-chiefs of the Kwahu region, with authority over Obo and seventeen other villages. The Nifahane received them in a courtyard, seated on a throne, shaded, British-style, by an umbrella held by an attendant (though there was no sun), and surrounded by village elders, all men. Although the chief spoke English, protocol dictated that he address his visitors through his "linguist," which he did. [21]

After mutual greetings between the men, Murray announced that she and the Carrolls had African ancestors, which pleased the chief, who welcomed them home. Noting that the women of the tribe stood back shyly in the doorway, Murray took the risk of announcing that she and Mrs. Carroll brought greetings from the women of America to the women of Obo, and the village women happily approached to shake their hands. Frank Untermeyer then delivered a speech in which he said he had never met people who were so friendly or who made him feel so at home. He added that just as their young man had come to the United States to study American ways, Americans were now coming to Ghana to study African ways so that each country could help the other. The chief responded that he was honored that Mr. Untermeyer would put on and wear kente; only once before had a white man done so.[22]

Figure 10.1 Pauli Murray, standing, fourth from left, dressed in kente cloth on a visit to the Kwahu village of Obo, Ghana, over Easter weekend, April 1960. The only member of the group not in native dress is Mprensem (kneeling in front of Murray), the member of the tribe who had returned to Ghana after studying in the United States. Estate of Pauli Murray, Schlesinger Library, Radcliffe Institute, Harvard University.

At the end of the ceremonies, which involved pouring some of the visitors' gift of gin on the ground to honor the god of the tribe, the Americans returned to Accra with Mprensem, who seemed to have been a little embarrassed by the whole affair. He alone had remained in Western dress during the afternoon, and Murray detected in his apologies throughout the day something of her own revolt against the customs and attitudes of her Fitzgerald relatives when she was young. "He could not know the irony of the situation," she reported in one of her "Newsletters" home; "what limited him and made him slightly ashamed had quite a different effect upon us. For here we were seeing the dignity and majesty of people who had been untouched by American slavery and its dehumanizing aftermath. What was enslavement for him was reassurance and a kind of liberation for us."[23]

Murray had one other experience of liberation from the shame of her slave ancestry, gained from a trip to Elmina Castle, ninety miles up the coast from Accra. One of the slave-trading strongholds along the West Coast of Africa, Elmina Castle was surrounded on three sides by water. Murray crossed a drawbridge over a moat to reach a stone courtyard and climbed narrow, winding stairs to the high-ceilinged room in the wing that faced the ocean. Here slaves, captured in the interior and driven to the coast by other Africans, had been sold to European traders for the slave markets in the Americas. Retracing the steps of the captives "through the dark, muggy dungeons, tunnel-shaped rooms, and small courtyards where they were stored like wine barrels awaiting shipment," she imagined the bewilderment and anguish of people being herded "under cover of night" through a small opening in the wall to waiting canoes, which transported them to slave ships anchored offshore and to "unknown destinations."[24]

Murray felt "shock" as she listened to a "local chief" boast that his great-grandfather and grandfather "used to catch and sell slaves" and "how his grandfather often wondered what happened to those slaves he sold." The experience left her "deeply shaken" when she realized the extent to which many Africans participated in the slave trade, but it also left her with a new respect for the millions who survived the ordeal. Through reimagining their travails and their triumph in survival, she felt that she had taken another step toward exorcising the lingering ghosts of her past.[25]

Women's Conference

The year 1960 featured conferences across Africa, as seventeen countries in sub-Saharan Africa won their independence from colonial rule and celebrated with meetings to consider the future. One of the most interesting was a conference on women, the first of its kind ever mounted on the continent. Held in July at University College in Accra, the Conference of Women of Africa and African Descent drew thirty-odd delegates and observers from ten nations, with at least half a dozen from the United States. To Murray's delight, the group included several good friends: Harold Isaacs, on a trip with his wife, Viola, to conduct research for his book; Dr. Dorothy Ferebee, Murray's friend and employer from Howard (now the director of the university's health services); and, best of all, her dear friend Anna Arnold Hedgeman, who was scheduled to give the keynote address. Modeled on meetings of the United Nations' Commission on the Status of Women, held regularly since 1947, the conference promised to discuss the legal status of women, the development of women's leadership, women's educational opportunities, women's health education, women in intellectual and cultural life, problems of social change, and problems common to women of Africa and African descent.[26]

President Kwame Nkrumah opened the conference with a plea to the assembled women that they join the struggle to create a Union of African States. The men alone, he declared, could not complete the gigantic task they had set themselves, one in which the "artificial boundaries which separate brother from brother and sister from sister must be wiped out." Nkrumah said nothing of the "artificial boundaries" that separated brothers from sisters, allowing the former to enjoy greater power and prestige in African society.[27]

Murray, for one, was dubious about the depth of Nkrumah's commitment to improving the status of women. True, he had been educated in the United States at Lincoln University, where Grandfather Robert Fitzgerald had studied when it was still Ashmun Institute. Nkrumah had gone on to embrace socialism and to support legislation important to women. Most recently, he had approved an act that added ten women's seats to the 104 already held by men in Parliament, but Murray regarded it as "a farce." Its goal was to expose women to political life, not to give them a voice in government, nor to make their representation permanent. The act made no provision for filling a vacancy of a woman member and had already been repealed.[28]

Nkrumah's cavalier treatment of women in government struck Murray as an ominous sign, part of a drift away from democratic rule. The new constitution had just been rushed through without a drafting convention. As written, it made the president "virtually a dictator." Questionable tactics had been used at the polls. Nkrumah was using preventive detention to silence his critics. A new law provided for censorship of the press. In this context, Nkrumah's opening remarks at the conference constituted less a promise to address women's needs, Murray believed, than a stump speech in his campaign to suppress the power of tribal chiefs in Ghana and to unify the continent under his rule.[29]

The task of looking more closely at how the lives of African women might be improved fell to Anna Arnold Hedgeman. Having devoted her entire career to the welfare of black women, through leadership in the YWCA; service in the Department of Health, Education, and Welfare; and most recently in a goodwill mission to India, Hedgeman proved more sensitive to the concerns of the women in the audience. Although her address was entitled "Women in Public Life," she began with a discussion of women in the family. All women, including housewives, she emphasized, contributed to public life in ways largely unrecognized but essential to public well-being.[30]

Hedgeman called for an examination of women's lives as they were actually lived and how those lives related to proposed reforms. The task was far more complex than anyone appreciated at the time. The Ghana Education Act of 1960, for instance, mandated free education for all. Many participants, including Murray, regarded this act as an essential precondition to Ghana's economic development and women's upward mobility. Most mothers disagreed. As farmers, traders, and custodians of family history, they enjoyed a level of economic independence and political influence that formal kinship structures did not recognize, but they rarely encouraged their daughters to aspire to individual autonomy. Mothers, especially the three quarters of them who lived in rural areas, needed their daughters at home to care for babies, haul water, and gather wood. As a consequence, illiteracy rates and, inevitably, birth rates were high. Rural mothers had seven to eight children. Murray had glimpsed the skeptical rural attitude toward the education of women on her visit to the matrilineal Obo. When she mentioned to the Nifahene that she was descended from slaves but had trained as a lawyer, the chief said that he was "surprised" that a woman would be so highly trained. He then volunteered, "the girls around Obo did not do so well in their studies."[31]

In short, Ghana in 1960 remained a tribal and heavily rural society in which individual desires mattered less than kinship responsibilities, and motherhood constituted women's most honored role. In this context Murray—alone and childless—was a woman worthy less of admiration than pity. Although Ghanaians politely overlooked this shortcoming by calling her "Mammy," or more intimately "Ma," the reforms that might produce more women like her came to naught.[32]

Curiously, the issue that produced the most intense controversy at the conference on women appeared to have little to do with women per se. One of the delegates proposed a resolution that condemned the United States and South Africa for their oppression of racial minorities. Hedgeman protested equating the two countries, but some participants, including US observer Shirley Graham DuBois (soon to join the growing number of radical expatriates in Ghana with her husband, W. E. B. DuBois), supported the resolution. In the ensuing debate, Murray sought to clarify distinctions between apartheid in South Africa and racial discrimination in America. She pointed in particular to the history of the American Constitution, the post–Civil War amendments, the two-party system, and the division of power among a president, Congress, and the Supreme Court "as basic to our struggle for freedom." In the final vote, Hedgeman and Murray prevailed, but the passions aroused by the debate underscored the growing disillusionment among the conferees not only with European colonial power but also with the United States. Many African women and women of African descent had lost patience with the legally constrained slog toward a better life in

America. These dissidents implied that anyone who sought to draw distinctions between the United States and South Africa was, as Murray ruefully put it, a "stooge of American imperialism."[33]

This view stemmed in part from events in neighboring Congo. Belgium had just granted Congo its independence, and Patrice Lumumba, a close friend of Nkrumah, had become the country's first premier. Both leaders supported "positive neutralism" as an independent stance between the United States and the Soviet Union, as they worked to support independence movements throughout Africa.[34]

Murray had just traveled to Leopoldville in mid-June to secure information for the Ghanaian government on how safely to rescue a group of South Africans at risk of arrest for their role in protesting apartheid. Although she hoped that the trip, which had been dangerous and difficult, would establish her "good faith" with the Ghanaian government "as a liberal and person of character," liberalism and character carried less and less weight in a country hurtling toward autocratic rule. Her outspoken commitment to civil rights and civil liberties, which had long made her a pariah to conservatives in the United States, made her seem too identified with the US government in the context of the struggle between East and West for influence in Africa. To be cast as an apologist for American foreign policy galled Murray. The Cold War had brought nothing but misery to her life, except insofar as it gave civil rights advocates leverage. Throughout her stay in Africa, she sought to drive home this point. If the United States hoped to best Russia, she declared in an unpublished letter to the New York Times, it had better address "its unsolved race problem." She approved when US policy makers spoke to the Soviet Union in words that were "sharp, precise, without bluster," but she wanted officials to be "equally blunt" with the Belgians.[35]

Murray particularly objected to American policymakers using blacks as pawns in the Cold War struggle. When some pundits began to suggest that the United States appoint American blacks to positions in "sensitive, race-conscious Africa," she objected. Although she had long called on the State Department to appoint blacks to positions of responsibility, she refined her view in the context of the fighting in Congo and her experience in Ghana. "I am not at all sure that we can pull this chestnut out of the fire for Uncle Sam," she mordantly observed. "Government officials in Africa are very status-conscious. When the chips are down, a second-class citizen in the United States will be a third-class citizen here." Moreover, she continued, "if Negroes have to spend their energies acting as apologists for United States racial policies, they will hardly be able to project the kind of image which will make an impact upon the Africans." Although Murray was coming to fear the drift toward authoritarianism in Ghana, she agreed with at least one comment Nkrumah was rumored to have made. Until such time as the United States sent black ambassadors to London, Paris, and Rome, its ambassador to Accra should be white.[36]

Anna Hedgeman, seeing Murray's dismay over the political battles that played out at the women's conference and in the weeks that followed, urged her not to "torture" herself. Murray tried. With the school year about to begin, she endeavored to shake off her discouragement and redoubled her efforts to succeed as a law professor. But even that goal proved more difficult to achieve than she had anticipated.[37]

Teaching Law under Surveillance

As Murray prepared her course materials for the fall, she audited classes to learn the customary law that still regulated most activity in Ghana. Interesting as she found the work, she grew increasingly dismayed by what she regarded as a complete lack of system at the Ghana School of Law. There were no faculty meetings, no organization, no sense of direction. She would have loved to impose American-style order, but by September she had learned an important lesson: the "missionary type," however well intentioned, was unlikely to succeed. The idea that one could come to Africa and help one's "Brothers" was an impulse that "articulate Africans . . . resent."[38]

If Murray had faced only administrative disarray she might have shrugged off her "missionary" impulses and focused on her own work, but added to her concerns about the law school were worries about Ghana's government. Committed to civil liberties as essential to any democratic order, she watched with mounting distress as Nkrumah ordered dissidents, many his former colleagues, arrested and thrown in jail. Murray was sufficiently worried that she, too, might face arrest that she sent all her course notes to the Central Intelligence Agency (CIA) through Earl Link at the US embassy as evidence against any charge that she was seeking to proselytize her students. In addition, she made sure Link knew where she was whenever she left the capital in case she needed to be rescued.[39]

Maida Springer, on a trip through Africa for the AFL-CIO that fall, stopped over in Accra to see Murray for a few days and was alarmed by what she found. Murray, in deep distress, complained that she lived in a police state. Springer defended Nkrumah, arguing that allowances should be made in this moment of decolonization to ensure that Ghana and other new states did not succumb to a bloodletting at the hands of warring tribal chieftains. Murray strongly disagreed. As Springer later told her biographer, "My passionate feeling about Africa she certainly did not share. She was too cool-headed and intellectually searching and was unwilling to make any compromise for undemocratic practices in Africa. . . . We never agreed."[40]

For a time, the demands of the new school year distracted Murray from the political turmoil around her. She had expected, on the basis of conversations with Arthur Sutherland at Harvard, that her students, though not college graduates, would have at least a year of college preparation. As she reviewed their records, she discovered that the overwhelming majority had never gone to college and that they were working to support themselves. Given her students' lack of education, she abandoned any idea of lecturing and settled on a discussion format as a way of connecting with them at whatever level they seemed ready to perform. With the help of Joyce Markham, secretary to John Lang, she compiled a casebook, bound in blue, designed to introduce students to British, American, and African tribal law.[41]

On the first day of class she "nervously faced several rows of young men whose impassive expressions" gave her "no hint of their reaction to the unique experience of having a woman professor from the United States." The twenty students expected a lecture and looked "surprised" when Murray distributed the blue-bound lecture notes and explained that she expected them to read the materials in advance and come to class prepared to discuss them. They were even more surprised at the next class, when Murray had them arrange their tables in a square, seminar-style, so that they could exchange their ideas more easily. Progress was slow in the beginning. The students had no experience in expressing their opinions, and their initial efforts proved stumbling and unclear. Murray "never rejected a student's offering but instead rephrased it until the student agreed she had captured his meaning." They often asked her opinion, but rather than give it, she outlined the principles from which the students might answer the question themselves.[42]

Once the students had mastered class discussion, she taught them how to support their arguments with judicial authority based on their own independent research. For examples, she showed them the majority opinions and dissents in the line of cases that had culminated in *Brown v. Board of Education* (1954). The students embraced her techniques, indeed asked for more class hours to cover all the material. She relaxed a little, but late in the term she had a shock. Walking into class one day she found six uniformed members of the Criminal Investigation Department seated in her classroom. Accepting them as visitors, Murray conducted discussion in the usual manner. The investigators left without a word, but Murray grew increasingly worried about what their appearance might portend.[43]

Fortunately, she had recently made a friend who offered a way out of what seemed an increasingly untenable situation. A couple of months earlier, Professor Fowler V. Harper of Yale Law School had delivered a series of lectures at the Ghana School of Law. An uncompromising supporter of civil liberties, Harper had long campaigned for the abolition of the House Un-American Activities

Committee. He also opposed legislation that would allow wire-tapping and sought to overturn laws that restricted the use of contraceptives. At Accra with his wife Miriam as part of a trip to Africa under the auspices of the United States Department of State, Harper had talked to the law students about civil liberties in the United States and had shown a film that reenacted several of the cases Murray had just discussed in class. Pleased by the familiarity demonstrated by some of the students with the legal issues raised, Harper asked to meet their teacher. He liked Murray immediately. Impressed to encounter someone in Africa as committed to civil liberties as he was, Fowler accepted Murray's invitation that he and his wife stay at her house at the end of their African tour.[44]

In early January, shortly after the visit by state investigators to Murray's class, the Harpers returned to Accra, on their way back to the United States. They stayed with Murray for several days and in the course of conversation, Harper sought to persuade her to return to the United States. Convinced that the visit from the investigators meant that Nkrumah was simply waiting for an opportunity to get rid of her, he urged her to come to Yale for the doctorate in law she had once hoped to win. Doubtful at first that the dream of the past fifteen years might really be achievable, Murray objected that she thought she was too old and that, furthermore, graduate study would, in her case, accomplish nothing. Men with graduate degrees could expect to win a position on a law school faculty. A woman could hold out no such hope. Harper pointed out that there were currently two women on the faculty at Yale Law School and that Murray would have "solid support" from the faculty. Thus reassured, she applied to Yale Law School for graduate study and fellowship assistance.[45]

While she awaited a response, Murray threw herself into her teaching and a book project on Ghana. A colleague at the law school, Dr. Leslie Rubin, had been in touch with Sweet & Maxwell, a London publisher interested in putting out a series of books on law in Africa. A former senator in the South African Parliament who had left his country rather than support apartheid, Rubin proposed that Murray work with him to produce a book on Ghana's constitution and evolving laws as soon as possible.[46]

Over spring break in 1961, Murray flew to Holland, where she met Caroline Ware and Gardner Means, who were on their way back to the United States from a lecture tour in Yugoslavia. With them she enjoyed a lawyer's holiday, as they visited the opening session of the International Court of Justice in the Hague and, following a flight to London, a week wandering through the Inns of Court, before Ware and Means returned home and she flew back to Accra. Several weeks after her return, Murray received a cable from Yale Law School announcing her admission to graduate study and offering her fellowship support for the coming school year. Not yet finished with the book on Ghana law, Murray turned her teaching over to Keith Highet, a recent Harvard Law School graduate, in Ghana on a year's grant from the Maxwell School at Syracuse University. Highet had originally been assigned to the attorney general's office but was given nothing to do there. Learning of his frustration, Murray urged him to switch to the law school in the fall of 1960, and he began to teach some of her classes. With time limited, she handed over even more of her teaching to him so that she could complete the book on the constitution and government of Ghana and prepare to leave the country. [47]

Just before Murray and Highet left Ghana in the summer of 1961, they found themselves drawn into a civil liberties battle in Ghana that would surely have led to their deportation had they not already been scheduled to leave. In the wake of Lumumba's assassination and fearing an attempt on his own life, Nkrumah ordered eight arrests under the Preventive Detention Act of 1958. The detainees enlisted Dr. J. B. Danquah, the most distinguished lawyer in Ghana, to represent them. A member of the royal family of Akyem Abuakwa (a province of Ashanti), the first African to earn a doctorate from a British university, and an early advocate of independence for Ghana, Danquah had been instrumental in bringing Nkrumah back from England to help lead the struggle for independence after World War II. When his protégé adopted repressive policies, however, Danquah broke with him and joined the opposition. [48]

In seeking to free his clients, Danquah wanted to attack the constitutionality of the Preventive Detention Act. Consulting one of Murray's students, Kwaku Baah, he learned that Murray and Highet might be able to help draft an argument. They did so over the weekend before Danquah had to appear in court. Highet and Murray argued that Nkrumah's arrest of political opponents violated his duty under the new constitution to pledge to protect freedom of speech and assembly. Murray was back in the United States before the Ghanaian Supreme Court issued its opinion, which dismissed the argument she and Highet had made. The Court held that the president's pledge did not constitute a legal requirement enforceable by the courts. If the public thought that the president was not doing enough to ensure freedom of speech, they could vote him out of office, the court concluded. Two weeks later, Dr. Danquah was arrested. Released after a year, he was rearrested and died in prison. [49]

Although relieved to be out of Ghana, Murray regretted leaving her students behind. Kwaku Baah, having served as liaison between her and Dr. Danquah, was in real danger. Indeed all her students were in trouble, both because of their association with her and the change she had nurtured in their thinking. Joseph Musah, from a poor region in the north where there had never been a lawyer, told her, "We used to accept without questioning whatever the lecturer told us. Through your class we have now learned to inquire." To compensate for the danger in which they now found themselves, she did everything she could to bring them to the United States for graduate legal training. [50]

What Is Africa to Me?

Throughout her time in Ghana, Murray continued to reflect on Countee Cullen's question: What is Africa to me? As the months passed, she found herself giving increasingly hostile answers. Part of the problem was political. She hated the arrogance of those in power, the way they would "lord it over" others, the way they looked down on American blacks. She despaired over the state-controlled newspapers, with their "sloganizing, the hysterical screaming, vituperative, unrestrained quality of the statements and articles." She resented having to smuggle her letters out with the US Embassy mail, un-postmarked, to avoid having them censored. She particularly resented the comment of one African leader, reported in a story in the *New York Times,* that Ghana had "won its independence in five years," as he told American black friends. "You have not achieved equality in 100 years."[51]

She liked the ordinary people, whom she found uniformly "kind and friendly" and with whom she believed she shared an understanding of how it felt to be oppressed. Otherwise, she felt little connection. "I am not African and have little feeling of kinship with things African per se," she concluded seven months into her stay. The culture was too different from her own.[52]

This is not to say that Africa did not in some important ways appeal to her. Like most American blacks who traveled there she appreciated being in a place where she was not forever wrestling with color consciousness, where race was a unifying, not a dividing factor. In this place where common people felt dignity in their ancestry, she began to do so also. She never discovered the tribe or tribes of her African forebears, but meeting people whose sense of self worth had not been undercut by slavery gave her new respect for this part of her heritage.

Living in Africa and experiencing that respect also raised her expectations. She wanted more from American whites. Practicing on this audience in her journal, she announced, "I want you to accept me as an American, as a Negro, but also I want you to respect my African background." She had never felt this way before, in part because she had always clung so tenaciously to the promise of integration. She realized that she had become "so integrated, I had merged into American life and lost all sense of African roots." Coming to Africa had encouraged her to recognize those origins.[53]

Murray found much to admire in Africa, but she believed more strongly than ever that her future lay in the United States. "I am prepared to accept fully that Africans had a glorious past, that they can and will master the art of modern political institutions and technology that they will unify the continent and build a powerful black nation," she wrote in a rare burst of optimism. "Having accepted this I want to get on with the business of being an American. For if Africans are trying to prove something to the world, so are we. We are trying to prove that an idea is more powerful than blood or race or past achievements." Of course, blood and race were ideas also, as she was usually the first to declare, but they had been used so often for evil purposes that she could not imagine them as liberating concepts. She believed that the idea of freedom from arbitrary classifications based on skin color or gender characteristics promised a surer avenue to human betterment than any idea of racial unity ever could. "We [Americans] are engaged in a spiritual struggle, first with ourselves," she wrote in humanistic inclusiveness; "in many ways we are on a spiritual frontier. We have the vision of a dream not yet fulfilled, vague and elusive even to ourselves, but it is there and it is pervasive in all our institutions."[54]

Murray worked these thoughts into an article she called "What Is Africa to Me?—a Question of Identity." It went through multiple drafts, as she sent it for comment to Caroline Ware, Maida Springer, Helen Lockwood, and Harold Isaacs.[55]

Murray had talked at length with Isaacs when he and his wife stayed with her. She told him how it felt to be an American black in Africa, "neither wholly welcome nor at ease." Here she was, trying to help build a new nation, while under suspicion of "acting on [her] government's behalf to further American influence." He encouraged her to write an article about her experience. After he left, she sent him a draft of "What Is Africa to Me?" She told him he was the "Godfather" of the essay and credited him with some of the ideas expressed therein—indeed, some of "his very expressions." She shopped it around and an editor at *Harper's* liked it, but the magazine already had too much on race and Africa scheduled for publication over the next twelve months. Having heard nothing further from Murray, Isaacs wrote in early 1961 to warn her that James Baldwin had secured a commission to travel to Africa and write a book. Isaacs urged her to "get on it."[56]

In the meantime, Patrice Lumumba, prime minister of the Democratic Republic of the Congo, was assassinated, and violent demonstrations at the United Nations inspired Isaacs to write his own article. It appeared in the May 13, 1961, issue of the *New Yorker* under the title: "A Reporter at Large: Back to Africa." Writing to Murray soon after its appearance, Isaacs again urged her to publish her own reflections. "I expect to have a need for your strong prose on this same subject—nobody's writing much hard sense on this matter these days, or talking it either."[57]

In the midst of packing for her return to the United States, Murray replied, "I don't know whether to congratulate you for doing an excellent job or to chide you for stealing most of my thunder." But she added, "I think that the things you said had to be said and that they come with better grace from your pen than mine at this stage. If I have anything further to say, you have broken the ground. I have only one minor criticism. To have made the picture complete, you should have stressed the point of view you know I hold, and that is Africans and Africa have given to some of us a perspective on the United States, and that in that respect is a positive gain. You left the picture almost hopeless."[58]

Caroline Ware was not so forgiving. She accused Isaacs of plagiarism. Recognizing Murray's ideas in his article, she told him bluntly that she hoped he had shared the payment with Murray. For Ware the matter was deeply personal, not only because she cared about Pauli but also because she was Murray's lender of last resort when funds ran low. Isaacs sent a chilly reply, noting that Murray had called him the "godfather" of her piece. He had used only one story involving her, about her epiphany at Elmina Castle. The weakness in Murray's article as drafted, he believed, was that it was too vague and included too little about herself. He was encouraging her to build on what he had written with that in mind. "Pauli and I esteem and value each other," he told Ware. "You really ought to look before you leap to make statements which are a gratuitous insult to us both."[59]

Encouraging Murray to put more of herself into her article was a way of suggesting that she consider a topic someone interested in Jane Crow might well have considered, and she had not: What Is Africa to Me, when the "Me" is a black woman? Isaacs had included a variation on the question in his interviews. Talking to American women of African descent who had moved to Ghana in the hope of finding a better, less color-conscious life, he concluded that—at least in the case of those who married African men—American black women had traded a reduction in color trouble for a sharp increase in gender trouble. Raised in a culture that honored companionate marriage, women who married African men found themselves part of a society that valued the needs of kin over the rights of wives, especially when those wives were "strangers" from America. Believing that women had the right to talk back to their husbands, American wives were not prepared for husbands who believed that women should accept a subordinate place. Having grown up with Planned Parenthood, and therefore expecting to rely on contraception within marriage to space their children and to continue to enjoy exclusive sexual relations with their husbands, they found that birth control in Africa was typically achieved by imposing at least two years of abstinence on new mothers, during which time new fathers enjoyed license to satisfy their sexual desires elsewhere.[60]

In answering Isaacs's question, Murray had considered neither the special problems of married women nor, more surprisingly, the difficulties encountered by women outside of marriage. One might have expected that the slights Murray had encountered from men at Howard, Harvard, and to a lesser extent at Paul, Weiss—slights indisputably based on her gender—might have primed her for a consideration of gender discrimination in Africa. And yet, she wrote barely a word in her journal, newsletters, or private letters on the subject. While in Africa, she tended to attribute any discrimination she encountered to her status as an American in Africa or to her not sufficiently black, tawny, skin color. Perhaps because she lived and worked as a male in Ghana's legal community, perhaps because she lived as a solitary householder cared for by her male steward, she did not encounter the level of culture shock experienced by women forced to navigate the heterosexual social world in Africa where feminist ideas about equal rights and American-style companionate marriage were unknown, or if known rejected.

Murray participated in the women's conference in July 1960, but—except for a fleeting reference in her private journal to "the farce" of women's representation in Parliament—she never wrote about the discussions of women's status that occurred there. Only after her return to the United States, where considerations of gender did not get lost for her amid the distractions of Africa's cultural differences and political struggles, could she once again meditate on the meaning of Jane Crow.

PART V

A CHANCE TO LEAD, 1961–1967

Making Sex Suspect

"Your Experience Would Be Invaluable"

Murray was relieved to be back in America and exhilarated to be headed to Yale Law School. Finally, she would earn a doctorate in law, the credential that might make up for the deficiencies in her prior training and compensate for her double disability of race and gender. She still harbored doubts. As she had told Fowler Harper in Africa, she feared that even this added certification would make no difference in the world of American law schools, that no faculty would be willing to hire a middle-aged black woman as a law professor. Harper had reassured her that times were changing.[1]

Murray spent the final weeks of the summer of 1961 in search of an apartment in New Haven. She would have preferred to live in New York, near Renee, but it made more sense to live close to the law school, which would absorb most of her time for the next several years. Renee would visit on weekends. Friends arranged for Marjorie Ulman, an experienced member of a local interracial committee, to show Murray around New Haven. They found an apartment near the campus in Murray's price range that looked fine and, as luck would have it, Ulman knew the rental agent as a friend. But when Murray and Ulman arrived at the rental office, the agent turned her down cold. He had nothing against her personally, he assured them, but "he simply could not risk renting an apartment to a colored person." Stunned, Murray felt as though she had suddenly been cast back to Los Angeles in 1944. How could the liberal community of New Haven still be engaged in the same discriminatory rental practices that had made life so difficult seventeen years before? Outraged, Ulman filed a complaint against the real estate agent with the local anti-discrimination agency, notwithstanding their friendship, and helped Murray find another apartment.[2]

Bitter and angry, Murray nonetheless forged ahead. Eager to complete her doctorate as quickly as possible, she enrolled in four law school classes, while hammering out a dissertation proposal on the constitutional protection of human rights in emerging African nations. All went as planned until early April

1962, when Murray received a telegram from Eleanor Roosevelt. "WOULD APPRECIATE YOUR SERVING AS MEMBER ON COMMITTEE ON POLITICAL AND CIVIL RIGHTS OF THE PRESIDENT'S COMMISSION ON THE STATUS OF WOMEN. YOUR EXPERIENCE WOULD BE INVALUABLE IN ANALYSIS OF PROBLEMS AND PREPARATION OF RECOMMENDATIONS." Murray had been concerned about gender discrimination since the early 1940s, when she confronted open and unabashed sexism, first at Howard, then as an applicant to Harvard Law School, and most painfully as she had struggled to establish herself as a lawyer. "Being a woman in the field of law," she had lamented to Aunt Pauline, "is as bad as being a Negro and the combination is pretty awful." Her gender battles had been much lonelier than her civil rights protests; in the latter, she could at least appeal for support to national groups, such as the NAACP. Not until Roosevelt's invitation to serve on John F. Kennedy's newly established commission on women did she have the opportunity to bring her civil rights experience and legal training to bear on behalf of women before a group with the power to take decisive action.[3]

The question of gender equity was hardly new, but the women's movement had been stalled, ever since women won the right to vote in 1920, over the question of how best to advance the interests of women. Some, led by Alice Paul's National Woman's Party (NWP), wanted to fight for an Equal Rights Amendment (ERA), which would eliminate legal distinctions between women and men. Others, led by Consumers League President Florence Kelly, opposed such an amendment on the grounds that equality in theory would lead to inequality in fact. For decades, Kelly and other reformers had fought to pass "specific bills for specific ills" to protect women from spousal abuse and employer exploitation; the ERA would likely ban them all. That was fine with Alice Paul. She regarded protective labor laws not as a boon to women workers but rather as a barrier to those who sought the better paying jobs dominated by men.[4]

By later standards, the two groups occupied counterintuitive political ground. ERA supporters tended to be political conservatives, who found common cause with racist southern Democrats and business-minded northern Republicans hoping to eliminate all labor laws. ERA opponents, by contrast, allied themselves with liberal northern Republicans and Democrats who regarded the proposed amendment as a cover for the exploitation of vulnerable women workers. At loggerheads, women's organizations were having trouble getting anything done. Here was a chance to break the logjam. Who better to mediate this debate, and possibly reframe it, than Pauli Murray, who had lived her whole life in a state of race, class, and gender in-betweenness—a mixed-race person who had lived much of her life in a white world, a professional who had endured poverty, a woman who thought she should have been a man, a supporter of both labor laws and equal rights? In 1953, Roosevelt had declared in *Ebony* that Murray was "ready to be of real use." A decade later, the former First Lady believed that the country was ready for Murray. Pauli accepted her political mentor's invitation without a second thought.[5]

"Sex" at Yale

Course work at Yale Law School, for all its intellectual challenges, offered Murray little guidance for the project ahead. "Constitutional Litigation" focused on recent cases dealing with whether the federal government had exceeded its constitutional powers in prosecuting Communists. "Political and Civil Rights" covered some of the same cases but also ranged more broadly over obscenity, the right of labor to organize, and the extent to which the Equal Protection Clause protected blacks against discrimination. Neither class offered any discussion of gender discrimination. Even the proposed paper topics for "Political and Civil Rights" gave no guidance. One list of subjects, suggested by lawyers at the ACLU, included the rights of parole violators, military personnel, criminal defendants, and black Muslims in penal institutions. Ideas proposed by lawyers at the NAACP included school desegregation, the utility of class action, efforts to enjoin state criminal prosecutions against civil rights activists, and thirty-two other topics. None concerned women except, indirectly, a proposed topic on whether anti-miscegenation statutes were constitutional. In accepting her assignment to the PCSW's Committee on Civil and Political Rights, Murray entered largely uncharted terrain.[6]

The silence of Murray's law school classes on the question of equal rights for women is not surprising. While the Supreme Court had moved decisively to ensure the racial integration of public accommodations and had taken its first tentative steps toward protecting the rights of the accused, it had refused, thus far, to extend equal rights to women as a class under any circumstances. The previous year, the Court had upheld a Florida law in *Hoyt v. Florida* (1961) that made it easier for women than for men to avoid jury duty, a disheartening defeat for the small band of lawyers who were seeking to advance equal rights (and responsibility) claims for women in jury service.[7]

Despite this recent defeat and the absence in law school classes of any discussion of gender discrimination, a few faculty members voiced support for the idea of equal rights for women, chief among them Murray's adviser, Fowler Harper, and his colleague, Thomas Emerson. So, too, did their wives Miriam Harper and Ruth Emerson. Fowler Harper worked with the local Planned Parenthood Clinic to challenge Connecticut's law banning the distribution and use of contraceptives. Ruth Emerson, a 1950 Yale Law School graduate, helped him. Thomas Emerson, a specialist in the First Amendment, would soon be involved himself.[8]

Murray also enjoyed the fellowship, and admiration, of the female students who gravitated around her. The group included young women who would go on to be leaders in the legal profession: Barbara Babcock, Eleanor Holmes, Marion Wright, and Inez Smith. At a time when female law students remained rare and female faculty members rarer still, Murray provided inspiration and encouragement. "A much underappreciated figure," remembered Eleanor Holmes, who found in Murray an unexpected source for a history paper entitled, "World War II and the Beginning of Non-Violent Action in Civil Rights." Despite their appreciation, Holmes and her friends had reservations. Murray's "feminism seemed way out to us then," she admitted. More than that, the older woman seemed "eccentric" to students who, for all their unconventional career ambitions, tried to fit into the gendered expectations of their day in other ways. She "was not married, kept impeccable records that she moved everywhere she went, and had a beloved . . . dog," all of which "was a bit much." Although Eleanor Holmes "admired" her mentor and strove to "catch up with her," she hoped to do so "without all of her eccentricities."[9]

Holmes regarded Murray as eccentric (a synonym for "queer") out of discomfort over Murray's unsettling divergence from what would later be known as "heteronormativity." Holmes loved to party; she later married and had children. She dressed stylishly and wore earrings. In a bow to professional convention, Murray occasionally wore lipstick and donned a skirt, but she avoided all other feminine adornment. Holmes admitted that Murray seemed "happy as a single woman and early feminist, alone in the world of her ideas and work," but the younger women found it hard to imagine happiness on those terms. It would take them a few years to appreciate how much Murray was doing on their behalf and how satisfying her work on behalf of women could be.[10]

Murray seemed eccentric to her younger friends, but she was settled as never before. The long-term effects of her 1954 thyroid operation, her ongoing psychotherapy, the satisfaction of being at Yale, and the steady emotional support of Renee Barlow all helped. She still felt in-between, but whereas she had once experienced that in-betweenness as an unbearable conflict that must be resolved medically, she had come to feel that it allowed her to challenge boundaries that seemed natural to others. No longer subject to the collapses that had regularly derailed her in the past, Murray channeled her abundant energy into her work at the Law School and on the President's Commission.[11]

The President's Commission on the Status of Women

The Women's Bureau, part of the United States Department of Labor, had been asking Congress to establish a commission on the status of women since 1946, without success because of conditions set by Alice Paul and her followers in the NWP. Paul insisted that the NWP would support the creation of a commission only if the Women's Bureau supported passage of the ERA. Leaders of the Women's Bureau, fearful that passage of the ERA would spell the death of protective labor laws for women, had long since abandoned their effort to seek a commission through Congress.[12]

In 1961 Secretary of Labor Arthur Goldberg suggested that the Women's Bureau avoid Congress altogether and seek an Executive Order instead. The idea was an old one, but until Kennedy's election no president had thought it worth pursuing. The new president proved sympathetic in large part because of his long association with Esther Peterson, whom he had just appointed head of the Women's Bureau. Peterson had worked closely with Kennedy since he entered Congress in 1946. Male labor leaders, having concluded that young Kennedy was just a rich man's son who was going nowhere, assigned Peterson to represent labor in his office. When Kennedy's career took off, she stuck by him, and in the nail-bitingly close election of 1960, she delivered the female labor vote. Peterson wanted a commission on women, and she turned to two assistants to make the commission happen: Katherine Ellickson, formerly assistant director of the Social Security Department of the AFL-CIO, and Murray's longtime friend Dollie Lowther (now Robinson), who had become the leading African American woman labor leader in the Democratic Party.[13]

The commission membership reflected Peterson, Ellickson, and Robinson's desire to advance women's interests without being hung up over the Equal Rights Amendment. Of the eleven women and fifteen men chosen to serve under Eleanor Roosevelt, eleven came from government, including Peterson as executive vice chair, Attorney General Robert F. Kennedy, and four members of Congress. To that group they added two commissioners from labor, and one from business. Another half dozen represented women's organizations. Among them was Dorothy Height, Murray's friend from the Harlem YWCA, now president of the National Council of Negro Women, the umbrella organization for the country's leading black women's groups. To provide scholarly expertise, the organizers called on four academics, including historian Caroline Ware. In an effort to be fair to supporters of the ERA, or at least to give the appearance of fairness, the commission organizers invited two past presidents of the Federation of Business and Professional Women: Margaret Hickey of *Ladies Home Journal*, a likely supporter of the ERA, and Marguerite Rawalt, a longtime attorney in the Department of the Treasury, past president of the Federal Bar Association, and an open supporter of the amendment.[14]

Kennedy announced the creation of the commission on December 14, 1961. He called on the group to make studies of "all barriers to the full partnership of women in our democracy" and asked that it report by October 1, 1963, on what remained to be done to "demolish prejudices and outmoded customs." Murray was tremendously excited: "No such concentration on women's problems by prominent people had ever occurred before."[15]

The commission met only eight times in two years, and therefore the staff, especially Ellickson and Robinson, whom Peterson assigned to full-time work on the project, exercised considerable influence. Much of the work was done in committees, of which there were seven: Civil and Political Rights, Protective Labor Legislation, Federal Employment, Social Insurance and Taxes, Home and Community, and Education. Peterson promised that the ERA would be examined objectively, but she took the precaution of turning the issue over to the Committee on Civil and Political Rights (CCPR), thereby leaving other committees free to consider their issues without distraction. With the support of Dollie Lowther Robinson, Caroline Ware, and Eleanor Roosevelt, Murray's appointment to this sensitive position had been assured.[16]

Murray later recalled that she followed the early stages of the body's work through Ware, who prepared a working paper, "Women Today—Trends and Issues," to guide the commission's initial discussions. Ware stressed the "profound confusion" that existed at the beginning of the 1960s as to "what is expected of women in today's world." At one extreme "many men and women [conceived of the typical woman] as wife and mother in an old-fashioned home in which most of her adult years were devoted to child-bearing and child care." At the opposite extreme were those who saw women "as individuals with varied capacities, interests and talents—as varied as those of men. To this latter group, the biological function of child-bearer," Ware wrote, "is seen as incidental to the broader concept of woman as a human being and a member of democratic society."[17]

Demographic changes taking place in the United States in the prior decade suggested a dramatic shift toward the latter view. The number of bachelor's degrees and first professional degrees earned by women had increased by 48 percent, compared to men's 15 percent gain. Women had also made dramatic gains in employment. Their workforce participation had risen 29 percent, compared with men's increase of only 6 percent. The biggest increase came with married women whose workforce participation rate jumped 43 percent. By 1960, 30 percent of married women were employed and 39 percent of all mothers with school-age children were in the workforce. But for the most part, women found themselves confined to a female labor ghetto.[18]

The day Murray received her telegram from Eleanor Roosevelt, the *New York Times* ran page after page of classified ads: "Help Wanted: Female." The classifieds signaled not only the explosion of the white collar and service sector of the economy with its seemingly unquenchable thirst for educated, low-cost workers, but also the dearth of positions open to women above the level of secretary. The *Times* placed ads for better-paying employment in a separate section, under "Help Wanted: Male." No matter how much education a woman acquired, discrimination relegated her to lower-level jobs with no future, while men had ready access to trainee positions with the prospect of promotion. Women with college diplomas still earned less than men with only high school degrees.[19]

The Committee on Civil and Political Rights

Shoehorning the work of the Committee on Civil and Political Rights into her academic schedule, Murray raced down to Washington for the first meeting on May 28, 1962. Meeting her fellow committee members, she realized she would have to draw on all her strengths as a creative thinker and diplomat. Oregon Democratic Congresswoman Edith Green, who chaired the committee, opposed the ERA; Treasury Department attorney Marguerite Rawalt, who took over when Green was gone, supported it. The rest of the committee was made up of two representatives of labor unions, six lawyers, and three presidents of pro-ERA organizations. The president of the NWP was invited but refused to participate in what she viewed as a committee stacked against a new amendment. Murray well understood the difficulty she faced in hammering out a compromise that would be acceptable to both those who favored the amendment and those who opposed it.[20]

Like other committees, the CCPR relied heavily on staff, especially the technical secretaries, loaned from governmental agencies. Mary O. Eastwood, from the Justice Department, served as technical secretary to the CCPR. Five years Murray's junior, Eastwood, a graduate of the University of Wisconsin Law School, had joined the Justice Department's Office of Legal Counsel in 1960. For the CCPR, Eastwood took charge of the accumulation of data, including answers culled from questionnaires given to women's organizations on both sides of the ERA controversy. She then followed up with further research and draft papers on the topics to be considered. An able diplomat, Eastwood worked well with members across the political spectrum. She and Murray became close friends as the months wore on.[21]

Murray spent the summer of 1962 reading in the Yale library and talking to those who might be able to help. Thomas Emerson offered advice, as did Phoebe Morrison, a former judge, who taught constitutional law at Barnard College and lived nearby in Connecticut. Morrison had accumulated more degrees than most of her male peers in her effort to overcome the discrimination against female lawyers in her generation. Following graduation from Vassar, she had earned a law degree at George Washington University and then a doctorate in law at Yale, the same degree that Murray was pursuing. Both Emerson and Morrison were open to new ways of approaching the topic of equal rights, and they encouraged

Murray as she labored away in un-air-conditioned Sterling Library through the hot summer of 1962.[22]

Eleanor Roosevelt also cheered her on. At Yale to give a speech to a group of foreign students, she visited with Murray and invited her to lunch at Val-Kill Cottage on July 14. Roosevelt had organized a picnic lunch for some UN families from India and Haiti and had space for a few more guests. Pauli brought her brother Raymond, his wife, and three children. At the gathering, Murray realized almost immediately that something was wrong when Mrs. Roosevelt asked Pauli to get her a glass of lemonade, a request that was totally out of character for a woman accustomed to serving others rather than being served. At the end of August, Mrs. Roosevelt wrote that she had had a "miserable summer" and had spent a week in the hospital. Murray began to worry about her mentor's health. In fact, she was suffering from a rare form of tuberculosis, which had spread to her bones, but Murray was too preoccupied with the task before her to give the matter much thought.[23]

Murray believed that the solution to the problem of discrimination lay in an expanded understanding of the Equal Protection Clause of the Fourteenth

Figure 11.1 Pauli Murray, pictured with Eleanor Roosevelt, on a visit to Val-Kill Cottage, Hyde Park, July 1962. Photographer: Raymond Murray. Estate of Pauli Murray, Schlesinger Library, Radcliffe Institute, Harvard University.

Amendment. If the Supreme Court was willing to concede that race was an unreasonable basis for classification under the Equal Protection Clause, as it had in *Brown v. Board of Education*, then why could it not be persuaded that "sex" was also? Lawyers often resorted to analogy in making a novel argument. Why not argue that "sex" characteristics are like race characteristics? Both are immutable. Both mark people as members of a group regularly discriminated against.

The problem, of course, was that women were not only the victims of discrimination; they were also the beneficiaries of a number of protective laws. The main reason that liberal politicians and labor leaders had always opposed the ERA was that it promised to fight discrimination in such a sweeping way that it would jeopardize protective labor laws. Murray would have to persuade those liberal skeptics that the Equal Protection Clause would offer a way for women to combat discrimination without losing those protections.[24]

On August 24, 1962, Murray returned to Washington to present a draft memorandum to the Committee on Civil and Political Rights in support of the idea that equal rights for women could be better pursued through litigation than by either a constitutional amendment or legislative efforts. But the day's discussion ranged so widely, from the need to encourage women in New York to volunteer for jury service to ongoing studies of discrimination against women in inheritance and property taxation, that her ideas received scant attention, apart from a negative comment from Harvard Professor Frank Sander, who responded immediately that he did not like the idea of the commission, or any other governmental agency for that matter, engaging in litigation. In response, Harriet Pilpel, a friend of Thomas Emerson, a newly appointed member of the Board of the ACLU, and one of the small band of lawyers active in litigation over reproductive rights, came to Murray's defense. The Federal Communications Commission, Pilpel noted, regularly intervened in court proceedings. Having done nothing but air a smorgasbord of ideas, the committee agreed before adjourning that it would devote its next meeting, in January, to a full discussion of the Equal Rights Amendment and related issues, including protective labor laws and the Fourteenth Amendment. On reflection, however, Edith Green did not want to wait until January. She believed that Murray's idea held promise for breaking the deadlock over the ERA and suggested to Peterson that Murray be invited to present her proposal to the full commission at its October 1–2, 1962 meeting.[25]

A Fourteenth Amendment Strategy

When Murray arrived on the morning of October 1, she discovered to her distress that Eleanor Roosevelt, whom she had expected to chair the meeting, would not be present. Roosevelt's condition had worsened, and she was in the hospital. Caroline Ware was also absent, having accepted an invitation from a school of social work in Chile to teach for a few weeks. But Murray's old friend Dorothy Height was there, as was Grace Hewell from the Department of Health Education and Welfare. As black women who had devoted their careers to the problems of women, both Height and Hewell would understand what she was about to say. How the other forty-two commissioners and staff would react, she could only guess.[26]

Beginning in self-effacing fashion, Murray conceded that she was a "Johnny-come-lately" to the issue of women's rights. Though she had "stood her ground" when personally confronted with "sex" discrimination, she had "not been involved in any of the organizations which have been seeking to advance women," as many of those sitting around her had. But she believed that her experience as a victim of both race and sex discrimination, together with her expertise in civil rights law, gave her a valuable perspective on the challenges the committee faced as it sought to emancipate women. For years civil rights lawyers had fought against "Jim Crow." The time had come for women's rights lawyers to attack "Jane Crow." Lawyers needed simply to recognize that there was a "very close parallel between the status of women and their struggle for equal opportunity and the status of Negroes for the same objective." Murray conceded that race and sex were not completely analogous, that some gender-based laws were desirable. The challenge would be "to remove legal restrictions which are not grounded in biological and life-serving functions," she argued, "without at the same time endangering protective legislation which still has a rational basis in law and in fact."[27]

Because women's advocates disagreed over which laws were restrictive and which were protective, Murray urged her audience to unite around issues on which they could agree. All believed that women should not experience "civil death" upon marriage, that the "inferior nature of women" was a "myth," and that women's political inequality was at odds with core values of the Constitution and the Declaration of Independence. Lawyers should focus on these areas of common agreement.[28]

How to proceed? Murray regarded legislative reform at the state level a waste of effort. Under the best of circumstances it would take a long, long time to repeal all the laws that restricted women's freedoms, especially in southern states where women lacked political power. The Equal Rights Amendment posed its own challenges. Advocates would have to win the support of two-thirds of Congress and then persuade super majorities in three-quarters of the states to achieve ratification. Even if the ERA should pass, its language was so broad that there would still be litigation over its meaning and application. Given how divided women's advocates now were over the wisdom of pursuing the ERA, it seemed unlikely that the proposed amendment would elicit the kind of enthusiastic support that would be necessary for passage within the next generation. Murray believed that her Fourteenth Amendment strategy offered a better approach, because it would allow a targeting of the "the most restrictive laws" for Court review.[29]

Moreover, she believed that the current climate for such a strategy was propitious. There had already been "gradual elimination of restrictive sex legislation on the State level." The justices had begun to recognize the "changing status of women," though mostly in dissents. Debates then taking place in Congress on the proposed Equal Pay Act revealed that a growing number in Congress admitted the existence of "discrimination on the basis of sex alone." Half a century of litigation and legal commentary over the meaning of the Fourteenth Amendment demonstrated that the Equal Protection Clause had in some instances been expanded to apply to groups other than blacks. Moreover, the United Nation's Declaration of Human Rights, the Cold War rhetoric of freedom, the demonstrated willingness of the Supreme Court to reverse itself, and the growing numbers of women lawyers and judges all boded well for the future.[30]

Murray concluded by pointing out that half a century before, Louis Brandeis had written a brief on behalf of the state of Oregon's law restricting the number of hours that laundresses could work (*Muller v. Oregon,* 1908). That brief had been filled with sociological evidence aimed at supporting the proposition that women, as future mothers, constituted a class deserving protection from exploitative working conditions. The time had come, Murray declared, for a modern Brandeis brief, one that demonstrated how women's status had changed and why laws once justified by belief in women's inferiority could no longer pass constitutional scrutiny.[31]

Following a round of applause, Anne Draper, representing the AFL-CIO, declared that Murray had just given the "most magnificent presentation I ever heard." Not everyone was happy. Marguerite Rawalt had grown flushed and angry even before Murray finished. She quickly interjected that the commissioners would hear other views as well. Peterson responded that of course there would be further discussion, but Murray had carried the day.[32]

"We were very much impressed by your presentation," Katherine Ellickson wrote a few days later. Ellickson quickly added, however, that she hoped Murray would clarify her position on protective labor legislation. "Some people interpreted your remarks as meaning that you considered protective labor legislation discriminatory and subject to invalidation under the Fourteenth Amendment. This is not my understanding of your position from hearing you talk at the committee meeting." Hoping to calm the fears of the labor feminists, Murray responded, "My position on labor legislation protective in nature is that it should not be disturbed." In fact, she had not thought through her position on protective labor laws, but she promised to give the matter further consideration and to "consolidate all of my thinking and documentation in a complete memorandum" for distribution to everyone on the Commission.[33]

Caroline Ware mailed Murray her own reactions, having received a copy of Murray's draft memorandum in Chile. She thought the memo "excellent," but recommended that Murray stay away from the "'equal rights amendment' controversy." Even without being present at the PCSW session, she knew that ERA supporters Marguerite Rawalt and Margaret Hickey would be dismayed by Murray's criticism. She worried that it would inevitably "invite opposition from a quarter which will support you if you keep strictly silent on the 'equal rights' issue." That caveat aside, Ware concluded, "More power to you. I think that you are on a <u>most</u> important track, perhaps the most strategically important of any which the Commission is pursuing."[34]

Murray devoted October and November to working out her Fourteenth Amendment strategy. She hoped both to reassure Ellickson about her support for protective labor legislation and to bring Frank Sander and Marguerite Rawalt around to her view that a targeted program of litigation would provide the best means of improving women's status. As she labored, she worried about Eleanor Roosevelt. The newspapers reported that she was "resting comfortably" at her apartment in New York, where she had asked to go when it became clear that the doctors could do nothing more for her in the hospital. On November 7, 1962, she died of complications of tuberculosis in her apartment on East 74th Street in Manhattan. Three days later Renee Barlow took the train to New Haven and drove with Murray to the funeral at Hyde Park. Standing in the Rose Garden under "low-hanging clouds and intermittent heavy rain," as Eleanor was buried next to Franklin, Murray felt bereft: "She had filled the landscape of my entire adult life. The only way I knew to serve her was to pour myself into completing the memorandum." Three weeks later Murray submitted her proposal for litigation under the Fourteenth Amendment.[35]

"Maternity Legislation Is Not Sex Legislation"

Beginning with an examination of the common law, Murray pointed to the ways in which women had been cast as both "an object of special concern" and "an inferior person" from the earliest days of American legal history. *Muller v. Oregon* (1908) had incorporated this common law tradition into the Constitution. Holding that because of a combination of physical limitations, "the burdens of motherhood," inferior education, and political incapacity, "she is properly placed in a class by herself," the Court created a "basis for legislative classification" that has "permitted sex inequalities in the law to continue down to the present." Over the intervening decades, Murray continued, the Court had permitted "a policy originally directed toward the protection of a segment of a woman's life to dominate and inhibit her mature development as an individual."[36]

A state, Murray granted, could make distinctions between classes of persons in the legislation it enacted. But each law must be "based upon some reasonable ground—some difference which bears a just and proper relation to the attempted classification—and is not a mere arbitrary selection." Children could be classed separately as immature and therefore justifiably restricted in their activities. But women were not children, although they were often treated as though they were. Here is where race came in. Murray saw a much clearer analogy between gender and race (on the basis of which classifications were almost always unreasonable) than between gender and age (on the basis of which classification was often acceptable).[37]

Murray was not the first lawyer to draw the analogy of gender to race. Legal commentator, and NWP member Blanche Crozier had argued in a 1935 article in the *Boston University Law Review* that gender discrimination was no more permissible than race discrimination when it came to jury service. The Court had struck down a state law barring blacks from jury service in *Strauder v. Virginia* in 1878. The Court should do the same where states banned women from serving as jurors. "Race and sex are in every way comparable classes," wrote Crozier, "and if exclusion in one case is a discrimination implying inferiority, it would seem that it must be in the other also. And if such discrimination implying inferiority is a violation of the equal protection of the laws in the case of one of these classes, it ought to be also in the case of the other."[38]

The Court raised the bar to treating gender like race three years later, however, when it indicated in a footnote in *Carolene Products v. United States* (1938) that it would generally allow states great latitude in their legislating (and therefore classifying) unless they passed laws that limited the rights of "insular minorities." Given the fact that women constituted a majority of the population, it was difficult to argue that they were a minority, much less an insular one. Murray did not mention *Carolene Products* explicitly, and yet she was clearly mindful of its significance when she pointed out that women were, like blacks, "an easily identifiable group, to a large degree unrepresented in the formal decision-making processes, and thus easy targets of both public and private discrimination." In this context, she believed, "constitutional principles applied to enforce the rights of other minorities seem equally relevant to the rights of women."[39]

Others had seen the possibility. Only a couple of years before, Raya Spiegel Dreben, a 1949 white graduate of Harvard Law School and member of the team that appealed Gwendolyn Hoyt's conviction for murdering her husband in *Hoyt v. Florida* (1961), had wanted to argue that limiting women's service on juries because of their gender was analogous to limiting the service of blacks because of their race. But Dreben could not persuade her male superior that the analogy was apt and the Supreme Court never heard the argument. Murray had a better chance. She was a mature, black woman, appointed by Eleanor Roosevelt to a presidential commission in search of new ideas. She could be assured, at the very least, of a respectful audience.[40]

There remained another problem. One could still argue that gender discrimination was not within the reach of the Equal Protection Clause because the Fourteenth Amendment had been enacted to overcome racial discrimination. But a 1954 jury discrimination case, *Hernandez v. Texas,* had made it clear that the Fourteenth Amendment covered all arbitrary class determinations, not just those involving race. In *Hernandez,* a Mexican defendant had been found guilty by a jury from which Mexicans, classed as white, were barred. The question before the Court was whether a white person could be barred from jury service on account of being Mexican. The Court said no, that a group deserved constitutional protection under the Equal Protection Clause not only on grounds of race discrimination but also, more broadly, when it suffered subordination. "Differences in race and color have defined easily identifiable groups which have at times required the aid of the courts in securing equal treatment under the laws," but "community prejudices are not static, and from time to time other differences from the community norm may define other groups which need the same protection." "The Fourteenth Amendment is not directed solely against discrimination due to a 'two-class theory'—that is, based upon differences between 'white' and Negro."[41]

Primed by her work on *Mendez v. Westminster,* back in 1946, Murray zeroed in on *Hernandez* as the critical link in establishing her race-gender analogy. *Hernandez* demonstrated that "the difficulty of asserting women's rights" did not lie "in the limited reach of the Fourteenth Amendment but in the failure of the courts to isolate and analyze the discriminatory aspect of differential treatment based upon sex." Gender had served as a judicially approved basis for classification in a wide variety of cases, including jury service, wage and hour legislation, employment in certain occupations, property rights, and education. Building from *Hernandez,* the central constitutional challenge was to determine "the reasonableness of each legislative classification based upon sex within the concept of equal protection of the laws."[42]

But how was one to determine which laws were reasonable and which were not? Murray found the answer in sociology, where the theory of functionalism had gained ascendancy in the years after World War II. In reaction to the biological determinism that had characterized early work in the field, modern sociologists had come to see human attributes and needs as a product of one's place in the social order rather than one's physiological characteristics. Murray built on this approach to argue that what was "needed to remove the present ambiguity of women's legal status is a shift of emphasis from their class attributes (sex per se) to their functional attributes and to redelineate the boundaries between social policies which are genuinely protective of the family and maternal functions and those which are unjustly discriminatory against women as individuals." Drawing the line,

Murray conceded, would not be easy, but the effort must be made, for the courts had been too ready to accept "the doctrine that sex forms the basis of a reasonable classification and to ignore the fact, [as Caroline Ware had shown in her paper], that 'women vary widely, and the vast majority function in many different ways at different stages of their lives.'" Just as race as a basis for classification in the law had come to be viewed with suspicion by the Supreme Court, so too should gender.[43]

But were gender and race truly analogous? Most legal commentators had come to believe that classification by race was never acceptable, except to make up for past discrimination, but biological differences between men and women seemed to justify greater legal recognition. Murray conceded the existence of sex differences, but she believed that legislators and judges had accorded them too much significance. For example, ever since *Muller*, the Court had tended to class all women as either mothers or potential mothers. But "maternity legislation," Murray countered, "is not sex legislation." Murray, the functionalist, argued that the Courts must distinguish between sex (biology) and what people did (function). In this view, maternity benefits should be viewed like veterans' benefits. While 98 percent of veterans were men, they received benefits because of the role they played as soldiers, not because of their gender. By analogy, laws related to maternity should apply narrowly to mothers, not to women as a class. The emphasis, she stressed, should be on benefits, not restrictions. Requiring special facilities for nursing mothers should be allowed; firing women who became pregnant should not.[44]

Murray's point that maternity legislation was not sex legislation was inspired by an article by an influential member of the National Woman's Party, who had used this same argument in 1952 in support of the Equal Rights Amendment. But Murray hoped that the distinction between maternity and sex legislation would now have greater force as a combination of increased economic opportunity for women, wider access to contraception, and greater longevity meant that motherhood had become a less defining part of the lives of women as a group.[45]

What about other forms of protection aimed at women, especially hours laws? Murray believed that analysis of this question should begin with *Muller*. Although *Muller* was a "police power," not an "equal protection," case, it was central to any analysis of sex discrimination because it was with *Muller* that the Court first announced that sex was a legitimate basis for classification. *Muller* upheld the constitutionality of an Oregon maximum-hour law for women on two grounds. The first was public health, that is, the interest that the state had in protecting the health of mothers or potential mothers to ensure the "strength and vigor of the race." The second was women's relative lack of economic and political power in American society. Maximum hours laws for women helped compensate for women's unequal bargaining position. Working from that principle, wage and hour laws could be justified so long as women lacked economic and political power relative to men, which Murray believed they still did.[46]

In making this argument, Murray drew a distinction between those laws that singled a group out for unfavorable treatment and those that protected a right (e.g., to control the hours one was forced to work) that a group, because of its disadvantaged position, had been unable to assert. Because mothers continued to have responsibility for child-bearing and rearing and because they did not yet enjoy equal opportunity in the larger world, Murray believed that the intervention of government was justified to compensate them for their special services and protect them in assertion of their rights. Breaking ranks with supporters of the ERA, she went so far as to say that legislatures might reasonably classify women who had "custody of children under sixteen years of age" or, to protect future mothers, might "reasonably classify women of child-bearing age." Murray also approved of differential treatment that did not imply inferiority. Separate bathrooms for women and men, and probably separate athletic teams, would pass constitutional muster under this principle. By contrast, "a governmental policy differentiating between men and women which does not meet these criteria," Murray concluded, should be judged by the courts to be "based upon a classification of sex *per se*" and therefore "arbitrary and unreasonable within the meaning of the 14th Amendment."[47]

In focusing on the ways in which pregnant women and mothers might be protected, Murray ignored the potential risks to these women in her Fourteenth Amendment strategy. What if employers declined to hire women who had custody of small children? What if they refused to include pregnancy benefits in their insurance coverage? What if they objected to state laws that required them to offer maternity leaves? These were problems that later feminist lawyers would have to square with Murray's strategy, but first Murray had to establish that motherhood was no longer the defining characteristic of women's lives, if ever it had been. Women, like men, were a varied lot; indeed, they differed more among themselves than they differed from men. It was time to stop treating them as though they were in a class by themselves.[48]

Murray conceded that no one could know at the start how her approach would work in practice, but precisely because society was changing, "the development of standards in a case-by-case approach" provided "the flexibility which permits the evolution of a more realistic application of the Fourteenth Amendment to protect both the maternal and family functions" than an ERA could. Putting her plan into action would not be easy, she conceded. Gender prejudice remained strong, especially among men. Moreover, social scientists had yet to make a concentrated effort, analogous to that made in school desegregation cases, to bring before the courts knowledge about the capacities of women that would challenge widespread belief in female inferiority. As a result, many judges remained "blind to the real meaning of discrimination against women and to its common features with other types of discrimination." Unfortunately, law schools themselves were also a problem. "Little or no emphasis is given to women's rights in law school courses on constitutional law or civil and political rights," wrote Murray.[49]

That said, there was a basis for optimism. Murray pointed to a growing emphasis on human rights around the world, a "revival of interest in the status of women," a "gradual elimination of restrictive laws" in states across the country, and an "increasing demand for trained efficient personnel," which women with their ever higher levels of education were increasingly ready to meet. Murray also saw promising developments in the law. Judges showed a growing awareness that "discrimination solely because of sex cannot be justified under any theory of law." One especially good sign came from the Appellate Division of the New York Supreme Court, which had just ruled that the New York City Police Department had violated its own regulation in denying a policewoman the opportunity to take an exam for promotion to sergeant. In doing so, the department had imposed a construction that was "suspect." That a judge was ready to read as "suspect" a state action that discriminated on the basis of sex encouraged Murray to think that her strategy could work. That the white policewoman, Felicia Shpritzer, had been one of Murray's classmates from Hunter made the victory all the sweeter.[50]

Murray called for a thorough review of all laws relating to women, with the goal of selecting those best suited to judicial review. She thought it important to focus on those laws that were clearly discriminatory rather than those that were arguably protective or compensatory. She recommended, specifically, that litigators begin by challenging laws that discriminated against women in jury selection, education, hiring, and pay. To succeed, lawyers would have to develop constitutional arguments, along the lines she was suggesting, and collect supporting research. She anticipated the need for a "specialized body," like the legal branch of the NAACP or the ACLU, which could focus its "attention on the problems of constitutional litigation." Bringing cases was important but not enough. As long as men dominated the courts, women's concerns would not be addressed. "One of the greatest obstacles to achieving insights into the issue of discrimination against women," Murray warned in conclusion, "is that the courts which pass upon this issue are overwhelmingly male and have little understanding of the problem." Until women could take their place alongside men in political office and on the bench, real progress toward equality would be difficult. In the meantime, however, Murray offered her approach as a place to start.[51]

Reactions

Esther Peterson responded warmly to Murray's proposal. "You must know how grateful I am to you for this work," she wrote. "I feel in my bones that you are making history." But Katherine Ellickson still had reservations. Writing in February to let Murray know that her paper had been distributed to members of the commission for review, she queried, "Is it practical to have protective labor laws apply only to certain groups of women, such as mothers of young children? Could the employer be expected to distinguish himself and how would a poorly staffed State agency administer such a law?"[52]

Some of the constitutional experts who reviewed Murray's proposal had further doubts. Dean Erwin Griswold of Harvard Law School wrote Murray, "Somehow or other, it has always seemed to me that there are differences in sex and that these differences may, in appropriate cases, be the basis of classification

Figure 11.2 Pauli Murray and Esther Peterson, 1962. Estate of Pauli Murray, Schlesinger Library, Radcliffe Institute, Harvard University.

for legal purposes. Generally speaking, I dislike carrying any argument to extremes, and your proposal does seem to me at times to carry a good thing, perhaps a little bit too far." Griswold's colleague Paul Freund agreed. He supported the idea of litigation but warned that the "comparison with desegregation litigation, or course, cannot be pressed too far. The issues here are more subtle and complex. For example, it is easier to attack the separate but equal doctrine all along the line in the case of racial discrimination in the public schools than it would be in the case of separation of the sexes; an obvious illustration would be the composition of athletic teams."[53]

Even some of Murray's friends among the small band of female law students at Yale had reservations about Murray's approach. Barbara Babcock took particular exception to the idea that pressure should be exerted to win women seats on the bench. She did not like the implication that female judges would naturally "come through for their own kind." Murray's depiction of gendered favoritism was, in Babcock's view, "not a flattering and I hope not a realistic view."[54]

Knowing that Murray's proposal was controversial, the PCSW staff invited representatives from fifteen women's organizations, including the NWP, to the March 1963 meeting of the Committee on Civil and Political Rights to discuss it. The reaction was not encouraging. The American Association of University Women still preferred a state-by-state legislative effort. The representative of the American Nurses Association reasserted its opposition to the ERA, but did not feel qualified to evaluate Murray's proposal. Mrs. Samuel Brown of the National Council of Jewish Women repeated her organization's opposition to the ERA but also warned against Murray's approach as "time-consuming, costly, and laborious without any assurance that the results will be entirely satisfactory." Brown found two particular faults. She objected to the equation of sex with race, which was always bad, and differential treatment based on sex, which was sometimes desirable. Moreover, she saw no reason to believe that women's organizations, which had never been able to agree on what constituted discrimination, would now be able to unite on a definition.[55]

Those who supported the Equal Rights Amendment were no more willing to endorse Murray's alternative approach. Representatives from the American Medical Women's Association, the Business and Professional Women, and the National Association of Women Lawyers all pointed out that the Supreme Court had been given the chance to adopt the Equal Protection argument and had not done so. Members of the National Woman's Party went further. Publicly, Miriam Y. Holden, one of the founding members of the NWP, characterized the Fourteenth Amendment strategy as "wishful thinking." Privately, she questioned Murray's motives. In a letter to fellow NWP member Anita Pollitzer, Holden worried about Murray's ties to the civil rights movement and her "preoccupation" with the "Negro problem." Murray's "primary purpose," she observed, in a marked misreading of current political conditions, "seems to be an attempt to hitch that wagon to our Equal Rights Amendment star."[56]

The only group to support Murray's Fourteenth Amendment strategy was the National Council of Catholic Women, but the council did not seem to understand what Murray was proposing. While championing women's progress in employment and politics, the council cautioned, "It must be remembered that the most important function of woman will always be associated with home and family." At the end of the day, the various women's organizations remained stuck where they had been at the beginning.[57]

As the members of the Committee on Civil and Political Rights listened to the various viewpoints being expressed at their March meeting, however, they came to conclude that Murray's Fourteenth Amendment approach offered the best chance to guarantee women the protection of both the Constitution and state labor statutes. Committee members believed that the courts would uphold laws that required husbands to support their families, which the ERA would presumably not allow, and, at the same time, would strike down discriminatory laws, such as those that banned women from juries in Alabama, Mississippi, and South Carolina. More than any other member, Frank Sanders proved critical to the shifting view on the committee. Despite his initial hostility to Murray's ideas, the more he considered the comparative merits of her litigation strategy and a constitutional amendment, the more he came to believe that Murray's case-by-case approach was the better choice.[58]

In addition to the growing support of her colleagues on the Committee on Civil and Political Rights, Murray won a ringing endorsement from Dorothy Kenyon and the American Civil Liberties Union. As John de J. Pemberton, executive director of the ACLU, wrote to Esther Peterson, "It is Judge Kenyon's view, in which our office concurs, that the Murray memorandum is an excellent piece of work which does offer additional insights into how the equal rights for women problem can be resolved through litigation brought under the Fourteenth Amendment. We believe that litigation action should be pursued rather than the old Equal Rights Amendment which has been before the Congress for a number of years." The ACLU had relied on the Equal Protection Clause itself in its effort to strike down laws that discriminated against women as prospective jurors, but it had not yet developed the race-sex analogy that Murray proposed. Kenyon believed that Murray's ideas offered a genuinely new and helpful approach. Shortly thereafter, Dorothy Kenyon wrote directly to Murray, offering congratulations on her Fourteenth Amendment memorandum and holding out the hope that with Felix Frankfurter newly retired from the Court and with Arthur Goldberg and Byron White newly appointed, women would fare better.[59]

There remained the problem of what to say about the Equal Rights Amendment. After much discussion, a subcommittee including Sanders, Murray, and Rawalt hammered out a compromise, which they persuaded the commission to adopt. The PCSW would "not take a position in favor of the equal rights amendment at this time."[60]

Not everyone rejoiced in the committee's compromise. Most members of the NWP continued to hold out hope for the ERA. Labor leaders, for their part, remained nervous that Murray's approach, in the wrong hands, would scuttle wage and hour laws. Some religious leaders feared that Murray had laid out a plan that would destroy the family. The majority of the commissioners concluded, however, that determining the reasonableness of sex as a basis of legal classification, one case at a time, offered the best way to win equal rights for women. Within the Committee on Civil and Political Rights, Murray had solidified friendships with both Mary Eastwood and Marguerite Rawalt. Murray had done it. She had charted a new course to equality for women.[61]

The Consultation on Negro Women

For all her talk of Jim Crow and Jane Crow as analogous systems of oppression, Murray well understood the limitations for black women of the parallel she drew. When most people talked about "sex" they meant white women, and when they talked about "race" they meant black men. Black women figured in public discourse not as a group doubly oppressed, but as a problem. Just at the moment when male psychologists and sociologists were beginning to reconsider their post–World War II tendency to blame white mothers for their children's problems, a growing chorus of complaints against black women as "matriarchs" began to appear. Black mothers, the social scientists contended, dominated their families and emasculated their sons. Following the submission of her report on the Fourteenth Amendment to Peterson, Murray turned, with mounting concern, to what she saw as a crisis that escaped nearly everyone's attention. As a stereotype, black women were being demonized. As real people, they were ignored.[62]

Esther Peterson had sought from the start to ensure that race would be part of the PCSW's deliberations about women's status. She named black women to key positions and made attention to race part of every committee's discussions. But as the civil rights movement called increasing attention to the inequality blacks faced in America, Peterson began to think that her strategy did not go far enough. PCSW commissioner Dorothy Height agreed. In a memo drafted in February 1963, Height urged that special attention be given to the "double jeopardy" that black women faced due to the combination of race and sex discrimination. Hurriedly, Peterson arranged a "consultation" to investigate the problems of women in minority groups. Although Mexican American and Indian women were included as topics, the focus was on the special problems faced by African American women. Peterson named Height to head the consultation and to write its report, the final title of which was simply "Problems of Negro Women."[63]

As the longtime president of the National Council of Negro Women (NCNW), a 3 million member umbrella group for the country's black women's organizations, Height exercised enormous influence. Born in Richmond, Virginia, in 1912, she had grown up in Pennsylvania, attended New York University, and trained in social work at Columbia. In 1937, as assistant director of the Harlem YWCA, she was assisting Eleanor Roosevelt at a meeting of the National Council of Negro Women when NCNW president Mary McLeod Bethune spotted her. Twenty years later Height assumed the presidency of the organization herself. No one was better positioned to lead a conversation about the compounding handicaps of race and gender discrimination.[64]

Height and Peterson invited eleven African American leaders, seven women and four men, to join the consultation. The consultants included social workers, academics, and journalists as well as representatives from government and civil rights organizations. Esther Peterson, Dollie Lowther Robinson, and three other PCSW staff members also attended, as did several representatives from the Department of Health, Education, and Welfare, including Grace Hewell. Commissioner Caroline Ware represented the commission. Murray did not participate, but she took a special interest in the consultation's work.[65]

To help the consultants prepare, Katherine Ellickson drafted a memo, which identified the particular challenges faced by black women and how recommendations already agreed to by the commissioners would help them. In the introduction to the memo, Ellickson stressed, "Negro women carry a very special load." In the face of job discrimination, "which has consigned their husbands to low status and low paid jobs, and of social discrimination which undermines self esteem and ambition, they have had to sustain the morale of their families and give their children security and purpose." In addition, to "compensate for the low and uncertain income of their husbands . . . they have often had no choice but to go to work." In all groups, women outnumbered men, but in none was that disparity greater than among blacks, a fact that guaranteed that black women, even under the best of circumstances, would more often have to support themselves, as well as children and aging relatives, on their own. Moreover, they would have to do so with only 63 percent of the wages that employed black men then earned. The commission's recommendations for specific action for all women, therefore, had special meaning for black women: equal opportunity in federal employment and government contracts, improvements in widow's benefits and unemployment insurance, the expansion of protective labor laws to cover jobs (such as domestic work and service industries) in which black women were concentrated, expanded child care services, better education, and access to apprenticeship programs.[66]

Circulated among staff members and others in related governmental departments, Ellickson's paper provoked a sharp attack from Daniel Patrick Moynihan, the thirty-six-year-old liaison between the Department of Labor and the PCSW. Moynihan scoffed at Ellickson's account of the special problems of black women, as well as the commission's suggested solutions. "I just don't believe anyone is interested in, listens to, or is in any way impressed by the standard liberal sentiment which we insist on pouring over our offerings like chocolate fudge over an ice cream sundae," he wrote. Discrimination and poverty were not the problem. The structure of the black family was to blame. "To my limited understanding," he argued, "and I could be quite wrong—Negro society in America is still substantially a matriarchy. This has enormous consequences to the lives of Negroes and may in fact be one of the principal keys to understanding and resolving the Negro problem." For Ellickson, the purpose of the consultation was to discuss how race discrimination compounded the problem of sex discrimination for black women. For Moynihan, the purpose should be to focus on the danger posed to the African American community by the black matriarch. In his view, black mothers dominated their families, drove away their husbands, and prevented their sons from reaching independent manhood. Juvenile delinquency, unemployment, and poverty were the inevitable result.[67]

Moynihan had grown up in a poverty-stricken, fatherless home in New York. From the age of ten he had worked as a shoeshine boy in Times Square. He attended the public schools of New York, enlisted in the US Navy, earned college and graduate degrees at Tufts on the GI Bill, entered politics, supported fellow Irishman John F. Kennedy, and won an appointment to the Department of Labor in 1961, just as Esther Peterson was taking over the Women's Bureau. In the spring of 1963 he rose to the position of assistant secretary of labor for policy and research. His March 1963 letter to Peterson, insisting that due attention be given to the problem of "matriarchy," was his first foray into policymaking. Moynihan owed much of his understanding of family structure to sociologist Nathan Glazer, with whom he had just published *Beyond the Melting Pot* (1963). Glazer had come to see the black family as a victim of slavery. Forbidden to marry, psychologically damaged, blacks had developed a matriarchal family structure that made success in the modern world impossible.[68]

Ellickson's memo and Moynihan's response highlighted the differences among those concerned with the problems faced by minority women in the United States in the 1960s. The makeup of the group that gathered in Washington on April 19, 1963, reflected those differences, although no member was as extreme as Moynihan (who did not attend) in his belief that the black community was essentially a matriarchy that undermined racial progress. In fact, the subject of "matriarchy" came up only briefly. Cernoria Johnson of the Urban League called attention to "the implications of the matriarchal family." In her view, the goal of the commission should be to shore up the "acceptable average family," one in which "there is a father and mother in the home." Deborah P. Wolfe, from the Committee on Education and Labor of the House of Representatives, urged that the effect of fatherless households on the development of children's sense of masculinity and femininity be examined. Ruth Whaley of the New York City Board of Education thought that the chief problem blacks faced was the "lack of [an] open road for the male." But all told, only 5 percent of the day's discussion centered on "matriarchy" as a problem. The rest dealt with concrete ways to help black women shoulder their family responsibilities.[69]

Dollie Lowther Robinson, speaking for the PCSW staff, argued that the main problem that black women faced was the lack of educational and employment opportunity. Caroline Ware noted that many apprenticeship programs discriminated not only on the basis of race but also gender. Dr. Grace Hewell, liaison to the PCSW from the Department of Health, Education and Welfare (HEW), spoke forcefully on behalf of single black mothers. In the years since World War II, welfare specialists had abandoned the model of the family in which a father worked for wages and a mother stayed home to care for the children. Their reasons were practical: more than 90 percent of their clients (the majority of them white) were either unmarried or divorced single mothers. Welfare specialists had therefore come to view the single-mother household as a valid, if imperfect, mode of family life. To help these families, these specialists believed that Aid to Families with Dependent Children (AFDC) must provide income support, social and psychological services, work experience, and better jobs.[70]

Four days later, the commissioners of the PCSW met to hear reports of the various consulting groups. Unable to attend, Height asked Caroline Ware to report on the meeting of the Consultation on Minority Women. Speaking off the cuff, Ware began by noting that black women faced "congeries of problems," which "stem basically from the lack of opportunity of Negro men." Because "men can't find decent jobs and can't make decent wages," she explained, "the women are forced into the labor market," where the combination of race and gender discrimination forced them into jobs overwhelmingly at the bottom of the economic ladder. There they worked for longer hours than any other group, without legal protection. Long hours at low pay made it more difficult for them than for more privileged women to care for their families and participate in their communities. To those who objected that black women's problems were no different from those of whites, Ware responded that black women "can't take all the same things for granted" that white women can. "Many of the things that they can't take for granted," Ware stressed, "are not minor." For all the discrimination that white women faced, they enjoyed educational and job opportunities, protective labor laws, and a level of economic and moral support from male relatives of which black women could only dream.[71]

But in the end, Ware's call for special attention to the problems of black women came to nothing, for Dorothy Height wrote the consultation's final, published report. In Height's telling, the danger of "matriarchy" took center stage. Allowing that the problems faced by black women were complex, Height nonetheless concluded, "If the negro woman has a major concern it is the negro man and his status in the whole community and his responsibility and feeling himself a strong person making his contribution in the whole society, in order that he may make it in the home." Gone from the final report were Ellickson's income figures, which showed that the median income for black women was 63 percent of that for black men. Instead, the report declared that "the Negro wife . . . often earns more than her husband." Gone was Ware's argument that black women could not take for granted the advantages enjoyed by white women. Instead, Height emphasized black women's power, contending that Negro families tended to be "matriarchal," a condition that resulted in "insecurity" for black men and created "problems to Negro children, both boys and girls, in developing their masculine or feminine roles."[72]

Height's framing of the discussion constituted a huge missed opportunity. She could have highlighted the ways in which race discrimination compounded gender discrimination, driving black women to the very bottom of the economic ladder, below white men, black men, and white women. She could have provided a blueprint for federal intervention: to improve educational programs and job opportunities for those who needed them most. Instead, Height's summary of the consultation's work gave Moynihan license to press forward with his idea that the problem of blacks was rooted in the matriarchal structure of the black family and its damaging psychological effects on black men and children.[73]

Murray was dismayed. Peterson had handed the Consultation on Minority Women a rare chance to highlight the double discrimination faced by African American women, and Height had squandered it. Just when Betty Friedan's newly published *Feminine Mystique* condemned social scientists for their role in the oppression of white mothers, Height blamed black mothers for the ills of black America. At the very moment that Friedan called on white mothers to leave the "comfortable concentration camp" of the suburban home for the world of paid labor, Height blamed black women's labor force participation for undermining black men's self-esteem. Murray felt that she had succeeded against tremendous odds in her own work at the PCSW. She had taken a significant step toward making sex suspect, but given Height's report, it looked as though sex would be suspect for white women only—unless Murray took corrective action.[74]

12

Invisible Woman

The March on Washington . . .

As Murray wound up her work for the President's Commission on the Status of Women in the summer of 1963, a series of events shook her faith in the civil rights movement as a friend to black women. Shortly before the March on Washington in August 1963, she learned that A. Philip Randolph, the inspiration behind the march, had accepted an invitation to speak at the all-male National Press Club. The club excluded women from membership; worse, it decreed that women could attend events only by sitting in the balcony. Black and white newswomen asked Randolph to cancel his speech. He declined to do so. When Murray read in the *Washington Post* of Randolph's decision, she fired off a letter to the editor. Randolph failed to understand, she charged, that it was just as "humiliating for a woman reporter assigned to cover Mr. Randolph's speech to be sent to the balcony as it would be for Mr. Randolph to be sent to the back of the bus."[1]

Not willing to let her feelings of betrayal rest with a letter, Murray persuaded Maida Springer to make her Washington apartment available to protesters who wanted to discuss how to respond. Springer, still working at the AFL-CIO International Affairs Department, was preoccupied with hosting a Guinean delegation, which she planned to take to the march. Returning home at the end of the day, she found that Murray "had set up shop in the foyer and living room of my apartment as a combination of secretariat and public relations office." The two friends greeted one another, and Murray briefed Springer on plans to picket Randolph if he spoke at the Press Club. "After a passionate exhortation about this unwise decision by our great man Randolph," Springer later recalled, "She asked me, 'You will join us, if it comes to that, won't you?' " "No," Springer replied, "I will not join you in a picket line to picket A. Philip Randolph a week before the March on Washington." Murray, angered by Springer's privileging of race over gender, retorted that she had finally found Springer's "Achilles heel." When Springer next returned home, she found that her friend had cleared out of her apartment. A long time would pass before these allies could speak to one another again.[2]

Murray's outrage over Randolph's insensitivity to gender discrimination at the National Press Club compounded another slight. Her longtime friend Bayard Rustin, Randolph's lieutenant and the executive director of the March on Washington, had all but shut women out of the day's events. Despite women's leading roles in the civil rights movement, no woman would be marching alongside A. Philip Randolph, Martin Luther King Jr., Roy Wilkins, or any of the other "Big Ten" male leaders. Nor would any woman be meeting with President Kennedy to press the case for economic justice and civil rights. Most distressing of all, no woman would be giving a speech that day. Not Dorothy Height, head of the National Council of Negro Women and a recognized orator. Not Ella Baker, national field secretary for the NAACP. Not Rosa Parks, who had inspired the Montgomery Bus Boycott. Not Diane Nash, fiery young leader of the Student Nonviolent Coordinating Committee (SNCC). Not Fannie Lou Hamer, the fearless voting organizer, who had faced down violence in Mississippi. Not Myrlie Evers, who had spoken movingly to the press following the assassination of her husband in Mississippi just a few weeks before. Not even Anna Arnold Hedgeman, the sole female member of the march's organizing committee, the first to protest the exclusion of women from the day's events and the one who had spread the word of women's exclusion to others.[3]

The day before the March, Murray protested to the male leadership. "In 1963," she declared, "no civil rights campaign can be permanently successful which does not stand foursquare for *all* human rights." She felt especially aggrieved that black women "have had to bear the dual burden of 'Jim Crow' and 'Jane Crow'" only to "find that the 'second class equality' they have shared with Negro men is dissolving and they are being frozen out of the positions of leadership in the struggle which they have earned by their courage, intelligence, militance, dedication, and ability."[4]

"Even on the morning of the march there had been appeals to include a woman speaker," recalled Dorothy Height, one of those Hedgeman contacted. "But Bayard Rustin refused, insisting that women were part of all groups—the churches, the synagogues, labor—represented on the podium." In a last-minute compromise, a few women leaders were included among those to be seated on the platform, and Randolph agreed to pay tribute to them in his own remarks. None of them, however, would be allowed to give a speech. "That moment was vital to awakening the women's movement," Height remembered.[5]

It was also the first step in the feminist awakening of Dorothy Height. "Mr. Rustin's stance showed us that men honestly didn't see their position as patriarchal or patronizing. They were happy to include women in the human family, but there was no question as to who headed the household!" For many years, Height had been one of the few women among the leaders of major civil rights organizations. She had always felt that she was treated as a peer until

Murray and Hedgeman made her recognize her second-class status. Even the last-minute concession made by the male leaders that Height be allowed to join them in their visit to the White House ended by reinforcing this fact. In news accounts of the day, the men's names and affiliations were all included. Height was not mentioned. For Murray, the accumulated slights surrounding the march drove home a lesson: human rights, rather than civil rights, which under pressure had devolved into rights for black men only, must be her focus. Otherwise, the black woman would always be invisible.[6]

. . . For Jobs and Freedom

The idea for the march had grown out of a meeting between Randolph and Rustin the prior December. As the two men reviewed the state of race relations in America, they worried over the deteriorating economic situation for blacks, especially black males. The postwar promise of economic opportunity in the expanding industrial sector had soured amid continuing discrimination by labor unions and the steady advance of automation. Black women could still find jobs as domestic servants and in the expanding service sector, but black men, more likely to work in unionized, heavy industry, experienced rising rates of unemployment. A generation before, black male unemployment roughly equaled that of whites; by the early 1960s, black men were twice as likely as whites to be out of work. With the centennial of the Emancipation Proclamation at hand, Randolph and Rustin decided it was time to revive the idea of a March on Washington, threatened in 1940 and then abandoned when FDR agreed to establish the Fair Employment Practices Committee in 1941. They called for a March on Washington for Jobs.[7]

At first, planning proved difficult. Interest in civil rights was waning with the end of the sit-ins and freedom rides of the early 1960s. Hoping to rekindle the movement, Martin Luther King Jr. moved the organizing efforts of the Southern Christian Leadership Conference to Birmingham. Known widely as the toughest town in the South, Birmingham was famous for its brutally racist police chief, Bull Connor, the same man who had enforced segregated seating at the first meeting of the Southern Conference for Human Welfare in 1938. Demonstrations against Birmingham's segregated businesses began in early April, during Easter Week. At first, Connor kept officers under tight control, and protesters lost steam after three weeks of nightly mass meetings followed by orderly arrests the following day. Then, in early May, hundreds of students, some as young as six, joined the protests at the end of each school day. At first Connor simply arrested them. But when the jails were full he told the police to disperse those who came after. Police dogs tore into the marchers and high-powered hoses knocked them down. News photographers captured the scene, and, suddenly, the eyes of the world were on the city.[8]

The violence in Birmingham ignited "brushfires of rebellion," Murray observed, in cities across the country. It also spurred her to rethink her dissertation. She had returned from Africa intending to write her doctoral thesis on comparative constitutionalism in Africa, but with civil wars, autocratic government, and assassinations wreaking havoc in one country after another, her proposed topic began to seem "premature." Meanwhile, she realized that she was in the midst of an American revolution that cried out for analysis. "From May to August, 1963, at the height of the national protest," Murray noted, by way of explaining her shifting interests to her adviser, Fowler Harper, "the United States Attorney General's Office counted at least 1,412 demonstrations which had occurred in 283 cities throughout 36 states and the District of Columbia." Murray wanted to explore the roots of these events and to assess their policy implications.[9]

She agreed with Randolph and Rustin, as she had since the 1930s, that the racial problems in America required the "restructuring of American economic life to eliminate the general threat of economic displacement and consequent deprivations." In her mind, the civil rights battle was first and foremost an economic struggle. But she differed from the male leaders on women's place in that battle. Murray believed women should occupy center stage. Women might find work more easily than men, but that work paid far less and demanded longer hours than the work available to men. Any restructuring of the American economy, she believed, had to put the needs of black women alongside those of men. Women were raising the next generation, increasingly alone. To ignore them was to invite, in James Baldwin's words, "the fire next time."[10]

The violence against blacks in Birmingham made organizing the March on Washington easier, but at a cost, especially for women. What Rustin and Randolph had envisioned as a March for Jobs became, with the expanding coalition of civil rights leaders a March on Washington for Jobs and Freedom. Rustin quickly recruited the "Big Six" male leaders of civil rights organizations. Before he was done, the "Big Six" had mushroomed to a "Big Ten," with additions from interracial religious and labor groups. As the coalition of leaders grew, the emphasis on economic justice, "Jobs," shifted to a call for "Freedom." The change disappointed Randolph and Rustin; it dismayed Murray. However, success required a goal on which the largest number of black and white male leaders could agree.[11]

Predictably, the intense organizing efforts provoked a backlash from conservatives. Convinced that civil rights activity succeeded only where Communists held sway, FBI director J. Edgar Hoover tried to discredit Bayard Rustin and the march by feeding incriminating material to Senator Strom Thurmond of South

Carolina. Whereas Thurmond would generally have been content to issue warnings of the left-wing threat posed by civil rights organizing, he upped the ante by
naming Rustin a sexual pervert in the *Congressional Record.* Thurmond's public
humiliation of Rustin must have sent a bolt of fear through Murray, who lived
in constant dread of exposure. What would Randolph do? He had no choice.
With the future of the march at risk, he came immediately to Rustin's defense,
declaring his "complete confidence" in Rustin and dismay that Thurmond would
"mutilate most elementary conceptions of human decency, privacy and humility
in order to persecute other men." Randolph's steadfast support of Rustin rallied
the other male leaders to the cause and guaranteed the march's ultimate success,
but the anger many black women felt toward the patronizing treatment they had
received in an event billed as a march for jobs and freedom would grow. Murray,
for one, promised to see to that.[12]

In the meantime, Murray refused to let her anger at the male leaders prevent
her from joining the quarter million people who descended on the Washington
Monument on the morning of August 28. As the gathering crowd headed
toward the Lincoln Memorial, where platforms stood ready for the concerts and
speeches later that afternoon, Murray felt herself swept along by the waves of
marchers, two thirds of them black. She marched twice, first under the banner
of the Washington chapter of the American Civil Liberties Union with her niece
Bonnie Fearing Alexis (Mildred's daughter) and old friend Pat Harris, who had
been one of the Howard undergraduates she had mentored in her time at law
school. The three women made plans to have lunch downtown in a few days to
celebrate the twentieth anniversary of the first restaurant sit-ins, and the tenth
anniversary of their effort's eventual success in court-ordered desegregation.
When they reached the Lincoln Memorial, just behind the march's male leaders, Pauli and Bonnie reversed course and walked back toward the Washington
Monument, "to witness the miracle of the oncoming multitudes," as Murray
later recalled. When Murray caught sight of Renee Barlow and their friends from
St. Mark's Church in New York, she and Bonnie fell in line again for a second
march to the Lincoln Memorial. The sense of interracial solidarity imparted by
the crowd lifted Murray's spirits, despite her dismay at women's marginalization,
evident even in the otherwise uplifting words of Martin Luther King Jr. His "I
Have a Dream" speech addressed America's failure to keep its promise of equal
rights to "black men." He said nothing about black women.[13]

"The Negro Woman in the Quest for Equality"

The day following the historic event, August 29, Murray joined Height and other
key women at the offices of the National Council of Negro Women (NCNW)

to review the events of the prior week. Murray was so upset about the multiple injustices done to women that she insisted the time had come to take a strong stand against the way men were treating women in the civil rights movement. In response, Height invited her to give the keynote address at the upcoming convention of the NCNW.[14]

In a session devoted to the theme of "Leadership," Murray shared the platform with two other black women, HEW representative Grace Hewell and New York University Professor of Education Jeanne Noble, before an audience of 300 leaders of black women's organizations. They spoke with one voice. Hewell attacked the idea that matriarchy lay behind black poverty and called for social services, training, and jobs for single, black mothers to guarantee their own economic independence and security for their children. Noble dismissed the idea that marginalizing women would elevate the status of men: "A male doesn't become adequate by making a female feel inadequate," she quipped. Noble stressed, instead, the central role of college-educated women to the creation of a more democratic family structure and to the welfare of the black community. Murray incorporated these themes in her own challenge to the idea that black America was essentially a matriarchy and that the remedy for black poverty in America was the marginalization of black women in the home, the workplace, and the civil rights movement.[15]

Negro women, Murray began, had historically borne a double burden of Jim Crow and Jane Crow. That burden meant "not only have they stood shoulder to shoulder with Negro men in every phase of the battle, but they have also continued to stand when their men were destroyed by it." In the course of their struggles, Murray continued, Negro women had fought against two stereotypes: the first of "female dominance," now generally referred to as "matriarchy"; the second of "loose morals." These stereotypes grew out of leadership roles forced on black women by slavery and sustained through Jim Crow, but neither captured the reality of black women's lives. What critics took to be female dominance in family life was simply the self-sufficiency created by the need to earn a living. Negro women were triply handicapped in this effort. They were concentrated in nonunion employment, discriminated against on the basis of both race and gender, and denied an equal education. No wonder the government's annual earnings reports listed white men first, black men second, white women third, and black women in distant fourth place.[16]

Why were black women so often alone in this struggle for survival? Not from any inherent propensity to dominate their husbands and sons, Murray insisted, but, in part, because black women greatly outnumbered black men in all age groups. Just as successive wars had left generations of European women without the possibility of marrying, so too had generations of racial violence in the United States, together with conditions that led to poor health, lowered the number of males relative to females in the black community. The fact that inter-racial marriage remained taboo, if not actually illegal, in the United States meant that black women could not overcome these adverse statistics by marrying out-side their race. "The point I am trying to make here," Murray declared, "is that the Negro woman cannot assume with any degree of confidence that she will be able to look to marriage for either economic or emotional support. She must prepare to be self-supporting and to support others, perhaps, for a considerable period or for life."[17]

The barriers black women faced in seeking self-support included woefully inadequate educational opportunities, which in turn, Murray contended, helped explain the rise of illegitimacy in the black community. Black women were sim-ply not as informed about contraception or the availability of abortion as were white women. Moreover, because black female relatives were generally willing to help care for any child who was born and because they looked with disfavor on adoption, the stigma attached to illegitimacy was much more limited among African Americans than it was among European Americans. Black women were no more immoral than white women; they were simply more likely to become pregnant and to keep the children who resulted from their sexual relations.[18]

Looking to black men for help in challenging the stereotypes of "female dom-inance" and "immorality" seemed fruitless at the moment. Even women's most valued friends among the male leaders were proving to be unreliable supporters. Sustaining an alliance with black men had proved difficult, Murray lamented, because black men, in their struggle to wrestle "the initiative of the civil rights movement from white liberals" and thereby demonstrate their manhood, had developed a new "aggressiveness" toward everyone, black women included. The news media compounded the insult when they "selected Negro men almost exclusively to articulate the aspiration of the Negro community."[19]

Why could not black women unite with white women in the fight against sex discrimination? Segregation had kept them from forming an alliance. And yet, white women were beginning to hold out a hand to black women. Murray urged her black sisters to take that hand, even as she recognized the difficulty many found in doing so. Throughout history, whites had proven to be fair-weather friends. It was hard to trust them. Still, something had to be done, and quickly. "The Negro woman," Murray announced, "can no longer postpone or subordi-nate the fight against discrimination because of sex to the civil rights struggle but must carry on both fights simultaneously." She refused to believe that black women must be subordinated to black men as the price of racial advance and closed with a quotation from playwright Lorraine Hansberry: "For above all, in behalf of an ailing world which sorely needs our defiance, may we, as Negroes or women, never accept the notion of 'our place.' "[20]

Murray, Hewell, and Noble may not have persuaded everyone at the conference that matriarchy was a myth, but they did prepare this audience of the largest black women's organization in the country to approach the idea of matriarchy with a more critical eye. A measure of their success was manifested at a program that followed the concluding banquet of the conference. Some of the country's leading male civil rights leaders, A. Philip Randolph among them, distributed awards to twenty-five women.[21]

It was a start, but one undertaken in the face of heavy headwinds. The male civil rights leaders to whom Murray gave copies of her speech continued either to see women as a threat to racial equality and family stability or to deny the seriousness of any discrimination that might exist. Whitney Young, the executive director of the National Urban League (NUL), held to his organization's previously stated position: "For the purposes of improving the stability of our Negro family life . . . I would think that Negro women leaders . . . should make their primary goal the lifting of the social, economic, and educational status of their men." Murray's old friend James Farmer agreed that Murray's charge of discrimination was "essentially correct," but he doubted "that discrimination against women is a matter of design in any but a few cases."[22]

As 1963 drew to a close, Murray felt deeply discouraged. Even her major success of the year—persuading the PCSW to endorse her Fourteenth Amendment strategy—had yet to produce any concrete action. Barnard Professor of Government Phoebe Morrison had warned her not to expect a quick success in court. The reason was simple. "There is no pressure group like NAACP to press litigation," Morrison reminded her. "Or rather . . . there are several women's groups which might—and there is no agreement among them—so that there is lacking the solid front which NAACP managed to present."[23]

Morrison was right. The PCSW, controlled as it was by the Women's Bureau had given a false sense of unity with its report. The National Woman's Party (NWP), largely excluded from the commission, remained bitterly opposed to Murray's approach, which it viewed as an inferior and needlessly complicated alternative to the ERA. Even those sympathetic to the commission's findings had doubts. Many members of the women's labor movement, for instance, feared that the Fourteenth Amendment, in the wrong hands, might prove as dangerous as the ERA to protective labor laws. Moreover, despite Murray's best efforts, some black women leaders continued to believe that black men deserved to be the focus of economic reform efforts. Somehow, Murray would have to persuade the remaining dissenters in all camps that her Fourteenth Amendment strategy's pick-and-choose method would advance the interests of everyone: black and white, women and men, rich and poor. While Murray worked on her doctoral thesis, she devoted every spare moment to that campaign of persuasion.

Adding "Sex" to Title VII

Murray faced not just divided women's and civil rights movements but also a problem inherent in the Fourteenth Amendment. The Equal Protection Clause covered only state action, that is, discriminatory laws and official behavior that stemmed from state laws. Far more pressing to most women were the barriers they faced in private employment. Murray had experienced private job discrimination all her life, though she could rarely be sure whether race or gender played a larger role in holding her back. She had suggested possible legal remedies for both as far back as 1945 in correspondence with Ware and in her *California Law Review* article on employment law. That article focused on ways to combat race discrimination in hiring, but Murray suggested parallel action against gender discrimination at every opportunity.[24]

Thacher Clarke, Murray's young friend from Paul, Weiss, homed in on the problem of private employment discrimination when Murray sought her comment on Murray's Fourteenth Amendment proposal. Thacher was by then married to the Reverend John Anderson, whom she had met in 1959 at the founding conference of the Episcopal Society for Cultural and Racial Unity (ESCRU), an organization aimed at ending race discrimination in the church. By 1962, Thacher was a mother on unpaid leave from a job she had taken at the New York State Division of Human Rights. She agreed with Murray's arguments in her Fourteenth Amendment memorandum, but her work at the Division of Human Rights persuaded her that the bigger problem was private employers. New York, along with more than a score of northern and western states, had passed a Fair Employment Practice law in the years since World War II. As of 1964, however, the state still allowed discrimination in employment on the basis of gender; indeed, only two states—Wisconsin and Hawaii—barred private businesses from discriminating against women. Anderson urged Murray to broaden her equal rights efforts to encompass sex discrimination in the private sector.[25]

Alice Paul, head of the National Woman's Party, agreed. Although Paul continued to believe that women needed an Equal Rights Amendment above all else, she turned her attention to the civil rights bill pending in Congress, when the PCSW declared in its final report on October 11, 1963, that the ERA "need not now be sought." If the ERA remained out of reach, Paul reasoned, then the NWP might at the very least seek equal rights to jobs in the private sector. As initially drafted, the civil rights bill proposed only to protect voting rights and to end racial segregation in public accommodations. Under pressure from civil rights organizations, however, Brooklyn Democratic Representative Emanuel Celler, chairman of the House Judiciary Committee (which was holding hearings on the bill), added Title VII to grant equal access to private employment without regard to national origin, religion, race, or color. Paul vowed to add "sex" to that list, and on December 16, 1963, the NWP unanimously adopted a resolution to do so. In language notable for its implicit racism, anti-Semitism, and xenophobia, the resolution condemned the civil rights bill in its current form, on the grounds that it would not "give protection against discrimination because of 'race, color, religion, or national origins' to a *White Woman*, a *Woman of the Christian Religion,* or a *Woman of United States Origin.*" To remedy this lapse, Paul turned to a long-time NWP ally: Democratic Representative Howard Smith of Virginia, chairman of the House Rules Committee, the final committee through which bills passed before being considered by the full House.[26]

The NWP had been cultivating Smith for years. Virginia, like many other southern states, had persuaded the textile industry to move south by offering cheap female workers who toiled long hours in sweatshop conditions. Recently passed protective labor laws for women endangered the mills' profit margins. When NWP members visited Smith and his southern colleagues, they never failed to stress that the ERA would invalidate laws that limited the hours that employers could require women to work. By 1945, the NWP had persuaded Smith to be a congressional sponsor of the amendment. Not that the Virginia Democrat ever became a feminist; he proved, at best, a chivalrous opportunist. In 1950, he defeated a Fair Employment Practice bill by adding "sex" to it. In 1956, he approved the addition of "sex discrimination" in the jurisdiction of a proposed Civil Rights Commission, with the statement, "if this iniquitous piece of legislation is to be adopted, we certainly ought to try to do whatever good with it that we can." The bill failed.[27]

With this history in mind, Paul urged Nina Horton Avery, chairman of the Virginia Committee of the National Woman's Party and an ardent foe of the civil rights bill, to urge Smith to add "sex" to Title VII. Avery obliged. Smith responded that nothing could be done while the bill was before the Rules Committee, but on January 9, during Rules Committee hearings, Smith did ask Emanuel Celler why sex had not been included in the bill from the beginning. Celler asked, "Do you want to put it in, Mr. Chairman?" To which Smith replied, "I think I will offer an amendment. The National Women's [*sic*] Party [is] serious about it." Shortly thereafter, a coalition of northern Democrats and liberal Republicans forced the bill out of the Rules Committee and Smith took action. On February 8, 1964, he rose on the floor of the House to amend the Civil Rights Act to include "sex" as a prohibited ground of discrimination under Title VII.[28]

Many later commentators described Smith's action as a last-ditch, surprise move, played for laughs and aimed not at advancing the interests of women but rather at defeating the bill. It is true that Smith sparked laughter from his male colleagues, when, in addition to deploring the discrimination that all women faced in the workplace, he read from a letter he had recently received from a woman who had heard he planned to offer an amendment barring sex discrimination. She had jokingly proposed that he also offer an amendment correcting the imbalance between the number of men and women in the United States. "Just why the Creator would set up such an imbalance of spinsters, shutting off the 'right' of every female to have a husband of her own, is, of course, known only to nature. But I am sure you will agree that this is a grave injustice." Smith elicited widespread laughter from the chamber as he made his point that those who sought racial equality through legislation, like those who sought gender balance by such means, were defying natural law.[29]

Commentators erred, however, in characterizing Smith's amendment as either a surprise or an entirely insincere addition. Smith had been under pressure not only from the NWP but also from many of his female colleagues in the House—then eleven in number—to do more for women. The Equal Pay Act, passed the year before, had sparked many months of testimony on the discrimination in pay suffered by women who performed the same work as men. Since few women then worked in jobs held by men, the bill had limited effect, a fact that made opening male jobs to women the obvious next step. Smith took that step, knowing full well that his amendment would divide the civil rights bill's supporters and perhaps lead to its defeat. Failing that, he would at least have helped white women. Two weeks before Smith proposed his amendment, he had appeared on *Meet the Press,* where May Craig, the White House reporter for the Portland, Maine, *Press Herald* and a member of the NWP, asked Smith whether, as rumor had it, he intended to add "sex" to Title VII. "I might do that," he replied. Everyone on both sides of the debate knew what was coming.[30]

As Smith expected, his divide-and-conquer amendment to Title VII provoked vigorous dissents from longtime ERA opponents Emanuel Celler and Edith Green. Celler read from a letter by Esther Peterson that reiterated the position taken by the PCSW a few months before against adding sex to any Fair Employment Law out of fear that doing so would invalidate protective labor laws: "We [in the Labor Department] are of the opinion that the attempt to amend H.R. 7152 would not be to the best interest of women at this time." Representative Green, suspicious of Smith's motives and primed by administration officials to resist any amendment that might jeopardize the bill, warned that the amendment might later "be used to help destroy this section of the bill by some of the very people who support it."[31]

Despite strong statements from Celler and Green, sentiment in the House favored the "sex" amendment, in large part because of the support organized on its behalf by Democratic Representative—and NWP member—Martha W. Griffiths of Michigan; indeed, by prior arrangement Griffiths had urged that Smith, rather than she, offer the amendment. She had a simple reason: Smith had the power to secure a hundred southern votes for it; she did not. Griffiths

now rose to endorse Smith's addition. She began by castigating her male colleagues for laughing at Smith's joke that what women really wanted was a bigger
pool of men from which to select husbands. "I presume that if there had been
any necessity to have pointed out that women were a second-class sex, the laughter would have proved it," she declared indignantly.[32]

Griffiths then proceeded to support Smith's amendment. In doing so, she
made explicit what Smith had left unsaid. Without the addition of "sex," the
bill might protect black women, but it would leave white women defenseless.
A "vote against this bill today by a white man is a vote against his wife, or his
widow, or his daughter, or his sister," Griffiths declared. "It would be incredible
to me that white men would be willing to place white women at such a disadvantage." After only two hours of debate, Smith's amendment passed 168–133, with
most of Smith's southern colleagues voting for it and, among the twelve women
in the House, only Green voting no. Two days later, the House passed the civil
rights bill.[33]

The Murray Memo

The bill then moved to the Senate. Normally, bills from the House went first to
the Senate Judiciary Committee, chaired by Mississippi Senator James Eastland.
If the bill concerned civil rights, it died there or suffered so many changes that it
emerged an empty shell. But when Republicans from the Midwest learned that
nuns and clergymen from the North were being arrested in the South for taking
part in nonviolent demonstrations, they abandoned their longtime opposition
to civil rights bills; indeed, they took steps to save this one. Faced with a rapidly shifting political landscape, Republican Everett Dirksen, the conservative
minority leader from Illinois, agreed to work with the liberal Democratic vice
president, Hubert Humphrey of Minnesota, to bring the bill to the floor. Behind
the scenes, the two men sought to hammer out a compromise. The bill's prospects brightened, until Dirksen told reporters he needed "40 changes" to secure
the Republican votes needed for passage.[34]

To feminists' dismay, Dirksen's proposed changes included the removal of
"sex" from Title VII. The informal network of Washington women Murray had
met through the PCSW kept her abreast of the bill's rollercoaster ride through
Congress. The group included Catherine East, Mary Eastwood, and Marguerite
Rawalt. All were government employees and therefore limited in what they
could do politically. When they learned that Dirksen was going to try to remove
"sex" from Title VII, they called on Murray. As someone outside government
who was directly affected by both race and gender discrimination, she was ideally placed to draft a memorandum in favor of retaining "sex" in Title VII.[35]

Murray was in New Haven, working on her thesis, when she got word she was needed. The irony of the situation did not escape her. Representative Howard Smith stood at the forefront of the southern white political establishment whose power derived from the white primaries and poll taxes that had disenfranchised black voters and worse. Odell Waller, convicted by a poll-tax jury, had gone to his death in 1942 in Smith's home state. New Deal liberals, including her friends Caroline Ware and Dorothy Kenyon, had run afoul of the Smith-inspired inquisition, aimed at keeping those sympathetic to the labor and civil rights movements out of government, from the late 1930s onward. And here Smith—through Dirksen—had handed her the opportunity to redress those wrongs. She had to do what she could to ensure that this chance would not be lost. In the process, she had to overcome the view of the "sex" amendment as a favor to white women and present it as essential to securing the rights of the women who needed them most, African American women.

Drawing on her Fourteenth Amendment proposal, Murray drafted a memorandum that detailed the parallels between discrimination based on race and that based on gender. Just as there were few, if any, jobs for which an employee's race could be considered relevant, she declared, so too were there few, if any, jobs for which an employee's gender had any bearing. The fact that some women were mothers and homemakers did not change "the basic principle that the right to a job without arbitrary discrimination is a fundamental and individual right."[36]

As for Representative Griffith's fear that without the "sex amendment," white women would be the last to be hired, Murray responded, "What is more likely to happen . . . [is that] in accordance with the prevailing patterns of employment *both* Negro and white women will share a common fate of discrimination, since it is exceedingly difficult for a Negro woman to determine whether or not she is being discriminated against because of race or sex." In fact, Murray urged, "A strong argument can be made for the proposition that Title VII without the 'sex' amendment would benefit Negro males primarily and thus offer genuine equality of opportunity to only half of the potential Negro work force."[37]

Drawing on the history of the women's movement, Murray raised the additional danger that if the "sex amendment" were removed on the grounds that "rights to Negroes" should take precedence, the country would witness a return to the time after the Civil War when the suffrage movement split apart over that same privileging of race over gender. The " bitter memories" of that earlier betrayal, Murray warned, made all women "understandably apprehensive and resentful" of any attempt to exclude them from the equal employment provision of Title VII.[38]

Murray had one final concern: how to respond to the worry, raised by Emanuel Celler and Edith Green, that Title VII would overturn protective labor laws. For guidance, Murray turned for to Mary Eastwood. What effect, Murray asked Eastwood, would the addition of "sex" have on Title VII? The answer, Eastwood declared, was a simple and emphatic "none." Copying Eastwood's argument, verbatim, into an appendix, Murray reassured readers that section 708 of Title VII would allow protective legislation to remain in force as a benefit that could coexist with equal opportunity.[39]

Section 708 had its roots in section 18 of the Fair Labor Standards Act (FLSA) (1938), wherein Congress had reassured progressive states that their higher standards would not be trumped by the new federal legislation. For instance, if a state had a higher minimum wage than that provided by the FLSA, then the higher wage would prevail. To grant equality as required by Title VII, Murray argued, employers could simply extend protective laws to cover men as well as women—raising the floor on minimum wages where necessary, opening (voluntary) overtime to all, and leaving maximum hours laws in place for those currently in positions.[40]

Murray sent the completed memo to Mary Eastwood and Marguerite Rawalt to be copied and distributed to Attorney General Robert F. Kennedy, Vice President Hubert Humphrey, Senate Minority Leader Everett Dirksen, Republican Senator Margaret Chase Smith, and a few others. Rawalt knew Lady Bird Johnson personally, so Murray sent the First Lady a copy as well, with a cover letter that urged her to talk to the president about it. Looking beyond the need to contact these key political figures, Murray told Rawalt that she thought women should begin to organize on their own behalf. "For some time I've been thinking that we needed a private organization of women to make our point of view felt, something a little more attuned to the Space Age than the NWP, and it may be that the time is nigh."[41]

Two weeks later, Murray received her first response, a letter from Senator Smith, which reported the results of a recent Senate Republican conference. Senator Dirksen had sought support from his fellow Republicans for the amendment he had drafted to strike "sex" from the bill as passed by the House. Senator Smith, who had taken no role in the campaign to pass the Equal Pay Act the year before, told Murray that she "stood up and opposed and argued against his amendment." In doing so, she "marshaled so much Republican opposition to it that Senator Dirksen decided not to introduce [it]." Smith did not credit Murray with inspiring her to action. Pressure came from so many different sources in the spring of 1964 that no one person kept "sex" in Title VII. A veritable avalanche of letters from members of the NWP and other professional women's groups swept over Senator Smith's desk that spring. Martha Griffiths, having mounted her own campaign in the House, monitored progress in the Senate and brought pressure where necessary. But Smith praised Murray's memorandum, which she had read "with much interest and deep admiration." Murray's lesson— that sex and race discrimination operated to reinforce one another—provided new ammunition to anyone who might otherwise have hesitated to take sex discrimination seriously, or who might, following the lead of the NWP and Representative Griffiths, have been tempted to treat black women as the enemy of white women's ambitions.[42]

Next came a letter from Bess Abell, Lady Bird Johnson's secretary. Abell reported that the First Lady had found Murray's memo "convincing and persuasive." Moreover, Abell had consulted the president's staff on that matter. As "far as the Administration is concerned," she reported, "its position is that the Bill should be enacted in its present form." Johnson said as much in a letter to the Texas Business and Women on April 23.[43]

Lyndon Johnson knew the Senate better than any other figure except his mentor, Georgia Democrat Richard Russell. Russell knew all the rules, and Johnson knew that Russell would use those rules to filibuster the civil rights bill to death on the Senate floor. The best way to extend the filibuster indefinitely would be to accept amendments, because each amendment would then be subject to debate. Endless debate. Determined to pass a strong bill, Johnson deployed his considerable experience and legendary force of personality to persuade Dirksen to drop all amendments, "sex" included.[44]

Putting an end to a Russell-led filibuster took more than hanging tough on additional amendments. Johnson and Humphries had to persuade enough conservative and moderate Republican midwesterners to join liberal Democratic northerners to cut off further debate through "cloture," by which debate could be ended by a vote of two thirds of the Senate. Senators had never invoked this device in debate over a civil rights bill, and through a fifty-seven-day filibuster, the longest in history, they resisted doing so in 1964. But the midwesterners were under heavy pressure from the National Council of Churches (NCC), where Anna Arnold Hedgeman organized delegations of religious leaders to lobby their congressmen on behalf of the Civil Rights Act of 1964. In the end, enough conservative midwestern Republicans joined liberal Democrats to muster the sixty-seven votes needed to pass a cloture motion on June 10.[45]

With the threat of filibuster out of the way, several amendments were proposed, debated under the strict time limit that could be imposed once a filibuster was ended, and quickly passed. One reassured both labor and employers that Title VII would not lead to racial quotas. A second weakened the power of the Equal Employment Opportunity Commission (EEOC), the agency tasked with enforcing the law; the EEOC could hear complaints and attempt conciliation between parties, but it would no longer be empowered to bring suits. On June 19 the Senate passed the bill 73–27. On July 2, 1964, the House waived the customary conference committee, accepted the Senate version as written, with "sex" still in it, and voted 289–126 in favor. As Representative Edith Green had predicted, the southerners who originally supported Smith in adding "sex" now voted against the bill. But they did not have the votes to defeat it. Later that day Johnson signed the Civil Rights Act of 1964 into law.[46]

Taking On Moynihan

Having dispatched her memo in favor of retaining "sex" in Title VII, Murray dove back into her doctoral thesis. A wide-ranging, interdisciplinary search for the roots of the "race hatred" that had exploded in Birmingham in May 1963, the thesis, entitled "Roots of the Racial Crisis: Prologue to Policy," sought to integrate the experiences of black women into the history of slavery and Jim Crow. Professor Fowler Harper, who had brought Murray to Yale and served as her thesis adviser, helped as much as he could, but, stricken with cancer, he died before she finished. Murray turned for advice to Professor Thomas Emerson and his wife Ruth Emerson, also a lawyer, whose knowledge of current research in psychology proved helpful. As always, Murray relied heavily on Caroline Ware, whose long career in social history proved most helpful to what was essentially a gender-minded history of the black experience. Ware worked hard to help Murray hammer her material into shape, but she never fully succeeded. At over 1,300 pages of text and notes, the thesis was a sprawling, often undigested, mass of overly long quotations.[47]

It took Murray two years to complete "Roots of the Racial Crisis." A Yale teaching fellow award paid for the first year; a Ford Foundation grant supported her through the second. Had she had the benefit of one more year and a firmer adviser, she might have been able to pare away the endless supporting material that clouded her main contribution: a highly original critique of the belief, soon to be made famous by Daniel Patrick Moynihan, that the economic crisis that confronted black America stemmed from the emasculation of black men by black women. Murray showed good instincts. As she systematically laid out the economic, historical, sociological, and psychological literature on slavery, Jim Crow, and the black family, she remained consistently attuned, as no one else had yet been, to the intersection of race and gender. When news of Moynihan's forthcoming report on the black family began to leak out of the Labor Department in the summer of 1965, she was ready to respond.

Moynihan's Report, entitled "The Negro Family: The Case for National Action," blamed a "tightening tangle of pathology" in the black community on female-headed households. Single mothers imparted female culture to their children and, in the process, diminished male children's chance of healthy gender-role development. The results were disastrous: a quarter of marriages failed, a quarter of births illegitimate, a quarter of Negro families headed by women, and a "startling increase" in welfare dependency. In Moynihan's view, black men needed to be removed to an "utterly masculine world," run by men of authority, ideally in the United States Army, where they could begin "to feel like a man" and recapture the universal male impulse "to strut." Not that the army alone could solve the problems of the black community. Only a broader jobs program, one that put men into jobs currently held by women, would restore a patriarchal family structure. America was built, Moynihan insisted, on the foundations of the male-headed family. As long as black Americans lived in the more primitive matriarchal family form, they would never enter the mainstream.[48]

Murray accepted the idea that blacks (as well as whites) had been damaged by America's racial history. In long chapters on psychology, she developed the idea that slavery and Jim Crow had devastating consequences for black self-esteem. Whereas Moynihan saw the damage as a function of family structure, however, she found the sources of that damage in the historical circumstances of slavery and Jim Crow.[49]

As she raced to finish her thesis, Murray reached out to others working on related topics. Chief among them was white southern historian Willie Lee Rose, whose work on blacks in the Sea Islands of Georgia following slavery demonstrated how quickly social patterns could change under altered circumstances. Rose thanked Murray for sharing with her the concept of Jane Crow and agreed that the negative views of blacks paralleled to a striking extent the negative views of women. She wondered, however, whether women would ever be as successful in protesting their oppression as blacks, as a group, were now being. Citing the work of pioneer women's historian Anne Firor Scott, Rose observed, "Women are the only subordinated group who actually live with the 'Master Class!'" Among slaves, only those who lived in the slaveholders' houses shared an experience that was at all similar to that experienced by most women. The result was difficulty in protesting their own oppression.[50]

Rose's letter delighted Murray. No other missive had ever done so much to validate her life. In response, she conceded that "as a single woman I have overlooked the fact that women generally do live with the 'superior' class," but she quickly added that this fact "accounts for why single women are more aggressive and militant on issues of sex. Thank you for pointing it up." Murray was, of course, speaking for herself. Apart from the few years she had spent in the same house with her father and then grandfather, she had lived her whole life either alone or with other women. Single women had long played a disproportionate role in the battle for women's rights. What Murray did not tell Rose was that she believed she brought one other characteristic to the battle, a characteristic just as important as being single. As a person who occupied an intermediate gender status, she had always seen more clearly and responded more aggressively to gender oppression. That very fact meant that she had a special role to play in liberating others.[51]

Completing her thesis, Murray laid out what she believed to be the policy implications of her analysis. She agreed with those who focused on the need in the black community for more and better jobs. Fighting unemployment and underemployment had to be the first priority. Education came second. "Earn, then learn," she insisted, for women as much as for men. At every step the emphasis must be on human rights. Patriarchy must be avoided and matriarchy, if it could even be said to exist, understood in positive terms, as a steppingstone to a more democratic society.[52]

Dr. Murray

June 14, 1965, in New Haven dawned chilly and overcast, with a threat of rain, but nothing could dampen Pauli Murray's joy as she donned her blue Yale doctoral robe, with its purple hood, and walked across the platform to receive the degree of Doctor of Juridical Science from Dean Eugene V. Rostow of the Yale Law School. The first black person—male or female—to earn a J.S.D. from Yale, Murray felt that she had finally arrived. Best of all, she could now cast aside the hated "Miss" and place "Dr." before her name. For her male peers, that academic honorific signaled only an upgrade in status; to Murray it symbolized something more. No longer would her name be preceded by the feminine (worse, girlish) honorific she so disdained.[53]

As the celebratory spirit of the day faded, however, Murray returned with Renee Barlow to her humble apartment to face the fact that, for all her elite schooling, she had not yet landed a job. She had hoped that Yale Law School might offer her a permanent position, but it did not. She applied to other schools. Nothing. Nearly half of all students who earned graduate law degrees at Yale did, in fact, secure law faculty appointments, but Murray was not among them. In the end, Methodist women once again came to her rescue. For the year following her graduation, she supported herself by writing a monograph entitled "Human Rights U.S.A.: 1948-1966" for the Women's Division of the Methodist Church, on a contract negotiated by her old friend Thelma Stevens.[54]

Murray's doctoral work had one immediate effect. On August 9, 1965, an article summarizing the unpublished Moynihan report appeared in *Newsweek*. Prepared by two years of research and analysis, Murray immediately fired off a critical letter, the first in what would become a barrage of protest, but different from the rest. Other critics would soon castigate Moynihan for its denigration of black men; Murray kept her focus on black women. Moynihan's report and the article about it, Murray wrote, did a "great disservice to the thousands of Negro women in the United State who have struggled to prepare themselves for employment in a limited job market which is not only highly competitive but

Figure 12.1 Pauli Murray, upon earning her J.S.D. from Yale Law School in 1965. Estate of Pauli Murray, Schlesinger Library, Radcliffe Institute, Harvard University.

which, historically, has severely restricted economic opportunities for women as well as Negroes." At a time when public policy emphasized the importance of education, she continued, "it is bitterly ironic that Negro women should be impliedly censured for their efforts to overcome a handicap not of their making and for trying to meet the standards of the country as a whole." She found most offensive Moynihan's suggestion that women be taken out of their jobs to give men full employment. The adoption of this approach, she charged, pitted "Negro males" against "Negro females in a highly competitive instead of a cooperative endeavor."[55]

Murray's concern about deteriorating employment prospects for black women soon found confirmation from others. Mary Keyserling, who had taken over from Esther Peterson as director of the Women's Bureau, complained that the director of a work-training center in Washington, DC, had declared, "We're not encouraging women. We're trying to reestablish the male as head of the house." Congresswoman Edith Green encountered the same problem in grilling Sargent Shriver of the Jobs Corps. He freely admitted that his program was favoring men in obvious violation of Title VII.[56]

Murray warned that such examples of discrimination against black women would multiply unless women's advocates took strong action to make equal rights for black women the touchstone for any equal rights campaign. As Murray's experience in the civil rights movement had taught her, to speak only of race risked winning rights for black men only. Race equality without sex equality rendered the black woman invisible.

13

Toward an NAACP for Women

"Sex" at the EEOC

As of the summer of 1965, the prospects for gender equality looked bleak. Not a single federal case had emerged that might allow a test of Murray's Fourteenth Amendment strategy, nor did any institutional structure exist that might help her pursue such a case should it arise. Civil rights leaders, encouraged by Moynihan's report, increasingly viewed black women's workforce participation and educational attainment as a threat to family stability and therefore to racial equality. Moreover, the "sex" provision of Title VII, which went into effect on July 2, looked as though it would come to naught, as newspaper coverage of the new federal policy against sex discrimination turned the reform into an occasion for jokes and ridicule, while government officials did little to defend the new law.[1]

The mainstream press led the way, zeroing in on Section 703 (d) of Title VII, which permitted employers to hire a person of a particular race or gender if that characteristic constituted a "bona fide occupational qualification" (BFOQ). In June, the *Wall Street Journal* quoted an airline executive as saying, "We're not worried about the racial discrimination ban—what's unnerving is the section on sex." "What are we going to do now," he asked, "when a gal walks into our office, demands a job as an airline pilot and has the credentials to qualify? Or, what will we do when some guy comes in and wants to be a stewardess?" President Johnson, who had thrown the full weight of his presidential power into the passage of a strong civil rights bill the year before seemed indifferent to enforcing it. Eleven months passed before he settled on Franklin D. Roosevelt Jr.—a man with an illustrious name but little administrative experience and less drive—to head the Equal Employment Opportunity Commission (EEOC). With only four weeks to assemble a skeletal staff, Roosevelt began by taking a week's vacation on his yacht. When a reporter asked him on his return how he intended to enforce the sex provision of Title VII, he admitted that the commission had "yet to come to grips with most of the problems involved."[2]

To Murray's dismay, only one of the other four commissioners was a woman, a Howard University graduate, as it happened. Aileen Hernandez, born Aileen Clarke in Brooklyn in 1926, was the daughter of Jamaican parents. She had gained her Spanish name through marriage. An undergraduate at Howard during World War II, she was one of Murray's picketers outside Thompson's restaurant in 1944. As a Democrat with strong union ties and a commitment to women's rights, she had served three years as the assistant to the chief of the California FEPC. Hernandez could count on the support of only one other commissioner on votes that concerned women, a liberal Republican, Richard A. Graham, who had served as head of the Peace Corps in Tunisia under Kennedy. Hernandez and Graham regularly found themselves outvoted by their more conservative colleagues on the commission: Franklin Roosevelt Jr., Luther Holcomb (a white minister from Texas), and Samuel Jackson (a black former member of the NAACP board of directors).[3]

EEOC staff members had no experience with women's problems in the labor force and less sympathy. A few weeks before taking office, the new executive director, Herman Edelsberg, told a conference on labor relations that the addition of "sex" to Title VII was a "fluke" that was "conceived out of wedlock." Another new staff member, Richard Berg, referred to the "sex" provision as an "orphan" and argued that employers should be able to bar women, under the "bona fide occupational qualification" exception, from jobs that required "close contact with fellow workers or customers."[4]

"Jane Crow and the Law"

Alarmed by this backlash against the "sex" provision in Title VII, Murray wrote Mary Eastwood and Marguerite Rawalt that unless they mounted a coordinated effort they were going to lose whatever gains they had made. Murray took the first step by revisiting a law review article on sex equality she had begun with Eastwood two years before. Spurring Eastwood forward, Murray predicted, "If we pull it off, we'll be cited to kingdom come." Tentatively entitled "Jane Crow and the Law," the article had three parts. The first, on the Fourteenth Amendment, was principally Murray's work. It laid out the same arguments she had made before the Committee on Civil and Political Rights in the fall of 1962. The second section, on BFOQs, appears to have been coauthored. The third, on protective labor laws, was Eastwood's work.[5]

In her section on the Fourteenth Amendment, Murray once again identified the ways in which discrimination on the basis of gender paralleled discrimination on the basis of race. Both were rooted in stereotypes and myth rather than reason and experience. As for state protective labor laws, they should be extended to cover men where they now covered women only, just as the report of the PCSW had proposed. If employers had a problem with this, they could always litigate the question in the courts.[6]

The article then shifted to a discussion of how to treat bona fide occupational qualifications (BFOQs). Thus far the EEOC was giving BFOQs the widest possible interpretation. The commission permitted airlines to hire only young, single women as stewardesses because male business travelers preferred them; moreover, the airlines could force female, but not male, employees to quit when they married or reached the age of thirty-two. Any employer could deny jobs to mothers of young children on the assumption that their child care responsibilities would interfere with paid work. Newspapers could run sex-segregated "Help Wanted" ads, as a service to their readers. Both Murray and Eastwood believed that such loose interpretations of BFOQ threatened to subvert Title VII. Any exception should be "extremely limited." Though they gave no examples, they no doubt agreed with Sonia Pressman, a newly hired white lawyer at the EEOC and a friend, who later remembered arguing to her superiors that the only sex BFOQ she could think of was "wet nurse."[7]

Thus far, "Jane Crow and the Law" tracked Murray and Eastwood's earlier writings, but two thirds of the way through, where the article moved to the possible conflict between Title VII and state protective labor laws for women, its argument shifted sharply. Whereas Eastwood had assured Murray in April 1964 that the impact on Title VII on state protective laws would be "none," she had reconsidered that position. The section on Title VII began with a recapitulation of Murray's recommendation that states extend current protections to cover men. For instance, where states required rest periods and special facilities, such as seats, dressing rooms, or restrooms, for women, they would have to do the same for men. Maximum hours laws, however, raised a special problem. Employers and male workers strongly opposed the extension of maximum hours laws to cover men.[8]

The culture of male labor had shifted over the past century, from one that emphasized the importance of securing more leisure to one that emphasized more pay. With that shift came a movement away from maximum-hour limits to time-and-a-half pay for overtime. The passage of the Fair Labor Standards Act in 1938, with its premium pay provision for work in excess of eight hours a day, signaled that the concept of overtime would be the principal means by which the federal government would discourage employers from exploiting their workers. Esther Peterson and the majority of commissioners on the Presidential Commission on the Status of Women (PCSW) had concluded by 1963 that overtime pay was the "best way to discourage excessive hours for all workers."[9]

As of 1965, the FLSA excluded two thirds of all women workers, including most low-income workers (laundry, hotel, restaurant, domestic workers, employees of small stores, farmworkers), but broader coverage looked imminent. A bill before Congress would reduce exclusions to less than half of the female workforce. If that bill succeeded, and if FLSA-mandated premium pay for overtime prevented employers from exploiting their workers, maximum-hour laws might become increasingly irrelevant. Pointing out that some state commissions were already recommending that protective labor laws be abolished, Eastwood persuaded Murray that "relatively little harm would result if employers were relieved of complying with the state laws under section 708 of the Civil Rights Act." Moreover, much good would follow: employers could no longer refuse to hire women for the best paying jobs on the grounds that state law prevented them from working overtime.[10]

Murray and Eastwood tried to place their article in the *Yale Law Journal,* but co-editor Raymond Clevenger found their treatment of BFOQs unpersuasive. It did not take the authors long, however, to find a willing editor elsewhere. The *George Washington Law Review* published "Jane Crow and the Law" in its December 1965 issue. Just as Murray had predicted, the article would eventually be cited "to kingdom come"[11]

A New March on Washington

While she sought a publisher for "Jane Crow and the Law," Murray agreed to speak to the annual meeting of the National Council of Women (NCW). Founded in 1888 by early suffragists, including Elizabeth Cady Stanton and Susan B. Anthony, the NCW reached out to women "irrespective of race or creed," from countries around the world to pursue human rights both at home and abroad. Radical at the time of its founding, the council had devolved over the decades into a relatively staid organization that specialized in public interest seminars. In October 12, 1965, at the Biltmore Hotel in New York, the annual meeting returned the organization to its radical roots.[12]

Billed as "a Title VII Seminar," the meeting pitted Murray against EEOC Chairman Franklin Roosevelt Jr. The chairman defended the commission's go-slow approach as it sought to determine which practices violated Title VII. Murray called for immediate action. She criticized, in particular, Roosevelt's support of sex-segregated "Help Wanted" ads in the nation's newspapers. He called them a "convenience" to the reader. She labeled them a clear violation of Title VII. Shocking the audience, she proposed a "March on Washington" for equal rights for women.[13]

Long-time *New York Times* reporter Edith Evans Asbury witnessed Murray's call to action. Having covered the civil rights movement for a decade, she knew a good story when she saw one. "PROTEST PROPOSED ON WOMEN'S JOBS; Yale Professor Says It May Be Necessary to Obtain Rights," read the headline for her article the next day. Murray felt embarrassed to see herself described as a "Yale Professor," when in fact she had never been a professor and was currently unemployed. But she recognized the value of that headline. The mis-designation gave her message "extra clout."[14]

One of those who saw the story was Miriam C. Holden of the National Woman's Party (NWP). Less than three years before, Holden had denigrated Murray for trying to "hitch" civil rights to the "Equal Rights Amendment star," but much had changed since then. Murray's memorandum in support of adding "sex" to Title VII and her speech to the NCW persuaded Holden that civil rights and women's rights could be mutually supportive movements. Holden wrote to Alice Paul in praise of Murray's "excellent" speech and the "objective and courageous position" she had taken in attacking the EEOC's chairman. Not all NWP members viewed Murray's position so favorably. Some criticized her for failing to endorse the ERA, but Murray was making headway in her effort to bridge the gap between the competing wings of the women's movement.[15]

Murray's acceptance of a brooch from the daughter of her friend Betsy Graves Reynau underscored her commitment. Murray had long admired Reynau's pin, one of several modeled on a jail door with a lock and chain, which Alice Paul had given to Reynau and the other women jailed in 1917 for picketing at the White House on behalf of women's suffrage. Reyneau's daughter Marie gave Murray the ornament when Reyneau died in 1964. To Murray, the "pin became one of my most cherished possessions," a symbol of her part in the long history of women's fight for equal justice.[16]

Another person who saw the article on Murray's speech to the NCW was Betty Friedan. Already famous as the author of *The Feminine Mystique*, Friedan had embarked on a new book on the women who were beginning to move beyond lives centered on domesticity. She tracked Murray down in New Haven, as the "Yale Professor" was preparing to move. Murray had decided to return to New York, "to renew my spiritual resources and get a fresh start," as she put it, as well as to be closer to Renee Barlow.[17]

Friedan and Murray spoke by phone as Murray packed. That conversation, followed by other calls and subsequent meetings, led beyond Friedan's planned book to more extended discussions about women in America and what Murray called the "shoddy treatment we were getting under Title VII and what we should do about it." Murray put Friedan in touch with the women she had met in the course of work on the PCSW and with whom she was in contact regarding enforcement of the Civil Rights Act, especially Mary Eastwood, Marguerite

Rawalt, and Sonia Pressman. She also introduced Friedan to Catherine East, at the Civil Service Commission, who had been the technical secretary of the Committee on Federal Employment for the PCSW and who had gone on to serve as the executive secretary of the Interdepartmental Committee on the Status of Women and the Citizens' Advisory Council on the Status of Women. The PCSW had established these organizations to ensure that its recommendations would be implemented once it submitted its final report to the president in 1963. East was the central figure in what Friedan came to call the "Washington underground network," women whose staff positions in the government allowed them to gather and disseminate information to women's organizations around the country.[18]

As Friedan made the rounds, she kept hearing the same thing: there needed to be "an NAACP for women," an independent group that could make government agencies take sex discrimination seriously. For the time being, however, no one was willing to act. The government women could not be openly identified with a group dedicated to pressuring the government. Friedan, who had the advantage of having broad name recognition, insisted that she was a writer, not an "organization person." Murray did not want to form a group that would compete with existing women's groups. Perhaps, with a little more time, the State Commissions on the Status of Women could pressure the government to defend women's newly acquired rights.[19]

In the meantime, Murray moved back to New York City. She found an apartment at 245 East 11th Street, on the corner of Second Avenue in the East Village, the low-cost heart of the Beat culture of the 1960s in New York. To her delight, the apartment overlooked the churchyard of St. Mark's Church in-the-Bowery, the Episcopal church she had joined with Renee Barlow before leaving for Africa. The second oldest church in the city, St. Mark's served not only as a house of worship but also as an avant-garde cultural and civil rights center. Among other projects, it supported the work of the Episcopal Society for Cultural and Racial Unity (ESCRU), dedicated to civil rights work in some of the most dangerous parts of the South.[20]

Smokey, Murray's companion for thirteen years, had recently died of a heart ailment, but Murray found a new dog at the pound to keep her company in her new home. She called him, alternately, "Doc" (in celebration of her new title from Yale) and "Black-and-White-Together-We-Shall-Overcome" (in recognition of her civil rights commitments). Side by side, they regularly walked the twelve blocks to visit Renee and her mother at their apartment in Peter Cooper Village at 23rd Street and the East River Drive. The Barlows had been lured there by the building's elevator after Mary Jane Barlow had grown too frail to manage the stairs at their midtown walk-up. Light and airy, the apartment had a view of the East River.[21]

American Civil Liberties Union

Moving to New York brought Murray more than proximity to Renee Barlow. No sooner had she settled into her new apartment than the American Civil Liberties Union invited her to stand for election to its national board of directors. The position carried no salary; indeed, board members at major nonprofits were generally expected to make significant monetary contributions. Executive Director John de J. Pemberton reassured Murray that she would not be expected to do so: "What our Board members do is work!"[22]

Since the ACLU's founding at the end of World War I, the board had been dominated by white men from New York City dedicated to protecting free speech. In the organization's early years, the closest it came to acting on women's behalf was in cases involving the First Amendment. In the 1920s it defended Margaret Sanger's right to speak publicly about birth control and Marry Ware Dennett's right to send her pamphlet "The Sex Side of Life" through the mails. When Kenyon joined the board in 1930, she lobbied her brethren, with modest success, to broaden their conception of civil liberties. But she felt for the most part like a "Cassandra crying out in the A.C.L.U. wilderness against the crime of our abortion laws and man's inhumanity to women." Then, in 1961, Kenyon scored a major victory when the ACLU board agreed to intervene in the appeal to the Supreme Court of a lower-court decision in *Hoyt v. Florida,* in which an all-male jury had convicted a Florida woman of murdering her husband. By that time, only three states, South Carolina, Alabama, and Mississippi, still excluded women from jury service by law, but twenty-one others, including Florida, limited female service to those who volunteered or who refrained from seeking exemptions not available to men. In her brief in the *Hoyt* case, Kenyon protested Florida's jury selection process as a denial of a woman's right under the Fourteenth Amendment to a jury of her peers. The Supreme Court disagreed. In a unanimous decision, the justices declared Florida's jury selection system to be "reasonable," because "woman is still regarded as the center of home and family life."[23]

The outcome in *Hoyt* notwithstanding, the social reform movements of the early 1960s raised Kenyon's hopes for the future. In 1962 Harriet Pilpel, a member of the PCSW and a leading figure in the movement for birth control and abortion rights, joined the ACLU board. The following year civil rights leader James Farmer did. In 1963, when Murray sent Kenyon her memorandum to the PCSW on the analogy of sex to race discrimination and its implications for litigation under the Equal Protection Clause, Kenyon persuaded the ACLU board to endorse Murray's approach. In 1964 the board increased the ACLU's budget by almost a third to open a southern office in Atlanta. And in the summer of 1965, the national office hired Murray's Yale Law School protégé Eleanor Holmes, now Norton, who had just completed a clerkship for black Federal District Court Judge Leon A. Higginbotham Jr. as one of its two staff attorneys. These changes primed the men of the ACLU to give greater attention to an argument that Kenyon had been making for many years, that civil liberties should be understood to include equal rights for women.[24]

Kenyon had kept in touch with Murray since 1946, when Murray began her search for work as a lawyer in New York. Now the older woman saw the perfect person to help push her agenda. Looking back later, she characterized their partnership: "Pauli and I, she out in front with her double discriminations, I at the rear with my years of experience behind me and the prayer that the young ones may start out differently from us." Together with James Farmer, Kenyon nominated Murray to the board in November 1965. The timing mattered. Murray had signed on to what was then the ACLU's most important litigation: a case in Lowndes County, Alabama, in which the lead plaintiff was a black woman.[25]

"Massive resistance" to the civil rights movement reached a murderous peak in Lowndes County in the summer of 1965. In response to the Civil Rights Act of 1964, Governor George Wallace urged whites in Alabama to "stand up for segregation." Those in "bloody" Lowndes did so by turning on the black majority. Thugs beat those who tried to integrate public accommodations; policemen arrested those who picketed; planters fired those who registered to vote; white juries acquitted the rare white person charged with murder of a civil rights worker.[26]

In the summer of 1965, Congress passed the Voting Rights Act, which provided for federal oversight of voter registration and gave much needed encouragement to civil rights workers in Lowndes. As local whites watched federal agents help blacks register to vote, their anger at "outside agitators" mounted. On August 14, 1965, policemen in Fort Deposit, Lowndes County, arrested Jonathan M. Daniels, a twenty-six-year-old white Episcopal seminarian from Keene, New Hampshire, together with twenty-six-year-old white Catholic Father Richard Morrisroe and others, for picketing local stores. Released without explanation on August 20, the prisoners were alarmed to see that no one had come to pick them up. But someone was waiting: Tom Coleman, the white local deputy sheriff. Coleman shot Daniels and Morrisroe as they tried to buy a Coke in a local store. Morrisroe was paralyzed; Daniels died.[27]

Learning of Daniels's murder later that day, the white Reverend John B. Morris, executive director of ESCRU (headquartered in Atlanta) and responsible for Daniels, called the US Justice Department to ask for help, without success. He then walked down the hall to the office of Charles Morgan Jr., a white lawyer and the new Southern Regional Director of the ACLU.[28]

Morgan had grown up in a liberal home in Birmingham, Alabama, and become a lawyer. He worked with black as well as white lawyers and represented black as well as white clients. Disturbed by Alabama's all-white jury system, he challenged it in court—without success. The bombing of a black church in Birmingham that killed four black girls in 1963 drove Morgan to more dramatic action. In a speech the following day to the Birmingham Young Men's Business Club, a progressive group to which he belonged, he laid blame for the atrocity at the feet of the white establishment. Who threw that bomb? "We all did it," he told his startled listeners. Morgan did not stop there. The following week he was at Yale Law School, where Murray and 750 others packed the law school auditorium to hear him declare the urgent need for the intervention of northern lawyers and business leaders in the civil rights struggle. Within a year, ACLU director John Pemberton persuaded Morgan to move to Atlanta to set up a southern office for the civil liberties organization. When the Reverend Morris appealed to Morgan for help, following the murder of Jonathan Daniels, the ACLU director swung into action. He believed that a jury case out of Lowndes County could produce a breakthrough. Delegating Orzell Billingsley Jr., one of the young black lawyers with whom he had worked in Birmingham, to find him plaintiffs, he then called Pauli Murray at Yale.[29]

As Morgan was well aware, women had long played an important role in the civil rights movement. In the current voter registration campaign, more than half the organizers were women; and yet they suffered more blatant discrimination than men when it came to jury service. Alabama kept black men off juries by tradition; it barred women by statute. That difference presented an opportunity. Under the federal rules of civil procedure, Morgan could demand a hearing before a three-judge federal court and from there go straight to the Supreme Court. He had merely to show that his case hinged on a state statute that conflicted with the Constitution. By arguing that Alabama's law barring women from jury service violated the Equal Protection Clause of the Fourteenth Amendment, he had a shot at swift justice. Taking his lead from Murray, Morgan believed he could win by linking race and gender discrimination.[30]

White v. Crook

Morgan quickly identified the obvious lead defendant in the case: Bruce Crook, the Lowndes County jury commissioner. This was the man who had systematically robbed black men of their right and responsibility as citizens to serve on juries. Identifying the lead plaintiff took a little longer, but as Morgan scanned Billingsley's list of "brave" people willing to challenge the Lowndes County jury system, he fastened on the name Gardenia White. The thirty-six-year-old black wife and mother belonged to an extended clan devoted to civil rights. Her grandmother, Rosie Steele, had donated her farm as a campsite to those who had come to Alabama for the Selma march for voting rights in March. Gardenia worked on behalf of the Lowndes County Christian Movement for Human Rights (LCCMHR), the local voter registration group. Starting with zero registrants at the beginning of the year, these grassroots organizers had signed up more than a thousand by the end of the summer. Though not as prominent in the movement as several other plaintiffs, her name underscored the arbitrariness of both race and gender discrimination, while contributing a bit of puckish humor to the serious business at hand. Thus began the case of *White v. Crook*.[31]

To Murray's delight, Morgan asked that she and Kenyon join the team that would represent Gardenia White in federal court. Here was the chance for which she had long been waiting. Not only did *White v. Crook* put the intersection of race and gender discrimination front and center but it also had the support of an institution—the ACLU—with the resources to take it all the way to the Supreme Court. As a bonus, it allowed her to work on behalf of ESCRU, to which she and Renee Barlow were devoted.[32]

Murray knew that Gardenia White had at least two friends among the three federal judges who would decide the case. Frank M. Johnson had ordered Governor Wallace to allow the Selma march to go forward. Richard Rives had been one of the Fifth Circuit judges who had worked to implement *Brown v. Board of Education*. Both Johnson and Rives had suffered death threats for their decisions. But neither Rives nor the more conservative Clarence Allgood wanted to tackle the question of whether women's exclusion from juries violated the constitution. Rives initially thought that the Supreme Court had already resolved that issue in *Hoyt*. He soon realized, however, that Alabama, by barring women from jury service by statute presented a clearer case of constitutional conflict than Florida, which made female service voluntary. After hearing oral arguments, Rives gave the parties two weeks to submit briefs.[33]

Morgan asked Murray to write the part of the ACLU brief that addressed the intersection of race and gender discrimination. Devoting every waking hour to this task in the days that followed, Murray laid out the parallel struggle of African American men and all women for simple justice—through the abolitionist, civil rights, and women's rights movements. She questioned how, in a democracy, a state could bar 55 percent of its otherwise eligible citizens from jury service, solely on the grounds of gender. She argued that given the similarity between gender and race discrimination, and given further that the Supreme Court had already ruled that any law that discriminated on the basis of race must be subject to "close judicial scrutiny," the same standard must be applied to any discrimination based on gender.[34]

So far, Murray was recapitulating material she had written many times. The clincher came near the end, where she and Kenyon helped Morgan show the arbitrariness of Alabama's practice with respect to women. A woman, State Auditor Bettye Frink, audited the accounts of Alabama's government. Women served as both secretary of state and state treasurer. Best of all, a woman, Annie Lola Price, presided over the State Court of Appeals. More than any other official, Price epitomized the arbitrariness of women's exclusion from jury service: "She can reverse the verdict of a jury. She could resign and practice law before a jury. But solely because she is a woman, she is not eligible to serve on a jury." Morgan, pressed for time and wanting to drive home Murray's sex-race analogy, appended a prepublication copy of "Jane Crow and the Law," and rushed the papers to Montgomery.[35]

The brief that Morgan hastily stitched together from their joint efforts was a "mish mash," Kenyon lamented, "with bits and pieces about women all through the thing." But it worked even better than they dared hope. Morgan, Kenyon, and Murray had expected to persuade the two liberal judges, Rives and Johnson, but they won over Allgood too. On February 7, 1966, the three-judge court ruled unanimously for Gardenia White and her fellow plaintiffs. After finding that the jury commissioner had discriminated in the selection of jurors on racial grounds, they ruled that the state statute that barred women from jury service violated the Equal Protection Clause of the Fourteenth Amendment. The time had come, the court declared, "when a state's complete exclusion of women from jury service is recognized as so arbitrary and unreasonable as to be unconstitutional."[36]

"Sound the tocsin!" exclaimed Marguerite Rawalt, who only a few years before had believed that only the ERA could provide the vehicle for winning equal rights for women. Murray was jubilant: "I conceive of *White v. Crook* as the *Brown v. Board of Education* for women in this country," she declared, "and while the Supreme Court has not spoken it is unthinkable that it could say any less." Mary Eastwood called the decision "far better than I dared hope for. It's the most important thing to happen to women since the Nineteenth Amendment." Perhaps the ERA would not be necessary after all. The effort to insert "sex" into Title VII and to keep it there had been a joint effort of traditionally competing women's groups. Now *White v. Crook* promised to bring them closer together. As Murray wrote ERA supporter and NWP member Alma Lutz, "We differ not so much in our objectives as in our strategy. It is just possible that through court interpretation the Equal Rights Amendment will be written into the Constitution."[37]

Murray's prediction proved premature. Her dream of seeing the case go to the Supreme Court was dashed when Alabama Attorney General Richmond Flowers declined to appeal the decision against his state. One of the few liberal officials in the South, a man who privately supported jury service for women and was about to enter a race for governor, Flowers had no desire to see his name attached to what he believed would be the losing side of a landmark women's rights case.

Better to let a state official somewhere else—perhaps in Mississippi or South Carolina, where state law continued to bar women from jury service—assume that dubious distinction.[38]

Anticipating a case from one of those two states, Murray asked Morgan to allow her not just to help write the brief but also to join in the oral argument at the next opportunity. Part of the "winning of equality and dignity by women is that women participate in the argument of constitutional cases," she emphasized. But no such case emerged. Inspired by the federal court ruling in *White v. Crook,* reformers in the state legislatures in South Carolina and Mississippi legislatures forced a revocation of their statutes barring women jury service in 1967 and 1968, respectively.[39]

Founding NOW

Flowers's decision to take a pass on an appeal to the Supreme Court left Murray feeling dejected. Her Fourteenth Amendment strategy had stalled in Alabama, and no other test case emerged. The Moynihan Report, released in July 1965, stated explicitly that the government should focus on finding jobs for black men, taking them from black women if necessary. Government officials agreed, as they directed Johnson's newly announced War on Poverty explicitly to black men. Murray's one hope for change was the EEOC, but the enforcement agency gave little indication that it was prepared to take sex discrimination seriously.[40]

The EEOC did not ignore women's concerns entirely. Its very first ruling, announced in September 1965, dealt with sex, not race discrimination. It held that under Title VII, employers could no longer fire female employees when they married. In April 1966, the commission went further. After hearing testimony, it accepted the recommendation of the Citizen's Advisory Council that it give a narrow interpretation to the bona fide occupational qualification provision. BFOQ exemptions would no longer be allowed "based on stereotypes of characteristics of the sexes; the preferences of the employer, coworkers, clients, or customers; or assumptions of the comparative characteristic of women (or men) in general."[41]

So far, so good, in Murray's view. She was dismayed to learn, however, that the commission rejected the council's additional suggestion that newspaper sex-segregated "Help Wanted" columns be outlawed. The EEOC banned companies from declaring race or sex preferences in their ads, but the American Newspaper Publishers' Association forced the commission, on First Amendment grounds, to accept their display of these ads in sex-segregated columns. Newspapers had ended racially segregated columns without discussion, but they insisted on maintaining sex-segregated columns as a service to their readers.[42]

The want-ad controversy sparked an angry reaction not only from Murray, but from others—most vocally, Martha Griffiths. On June 20, 1966, Griffiths delivered an angry speech on the floor of the House of Representatives, in which she charged that the EEOC's failure to strike down sex-segregated, help-wanted ads constituted "nothing more than arbitrary arrogance, disregard of law, and a manifestation of flat hostility to the human rights of women." Even where the EEOC led, employers often failed to follow. For instance, airline stewardesses were still being forced to leave their jobs when they married or reached the age of thirty-two. Although women leaders continued to disagree about the fate of protective labor laws, their outrage over what they saw as agency conservatism, especially on the subject of help-wanted ads, pressed them to take action.[43]

Anger also mounted over the fact that the leadership of the EEOC seemed in disarray. Franklin D. Roosevelt Jr. resigned only a year into his job to run (unsuccessfully) for governor of New York. Aileen Hernandez, frustrated that she and Richard Graham were the only commissioners who saw gender discrimination as a serious problem, threatened to quit. Graham's one-year term was about to expire, and rumors had spread that his independence on the gender issue had destroyed his chances of being reappointed.[44]

Resentment against the EEOC boiled over at the end of June 1966 at the Third Annual Conference of State Commissions on the Status of Women, held in Washington. Murray was scheduled to participate on a panel entitled "Sex Discrimination—Progress in Legal Status." Friedan attended as a writer observer. Over the past months, Catherine East had persuaded Friedan that she was the best person to organize an independent women's group that could apply the pressure necessary to get the government to enforce women's right to equal opportunity. Before taking such a fateful step, however, Friedan wanted to sound out the women from the various state commissions on the status of women. No more than Murray did she want to generate bad feeling by appearing to compete with these existing groups.[45]

By the end of the second day, June 29, Friedan and Murray resolved to act. Friedan invited about fifteen women to her hotel room that evening. Murray knew only five of them: Friedan, Eastwood, Dorothy Haener of the Women's Department of the United Automobile Workers, Catherine Conroy of the Communication Workers of America, and Kathryn Clarenbach, chair of the Wisconsin Commission on the Status of Women. Murray argued that it was time for a new organization, but Clarenbach and Conroy believed that the existing state commissions could deal with their concerns. Over Murray's objection, they insisted that they be allowed to present a resolution at the closing luncheon the next day, one that would urge the EEOC to enforce the sex provision of Title VII and reappoint commissioner Graham.[46]

Upset at what seemed to her a missed opportunity, Murray considered leaving the conference following her panel the next morning. When she heard, however, that conference officials had rejected Clarenbach and Conroy's proposal on the grounds that it was inappropriate for "government commissions to take action against other departments," she decided to stay. By lunchtime, Clarenbach and Conroy had agreed to go ahead with a new organization. Joining the other renegades at two tables near the rostrum, where dignitaries were making speeches, they whispered their agreement that the new group should be called the "National Organization for Women." Friedan scribbled its purpose on a paper napkin: "to take the actions needed to bring women into the mainstream of American society *now* . . . in fully equal partnership with men." The next day a telegram bearing twenty-eight names went to the White House; it demanded the reappointment of Graham. Night letters went out to the EEOC commissioners urging that sex-segregated want-ads be ruled unlawful. The group named Kay Clarenbach temporary coordinator of NOW. Murray and Caroline Ware were named to a six-person "temporary coordinating committee" to assist Clarenbach over the summer to develop a framework for a permanent organization.[47]

In the weeks that followed, Betty Friedan drafted a statement of purpose for the new organization. Initially, it focused on white, middle-class professional

Figure 13.1 The organizers of NOW at their first meeting in October 1966. Pauli Murray is in the back row, third from left. Betty Friedan is in the first row, first on the right. Records of the National Organization for Women, Schlesinger Library, Radcliffe Institute, Harvard University.

women and the abstract goal of equal rights, but when the drafting committee met to discussed revisions, Murray objected to the emphasis on legal rights to the exclusion of the broader goal of economic justice. The committee agreed to her request that she redraft that part of the statement. Whereas Friedan had written that NOW would give "active support to the common cause of equal rights for all groups," Murray substituted, "We realize that women's problems are linked to many broader questions of social justice." By "social justice," she meant "active support to the common cause of equal rights," not only "for all those who suffer discrimination," but also "for all those who suffer deprivation." Murray always worried that male civil rights leaders would forget women. She now feared that white professional women would forget about the poor, people who were disproportionately women and children of African descent. Other members of the committee readily agreed to her revision of Friedan's draft. The next day, October 30, 1966, the thirty-two charter members set up the permanent organization for the National Organization for Women (NOW) in Washington, DC.[48]

Consultant to the EEOC

Ironically, Murray's participation in NOW's organizational meeting marked the end of her influence on the nascent organization. On September 26, 1966, she landed a job at the EEOC. Charles B. Markham, a liberal Republican lawyer from Durham, NC, and director of the Office of Research at the commission, had been trying for a year to hire her as "Chief of Studies," but it took that long to secure authorization. When approval finally came through, it was only for a position as a consultant. With nothing else in hand, Murray accepted. Doing so meant giving up a chance to hold an executive position at NOW, because conflict of interest rules barred her from playing a leadership role in an organization gearing up for war against her new employer.[49]

Wanting to keep her New York apartment for weekend visits home to see Renee, Pauli asked Mildred if she could stay in a spare room at her house in Washington during the week. Mildred agreed, and Pauli set to work. Initially, she felt excited at the prospect of burrowing from within, but she soon found herself hamstrung by the agency's limited powers and inadequate funding. Congress had not only denied the EEOC the basic power to issue cease and desist orders when it discovered discrimination in private business, but it also underfunded the agency. In its first year the commission received 8,854 complaints, but conservatives in Congress, worried about creating too powerful an agency (along the lines of the National Labor Relations Board), provided only enough funding to handle 2,000 cases.[50]

Poor administration and low morale exacerbated the EEOC's limited powers and inadequate funding. When Murray arrived, the commission had been leaderless for four months. Roosevelt had not been replaced, nor had Graham. Hernandez, increasingly frustrated by the inaction of the remaining two commissioners, despite her repeated requests for decisions, resigned a few weeks after Murray's arrival. Five top staff positions remained vacant. One had never been filled; the others had been created by a rash of resignations.[51]

It fell to Murray to organize much of the early statistical work done at the agency—to prepare the EEO-3 forms on which labor unions reported the gender and race composition of their members, to analyze the complaints flowing into the agency, and to organize the forms for data processing. The EEOC commissioners continued to treat women's problems as relatively unimportant, but more than a quarter of all the complaints in the first year were of gender discrimination. Overwhelmed by the flood of paper, Murray set herself a task that could be completed in a short period of time: a study of the EEOC itself. She quickly found that it had failed to follow its own guidelines with regard to gender discrimination. Her analysis of staff positions at the commission revealed that "not one woman held a senior staff position. Males held 24 of the 25 top civil service posts (Grades 15–18) and almost ninety percent of all jobs in Grades 12–18."[52]

The most nettlesome problem the EEOC faced in 1966 was protective legislation for women, the one topic on which women leaders remained deeply divided. At one end of the spectrum, the NWP contended that all protective laws should be abolished. They were joined by a number of other NOW founders, including Mary Eastwood and Marguerite Rawalt, as well as many women in male-dominated industries who found themselves stuck in low-paying jobs because their states barred them from lifting weights above a set level and from working more than a fixed number of hours each day. At the other end of the spectrum stood Mary Keyserling of the Women's Bureau, joined by Caroline Ware, Dorothy Height, a number of women's groups, and many service union leaders, who believed that the protective laws for women should be upheld for women and extended to cover men. Murray found herself in the middle. As she wrote Kay Clarenbach, she believed with Ware and Keyserling in "revising upward" protective laws where possible. She also believed, however, in voluntary overtime. In states such as California, women were being denied promotion to jobs for which they were qualified, because the jobs required overtime work and those states barred them from working more than eight hours a day.[53]

Uncertain how to resolve these differences, the EEOC commissioners initially shifted responsibility to the states, asking that each one review its laws to decide whether or not they conflicted with Title VII. State legislatures obliged, beginning in 1965 with Delaware, which struck down its maximum-hour law. In the meantime, the EEOC urged complainants to sue their companies in federal court as a way of winning a speedier resolution of their claims. In the spring and summer of 1966, women barred from higher paying, traditionally male jobs in Georgia, Indiana, and California did so.[54]

Voluntary Overtime

On the lookout for a claim that might vindicate her Fourteenth Amendment strategy, Murray followed these cases closely, even before she reached the EEOC, through Sonia Pressman. Angry about what she regarded as foot dragging by male colleagues, Pressman reported early complaints of sex discrimination to members of the Washington underground. One case, in particular, captured Murray's attention, that of Velma Menglekoch, an aircraft worker in Long Beach, California.[55]

Mengelkoch wanted to sue California for barring her from overtime work. She had objected first to the United Auto Workers in January 1966, and then to the EEOC in February, that men doing the same electronics assembly work as she at the Autonetics Division of North American Aviation could earn overtime pay, but she could not. A widowed mother of three, she argued that the California law was especially hard on female heads of households. "I had to raise three children on my salary," she told a reporter indignantly. In fact, to cover her expenses she had worked two full-time jobs while her children were growing up. California's eight-hour law had not protected her from excessive hours; it had simply forced her to work for eighty hours to achieve what she could have earned, with overtime pay, in fifty-four. "We want the right to be asked for overtime and the right to refuse it without detriment to our jobs," she concluded. When asked if overturning the California law might open other women workers to exploitation, she responded, "There's no chance of going back to forced labor and sweatshops." Mengelkoch assumed, naïvely, that overtime would always be voluntary. Proceeding on that faith, she organized other women workers at her plant and approached a local lawyer, Phil Poppler, about filing a case. Poppler, following Chuck Morgan's strategy in *White v. Crook*, advised Mengelkoch to claim that California's hours-law violated the Fourteenth Amendment. If she did that, she could request a three-judge court and from there go straight to the Supreme Court.[56]

In Mengelkoch's story, Murray saw the possibility of picking up where *White v. Crook* had left off. It was a risky move. Challenging a state law that barred women from jury service was one thing; all but three states had already made jury service available to women under at least some conditions. Going after state protective laws was another matter altogether. Forty-two states, including a few in the South, had enacted such laws under pressure from reformers. The Supreme

Court would not be eager to take up a question that appeared to be well settled throughout much of the country, especially given that so many women's groups and labor unions continued to support protective labor laws for women.[57]

To complicate matters, Murray learned of the case only a few weeks before taking her job at the EEOC. She therefore tried to interest either NOW or the ACLU in representing Mengelkoch. Caruthers Berger, an attorney in the office of the solicitor, Department of Labor, presented the case at the organizational meeting of NOW at the end of September 1966. A debate ensued. Caroline Ware objected that the case would jeopardize protective labor legislation and force women to work excessive hours. Murray conceded that it might, but that the time had come to challenge hours laws as limiting women's economic prog-ress. With the FLSA now extended to cover more than half of all female work-ers, the requirement that employers pay time and a half for overtime, Murray believed, would inhibit employers from enforcing excessive hours of work. In addition, Murray saw in the *Mengelkoch* case a chance to make common cause with working-class women. The new members voted to create a legal committee that would decide what to do. Murray also approached the ACLU, but Kenyon, like Ware at NOW, objected that the case posed too great a danger to protective labor laws. In the end, the ACLU begged off, but Marguerite Rawalt offered her assistance on behalf of NOW, which (overriding the objections of Ware and oth-ers) predicted that the *Mengelkoch* case "may well result in a landmark decision in civil rights for women comparable to the historic decision of *Brown v. Board of Education.*"[58]

General-Counsel Designate and the FBI

The saga of *Mengelkoch* had barely commenced when Murray learned of a won-derful opportunity. In November, the EEOC general counsel, Charles Duncan, left his position to become corporation counsel in Washington, DC. Stephen Shulman, the newly appointed EEOC chairman and a white lawyer, told Murray that he intended to appoint her to replace Duncan, who was black. A position at that level required FBI clearance, appointment by the president, and confirma-tion by the Senate, but Shulman did not expect that to take long.[59]

The prospect thrilled Murray. Of all the positions at the EEOC, only the five commissioners exercised more influence than the general counsel. As much as Murray relished the possibility of promotion, however, she feared the FBI investigation required by a job at that level. Her struggle to win admission to the New York State Bar in 1948, and even more her failure to win the research posi-tion at Cornell in 1952, made her all too aware of the risk she ran from any inves-tigation. For a few weeks, she put off work on the necessary forms. She had most of the information she needed from the records she had saved from her prior applications for legal work. Updating it would not be difficult; indeed, it would be satisfying to list her achievements since the disappointment at Cornell. She just hoped that the Red Scare of the postwar years had subsided enough and that her professional success since then—the publication of *Proud Shoes,* her work as an associate at Paul, Weiss, her teaching and writing at Ghana Law School, and her doctoral work at Yale Law School—would outweigh any evidence of youthful indiscretions. Nonetheless, she took great care in explaining the points in her past most likely to raise concerns.[60]

At least she had not followed up on a possibility that had once seemed like the only way out of her gender-identity torment. When Murray first sought hormone therapy to transition from female to male, the medical community had no name for her condition other than "schizophrenia." That changed in 1949, when Ohio psychiatrist Dr. David Cauldwell coined the term transsexual. By the mid-1960s Dr. Harry Benjamin was giving hormones to hundreds of patients, one of them, Reed Erickson, a wealthy female-to-male (FTM) transsexual, seven years Murray's junior. At Benjamin's urging, Erickson funded a Gender Identity Clinic to provide sex-reassignment surgery at Johns Hopkins University Hospital in 1966. Murray no doubt followed this well-publicized innovation closely, as well as Benjamin's newly published treatise, *The Transsexual Phenomenon* (1966). Had the treatment been available in the 1930s or 1940s, she almost certainly would have pursued it. But she had long since given up any thought of following through on such a plan. If reading about the new Gender Identity Clinic prompted second thoughts, her nomination to the position of general counsel at the EEOC squelched them. She knew that she would have enough trouble passing the FBI review of her case as it was. To add to her checkered political and personal past the news that she was undergoing sex reassignment treatment would have ended any hope she had of a position that came to her, in part, because of her public identification as female.[61]

The FBI completed its investigation in February 1967, and Cartha DeLoach, the bureau's deputy director and liaison to the White House, reported the findings to President Lyndon Johnson in March. Assuming that the investigation would soon reach a favorable completion, Shulman announced in a staff meeting in late March that Murray would be the new general counsel. Stories began to appear in the press, and letters of congratulation—one from a delighted Aileen Hernandez—arrived at Shulman's office.[62]

Then the ax fell. DeLoach sent the FBI report to Shulman, who met with DeLoach and another official at FBI headquarters. Most of those consulted had praised Murray's work, her intelligence, and her loyalty, but the very problems about which Murray had worried caught the eye of investigators. Shulman was not sure how to proceed. DeLoach emphasized that it was not for the FBI to say. When Shulman called the president, however, he realized he had no choice. Johnson refused to risk political capital on a candidate with Murray's past.[63]

On April 18, Shulman called Murray into his office and delivered the bad news. In her autobiography, Murray stated simply, "The job of General Counsel was treated as a 'Sensitive Position' and the Administration feared my activist background would draw fire from EEOC's opponents in Congress." It was actually worse than that. The FBI's investigation had turned up a series of problems, some political, others more personal, which Shulman laid out for Murray when he explained why he could not promote her, even though he had announced that he would: her "unconsummated marriage," her work for Open Road, her arrest for picketing, her membership in the Communist Party Opposition, her work for the Negro People's Committee to Aid Spanish Refugees (NPC), the time she was picked up in Rhode Island by the police and taken to Bellevue and diagnosed as "schizophrenic," her arrest for creating a disturbance on a bus in Virginia and subsequent jail term, and her membership in the Socialist Party. As Murray's friend Sonia Pressman later told her, Murray had been "incredibly naïve" not to have anticipated that her activism (Pressman knew nothing of her personal travails) would pose a problem, given the fact that her nomination would have to be vetted by a Senate where opposition to the EEOC remained strong.[64]

There was more. Although Murray's references had generally praised her work, an attorney who had supervised her work at Paul, Weiss faulted her for being more interested in sociology than in law. Murray might have corrected this problem in her graduate work at Yale Law School, but her dissertation had focused on social policy, not legal issues. Could she separate her policy views from her legal responsibilities as general counsel? Shulman had concluded that he could not risk finding out that the answer was no.[65]

Fearing the public relations disaster that would attend his failure to promote Murray, Shulman quickly devised a back-up plan. He offered her the position of deputy general counsel, a job that did not require Senate approval. Humiliated and angry at being denied, once again, a position for which she considered herself uniquely qualified, Murray refused Shulman's olive branch. More than wounded pride prompted her decision. She feared being trapped in work she felt least able to do well—the writing of memos in support of decisions she strongly opposed. As she considered her situation further, she realized that the position of general counsel, which she had wanted so much, would have posed the same problem. "I knew from the beginning that if I belonged anywhere at all in this agency, it was as a Commissioner and not as a staff member," she admitted to her diary. It had been foolish of her to "try to be what I am unable to be well—a subordinate." She had to go. Within a week, she resigned from the agency, cleared out her office, and returned to New York. Renee Barlow met her at her 11th Street apartment and helped her move back in. Pauli talked of writing another book, but Renee gently pointed out that she was in no state for such work. She needed the structure of a job, not the isolation of an as yet undefined writing project.[66]

Returning to the South

Perhaps, Murray thought, she would be happier working in a religious institution. She spoke to her friend Anna Arnold Hedgeman at the National Council of Churches, who put her in touch with Dr. Benjamin F. Payton, the new executive director of her office, the Commission on Religion and Race within the Department of Social Justice. Payton, a black, thirty-four-year-old Baptist minister from South Carolina, with degrees from Harvard, Columbia, and Yale, had just been appointed president of Benedict College, a small black Baptist college in Columbia, South Carolina. After meeting Murray, he offered her a job as vice president for curricular development.[67]

Founded by Baptists in 1867 to educate former slaves, the college, open to both women and men, remained segregated and poor. If it was to survive, it needed help, someone with Murray's background who could raise its students' educational level. Having fled the segregated schools of the South four decades before, Murray had never wanted to return. But she had long hoped for an academic position, one in which she could fight for what she believed in and have the freedom to speak her mind. If she really believed in human rights and the fight against poverty, what better place to make a contribution than at a beleaguered school like Benedict? Hedgeman urged her to accept the position. Murray flew down to South Carolina to explore what the job would require and concluded that it might be just the thing.[68]

Before Murray left for her new job in late July, however, Barlow was diagnosed with breast cancer. Renee, who no longer worked at Paul, Weiss, had just been appointed personnel director at the Executive Council of the Episcopal Church. During the routine physical exam required of all new employees, the examining doctor discovered a lump. Tests confirmed a malignancy and the doctor urged immediate surgery. Barlow feared that if anyone other than Murray learned of her condition, she would never be able to work again. As the fifty-three-year-old sole support of her mother, Barlow decided to keep her illness a secret even from her. Mrs. Barlow had already lost two daughters to cancer, and Renee thought it better to tell her mother that she had decided to have surgery on her varicose veins than to reveal the truth. The surgery took place at Columbia-Presbyterian Hospital on June 16. Complications ensued. Renee developed a severe case of hepatitis from a blood transfusion. Weakened, she developed pneumonia. A wound on her leg, from which tissue had been removed for skin grafting, failed to heal. She remained in the hospital for months. Murray found herself shuttling back and forth between the hospital to comfort Renee and the Barlow apartment to reassure Mrs. Barlow that everything was fine, just taking a little longer to heal than originally thought. Pauli had to leave for South Carolina six weeks into Renee's recovery, but at least by that time Barlow was able to take short walks along the hospital corridor. The Episcopal Church held her job for her and by mid September she returned to work part-time. Gradually, she increased her hours to full-time, and by Christmas the two were able to celebrate her improved health with a trip Jamaica.[69]

Breaking with NOW

Before Renee Barlow's diagnosis, Murray had considered becoming more actively involved in NOW. No longer at the EEOC, she need not worry about a conflict of interest. But she had begun to "sour" on the organization she had worked so hard to found. When she attended the annual meeting in Washington in November 1967, a couple of months after beginning her new job in South Carolina, she realized that NOW had moved away from the vision she had initially had of a group dedicated to human rights.[70]

At its first meeting in October 1966, the NOW Board had established a series of task forces to develop policy for the organization and appointed Murray head of Equal Rights and Responsibilities as Citizens. When Murray's appointment to a job at the EEOC prevented her from taking charge of the Equal Rights Task Force, the officers established a "Subcommittee on Constitutional Protections of Women" in February 1967 to discuss whether to focus on Murray's strategy, support the passage of the Equal Rights Amendment, propose a new amendment, or pursue some combination of these.[71]

By this time, membership in NOW had grown to include at least some leaders of the National Woman's Party, including, most importantly, Alma Lutz. Following Murray's call to action at the National Council of Women in October 1965, Lutz had written to praise her speech but also to inquire why she had not endorsed the ERA. Murray responded that the Fourteenth Amendment offered a better alternative—already in place and easier to tailor to the needs of the time. In the next six months, Lutz continued the correspondence, trying in each letter to persuade Murray that only the ERA would do.[72]

Sometime between NOW's founding conference in October 1966 and February 1967, Lutz joined the new organization. When the officers formed the "Subcommittee on Constitutional Protections of Women," she secured a spot. The subcommittee also included Marguerite Rawalt, who continued to support the ERA but had come to regard Murray's approach as the best immediate option, and Mary Eastwood, who had come in recent months to believe the ERA was necessary. By September 1967, in large part because of the shift in Mary Eastwood's position, the officers agreed to devote a substantial part of the second annual meeting, in November, to an all-conference debate over whether NOW should endorse passage of the ERA. Murray knew that a major policy change was under way. A few weeks before the November meeting, Eastwood informed her of her own shift, specifically that she thought the Fourteenth Amendment strategy could be pursued in tandem with an Equal Rights Amendment, and that any success achieved through one would help the other. Murray disagreed. She feared that support for the ERA would divert attention not only from litigation under the Equal Protection Clause but also from the work of the other task forces, especially Anna Arnold Hedgeman's Task Force on Poverty.[73]

By the fall of 1967, Murray had come to regard poverty, which disproportionately affected women—and especially African American women and their children—as the country's most pressing concern. Unfortunately, civil rights leaders, encouraged by the Moynihan Report, had come to see African American women as a threat to the family and thus a cause of that poverty. To Murray's great satisfaction, she had finally won over Dorothy Height to her view that the government should not privilege black men. In early June 1966, a task force that included Height and Caroline Ware presented a paper at a White House Conference entitled, "To Fulfill the Rights of Negro Women in Disadvantaged Families," in which they argued—in sharp contrast to Moynihan and a growing number of civil rights leaders—that the government must provide jobs, training, and economic assistance to women, not just men, if poverty was to be overcome. The report was widely circulated, but it made little headway in policy circles.[74]

At NOW, Hedgeman and Murray both worried over reports that government officials were shutting women out of job training and other poverty programs. Far from pushing back against this anti-women campaign, NOW leaders talked of making passage of the ERA, long associated with elite professional women, its top priority. Murray and Hedgeman's campaign to keep the new organization focused on economic issues grew more difficult when Anna's husband, the opera and folk singer Marritt A. Hedgeman, fell ill. Anna missed the critical September 1967 meeting and feared that she might be called away from the annual meeting in November should his condition worsen. In desperation, she asked Murray to represent the Task Force on Poverty at the annual meeting, if she could not attend.[75]

On November 18, 1967, at the second annual NOW conference, Murray found herself trying to do two things at once: represent Hedgeman and stave off endorsement of the ERA. In the end, debate over a possible constitutional amendment consumed most of the time available for general discussion. Labor leaders Caroline Davis and Dorothy Haener asked for time to persuade their unions. Phineas Indritz, a longtime lawyer for civil rights causes, warned that the ERA had no chance of passing Congress. He urged instead that NOW continue Murray's Fourteenth Amendment strategy. Murray warned that support for the ERA would "alienate organizations who have given us support until now." She urged a seven-month delay so that members could choose among three alternatives: endorse the ERA as it was currently worded; endorse an alternative amendment with different wording; or pursue the Fourteenth Amendment strategy as before. According to minutes from the meeting, "much discussion followed," but Murray mustered only fifteen votes, while eighty-two voted for NOW's immediate endorsement of the ERA.[76]

Murray left the conference "deeply disillusioned." Two days later, in a letter to Kay Clarenbach, she withdrew her name from nomination to the NOW board of directors. In despair, she predicted that NOW's single-minded focus on the ERA would limit the movement "almost solely to 'women's rights' without strong bonds with other movements toward human rights" and "might develop into a 'head-on collision' with Black civil rights and other struggles." It all came down to the fact that she could not fragment herself "into Negro at one time, woman at another, or worker at another." She did not mention her inability to fragment her gender identity into a man at one time, woman at another, but surely she was thinking of that, too. She left the conference feeling "like a stranger in my own household . . . passé, old, and declassed." In her absence, Murray's NAACP for women had turned into an NAACP for professional, white women. Gradually, NOW gave up altogether on protective labor laws—even gender neutral ones. As long as Murray fought for the principle of freedom, white women listened, but when she voiced concern over economic injustice, she lost that audience.[77]

In coining the term "Jane Crow" in the early 1940s, Murray had meant not only to emphasize the parallel nature of race and gender discrimination but also to convey the compounding effect of gender plus race discrimination for women of color. In her 1964 memo in support of keeping "sex" in Title VII and her article "The Negro Woman in the Quest for Equality" Murray moved back and forth between the parallels between race and gender, on the one hand, and the "interrelatedness" of this "dual burden" in the lives of black women, on the other. She tried to establish common cause with white women, even as she underscored the particular plight of black women. As of the fall of 1967, she had succeeded more in the former than in the latter effort. Moynihan had spread the illusion that black women were better off financially than black men. The truth was very different. In 1967, the median income of black women was only 71 percent that of white women and only 66 percent of that for black men. Women as a group did poorly compared to men as a group, but black women fared worst of all. The National Woman's Party had successfully used Murray in its campaign for freedom, but for Murray, as for the majority of African American women, freedom was not enough.[78]

PART VI

TO TEACH, TO PREACH, 1967–1977

Professor Murray

Benedict College

Murray embarked on her job at Benedict College with high hopes. She looked forward to assuming her position as vice president in charge of curricular reform and to working with President Benjamin Payton, whose intelligence and idealism impressed her when they met in New York. Payton persuaded her that schools like Benedict represented the new frontier in civil rights, places where one could do the most to close the educational gap that separated blacks from whites. The future seemed bright, until, a few months into her new job, Murray again discovered she had made a serious mistake.

The problem, ironically, was not the South. Before school started, she attended an educational conference at a small black boarding school in Columbus, Mississippi. There, she met and got to know Fannie Lou Hamer, a national celebrity following her testimony on behalf of the Mississippi Freedom Democratic Party at the 1964 Democratic Convention. The local motel welcomed Murray without incident, as did the cafeteria on the main street of town, where she dined with an interracial group of conferees that included three whites and another black person. She had similar experiences when she reached her new home in Columbia, South Carolina. Although the Confederate flag flew above the state capitol, only a few blocks away, local storekeepers treated her with courtesy.[1]

The problem was President Payton. Once installed as president of Benedict College he turned into an "Osagyefo" (the name Nkrumah's admirers gave him, when he declared Ghana's independence from Britain and embarked on a course of military rule). Payton treated her not with the respect due her greater age, experience, and wisdom, but with a high-handed condescension that infuriated her. Born a generation later, he had enjoyed a fast track to the Ivy League education she had only partially, and belatedly, achieved; and yet, he displayed none of the generosity of spirit that, in her mind, should have accompanied that privilege. He claimed for himself the plaudits that came from her hard work and bridled at the least show of independence. When she asked the phone company to install a private line in her campus residence, at her own expense, to stay in touch with Renee Barlow, Payton ordered the line removed.[2]

Murray understood that the new president, coming as he did from a patriarchal black Baptist family in the rural South, had certain expectations about the place of women. She understood further, that as a young man in a new job he felt defensive about his authority. One had to make allowances. But there were limits. In addition to alienating her, he had, in a few short months, undone the excitement that had attended his arrival by castigating newly recruited faculty from the North and West as "hippies" and "white liberals," who discussed only "sex" and "Black Power" in their classrooms. By November, Murray had had enough but would see out the school year. She tendered her resignation, effective July 31, 1968.[3]

Shortly thereafter, while waiting for a plane to take her to the ill-fated November NOW convention in Washington, Murray unburdened herself in a letter to Laura Bornholdt, a friend from her time in Ghana. Murray had met Bornholdt when Kwame Nkrumah had invited the latter, then dean of women at the University of Pennsylvania, to visit Ghana as an educational adviser. "Osagyefo," as Bornholdt well knew, had strongly negative meaning for Murray. Murray feared she had once again fallen prey to the kind of autocratic power that had driven her from her law school post in 1961. She had always bridled at such treatment, especially from black men in the civil rights and Pan-African movements. Bornholdt was one friend to whom she could write candidly on the subject. Having left the University of Pennsylvania in 1961 to become dean of Wellesley College and having joined the Danforth Foundation in 1964, Bornholdt took a particular interest in the travails of academic women as well as the plight of black colleges, which in the post-*Brown* era found themselves in a battle for their very survival.[4]

Having announced that she would leave Benedict after the 1967–1968 academic school year, and having grown disillusioned with NOW after the 1967 convention in which it voted to support the ERA, Murray turned her attention to the job at hand: to develop new educational programs at Benedict and to fund them through external grants. With a grant from the Department of Housing Education and Welfare (HEW), she pioneered a reading center and pilot math project. They proved so successful that some first-year students made a leap of more than four years between September and May. The median advanced almost two years. Murray also won a grant from the Ford Foundation for a six-week summer institute for teachers of freshman English. Anna Hedgeman, who oversaw the program, marveled at the teachers' excitement as they talked about new approaches to teaching their subject. For Murray, the institute represented a return to the tradition, initiated in her grandfathers' time and carried on in her

Figure 14.1 Pauli Murray playing with her dog Doc at Benedict College, South Carolina, 1967–1968. Estate of Pauli Murray, Schlesinger Library, Radcliffe Institute, Harvard University.

father's and aunts' generation, of southern black teachers who attended annual summer schools to better themselves and their students.[5]

The South was changing, and yet violence "smoldered beneath the surface, ready to flare up at any moment," Murray discovered. Even on her otherwise uplifting trip to Mississippi before starting at Benedict, she discovered that the interracial conference was under surveillance. One night the attendees saw a string of headlights snaking up the road to their hillside-meeting place. Only after they moved their own cars to the head of the road and trained their headlights downward did the approaching vehicles shift direction and move away.

Much worse was to come. In February 1968, police shot and killed three black students and wounded more than thirty people at nearby South Carolina State College during a protest against a segregated bowling alley. Two months later, Martin Luther King Jr. was assassinated in Memphis, Tennessee.[6]

Murray had often resented King's condescension toward black women in the movement, but she had always been "passionately devoted" to King's cause and was stricken by his death. She felt a little better when she learned that she had been part of one of the memorials to the fallen leader. Sarah Dalkowitz Kaplan, a friend from International House in New York who had moved to Seattle, wrote that she had been one of 10,000 people at a ceremony to honor King in Seattle's Memorial Stadium on Sunday, April 7. The multiracial crowd sang "We Shall Overcome," and the governor spoke. Closing the ceremony, Olivia Cole, an actress with the Seattle Repertory Theater, read a passage from Murray's poem "Dark Testament":

> Then let the dream linger on.
> Let it be the test of nations,
> Let it be the quest of all our days, . . .
> Until the final man may stand in any place,
> And thrust his shoulders to the sky,
> Friend and brother to every other man.[7]

The power of Murray's words at that moment led finally to the publication of her collected poems as *Dark Testament* two years later, but in the spring of 1968, her dream of universal brotherhood proved hard to sustain. Riots broke out across the nation. At Benedict, Murray's relations with her boss deteriorated further. By the end of May, she returned to New York City, mindful that for the second time in only two years, she had left a job on which she had pinned high hopes. To her diary she confessed a fear that she lacked "the ingredients of steady success."[8]

Brandeis University

To Murray's astonishment, a new opportunity arose only a few days later. On June 10, Morris B. Abram, the newly named president of Brandeis University, called Murray at her New York City apartment. He wanted to know whether she would be interested in a faculty position. Following Martin Luther King Jr.'s assassination, African American students at Brandeis—in common with others across the country—had demanded more black students, black faculty, and black courses. Outgoing university president Abram Sachar and a small group of faculty members had worked with Abram to do all three. Their efforts took on fresh urgency when on June 6, Robert F. Kennedy was shot and killed in Los Angeles the night he won the California Democratic primary for the presidency. Feeling guilty that she was not pulling her "own weight in helping to resolve some of the chaos of our time," Murray saw in Abram's call a way to do so.[9]

Murray greatly admired Abram, a small-town civil rights attorney from Georgia, best known for his winning argument in the 1963 voter-rights case *Gray v. Sanders*. Abram persuaded the Supreme Court that Georgia's electoral system violated the Equal Protection Clause of the Fourteenth Amendment by giving greater weight to ballots cast in predominantly white rural areas than to those cast by urban blacks. In a historic opinion, Justice William Douglas declared, "The concept of political equality . . . can mean only one thing—one person, one vote." That same year Abram and his family moved to New York, where he became president of the American Jewish Committee and, two years later, United States representative to the United Nations Commission on Human Rights. He also joined Paul, Weiss, where he got to know Lloyd Garrison. Following the racial turmoil of the spring of 1968, he sought Garrison's recommendation of someone who could build a program in "Black Studies" at Brandeis. Garrison suggested Murray. Abram liked the idea of a civil rights lawyer in the job.[10]

For Murray the name Brandeis held a certain "magic." Harvard-trained Louis D. Brandeis had created the "Brandeis Brief," an indispensable model for civil rights advocates faced with weak law but strong facts. He was also the first Jew, as well as one of the most distinguished justices, ever to serve on the Supreme Court. The university that bore his name was founded in 1948—the same year as Israel—as a nonsectarian university under Jewish auspices. Most impressive to Murray, the university was open to all, without regard to religion, race, or gender—in contrast to such elite institutions as Harvard, Yale, and Princeton, which had long discriminated against Jews and women. Murray also admired the fact that in 1949 the twelve-member board of trustees of the university had asked Eleanor Roosevelt to be their first female trustee. Accepting their offer, Roosevelt declared her wish for the new university: "that it will fulfill the hopes of all those who have suffered in minority groups." For the rest of her life, as a trustee and occasional visiting lecturer in international relations, she worked to ensure that it would. Feeling keenly the pull of that legacy, Murray traveled to Brandeis, thirteen miles west of Boston, to meet with Dean of the Faculty Peter Diamandopoulos and several professors.[11]

One of those professors was Larry Fuchs, a political scientist who headed the American Civilization Program at Brandeis. He had once taught a course with Eleanor Roosevelt on international relations, and Roosevelt had spoken warmly to him of Murray. When Murray arrived on campus, he liked her immediately and talked about the contribution she could make to Brandeis through interdisciplinary courses not only on the black experience but also in legal studies for undergraduates. His warmth and enthusiasm encouraged Murray to think she might fit in.[12]

Nothing was resolved during these initial talks, but later that summer, while Murray was in Sweden at a meeting of the World Conference of Churches, a telegram arrived from Dean Peter Diamandopoulos offering her a one-year visiting professorship in the Department of Politics and the American Civilization Program. She hesitated. Ever since Abram's initial call she had been having second thoughts about leaving Renee Barlow and New York City. She also feared that at Brandeis, as at NOW, she would be judged "passé." Worse, she might not be up to the challenge of teaching at so demanding an academic institution, and, even if she was, she might not be able to prove her competence in just one year. And yet, the prospect of having a job was tempting. She cabled her acceptance.[13]

Murray experienced one more crisis of confidence in August, while vacationing in Maine with Caroline Ware, Gardner Means, and others. To everyone's surprise, Murray announced that rather than teach at Brandeis, she wanted to write a memoir. She would call it "Jane Crow." Skipper and Gardner, recognizing a familiar case of nerves, told her that she was going to love Brandeis as well as the Boston area, with its dozens of colleges and universities, seminaries, and cultural attractions. She should buckle down, earn tenure, and then spend her summers writing the book. Mary Norris (the daughter of one of Ware's friends and a Radcliffe student) promised to help her find an apartment in Cambridge and act as a guide to local attractions. Calmer, Murray drove back to New York with her nephew, Michael Murray (Raymond's son), stopping along the way at Hyde Park, to draw renewed courage from a visit to the graves of Franklin and Eleanor Roosevelt.[14]

By September, Murray felt better. Hopeful that her new position would become permanent, she gave up her apartment in New York and packed her dog, Doc, together with as much else as she could, into the Volkswagen she and Barlow had bought together. Murray then stacked as many boxes as she dared into a luggage rack on top. A moving van, which carried a half-dozen file cabinets, dozens of cartons of books and papers, and a few household effects, followed. For decades, Murray's correspondence, diaries, pictures, and other personal papers had been her most prized possessions; by 1968, even with periodic pruning, they comprised the vast bulk of her property.[15]

Murray's first day at Brandeis—Friday, September 13—began inauspiciously. Famished, she found the student cafeteria, where she asked for bacon and eggs. "We don't serve bacon here," the server responded. Though a secular institution, Brandeis observed Kosher dietary laws out of respect for Jewish students. Mortified by her "boner," Murray felt like sinking through the floor. And thus began what would be "the most exciting, tormenting, satisfying, embattled, frustrated, and at times triumphant period" of her life thus far.[16]

American Civilization

In hiring Murray, Abram had executed an end run around Brandeis's customary faculty-search procedures. There had not been enough time, in the spring of King's assassination and the protests that followed, for a regular search. Even if there had been, what department would have her? Murray lacked graduate training in history, English, or politics, the disciplines most closely associated with American Civilization Programs. Needing to place her somewhere, Dean Diamondopolous persuaded a reluctant Roy C. Macridis, chair of the Department of Politics, to give her a one-year "courtesy appointment" in his department, while an enthusiastic Larry Fuchs offered to assume primary responsibility for her in the American Civilization Program.[17]

Those drawn to American Civilization often supported progressive politics and sought in their academic life to bring more attention to indigenous peoples, blacks, the working class, and women. No one assigned *Moby-Dick* in English departments before E. O. Matthiessen, the secretly gay, Communist founder of American Civilization at Harvard, began to do so in the 1930s. He taught students to see the Pequod as America in miniature, with its racial diversity, capitalist tyranny, and oppressed crew. To Matthiessen, the interdisciplinary study of history and literature offered a way to critique the undemocratic aspects of American society. Not all those attracted to these programs were leftists. During the Cold War, some saw in them as an opportunity to teach students to appreciate American values associated with private enterprise. At Yale, for instance, the program became a vehicle for recruiting students to the Central Intelligence Agency (CIA). Brandeis, filled with Harvard-trained faculty, resembled Harvard more than Yale. For Larry Fuchs and others the program offered a chance to experiment with new ways of understanding American culture, particularly the African American experience.[18]

Murray was delighted by the opportunity to be part of American Civilization and to develop interdisciplinary courses on law and the black experience. Early in the new term, she submitted a proposal to Larry Fuchs and other interested parties for a program in legal studies, as part of what she suggested Brandeis call American Studies, to emphasize its interdisciplinary nature and to dispel any implication that America possessed a "civilization" that was "exceptional" or more elevated than any other. The opportunities provided by Murray's new home in American Civilization excited her, but she well knew that they came as an incidental byproduct of the protest that had brought her to the university.[19]

She had been called to Brandeis on behalf of the black students. Through intense recruitment, the university had doubled black enrollment over the summer—from 58 to 120 in a student body of 2,600. More than a third of the increase came from a new project, inspired by Daniel Patrick Moynihan, called the Transitional Year Program (TYP). Designed to bring inner-city males to Brandeis for a pre-college year to correct their educational deficits and see what college was like, the TYP offered a fully funded year of residence on campus to twenty-six males, twenty-three of them black. A number were high school drop-outs from Roxbury, the black neighborhood in southern Boston beset by riots following the death of Martin Luther King Jr. TYP students were to take three remedial courses. If they completed the program successfully, they would win admission to the university. In addition, each student would be permitted to take a regular course, to get a foretaste of college work and competition with regularly admitted undergraduates. If they passed they got credit. If they failed, the grade would not be recorded.[20]

Murray thought the program "a bold, imaginative idea," but she deplored the fact that no women had been recruited. Moreover, she worried that the university had made a serious mistake in targeting students who did not have the background or study skills necessary to handle college work. It would have been better, she believed, to enroll students from traditionally black southern schools like Benedict, where they had been exposed to the discipline of college study. Murray would have a chance to consider these issues in some depth, since the college administration had authorized a concentration in African and African American Studies and had appointed her to the committee of faculty and student representatives charged with overseeing it.[21]

A generation older, reared in the South, the product of a middle-class background and many years of hard-won, elite education, Murray had little in common with the black students arriving at Brandeis in 1968, except for the single racial category to which American society had assigned them. Murray later recognized that she would have been in the "same predicament as a member of the faculty of Cornell, Swarthmore, Harvard, Yale, Columbia." Across the country liberals like her, who sought reform, proved to be as vulnerable to attack as the racial bigots who resisted change. "In the agony of breaking free from the bondage of past untouchability," she ruefully learned, "its victims flailed at friends and enemies alike." At the time, however, she believed she could win acceptance.[22]

Murray had two weeks to learn about her new committee assignment and develop the seminar Larry Fuchs had asked her to teach on "Law as an Instrument of Social Change" (shortened to "Law and Social Change"), scheduled to meet twice a week. In haste, Murray drew up a syllabus for seniors with strong backgrounds in history and politics. She planned to use statutes and court cases as primary documents, provide historical context through lectures, and lead the class in a discussion of the possibilities and limits of legal action as a vehicle for achieving racial justice, consumer protection, participatory democracy, and women's rights as well as solutions to urban problems and remedies for poverty. Introduced too late to appear in the course catalogue, the course was publicized by word of mouth, notices posted on bulletin boards in classroom buildings, and an announcement at the first fall meeting of the Afro-American Students Association. Murray waited nervously to see if anyone would show up.[23]

"Black Male Power"

On the first day of class, Murray walked down the hall from her office in Ford Hall and entered the seminar room assigned to "Law and Social Change." There she found fourteen students seated behind tables arranged in a U-shaped formation, facing a teacher's desk. From their enrollment cards, she learned that the students included eight seniors (including one black woman) and two juniors. They all had strong backgrounds in political science, and several were considering law school. These students had seated themselves along the sides of the U. The remaining four, all black males, sat together in the rear. To her dismay, she learned that they were from the TYP project. The students she had taught in Ghana and helped at Benedict had all suffered from weak preparation, but at least they had that handicap in common. How was she to bridge the educational gap between some of the best students at Brandeis, all but one of whom were white, and these four black male pre-freshmen?[24]

Beset by first day jitters, Murray had barely begun her overview of the course and requirements when one of the TYP students interrupted her with a question: "Why do you keep saying 'Knee-grows' when you're talking about *black* people?" Murray groped for an answer. Finally, she responded that "'Negro' was a legitimate usage, a proper noun adopted by scholars and official government publications, and was preferred by many people," including her. Murray had engaged in her own protest as a student, going through her textbooks and professors' comments on her papers, crossing out every lowercase "n" in "negro" and inking in a capital "N," as a way of dignifying a term regularly used to belittle people of African descent. A generation later the students before her were seeking dignity by embracing the English variant, "black," and ridiculing as a symbol of slavery and segregation its Spanish and Portuguese version, "negro." Murray no doubt appreciated the parallel between her own youthful rebellion and that of the young man seated before her, but she saw a larger political point at stake. She was being challenged in a disrespectful manner because of her gender to adopt a term that she and the students both associated with a reductionist view of skin color and a separatist vision of racial life, a political stance that went against everything she had fought for all her life. Nevertheless, she offered to compromise. Henceforth, she would use "Negro" half the time and "black" the other half.[25]

In the early weeks of the class, Murray focused on trying to engage the pre-freshmen, but her lectures went over their heads. To make matters worse, several of the seniors, all women, came to her office to complain that the class was being pitched at too simple a level. If Murray did not make it more challenging, they threatened to drop out. Deeply worried, Murray turned to Kathryn "Kitty" Preyer, a professor of history at Wellesley College and her next-door neighbor in Cambridge, where she had rented an apartment. Trained by the pioneer social historian Merle Curti at the University of Wisconsin, Preyer had been teaching early American social and legal history for the past thirteen years and was head of the Afro-American Studies Program at Wellesley. Preyer offered some suggestions. To engage the TYP students, Murray needed to lecture less and introduce some well-crafted prompts to spur discussion. To retain the interest of the juniors and seniors, she should provide more challenging readings and writing assignments.[26]

Preyer's suggestions helped Murray turn the class around. Reporting to Renee Barlow two days later, Murray wrote, "I started the kids off with 'Reflect a few minutes on what it meant to be a slave.' Got the tip from my next door neighbor, Mrs. Preyer.... She also spent an hour talking with me Sunday night and gave me sources and all kinds of tips." Murray followed up the discussion on slavery by handing out a six-page bibliography of secondary readings for the course and a two-page bibliography of primary sources for the lectures on the background and law of slavery. She summarized each book and primary source on the list and explained why she recommended that the students read it. "I guess that will hold them for a while," she continued to Barlow, with whom she had been anxiously conferring by phone. "You're right. Some of them needed to be overwhelmed . . . and they are beginning to seem impressed," she wrote of the seniors. Just as encouraging, "Three of the Negro kids followed me back to my office and hung around until I had to throw them out to go to a meeting. But they know they are welcome, and that I shall do all I can to help them."[27]

In the early weeks of the course, Murray organized her lectures and assignments around the *Dred Scott* case (1857). She introduced the students to the South's slave laws, including most particularly the law that prohibited teaching slaves how to read or write. She provided historical, economic, and anthropological context, striving all the while to make "the period come alive for them." She stressed "the continuous protest against enslavement, the long slow torturous cases through the courts, lasting sometimes 10 to 20 years." Most of the students were aware of violent slave revolts and the Underground Railroad. What they did not know was that *Dred Scott* was merely the most famous of hundreds of legal challenges to slavery.[28]

"My students are responding," she reported to Barlow with relief. One chose to write on Thurgood Marshall's role in *Brown*; she urged him to try to get an appointment with Marshall and interview him. Another wanted to write about the current controversy over community control of public schools, and she suggested that she write to the lawyer whose letter had just appeared in the *New York Times* to get the briefs and other documents in the case. One of her pre-freshmen wanted to write on a "Separate State"; she helped him see that the subject was too difficult to be done in a semester and guided him to a more manageable subject.[29]

"A little levity is being introduced on the use of 'black' and 'Negro,'" Murray reported to Barlow. "One of my pre-Freshmen [Leonard E. Carson], sits at the end of the seminar table facing me. . . . Yesterday, I said something about 'Negro,' I mean 'Black'—Mr. Carson, I see you down there at the end of the table looking at me like the angel Gabriel, at which point the class breaks up." In a darker mood, she complained in her midterm report on the class that the TYP students had been challenging her ever since the first day. Carson kept score of the number of times she used "black" and the number of times she used "Negro."[30]

She tried to make the students see that she cared about them individually by bringing in material from outside of class. One day she brought in something that related to a comment made by a black student, another day a document about an idea on which a white student had commented. She also strove to get across an appreciation for legal processes "however frustrating and time-consuming these are, and a recognition of the dangers involved in sweeping away these procedures." To reinforce her individualized concern, and to help bridge the educational gap between the TYP students and the upperclassmen, she held six office hours a week, three times the expected number.[31]

Throughout the semester, she divided subjects by topic, but never by race or gender. She talked about white indentured servants before mentioning black slaves. When she raised the question of the possible liberation of women, she inquired what the liberation of men would look like. The latter topic, in particular, startled the TYP students. "They're males, and all full of 'Black Male Power,'" she told Caroline Ware halfway through the term.[32]

The senior women who had threatened to drop the course offered to tutor the TYP students, who were obviously struggling. Murray, worried that the black men would feel humiliated to be tutored by white women, thought of a better way to present the offer. Remembering her first days at Paul, Weiss, when she felt unable to do the work expected of her, she entered class one day and told the students that the class had reached that point in the term when it was time to move on to the preceptor system. This was the method, she explained, used at elite law firms to get the work done. Every time the firm hired a new associate, it assigned a senior attorney to show the new person "the ropes." If any one of the new students would be interested she would assign him to a precep-tor. Nothing happened for several weeks, and then Carson and Myers, the most promising of the four TYP students, came to her office to inquire about "what did you call them—pre- pre-something?" Murray felt like weeping with relief. She put the two men in touch with two female seniors who had volunteered. "It began to work!" The students began to meet outside of class and to discuss some of the sensitive racial issues. Murray noticed a more relaxed atmosphere in the seminar.[33]

By November, Murray felt she had turned a corner. Larry Fuchs called to say that he had been hearing "wonderful things about the course." One of his better students, a transfer from Goucher College, had come to thank him for recom-mending the class. She told him it was the "best course she had taken; that it was pulling together many things for her." Others were "saying similar things," Fuchs reported. In addition, Morris Abram, learning of her success at Benedict in rais-ing grant money, asked if she would do the same at Brandeis.[34]

Murray felt that she was succeeding with her students, but she heard rumors of a movement afoot to boycott the seminar as too uncritical of American soci-ety, when she gave it again in the spring. She feared that the boycott had started already, inasmuch as she had only one black student among her upperclassmen. To Barlow, Murray lamented, "There are a group of Afro-headed women who are members of the Afro-American Student Association and none of them come near me." This troubled her in part because she had been bold enough to wear her hair in a close-cropped, natural style from the time she was a young adult. Sometimes, she despaired. "Despite every subtle overture and a plea that we keep the dialogue going," these students looked upon her with "obvious dis-trust." She felt herself "a Negro Brahmin, dealing with Northern Ghetto prod-ucts . . . alien to my entire upbringing and lifestyle and who cannot (yet) identify with me as a model of achievement." Deeply distressed, she wondered: "How can one make these youngsters see that they are—<u>not</u> dealing with a mono-lithic white society arrayed against them like a consuming fire but that they are dealing with social forces and structures, some of them impersonal, and that unless they analyze and understand these forces and learn to manipulate or help to control them, they will help to sweep themselves and the rest of us into the chaos?' "[35]

The Seizure of Ford Hall

In the final weeks of the semester, chaos arrived. On Wednesday, January 8, 1969, Murray had just begun class, her third to last of the fall term, when "Around 2:05" two "Negro girl students" ran through the halls shouting, "Everybody out of the building." Since "there was no indication of fire or other emergency, my class continued until 3:15 when a Negro male student opened the door and declared, 'The black students have taken over this building. Will you please leave.'" Murray asked the young man why. "No explanation was forthcoming." She then asked the students what they wanted to do, seeking in particular the view of Stephen Deitsch, vice president of the Student Council. Since only ten minutes remained, the class decided to leave the building.[36]

As Murray would soon learn, fifteen members of the Afro-American Society had seized Ford-Sydeman Hall, which housed, in addition to faculty offices and classrooms, laboratories, a computer, and the campus switchboard. When the protesters asked the switchboard operators to leave, communication within the university was effectively severed. By the end of the day the number of protestors had risen to sixty-five or seventy, about half the black students on campus. They issued ten demands, which included a call for a Department of Afro-American Studies, with its own budget; more black students, black leaders of TYP, and black student recruitment; more black faculty; and an Afro-American Center, designed by the black students. That evening a committee of nine faculty members entered the building in an attempt to establish negotiations, but they were rebuffed.[37]

President Abram, startled by the demands, declared that almost all were either "existing policy or being implemented." He had met several times in the fall with the Afro-American Society and even when he had not agreed with them had expressed his desire to keep the dialogue going. The university had already embarked on a vigorous program of recruiting more black students and black faculty. It had raised ten Martin Luther King scholarships and dedicated thirty other scholarships to financial aid for black students. He had also approved a concentration in Afro-American Studies, overseen by the student-faculty committee on which Murray served. The sticking point was the protesters' demand—made also at San Francisco State College and at Queens College in New York—for a separate Department of Afro-American Studies, to be controlled by students. That demand violated the faculty's responsibility as guardian of the academic quality of the institution. Abram met with the protesters and asked them to leave the building so that negotiations could take place without the threat of coercion.[38]

The takeover appeared to have been inspired by a visit to campus of a black student and professor from San Francisco State College (SFSC). They had come to Brandeis to seek support for a strike at SFSC, begun when President S. I. Hayakawa refused a demand to establish a black studies department and called in the police to disperse the protesters. The Brandeis protestors preceded their list of demands with an announcement of support for the San Francisco State College strikers, as well as a protest against the Boston School Committee's handling of the Martin Luther King School, which had been beset by racial troubles.[39]

Abram secured a temporary restraining order from the Middlesex Superior Court, ordering the students to leave Ford Hall, but he declined to call in the police to enforce it. He did not want a repetition of the recent violence at SFSC or the violence the previous spring at Columbia University, when President Grayson Kirk had called in police to clear buildings that had been taken over by students protesting the university's involvement in defense research and actions affecting the largely black community adjacent to the university. Abram suspended all the students involved, but he also declared that he recognized "the deep frustration and anger which black students here and all over the country feel at what must seem—and often is—the indifference and duplicity of white men in relation to blacks." The Brandeis Faculty voted 153 to 18 to "condemn the forcible takeover of the university premises" and demanded that the students involved "vacate Ford Hall and enter negotiations of any grievance with the university administration." White students were divided. About 500 held a mass rally to demand amnesty for the black protestors. But when those involved in the takeover urged them to support their demands by calling a strike, most responded by returning to class. Final exams would be given in a matter of days and they dared not miss the concluding sessions of the term.[40]

Outside the university, a firestorm of disapproval rained down on the protesting students. Roy Wilkins, executive director of the NAACP, told the leaders of the organization "that any effort to set up a black studies department which would be wholly autonomous—with students picking the teachers and having control of the budget—represents setting up Jim Crow schools." Moreover, he threatened "court action," if any university gave into this demand or to the call, also being made at several schools, "to set up separate dormitories." Rather than pursue this separatist vision, he advised the students to go back to their classrooms, graduate, and help the NAACP in its work. The negative reaction included many of the protestors' parents. One mother, Aloisa Scull, a night hospital worker from nearby Dorchester, stormed Ford-Sydeman Hall. "Christopher Colombo, you come out of there," she demanded as she banged on the doors and windows with an umbrella. Allowed by one of the protestors to enter, she emerged with three students, including her son. "She'd do anything for that boy," a neighbor said.[41]

The next day, Murray arrived at class, which had been moved to another building, for the final session of her seminar. To her surprise, one of the TYP students, Joseph Reese, who had been absent since Thanksgiving, left Ford Hall and came to class. Although Murray had prepared a detailed outline for class discussion, she laid it aside. "It seemed more important that I have him present the class with the views of the students in F. H. and make as many observations as he wished to, or answer the many questions the members of the class wanted to put to him," she wrote in her diary. Reese replied that he had left because "the controversy had reached a stalemate." He had advocated taking over another building, or some other dramatic action to force the administration to act. Since he had failed to persuade the others to do so, he thought it pointless to remain. Moreover, he had tired of the rivalry among the protestors over "who is the blackest." Having been arrested and jailed, following a riot near his home in Florida, he felt that he had fully established his blackness. Let out of jail to attend Brandeis, he feared that if he stayed inside Ford Hall, he might be sent back to the South and to jail, thereby losing both his freedom and this educational opportunity. A hard-nosed realist, he was not willing to risk his future for no reward. After class, Reese walked Murray back to her car, carrying her briefcase. When she dropped him off at his dormitory, he told her, "I'm sorry it took me so long to wake up."[42]

That same day a group of black women students entered the Reserve Reading Room in the library and swept the books from the shelves, an act of vandalism that more than any other dismayed Murray. But three days after life at Brandeis reached this new low, the black protestors left Ford-Sydeman Hall without incident. Abram eventually granted the students complete amnesty. The administration also agreed to the establishment of a Department of African American Studies and promised the students a voice in the selection of the department's chair, but Abram insisted that the faculty control the new department. Pauli Murray refused to teach there, preferring to stay in American Civilization. Committed to color-blindness, she refused to accept racial separatism. [43]

Partner

Murray's alienation from the black students she had been brought to Brandeis to teach left her lonely and depressed in the spring of 1969. Her dog, Doc, sustained her, but he was almost fourteen years old, and his death in May left her grief-stricken. Caroline Ware continued to serve as a sounding board, by letter, phone, and occasional visits. Murray's new young friend Mary Norris helped by giving her perspective on the young and disaffected. Beneath the angry rhetoric of many black students, Norris believed, was an attempt to retrieve "a communal history that had long been ignored" and to affirm "a positive identity after centuries of denigration." Norris also helped Murray to understand that much of the distress she felt was anger at "crude sexism" she perceived in many of the male leaders of the Black Revolution. As Murray's memory of the searing experience of the strike began to recede, she came to feel a measure of sympathy for the black student protesters. They felt isolated on this foreign, overwhelmingly white campus. She felt that too, suffering as she did the condescending attitude of the senior faculty. For these insights, she owed Mary Norris a great deal. But it was Renee Barlow, the person Murray referred to as her "partner," who did the most to pull her through that difficult time. They talked frequently by phone and followed up with letters. To Barlow, Murray confided her doubts about her ability to challenge her most brilliant and accomplished juniors and seniors. Barlow gave her the perspective and encouragement she desperately needed.[44]

The partners yearned to spend time together, but that proved difficult. Murray's Cambridge landlord dragged out the simple repairs and installation of bookshelves so long that Murray despaired of ever being able to unpack the dozens of boxes of books that choked the apartment. They visited in Renee's New York apartment, but the presence of Renee's mother, Jennie Wren, made intimacy impossible. Occasionally, they met in hotel rooms and then felt terrible about the wasted funds. Murray's income, $20,000 for the year, was more than she had ever earned, but the cost of living in Cambridge was so great that she found she could not put aside savings, as she had always managed to do before, when employed.[45]

By the end of her first year at Brandeis, Murray began to feel a little better. Her students' "excellent" papers for the second semester of "Law and Social Change" delighted her. She recognized in their quality an "implied tribute" to her, one that made "all the anxiety, the hours of preparation worthwhile." The students were as happy about Murray's performance as she was about theirs. Looking back on their experience in her class, former students praised her "as a teacher and a person." She "prepared meticulously" for each class, "cared deeply and seriously for her students," was "thoughtful and analytical," but also "approachable from a student's point of view," recalled one student. She was also exacting. She was "a tough professor," a "tough critic . . . who commanded respect." "I think you have a good brain in your head but you need to apply it," Murray told one student, by way of encouragement. "She was special."[46]

A visit from Barlow at the semester's end also boosted Murray's spirits: "It was a healing process—healing of the loneliness and desolation. Our times together are so few and long spaces between." By then, she had learned that Brandeis would extend her contract as visiting professor another year. She felt disappointed not to secure a permanent position, but she had no alternative employment. Murray sometimes fantasized that Yale or Harvard Law School would offer her an appointment and that she could then afford an apartment large enough to make visits from Barlow more comfortable, but no offer came. Law schools remained heavily male institutions, with barely any female faculty and only a handful of female students. In her brief time at Brandeis, Murray had come to appreciate the coeducational environment there. Many of her best students were women, and she valued their company. She realized that she was less lonely at Brandeis than she would be anywhere else, except in New York City, with Renee.[47]

Deciding to make do by moving to a less expensive apartment, Murray took comfort in the fact that for the first time in four years she could enjoy a summer without uncertainty about a new job. By the middle of June she had moved to a "cozy" apartment at 8A Forest Street Cambridge, close to Radcliffe. A bit later Caroline Ware visited for a few days. Mary Norris joined them for dinner. Murray began to think that she would succeed at Brandeis after all.[48]

Murray spent more time with Barlow that summer while she worked on a new course in what she was coming to call American Studies, an academic space that felt increasingly like home. The program encouraged interdisciplinary work on all the peoples who made up America, unlike Afro-American Studies, which exhibited a narrow race-consciousness she found alienating, and unlike the Department of Politics, which she knew would never grant her more than a courtesy appointment, in part because it evidenced no interest in the subject that she found increasingly important: women.

Women's History

In the fall of 1969, Murray joined half a dozen professors around the country who had begun to experiment with courses in women's history. Murray planned her class as a contribution to American Studies, where it became the foundation for what would become Women's Studies at Brandeis. Unusual among those who taught one of these pioneering courses, Murray approached her topic not from the perspective of the white middle-class women of the early women's rights movement, but rather from the vantage point of black women.[49]

As she had done in writings dating back to the mid-1940s, Murray discussed the "similarities" and "differences" between "Jim Crow" and "Jane Crow." She assigned readings not only on Elizabeth Cady Stanton and Susan B. Anthony, but also on Sojourner Truth and Harriet Tubman. She urged students to reflect on the common oppression of black women and men. "If black males suffered from real and psychological castration," she told them, "black females suffered from real and psychological rape." The course ranged across the emerging literature on gender, race, and class in psychology, sociology, anthropology, and history. It covered the psychology of minority group oppression and the interconnection of the civil rights, labor, and women's movements. Given the wide-ranging nature of the topics covered and the intimidating, seven-page, single-spaced reading list, Murray scheduled extra office hours each week to discuss possible research projects with each member of the class.[50]

The student evaluations for this course, for which the readings changed each year as more articles and books became available, were mixed. Some complained that the "classes were not well-organized and formed no logical sequence." And yet, even the complainers responded that Murray was "worth knowing and emulating." She was "part of what's happening now and needs to be experienced if one is interested in this area."[51]

"What's happening now" was a seismic shift in women's lives. By 1970, fifty years after the passage of the Nineteenth Amendment, the women's movement hit flood tide. In the process, black women gained recognition never before accorded them. In 1970, Murray's protégé from Yale Law School, Eleanor Holmes Norton, became the first black woman to head the New York Commission on Human Rights. Aileen Hernandez became the first black woman to head NOW. Libby Koontz, a teacher who had grown up near Murray in North Carolina, became the first black woman to head the Women's Bureau. And in the cascade of feminist writings that reached print that year, Murray finally saw her long campaign against "Jane Crow" bear fruit, not just in her classroom, but in the writings on women that began to pour forth from the nation's publishers.

In 1970, Murray published "The Liberation of Black Women" in *The Voices of Feminism,* edited by white feminist Mary Lou Thompson. The twelve other authors included Betty Friedan, Martha Griffiths, Mary Daly, Alice Rossi, and Shirley Chisholm. An updated version of her 1964 article, "The Negro Woman in the Quest for Equality," Murray's essay revisited her argument that black women had historically borne the double burden of "Jim Crow and Jane Crow." Murray attacked once more the stereotype of the black matriarch as a distortion of black women's "qualities of strength and independence," qualities needed in a community that has had to "draw on the resources of all its members to survive." She deplored the fact that whereas black women had been at the forefront of the struggle for human rights for more than a century, the history of black women had been largely ignored. She stressed the multiple sources of oppression black women faced—economic exploitation, sexism, and racism—each interacting with and amplifying the others. "Because black women have an equal stake in women's liberation and black liberation," Murray declared, "they are key figures at the juncture of these two movements." Focused on legal reform and practical goals, she called for "adequate incomes maintenance, and the elimination of poverty, repeal or reform of abortion laws, a national system of child-care centers, extension of labor standards to workers now excluded, cash maternity benefits as part of a system of social insurance, and the removal of all sex barriers to educational and employment opportunities at all levels." The biggest change in the article, compared to Murray's previous writings, was the use of "black," apparently at the insistence of Thompson, in place of Murray's preferred "Negro."

Murray did not agree to a complete substitution. Following her practice with her former TYP student, she retained the Negro usage about half the time, and when using black, pleaded (with limited success)—"please, Madam editor"—that it be capitalized.[52]

Just as gratifying as the publication of her own essay, with those of other leading feminists, was the appearance that year of essays from a younger generation of black women who embraced her argument that black women were doubly oppressed. One example, by Frances Beal, was entitled "Double Jeopardy: To Be Black and Female." It appeared in *Sisterhood Is Powerful*, a collection of essays edited by white feminist Robin Morgan. A founding member of the Women's Liberation Committee of the Student Non-Violent Coordinating Committee (SNCC) and a member of the Third World Women's Alliance, Beal argued that black women suffered a particularly intense disadvantage because of the way that sex discrimination compounded race discrimination: "As blacks they suffer all the burdens of prejudice and mistreatment that fall on anyone with dark skin. As women they bear the additional burden of having to cope with white men and black men." Though thirty years younger, Beal shared much with Murray. Both came from mixed-race backgrounds and were strongly influenced by Jewish, Communist, and Socialist traditions. Beal's mother was Jewish, her father an Afro-Euro-Native-American. Beal had been one of the women in SNCC put off by the machismo of the black men who turned toward Black Power.[53]

Beal, following closely the points Murray had been making in print since 1964, argued that the liberation of any group was not possible without the liberation of its women. She attacked the myth of matriarchy and the idea that the aspirations of black men should take precedence over those of black women. She celebrated the contributions of black women (from Sojourner Truth to Fannie Lou Hamer) to the struggle for human rights. She condemned black men who sought their own liberation but denigrated women and she used US Department of Labor statistics to show that black women earned less than white men, black men, and white women—in that order. Beal split with Murray, however, on one crucial point. Unlike the older woman, who saw "sex bias [as] more formidable than race bias" and therefore urged black women to recognize white women as "natural" allies, Beal could not find common cause with a group of mostly middle-class white women who, she charged, participated in the exploitation of working-class women of color, supported imperialist policies, engaged in racism, and endorsed capitalism. Better for her an alliance with the black liberation movement, for all its male-dominating faults.[54]

Murray must have recognized her own youthful revolutionary ardor in Beal's writing and that of other young black women, but she had long since abandoned sweeping calls for the destruction of capitalism as naïve, and she had never favored black separatism. Murray's legal training and her belief that white women were the "natural" allies of black women distanced her from younger black feminists, but her argument that gender oppression compounded racial exploitation had finally found traction. Never again would she be a voice in the wilderness. A new generation had joined her in the battle against Jane Crow.

15

Triumph and Loss

The ACLU as a Feminist Force

While she developed new courses at Brandeis, counseled students, and advanced her theory of the conjunction of race and sex, Murray maintained a heavy schedule of public speaking and activism. She had hoped that NOW would be her NAACP for women and her activist home, but following her disillusionment over the organization's endorsement of the ERA in November 1967, Murray shifted her energies to the American Civil Liberties Union, where she remained a member of the national board. The ACLU was the one group that fought for civil liberties and rights broadly, including what she began to call the rights of "social minorities," the term she used in public to cover lesbians, gays, bisexuals, and transsexuals.[1]

The term "social minorities" came from the work of sociologist Louis Wirth, the leading theorist of minority groups in the United States in the 1930s and 1940s. Wirth acknowledged "minority" as traditionally meaning a group that constituted less than half the population. But he taught sociologists to use the term more broadly to refer to any group, large or small, that lacked power. Encountering the concept through sociologist Helen Mayer Hacker, a close friend with whom she regularly lunched when in New York, Murray cited Hacker's "Women as a Minority Group" in many of her papers and assigned it in her Women's History course at Brandeis.[2]

Women constituted an example of a group that was a numerical majority but a minority in terms of its social power, whereas homosexuals, bisexuals, and transsexuals constituted small and vilified groups, minorities in both their numbers and power. Of these latter groups, transsexuals constituted the smallest and most vilified of all, as revealed in the rapidly growing coverage given them in the press. Male to female transsexuals attracted more scorn, but those who had been identified as female at birth had the harder time seeking treatment and acceptance, not to mention the legal rights that would have flowed from being recognized as male. Some specialists doubted that females who identified as male qualified as transsexuals; those who recognized their existence thought that they constituted only a small fraction of this group. Doctors generally refused to treat them. All other advocacy groups in which Murray participated left out one of the minority groups to which she belonged, and thus some part of her identity. The ACLU was the only one to include them all.[3]

The civil liberties organization was not without limitations as a home. As one of only five women on a national board of seventy-six, Murray often found her concerns minimized and sensibilities ignored. Fellow board member Floyd McKissick, who, inspired by Murray, had been the first black to finally win acceptance to the University of North Carolina Law School in 1951 and who had recently replaced James Farmer as head of CORE, met her in the elevator one day on the way to attend a meeting of the Equality Committee. Accompanied by his second in command, Roy Innis, McKissick introduced Murray, adding, "This chick really has something on the ball." Murray believed that he meant the comment as "a high compliment," but the sexist, demeaning remark gave her "a jolt" from which she did not soon recover.[4]

Murray also encountered stiff resistance from some of her ACLU colleagues on the subject of affirmative action, a difficult topic especially for the Jews on the board who had been kept out of Ivy League universities on the basis of quotas. At the very first meeting of the Equality Committee she attended in February 1966, she got into an argument with Will Maslow, head of the American Jewish Congress, over the issue of "compensatory treatment" as a remedy for past discrimination. Maslow believed strongly that this was inevitably a form of discrimination. Murray disagreed: "Until we grow up a generation of Head Starts, until people come into the job market more prepared, we have a problem which we can't ignore."[5]

Murray nonetheless continued to appreciate the ACLU as the one organization that took human rights, in their multiple forms, as seriously as she did. Funded by dues and foundation grants, and having affiliates throughout the country, the organization also had more resources to fight for individual rights than any other advocacy group. As a member of the national board and as a faculty member at Brandeis, Murray felt she had real power, especially to advance the interests of women within education.[6]

The Women of the Ivory Tower

Dorothy Kenyon had wanted the ACLU to attack sex discrimination in education ever since 1958, when she learned of a case brought by two women against Texas A&M. The women, who had applied for admission to the all-male public college, sued when they were rejected because of their gender. They won at the district court level, but lost at the court of appeals. Kenyon judged the case a good candidate to establish equal access to public education for women under the Fourteenth Amendment. But the Supreme Court refused to take it, letting the court of appeals decision stand.[7]

Education proved a tricky subject. Texas had a number of coeducational colleges, so, unlike the defendants in *Brown v. Board of Education*, lawyers for the state school could argue that Texas offered women other options. Moreover, single-sex education had a long tradition, in both public and private settings, and deep support from women as well as men. The Civil Rights Act of 1964 excluded education from coverage, which left colleges and universities, Brandeis among them, free to discriminate on the basis of gender. Many, perhaps most, welcomed women as students but ignored their particular concerns and rarely advanced women to the upper faculty and administrative levels.

The person who did the most to call attention to this problem was Bernice Sandler at the University of Maryland. Having raised two children and earned a Ph.D. in clinical psychology at the University of Maryland, Sandler decided to return to full-time work. She applied for a position at the university's department of counseling and personnel services, but even though the department had seven openings, she was rejected. When she asked the reason, she was told that she "came on too strong for a woman." Sandler's husband, a lawyer, believed that she was a victim of blatant gender discrimination, but he counseled that there was not much she could do because federal legislation against employment discrimination exempted institutions of higher education. She could not sue on her own behalf, but, he suggested, she might be able to bring pressure on the University of Maryland to treat women fairly, because the university was a "government contractor." If she could show that the university discriminated against women, she might get the federal government to terminate the university's contracts, or at least threaten to.[8]

Sandler, following research into hiring practices, first at the University of Maryland and then elsewhere, drafted a blanket complaint against the nation's colleges and universities. On January 31, 1970, she filed it with the Department of Labor, which forwarded it to the Department of Health, Education and Welfare. At the same time she began to pressure Congress to pass a law that would protect women more directly. Her chief ally was Edith Green, one of the highest-ranking members of the House's Committee on Education and Labor. For years Green had watched helplessly as various civil rights measures had exempted institutions of higher education from coverage. In 1970 her committee considered an omnibus educational reform bill. She was determined that, this time, women would be protected against discrimination in education. She appointed Sandler to her staff and prepared for hearings on the bill in the summer of 1970.[9]

By 1970, Murray and Green were old friends, and when Green called on Murray to testify before her committee in support of legislation that would protect women against discrimination in academe, Murray eagerly accepted. Speaking as a member of the National Board of the ACLU, Murray told Green's committee on June 19, 1970, that the women's movement was part of a world-wide revolution in human rights, a revolution that included "blacks, women, youth, various economic and social minorities, and the handicapped." Murray inserted her favorite, sociologically distancing term, "social minorities," to the list of those "demanding to be accepted as <u>persons</u> and to share fully in making the decisions which affect their destinies," because she could not yet say "homosexuals" and would never be able to utter "transsexuals" in a public statement.[10]

Murray was well aware of the battle that had broken out over the place of lesbians in NOW. The year before, Betty Friedan had publicly worried that any attention to lesbian rights would hamstring feminists' ability to achieve the political change already on their agenda. She fretted, moreover, that stereotypes of "mannish" and "man-hating" lesbians would provide an easy way to dismiss the movement. Still president of NOW, Friedan did what she could to distance the organization from lesbian causes, calling them a "Lavender Menace." In anger over this slur, lesbian feminist Rita Mae Brown resigned her administrative job at NOW in February 1970. In March, straight radical feminist Susan Brownmiller popularized the term "Lavender Menace" in an article in the *New York Times*. By the time Murray testified before the House in June, conflict over the role of lesbians in NOW threatened to tear the organization apart.[11]

Murray carefully skirted the issue in her testimony. Privately, she agreed with Friedan. She feared that the young radical lesbians would turn NOW into a single-issue group. As she later wrote Julie Lee of the Daughters of Bilitis, "We differ on the basic issue: in your words 'lesbian is the epitome of feminism.' This is not what NOW is all about, and never was. It is for the equality of women in true partnership with men. . . . I support the right of consenting adults to make choices as to the sex [sexual orientation] they prefer, but I see this as a private personal matter in the same way that I see all sex relationships—personal matters between two people." Murray wished that the Daughters of Bilitis and other activist lesbians would follow the model of the ACLU, which had been treating gay and lesbian rights as a civil liberties issue for a decade. The problem with Murry's individualistic emphasis on the matter of homosexuality, as she had known when she called for an NAACP for women, is that individuals are rarely successful in advancing their interests against concerted opposition unless there is an organized group behind them. But Murray had been burned too often to follow this principle to its logical conclusion where gender and sexual nonconformity were concerned. As a professional woman, especially a woman hoping to win tenure at a major university, she faced particular perils. The gender difference she lived shaped her thinking and fueled her restlessness, but not her action, at least not directly. The taboo remained for her too great.[12]

Some of those close to her suspected she was hiding something. Her friend Mary Norris wondered if Pauli and Renee might be more than close friends, but Norris never imagined that Murray had any doubts about her gender identity. Moreover, in a sign of how guarded those with personal secrets remained, even in the midst of the emerging lesbian-feminist movement, Norris and Murray never discussed the fact that both had had intimate relationships with women.[13]

At Brandeis, Larry Fuchs, the father of a lesbian daughter, made clear to Murray that he loved his daughter all the more for having the courage to be who she was. Murray did not take his lead. The most personal comment she ever made was in a conversation one day in which she advised Fuchs to drink eight glasses of water a day to avoid constipation. This piece of advice from so reserved a woman stunned Fuchs, but it made perfect sense. Her emotional turmoil over her gender identity—from her earliest years—had manifested itself somatically, often in the form of constipation. Water was the one way she could deal with that turmoil. Her earlier, open discussions about her gender identity had brought only rebuff from doctors or, worse, outright rejection. Suspicions about her personal life had often led to grief, most recently at the EEOC. She dared not risk exposure at Brandeis. Murray had concluded it best not to refer to matters of gender identity except through advice on best dietary practices and the distancing language of sociology.[14]

Sociology helped in other ways. Using sociological research, she blasted Moynihan in her congressional testimony for encouraging Brandeis to limit TYP to male students. Moreover, she criticized universities in general, and Brandeis in particular, for discriminating against women in hiring and promotion on college faculties. The ACLU had just won a case against the University of Virginia, which had previously agreed to accept women, but on a timetable that stretched out over many years. Moreover, the university had limited the percentage of women accepted. The victorious plaintiffs won a court order to admit women immediately and to eliminate quotas that restricted their numbers. The trend in the South more broadly, however, spelled trouble. Faced with orders to integrate schools by race, local school boards had begun to segregate by sex. Without new legislation, Murray warned, black schoolgirls would simply face a new kind of segregation. Only through federal legislation could girls and women be protected from discrimination in education everywhere.[15]

Fighting on Behalf of Women Workers

United on education, Murray and the ACLU remained divided over how to pursue equality in employment until 1970. In 1966, having failed in her effort to persuade Kenyon to take on *Mengelkoch* as a Fourteenth Amendment case, Murray watched Marguerite Rawalt carry on that battle on behalf of NOW. To Murray and Rawalt's joint dismay, the three-judge strategy, intended to speed *Mengelkoch* to a hearing before the Supreme Court, failed. With the country deeply divided over the question of whether sex-specific protective labor laws helped or hurt women workers, the courts proved reluctant to subject that question to a constitutional test.

In May 1968, nineteen months after Vilma Mengelkoch commenced her suit against California for denying her the right to work overtime, the presiding judge denied jurisdiction; *Mengelkoch* did not present a "substantial" issue. In the judge's view, the question of hours limitations for women had been settled back in 1908 by *Muller v. Oregon* and had not since been seriously questioned. Rawalt appealed, but not until 1971 did the Ninth Circuit declare that the three-judge court had been wrong, that the issue presented in *Mengelkoch* was indeed "substantial," and that the case should be remanded to the three-judge court for further consideration, consistent with the appellate court's ruling.[16]

By that time, Title VII suits brought by women against employers in district courts around the country, together with new rulings from the EEOC, had taken much of the wind out of Mengelkoch's sails. After some initial hesitation, federal judges coalesced around the view that Title VII, a federal law, superseded state protective labor laws that prevented women from being hired or promoted into jobs for which they were otherwise qualified.[17]

In 1969, influenced by the success of these Title VII cases, the EEOC issued guidelines under which employers could no longer declare sex a bona fide occupational qualification (BFOQ) under sex-specific protective labor laws. State legislatures made the EEOC's change of heart easier. In the increasingly conservative political climate of the late 1960s, labor laws came under fire as being needless governmental regulation. State legislatures around the country that had not already repealed their hour laws began to do so. Where state legislatures were slow to act, a growing number of state attorneys general declared their state protective laws null and void. By the early 1970s, maximum hours had been struck down by the courts in nine states, repealed by state legislatures in twenty-one, and ruled against by attorneys general in twenty-three. The states with the most complete coverage, New York and New Jersey, were among the first either to limit coverage or repeal their laws.[18]

On top of this state action, President Richard Nixon took advantage of his federal power to fill judicial vacancies with conservatives who were even less likely than their liberal predecessors to extend the scope of the Fourteenth Amendment. In this context, support for pressing the *Mengelkoch* case waned, and Murray began to lose hope that her Fourteenth Amendment strategy would ever be fully tested. The only way to win women a constitutional guarantee of equal rights, she reluctantly concluded, might be to pass an Equal Rights Amendment.[19]

In coming to the view that she would have to support the ERA, Murray did not give up on protective labor laws. Unlike members of the National Woman's Party, she continued to think protective labor laws were necessary, but she thought they should apply to men and women equally. In 1965, Murray had accepted Eastwood's view that the threat of premium pay under the Fair Labor Standards Act would keep employers from exploiting their workers. But by 1970, Murray had developed doubts. A growing body of evidence demonstrated that employers found it more economical to force workers into overtime than to hire additional, full-time workers, to whom they had to pay benefits. Murray took up the suggestion offered by Susan Deller Ross, a fellow at NYU Law School who had just accepted a job at the EEOC, that the country needed a model labor code for the states, one that, at best, would provide rest periods and safety protections for all workers, and, at the very least, would protect employees from dismissal if they preferred not to work overtime. States that abolished their laws for women, however, showed less interest in gender equality than in scuttling government regulations altogether. The country seemed to be reverting to the 1920s.[20]

Under these conditions, and with her Fourteenth Amendment strategy an apparent failure, Murray lobbied Kenyon and other members of the ACLU board to endorse the ERA. The need to win equal rights for women to better jobs, she argued, outweighed whatever diminishing benefits women-only laws provided. She continued to believe in the need for protective labor laws, but unlike many of her colleagues in the labor movement, she was no longer willing to allow what appeared to be a long, drawn-out battle for a model labor code to stand in the way of progress toward formal equality.[21]

Even before she had brought the ACLU board around to her position, Murray submitted testimony in September 1970 to the Senate committee that was considering passage of the ERA. She spoke once again as a member of the ACLU board but also as a black woman. At the outset she conceded that she had been atypical of black women in her attainments. She stressed, however, that she had traveled the same road as her sisters. "The Negro woman has suffered more than the addition of sex discrimination to race discrimination," she told the senators; "she has suffered the conjunction of these twin immoralities. . . . The Negro woman remains on the lowest rank of social and economic status in the United States. The black male, at least, can identify and aspire to the dominance of his white counterpart." She had changed her mind on the ERA because she had come to conclude that it was the only way that the country's most disadvantaged group could improve its lot.[22]

The biggest impediment to achieving equal rights for all minorities, she believed, was the propensity of all people to classify. She conceded that this tendency helped people to make sense out of "the myriad stimuli of experience," but it inevitably led to stereotypes. In a statement that came close to calling for tolerance of transsexuals, she declared that the stereotype imposed on women created serious problems for those who varied in their "body structure, strength, musculature, physical and emotional capacities, aspirations and expectations, just as men do."[23]

Murray believed that the constitutional grant of equal rights to women would enhance their political and economic power and lead to a better world. "A Congress of the United States in which one-third or more are women (if one uses the percentage of the labor force that are women) and the unique experiences of this untapped resource are likely to accelerate our progress toward the solution of such massive problems as pollution, poverty, racism, and war." The same would hold for all other institutions in which power was concentrated. "The presence of women would also accelerate the presence of other groups in our heterogeneous population and bring into play a variety of human experiences and wisdom which would enrich the entire process." In a hopeful peroration she concluded, "Women may well hold the key to the reconciliation of the races, the generations and the social and economic classes."[24]

The ERA won the requisite two thirds vote from the US House of Representatives the next year. In March 1972, the US Senate approved the amendment and sent it to the states. Hawaii was the first state to ratify what would have been the Twenty-Seventh Amendment, followed by some thirty other states within a year. By the mid-1970s, however, a conservative backlash eroded support for the amendment and it failed to achieve ratification by the requisite thirty-eight, or three fourths, of the states before time ran out in 1982. Ironically, the ERA, which Murray supported because her Fourteenth Amendment strategy had failed, itself failed in the end. In the meantime, the Fourteenth Amendment approach began to bear fruit.

Reed v. Reed (1971)

At the June 1970 Biennial Conference of the ACLU, a group of younger members organized a Women's Rights panel. The purpose, according to Suzy Post of the Louisville, Kentucky, affiliate, was to put some "troops in the field" to support Murray, Kenyon, and Pilpel in their work on the ACLU board against sex discrimination. The conference marked a turning point in the battle for women's rights. From that moment, affiliates were on high alert for a case that could bring Murray's Fourteenth Amendment strategy to the Supreme Court.[25]

A case in Idaho had already captured the attention of Marvin Karpatkin, head of the ACLU Equality Committee, who read about it in Law Weekly in

March 1970. The case, *Reed v. Reed*, began in 1967, when sixteen-year-old Richard Reed died intestate. Richard's mother, Sally, petitioned the probate court to serve as administrator of her son's estate, which consisted chiefly of clothes, phonograph records, a clarinet, and $495 in savings. Richard's father, Cecil, from whom Sally was divorced, filed a competing application. At a hearing, the probate judge awarded Cecil the position, based solely on an 1864 state law, which provided that when more than one person was entitled to serve, "males must be preferred to females."[26]

Outraged that the court gave her no chance to demonstrate that she was the better person for the position, Sally fought back. According to Sally, Cecil was an abusive husband and father who had abandoned the family when Richard, their adopted son, was a young child. The couple divorced in 1958, and the court awarded Sally custody through Richard's "tender years." She supported her son and established a college savings account for him with money she made baking, babysitting, and caring for disabled people in their homes. When Richard became a teenager and got into some trouble with the law, the court altered the custody arrangement, despite Sally's objections that Cecil was a bad influence. During a visit to his father's home in 1967, Richard died, apparently having shot himself with one of his father's rifles. The death was ruled a suicide, but Sally held Cecil responsible. When the probate judge named Cecil administrator of Richard's estate, Sally appealed to a number of lawyers to represent her in a challenge. After sixteen failed attempts, she reached Allen Derr, who advised her, as had all previous lawyers, that she would likely lose. Derr nonetheless thought she had a legitimate claim under the Fourteenth Amendment and agreed to represent her. Sally won in the state district court, but lost in Idaho's Supreme Court, which declared, "men are better qualified to act as an administrator than are women" and "nature itself had established this distinction."[27]

To lawyers at the ACLU, the Idaho law that gave the father preference in *Reed v. Reed* constituted a perfect example of arbitrary sex discrimination. Melvin Wulf, legal director of the ACLU, offered Allen Derr the organization's legal services to take the case to the Supreme Court and enlisted the help of a childhood acquaintance, Ruth Bader Ginsburg, to write the appellate brief.[28]

Following law school, Ginsburg had faced difficulty finding a job. Paul, Weiss had already declined to offer her a full-time position. No other firm would consider her. Finally, Gerald Gunther, Columbia's professor of constitutional law, persuaded Judge Edmund L. Palmieri, a federal judge in the Southern District of New York, to take her, with the promise, as Ginsburg later reported, that "if I didn't work out, he would find a male lawyer to replace me." After her clerkship, Ginsburg opted for a fellowship at Columbia to write her first book, a study of civil procedure in Sweden. Traveling to Sweden and learning Swedish, she immersed herself in a legal culture strikingly different from her own. Whereas women in the United States constituted less than 5 percent of all law students, between 20 and 25 percent of the law students in Sweden were women; moreover, women were commonly seen in court. Ginsburg later recalled attending "one proceeding in Stockholm where the presiding judge was eight months pregnant." She also remembered "a journalist who wrote a column in the Swedish daily paper: 'Why should women have two jobs, and men only one?' . . . [I]t was the woman who was expected to buy the kids new shoes and have dinner on the table at 7." Delighted though she was to see that she and her husband were not alone in bucking conventional gender norms in their private lives, Ginsburg remained focused on her legal career as a specialist in civil procedure. Returning to the United States, she accepted a position as assistant professor of law at Rutgers in 1963.[29]

Not until 1969, when some women students asked her to teach a course on women and the law, did Ginsburg's attention shift decisively to gender inequality. Reading everything she could find on the subject, she quickly discovered Murray and Eastwood's "Jane Crow and the Law," an article she found to be "an enormous eye opener." Inspired by Murray's racial analogy, she proceeded to review every gender discrimination case then wending its way through the courts. One of those cases was Sally Reed's in Idaho.[30]

Melvin Wulf visited Ginsburg at her office in the spring of 1970, on a day he was at the law school to give a talk. They talked about *Reed*. She offered to help. At first he demurred, but she peppered him with ideas on how best to proceed until he relented. In his mind, he "plucked her from obscurity"; in fact, as he later conceded, she plucked herself and became the principal author of the brief in *Reed*.[31]

Building on Murray's analogy of gender to race and drawing on Murray's past work, Ginsburg wrote a sixty-eight-page Brandeis Brief that laid out the ways in which discrimination against women mirrored discrimination against blacks. She then detailed the ways in which women's educational and workplace progress since 1864, when Idaho passed the law in question, cast doubt on the law's underlying assumption that women were less qualified than men to administer estates. Thus far, the brief tracked Murray and Kenyon's earlier work. But, when it came to an analysis of the law in question, Ginsburg insisted on a different tack. Murray and Kenyon had argued, in their contribution to the ACLU brief in *White v. Crook*, that the court should subject "sex" to the same "strict scrutiny" accorded to race. In *Reed*, Ginsburg opted for a more cautious approach. She advanced three legal arguments, each an alternative pleading to the one that preceded it. First, she argued, "sex" should be subjected to "strict scrutiny," as Murray and Kenyon had successfully argued in *White* and as the California circuit court had done only months before in *Sail'er Inn*, a case that struck down a law that barred women from working as bartenders. But Ginsberg did not count on the Supreme Court going so far; it had never struck down a state law that discriminated on the basis of gender.[32]

She therefore argued, in addition, if the Court was not ready to apply "strict scrutiny," it should apply a somewhat lesser standard; she called it an "intermediate" test: one that shifted the burden of proof from the plaintiff to the state. Rather than require that Sally Reed prove that the estate administration statute was discriminatory, the Court should require that the state prove that the law being challenged was not discriminatory.[33]

If the Court was not ready even for this lesser, "intermediate" step, Ginsburg concluded (in her third argument in the alternative), it should, nevertheless, strike down the Idaho law because it did not pass the test of simple rationality. Ginsburg reached back to a decades-old, seemingly irrelevant case, *Royster Guano v. Virginia* (1920), to support this final argument. In *Royster,* a tax case, the Court had considered whether a state could tax some businesses and not others engaged in closely related activity. To answer this question the court imposed the following test: "the classification [in this case, of business activity singled out for taxation by the state] must be reasonable, not arbitrary, and must rest upon some ground of difference having a fair and substantial relation to the object of the legislation, so that all persons similarly circumstanced shall be treated alike."[34]

The best argument that Idaho could make in favor of a law that automatically preferred males to females was that it saved probate judges from having to hold a hearing on whether one applicant might be better qualified than another. "Surely," Ginsburg wrote, in clear reference to the relative merits of Sally and Cecil Reed as potential administrators, "this Court cannot give its approval to a fiduciary statute that demands preference for an idler, because he is a man, and rejects a potentially diligent administrator solely because she is a woman." Where gender was concerned, the government had to make a better argument than administrative convenience. Going out of her way to give credit to the two ACLU board members who had provided the basic framework for her brief, Ginsburg went beyond extensive reliance on their work; she added the names of Pauli Murray and Dorothy Kenyon as coauthors.[35]

The question remained as to who should represent Sally Reed in oral argument before the justices of the Supreme Court. Wulf wanted a woman. He apparently did not consider Ginsburg. She had proven an excellent brief writer, but she had never argued a case in court. Nor, for the same reason, did he consider Murray, who had never argued an appeal and was no longer a practicing lawyer. Kenyon was by then too old and stricken with cancer. He settled on his long-time legal associate and Murray's protégée, Eleanor Holmes Norton. Better that this black woman, who embodied the race-sex link and who had extensive experience in oral argument, face the justices and deflect any untoward locker-room humor than Allen Derr, a white male who had never before set foot in the Supreme Court. Despite Wulf's strong recommendation, Sally Reed opted to stay with Derr. Nervous and shaking, Derr proved unable to parry questions from the bench; moreover, he made his supporters cringe in embarrassment when he suggested that *Reed* would do for women what *Brown v. Board of Education* had done for "Colored people." Justice Blackman assigned him a D for his performance. If Sally Reed was to prevail, she would do so solely by virtue of the ACLU brief.[36]

The brief was enough. On November 22, 1971, Chief Justice Warren Burger, writing for a unanimous Court, ruled in Sally Reed's favor. He began by reiterating the Court's long-standing view that states have the right "to treat different classes of people in different ways." But, quoting from *Royster Guano*, as cited in Ginsburg's brief, he added that a classification "must be reasonable, not arbitrary, and must rest upon some ground of difference having a fair and substantial relation to the object of the legislation, so that all persons similarly circumstanced shall be treated alike." The Idaho probate law failed this test. In Burger's words, "to give a mandatory preference to members of either sex over members of the other, merely to accomplish the elimination of hearings on the merits, is to make the very kind of arbitrary legislative choice forbidden by the Equal Protection Clause of the Fourteenth Amendment."[37]

Burger did not give Ginsburg, Murray, and Kenyon all that they wanted. He did not say that "sex," like race, should be treated with "strict scrutiny," or even that it warranted an "intermediate" level of scrutiny, but for the first time the Supreme Court ruled that a state law that discriminated against women violated the Fourteenth Amendment, and it did so by raising the bar on what the Court deemed "reasonable" when it came to gender discrimination. A disappointed Murray called it a "baby step," but it provided an important foundation for future cases.[38]

Victory in *Reed* gave the women at the ACLU new energy. In 1972 Ginsburg established the ACLU Women's Rights Project, which quickly dominated the field of women's rights litigation. That same year, Columbia Law School's new dean, Michael Sovern, recruited Ginsburg to be the school's first tenured female professor. Ginsburg extracted a stiff price. She would accept Columbia's offer only if she were granted a half teaching load and allowed to devote the rest of her time to the Women's Rights Project.[39]

By 1974 the ACLU affiliates had embarked on more than 300 women's rights cases. Between 1969 and 1980, the ACLU participated in more than 65 percent of the gender-discrimination cases that reached the Supreme Court, twice as many as NOW. The ACLU's network of affiliated groups allowed them to identify and develop cases that might never have reached the attention of the courts. The ACLU's prestige enabled it to secure foundation

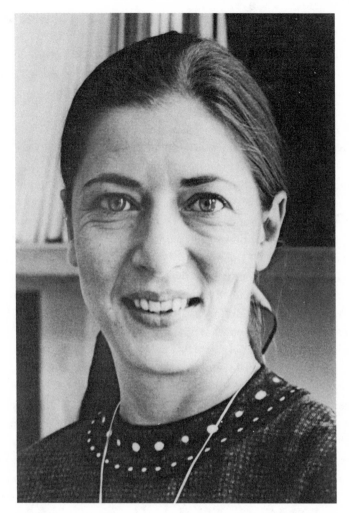

Figure 15.1 Ruth Bader Ginsburg, 1972. Courtesy of Columbia Law School.

grants and bequests not available to newer organizations, and these grants supported large numbers of attorneys who could not otherwise have afforded to work on many of the cases.[40]

The Battle for Tenure

By 1970, the year Murray testified before both houses of Congress and saw the ACLU take on *Reed v. Reed*, she was easily the leading black female academic in the country. Having won a second one-year contract as a visiting professor at Brandeis for the 1969–1970 academic year, she demanded promotion to a permanent, tenured position. She would turn sixty in November, and she worried about her financial future. According to her calculations, she needed five more years of financial stability to achieve anything close to a secure retirement. Demanding tenure after only two years of teaching took nerve. Larry Fuchs tried to talk her out of it, but she was determined. To Fuchs she wrote, "Increasing numbers of women today are going for all the marbles, and I am a woman." Either tenure or she would leave.[41]

Murray could not have asked for a tenure decision at a worse time. Across the United States, colleges and universities suffered serious financial reverses in the late 1960s. The Vietnam War diverted government money away from research and graduate fellowships to the Defense Department. The problems of the inner cities diverted the funds of private foundations away from academic support to poverty programs. In December 1969, a recession struck, reducing the value of endowment portfolios at universities across the country. Inflation, which had stood at a manageable 1.31 percent in 1964, grew to 5.46 percent (and rising) five years later. All academic institutions suffered during the financial reversals of the late 1960s, but none suffered more than Brandeis, a relative newcomer to the higher ranks of research universities. With a tiny endowment of only $29 million, it had no margin. When Morris Abram assumed office, he faced the need to make budget cuts at the very time that he wanted to make new appointments and spend more on financial aid for minority students. In that environment, the university could ill afford promotions to tenure.[42]

Undaunted, Murray approached Roy C. Macridis, chair of the Department of Politics, and asked for his support. After meeting with the senior members of the department, Macridis informed her that they were willing to extend her another "courtesy appointment," but they declined to consider a tenured appointment in their department. The reason was simple: "We do not need somebody of your talents in the Department." He urged her to see the dean to determine whether she might have some other option. Thwarted in Politics, Murray urged Diamandopoulos to solve her problem by elevating American Civilization (renamed American Studies) to departmental status. Six months later, Diamandopoulos did so.[43]

Larry Fuchs immediately informed Diamandopoulos that he intended to recommend Murray for tenure and sent out requests for recommendations. Within a few days, letters arrived from Caroline Ware, Thomas Emerson, Eugene Rostow, William Hastie, and Lloyd Garrison. All wrote glowingly of Murray's abilities and accomplishments. All urged that she be promoted to full professor with tenure. In early June, Diamandopoulos named an ad hoc committee of five faculty members to consider Murray's case. The committee included Professor of Philosophy Henry D. Aiken, Professor of Music Seymour Shifrin, Professor of Physics Edgar Lipworth, and Professor of Human Relations (at the Brandeis

Graduate School of Social Work) Morrie S. Schwartz. Typically, ad hoc committees on tenure do not include the person presenting the case, but procedures at Brandeis were an exception. The fifth member of the committee was Professor of Politics and American Studies Larry Fuchs.[44]

Two weeks later, the Ad Hoc Committee met. To Fuchs' dismay, only one of his colleagues joined him in voting for Murray's tenure. Two others voted no and the fifth member abstained. Everyone apparently agreed that Murray made a valuable contribution to Brandeis. She was an exemplary teacher and a conscientious, principled citizen of the university. The problem was her publications. A journalist, memoirist, lawyer, and poet, she showed scant evidence of scholarly distinction. She had no scholarly monograph and her one law review article—not obviously relevant to American Studies—was jointly authored. In the judgment of the dissenters, Murray lacked the basic scholarly credentials expected of a tenured professor. Even were they to relax their standards and accept the publications presented in lieu of the expected scholarship, they could not vote for tenure. In their judgment her work lacked "brilliance," "flair," and "conceptual power." Without Fuchs's vote, Murray would have lost outright. The committee offered Fuchs one consolation. It voted unanimously to appoint Murray to a term full professorship for three years.[45]

Fuchs, unwilling to accept defeat, and believing Murray's threat that she would leave Brandeis if not granted tenure, appealed to Diamandopoulos, to whom the ad hoc committee's report was merely advisory. Stressing that Murray was an exemplary teacher who had attracted some of the very best students at Brandeis, Fuchs reminded the dean of her unique value to the university. She taught courses not only in civil rights and law, but also on women—a subject increasingly in demand and barely addressed elsewhere in the university. In a period of unprecedented strife and arrogant posturing, she had demonstrated an optimistic spirit, as well as a becoming modesty—even though she was the "most distinguished sixty-year-old Negro woman in the country today in any field of scholarship." To what other professor on campus, Fuchs asked, could either a black or white student, skeptical of the "Afro point of view," talk about his or her misgivings? "We need her."[46]

Fuchs conceded that Murray was not "brilliant." Nor did her work show "an unusually creative power of analysis or conceptualization." But he believed that "everyone acknowledges its excellence." To buttress his appeal, Fuchs offered Murray's three-volume doctoral thesis into evidence. True, it had not been published, but Fuchs believed that it showed a "quality of thoroughness, integrity, and excellence which comes through all her writings," qualities that underscored her value as an undergraduate teacher (the job for which she had been hired), if not a graduate researcher (a role for which the dissenters found her wanting).[47]

"Switch Hitter"

Typically, tenure considerations at private universities are confidential. Candidates have access neither to letters of recommendation, committee reports, nor even the identity of those who deliberate on the case. To Murray, such a process amounted to a "star chamber" proceeding. As a lawyer, she insisted on full disclosure. Dating back to her law school days, she had always asked recommenders to send her copies of any letters sent on her behalf, which she retained in her personal files. She continued this practice for her tenure case. She also demanded that Larry Fuchs share with her all relevant documents and that he divulge the details of the committees' deliberations. How fully Fuchs cooperated with her is difficult to say. He clearly revealed the arguments against her, but she learned much more.[48]

Just as she had once kept abreast of developments in the federal government through the female staff in the Justice Department and EEOC, Murray turned for intelligence on her tenure case to the Brandeis "underground," female secretaries and other support staff at the university who copied all letters and reports for confidential distribution to the dean and members of ad hoc committees. Murray did not hesitate to engage in this subterfuge. She believed she had been subjected to a process that violated the basic guarantees of due process. Tenure proceedings, she believed, ought to be reformed, made more open and transparent.[49]

Reading the documents provided by the "underground," Murray felt a mounting fury. "BASTARDS!" she exclaimed, to which Barlow added the more British "BLAST!" Once she had absorbed the news, Murray conveyed her outrage in a letter to her Yale friends Ruth and Tom Emerson. Fuchs's letter of support upset her nearly as much as the ad hoc committee's report. His concession that she was no more than an undergraduate teacher who lacked conceptual power made her feel "downgraded." She knew the rule "Publish or Perish" and realized she would have a stronger case if she could have published her thesis, but she had devoted her time to developing four innovative courses. She noted that American Studies had "won—THIS SPRING—its fifteen-year old struggle to become an independent department in its own right," and she claimed a good bit of the credit for the result. She criticized the tenure system for keeping out mavericks, suspected unconscious race and sex discrimination, and condemned the lack of flexibility shown by the committee in evaluating her unusual credentials.[50]

Murray reminded the Emersons (who needed no reminding) that men and women, not to mention blacks and whites, had been exposed to different "cultural conditioning," the result of which was different perspectives. That was a good thing, she believed, "the essence of the integrative process," something needed to make "the academic process whole." She insisted that she *did* have unusual powers of "conceptualization," but they came from "poetic" insight, born of her experience. They had to be "fleshed out by a more pedestrian approach," a quality, she conceded that she had never developed. Since no reply from the Emersons exists in Murray's files, it seems likely that they phoned her with their advice. Judging from the letter she sent to Fuchs a few days later, they urged her to provide him with better evidence of her "conceptual power."[51]

In a six-page, single-spaced letter, Murray did. Without blaming Fuchs for sabotaging her case, she urged that he reconsider his concession that her work lacked "flair, brilliance, and conceptual power." Perhaps, if one judged her as a historian or a literary critic, that concession might be justified. But she was neither and had never claimed to make original contributions to those fields. She had trained as a lawyer, and as all of her referees had made clear, her conceptual power lay there.[52]

She had been one of the first to challenge the long-settled view that racial segregation was constitutional under the Fourteenth Amendment. Drawing on diverse anthropological, psychological, and sociological sources, as well as her own experience, she had declared in 1944 that racial segregation was per se unequal. Howard students and teachers alike laughed at her, but a decade later the Supreme Court accepted her view. At Boalt Hall, she had challenged the constitutionality—under the Thirteenth Amendment—of private discrimination in the sale or rental of housing. McGovney had found her argument "inconclusive," but in 1968 the Supreme Court accepted the same reasoning in *Jones v. Alfred H. Mayer Co.*, holding that such discrimination was among the "badges and incidents of slavery." Forced to research and write a second master's thesis at Berkeley to win her degree, she had explored the possibility of using federal legislation to protect blacks from employment discrimination. Twenty years later, Congress did so through Title VII.[53]

Murray had also been the first (after Blanche Crozier) to see integral connections between gender and race. In her work before the President's Commission on the Status of Women in 1962–1963, she had advanced the theory of a "functional approach to sex discrimination." Published as the article "Jane Crow and the Law" in 1965, it had caught the attention of law professor Leo Kanowitz, who called the idea "seminal" and made it the centerpiece of his influential 1969 book *Women and the Law*.[54]

Far from repeating "the obvious," as the committee members accused her of doing, Murray saw herself as having been "on the frontier of reconceptualization" over several decades. Committee members should understand that what seemed obvious to them—for instance, that segregation was unequal per se—had been unthinkable until she and a few others challenged the "obvious" assumptions that underlay segregation and then proposed the sociological, anthropological, and psychological evidence for a Brandeis Brief that could overturn settled opinion in the courts. Identifying the link between race and sex, Murray had embarked on a similar analysis of gender discrimination.[55]

Murray had been able to do this, she believed, because she was different. She was black in a white society, female in a male culture, and left-handed in a right-handed world. But there was something more. "Unless one understands that my peculiar personality type is analogous to a 'switch-hitter' on a baseball team, it would be easy to dismiss the creativity of ideas as 'lacking in conceptualization.'"[56]

It is impossible to know how Fuchs read this statement, but in 1970 "switch hitter" meant more than a baseball player who bats both right and left-handed, or a versatile person. In urban slang it meant being bisexual. Based on her reading in the 1930s, Murray understood "bisexual" to refer not only to a person who was sexually attracted to both men and women (which she was not), but also a person who occupied an intermediate place along a continuum from female to male (in her case more male than female). Up to that point, the closest Murray had ever come to divulging the details of her well-guarded privacy was to reveal to Fuchs that she drank eight glasses of water a day. In the midst of her tenure battle, she went further. Murray told Fuchs that those on the sexual as well as the gender and racial margins of society had an angle of vision and conceptual advantage that those in the mainstream lacked.[57]

Murray knew full well that she had a tendency to get ahead of herself, not to develop her ideas fully, to leave that "pedestrian" (most writers would say essential) task to others. That said, she had indeed sparked an extraordinary number of important lines of inquiry, both in the law and beyond. *Proud Shoes* (1956) later became a staple of American Studies courses. Professors assigned it for its black-child's-eye view of Jim Crow and slavery's other remnants, its attention to America's multiethnic make up, its treatment of both rape and consensual sex across the color line, and its melding of storytelling with careful historical research. "Jane Crow and the Law" (1965) inspired a generation of younger attorneys, led by Ruth Bader Ginsburg, to use the Equal Protection Clause to win new rights for women. Murray's theory of "the conjunction of race and sex" became a staple of black feminist scholarship in legal circles, as well as scholarship in many other fields, in the decades to come.[58]

Murray's letter to Fuchs had a dramatic effect. Five days later, he sent off one final, impassioned appeal to Diamandopoulos. Fuchs reminded the dean how important Murray was to the university and to the students, but this time he mounted a powerful case for her conceptual power and the influence of her ideas. She was a visionary. Others filled in the gaps. Her unique experience gave her insights no one else had.[59]

And then they waited. Diamandopoulos deferred the decision for months. He felt torn. Much as he admired Murray, he was also a member of the philosophy department, to which he would soon return, following his term as dean. Professor of Philosophy Henry Aiken had cast one of the two votes against Murray on the ad hoc committee. Diamandopoulos could not ignore that vote of no confidence. Moreover, Brandeis's financial situation had deteriorated further, and the trustees had ordered a tenure freeze. Making matters still worse, President Abram, who had brought Murray to Brandeis, had resigned to run (unsuccessfully) in New York for a seat in the Senate. The one good piece of news was that Abram's replacement, Charles Schottland, was a man with whom Murray had served long ago on the President's Commission on the Status of Women. She believed he thought well of her, but that did not necessarily translate into a speedier decision or a favorable one.[60]

Finally, eight months after the ad hoc committee deadlocked on Murray's tenure case, Diamandopoulos recommended that the board of trustees grant her tenure, and they agreed. Several months later, she won appointment to the newly created Louis Stulberg Chair of American Studies, named for the president of the International Ladies Garment Workers Union (ILGWU). Murray could not have been more delighted. Her long association, through Maida Springer, with the ILGWU and Stulberg's predecessor, David Dubinsky, made this honor all the more meaningful to her.[61]

Suing Brandeis

Even as Dean Diamandopoulos and President Schottland struggled to find the funds to grant tenure to Murray and to retain her thereafter, they faced a related problem: the mounting fury of academic women at Brandeis and across the country over what they believed to be blatant gender discrimination. The US Department of Education threatened to withhold federal contracts from any university that failed to prove that it was not discriminating against minorities and female faculty and staff in hiring, promotions, and salary. Even before the board of trustees voted to approve tenure for Murray, she and Assistant Professor of French Jane Pollack, leaders of the newly formed Women's Faculty Caucus, met with Diamandopoulos to discuss women's grievances against the university. He agreed that their complaints were just and promised corrective action.[62]

Only a couple of weeks after Murray won tenure, she and Pollack met with President Schottland to repeat their concerns to him and demand action. A few weeks after that Diamandopoulos asked Murray to serve on a committee on the status of women. Above all, Brandeis administrators wanted to avoid the very real danger that the federal government would terminate university contracts for noncompliance with the Executive Order 11375, which required all government contractors to provide evidence that they did not discriminate of the basis of either race or gender. If Brandeis could not do so, it risked the loss of federal funds, without which research in much of the university would grind to a halt.[63]

The figures at Brandeis, as at other elite research universities, did not look good. Whereas a little over half the university's undergraduates and slightly less than a third of its graduate students were female, only 11 percent of Brandeis's full-time faculty and 6 percent of its tenured faculty were women. The hiring figures for the "high administration" were no better. Comparing Brandeis to other academic institutions, Murray and Pollack dryly observed, "This failure to utilize the skills and talents of women is exceeded, in the Boston area, only by Harvard's record." Moreover, the two as yet untenured faculty members complained, "It has been our experience that the credentials and aspirations of women in faculty positions have been scrutinized much more stringently than those of their male counterparts."[64]

Women who won faculty positions reported discrimination in pay. Murray's jubilation over winning tenure turned to anger when she discovered that, just five years from retirement, her salary of $22,350 was $400 below the median for all full professors. She could not understand how a person of her accomplishments and influence, someone who was changing American law at the highest levels, could be so undervalued.[65]

In 1972 women's complaints intensified against Brandeis and other universities around the country. NOW filed a complaint against Brandeis in March. The Brandeis Committee on the Status of Women filed a damning report the following February 1973. Murray sued Brandeis and TIAA-CREF, the pension fund for academics, charging that Brandeis engaged in sex discrimination in the determination of salaries and that the pension fund paid out lower annuities for women than for men. TIAA-CREF granted that was true but defended this difference on the ground that women lived longer than men. In the end, however, TIAA-CREF agreed to stop classifying annuity payments according to gender.[66]

Losing Renee

Murray's struggles at Brandeis played out against the backdrop of an alarming setback in the health of Renee Barlow. Although Barlow had been cancer free for five years by the summer of 1972, Murray could not help but notice that whenever Renee visited her in Boston, she spent most of the weekend sleeping. When Murray and Barlow were not together they kept in close touch by phone. In one call, Barlow reported that there was something wrong with her hand. "I can't type." Another time Barlow complained that she had tried to reach Murray a number of times but had kept getting the wrong number. Something was amiss. When Murray visited Barlow at Thanksgiving, she was alarmed by her appearance, but Renee responded that she just needed a little rest, perhaps a trip to Jamaica. Murray could not get away before the end of the term in February, so Barlow went with a mutual friend. On the flight Barlow suffered terrible vertigo and had to return to New York. She tried to work, but when she began to have trouble walking, Murray insisted that she contact her doctor. At first, Barlow refused, but as her condition worsened she relented. On January 10, 1973, she agreed to enter Columbia-Presbyterian Medical Center, where doctors discovered an inoperable brain tumor.[67]

Barlow had long ago given Murray her power of attorney in case she was ever incapacitated. Murray agonized over what to do. In those days, patients were not automatically informed of their medical condition. Murray refused to follow this tradition. Throughout their sixteen years together, they had always been open with one another. Murray insisted that the doctors speak frankly to Barlow and that she be allowed to make decisions concerning her care as long as she was able. Barlow agreed to steroids, followed by cobalt treatment to shrink her tumor. Not able to care for her mother, then ninety-three, Renee called on a sister in Connecticut to come to get her.[68]

The steroids had an immediate effect. Barlow regained her speech and good humor. She then began cobalt treatments on January 22, 1973, the day Lyndon B. Johnson died and the Supreme Court handed down its decision in *Roe v. Wade*. The doctors were hopeful that this treatment might extend Barlow's life by six months or a year—perhaps two years. At first their optimism was born out, and Murray returned to Brandeis for the end of the fall semester. Then Renee suffered a setback. Pauli rushed back, but Renee slipped into a coma and died on February 21.[69]

Murray was devastated. Planning Barlow's funeral fell to her. The service took place in Calvary Episcopal Church on East 21st Street in Manhattan, the church to which they had moved following a rift over treatment of women at their former church, St. Mark's Church in-the-Bowery. Lloyd Garrison spoke, as did several other friends. Everyone sang "We Shall Overcome," but Murray was not at all sure she could overcome the "inconsolable grief" that swept over her following the death of her "silent partner," the "closest person" in her life.[70]

Murray knew herself well. As a "firebrand," "involved in public causes and constantly subject to impulsiveness, combativeness, misjudgment of character," she recognized that she had lost her "guiding hand." Barlow's death was "a personal disaster" that made it impossible to continue as before. Murray returned to Brandeis to finish out the spring term of 1973, but she spent those months in a spiritual quest.[71]

16

The Reverend Dr. Murray

Grief

For sixteen years, Irene Barlow had been Murray's emotional anchor. Overwhelmed by grief, Murray turned for solace to the Episcopal faith they had shared throughout their life together, most intensely through the crisis of Barlow's final illness. Everything else—professional commitments at Brandeis, work at the ACLU—suddenly seemed trivial. Although she returned to Brandeis following Barlow's funeral, Murray began to discuss the possibility of reducing her commitment to one semester a year going forward. She told Larry Fuchs that she needed time alone to write.[1]

Murray's closest friends were "appalled" by this sudden about-face, and Murray herself sensed that her impulse to withdraw posed a danger. She had exhibited certain worrying propensities all her life: a bit of the "manic-depressive," manifested by "high creativity followed by uncommunicative states of silence and withdrawal, . . . refusal or neglect to eat, keeping odd hours." Losing Barlow made matters much worse. She knew that she needed "community"—more community, in fact, than Brandeis could provide. When depressed, she had found it all too easy to limit her appearances on campus to two days a week.[2]

Murray began to think about leaving academe altogether. She had never before stayed with any one employer for more than two or three years. Her five years at Brandeis constituted a lifetime record. Even without Barlow's death, she might have felt impelled to move on. She had beaten down the doors that barred women's access to the legal profession and professoriate. For her, there remained only the Episcopal priesthood as a final challenge. Other Protestant denominations had ordained women, some as early as the nineteenth century. The Reform Movement in Judaism ordained its first female rabbi in 1972, and women were bringing pressure on conservatives and orthodox rabbis to do the same. Within Christianity, only the Episcopal and Catholic churches remained intransigent on the subject of women's ordination.[3]

Murray had grown up in the Episcopal Church. She had spent much of her childhood reading from the precious Bible that Granma Cornelia had inherited from Mary Ruffin Smith. Granma requested two passages so often Pauli knew them by heart: Daniel in the lion's den and Ezekiel in the valley of the dry bones—both tales of triumph in captivity. These were the stories Murray turned to in the opening chapter of *Proud Shoes* to convey Pauli's ability as a little child to calm her grandmother in the midst of a rant against neighbors, a rant born of her tormented relationship to slavery and whiteness.[4]

Murray's aunts were almost as important as her grandmother to her religious education. Aunt Pauline and Aunt Sallie had been prime movers in the formation of St. Titus Church in Durham, North Carolina. The church and adjoining rectory became her second home when Aunt Sallie married the Reverend Small. Pauli's fondest memory of her summer visits to the Smalls was of making the rounds of the neighboring Episcopal churches each Sunday with her uncle. Beyond her immediate family, the Right Reverend Henry B. Delany, the black suffragan (assistant) bishop of North Carolina, exercised the most powerful influence on Murray as a child. Bishop Delany had taught her aunts, confirmed Pauli in the church when she was nine, and, on his deathbed, blessed her as "a child of destiny."[5]

In the midst of the Great Depression Murray lost her faith, but by the time she was thirty, she had return to the fold, prompted by her need for help in parenting her two nephews. She never again left the church. Her friendship with Eleanor Roosevelt gained strength from their shared Episcopal faith. With Barlow, the church had taken on a deeper importance. Together they had tried to make it a better, more inclusive place, open to "the least of these," as they liked to say, quoting Mathew 25:40.[6]

Women in the Episcopal Church

Murray and Barlow had no doubt been cheered when a coalition of liberal churches passed a resolution at the 1958 General Convention of the Episcopal Church recognizing "the natural dignity and value of every man, of whatever color or race, as created in the image of God." In the years that followed, the Episcopal Church increasingly welcomed black men to the priesthood, but women, whatever their race, enjoyed no such acceptance, despite mounting pressure from laywomen.[7]

Murray and Barlow's own church, St. Mark's Church in-the-Bowery proved no exception to the church's resistance on the subject of gender. In early 1966, as Murray talked with Betty Friedan and others about founding an NAACP for women, she felt a mounting anger at the exclusion of women and girls from religious ceremonies at St. Marks. On Sunday morning, March 27, her anger boiled over. Attending services, she kept asking herself, "Why is not one of the candle bearers a little girl? Why cannot the crucifer be a girl or woman? Why cannot the vestmented lay reader be a woman of the church? Why cannot women and men, boys and girls, participate equally in every phase of church activity?" The congregation appeared to be more than half women. Murray thought it likely that women contributed half, if not more, to the financial support of the parish. Was this not "taxation without representation?" she asked in an angry letter to the members of the vestry. Not satisfied with their response, Murray and Barlow moved uptown to the more welcoming Calvary Episcopal Church, where Eleanor Roosevelt had been baptized.[8]

Over the next few years, work at the ACLU, Benedict, and Brandeis occupied most of Murray's energies, but successes in those arenas—her promotion to tenured professor, the victory in *Reed v. Reed*—served to highlight continuing discrimination in the church and prompted her to throw herself into the battle for gender equality there as well. She had already become friends with women at the Episcopal Theological Seminary in Cambridge, who were as passionate on the subject of women's ordination as she was. In the spring of 1970, she attended a weekend conference of forty-five Episcopal women at Graymoor Monastery in New York state that called for equality for women at every level of the church. Later that spring she met with Henry H. Rightor, a lawyer-priest and professor of pastoral theology at Virginia Theological Seminar and a supporter of women's ordination. With Rightor she embarked on an exhaustive study of the constitution and canons of the Episcopal Church. Finding no language that specifically prohibited women from ordination, they issued a report calling for immediate action at the next meeting of the General Convention of the Episcopal Church. Murray and Rightor met with partial success. In October 1970, in Houston, the General Convention of the Episcopal Church, which convened every three years, accepted its first female delegates and voted to admit women to the offices of deacon and elder on equal terms with men. The Convention remained opposed, however, to the ordination of women as priests.[9]

Murray continued her activism within the church in the years that followed the 1970 General Convention. Initially, she fought for others, but with Barlow's death, she fought for herself as well. Barlow had been her partner in a religious journey. With her partner gone, Murray could imagine no alternative but to carry that journey forward. They had done all they could as laywomen. Murray wanted to become a priest or, at the very least, to enter a seminary to prepare herself for that calling. The Reverend Alvin "Al" Kershaw of Emmanuel Church in Boston, which she had begun to attend after moving from Cambridge to Boston three years before, encouraged her. Father Kershaw directed her to the Right Reverend John W. Burgess, bishop of the Diocese of Massachusetts, to whom she applied for admission to holy orders. Burgess turned her over to the suffragan bishop, Morris "Ben" Arnold, who supervised the candidates for ordination in the diocese. Arnold had made his first speech to the House of Bishops the year before, during a debate over women's ordination. Encouraging Murray to press forward, he told her that he had suggested to his brethren that the Second Coming of Christ "would not necessarily be represented by someone of the same race or sex as the First Coming."[10]

Murray also spoke to the Reverend John Anderson, husband of her longtime friend Thacher Clarke Anderson. John had prepared for ordination at the General Theological Seminary (GTS) in New York, the country's oldest Episcopal training ground. GTS had admitted its first woman in 1972 and seemed ready for change. Murray applied to both the Episcopal Theological Seminary (ETS) in Cambridge and GTS in New York. Staying in Cambridge seemed the obvious choice, but when Murray visited GTS, she knew immediately that the small, jewel-like campus, nestled in Chelsea Square, on West 20th Street at Ninth Avenue, was where she wanted to be. New York felt like home, her interviews went well, and she was offered an apartment in the seminary's "Close" on her first visit. Drowning in sorrow, she felt buoyed by the welcome she found there.[11]

General Theological Seminary

Leaving a tenured professorship to enter a seminary required a radical reduction in Murray's standard of living. In 1972, she earned $26,000 from her Brandeis salary and another $1,000 from speaking engagements. The salary ended in June 1973. From that point forward, Murray, aged sixty-two, lived on a budget of about $6,000 a year, pieced together from half a dozen sources: royalties of about $500, honoraria from speaking engagements of about $1,000, a few hundred dollars from teaching the occasional class at the New School, and income from a $26,500 annuity, purchased with a loan from Caroline Ware and Gardner Means, which they forgave over the next five years. Murray had also inherited $6,300 from Barlow, with which she hoped to handle expenses not covered by other sources until she reached sixty-five, at which point she would apply for benefits under her retirement plan and to begin to collect Social Security.[12]

In August, Murray packed up her Boston apartment and moved to GTS. Her ground floor rooms comprised a kitchenette and two rooms; one (normally a bedroom, with two windows on an airshaft) she dedicated to her books and papers; the other (with two windows on the street) she turned into a bed-sitting room-study. Hot and exhausted the day she arrived at the un-air-conditioned apartment, Murray steeled herself for the work ahead. Even after paring her possessions back to "essentials" and donating several boxes of her personal papers to the Schlesinger Library on the History of Women at Radcliffe College, Harvard University, she had boxes stacked to the ceiling. Roaches roamed the floors, the walls, and the ceiling. Chelsea, later one of Manhattan's most sought after neighborhoods, was an undesirable part of the city by common measures of cleanliness and safety in 1973. Even with her new dog, Roy, to protect her, Murray feared a break-in. She would have to get bars for her windows. What to do about her car? In Manhattan, car owners had to spend several hours each week moving their automobiles from one side of the street to the other to allow for street cleaning and avoid parking tickets. She finally found a $15-a-month space in a parking lot in the Bronx, an hour's subway ride away. By September, she had done what she could to reduce her living costs and prepare for the challenge ahead.[13]

As usual, that challenge proved greater than Murray had anticipated. Having exchanged her Boston apartment for rooms in the Close, she entered a fishbowl existence, subject to the close and continuous scrutiny of instructors and classmates, as she labored to master a whole new field of knowledge.[14]

For Murray the challenge of adapting to the seminary was compounded by her personal status. Having reached the apogee of academic life, as a chaired professor at a research university, she found herself under the tutelage of faculty many years her junior, alongside classmates less than half her age. And then there was the uncertainty of her future. Most seminarians looked confidently toward the priesthood at the end of three years of study. Murray did not know whether she would ever be ordained. Upon arrival, she hoped that the 1973 General Convention, scheduled to meet in a few weeks in Louisville, Kentucky, would vote to accept women as priests. The vote was closer than it had been three years earlier, but it fell short of approval. Murray would spend her entire training in doubt about the eventual outcome of women's campaign for the right to be priests.[15]

GTS was an especially difficult place to wait. Despite the warm welcome Murray had received when she first visited, and despite the support she found from some faculty and students throughout her time there, GTS was the country's most conservative seminary. Many professors and students passionately opposed women's ordination. Twenty-three all-white, all-male faculty (plus one half-time female) taught 133 seminarians, of whom only ten were women. Brandeis had been far from perfect, but 11 percent of its full-time faculty was female as were more than half the undergraduate students. The racial makeup of the seminary compounded her sense of isolation. She was one of only three black students enrolled at the school. In ways large and small, she struggled to fit in.[16]

For starters, she had trouble dressing the part. Given her height, now barely five feet, she had trouble finding vestments. Even the smallest size for men proved too large for her. She tried to hike up her robe with a "rope cincture," but often the cord came lose. She kept tripping on her hem as she served the priest, sabotaging her dignity and risking worse. In one of her periodic updates to her supervisor, Bishop Ben Morris, in Boston, she wrote, "I need a cassock (black) which fits, a surplice which fits, and a 'Cassock-Alb' for service at Calvary," the church she had attended with Barlow in the years before she died and where as a seminarian Murray volunteered to help in services. Murray calculated that she needed $155.25 to outfit herself respectably. Morris immediately sent funds, and Murray found a solution, the same she had been using since she was eight years old: boys' clothes. She found a choirboy robe, size 14, perfect for this "E-pixie-palian," as she jokingly referred to herself.[17]

In addition to worry over vestments, Murray fretted over cosmetics. The one concession she had made to feminine fashion upon becoming a lawyer, thirty years before, was lipstick, but woe to the man who complimented her shade. One morning a hapless senior, Paul Goranson, did so, and a few days later Murray fired off a letter intended to raise his "consciousness" about "that crack about 'lipstick' the other morning at breakfast." She seized on his comment as "an opportunity" to teach him something. "You may not have meant it as a sexist remark," Murray allowed, "but many liberated women would take it as such— that it is necessary for a woman to wear lipstick to be attractive. To whom? For what purpose? As sex objects?" As a person of mixed, Cherokee, African, and European descent, Murray chose to regard "lipstick as <u>war</u> paint, and [to] wear it when I am either on the warpath or want to protect my lips from chapping. A true woman does not need lipstick to make her attractive, any more than a true man needs it." Nonplused, Goranson responded that Murray had misinterpreted his compliment as a crack; that she was being petty and overly sensitive; and that she was better at talking than at listening.[18]

Many at the seminary shared Goranson's view. Evaluating Murray's performance in the Junior Tutorial Seminar at the end of the Michaelmas [Fall] Term, 1973, Professors James A. Carpenter and Richard W. Corney praised her preparation for tutorial and seminar discussions, for "frequently going beyond requirements," and for, overall, putting in a "superior" performance. They noted further that she had "participated well in the field education segment of the program." However, they pointedly added, Murray's "adversary approach in the reflective portion of that segment was perceived by some as overly argumentative."[19]

This "adversary approach" did not abate the next term. Student complaints became so insistent that Murray felt the need to make a public apology: "Two members of this morning's preceptorial group," she began her open letter, "have brought to my attention in loving brotherly manner the fact that, in my enthusiasm for the subject-matter today, I dominated the class discussion and others who wished to comment were crowded out. I am very sorry that I was not more sensitive to recognize their need to speak."[20]

Murray regretted her growing unpopularity at GTS, but that did not stop her from arguing with professors and classmates, frequently to the point of speaking over them. She had no idea that she was doing so, until a woman friend urged her to see a doctor. Tests revealed she had lost 30 percent of her hearing. Helped somewhat by hearing aids, Murray nonetheless complained that the devices, good for amplifying the voices of those near her, amplified ambient noise as well, thereby undermining their effectiveness. Hearing-assisted to only modest effect, Murray continued her campaign to raise the consciousness of her fellow seminarians, but she felt as though she had been catapulted back to the 1940s. Then the discrimination that mattered most to her was race; now it was gender.[21]

Protest by Typewriter, Renewed

In the tradition of Martin Luther, Murray regularly thumbtacked her typed indictments of church practices to the seminary's bulletin board. She was proudest of her letter to the community, accompanied by an op-ed piece by Andrew Young on the occasion of what would have been Martin Luther King Jr.'s forty-fifth birthday on January 15, 1974. The title of Young's essay, "But His Truth Is Marching On," was lifted from the final line of the chorus to the "Battle Hymn of the Republic," written for the Union Army in 1861 by abolitionist and early feminist Julia Ward Howe. Young called on the country to carry on King's religiously inspired, nonviolent movement for racial and economic justice.[22]

Despite Murray's dislike for King in his lifetime over what she perceived to be his mistreatment of women, she never missed an opportunity after his death to stress that she "walked in his tradition." She attached an "Open Letter to the Board of Trustees of General Theological Seminary," knowing that the trustees were due on campus in a few days for their mid-year meeting. After laying out the dismal statistics on the gender and racial composition of the faculty and student body at GTS, Murray lamented, "This means that our community is woefully incomplete and lacks the enrichment and insights which a more inclusive faculty and ministry would bring to our daily life and devotions."[23]

Murray lamented, further, that the seminary's search for a new member of the faculty that year had failed to improve matters. "Recently, a qualified woman candidate was considered for a position in New Testament. She was apparently not recommended for appointment because she was competing with a male candidate who is both a priest and has had more academic experience," Murray observed. Then she pointed out the inevitable consequences of past discrimination on seminary searches. "Because of past exclusionary policies, this will always to be true unless the Board of Trustees has both the will and the imagination to take affirmative action and to find the necessary funds to train women (and minority) faculty members in accordance with their potential."[24]

Murray attacked the failure of GTS to hire a qualified female to the faculty just as she was wrestling with a critical question before the Supreme Court. Should universities make use of racial or gender quotas in admissions to make up for past discrimination against blacks and women? Committed to affirmative action, Murray nonetheless disapproved of quotas. In her view they reinforced group identity in a way that she found needlessly divisive and inevitably stigmatizing. But as long as prior discrimination barred blacks and women from presenting qualifications as strong as those of white males, how could one ensure equal opportunity?

In early 1974 Murray retired from the last of her secular commitments, the National Board of the ACLU, and recommended that Ruth Bader Ginsburg succeed her. Before doing so, she addressed the subject of qualifications and racial preference in the context of law school admissions in one of her final memos to the Equality Committee of the Board. She urged that the Board lay "down a policy which protects the rights of <u>individuals</u>, which gives notice to applicants in advance that LSAT scores and academic records are only two of many criteria in the selection of students." She believed that opportunities should be made to as many different kinds of "disadvantaged students" as possible, including "poor white, Indian, women, etc., etc., as well as Black students." This approach would "maintain the general policy of equal protection of equal opportunity for all and at the same time include those members of racial minorities whose personal life histories show deprivation growing out of racial status."[25]

A case before the Supreme Court, in the spring of 1974, addressed the constitutional limits on affirmative action squarely. In *DeFunis v. Odegaard*, an unsuccessful white male applicant to the University of Washington Law School argued that the school's race-based affirmative action policy had discriminated against him. In private correspondence about the case with Thurgood Marshall, Murray argued, "The moral question, it seems to me, is how do we facilitate the overcoming of past discrimination—its results—without violating the rights of the individual person. Is there no standard which would reach the same result without making race or sex the criteria?" She asked Marshall to send her a list of amicus curiae so that she could request copies of the briefs.[26]

One amicus brief, from Harvard, caught the attention of everyone interested in the subject. Written by Archibald Cox, the Harvard brief insisted on the right of admissions officials to assemble a "diverse" group of students for the benefit of all. The ideal of diversity had deep roots in the Episcopal Church. In 1882, Dean of Canterbury Frederic William Farrar, made it a keystone of Episcopal faith: "Unity does not exclude diversity," he declared; "nay more, without diversity there can be no true and perfect unity." For Murray the idea of diversity became a central feature of her approach to theology during her seminary training and in her protests against student and faculty attitudes and practices.[27]

Murray's position placed her on the more conservative end of the civil rights spectrum at a time when Black Power remained ascendant. But within the GTS, her outspoken advocacy seemed beyond the liberal pale. Fellow student Earnest E. Pollock wrote Murray a long letter, accusing her of hurting the cause of both blacks and women by dominating discussions and diverting attention to herself. He told her that her use of the bulletin board angered him and urged that she listen more and speak less. "A person of your intellect and experience obviously has a great deal to offer a Seminary Community like ours. What you have done, however, due to your continual badgering and often rude interventions is turn off a great number of people." Pollock charged that Murray had failed to display the "sense of quiet reserve, taking time to seriously contemplate the responsibility that has been given you." In his view she needed a cause and the ordination of women had now become her cause. "You appear to be working for the glory of women, blacks and Pauli Murray, rather than to the Glory of God. I submit no advice, but rather a request that you re-evaluate your tactics and methods that have become quite tiring and cumbersome to many of the people for whom you say you have concern."[28]

Murray responded temperately, but firmly, "If you have to live with anger; I have to live with pain. I'll trade you both my pain, my sex, my race and my age—and see how you deport yourself in such circumstances. Barring that, try to imagine for 24 hours what it must be like to be a Negro in a predominantly white Seminary, a woman in an institution dominated by men and for the convenience of men, some of whom radiate hostility even though they do not say a word, who are patronizing and kindly as long as I do not get out of my place, but who feel threatened by my intellect, my achievements, and my refusal to be suppressed."[29]

Wanting to be more than someone intent on finding fault, Murray sought creative ways to make the seminary and wider religious world better. She gave her book collection in African history and American race relations to the seminary library, to free up space in her rooms but also to encourage greater understanding between whites and blacks at the school. When she learned from a white friend who taught at the Episcopal Master's School in Dobbs Ferry that black girls at the school felt alienated from the predominantly white population, she offered her help. Murray urged her friend to tell the girls that she would be honored to be invited to visit. The girls could serve as hostesses at a school reception for her as a way of "bringing about racial reconciliation."[30]

A "Thorn in the Flesh"

Grief-stricken, lonely, and beleaguered, Murray desperately needed a friend at the seminary, someone who understood and accepted who she was, as Renee Barlow had. Miraculously, one appeared. Page Smith Bigelow, two years ahead (though a decade her junior in age), was a wife and mother of three grown children. Unlike Murray, Bigelow commuted to the GTS from her home in Maplewood, New Jersey. Drawn to Murray's vitality and intellectual intensity, Bigelow warmly welcomed Pauli's contribution to the battle for women's ordination. She was the friend who sent Murray to a doctor to check her hearing. Bigelow represented an ally and more. Physically, she reminded Murray of Peg Holmes. "There are so many similarities . . . it almost scares me," Murray confided.[31]

Though she sensed, once again, the futility of her longing, Murray needed to tell Bigelow its basis. "I figure God created me," Murray wrote, "maybe two got fused into one with parts of each sex—male head and brain (?), female-ish

Figure 16.1 Page Bigelow, 1974. Estate of Pauli Murray, Schlesinger Library, Radcliffe Institute, Harvard University.

body, mixed emotional characteristics—borderline, marginal type." She might seem like a lesbian, but she had always felt like a heterosexual man in a "female-ish" body, and now she had fallen desperately in love with another heterosexual woman, just as she had forty years before with Peg Holmes. Murray regarded her strange inbetweenness, her "borderline, marginal type" as "a cross," a "thorn in the flesh": "it gets me into messes and complications,—just stating facts, not whining." Murray wanted Bigelow to know these details, to give her fair warn-ing. "This <u>had</u> to be said to you, because even though you are mature, perfectly capable of handling yourself, completely absorbed in your family, there is the fatal persuasiveness, the hunt, the chase, the call of nature—'THE FLESH' on my part . . . the intolerable dilemma of 'Admire with your eyes, but don't touch!'" Murray felt obligated "to be as honest as I can in these 'True Confessions' because you said, 'Don't be afraid to touch,' but dear Juliet, this Romeo is not made of angels' stuff, but very, very, human."[32]

Murray often found physical contact uncomfortable. With men, a hug rubbed in the unpleasant fact of her femaleness. With women, it too often provoked romantic feelings that threatened to destabilize her. Rather than risk such reac-tions, she typically begged off, with a veiled reference to the residue of racial oppression: "Don't touch me; I'm full of slivers." Murray judged Bigelow a strong woman: "practical, deliberate, down to earth . . . ruthless when you have to be." For her own part, Murray despaired, "I am more temperamentally flighty, tem-pestuous, daydreaming, mooning—very much like Roy Dog—he and I under-stand each other perfectly, that's why he's male and not female."[33]

Gently, Bigelow told Murray that she loved her, too, though not in quite the same way. As she explained after a brief separation, "Those few days I have missed your presence and the tangible visible audible knowledge you were about. Being one whose instinct is to hug those I care for, regardless of sex, and also generally having not the slightest sense of any sort of stimulating effect on the hormones in that affectionate embrace, I simply go ahead with my natural sense of wanting to show I care by touching my friends and loved ones. I suppose I should be more guarded but it just is not like me, and perhaps that is not all bad." Mismatched though they were, Murray and Bigelow established a friendship, the most inti-mate of Murray's years preparing for the ministry.[34]

Bellevue Hospital, Again

At the end of her first year at the GTS, Murray commenced her clinical pastoral training. Just as medical students supplemented classroom work with practical experience in teaching hospitals, so too did divinity students, who ministered to the sick and dying as the first step toward becoming priests. Enrolled in the

Pastoral Department, Murray was assigned to Bellevue Hospital, a half-hour walk across town.[35]

Entering Bellevue in May 1974 must have brought back painful memories of being picked up along the highway in Rhode Island and brought to Bellevue for psychiatric observation in 1940. She felt relieved that the Pastoral Department assigned her not to the psychiatric wing but rather to the emergency room and medical wards. Journal entries nonetheless reveal that the shadow of her earlier ordeal hung over her. To make matters worse, she was the only black, the only woman, and the only older person among the chaplaincy interns. She felt uneasy on the male ward: "the atmosphere was such I just couldn't penetrate it," she lamented. The black nurses saved her from complete humiliation by directing her to the black female patients. They, at least, seemed to accept her attentions. But she still had to face the weekly conferences with the other interns, who criticized her for being "abrasive." A month into the internship, Murray concluded it was better not to talk to her young colleagues, especially about women in the ministry. Opposition remained too great.[36]

In the midst of this sorry time, Murray's older sister Grace died. Pauli believed that her psychologically fragile sister, institutionalized (again) at the age of sixty-nine, had lost the will to live. And then there was her brother Bill (sixty-five), so mentally ill that he could not be left alone. Since his last institutionalization, his care had fallen largely to Mildred. Desperately in need of some time to herself, Mildred asked Pauli to take over for a week so that she could get away.[37]

Through this difficult summer, the debate over whether the Episcopal Church should ordain women as priests continued. Were it up to the bishops, women would have been ordained in 1970, but the House of Delegates, which voted first, continued to oppose ordination, though by ever narrower numbers. Discouraged by the slowness of the process, three retired bishops ordained eleven female deacons in Philadelphia on July 29, 1974. On August 16, Murray sadly recorded in her journal that the House of Bishops voted 120 to 9 with 10 abstaining to "invalidate" the ordination of the 11 women in Philadelphia and "mildly reproved" the bishops involved. The next day she added that the opposition to women's ordination "tends to reinforce one's sense of unworthiness." Murray felt increasingly isolated from the bishops, as well as from friends who were not members of the church. They simply could not understand what she was going through.[38]

As Murray entered her second year at the GTS, she concluded that she could not handle a repeat of the first, which had ended with a cautionary letter from Bishop Morris, provoked by charges of her "abrasiveness" at the seminary. She would simply have to be patient, learn to listen, refrain from debate, and focus on her studies. Quietly, she worked her way through her second year classes: "Liturgies," "New Testament," "Philosophy of Religion," and

"Prayer Course" in the fall term; "Church in the Modern World," "Gospel of St. John," and "Modern Theological Systems" in the spring. She avoided disputes and run-ins. She tried (with limited success) to cut back on smoking. She sought spiritual enlightenment. In February 1975, on the second anniversary of Renee Barlow's death, she turned to Reinhold Niebuhr's "Serenity Prayer" (1926): "Give me the serenity to accept the things I cannot change, the courage to change the things I can, and the wisdom to know the difference." By the end of the academic year, that prayer had inspired her to change one thing. She would take her senior year at the Virginia Theological Seminary (VTS) in Alexandria, Virginia.[39]

Virginia Theological Seminary

Murray had not anticipated how much living in the conservative environment of the GTS would wear on her. She especially disliked the pastoral department, from which she had received her harshest critiques. She may also have had reservations about returning to Bellevue, where the pastoral department had proposed that her next assignment be to the psychiatric ward. Money, too, played a role in Murray's thinking. The stock market collapse of 1973 had wiped out 45 percent of her retirement savings. She had to find a place to live where the cost of living was lower than in either Boston or New York. Finally, the Episcopal Church, which had grown dramatically in the 1950s, had begun to decline. The cultural revolutions of the 1960s and early 1970s, with their assault on established culture and authority, was draining membership from established churches at an accelerating rate. By 1975, the Episcopal dioceses of Massachusetts and New York reported trouble placing new priests.[40]

The VTS offered a faculty more supportive of women's ordination; indeed, the seminary had just hired Marianne Micks, the country's leading scholar on theological arguments in favor of women's becoming priests. The VTS faculty also included Henry H. Rightor, the lawyer-priest who had worked with Murray in the early 1970s to show that nothing in the Episcopal rules barred women from becoming priests. The VTS had more older students, the nucleus of a peer group for which Murray yearned. Most helpfully, in financial terms, the Virginia seminary offered a fellowship, dedicated to black seminarians. Unlike most fellowships it apparently imposed no age restrictions. If she did not win it, she would have to dip into her savings, until she began drawing retirement benefits when she turned sixty-five a year later.[41]

Fortunately, the Virginia-Maryland-Washington, DC, region seemed both more welcoming and affordable than either Boston or New York. Washington had a majority black population. Murray believed that she would stand a better chance there of finding work. She would also be nearer her extended family. As she watched her siblings grow more frail and die, she felt both a greater sense of responsibility to look out for the younger generation and a greater need for their attention. One sign that relocating to the VTS might have a long-term pay-off was the discovery that she could take her remaining pastoral education as a seminarian at St. Philip's in Aquasco, one of the rural churches in Maryland she had regularly attended with her uncle, the Reverend Small, as a child. St. Philip's had a majority black, minority white congregation, and was led by a white priest, Bill Jerr. She could easily imagine herself continuing after graduation as his assistant in a project of racial reconciliation. Finally, she could afford a two-bedroom apartment near the VTS campus and thereby regain some of the privacy she had given up by living in the Close at the GTS. For all of these reasons, she began to lobby Dean Foster at the GTS and Bishop Arnold in Boston to allow her to take her final year of seminary at the VTS, while retaining the right to graduate with her class at the GTS in 1976. Dean Foster persuaded the GTS faculty to allow Murray to accept this plan.[42]

Murray went to the VTS intending to write a master's thesis in defense of women's ordination. To do so she imagined a two-pronged strategy. First, she would highlight passages in the Bible that spoke of males and females in equal terms, passages such as the one in Genesis that declared, "male and female created he them; and blessed them, and called their name Adam, in the day when they were created." Another passage, attributed to her namesake Saint Paul, also supported the theme of equality: "There is neither Jew nor Greek, there is neither bond nor free, there is neither male nor female: for ye are all one in Christ Jesus." On balance, however, the Bible displayed a frankly patriarchal attitude. In those instances, only history would serve. Therefore, the second prong of her strategy would be to trace the patriarchal roots of women's subordinate status within the church to its origins. A group of female theologians—chief among them Mary Daly (Catholic), Rosemary Radford Ruether (Catholic), Letty M. Russell (Presbyterian), and Marianne Micks (Episcopalian) had begun that task. Daly and Russell had been inspired by Murray's own work on gender. Murray, in turn, drew on their books and articles to question certain interpretations of the Bible and to highlight others. Biblical criticism dated back to the Enlightenment, but it took on new urgency in the 1960s, with the rise of Liberation Theologies. The so-called new history with its search for a "usable past" offered these theologians of the oppressed a method.[43]

Murray began with Mary Daly's effort to turn God from a noun into an intransitive verb, from a male "Being" (set off against a female "other") to "Be-ing," an action without gender reference. Murray knew Daly from Boston College, the Jesuit institution, where Daly, a self-described radical lesbian feminist, taught theology, and where Murray taught a course at the law school in her final years at Brandeis. Daly and Murray shared not only an employer but also a publisher, Harper & Row. Among the first women to be trained as Roman Catholic theologians, Daly published *The Church and the Second Sex* in 1968, in which she argued that the Catholic Church had oppressed women for centuries. She then embarked on her second, and more famous, book, *Beyond God the Father: Toward a Philosophy of Women's Liberation* (1973). Daly credited Murray as the godmother of this latter work, a philosophical exploration of misogyny in religion generally. Murray appreciated the credit, though she did not like to think of herself as a godmother. Moreover, she found Daly's approach too abstract and vastly preferred the anthropological and historicist approaches of Micks, Ruether, and Russell.[44]

Eve, Hagar, and Mary

Taking her cue from Marianne Micks, Murray challenged the traditional reading of the story of creation, wherein Eve was created from Adam's rib, assigned responsibility for man's fall through her susceptibility to evil, and as a result demoted to a subordinate position under man's rule. Micks argued that recent biblical research had cast doubt on this interpretation. As Murray learned, "a careful reading of the original Hebrew text . . . shows that Adam, the first of God's creation, is generic, if not androgynous, that is, including within itself both sexes." Citing Micks, Murray declared, "Man as male does not precede woman as female but happens concurrently with her." She conceded that "we must deal with the myth as it has come down to us through patriarchal practice and church tradition," but for all of those conservative theologians who insisted on following original intent, Murray pressed the message that the original intent was not what conservatives had assumed. The meaning of the words had changed with altered historical conditions.[45]

Murray emphasized the significance of historical context in one of her first sermons, while still in New York. The occasion was "Father's Day," June 15, 1975; the place, St. Philip's in Harlem, was where she had worshipped when she first moved to Harlem in 1929. As in earlier times, so too in "the late twentieth century," she told the congregation, "the theologian must . . . speak to his or her own era, and it is my understanding as a student of theology that God is not limited by any man's notion of sex, or gender, or race, or ethnic origin, or status— God is all inclusive." When she spoke of herself as "a child of God," therefore, she did not feel, as those before her often had, the "need to make a special pleading for my sex—male or female, or in-between—to bolster self-esteem." If everyone could feel that way, then they could look toward a time when they might all celebrate "Mother-Father Day."[46]

Murray turned next to the central stories of the Old Testament, most especially to a female figure she already knew intimately from her childhood, the story of Hagar. In *Proud Shoes,* Murray characterized the circumstance of her Grandmother Cornelia's birth as "a human story as old as the biblical narrative of Abraham and his bondwoman Hagar, and their son Ishmael." Like Hagar, Grandmother Cornelia's mother had been a servant [house slave] who by her master had borne a child. Like Ishmael, Cornelia was, metaphorically, cast out into the wilderness of slavery and, following slavery, into the indignity and terror of Jim Crow. But Grandmother Cornelia, as Ishmael before her, looked to God for ultimate salvation. For Murray the story of Hagar and Ishmael stood for the multiracial origins of all wanderers— of whatever origin—who peopled America. The story of Hagar and Ishmael was the quintessential biblical story of the New World.[47]

Finding gender equality in the Old Testament posed a daunting challenge. The New Testament provided more promising material, most especially in a story about a visit Jesus made to the home of a woman named Martha, who had a sister, Mary. While Martha scurried about, preparing and serving food, Mary "sat at Jesus' feet and heard his word." Upset that Mary did nothing to help her, Martha complained to Jesus, "Dost thou not care that my sister hath left me to serve alone?" To which Jesus responded, "Martha, thou art careful and troubled by many things, But one thing is needful: and Mary hath chosen that good part, which shall not be taken away from her." This passage had traditionally been interpreted to mean that one should seek spiritual rather than material fulfillment, but Murray saw a feminist message as well. As she explained to a congregation in Maryland, in one of her early sermons, Martha represented the human tendency, still common in "our own day," to be "caught up in the frantic search for security, for material comforts, for worldly success, for new experiences and more and more *things*." But Martha's scurrying represented something more: the felt need to follow "traditional custom in conformity with the position of women in her time. Women in Jewish culture were not permitted to study the Torah or to engage in theological conversation with a rabbi." Murray read Jesus's validation of Mary's decision "to give her undivided attention to the Lord" as an affirmation that he viewed women, as much as men, responsible for learning and spreading his message."[48]

"Black [Male] Theology and Feminist [White] Theology"

Murray's search for strong women in the Bible and her reinterpretation of their stories laid the foundation for her master's thesis on the biblical and historical case for the ordination of women. But when a book on that subject appeared, she had to identify another topic. She embarked, instead, on a comparative study of the two principal outgrowths of liberation theology in the United States: the black and feminist versions. Liberation theology emerged out of indigenous struggles in Europe and Latin America. It avoided the traditional dualism of body and spirit and looked instead to experience as a theological source. Not content to wait for the hereafter, liberation theology sought salvation in this life. Black theology was a homegrown, American version, as was its feminist counterpart. In black theology, God was black and focused on black concerns. He was also male, with no use for feminism.[49]

Murray found feminist theology more appealing, closer to imagining the conditions for widespread liberation, but she believed that it tended toward a too-easy universalism, especially in the case of Daly. Murray preferred the work of Ruether and Russell, which posited a feminism in dialogue with black theology. Murray admired Russell, in particular, for rejecting the all-too-common tendency to emphasize the redemptive potential of the black female victim. In Russell's view, as in Murray's, each person possessed elements of the oppressor and the oppressed. But not even Russell ventured beyond black and feminist theology to analyze the multiple ways in which oppression could work.[50]

In the early 1960s, Murray had talked about the ways in which gender was like race. She had also talked about how gender interconnected with race to create a more intense oppression for black women than that experienced either by black men or white women. In wrestling with theology, she argued once more that black and white women, by virtue of their subordinate status, held a unique potential to guide humanity toward liberation and reconciliation. But now she ventured beyond black and white, to include all women, as well as other forms of oppression. "By dint of sheer numbers and intimate interaction with men," she explained, all women "possess potential power to affect social structures and attitudes. Of necessity their concerns must embrace the whole of the human condition—sexuality, the family, marital and single status, economic well-being, youth, the aged, poverty, disease, war and peace." Murray had not worked out how women were to achieve the liberationist potential of this shared "embrace of the whole human condition," but her critique of binary thinking represented a pioneering achievement.[51]

On April 17, 1976, Murray finished her last term papers. Far from feeling elated, she experienced the depression and anxieties that frequently accompanied the end of academic years. Only this time she felt worse. With the battle over women's ordination at its peak, expressions of self-doubt, loneliness, and panic filled every page of her diary, until a series of graduation commitments forced her into a marathon road trip up and down the East Coast: to New York for a class picture at the GTS, on to New Haven for a dinner at Tom and Ruth Emerson's, up to Boston for physical and psychiatric evaluations and the final ordination examination. Then back to DC for a dinner honoring Maida Springer, who had remarried in 1965, and was now Maida Springer Kemp. And finally to

Durham on May 5 for the fiftieth reunion of the Hillside High School class of 1926. To Murray's delight, ten out of a possible seventeen classmates attended. Everyone was doing well; their children had succeeded. But she also felt, once again, passé. A talk at NC Central College that she had hoped would attract a good audience produced only a "complete fizzle of the 'big moment' in the 'hometown.'" Dejected, she returned to New York for her graduation from the GTS cum laude on May 19, then returned to Virginia the next day, glad to escape "the crowds of NYC and the anxieties I tend to feel there." There were two further celebrations to get through: her ordination as a deacon in Massachusetts (still her home diocese) on June 9, and graduation ceremonies four days later at Dartmouth College, where she received an honorary doctorate of law. By midsummer, there was nothing more for her to do but work on her memoir and follow the debate over ordination in the nation's press that led up to the General Convention of the Episcopal Church in September.[52]

The New York State Legislature, EEOC, ACLU, and *New York Times* all had an opinion. Former New York assemblywoman Constance E. Cook, who had been the coauthor of the law that legalized abortion in New York, led off. Cook took up the cause of the Reverend Betty Bone Schiess, one of the Philadelphia 11, ordained as an Episcopal priest by reformist bishops in 1974, only to be denied a license by Bishop Ned Cole of Central New York. Cook presented the case to the EEOC. Notwithstanding the principle of separation of church and state guaranteed by the First Amendment, she argued, the Episcopal Church was also an employer, required by Title VII to refrain from discrimination in hiring and promotion on the basis of sex. The EEOC ruled in Scheiss's favor. Edward J. Ennis, chairman of the National Board of the ACLU, disagreed, objecting that the EEOC lacked authority to intervene in church affairs. Murray hotly replied, in turn, that where employment was at issue, Title VII should govern—in the church as in the case of any large employer. The *New York Times* editorial board agreed with Ennis on the law but with Murray on the principle and urged the church to move quickly to resolve the controversy. And so it did. In September 1976, the General Convention of the Episcopal Church, meeting in Minneapolis, passed a resolution declaring that "no one shall be denied access" to ordination on the basis of sex, effective January 1, 1977.[53]

Ordination

Page Bigelow, following tradition, was ordained in her local parish in New Jersey on January 6, 1976. Murray took part in the ceremony as a deacon. Two days later, Bigelow was one of the priests who presented Murray for ordination to the Right Reverend William Creighton, Bishop of Washington, at the National Cathedral in Washington, DC. Assisting Bishop Creighton was the Right Reverend John T. Walker, scheduled to succeed Creighton in July 1977 as the first black bishop

of Washington. The unusual national ceremony was organized as a celebration
by the Washington diocese to mark the equal ordination of women and men and
to recognize Murray's accomplishment. The first black person to be ordained
in the Episcopal Church was Absalom Jones of Philadelphia in 1805; 172 years
later, Murray was the first black woman. It was a glorious day, shared with 1,450
well wishers. Bishop Creighton, a passionate supporter of women's ordination,
had imposed a moratorium on all ordinations in 1975 until qualified women
could be ordained. Once that happened, he presided over the ordination of six
priests, three men and three women, the last of whom was Murray. When sun-
light burst through the clouds and shone down into the sanctuary, Murray took
the sudden illumination as a sign that God approved.[54]

Not everyone approved. Fifteen picketers passed out leaflets and carried signs
deploring "priestesses." The protests were decorous. Having sent letters signaling
their opposition to the bishops and those being ordained, they held a silent vigil
outside on the steps of the church. The opponents felt "compelled to make their
position clear," as one organizer wrote Murray, "and yet chose to spare you and
others the further pain of 'interrupting' the service."[55]

Figure 16.2 Pauli Murray, center, accepting a Bible from the Right Reverend William
Creighton, Bishop of Washington, at her ordination in the National Cathedral in
Washington, DC, January 8, 1977. Photographer: Milton Williams. Estate of Pauli
Murray, Schlesinger Library, Radcliffe Institute, Harvard University.

The media noted the picketers but focused on the historic event itself. To the national wire services and television, Murray was "the first black woman priest." In Australia, she symbolized a new beginning: "History as Black Woman Ordained." Many claimed her as their own. To Boston newspapers, she was "Massachusetts' first." To the *Durham Morning Herald* she was the "woman priest from Durham." The *Afro-American* asserted its claim with the headline: "Baltimorian Is an Episcopal Priest."[56]

At the age of sixty-six, Murray had become a minor celebrity, "The Poet as Lawyer and Priest," as a reporter for the *Washington Post* described her. "She is barely 5 feet tall, somewhat fragile looking—and intense. Her modest garden apartment in Alexandria is dominated by books, pictures of family and friends, and meticulously organized file cabinets. Of the last, a friend says, 'Pauli has the most incredible files on everything and everyone. She has a strong historical sense, a sense that everything she does is part of history. She sees herself as an instrument for achieving things.' "[57]

Friends, relations, and reporters all wanted to know: what does one call a female priest? "Please don't call me Mother," Murray begged. "As for the clerical labels—I've received the following suggestions: 'Rabbi,' for teacher'; 'the Rev. Miss (!),' the 'Rev. Doctor, Doctor, Doctor' [to account for her actual and honorary degrees—Yale, 1965, Stonehill College, 1967, and Dartmouth College, 1976] for a start." She eventually settled on the Reverend Dr. Murray, as a descriptor,

Figure 16.3 The Reverend Dr. Pauli Murray at the desk in her Alexandria, Virginia, apartment, in 1977. Estate of Pauli Murray, Schlesinger Library, Radcliffe Institute, Harvard University.

and, for direct address, Dr. Murray, as she had asked others to call her since earning her J.S.D. degree at Yale Law School in 1965. In a lighter vein, Murray dubbed
herself the "pixie priest . . . getting into people's hair, raising people's blood pressure." But she must have taken secret delight when her close-cropped hair, slacks,
and clerical collar prompted a new parishioner to call her "Father."[58]

While she was on the subject of nomenclature, she offered a few further
thoughts. During the rise of Black Power, she had held onto "Negro," but she had
been given such a hard time over its growing obsolescence that she began to consider alternatives. She suggested that "people of color" would be a suitable alternative for the polarizing "Black" or "White." She also liked "Eurafroamerican,"
in fact she had been using the term in reference to her own family for at least a
decade and to describe all those in the United States of mixed African, European,
and Native American ancestry.[59]

Sexuality and the Church

The General Convention's decision to allow women to be priests was only one
of the innovations that rocked the Episcopal Church in the 1970s. Another was
the adoption of a modernized version of the Book of Common Prayer, a change
many opposed as a violation of tradition. And then there was the subject of
homosexuality. Ever since the 1969 Stonewall Riots in Greenwich Village catapulted the gay rights movement onto the front page of newspapers around the
country, and even more since 1973, when the American Psychiatric Association
removed homosexuality from its official *Diagnostic and Statistical Manual of
Mental Disorders* (*DSM*), gays and lesbians had been demanding equal rights
in the Episcopal Church. In 1976, the General Convention defeated a motion
that would have barred the ordination of homosexuals, but gay rights supporters
lacked the votes to grant them equal rights.[60]

Those in a position to decide Murray's future disagreed on the place of homosexuals in the priesthood. Al Kershaw, from Murray's home church in Boston,
welcomed them and had long been an unquestioning source of support to
Murray and others. The head of the Massachusetts diocese, Bishop Coburn,
hedged. Although he professed to have nothing against them in theory, he
opposed the ordination of "practicing homosexuals." Bishop John Walker, due to
replace Bishop Creighton as head of the Washington Diocese in July 1976, and
therefore the person with immediate authority over Murray, opposed homosexuality, practicing or not.[61]

Under these circumstances, Murray read with horror one of the many stories
about her ordination on January 8. "Episcopals to Ordain Black Woman, Lesbian,"
declared the *News American*. Although the story that followed made clear that the

headline referred to two different women—Pauli Murray and Ellen Marie Barrett (a leader in the church's gay and lesbian group, Integrity)—Murray dared not let the ambiguous headline stand. A week later, she had her way. "It has been called to our attention," the *News American* editors reported on page one, "that that some readers misinterpreted the headline on a Page 1 article published Jan. 8. The head-line, 'Episcopals To Ordain Black Woman, Lesbian,' referred to separate ordina-tions of two women. We regret the misunderstanding of the wording".[62]

The torment that Murray continued to suffer on the subject of her gender identity and sexual orientation came through in a letter to Bishop Walker that she drafted but never sent. "I hear that you have been making 'tut' 'tut' remarks about my sexuality, 'It's unfortunate that she's a "so-and-so!" ' " she began.

> While this gossip distresses me, I am glad to know about it for it explains in large part your behavior toward me in recent months. It also explains certain things about your character which puzzled me. My reaction has been mixed. I could let my African-Irish temper rage and phantacize [*sic*] about blacking both your eyes, but since you are bigger than I am I might wind up with black-and-blue eyes—not a pretty picture for a newly ordained 'first'! I could—and do—remind you that such gossip, if you said it, can make you vulnerable to a civil suit in slander. . . . But— you are the 664th Bishop of PECUSA in the line of succession, soon to become the first Black Diocesan Bishop in one of the most volatile jurisdictions of our Church! Since I am identified with you by color, it is to my racially identifiable group interest that you be a great Bishop— and if you go around putting such words about fellow clergy in the "street," you are going to fall flat on your face. So let me raise a question with you: 1. ~~What do you really know about sexuality = heterosexual-ity, bi-sexuality, homosexuality, transsexuality, unisexuality?~~ 2. What do you know about metabolic imbalance? The varieties of approach to mental health? When you become an expert in these matters, you can speak with authority. Otherwise, please keep your mouth shut! 3. ~~God made me as I am. Are you, Bishop of the Church, questioning God's handiwork?~~ Faithfully yours, Pauli Murray.[63]

Murray did not send this letter for good reason. The 1970s witnessed a growing acceptance of homosexuality within the church, as the debate at the General Convention attested. But a new priest risked unemployment by admitting to a nonconforming sexual orientation or gender identity, especially if that priest was also black, female, and rapidly approaching retirement age. To announce oneself a "transsexual" would have destroyed what little chance Murray had of finding work in the church.

The Reverend John Walker may not have known much about transsexuality, but the word "transsexual," which had long been familiar only to a small number of people, was suddenly big news. This surge in interest derived from several factors, including the growing interest in sex and gender fostered by the sexual revolution of the 1960s, as well as the gay rights and feminist movements of the 1970s. But there was another reason.[64]

In 1975, Richard Raskin, an ophthalmologist and patient of Dr. Henry Benjamin's associate Dr. Ihlenfeld, completed hormone treatment, underwent sex reassignment surgery, and took the name Renée Richards. As a man, Raskin had been one of the leading amateur tennis players in the male division of the United States Tennis Association (USTA). As a woman, Richards petitioned to play in the women's division. The USTA denied her the right to do so, but a federal judge ruled in her favor. At the US Open in 1977, Richards lost to the American champion, Virginia Wade, in the first round.[65]

News of Richards's transition must have stirred up old longings in Murray. But as a newly ordained priest in the Episcopal Church and the first black woman ever to have won this recognition, Murray did not wish to follow Richards's example. She believed her gender identity to be a private matter. Caroline Ware knew, as did Maida Spring Kemp, Page Smith Bigelow, and Peg Holmes Gilbert. In the 1970s, in the course of "sanitizing" the papers Murray intended to deposit with the Schlesinger Library, she reestablished contact with Peg, who was living in Southern California, married, with two grown daughters. Murray thought back to falling in love with her when they were in their twenties and to her effort "to overturn all the laws of nature" to win her. But with rare exceptions, even Murray's closest friends and family knew nothing of her struggle over gender identity.[66]

Murray's young friend Mary Norris never knew. Although she shared Murray's Boston apartment in the early 1970s and later recalled conversations about the bouts of depression that plagued them both, they never discussed either homosexuality or transsexuality. Norris knew of Murray's close friendship with Barlow and her grief after Barlow's death, but she assumed that this was one of the close friendships between women that had been so common in an earlier day. Even after Norris realized that she herself was a lesbian, she never thought that Murray was homosexual (much less transsexual) until one day, in a Philadelphia library, long after Murray's death, she came across a book on the history of lesbian, gay, bisexual, and transgender people. The book included a piece on Murray, which mentioned that she had "struggled with her same-sex desires and gender identity." "Astounded," Norris asked Maida Springer Kemp whether the biographical entry's characterization of Murray could possibly be true. Maida responded that Pauli had once confided that she felt more male than female, and that she had felt drawn to feminine, heterosexual women, not to men or lesbians. Maida, however, had dismissed this revelation as "ridiculous," and they had never discussed the subject again. The 1970s and '80s were an especially difficult time to claim an identity different from the one assigned at birth. To confess a belief that one was a member of the opposite gender was to accept the very binary thinking that feminists, including Murray, wanted to overcome. The closest she ever came to giving public expression of herself as more male than female was to assume the identity of an Episcopal priest (a person invariably male, until a few weeks before), draft the letter to Johnny Walker (which she never sent), and press the importance of diversity—including gender diversity—whenever the opportunity arose.[67]

Going Home

Five weeks after her ordination, Murray drove to Chapel Hill to preach at the Chapel of the Cross. The chapel held particular significance for her. In 1854, her great-great aunt, Mary Ruffin Smith, had brought ten-year-old Cornelia there to be baptized. This visit was a homecoming, as well as a healing and reconciliation. The Reverend Peter James Lee, who had invited her, welcomed Murray as "a priest, a pontiff, that Latin word that means 'bridge.'" The image of the bridge fit Murray perfectly, as someone who all her life had tried to bridge the racial, gender, and class (among other) chasms that divided her fellow Americans.[68]

The day was full of symbols. Murray spoke on Sunday, February 13, the day after Lincoln's birthday. She stood at the lectern given to the chapel in honor of Mary Ruffin Smith. She read from the Bible that Mary Ruffin Smith had given to Grandmother Cornelia, and she marked her place with the purple ribbons that had wrapped the flowers given her by Eleanor Roosevelt the day Murray graduated from Howard Law School in 1944. Reading from Luke: 17–18, Murray spoke of Jesus, standing before "a great multitude of people," gathered to hear him preach, and she marveled at the multitude before her, some 600 people of many hues, who had crowded into the small chapel on this historic occasion. Their presence and Luke's words took her back fourteen years to the joyous assemblage of peoples who made up the March on Washington—"men, women, and children, old and young, the lame, the halt, the blind, the Jew and Greek, the Black, White, Red, and Yellow—Republicans and Democrats, rich and poor." There had been "not a single instance of violence," she recalled, though opponents had predicted there would be many. She remembered marching with the ACLU, then starting over to march with her parish church, St. Mark's Church in-the-Bowery. That day had given new energy to the campaign to enact the Civil Rights Act, then languishing in Congress. But divisions persisted, as did violence throughout America.[69]

Murray hoped that January 1, 1977, the day that the Episcopal Church officially welcomed women into the priesthood, might represent the opportunity to
heal the wounds inflicted by those divisions and that violence. Choosing as the
topic for her inaugural sermon, "Healing and Reconciliation," she went so far as
to imagine a Second American Revolution—the beginning of "the reconciliation of groups of Americans now alienated from one another by reason of race,
color, religion, sex (gender), age, sex preference, political and theological difference, economic and social status, and other man-made barriers."[70]

By including "sex (gender)" and "sex preference" among the categories that
alienated Americans from each other, Murray took a major step. A few days
before coming to Chapel Hill, she had written to her former teacher at the GTS,
James A. Carpenter and his wife Mary: "It was you, Jim who taught me that we
bring our total selves to God, our sexuality, our joyousness, our foolishness, etc.,
etc." With that teaching in mind, Murray publicly included prejudice against a
person's "sex preference" or "homosexuality" as illegitimate "man-made barriers"
to reconciliation. She seemed hopeful. If the Episcopal church could welcome
into the priesthood not just women but a black woman—"the least of these," as
she put it, quoting Mathew 25:40—then perhaps, one day, American society
would be able to welcome those judged gender and sexual deviants as well.[71]

In the meantime, here she was, welcomed back to Chapel Hill, where the
University of North Carolina had rejected her on account of race in 1938. She
believed the invitation was a sign. " 'Deep in my heart, I do believe' that the
American South will lead the way toward the renewal of our moral and spiritual
strength and our sense of mission," she told her listeners. The light had passed
from the Pilgrims and the City on a Hill to places like Chapel Hill, "where we
are today witnessing to the reconciling of Isaac and Ishmael in the House of
Abraham."[72]

Grandmother Cornelia, the daughter of a slave and a slave owner, had taught
her the "Old Testament story of Abraham, Sarah, Hagar the bondswoman, Isaac
the legitimate heir, and Ishmael the outcast." It was a story that "comes alive in
our own time," she said. "The promise of the angel and the Lord to Hagar in the
desert to make Ishmael and his descendants a 'great nation' is being fulfilled.
And this great nation is the American nation—neither black nor white—but all
colors."[73]

"My entire life's quest," Murray concluded, "has been for spiritual integration,
and this quest has led me ultimately to Christ in whom there is no East or West,
no North nor South, no Black nor white, nor Red Christ . . . only Christ, the Spirit
and Love and reconciliation, the healer of deep psychic wounds, drawing us all
closer to that goal of perfection which links up to God our Creator and to eter-
nity. Let us pray":

O god, who created all peoples in your image, we thank you for the won-
derful diversity of races and cultures in this world. Enrich our lives by
ever-widening circles of fellowship, and show us your presence in those
who differ most from us, until knowledge of your love is made perfect
in our love for all your children, through Jesus Christ our Lord.[74]

Earlier in her life, Murray had believed with Justice Harlan that justice was color-
blind. She continued to oppose laws that categorized on the basis of race or gender, but she had come to worry that ignoring these groupings could lead to a
too-easy universalism. She now believed that people should be attuned to any
difference—of race, color, gender, age, or disability, for starters—used to justify
discrimination. But there was more. She had come to value difference—diversity
of every kind—as good in itself. Only through honoring diversity could healing,
reconciliation, and, ultimately, justice be achieved.

Epilogue

The Search for Work

Given her age, gender, and race, as well as the decline in church membership in the early 1970s, Murray's chances of attaining a full-time position as a priest seemed remote. Her hope of remaining at Aquasco in rural Maryland, where she had served as a seminarian while completing her final year at the VTS, ended when the church burned down in November 1976. Even had the church survived, she would probably not have secured a permanent place. Bishop Walker, she learned, had wanted to replace her supervising priest, Bill Jerr, with a black priest and to remove Murray.[1]

She would have loved to teach, and she believed the country's seminaries needed faculty like her. As she pointed out to GTS Dean Roland Foster, there were no brown faces and only one female face on his faculty. Although she assured him that she was not applying for a job—just pointing out facts— she would almost certainly have accepted an offer, had it been forthcoming. It wasn't. She received several nibbles from non-Episcopal schools, but she was already beyond retirement age for one and was within three years of retirement in two others. A seminary position appeared to be out of the question.[2]

She looked for a position as parish priest in Massachusetts, to no avail. Ditto New York and Washington. By June, she conceded the obvious. There would be no parish rectorship. As she told a reporter from the New Haven Register, she would instead "serve the church in a legal capacity and as a writer." Her one request: "Please don't refer to me as 'Mother Murray.'"[3]

This is not to say that she wanted for work. She became a minister without portfolio in and around Washington, DC, most often at St. Stephen and the Incarnation Church and the Episcopal Church of Atonement, where she filled in when the regular priest was unavailable—for services, weddings, and funerals. She volunteered at the Wisconsin Avenue Nursing Home twice a month. She served as priest and celebrant at special Women's Day services throughout Virginia.

She also lectured all over the country on college campuses, before women's groups, and at conferences. She gave the occasional class, including one for Dr. Marianne H. Micks's seminar "Adam and Eve" at the Virginia Theological Seminary. She developed a "floating congregation" that followed her from place to place. As women entered journalism in larger numbers, she achieved a measure of fame.[4]

She earned little for her priestly duties—only $25 to $35 for a sermon that took her ten days to write. In 1977, those efforts added up only to $750. She made more from other sources: $2,150 from speeches and college seminars, $500 from an award, $364 from royalties and permissions, and $3,600 from advances on two book contracts. Together with Social Security, her annuity from TIAA-CREF, and the annuity she purchased in 1973, her income came to around $10,000, not a lot in an economy in which inflation hit double digits in 1978–1979.[5]

Murray continued to live in Alexandria until 1980, when she learned her apartment complex would be converted to a condominium. Unable to purchase her unit, she moved to Baltimore. She had been spending more time there in recent months. Her niece, June Gwynn, Grace's daughter, was battling cancer. In January 1980 June died. Murray was with her at the end and served as priest at her funeral. June left behind a pregnant daughter, Karen Watson, and son-in-law, Dr. Terry Watson, a dentist. Karen, having lost both her grandmother and mother in quick succession, asked Murray to stay on. Terry offered to let her live in an apartment above his dental office. Facing eviction in Alexandria and feeling the need for family connection, Murray agreed. She lived above Terry Watson's dental office for the next four years, during which time she affiliated with the Church of the Holy Nativity and baptized two new great-great nephews, Erique and Ian Watson.[6]

Murray enjoyed one significant financial success after ordination. In 1978, she finally persuaded Harper & Row to reissue *Proud Shoes*. For years, the editors had refused on the grounds that in the modern era of Black Power there was no longer an audience for a book that celebrated a multiracial clan as the quintessential American family. But by the end of the 1970s, an audience had begun to develop. This time *Proud Shoes* made money, nowhere near as much as Alex Haley's *Roots*, with its tale of African forebears, but enough to allow Murray to indulge in the greatest extravagance of her life, a luxury automobile.[7]

Ever since the incident on the bus in Petersburg, Virginia, in 1940, owning a car had been an obsession. In 1960, newly arrived in traffic-choked Accra, Ghana, she had splurged on a Karmann Ghia. In 1967, she and Renee Barlow had bought a Volkswagen together. With royalties from the second edition of *Proud Shoes*, Murray strove for something grander. In 1980 she bought a 1974

Mercedes. Two years later, she sold the Mercedes to Maida Springer Kemp and purchased a two-year-old BMW, series 5, for $17,500.[8]

Murray proudly drove up and down the East Coast to university campuses and to churches of every denomination. In her sermons and lectures, as in her essays and the interviews she gave, she stressed the multilayered nature of oppression, the indivisibility of human rights, and the importance of serving as a "bridge" between people alienated from one another because of their differences. Drawing on her legal and theological training, she reminded her listeners how religion and the laws that flowed from it had structured relations between the men and women throughout history, ensuring the domination of men and the subjugation of women. Society needed a feminism attentive to human diversity to "reshape patriarchal religion" and to "establish a new humanity beyond patriarchy." Carrying on the work she had begun during World War II, when she had joined A. J. Muste's Fellowship of Reconciliation (FOR), she stressed the continuing need for "patience," "restraint," "forgiveness without limits," and, most important, "reconciliation" in the face of

Figure E.1 Pauli Murray and Maida Springer Kemp, 1979. Estate of Pauli Murray, Schlesinger Library, Radcliffe Institute, Harvard University.

continuing discrimination, war in the Middle East, and the threat of nuclear annihilation.[9]

Barriers to Reconciliation

Murray's writings and sermons staked out a vision of diversity and reconciliation, but her experience as a priest highlighted the distance that remained between that ideal and the reality of everyday life. As she moved from church to church, Murray came to see that her day at the Chapel of the Cross, in Chapel Hill, had been an anomaly. Reconciliation turned out to be far more difficult than she had dreamed it would be.

Part of the problem was the continuing decline in church membership, a worry throughout the Episcopal Church in the 1970s. At one time Holy Nativity had been an affluent church of more than 600 members with a parish house and rectory, offices, and rooms for day care, choir, vestry meetings, Sunday school rooms, a large kitchen, and a dining hall. By the late 1970s, church attendance had declined to the point that only a merger with a neighboring parish could sustain it. The church was now half white and half black—an ideal mix, from Murray's point of view. And yet there were difficulties. As she explained the situation to Page Bigelow, the church was "now almost top heavy with clergy 'types.'" Murray gave the "needed component of 'black' clergy," but did not wish to be a priest without authority. "The white elements of the church have apparently intimidated, not by design, the black elements who have withdrawn from activity around the altar," Murray reported. "They could use me as co-rector, but I do not know whether the active whites will accept black leadership, and the infusion of aggressive blacks to make the parish truly interracial. It cannot be done without pain, for we do in fact live in two worlds—particularly in Middle Atlantic and Northern communities, and until we recognize and deal with it and all the pain it entails, we will not move forward."[10]

After much debate, the vestry voted to have Murray serve as Priest-in-Charge at Holy Nativity in early 1982, but her tenure lasted only a few months. Under church rules, full-time priests had to retire when they reached seventy-two. Murray hit that milestone on November 20, 1982, after which she returned to her former status as a supply priest, available to fill in when needed. Even as a supply priest, Murray faced difficult challenges. In addition to the economic pressures that continued to plague Holy Nativity and the racial tensions manifest in a church that was half black, half white, Murray faced gender bias. Her greatest difficulty came in her relationship with the senior warden, a younger black woman. Never sure about the source of the conflict, Murray speculated that the warden envied her, but she wondered whether her subordinate's hostility had other roots. "How much of it was my fault?" she mused, "My style of dress? My free-dom from convention and the 'canons of respectability?'" Murray now dressed exclusively in slacks, an increasingly acceptable choice for women in informal settings, though not yet in the more conservative professions. Her assertive-ness troubled many. The fact that she was single raised suspicions that she was a lesbian. Gender tensions affected not only Murray's work at Holy Nativity but also relations in her own family. Her great nephew-in-law and landlord, Terry Watson, sided with the warden, charging her with "doing the devil's work dis-guised as a priest!"[11]

To Pittsburgh with Maida

Murray hated to leave her niece Karen and the children, but she decided it best to find another home. In early 1984, she moved to Pittsburgh, to live close to Maida Springer Kemp, who had settled in Pittsburgh to be near her son and daughter-in-law. That summer Pauli and Maida decided to tour the country together by Amtrak. The fact that two black women could travel throughout the country without restrictions revealed how much America had changed in their lifetime. As Murray reported in her year-end letter, they headed for "Seattle, stopping off en route to attend the Wingspread (Wisc.) Consultation of Black Women in preparation for the Nairobi Conference in 1985 marking the close of the Women's Decade." Murray's keynote address at the Seattle Urban League's Annual Dinner was "warmly received," and "Maida thrilled the Coalition of Labor Union Women at a luncheon held for her with reflections on her career as a trade unionist since the early New Deal." On the return trip, they stopped in Salt Lake City, where they visited with Elizabeth Lawrence Kalashnikoff, Murray's editor for *Proud Shoes*. They finished their grand tour with the "High Point of 1984—the Eleanor Roosevelt Centennial celebrations at Vassar College."[12]

In November, Pauli and Maida moved into a small, two-story, two-fam-ily house with twin apartments and a garage on Thomas Boulevard facing Westinghouse Park. Their new neighborhood was a racially integrated residen-tial area in the North Point Breeze section of Pittsburgh. Pauli took the upstairs apartment, Maida the one below. They shared a common basement. Pauli thought it the perfect solution to retirement living—independent, but with a friend downstairs. Better still, Maida had family nearby.[13]

At seventy-four, Murray enjoyed reasonably good health. She continued to be hard of hearing, and she suffered from occasional vertigo. She thought that she might have suffered a mild heart attack in 1980 but was not sure of the diag-nosis and had experienced no further episodes. In 1982, she had entered Johns Hopkins Hospital for treatment of a recurrence of the abdominal adhesions that had plagued her, off and on, since her thirties. Apart from these complaints, nothing slowed her down—until around Christmas 1984. Suddenly, she turned yellow.[14]

Suspecting pancreatic cancer, the doctor she consulted admitted her to Presbyterian University Hospital for a biopsy. The biopsy procedure had barely begun when Murray's heart stopped. The surgeons got it started again but dared not continue. They inserted a tube to bypass the blockage they found and drain fluids into the small bowel, in the hope that they could thereby reduce the jaundice, and sewed her up. In and out of consciousness in the hospital's intensive care unit, Murray finally woke up after a week. She had lost fifteen pounds from her already slender 100-pound frame. Dressing herself took several hours. She had to learn to walk all over again. While she remained in the hospital, Maida, with the help of family and friends, completed work on their new apartments. On March 8, Maida brought Pauli home to a "sparkling place," as Murray reported to friends and family. Maida had arranged for "flowers, and a 'fatted calf.' " The whole experience "reduced me to tears, and I don't cry easily," Murray confessed. For all her joy at being able to return to her new home, Murray knew the gravity of her condition: "from here on out, it's a day at a time."[15]

Murray hoped to attend graduation at Hunter College, where she was scheduled to receive yet another degree, a Doctor of Humane Letters, and to share the stage with Geraldine Ferraro, who the year before had been the first woman to run on the Democratic ticket for vice president. In the end, Murray was too weak to go. On Monday, July 1, 1985, she died, aged seventy-four.[16]

Legacy

At the time of her death, Murray was working with her editor on the final revisions of her autobiography. Years of meticulously saved correspondence, scrapbooks, diaries, notebooks, essays, poems, stories, letters to the editor, published articles, speeches, sermons, pictures, and organizational minutes allowed her to produce a model memoir. Like *Proud Shoes,* it provided an extraordinary level of detail, but it lacked the power of her earlier family history. Not wanting to embarrass those still living and unwilling to tackle personal topics that, made public, would risk ending the invitations to preach, teach, and participate in conferences, she revealed little of her inner self. She returned some letters and pictures to a few close friends, including Peg Holmes, to protect their privacy. After Murray's death, her sister Mildred apparently sanitized her papers further, thereby imposing serious obstacles to later researchers. And yet, enough remained to guide scholars to a deeper understanding of Murray's private struggles. By the mid-1990s, scholars were beginning to mine those papers for essays and later books that would make Murray's contributions and her struggles more widely known.[17]

The title of her autobiography remained uncertain. She had dropped the original, "Jane Crow," in favor of "The Fourth Generation of Proud Shoes," but her editors eventually selected "Song in a Weary Throat," from Murray's collection of poems, *Dark Testament*. The phrase "Hope is a song in a weary throat" evoked the long march toward equal rights for all, rights gained by breaking down arbitrary categories. Murray imagined more than destruction. "I speak for my race and my people," she liked to say; "the human race and just people."[18]

She had lived to see three of her lost causes won. Her use of the analogy of "sex" to race before the President's Commission on the Status of Women on behalf of her Fourteenth Amendment strategy had been vindicated. Over the course of the 1970s, the ACLU Women's Rights Project, led by Ruth Bader Ginsburg, achieved a series of victories by building on Murray's argument that gender discrimination paralleled race discrimination. With the defeat of the ERA in 1982, Murray's 1962 prediction that the Equal Protection Clause of the Fourteenth Amendment offered a surer path to legal gender equality proved correct. Although the Court declined to treat gender cases with the same "strict" scrutiny it applied to race, it did accept (with occasional lapses) Murray's argument, made in 1963, that government define its law and policy according to the function to be performed, rather than the gender of the performer.[19]

Murray's further argument that race and gender discrimination, as well as poverty, must be considered as "oppressions [that] are interconnected" was being advanced by a younger generation of black feminists. In 1982, Gloria T. Hall, Patricia Bell-Scott, and Barbara Smith published a collection of essays and course syllabi by black women. Entitled *All the Women Are White, All the Blacks Are Men, But Some of Us Are Brave*, the book condemned racism, sexism, and homophobia. Murray wrote the editors an appreciative note: "Dear Sisters, if *Newsweek* [which had run a feature on women's studies ignoring the contributions of black women] doesn't see the value of your work, here's an 'Old Timer' who does. So be encouraged. *It can be done*."[20]

Finally, Murray's early support for diversity as a legally justifiable goal for educational institutions had won widespread acceptance by the 1980s—not only as an alternative to quotas, but also as a way to foster tolerance for all groups who were unjustly maligned and discriminated against.[21]

Murray no doubt took satisfaction in seeing the idea of the interconnectedness of multiple forms of oppression as well as the importance of diversity embraced by younger scholars. She only wished that her pioneering role in developing these ideas and trying to sell them to a skeptical, even hostile older generation, could have been more widely recognized. When Bell-Scott asked her to serve as a consulting editor on a new journal, *SAGE: A Scholarly Journal of Black Women*, in 1983, Murray applauded the new enterprise but declined the invitation, citing other obligations. When she had more time, she promised, she would help: "You need to know some of the veterans of the battle whose shoulders you stand on."[22]

Sadly, the cause that tormented Murray most—that of the transgender person—remained lost to her. Her genius was her ability to displace that torment into battles she had a better chance of winning and, in the process, to lay the groundwork for others to use those successes as stepping stones to later victories. Once she had convinced her colleagues at the NAACP that race should be challenged directly as an arbitrary category, and therefore unjustifiable under the Equal Protection Clause, she could then persuade the President's Commission on the Status of Women and, eventually, Ruth Bader Ginsburg that gender should be treated the same way. If the distinction between men and women was arbitrary, then the justification for discriminating against those judged sexual and gender deviants must eventually fail.

Two decades would pass before a significant part of American society would be ready to embrace all of her crusades. It began in 2008 with the election of Barack Hussein Obama to the presidency and continued with his reelection in 2012. Three years later the Supreme Court ruled in *Obergefell v. Hodges* (2015) that marriage was a fundamental right guaranteed to same-sex couples. In that opinion, Justice Anthony Kennedy forecast the extension of the Equal Protection Clause to transgender people, when he wrote: "The Constitution promises liberty to all within its reach, a liberty that includes certain specific rights that allow persons, within a lawful realm, to define and express their identity." The legal battle to break down arbitrary boundaries would continue, but the shift in popular culture was already well under way. In 2014, a cover of *Time* magazine pictured the trans woman Laverne Cox of the television series "Orange Is the New Black," with the declaration that America had reached a "tipping point" in the acceptance of transgender people. Resistance remained, but when in 2016 North Carolina passed a law barring people from using bathrooms that did not correspond to the gender they had been assigned at birth, Obama's Justice Department reacted by ordering all states to allow transgender students to use the bathrooms that match their gender identity.[23]

By then Murray's career had begun to attract the attention that had eluded her in her lifetime. She would have taken special delight had she lived to see her name engraved on a building at Yale University. Under attack because one of its residential colleges bore the name of John C. Calhoun, the antebellum southern senator and slave owner, infamous for arguing that slavery was a benign institution, Yale announced it would name one of two new residences Pauli Murray College. For Murray, who had championed "diversity" in all its forms, this honor would have felt like a vindication. In recognizing Murray in this way, Yale honored the decision she had made long ago to offer herself as a bridge, between black and white, male and female, northerner and southerner, left handed and right handed, old and young—an example of diversity in one body, on its way toward mutuality and reconciliation in a better world.[24]

NOTES

Frontmatter

1. On terminology, I have found helpful Susan Stryker, *Transgender History* (Berkeley: Seal Press, 2008), and Laura Erickson-Schroth, ed., *Trans Bodies, Trans Selves: A Resource for the Transgender Community* (New York: Oxford University Press, 2014).

Introduction

1. Interview with Pauli Murray by Genna Rae McNeil, February 13, 1976 (G-0044), in the Oral History Program Collection (#4007), Southern Historical Collection, Wilson Library, University of North Carolina at Chapel Hill, 17–18.
2. Pauli Murray, *Song in a Weary Throat: An American Pilgrimage* (New York: Harper Collins, 1987), 255 (for Murray's influence on Marshall), 365 (for Murray's influence on Friedan). Ginsburg acknowledged her debt to Murray, by adding Murray's name as a coauthor in her brief in *Reed v. Reed*, a highly unusual gesture.
3. Murray spoke of her "boy-girl" self in a letter to her Aunt Pauline in Lenie [Pauli Murray] to Mother [Pauline F. Dame], June 2, 1943, Pauli Murray Papers [hereafter PM Papers], Schlesinger Library, Radcliffe Institute, Harvard University, Box 10, Folder 253; she referred to her "queerness" in Pauli Murray to Helene Hanff, November 16, 1955, PM Papers, Schlesinger Library, Box 97, Folder 1732; she used "between" scores of times in Pauli Murray, *Proud Shoes: The Story of an American Family* (New York: Harper & Brothers, 1956); see, for example, 55, 66, 67, 158, 252, 257. For an insightful exploration of Murray's understanding of her gender identity, in the context of her family, community, race, and class, see the work of Doreen Marie Drury, especially "'Experiment on the Male Side': Race, Class, Gender, and Sexuality in Pauli Murray's Quest for Love and Identity, 1910–1960," Ph.D. diss., Boston College, 2000; "Love, Ambition, and 'Invisible Footnotes' in the Life and Writing of Pauli Murray," *Souls: A Critical Journal of Black Politics, Culture, and Society* 11, no. 3 (2009): 295–209; and "Boy-Girl, Imp Priest: Pauli Murray and the Limits of Identity," *Journal of Feminist Studies in Religion* 29, no. 1 (2013): 142–147. On the broader subject of transgender identity and sexuality, see Susan Stryker, *Transgender History* (Berkeley: Seal Press, 2008); Laura Erickson-Schroth, ed., *Trans Bodies, Trans Selves: A Resource for the Transgender Community* (New York: Oxford University Press, 2014); Joanne J. Meyerowitz, *How Sex Changed: A History of Transsexuality in the United States* (Cambridge, MA: Harvard University Press, 2002); Anne Fausto-Sterling, *Sexing the Body: Gender Politics and the Construction of Sexuality* (New York: Basic Books, 2000); Judith Halberstam, *In a Queer Time and Place: Transgender Bodies, Subcultural Lives* (New York: NYU Press 2005).
4. Murray first used the phrase "Jane Crow" in a note to Professor Leon Ransom at Howard: Pauli Murray to Leon Ransom, August 21, 1944, PM Papers, Schlesinger Library, Box 84,

Folder 1467. She first used "Jane Crow" in a published work in Peter Panic [Pauli Murray], "Little Man from Mars," *Sentinel*, date written in ink is 7-14-44, but publication date was likely later, because Murray did not start writing for the *Sentinel* until August; PM Papers, Schlesinger Library, Box 1, Folder 12. Most famously, Murray used "Jane Crow" in the title of her law review article, written with Mary Eastwood: Pauli Murray and Mary O. Eastwood, "Jane Crow and the Law: Sex Discrimination and Title VII," *George Washington Law Review* 34, no. 2 (December 1965): 232-256. For her use of "Jane Crow" as the provisional title of her autobiography see Pauli Murray, "Draft ms—Jane Crow," August 26, 1968, in bound diary, PM Papers, Schlesinger Library, Box 2, Folder 30. See also Sarah Azransky, "Jane Crow: Pauli Murray's Intersections and Antidiscrimination Law," *Journal of Feminist Studies of Religion* 11, no. 3 (2013): 155-160, and Britney Cooper, "Black, Queer, Feminist, Erased from History: Meet the Most Important Legal Scholar You've Likely Never Heard Of; Ruth Bader Ginsburg Is this Supreme Court's Liberal Hero, but Her Work Sits on the Shoulders of Dr. Pauli Murray," *Salon*, February 18, 2015.

5. Interview with Pauli Murray by Robert Martin, August 15 and 17, 1968, Pauli Murray Papers, Moorland-Spingarn Research Collection, Howard University, Washington, DC; Murray, *Proud Shoes.*

6. Pauli Murray, notes on conversation with Dr. Titley, Long Island Rest Home, December 17, 1937, PM Papers, Schlesinger Library, Box 4, Folder 71; Peter Marshall Murray, M.D. [no relation] to Pauli Murray, April 20, 1947, Box 4, folder 73.

7. For the significance she attached to the thyroid operation, see Pauli Murray to Joe Lasch, undated memo in Letters to Eleanor Roosevelt Folder, June 19, 1954, PM Papers, Schlesinger Library, Box 99, Folder 1780.

8. Pauli Murray to Katherine Clarenbach, November 21, 1967, PM Papers, Schlesinger Library, Box 51, Folder 899; Murray, *Proud Shoes*, 270-271.

9. Pauli Murray, "Should the *Civil Rights Cases* and *Plessy v. Ferguson* Be Overruled?" PM Papers, Box 84, Folder 1467; Murray, *Song in a Weary Throat*, 255; interview with Pauli Murray by Martin, 78-79.

10. Murray, *Song in a Weary Throat*, 183.

11. Pauli Murray, "The Liberation of Black Women," in *Voices of the New Feminism*, edited by Mary Lou Thompson (Boston: Beacon Press, 1971), 88.

12. Drury, "Boy-Girl, Imp Priest: Pauli Murray and the Limits of Identity," p. 41; Cornell Williams Brooks, president and CEO of the NAACP, "Pauli Murray: A Great American Hero," posted to MarriageEquality.org, February 2, 2015; Marcia M. Gallo, *Different Daughters: A History of the Daughters of Bilitis and the Rise of the Lesbian Rights Movement* (Emeryville, CA: Seal Press, 2007).

Chapter 1

1. Birth Certificate for Anna Pauline Murray, Pauli Murray Papers, Schlesinger Library, Radcliffe Institute, Harvard University, Box 1, Folder 1; "Family Tree," PM Papers, Box 12, Folder 328; Pauli Murray, *Song in a Weary Throat: An American Pilgrimage* (New York: Harper Collins, 1987), 1-3; Doreen Marie Drury, "'Experiment on the Male Side': Race, Class, Gender, and Sexuality in Pauli Murray's Quest for Love and Identity, 1910-1960," Ph.D. diss., Boston College, 2000, 14-19.

2. Agnes Murray to Sallie Fitzgerald, April 23, 1907, PM Papers, Schlesinger Library, Box 11, Folder 296; Murray, *Song in a Weary Throat*, 11-12.

3. Murray, *Song in a Weary Throat*, 7.

4. Pauli Murray, handwritten family tree of the Fitzgeralds, PM Papers, Schlesinger Library, Box 12, Folder 323; Murray, *Song in a Weary Throat*, 4; Pauli Murray, *Proud Shoes: The Story of an American Family* (New York: Harper & Brothers, 1956), 102-192, 38-54

5. Murray, *Proud Shoes*, 219-240.

6. Murray, *Song in a Weary Throat*, 5; Darlene Clark Hine, *Black Women in White: Racial Conflict and Cooperation in the Nursing Profession, 1890-1950* (Bloomington, IN: Indiana University Press, 1989), 16.

7. Pauli Murray, handwritten family tree, PM Papers, Schlesinger Library, Box 76, Folder 1352. On the prominence of the Murrays among upper-class African Americans in nineteenth-century Baltimore and Washington, see Willard B. Gatewood, *Aristocrats of Color: The Black Elite, 1880–1920* (Bloomington: University of Indiana Press, 1990), 41, 73, 74, 103.

8. William Murray, notes, n.d., PM Papers, Schlesinger Library, Box 10, Folder 230; Murray, *Song in a Weary Throat*, 3–4.

9. William Murray, notes, n.d., PM Papers, Schlesinger Library, Box 10, Folder 230; James D. Anderson, *The Education of Blacks in the South, 1860–1935* (Chapel Hill: University of North Carolina Press, 1988), 34–35, 188, 193.

10. William Murray, notes, PM Papers, Schlesinger Library, Box 76, Folder 1352; Anderson, *Education of Blacks*, 33–35.

11. Murray, *Song in a Weary Throat*, 5–6.

12. "Our Marriage Vow, the Service and Minister's Certificate," PM Papers, Box 10, Folder 225; Murray, *Song in a Weary Throat*, 6.

13. Interview with Pauli Murray by Robert Martin, August 15 and 17, 1968, PM Papers, Howard University Archives, 2–3; Roberta Fitzgerald to Pauline Dame and Sallie Fitzgerald, April 16, 1904, PM, Box 10, F 264.

14. Pauli Murray, "The Fitzgeralds," handwritten family tree, PM Papers, Schlesinger Library, Box 12, Folder 328; Roberta Fitzgerald to Agnes Murray, February 23, 1904, PM Papers, Schlesinger, Box 10, Folder 226; Roberta Fitzgerald to Pauline Dame and Sallie Fitzgerald, April 16, 1904, PM Papers, Schlesinger Library, Box 10, Folder 264.

15. Murray, *Song in a Weary Throat*, 14–15; Murray, *Proud Shoes*, see caption for picture of Tommie in collection of pictures between pages 202 and 203; fragment, with dates and places of marriage, births, and deaths of children, PM Papers, Schlesinger Library, Box 11, Folder 284; "Autobiography of Aunt Pauline," PM Papers, Schlesinger Library, Box 11, Folder 275; Murray, *Song in a Weary Throat*, 14–15. For more on the phenomenon of passing from black to white in these years, see Daniel J. Sharfstein, *The Invisible Line: A Secret History of Race in America* (New York: Penguin, 2012); Allyson Hobbs, *A Chosen Exile: A History of Racial Passing in American Life* (Cambridge, MA: Harvard University Press, 2014).

16. Agnes Murray to Robert and Cornelia Fitzgerald, August 22–24, 1905, PM Papers, Schlesinger Library, Box 10, Folder 226; Murray, *Song in a Weary Throat*, 31.

17. Introduction to poems of William Henry Murray, PM Papers, Schlesinger Library, Box 10, Folder 230; Interview with Murray, by Martin, 4–5.

18. Murray, *Song in a Weary Throat*, 2–3.

19. Pauline Fitzgerald Dame, notes written about her early care of Pauli, possibly in support of Murray's application to the New York State Bar, April 1, 1948, PM Papers, Schlesinger Library, Box 10, Folder 262; Murray, *Song in a Weary Throat*, 10–11.

20. Agnes Murray to Pauline Dame, October 21, 1912, PM Papers, Schlesinger Library, Box 10, Folder 264; Robert A. Margo, "Teacher Salaries in Black and White": Pay Discrimination in the Southern Classroom," in *Race and Schooling in the South*, edited by Robert A. Margo (Chicago: University of Chicago Press, 1990), 54.

21. Agnes to Pauline, October 21, 1912, PM Papers, Schlesinger Library, Box 10, Folder 264; Murray, *Song in a Weary Throat*, 2–3, 10.

22. Death Certificate for Agnes G. Murray, March 26, 1914, PM Papers, Schlesinger Library, Box 10, Folder 227; Janet Farrell Brodie, *Contraception and Abortion in Nineteenth-Century America* (Ithaca, NY: Cornell University Press, 1997), 253–294.

23. Ellen Chesler, *Woman of Valor: Margaret Sanger and the Birth Control Movement in America* (New York: Simon & Schuster, 1992), 44–73.

24. Mildred Fitzgerald Fearing's memories, recorded by Pauli Murray, PM Papers, Schlesinger Library, Box 76, Folder 1352; interview with Pauli Murray by Genna Rae McNeil, February 13, 1976 (G-0044), in the Oral History Program Collection (#4007), Southern Historical Collection, Wilson Library, University of North Carolina at Chapel Hill, 5; *A Poet's Notebook*, epigraph to first chapter of Murray, *Song in a Weary Throat*, 1.

25. Mildred Fitzgerald Fearing's memories, recorded by Pauli Murray, PM Papers, Schlesinger Library, Box 76, Folder 1352.

26. Interview with Murray by Martin, 1; Murray, *Song in a Weary Throat*, 1. The causes of gender dysphoria and gender variance have yet to be determined. See Jack Drescher and William Byne, "Gender Dysphoria/Gender Variant (GD/GV) Children and Adolescents: Summarizing What We Know and What We Have Yet to Learn, *Journal of Homosexuality* 59, no. 3 (March 2012): 501–510; and Anne Fausto-Sterling, who urges scientists to study gender identity formation within a dynamic systems framework that takes into account multiple factors: biological, psychological, and environmental: Anne Fausto-Sterling, "The Dynamic Development of Gender Variability," *Journal of Homosexuality* 59, no. 3 (March 2012): 398–421.

27. Murray, *Proud Shoes*, 27.

28. Murray, *Proud Shoes*, 27; interview with Murray by McNeil, 12; J. Morgan Kousser, *The Shaping of Southern Politics: Suffrage Restriction and the Establishment of the One-Party South, 1880–1910* (New Haven, CT: Yale University Press, 1974), 241.

29. Murray, *Proud Shoes*, 10–11, 25–26; Murray, *Song in a Weary Throat*, 19, 22.

30. Interview with Murray by McNeil, 12–13; Murray, draft manuscript for autobiography "Jane Crow," August 26, 1968, PM Papers, Schlesinger Library, Box 2, Folder 30.

31. Murray, draft manuscript for autobiography "Jane Crow."

32. Interview with Murray by Martin, 32; Murray, draft manuscript for autobiography "Jane Crow."

33. Interview with Murray by McNeil, 19; Murray, *Song in a Weary Throat*, 23.

34. Murray, *Song in a Weary Throat*, 16, 24, 26.

35. Interview with Murray by McNeil, 17–18; Lenie [Pauli Murray] to Mother [Pauline Dame], June 2, 1943, PM Papers, Schlesinger Library, Box 10, Folder 253; Pauli Murray to Page Bigelow, February 20, 1974, PM Papers, Schlesinger Library, Box 93, Folder 1623; it is difficult to document the names family members called each other in private. In her first letters to her Aunt Pauline, Pauli signed herself, "Your daughter" or "Babykins." Pauli first signed a letter "Lenie" in 1936, a name that she used along with "Your child" and "Pauli" thereafter.

36. Interview with Murray by McNeil, 17–18; Lenie [Pauli Murray] to Mother [Pauline Dame], June 2, 1943, PM Papers, Schlesinger Library, Box 10, Folder 253; Murray, *Song in a Weary Throat*, 16–17.

37. Pauli Murray, 1933 notes for a history of the family, PM Papers, Schlesinger Library, Box 76, Folder 1352; Murray, *Song in a Weary Throat*, 449.

38. Margo, "Teachers Salaries in Black and White," 54; interview with Murray by McNeil, 22.

39. Murray, draft manuscript for autobiography "Jane Crow"; Murray, *Song in a Weary Throat*, 62; Murray, *Proud Shoes*, 251.

40. Murray, *Proud Shoes*, 33.

41. Murray, *Proud Shoes*, 33–35; Interview with Murray by McNeil, 13.

42. Murray, *Proud Shoes*, 241, 248–255; E. M. Perdue, "Study of Pellagra; Conclusions Based on Research by Italian Scientists," letter to the editor, *New York Times*, August 18, 1921. Later, researchers would discover that soaking corn in hard water released the niacin (B3), without which those who subsisted on corn would develop pellagra.

43. Murray, *Proud Shoes*, 270. Murray's experience of color discrimination within the black community, and even within her own family was widespread, though by no means universal. For more on this subject, compare Wallace Thurmon, *The Blacker the Berry* (New York: Macaulay, 1929) and Sara Lawrence-Lightfoot, *Balm in Gilead: Journey of a Healer* (Reading, MA: Addison-Wesley, 1988). See also Joel Williamson, *New People: Miscegenation and Mulattoes in the United States* (New York: Free Press, 1980), 111–186; and Gatewood, "The Color Factor," in *Aristocrats of Color*, 149–181.

44. Murray, *Song in a Weary Throat*, 30.

45. Interview with Murray by McNeil, 13.

46. Murray, *Song in a Weary Throat*, 17–18.

47. Murray, *Song in a Weary Throat*, 20.

48. Murray, *Song in a Weary Throat*, 25–26.

49. Murray, *Song in a Weary Throat*, 22, 27. Murray's diaries and letters are a pleasure to read not only for their contents but for the clarity of her left-handed script; Murray, *Proud Shoes*, 271; interview with Murray by McNeil, 11.

50. Interview with Murray by McNeil, 9; E. Franklin Frazier, "Durham: Capital of the Black Middle Class," in *The New Negro*, edited by Alain Locke (New York: Albert & Charles Boni, 1925), 333–340; Nancy MacLean, *Behind the Mask of Chivalry: The Making of the Second Ku Klux Klan* (New York: Oxford, 1994), 3–22.

51. Murray, *Proud Shoes*, 257–265.

52. Pauli Murray, *States' Laws on Race and Color* (Cincinnati, OH: Women's Division of Christian Service, Board of Missions and Church Extensions, Methodist Church, 1950), 343–348.

53. Interview with Murray by McNeil, 10–12; Murray, *Proud Shoes*, 268.

54. Murray, *Proud Shoes*, 32.

55. Murray, *Proud Shoes*, 269.

56. Murray, *Song in a Weary Throat*, 32–33.

57. Murray, *Song in a Weary Throat*, 44.

58. Murray, *Song in a Weary Throat*, 42–45, 55; Drury, " 'Experiment on the Male Side,' " 19–24.

59. Kenneth T. Jackson, *The Ku Klux Klan in the City, 1915–1930* (New York: Oxford University Press, 1967), *passim*.

60. Murray, *Song in a Weary Throat*, 46–48.

61. Pauline [PM] to Mama [Pauline Dame] and Grandma [Cornelia Fitzgerald], from Croome, June 24, 1921, PM Papers, Schlesinger Library, Box 10, Folder 252.

62. Murray, *Song in a Weary Throat*, 58.

63. Pauline to "My Darling Mother," Croome, July 2, 1924, PM Papers, Schlesinger Library, Box 10, Folder 252.

64. Murray, *Song in a Weary Throat*, 59; Pauli Murray, Application of Pauli Murray for Admission to the Bar of the State of New York, May 8, 1948, Archives of the Appellate Division, Supreme Court of the State of New York, Second Judicial Department, Brooklyn, New York.

65. Anderson, *Education of Blacks*, 192–193, Table 6.1.

66. Newspaper clipping, n.d., PM Papers, Schlesinger Library, Box 15, Folder 366.

67. Hillside Yearbook, *The Eagle*, 1926, PM Papers, Schlesinger Library, Box 15, Folder 367; Murray, *Song in a Weary Throat*, 64.

68. According to report cards for the academic year 1923–1924, when Pauli turned thirteen, she earned (with virtually no exceptions) As in conduct, effort, personal appearance, language, literature, Latin, history, and algebra. In music and physical culture she got Bs, in science Bs and Cs, in sewing As, Bs, and a C, and in cooking As and Bs; PM Papers, Schlesinger Library, Box 15, Folder 365; interview with Murray by McNeil, 14–15; Murray, *Song in a Weary Throat*, 63–64; Hillside Yearbook "The Eagle," 1926, p. 17, PM Papers, Schlesinger Library, Box 15, Folder 367.

69. Murray, *Song in a Weary Throat*, 63; interview with Murray by McNeil, 25.

70. "The Outstanding Seniors of the Year," *Hillside SKI HI*, n.d., PM Papers, Schlesinger Library, Box 15, Folder 366; Ann Douglas, *Terrible Honesty: Mongrel Manhattan in the 1920s* (New York: Farrar, Straus and Giroux, 1996), 217–253; on Pauli's preference for pants in high school, see "Pauli Murray Reminisces in Letter to Friends in City," *Carolina Times*, March 23, 1946, PM Papers, Schlesinger Library, Box 4, Folder 91; Hillside Yearbook, *The Eagle*, 1926, p. 17, PM Papers, Schlesinger Library, Box 15, Folder 367.

71. Interview with Murray by McNeil, 19.

Chapter 2

1. Pauli Murray, *Song in a Weary Throat: An American Pilgrimage* (New York: Harper & Row, 1987), 66; *Barnard College Catalogue*, 1926.

2. Murray, *Song in a Weary Throat*, 67.

3. Murray, *Song in a Weary Throat*, 67.

4. Richmond High School transcript, Pauli Murray Papers, Schlesinger Library, Radcliffe Institute, Harvard University, Box 15, Folder 368; Murray, *Song in a Weary Throat*, 68–70; Murray recalled cessation of menstruation for five months when she was sixteen in notes to herself, December 14, 1937, PM Papers, Schlesinger Library, Box 4, Folder 71; Richmond High Yearbook, 1929, PM Papers, Schlesinger Library, Box 15, Folder 368.

5. Deed to the Homeplace of Robert G. Fitzgerald, October 3, 1927, PM Papers, Schlesinger Library, Box 273; "Teachers Contract" for Pauline Dame, May 10, 1927, PM Papers, Schlesinger Library, Box 11, Folder 269.

6. Felicia D. Miller, Affidavit of Character and Home Life, In the Matter of the Application of Pauli Murray for Admission to Practice as an Attorney and Counselor-at-Law, New York Supreme Court, Appellate Division, Second Department, June 11, 1948 [Hereafter, PM Application for Admission to NY Bar.]

7. Murray, Song in a Weary Throat, 70; Sarah and A. Elizabeth Delany, with Amy Hill Hearth, Having Our Say: The Delany Sisters' First 100 Years (New York: Kodansha America, 1993), 3.

8. Murray, Song in a Weary Throat, 71; Ruth Jacknow Markowitz, "Subway Scholars at Concrete Campuses: Daughters of Jewish Immigrants Prepare for the Teaching Profession, New York City, 1920-1940," History of Higher Education Annual 10 (1990): 35.

9. Murray, Song in a Weary Throat, 73.

10. Pauli Murray to Irene Barlow, August 26, 1960, PM Papers, Schlesinger Library, Box 5, Folder 138.

11. Murray, Song in a Weary Throat, 71.

12. Murray, Song in a Weary Throat, 88.

13. Murray, Song in a Weary Throat, 73-74; Gilbert Osofsky, Harlem: The Making of a Ghetto, 1890-1930, 2nd ed. (New York: Harper & Row, 1971), 130.

14. Anna Arnold Hedgeman, The Trumpet Sounds: A Memoir of Negro Leadership (New York: Holt, Rinehart, and Winston, 1964), 45; Dorothy Height, Open Wide the Freedom Gates: A Memoir (New York: Public Affairs, 2003), 80; Judith Weisenfeld, African American Women and Christian Activism: New York's Black YWCA, 1905-1945 (Cambridge, MA: Harvard University Press, 1997), 156-169.

15. Murray, Song in a Weary Throat, 74; James Weldon Johnson, Black Manhattan (New York: Alfred A. Knopf, 1930), 162-163.

16. Murray, Song in a Weary Throat, 74-75; Hedgeman, The Trumpet Sounds, 44; Height, Open Wide the Freedom Gate, 80; Barbara Ransby, Ella Baker and the Black Freedom Movement: A Radical Democratic Vision (Chapel Hill: University of North Carolina Press, 2003), 69-70.

17. Hedgeman, The Trumpet Sounds, 47-51; Ransby, Ella Baker, 64-71; Thomas J. Sugrue, Sweet Land of Liberty: The Forgotten Struggle for Civil Rights in the North (New York: Random House, 2009), 12-13.

18. Murray, Song in a Weary Throat, 75-76. On employment discrimination against those who were judged too dark, see Yevette Richards, Maida Springer: Pan-Africanist and International Labor Leader (Pittsburgh: University of Pittsburgh Press, 2000), 32.

19. See ticket stubs pasted into the scrapbook Murray kept during her college years: PM Papers, Schlesinger Library, Box 4, 83v.

20. Murray, Song in a Weary Throat, 76; on Murray's smoking, see Dr. May Chinn to Whom This May Concern, June 12, 1954, PM Papers, Schlesinger Library, Box 4, Folder 73.

21. Murray, Song in a Weary Throat, 77.

22. Murray, Song in a Weary Throat, 77; Mark Naison, Communists in Harlem during the Depression (New York: Grove, 1984), 11; for an advertisement for an Open Road trip to the Soviet Union see "Traveler's Notebook," The Survey, February 1, 1932, 502.

23. Murray, Song in a Weary Throat, 76-77; Susie A. Elliott, Affidavit of Character and Home Life, PM Application for Admission to NY Bar; Alfred Kinsey et al., Sexual Behavior in the Human Female (Philadelphia: W. B. Saunders, 1953), 299.

24. Certificate of Marriage of William Roy Wynn and Anna Pauline Murray at All Saints Episcopal Church, Richmond Hill, L. I., on November 28, 1930, Exhibit 3, PM Application for Admission to NY Bar (judging by their names, the witnesses were not family members); Murray, Song in a Weary Throat, 77; Pauli Murray, notes on conversation with Dr. Titley, Long Island Rest Home, December 17, 1937, PM Papers, Schlesinger Library, Box 4, Folder 71.

25. Murray, Song in a Weary Throat, 89; Kathleen A. Hauke, Ted Poston: Pioneer American Journalist (Athens: University of Georgia Press, 1998), 1-36; Ted Poston, "Age Meets Youth," in "Harlem Shadows," Pittsburgh Courier, January 24, 1931; Murray, Song in a Weary Throat, 89, 76-77. Pauli and Billy never met again, but in 1949 Murray had their marriage annulled

in Virginia, where William Roy Wynn (who had married a second time) then lived; for evidence, see James H. Raby to Carson DeWitt Baker, April, 29, 1949, PM Papers, Schlesinger Library, Box 3, Folder 70.

26. Murray, *Song in a Weary Throat*, 77; on Open Road, see John Rothschild to Committee on Character and Fitness, PM Application for Admission to NY Bar; on "running away," see Murray, notes on conversation with Dr. Titley, Long Island Rest Home, December 17, 1937, PM Papers, Schlesinger Library, Fox 4, Folder 71.

27. "Slip Brings Halt to Tour of Two Girls," March 25, 1931, a newspaper clipping pasted into the same scrapbook page with another story on a girl who had always dressed as a boy, encouraged by her mother, "Vagabondia" scrapbook, PM, Box 4, Folder 83v; Joanne Meyerowitz, *Women Adrift: Independent Wage Earners in Chicago, 1880–1930* (Chicago: University of Chicago Press, 1988), 120.

28. "Slip Brings Halt to Tour of Two Girls."

29. See names in Murray's "Vagabondia" scrapbook, PM Papers, Schlesinger Library, Box 4, Folder 83v. For official names, see PM, Application for Admission to NY Bar, May 8, 1948.

30. Pauli Murray, "The Song of the Highway," in Nancy Cunard, ed., *Negro: An Anthology* (New York: Continuum International, 1934), 69–70.

31. Murray, *Song in a Weary Throat*, 78; C. W. B. Hurd, "Legions of Transient Boys Create a National Problem: Children's Bureau Suggests Ways of Handling the Rapidly Increasing Numbers Forced to 'Take to the Road,'" *New York Times* August 14, 1932, clipping in Murray, "Vagabondia" scrapbook, PM Papers, Schlesinger Library, Box 4, Folder 83v.

32. Murray, *Song in a Weary Throat*, 78–81; Murray, "Vagabondia" scrapbook, PM Papers, Schlesinger Library, Box 4, Folder 83v; Pauli Murray, "Three Thousand Miles on a Dime in Ten Days," in Cunard, ed., *Negro*, 67–68.

33. Murray, "Three Thousand Miles on a Dime in Ten Days."

34. Murray, *Song in a Weary Throat*, 82; see "The Acrobat," posed in a backbend in "Durham 1931"; Pauli gives her fullest review of past conversations with Aunt Pauline in Pauli to Mother, June 2, 1943, PM Papers, Schlesinger Library, Box 10, Folder 253.

35. Murray, *Song in a Weary Throat*, 84; Cheryl Lynn Greenberg, *Or Does It Explode: Black Harlem in the Great Depression* (New York: Oxford University Press, 1991), 30–31. For the location of the apartment, as well as of every other place Pauli occupied before 1948, see PM Application Admission to NY Bar, May 8, 1948.

36. Murray, *Song in a Weary Throat*, 83.

37. Murray, *Song in a Weary Throat*, 85.

38. Ute Gacs, "Dorothy Louise Strouse Keur," in *Women Anthropologists: Selected Biographies* (New York: Greenwood, 1968), 181–185; on the influence of anthropology see Pauli Murray, response to "Questionnaire for *Harper's Bazaar*," n.d., PM Papers, Schlesinger Library, Box 94, Folder 1649.

39. Franz Boas, *The Mind of Primitive Man: A Course of Lectures Delivered before the Lowell Institute, Boston, Mass., and the National University of Mexico, 1910–1911* (New York: Macmillan, 1911), 149–158 and *passim*.

40. George Stocking, "Basic Assumptions of Boasian Anthropology," in Stocking, ed., *The Shaping of American Anthropology, 1883–1911: A Franz Boas Reader* (New York: Basic Books, 1974), 4–5; interview with Pauli Murray by Genna Rae McNeil, February 13, 1976 (G-0044), in the Oral History Program Collection (#4007), Southern Historical Collection, Wilson Library, University of North Carolina at Chapel Hill, p. 32; Murray, *Song in a Weary Throat*, 87–88.

41. Murray, *Song in a Weary Throat*, 88–89; special to the *New York Times*, "Jail Head Asks Troops as Mob Seeks Negroes: Riot Feared in Scottsboro, Alabama," *New York Times*, March 26, 1931; James Goodman, *Stories of Scottsboro* (New York: Vintage, 1995), 3–18, 25; Mark Naison, *Communists in Harlem during the Depression* (New York: Grove Press, 1984), 59–60.

42. "Communism Is More Effective Than Religion: Langston Hughes in Russia Talks to Afro Reporter; Poet Packs His Bags for Home: No Race Hate in Red Republic, *Afro American*, May 20, 1933, in Scrapbook, PM, Box 4, 83v; Arnold Rampersand, *The Life of Langston Hughes*,

vol. 1, *I, Too, Sing America, 1902–1941* (New York: Oxford University Press, 1986), 216–220; Murray, *Song in a Weary Throat*, 80–81; Murray explained her decision not to go to Russia in 1931—and her regret—in Pauli Murray, "Notes on San Francisco Conference," Friday, April 27, 1945, Berkeley, Boalt Hall of Law Library Attic, PM, Box 73, Folder 1271; Murray, *Song in a Weary Throat*, 88.

43. "Sigma Tau Delta Elects Eight New Members," clipping in Scrapbook, PM, Box 4, 83v. The journal of Sigma Tau Delta—*The Rectangle*—published "Song of the Highway" in May 1932, two years before it appeared in Nancy Cunard's collection *Negro*.

44. Pauli Murray, "A Working Student," *Hunter College Echo* (Christmas 1932): 42–44, in scrapbook, PM Papers, Schlesinger Library, Box 4, 83v.

45. "Session Ends at Hunter College," clipping in scrapbook; Cheryl Lynn Greenburg, *Or Does It Explode: Black Harlem in the Great Depression* (New York: Oxford University Press, 1991), 66.

46. Murray, *Song in a Weary Throat*, 93.

47. John Rothschild to Eugene K. Jones, July 7, 1932, PM, Box 4, scrapbook 83v; Poston: *Pioneer American Journalist*, 35; Murray, *Song in a Weary Throat*, 93.

48. Murray, *Song in a Weary Throat*, 88.

49. Interview with Murray by McNeil, 37; Pauli Murray, "Youth, 1933," in *Dark Testament and Other Poems* (Norwalk, CT: Silvermine, 1970), 51–53.

50. Pauli Murray, "The Newer Cry," in *Dark Testament and Other Poems*, 54–55; Murray, *Song in a Weary Throat*, 92.

51. Murray, Notes, July 18, 1933, PM Papers, Schlesinger Library, Box 76, Folder 1352.

52. Murray, *Song in a Weary Throat*, 93–94; Thomas J. Sugrue, *Sweet Land of Liberty: The Forgotten Struggle for Civil Right in the North* (New York: Random House, 2009), 35.

53. Murray, *Song in a Weary Throat*, 94–95; "May Edward Chinn," Black Oral History Project, 1976–1980, Columbia Oral History, Butler Library, Columbia University; on the history of Murray's health, see May Edward Chinn, To Whom It May Concern, June 12, 1954, PM Papers, Schlesinger Library, PM, Box 4, Folder 73; "Tera" stood for Temporary Emergency Relief Administration.

54. Thomas W. Patton, "'What of Her?' Eleanor Roosevelt and Camp Tera," *New York History* 87, no. 2 (Spring 2006): 229–247, esp. 234.

55. Murray, *Song in a Weary Throat*, 95.

56. Murray, *Song in a Weary Throat*, 96.

57. Murray, *Song in a Weary Throat*, 96; Natalie Gordon, "Gracious Ladies," *Boston Traveler*, November 7, 1945. Murray mentioned Margaret Holmes's birthdate as 1909 in a letter to her of February 8, 1977, PM, Box 96, Folder 1688.

58. Murray, *Song in a Weary Throat*, 96–97.

59. Murray reminded the First Lady of the episode in Pauli Murray to Eleanor Roosevelt, December 6, 1938, PM, Box 15, Folder 380; Jane Kahramanidis, "The She-She-She Camps of the Great Depression," *History Magazine* (February/March 2008), 13–16; Murray, *Song in a Weary Throat*, 97. For more on this incident and the friendship that later developed between Murray and Eleanor Roosevelt, see Patricia Bell-Scott, *The Firebrand and the First Lady: Portrait of a Friendship: Pauli Murray, Eleanor Roosevelt, and the Struggle for Social Justice* (New York: Knopf, 2016), 1–20 and *passim*.

60. Murray, *Song in a Weary Throat*, 98; Pauli Murray to Dr. Ruth Fox, July 25, 1942, PM, Box 4, Folder 71; New York Public Library electronic catalogue makes it possible to determine which books were available to readers in 1935. Murray likely followed up with reading at the New York Medical Library on Fifth Avenue at 103rd Street.

61. Gregorio Marañón, *The Evolution of Sex and Intersexual Conditions, translated from the Spanish by Warre B. Wells* (London: G. Allen & Unwin [1932]), 247; Otto Weininger, *Sex and Character: Authorized Translation from the 6th German ed.* (London: William Heinemann; New York, G. P. Putnam's Sons [1906?], 7–8; cited in Joanne Meyerowitz, *How Sex Changed: A History of Transsexuality in the United States* (Cambridge, MA: Harvard University Press, 2002), 23–24.

62. Ruth Benedict, *Patterns of Culture* (Boston: Houghton Mifflin, 1934), 190–191.

63. Magnus Hirschfeld, "Die Intersexuelle Konstitution," *Jahrbuch für Sexuelle Zwischenstufen* 23 (1923), 3; cited in Meyerowitz, *How Sex Changed*, 26.

64. Havelock Ellis, *Studies in the Psychology of Sex: Sexual Inversion* (London: University Press, 1897), 314–315; Ellis, "Sexo-Aesthetic Inversion," *Alienist and Neurologist* 34 (1913), 273, 279; Meyerowitz, *How Sex Changed*, 26–27. Murray raises the possibility that she might be a pseudo-hermaphrodite in notes to herself from the Long Island Rest Home, December 14, 1937, PM, Box 4, Folder 71. For the history of the idea of pseudo-hermaphroditism, see Alice Domurat Dreger, *Hermaphrodites and the Medical Invention of Sex* (Cambridge, MA: Harvard University Press, 2000), 145, and Anne Fausto-Sterling, *Sexing the Body: Gender Politics and the Construction of Sexuality* (New York: Basic Books, 2000), 37–38.

65. Pauli Murray to Peg Holmes Gilbert, February 8, 1977, PM Papers, Schlesinger Library, Box 96, Folder 1688; for feelings of "lust" see Pauli Murray to Page Bigelow, February 20, 1974, PM, Box 93, Folder 1623; Pauli Murray, diary entry, Saturday, April 27, 1935, PM Papers, Schlesinger Library, Box 1, Folder 25.

66. Pauli Murray, "Life and Times," scrapbook, PM Papers, Schlesinger Library, Box 1, Folder 21; Murray, diary entry, Saturday, April 28–29, 1935, PM Papers, Schlesinger Library, Box 1, Folder 25.

67. Murray, diary entry, Tuesday, April 28, May 7 and 24, 1935; Pauli Murray, list of addresses given in "Application of Pauli Murray for Admission to the Bar of the State of New York," May 8, 1948, Archives of the Appellate Division, Supreme Court of the State of New York, Second Judicial Department, Brooklyn, New York.

68. Pauli Murray, untitled fragment, 1935, PM Papers, Schlesinger Library, Box 83, Folder 1451.

69. Murray, *Song in a Weary Throat*, 98; Greenburg, *Or Does It Explode*, 3–6.

70. Ella Baker and Marvel Cooke, "The Bronx Slave Market," *The Crisis* 42 (November 1935): 330–331, 340; Barbara Ransby, *Ella Baker and the Black Freedom Movement: A Radical Democratic Vision* (Chapel Hill: University of North Carolina Press, 2003), 76–77.

71. "Newspaper Is Picketed: Dismissal of 9 in Harlem Brings Action by Guild Members," *New York Times*, October 10, 1935; Murray, *Song in a Weary Throat*, 99.

72. "Mayor Gets Strike Data: Caustic on Failure of Owners of Harlem Weekly to Meet Guild," *New York Times*, October 17, 1935; "Broun Joins Guild Pickets," *New York Times*, October 11, 1935; Hauke, *Ted Poston*, 84; Ransby, *Ella Baker*, 86; Pauli Murray, Rider to Question # 24 of New York State Bar Application, "Application of Pauli Murray for Admission to the Bar of the State of New York," May 8, 1948; Murray, *Song in a Weary Throat*, 99; "N. Y. Newspaper Discharges All of Its Writers: Amsterdam News Picketed by Locked Out Staff," *Chicago Defender*, October 19, 1935.

73. Murray, *Song in a Weary Throat*, 101; Hauke, *Ted Poston*, 65–71.

74. Interview with Murray by McNeil, 44; Ransby, *Ella Baker*, 72.

75. Ted Morgan, *A Covert Life: Jay Lovestone: Communist, Anti-Communist, and Spymaster* (New York: Random House, 1999), 2–67; Theodore Draper, *American Communism and Soviet Russia* (New York: Viking Press, 1957; with new material, New Brunswick: Transaction, 2004), 315; Murray, *Song in a Weary Throat*, 103; Barbara Ransby, *Ella Baker*, 96–97.

76. Jay Lovestone, "The Great Negro Migration," *Workers Monthly* 5 (February 1926): 182–184; Glenda Gilmore, *Defying Dixie*, 59–60; Morgan, *A Covert Life: Jay Lovestone*, 268–441; Miscellaneous Courses, PM Papers, Schlesinger Library, Box 15, Folder 379.

77. Ransby, *Ella Baker*, 93–94; Murray, *Song in a Weary Throat*, 104–105

78. Ransby, *Ella Baker*, 73–74; Glenda Elizabeth Gilmore, *Defying Dixie: The Radical Roots of Civil Rights, 1919–1950* (New York: W. W. Norton, 2008), 254; Jonathan D. Bloom, "Brookwood Labor College: The Final Years, 1933–1937," *Labor's Heritage* 2, no. 2 (April 1990): 24–43; Jonathan D. Bloom, "Brookwood Labor College," in *The Re-education of the American Working Class*, edited by Steven H. London, Elvira R. Tarr, and Joseph F. Wilson, Contributions in Economics and Economic History, Book 31 (Westport, CT: Greenwood, 1990), 73.

79. Murray, *Song in a Weary Throat*, 105–107; Lawrence M. Rogin [director of Education and Publicity of the Textile Workers Union and a teacher at Brookwood when Pauli was there], Affidavit of Character and Home Life, PM Application for Admission to NY Bar.

80. Pauli Murray, application to the Rosenwald Fund, February 25, 1937, PM Papers, Schlesinger Library, Box 72, Folder 1243; for Peggie Holmes's activities in this period see Natalie Gordon, "Gracious Ladies," *Boston Traveler*, November 7, 1945; for Murray's work at the Workers Education Project, see PM Papers, Schlesinger Library, Box 72, Folder 1236.

81. Pauli Murray, affidavit regarding membership in the Communist Party Opposition from the spring of 1936 to the fall of 1937, PM Application for Admission to NY Bar; Kate Weigand, *Red Feminism: American Communism and the Making of Women's Liberation* (Baltimore: Johns Hopkins University Press, 2001), 32.

82. Pauli Murray to Mother [Pauline Dame], May 6, 1948, PM Papers, Schlesinger Library, Box 10, Folder 255.

83. Pauli Murray, Notes to herself, written at the Long Island Rest Home, December 14–17, 1937, PM Papers, Schlesinger Library, Box 4, Folder 71.

84. Pauli Murray, Notes to herself, written at the Long Island Rest Home.

85. Pauli Murray, Notes to herself, written at the Long Island Rest Home.

86. Pauli Murray, Notes to herself, written at the Long Island Rest Home.

87. Pauli Murray, Notes to herself, written at the Long Island Rest Home.

88. Pauli Murray, Notes to herself, written at the Long Island Rest Home; Pauli Murray to Page Bigelow, February 20, 1974, PM Papers, Schlesinger Library, Box 93, Folder 1623; Fausto-Sterling, *Sexing the Body*, 37–38.

89. Murray, Notes to herself, written at the Long Island Rest Home.

90. Murray, Notes to herself, written at the Long Island Rest Home.

91. Murray, Notes to herself, written at the Long Island Rest Home.

92. Pauli Murray, "Summary of Symptoms of Upset," March 8, 1940, PM Papers, Schlesinger Library, Box 4, Folder 71.

Chapter 3

1. "Present Program in Harlem Area," as of November 4, 1938, Worker's Education Division of the Works Progress Administration, PM Papers, Schlesinger Library, Radcliffe College, Harvard University, Box 72, Folder 1236; Pauli Murray to Miss [Isabel] Taylor and Miss [Floria] Pickney, October 28, 1938, PM Papers, Schlesinger Library, Box 72, Folder 1237; see also notes on classes at the YWCA, St. James Church, Brotherhood of Sleeping Car Porters, and the Henry Street Settlement, Box 72, Folders 1235–1239.

2. Pauli Murray, *Song in a Weary Throat: An American Pilgrimage* (New York: Harper & Row, 1987), 107–108; Pauli Murray to Mother and Aunt Sallie, November 6, 1938, PM Papers, Schlesinger Library, Box 10, Folder 252. Among the lectures that Pauli gave in 1938 was one at the YWCA, on May 24, listed as "Fascism and Racial Prejudice" on a sheet marked "YWCA Class, Current Events," PM Papers, Schlesinger Library, Box 72, Folder 1239. The WPA did not in fact end until July 1939.

3. Murray, *Song in a Weary Throat*, 108; Jane Addams, "The College Woman and the Family Claim," *Commons* (September 1898): 3–7; Elsa Barkley Brown, "Womanist Consciousness: Maggie Lea Walker and the Independent Order of Saint Luke," *Signs* 14 (Spring 1989): 610–633.

4. For the phrase "minority of minorities," see A. McBean to the editor of the *New York Amsterdam News*, November 9, 1939, PM Papers, Schlesinger Library, Box 4, Folder 71.

5. Murray was not, in fact, qualified to teach, as she learned in Ruth Henry (from the Office of the Superintendent of Public Instruction) to Pauli Murray, June 26, 1939, PM Papers, Schlesinger Library, Box 72, Folder 1247; "Teacher's Contract" for Pauline F. Dame, August 1935, showed that Dame would earn $743 from the next year, or about $62 a month, 60 percent of Pauli's WPA salary. Black teachers made about 77 percent as much as white teachers in North Carolina at that time; see Anita Price Davis, "Keeping the School Doors Open," *Tarheel Junior Historian* (Spring 2010).

6. Interview with Guy B. Johnson by John Egerton, July 22, 1990 (A-0345), Southern Oral History Program (#4007), Southern Historical Collection, Wilson Library, University of North Carolina, Chapel Hill.

7. Howard W. Odum, *Social and Mental Traits of the Negro* (New York: Columbia University Press, 1910), 37–39; interview with Guy B. Johnson by John Egerton; interview with Guion Griffis Johnson by Mary Frederickson and Jacquelyn Dowd Hall, April 24, 1974 (G-0029-1), and interview with Guion Johnson by Frederickson, July 1, 1974 (G-00029-4) in the Southern Oral History Program Collection (#4007), Southern Historical Collection, Wilson Library, University of North Carolina at Chapel Hill; Anne Firor Scott, *Unheard Voices: The*

First Historians of Southern Women (Charlottesville, Virginia: University Press of Virginia, 1993), 38–44; William Ogburn, "Howard Odum," *American Sociological Review* 20 (April 1955): 237; William B. Thomas, "Howard W. Odum's Social Theories in Transition, 1910–1930," *American Sociologist* 16 (February 1981): 25–34.

8. Charles J. Holden, *The New Southern University: Academic Freedom and Liberalism at UNC* (Lexington: University Press of Kentucky, 2012), 97, 102, 106–107.

9. Pauli Murray to Frank Graham, January 17, 1939, and "Summary of Estimated Expenses of the Average Student [at UNC in 1937–38]," PM Papers, Box 15, Folder 381; "Cost In State Institutions for 1938," *News and Observer*, Raleigh, North Carolina, January 12, 1939, the University of North Carolina Digital Archive. Also see interview with Guy Johnson by Egerton for discussion of Johnson's graduate fellowship at UNC for $1,500, half for tuition and half for living expenses; Murray *Song in a Weary Throat*, 125.

10. Interview with Pauli Murray by Genna Rae McNeil, 13 February 1976 (G-0044), in the Oral History Program Collection (#4007), Southern Historical Collection, Wilson Library, University of North Carolina at Chapel Hill, 45; Murray, *Song in a Weary Throat*, 108, 125.

11. Murray, *Song in a Weary Throat*, 10; Pauli Murray to Frank Graham, January 17, 1939, PM Papers, Schlesinger Library, Box 15, Folder 381; Glenda E. Gilmore, *Defying Dixie: The Radical Roots of Civil Rights, 1919–1950* (New York: Norton, 2008), 255–260. North Carolina College for Negroes became North Carolina Central University in 1969. According to North Carolina Central University, "History," www.nccu.edu, NCCN won a grade "A" ranking in 1937; interview with Pauli Murray by Robert Martin, August 15 and 17, 1968, Moorland-Spingarn Collection, Howard University Archives, 35.

12. Charles H. Houston, "A Challenge to Negro College Youth," *Crisis* 45, no. 1 (January 1938): 14–15; Pauli Murray to Roy Wilkins, July 15, 1939, PM Papers, Schlesinger Library, Box 72, Folder 1235. Murray, *Song in a Weary Throat*, 30. Pauli Murray, "To the Oppressors," *Crisis* (January 1939): 18; Murray, "Quarrel," *Crisis* (October 1939): 306; Murray, "Words," *Crisis* (November 1939): 350; Murray, "Hate," *Crisis* (December 1939): 368.

13. For a useful timeline, see Pauli Murray to George T. Guernsey, February 6, 1939, PM Papers, Schlesinger Library, Box 15, Folder 381. Murray's earlier application for a Rosenwald Fellowship shows that her goal was a Ph.D.; see the typed list of courses in sociology and economics that Murray intended to take, copied from the University of North Carolina Graduate School Catalogue for 1937-1938, PM Papers, Schlesinger Library, Box 15, Folder 381. See also, Holden, *The New Southern University*, 109.

14. Thomas A. Krueger, *And Promises to Keep: The Southern Conference for Human Welfare, 1938–1948* (Nashville, TN: Vanderbilt University Press, 1967), 13–37.

15. John Egerton, *Speak Now against the Day: The Generation before the Civil Rights Movement in the South* (New York: Knopf, 1994), 188.

16. Egerton, *Speak Now against the Day*, 185–189; Gilmore, *Defying Dixie*, 271. Connor achieved notoriety in 1963 for jailing Martin Luther King Jr. and ordering fire hoses turned on peaceful protestors in Birmingham.

17. Eleanor Roosevelt, *This I Remember* (New York: Harper & Row, 1949), 173–174; John Egerton, *Speak Now against the Day*, 185–189; James R. Kearney, *Anna Eleanor Roosevelt: The Evolution of a Reformer* (New York: Houghton Mifflin, 1969), 89; *Proceedings of the Second National Conference on the Problems of the Negro and Negro Youth*, January 12, 1939, 89; "Mrs. Roosevelt Fights Shy of Segregation Issue in South; Refuses to be Drawn into Controversy," *Baltimore Sun*, November 23, 1938; "Mrs. Roosevelt's Answer," *Baltimore Afro American*, December 17, 1938; Winifred Mallon, "Black Hails Gains in Rights in South; Justice Receives Jefferson Medal," *New York Times*, November 24, 1938.

18. "As Roosevelt Sees Himself," *New York Times*, December 6, 1938, 1, PM Papers, Schlesinger Library, Box 1, Folder 383.

19. Pauli Murray to Franklin Delano Roosevelt, December 6, 1938, PM Papers, Schlesinger Library, Box 15, Folder 380.

20. Eleanor Roosevelt to Pauli Murray, December 19, 1938, PM Papers, Schlesinger Library, Box 15, Folder 380.

21. Pauli Murray to President Shepard, December 6, 1938, PM Papers, Schlesinger Library, Box 15, Folder 380.

22. She mailed the letter on December 8, according to a letter she later wrote: Pauli Murray to George T. Guernsey, February 6, 1939, PM Papers, Schlesinger Library, Box 15, Folder 381.

23. David Stout, "A Supreme Triumph, Then in the Shadows," *New York Times*, July 11, 2009; *Missouri ex rel. Gaines v. Canada*, 305 U.S. 337 (1938); Gilmore, *Defying Dixie*, 263–264; "For Human Rights," *New York Times*, December 13, 1938, PM Papers, Schlesinger Library, Box 15, Folder 383; Murray, *Song in a Weary Throat*, 115.

24. Murray, *Song in a Weary Throat*, 115; W. W. Pierson to Pauli Murray, December 14, 1938, should be in the PM Papers, Schlesinger Library, Box 15, Folder 380, but it is not there.

25. Pauli Murray to Frank Graham, December 17, 1938, PM Papers, Schlesinger Library, Box 15, Folder 380; Lenie (PM) to Lisha [Felicia Miller], December 17, 1938, PM Papers, Schlesinger Library, Box 15, Folder 380.

26. Pauli Murray to Lloyd Gaines, December 18, 1938, PM Papers, Schlesinger Library, Box 15, Folder 380.

27. Gilmore, *Defying Dixie*, 268.

28. Mother [Pauline Dame] to Lenie [Pauli Murray], January 6, 1939, PM Papers, Schlesinger Library, Box 15, Folder 380 (underlining in the original).

29. Interview with Guion Johnson by Frederickson, 52b.

30. Interview with Guion Johnson by Frederickson, 52b.; "Evidence against Chapel Hill Negro Fast Losing Ground," *Carolina Times*, December 17, 1938, 1, 8; "Mills of the Gods," *Daily Tar Heel*, January 7, 1939, PM Papers, Schlesinger Library, Box 15, Folder 382; "Black Justice," *Daily Tar Heel*, February 2, 1939, PM Papers, Schlesinger Library, Box 15, Folder 383; Glenda Elizabeth Gilmore, "From Jim Crow to Jane Crow, or How Anne Scott and Pauli Murray Found Each Other," in *Writing Women's History: A Tribute to Anne Firor Scott*, edited by Elizabeth Anne Payne (Oxford: University Press of Mississippi, 2011), 142–148. Gilmore estimates that these events occurred later, in the spring of 1939, but contemporaneous accounts place the events in mid-December 1938 and were still in the news when Pauli applied to UNC.

31. Lafitte Howard, "Officials Faced by Negro Entrance Application; New York Woman Seeks to Enter Grad School; Administration Is Confronted with 'Liberalism' Issue," *Daily Tar Heel*," January 5, 1939, PM Papers, Schlesinger Library, Box 15, Folder 382; Editorial, *Durham Morning Herald*, January 6, 1939, "Mills of the Gods," *Daily Tar Heel*, January 7, 1939, PM Papers, Schlesinger Library, Box 15, Folder 382.

32. Howard, "Officials Faced by Negro Entrance Application"; "Negress Applies to Enter Carolina U," *Durham Morning Herald*, January 6, 1939 [see note on Pauli's copy on this story for how much reference to "Negress" "hurt"]; Editorial, "Mills of the Gods";

33. Pauli Murray to Editorial Board of the Tar Heel," January 12, 1939, PM Papers, Schlesinger Library, Box 15, Folder 380.

34. Pauli Murray to C. B. Powel, editor of the *New York Amsterdam News*, December 31, 1938; Pauli Murray to P. B. Young, *Norfolk Journal and Guide*, January 13, 1939, PM Papers, Schlesinger Library, Box 15, Folder 380.

35. Letter to the Editor of the *Daily Tar Heel*, as quoted in *Crisis*, April 1939, 104, PM Papers, Schlesinger Library, Box 15, Folder 383. The 82 to 38 poll results were quickly challenged as unreliable by those who said the ballot box had been left unattended. It is certainly possible that the ballot box was stuffed with the votes of supporters, but it seems more likely that among the minority of graduate students who cared about the issue (likely those in the sociology, economics, history, and English departments), a clear majority favored integration. "Only One Negro Pressing to Register at Carolina" and "Graham Discusses Negro Application," *Durham Morning Herald*, January 10, 1939, and "Carolina Students Favor Admission," *Norfolk Journal and Guide*, January 21, 1939, PM Papers, Schlesinger Library, Box 15, Folder 382.

36. John Creedy to Pauli Murray, February 13, 1939, via Western Union, PM Papers, Schlesinger Library, Box 15, Folder 381; James T. Taylor, "Higher Education for Negroes," *Carolina Magazine* (February 1938): 2–4; Howard Odum, "What Is the Answer?" *Carolina Magazine*, (February 1938): 5–8; Holden, *New Southern University*, 42–44. Ever since 1927, *Carolina Magazine* had published an annual "Negro Number," an issue turned over to a black guest editor and guest writers. Over the years the magazine published the work of some of the

foremost poets of the Harlem Renaissance, including that of Langston Hughes and Countee Cullen.

37. Glenn Hutchinson, "They Call It Equal Opportunity," *Carolina Magazine"* (February 1939): 9–11. See also Hutchinson, "Jim Crow Challenged in Southern Universities," *Crisis* (April 1939): 103–105, PM Papers, Schlesinger Library, Box 15, Folder 383.

38. Howard K. Beale to the Editor of the *Daily Tar Heel,* January 11, 1939, PM Papers, Schlesinger Library, Box 15, Folder 382.

39. "Daniels Has No Objection to Entrance of Graduate Negroes," *Daily Tar Heel,* January 20, 1939, PM Papers, Schlesinger Library, Box 15, Folder 382; "Long Live Dean Russell," *Carolina Times,* February 25, 1939, PM Papers, Schlesinger Library, Box 15, Folder 383.

40. Louis Harris [the future pollster, then a freshman], "Inter-Racial Discussion Group Adopts Resolution to Admit Negro Graduates Immediately," *Daily Tar Heel,* February 16, 1939, PM Papers, Schlesinger Library, Box 15, Folder 383; Holden, *The New Southern University,* 115.

41. Frank Graham to Pauli Murray, February 3, 1939, PM Papers, Schlesinger Library, Box 15, Folder 381.

42. Howard Odum, "What Is the Answer?" *Carolina Magazine* (February 1939); "Negro Entrance to UNC Is Topic of Student Forum," *Daily Tar Heel,* January 26, 1939, PM Papers, Schlesinger Library, Box 15, Folder 382. Guion Johnson came to support integration after World War II, well ahead of her husband.

43. Murray, *Song in a Weary Throat,* 125–126.

44. Interview with Murray by McNeil, 47–48; Murray, *Song in a Weary Throat,* 126. Murray did not give a detailed account of the interview, but Marshall was a skilled cross-examiner, and he knew Pauli personally.

45. Pauli Murray, "Summary of Symptoms of Upset," March 8, 1940, PM Papers, Schlesinger Library, Box 4, Folder 71.

46. Murray, *Song in a Weary Throat,* 126; Kearney, *Eleanor Roosevelt,* 88–90.

47. For a discussion of the state legislature's actions see Pauli Murray to Carl DeVane, March 6, 1939, PM Papers, Schlesinger Library, Box 15, Folder 381; Carl DeVane to Pauli Murray, April 23, 1939, PM Papers, Schlesinger Library, Box 15, Folder 381; Murray, *Song in a Weary Throat,* 126; Pauli Murray, "Who Is to Blame for the Disappearance of Lloyd Gaines," clipping [late summer or fall of 1939], PM Papers, Schlesinger Library, Box 15, Folder 383.

48. Michael J. Klarman, *From Jim Crow to Civil Rights: The Supreme Court and the Struggle for Racial Equality* (New York: Oxford University Press, 2004), 160–161.

49. Murray, *Song in a Weary Throat,* 126–127; Robert A. Margo, "Teacher Salaries in Black and White," in *Race and Schooling in the South, 1880–1850: An Economic History,* edited by Robert A. Margo (Chicago: University of Chicago Press, 1990), 52–67.

Chapter 4

1. Mother [Pauline Dame] to Lenie [Pauli Murray], October 21, 1938, Sallie Small to Pauli Murray, September 11, 1939, and Sallie Small to Pauli Murray, September 11, 1939, Pauli Murray Papers, Schlesinger Library, Radcliffe Institute, Harvard University, Box 10, Folder 257; Lenie [PM] to Mother [Pauline Dame], November 6, 1938, PM Papers, Schlesinger Library, Box 10, Folder 252.

2. Pauli Murray, *Song in a Weary Throat: An American Pilgrimage* (New York: Harper & Row, 1987), 109; Pauli Murray to Walter White, April 17, 1939, PM Papers, Schlesinger Library, Box 98, Folder 1750; Pauli Murray to Jean [Gene Phillips] and Pan [Candace Stone], April 9, 1940, PM Papers, Schlesinger, Box 4, Folder 86.

3. Lenie [Pauli Murray] to Mother [Pauline Dame] and Aunt Sallie [Sarah Small], October 6, 1939, PM Papers, Schlesinger Library, Box 10, Folder 252.

4. Glenn Hutchinson, "They Call It Equal Opportunity," *Carolina Magazine* (February 1938): 9–11; Pauli Murray to Mr. Efron, October 3, 1939, PM Papers, Schlesinger Library, Box 13, Folder 340; Pauli Murray to Mother [Pauline Dame], January 10, 1940, PM Papers, Schlesinger Library, Box 10, Folder 253.

5. Pauli to Mother [Pauline Dame], November 11, 1939, PM Papers, Schlesinger Library, Box 10, Folder 252; "Pill 'Planted' in Boys Turns Weak, Effeminate Youths into Strong, Virile

Men," *World Telegram*, November 3, 1939, Pauli Murray to Dr. Richards, November 3, 1939, and Pauli Murray, "Summary of Symptoms of Upset," March 8, 1940, PM Papers, Schlesinger Library, Box 4, Folder 71.

6. A. McBean to the editor of the *New York Amsterdam News*, November 9, 1939, PM Papers, Schlesinger Library, Box 4, Folder 71; note that Mac gave an address different from the one where she was currently living with Murray.

7. Pauli Murray to Aunt Sallie and Mother [Pauline Dame], September 28, 1939, PM Papers, Schlesinger Library, Box 10, Folder 252; Pauli Murray to Peg Holmes, December 1939, PM Papers, Schlesinger Library, Box 83, Folder 1451; Pauli Murray, notes to herself at the Helen Rogers Hospital, March 8, 1940, PM Papers, Schlesinger Library, Box 4, File 71. Information on Margaret Holmes's move to California is from Natalie, Gordon, "Gracious Ladies," *Boston Traveler*, Wednesday, November 7, 1945, PM Papers, Schlesinger Library, Box 96, Folder 1688.

8. FBI interview with former probation officer of Providence, Rhode Island, January 4, 1967, FBI Report on Pauli Murray, secured through FOIA request; Pauli Murray, notes to herself at Rogers Hospital, March 8, 1940, PM Papers, Schlesinger Library, Box 4, File 71; Pauli Murray application to NYS Bar, 1948, Rider to #24; FBI Report on Pauli Murray, interviews January 3–4, 1967; the FBI investigation found that her diagnosis at Bellevue was "schizophrenia."

9. FBI File on Pauli Murray, interviews January 3–4, 1967, reported that Pauli had told hospital officials that Adelene McBean was her cousin; Pauli Murray's Certificate of Release from Bellevue Hospital into the custody of Adelene McBean, March 2, 1940, and Adelene McBean to Dr. Helen Rogers, March 14, 1940, PM Papers, Schlesinger Library, Box 4, Folder 71.

10. Pauli Murray, "Summary of Symptoms of Upset," March 8, 1940, PM Papers, Schlesinger Library, Box 4, Folder 71.

11. Mother [Pauline Dame] to Lenie [Pauli Murray], May 18, 1940, PM Papers, Schlesinger Library, Box 10, Folder 257; Pauli Murray to Pauline Dame, telegram, March 22, 1940, and Pauline Dame to Pauli Murray, c/o Mildred Fearing, March 23, 1940, Western Union Money Order, PM Papers, Schlesinger Library, Box 4, Folder 85; Murray, *Song in a Weary Throat*, 138.

12. Harold Garfinkel, "Color Trouble," *Opportunity* (May 1940): 144; Pauli Murray, "Summary of Facts Leading Up to Arrest of Pauli Murray and Adelene McBean," March 24, 1940, PM Papers, Schlesinger Library, Box 4, Folder 85.

13. Murray, "Summary of Facts Leading Up to Arrest"; Harold Garfinkel, "Color Trouble," *Opportunity* (May 1940): 144.

14. Murray, "Summary of Facts Leading Up to Arrest"; Murray, *Song in a Weary Throat*, 138.

15. Murray, "Summary of Facts Leading Up to Arrest."

16. Murray, "Summary of Facts Leading Up to Arrest"; "Jailed in Virginia; Jim Crow Bus Dispute Leads to Girls Arrest," *Carolina Times*, April 6, 1940, PM Papers, Schlesinger Library, Box 4, Folder 87.

17. Krishnalal Shridharani, *War without Violence: A Study of Gandhi's Method and Its Accomplishments* (New York: Harcourt Brace, 1939). Murray made reference to Satyagraha and gave a detailed account of the bus incident in a letter to "Jean [Gene Phillips] and [Candace Stone]," April 9, 1940, PM Papers, Schlesinger Library, Box 4, Folder 87. For an analysis of the connection between Gandhi's efforts in India and the early stages of the modern civil rights movement in the United States, see Nico Slate, *Colored Cosmopolitanism: The Shared Struggle for Freedom in the United States and India* (Cambridge, MA: Harvard University Press, 2012), 202–210.

18. Pauli Murray to Jean [Gene Phillips] and Pan [Candace Stone], April 9, 1940, PM Papers, Schlesinger Library, Box 4, Folder 87.

19. Ted Poston, "Two New Yorkers Ready for Appeal of Conviction in Greyhound Case," *Pittsburgh Courier*, April 13, 1940, PM Papers, Schlesinger Library, Box 4, Folder 87; Murray, "Summary of Facts Leading Up to Arrest."

20. Murray, "Summary of Facts Leading Up to Arrest."

21. Pauli Murray, scribbled note on lined paper, March 23, 1940, between 6 and 7 PM, PM Papers, Schlesinger Library, Box 4, Folder 85; Pauli Murray to Jay Walker, chairman, NAACP Branch, Durham, North Caroline, April 2, 1940, PM Papers, Schlesinger Library, Box 4, Folder 86; Murray, "Summary of Facts Leading Up to Arrest."

22. "Denounce Police Brutality in Richmond Mass Meeting: Raise Funds for Defense of Jackson Victim of Grocery Store Assault Thanks Public," *New Journal and Guide*, Norfolk Virginia, July 31, 1937, 13; "Lawyer Aids Police Brutality Quiz," *Pittsburgh Courier*, January 1, 1938, 3; Murray, *Song in a Weary Throat*, 142; "Jailed in Virginia; Jim Crow Bus Dispute Leads to Girls Arrest," *Carolina Times*, April 6, 1940, PM Papers, Box 4, Folder 87; Pauli Murray to Jean [Gene Phillips] and Pan [Candace Stone], April 9, 1940, PM Papers Box 4, Folder 87.

23. Pan [Candace Stone] to Pauli and Mac, March 26, 1940, PM Papers, Schlesinger Library, Box 4, Folder 86. Pan praises Pauli and Mac for going to jail for her principles; Caroline Ware to Pauli Murray, March 19, 1981, PM Papers, Schlesinger Library, Box 18, Folder 402; Murray, *Song in a Weary Throat*, 142–143.

24. Pauli Murray, "Prison," from "Notebook, Petersburg Prison," Monday, March 25, 1940, PM Papers, Schlesinger Library, Box 4, Folder 85.

25. Pauli Murray, "Prison"; handwritten copy of "Rules for Prisoners" PM Papers, Schlesinger Library, Box 4, Folder 86; Pauli Murray to Deputy, Petersburg Jail, "Requests Made of Petersburg Authorities," March 24, 1940, PM Papers, Schlesinger Library, Box 4, Folder 85.

26. Murray, "Prison"; "Notes from Negro Male Prisoners Slipped under Door of cell of Female Prisoners," PM Papers, Schlesinger Library, Box 4, Folder 85; Murray, *Song in a Weary Throat*, 143–145.

27. Pauli Murray, "Telegrams Sent—Collect," March 24, 1940, PM Papers, Schlesinger Library, Box 4, Folder 85.

28. Pauli Murray to Jay Walker, head of Durham NAACP, April 2, 1940, Box 4, Folder 86; Mildred Fearing to Pauline Dame, Wednesday, March 27, 1940, Box 4, Folder 86; Raymond J. Valentine, and Robert H. Cooley Jr., "Stipulations to Be Met in Accepting Power of Attorney for Murray and McBean," April 12, 1940, PM Papers, Schlesinger Library, Box 4, Folder 87; Cooley to Houston, March 24, 1940, PM Papers, Schlesinger Library, Box 4, Folder 86.

29. Pauli Murray to Jean [Gene Phillips] and Pan [Candace Stone], April 9, 1940, PM Papers Box 4, Folder 87; "Top Executives of Bus Systems Here for Opening," *Washington Post*, March 25, 1940; "Investors Guide; Greyhound System," *Chicago Daily Tribune*, April 24, 1940.

30. "NAACP Refuses Greyhound Buses for Annual Conclave," *Chicago Defender*, April 18, 1936. See also "Greyhound Line Admits Jim Crow Was a Mistake," *Afro-American*, November 2, 1935; "Wins $3500 Judgment from Greyhound Bus Co.," February 4, 1939 (case of a black passenger beaten by driver, arrested, and robbed by police in Blytheville, Arkansas); "Greyhound Bus Office Admits J. C. Over-the-Wheels Policy," *Afro-American*, October 5, 1935.

31. Ted Poston, "Two New Yorkers Ready for Appeal of Conviction in Greyhound Case," *Pittsburgh Courier*, April 13, 1940, PM Papers, Schlesinger Library, Box 4, Folder 87.

32. Mother [Pauline Dame] to Lenie [Pauli Murray], and David L. Clendenin to Pauli Murray, March 25, 1940, PM Papers Box 4, Folder 85.

33. Pauli Murray, "City Court House, 3/27" handwritten notes, PM Papers, Schlesinger Library, Box 4, Folder 86; Murray, *Song in a Weary Throat*, 146.

34. Pauli Murray to Jean [Gene Phillips] and Pan [Constance Stone], April 2, 1940, PM Papers, Schlesinger Library, Box 4, Folder 86; Pauli Murray to Walter White March 29, 1940, PM Papers, Schlesinger Library, Box 4, Folder 86.

35. Ted Poston, "Two New Yorkers Ready for Appeal of Conviction in Greyhound Case," *Pittsburgh Courier*, April 13, 1940, PM Papers, Schlesinger Library, Box 4, Folder 87; Pauli Murray to Walter White, March 29, 1940, PM Papers, Schlesinger Library, Box 4, Folder 85.

36. Pauli Murray and Adelene McBean to Jay Walker, chairman, NAACP Branch, Durham, North Carolina, PM Papers, Schlesinger Library, Box 4, Folder 86.

37. Pauli Murray and Adelene McBean to Robert H. Cooley, April 2, 1940, PM Papers, Schlesinger Library, Box 4, Folder 86.

38. Pauli Murray to Jean [Gene Phillips] and Pan [Candace Stone], April 9, 1940, PM Papers Box 4, Folder 87; Pauli Murray to Dave Clendenin, March 29, 1940, Morris Milgram to Pauli Murray, April 4, 1940, Pauli Murray to Morris Milgram, April 9, 1940, and Pauli Murray to Jean [Gene Phillips] and Pan [Candace Stone], April 2, 1940, PM Papers, Schlesinger Library, Box 4, Folder 86.

39. Pauli Murray to Morris Milgram, April 15, 1940, PM Papers, Schlesinger Library, Box 4, Folder 87.

40. "Jailed in Virginia; Jim Crow Bus Dispute Leads to Girls Arrest," and editorial, "Bus Accommodations for Negroes," *Carolina Times*, April 6, 1940, PM Papers, Schlesinger Library, Box 4, Folder 87; Ted Poston, "Tobacco Workers Combat Layoffs," *Pittsburgh Courier*, April 20, 1940; Ted Poston, "Two New Yorkers Ready for Appeal of Conviction in Greyhound Case," *Pittsburgh Courier*, April 13, 1940, a clipping in the PM Papers, Schlesinger Library, Box 4, Folder 87.

41. Cooley to Murray and MacBean [*sic*], April 8, 1940, Box 4, Folder 85; Malvina Thompson to Mildred Fearing, April 10, 1940, PM Papers, Schlesinger Library, Box 4, Folder 87, Murray, *Song in a Weary Throat*, 147; Pauli and Mac returned to New York on April 19 and then returned to Petersburg for the appeal on April 29, 1940.

42. Pauli Murray to Mother [Pauline Dame], April 25, 1940, PM Papers, Schlesinger Library, Box 10, Folder 253; Pauli Murray to Morris Milgram, April 29, 1940, Atlantic Coast Line, Richmond en route to Washington, PM Papers, Schlesinger Library, Box 4, Folder 85; Robert G. Bass, clerk of the court, "On Appeal from the Police Ct. for Misdme. Creating a Disturbance etc. Fine $5 and Costs, Pulli [*sic*] Murray," Virginia Hustings Court of the City of Petersburg, April 29th, 1940, Common Law Order Book, Vol. 37, Page 320, In the Matter of the Application of Pauli Murray for Admission to Practice as an Attorney and Counselor-at-Law, New York Supreme Court, Appellate Division, Second Department, June 11, 1948, Archives of the Appellate Division, Supreme Court of the State of New York, Second Judicial Department, Brooklyn, New York.

43. Murray, *Song in a Weary Throat*, 148.

44. Pauli Murray to Pan [Candace Stone] and Jean [Gene Phillips], May 16, 1940, PM Papers, Schlesinger Library, Box 4, Folder 88; Robert G. Bass, clerk, "On Appeal from the Police Ct. for Misdmr. Creating a Disturbance, etc. Fine $5 and Costs," Virginia: In the Hustings Court of the City of Petersburg, May 10th, 1940, *Common Law Order Book*, Vol. 37, Page 330; Pauli to Pan and Jean, May 16, 1940, PM Papers, Schlesinger Library, Box 4, Folder 88; Dave L. Clendenin to H. L. Fauntleroy, June 6, 1940, PM Papers, Schlesinger Library, Box 4, Folder 85 (in which the Workers Defense League [WDL] sought partial compensation from H. L. Fauntleroy, chairman of the Petersburg branch of the NAACP); Western Union Money Order Message from WDL to Murray in Petersburg City Jail, May 16, 1940, PM Papers, Schlesinger Library, Box 4, Folder 87.

45. Lenie [Pauli Murray] to Mother [Pauline Dame], May 17, 1940, PM Papers, Schlesinger Library, Box 4, Folder 88; Mother to Lenie, May 18, 1940, PM Papers, Schlesinger Library, Box 10, Folder 257.

46. Pauli Murray to Thomas H. Stone, May 14, 1940, PM Papers, Schlesinger Library, Box 4, Folder 88; Pauli to Pan [Candace Stone] and Jean [Gene Phillips], May 16, 1940, PM Papers Box 4, Folder 88; Lenie (Pauli) to Mother [Pauline Dame], May 17, 1940, Box 4, Folder 88.

47. Harold Garfinkel, "Color Trouble," *Opportunity* (May 1940): 144–1452; Pauli Murray and Adelene McBean to Robert H. Cooley Jr., n.d. [May 31, 1940], PM Papers, Schlesinger Library, Box 4, Folder 87, in which Murray asks whether Cooley thinks Hastie's apparent change of heart might be traceable to the Garfinkel story. See also Mother [Pauline Dame] to Lenie [Pauli Murray], August 10, 1940, in which Aunt Pauline tells Pauli that friends have told her about the article; she asks Pauli to send it to her and urges her to pray "for the devil is always busy," PM, Box 10, Folder 257.

48. Harold Garfinkel, "Color Trouble," *Opportunity* (May 1940): 144.

49. Pauli Murray and Adelene McBean to Robert H. Cooley Jr., n.d. [May 31, 1940], PM Papers, Schlesinger Library, Box 4, Folder 87; Harold Garfinkel, "Color Trouble," in Edward J. O'Brien, ed., *The Best Short Stories of 1941* (Boston: Houghton Mifflin, 1941). The story that preceded Garfinkel's was William Faulkner's "Gold Is Not Always." For evidence that Murray was trying to publish her own account of the Petersburg events, see Pauli Murray to Dave Clendenin, March 29, 1940, PM Papers, Schlesinger Library, Box 4, Folder 86.

50. Garfinkel, "Color Trouble," 144.

51. Compare Garfinkel, "Color Trouble," and Murray, "Summary of Facts."

52. Garfinkel, "Color Trouble," 145–146.

53. Mary C. Waters, *Black Identities: West Indian Immigrant Dreams and American Realities* (Cambridge, MA: Harvard University Press, 2001), 141.

54. Garfinkel, "Color Trouble," 146.

55. Garfinkel, "Color Trouble," 146.
56. Garfinkel, "Color Trouble," 148.
57. Garfinkel, "Color Trouble,"149–150.
58. Garfinkel, "Color Trouble,"152.
59. Garfinkel, "Color Trouble," 152.
60. *Morgan v. Virginia* 328 U.S. 373 (1946). Other lawyers included Spotswood Robinson and Oliver Hill. For details on the story behind the case see Yvonne Shinhoster Lamb, "Irene M. Kirkaldy; Case Spurred Freedom Rides," *Washington Post*, August 13, 2007.
61. For the Journeys of Reconciliation, and Pauli Murray and Bayard Rustin's role in them, see Pauli Murray to Eleanor Roosevelt, May 5, 1947, PM Papers, Box 99, Folder 1780; and John D'Emilio, *Lost Prophet: The Life and Times of Bayard Rustin* (New York: Free Press, 2003), 133–140. Not until 1961 would the Supreme Court reverse a conviction for "disturbing the peace" in a civil rights case. It did so in *Garner et al. v. Louisiana*, inspired by sit-ins in North Carolina, beginning February 1, 1960.

Chapter 5

1. Richard B. Sherman, *The Case of Odell Waller and Virginia Justice, 1940–1942* (Knoxville: University of Tennessee Press, 1992), 19.
2. Pauli Murray, *Song in a Weary Throat: An American Pilgrimage* (New York: Harper & Row, 1987), 150–151.
3. Pauli Murray, "The Waller Case and the Poll Tax," typescript, page 4, PM Papers, Schlesinger Library, Box 72, Folder 1255; Sherman, *Case of Odell Waller*, 65. Carl Raushenbush (chairman of the WDL), "Dear Reader," in *"All for Mr. Davis": The Story of Sharecropper Odell Waller*, by Pauli Murray and Murray Kempton (New York: Workers Defense League, 1940).
4. Sherman, *The Case of Odell Waller*, 9–11.
5. Pauli Murray to Morris Milgram, April 29, 1940, PM Papers, Schlesinger Library, Box 4, Folder 85; Sherman, *The Case of Odell Waller*, 24–25; By coincidence Stone was one of the lawyers who had joined in Murray's defense at the Petersburg Hustings Trial.
6. Sherman, *The Case of Odell Waller*, 32, 24–25.
7. Pauli Murray to Elmer Carter and Edward Lawson of *Opportunity Magazine*, December 2, 1940, PM Papers, Schlesinger Library, Box 72, Folder 1251 (an excellent summary of the case).
8. Gene Phillips was a member of the National Advisory Committee to the Workers Defense League, as well as its National Action Committee, according to the WDL's official list: In the Matter of the Application of Pauli Murray for Admission to Practice as an Attorney and Counselor-at-Law, New York Supreme Court, Appellate Division, Second Department, June 11, 1948; Murray, *Song in a Weary Throat*, 152–153.
9. Murray, *Song in a Weary Throat*, 161.
10. Murray, *Song in a Weary Throat*, 162; on February 15, 1941, Pauli submitted an application to Howard Law School; see copy of application, appended to Murray's New York State bar application, In the Matter of the Application of Pauli Murray for Admission to Practice as an Attorney and Counselor-at-Law, New York Supreme Court, Appellate Division, Second Department, June 11, 1948.
11. Murray, *Song in a Weary Throat*, 162–164.
12. Abstract, J. Holmes Smith Papers, Duke University Archives; "Methodists v. Viceroy," *Time*, April 22, 1940, p. 46, cited in Nico Slate, *Colored Cosmopolitanism: The Shared Struggle for Freedom in the United States and India* (Cambridge, MA: Harvard University Press, 2012), 208.
13. Slate, *Colored Cosmopolitanism*, 208–212; Joseph Kip Kosek, *Acts of Conscience: Christian Nonviolence and Modern American Democracy* (New York: Columbia University Press, 2009), 186.
14. Pauli Murray, diary, January 3, 1941 (Murray pledged $7.50 to $10.00 a week to the Ashram, depending on her income; she also pledged $5 to the FOR, $5 to the WDF, $5 to the NAACP, $10 to repay Agnes Martocci, who, with another friend, evidently had helped pay off the Rogers Hospital Bill; she still owed Spaulding $30), PM Papers, Schlesinger Library, Box 1, Folder 26; Slate, *Colored Cosmopolitanism*, 208–212; James Farmer, *Lay Bare the Heart: An Autobiography of the Civil Rights Movement* (New York: Arbor House, 1985), 149–152.

15. Murray, diary, January 3, 1941.

16. Sherman, *The Case of Odell Waller*, 44–57, 67.

17. [Vivian Odems] to Pauli Murray, January, 8, 1941, PM Papers, Schlesinger Library, Box 4, Folder 71. The letter was unsigned, but the writer identified the place of writing as "At the Office," in the upper-right-hand corner of the first page. According to Murray, *Song in a Weary Throat*, 164, Odems "ran the office"; the 1940 Census lists Odems as Negro.

18. Sherman, *The Case of Odell Waller*, 67; Murray, *Song in a Weary Throat*, 168.

19. Ted LeBerthon, "Night and Day," *Daily News*, Los Angeles, March 24, 1941, PM Papers, Schlesinger Library, Box 72, Folder 1256.

20. LeBerthon, "Night and Day."

21. LeBerthon, "Night and Day."

22. LeBerthon, "Night and Day."

23. Murray mentioned her plan to go to Iowa in Pauli Murray to Morris Milgram, August 26, 1941, PM Papers, Schlesinger Library, Box 72, Folder 1251; Pauli Murray to Leon Ransom, February 13, 1941, PM Papers, Schlesinger Library, Box 15, Folder 384.

24. Murray, *Song in a Weary Throat*, 180; Pauli Murray to Morris Milgram, August 26, 1941 (discussion of various work options; Murray needed to make $25 a week ($10 to go to her mother), Morris offered only $12), PM Papers, Schlesinger Library, Box 72, Folder 1251.

25. Murray, *Song in a Weary Throat*, 181; Pauli Murray to Agnes Martocci, September 8, 1941, and Pauli Murray to Morris Milgram, September 18, 1941, PM Papers, Schlesinger Library, Box 72, Folder 1251.

26. Sherman, *The Case of Odell Waller*, 95–174.

27. Interview with Pauli Murray by Dr. Thomas Soapes, February 3, 1978, FDR Library, Hyde Park, New York, p. 4. For a picture of the delegation that listened in on the party line see "Their Pleas Failed to Save Waller," *Afro-American*, July 2–6 1942, PM Papers, Schlesinger Library, Box 72, Folder 1257. It would take the Twenty-Fifth Amendment to the Constitution, which abolished the poll tax in federal elections in 1964, and a Supreme Court decision by a very different panel of justices to abolish the poll tax in state elections in 1966.

28. Herbert Garfinkel, *When Negroes March: The March on Washington Movement in the Organizational Politics for FEPC* (New York: Macmillan, 1969), 188–189.

29. Murray, *Song in a Weary Throat*, 175.

30. For biographical facts on Dollie Lowther, see the Fifteenth Census of the United States: 1930, Population Schedule, Elizabeth City, North Carolina; and information from Dowther's Social Security Card, available at Ancestry.com; Dollie Lowther Robinson, oral history by Bette Craig, Institute of Labor and Industrial Relations, Wayne State, University of Michigan, 1978, pp. 1–4; Karen Pastorello, *A Power among Them: Bessie Abramowitz Hillman and the Making of the Amalgamated Clothing Workers of America* (Urbana-Champaign: University of Illinois Press, 2008), 122.

31. Yevette Richards, *Maida Springer: Pan-Africanist and International Labor Leader* (Pittsburgh: University of Pittsburgh Press, 2000), 14–37.

32. Richards, *Maida Springer*, 75; Maida Springer Kemp, oral history, Institute of Labor and Industrial Relations, Wayne State, University of Michigan, 1978, p. 7.

33. Pauli Murray to Brother Randolph [A. Philip Randolph], July 24, 1942 [the five-page, single spaced letter was begun on July 24 but concluded after the march], PM Papers, Schlesinger Library, Box 72, Folder 1265; Yevette Richards, *Conversations with Maida Springer: A Personal History of Labor, Race, and International Relations* (Pittsburgh: University of Pittsburgh Press, 2004), 124; "Solemn Protest Parade Brings Injustice Home to Manhattan," *New York Amsterdam-Star News*, August 1, 1942; Murray, *Song in a Weary Throat*, 175–176.

34. Interview with Pauli Murray by Soapes, 11–12; Eleanor Roosevelt, "Freedom: Promise or Fact," *Negro Digest* 1 (October 1943): 8–9, PM Papers, Schlesinger Library, Box 99, Folder 1782; Patricia Bell-Scott, *The Firebrand and the First Lady: Portrait of a Friendship: Pauli Murray, Eleanor Roosevelt, and the Struggle for Social Justice* (New York: Knopf, 2016).

35. "First Lady Urges Sharecropper Aid," *New York Times*, March 6, 1940, clipping in PM Papers, Schlesinger Library, Box 18, Folder 399; Pauli Murray to Eleanor Roosevelt, March 15, 1940, PM Papers, Schlesinger Library, Box 4, Folder 85.

36. Pauli Murray to Franklin D. Roosevelt, July 23, 1942, PM Papers, Schlesinger Library, Box 99, Folder 1779.

37. Eleanor Roosevelt to "Miss Murray," August 3, 1942, PM Papers, Schlesinger Library, Box 99, Folder, 1781. For Eleanor Roosevelt's opposition to the camps see Allida Black, *Casting Her Own Shadow: Eleanor Roosevelt and the Shaping of Postwar Liberalism* (New York: Columbia University Press, 1996), 142–147; Murray, *Song in a Weary Throat*, 189–192.

38. On Murray as a "firebrand," see Eleanor Roosevelt, "Some of My Best Friends Are Negro," *Ebony* 9 (February 1953): 16–20, 22, 24–26; Murray, *Song in a Weary Throat*, 191–193.

39. Murray, *Song in a Weary Throat*, 194–195.

40. Pauli Murray, "A Stormy Relationship with Mrs. Roosevelt," n.d., typescript, p. 31, PM Papers, Schlesinger Library, Box 132, Folder 2406.

Chapter 6

1. Pauli Murray to Leon Ransom, August 21, 1944, PM Papers, Schlesinger Library, Box 84, Folder 1467; Pauli Murray, *Song in a Weary Throat: An American Pilgrimage* (New York: Harper & Row, 1987), 183; Interview with Pauli Murray by Genna Rae McNeil, February 13, 1976 (G-0044), in the Oral History Program Collection (#4007), Southern Historical Collection, Wilson Library, University of North Carolina at Chapel Hill, p. 65.

2. Murray, *Song in a Weary Throat*, 183; A. McBean to the editor of the *New York Amsterdam News*, November 9, 1939, PM Papers, Schlesinger Library, Box 4, Folder 71; Murray, *Song*, 183. Women fared no better in the wider world of law. In 1940 only two or three out of every 100 attorneys in the United States were female: Virginia Drachman, *Sisters in Law: Women Lawyers in Modern American History* (Cambridge, MA: Harvard University Press, 2001), Appendix 1, Table 3, p. 254.

3. *Brown* declared racial segregation in public schools unconstitutional; *Reed* declared discrimination on the basis of gender in determining who should administer an estate unconstitutional.

4. Interview with Pauli Murray by McNeil, 65; Murray, *Song in a Weary Throat*, 183.

5. Murray, *Song in a Weary Throat*, 183; Cynthia Fuchs Epstein, *Women in Law*, 2nd ed. (Champaign: University of Illinois Press, 1993), 65–66; Deborah Tannen, "The Power of Talk: Who Gets Heard and Why," *Harvard Business Review* (September–October 1995): 139–148; Drachman, *Sisters in Law*, 3; Joseph Eidelsberg to Pauli Murray, July 22, 1941, Box 4, Folder 71; Dr. Ruth Fox to Pauli Murray, July 31, 1942, Box 4, Folder 71; Pauli Murray to Dr. Mazique, July 29, 1944, all in PM Papers, Schlesinger Library, Box 4, Folder 73. To hear Murray's voice, listen to the recording of the interview with Pauli Murray by Genna Rae McNeil, February 13, 1967 (G-0044) audio, available online at the Southern Oral History Program, Southern Historical Collection (#4007), Manuscript Department, Wilson Library, University of North Carolina, Chapel Hill.

6. Murray, *Song in a Weary Throat*, 184. Note that, in one of her rare mistakes, Murray gave the name of her English honorary society, Sigma Tau Delta, as the name of the Howard legal fraternity. The legal fraternity was, in fact, Phi Alpha Delta. It did not admit women until 1970 but was the first legal fraternity to do so; see Laura Duncan, "Happy Birthday PADs," *Chicago Daily Law Bulletin*, November 13, 1992.

7. Murray, *Song in a Weary Throat*, 185–188. According to the list of grades Murray compiled after law school, she earned a 92.87 percent grade point average in the first year and a 90.74 percent average for the second: PM Papers, Schlesinger Library, Box 1, Folder 4.

8. Murray, *Song in a Weary Throat*, 218–219.

9. Pauli Murray to Lisha and Cat, September 11, 1941, PM Papers, Schlesinger Library, Box 15, Folder 384; Pauli Murray, "Budget—Howard Law School—Year 1941–42—10 month period," PM Papers, Schlesinger Library, Box 15, Folder 384; on work for Dr. Dorothy Ferebee, see Rider to No. 19, in "Application of Pauli Murray for Admission to the Bar of the State of New York," May 8, 1948, Archives of the Appellate Division, Supreme Court of the State of New York, Second Judicial Department, Brooklyn, New York; Pauli Murray to Caroline Ware, July 31, 1943, PM Papers, Schlesinger Library, Box 101, Folder 1816 (describes work as a waitress in summer of 1943); Pauli Murray to Jessie Overholt, August 29, 1941, and Jessie

Overholt to Pauli Murray, September 6, 1941, PM Papers, Schlesinger Library, Box 98, Folder 1762; Murray, *Song in a Weary Throat*, 182.

10. Pauli Murray to Dr. Ruth Fox, July 25, 1942, and Pauli Murray to Dr. Joseph Eidelsberg, July 13, 1942, and July 21, 1942, PM Papers, Schlesinger Library, Box 4, Folder 71.

11. Pauli Murray, Memorandum on PM, July 13, 1942, PM Papers, Schlesinger Library, Box 4, Folder 71.

12. Pauli Murray, Memorandum on PM, July 13, 1942.

13. Dr. Joseph Eidelsberg to Pauli Murray, July 22, 1942, PM Papers, Schlesinger Library, Box 4, Folder, 71.

14. Pauli Murray to Dr. Ruth Fox, July 25, 1942, PM Papers, Schlesinger Library, Box 4, Folder 71.

15. Dr. Ruth Fox to Pauli Murray, July 31, 1942, PM Papers, Schlesinger Library, Box 4, Folder 71.

16. John Randolph to Dr. W. Winters, July 31, 1942, PM Papers, Schlesinger Library, Box 4, Folder 71.

17. Murray, *Song in a Weary Throat*, 202.

18. Lenie [Pauli Murray] to Mother [Pauline Fitzgerald Dame], July 10, 1936, and Pauli Murray, "The Negro School and the Negro Student," footnotes and bibliography, PM Papers, Schlesinger Library, Box 10, Folder 252. Pauli first started to sign her letters home with the name "Lenie" after college. It is not clear when the family first called her by that name.

19. Ellen Fitzpatrick, "Caroline F. Ware and the Cultural Approach to History," *American Quarterly* 43, no. 2 (June 1991): 177–188, and *passim*, 173–187; Thomas Dublin, "Caroline Farrar Ware," *Notable American Women* (Cambridge, MA: Belknap Press, 2004), 662–664; Charles Ware Papers, Collection 109–1 to 109–2, Moorland-Spingarn Research Center, Howard University; Caroline F. Ware, *The Early New England Cotton Manufacture: A Study in Industrial Beginnings* (Boston: Houghton Mifflin, 1931); Landon R. Y. Storrs, *The Second Red Scare and the Unmaking of the New Deal Left* (Princeton, NJ: Princeton University Press, 2013), 26, 75–80. Dr. Caroline F. Ware, curriculum vitae, Howard University Archives (Ware was hired to teach at Howard part-time).

20. Murray, *Song in a Weary Throat*, 199.

21. L-o-n-e-l-y L'le Lamb (Pauli Murray) to Skipper (Caroline F. Ware), September 16, 1944, PM Papers, Schlesinger Library, Box 101, Folder 1816. On Murray's friendship with Ware, see Anne Firor Scott, ed., *Pauli Murray and Caroline Ware: Forty Years of Letters in Black and White* (Chapel Hill: University of North Carolina Press, 2006).

22. Dublin, "Caroline Farrar Ware," 198–200; Murray, *Song in a Weary Throat*, 198–199, 233.

23. Pauli Murray, diary, Thursday, February 19, 1942, PM Papers, Schlesinger Library, Box 1, Folder 26; interview with Murray by Martin, 47; Murray, *Song in a Weary Throat*, 185.

24. Mordecai W. Johnson, typed summary of Talk to University, Howard University Broadcast, April 30, 1943, Civil Rights Committee, Howard University Chapter: Announcements, Bulletins, etc., Pauli Murray Papers, Howard University Archives, Box 1, Folder 5; according to Carol McKinnon, Howard University Registrar, there were 3,644 students enrolled for the 1942–1943 year, and 4,196 the next year; Murray, *Song in a Weary Throat*, 200–201.

25. Rayford Whittingham Logan, *Howard University: The First Hundred Years, 1867–1967* (New York: New York University Press, 1969), 323–406; Wolfgang Saxon, "J. H. Herz, a Scholar of Diplomacy, Is Dead at 97," *New York Times*, December 28, 2005; Howard was not the only black institution to give refuge to Jews fleeing Hitler. Black colleges throughout the South did so; see Gabrielle Simon, *From Swastika to Jim Crow: Refugee Scholars at Black Colleges* (Malabar, FL: Krieger, 1993).

26. John D'Emilio, *Lost Prophet: The Life and Times of Bayard Rustin* (New York: Free Press, 2003), 50–51.

27. James Farmer, *Lay Bare the Heart: An Autobiography of the Civil Rights Movement* (New York: Arbor House, 1985), 106.

28. Murray, *Song in a Weary Throat*, 200–202.

29. Murray, *Song in a Weary Throat*, 202–203.

30. Murray, *Song in a Weary Throat*, 205–207.

31. Murray, *Song in a Weary Throat*, 207.

32. Murray, *Song in a Weary Throat*, 207.

33. Murray, *Song in a Weary Throat*, 208–209; Harry McAlpin, "Howard Students Picket Jim Crow Restaurant," *Chicago Defender*, April 24, 1943; "HU Student Pickets Force Restaurant to Drop Color Bar," *Baltimore Afro-American*, April 24, 1943, PM Papers, Schlesinger Library, Box 18, Folder 399; "Non-Violent Direct Action Breaks Jim Crow in Restaurant," *Baltimore Afro-American*, May 29, 1943.

34. Interview with Murray by McNeil, 51; Murray, *Song in a Weary Throat*, 208–209.

35. Pauli Murray to Jessie Overholt, June 9, 1943, PM Papers, Schlesinger Library, Box 98, Folder 1762.

36. Lenie [Pauli Murray] to Mother [Pauline F. Dame], June 2, 1943, PM Papers, Schlesinger Library, Box 10, Folder 253.

37. Medical Records from Howard University Infirmary, May 13–19, 1943, PM Papers, Schlesinger Library, Box 4, Folder 71; Lenie to Mother, June 2, 1943.

38. Quoted in Glenda Elizabeth Gilmore, *Defying Dixie: The Radical Roots of Civil Rights, 1919–1950* (New York: W. W. Norton, 2008), 390; Pauli Murray to Eleanor Roosevelt, May 4, 1943, Eleanor Roosevelt Papers on Microfilm, reel 14; Eleanor Roosevelt, "My Day," June 2, 1943; Lenie [Pauli Murray] to Mother [Pauline F. Dame], June 2, 1943, PM Papers, Schlesinger Library, Box 10, Folder 253. For a more complete story of the tea at the White House see Murray, *Song in a Weary Throat*, 195–197.

39. Lena [Caroline Ware] to Pauli, June 14, 1943, PM Papers, Schlesinger Library, Box 101, Folder 1816; Lenie [Pauli Murray]to Mother [Pauline Dame], June 4, 1943, PM Papers, Schlesinger Library, Box 10, Folder 253; Pauli Murray to Jessie Overholt, June 9, 1943, PM Papers, Schlesinger Library, Box 98, Folder 1762 (in which Murray reports that she is going to the endocrinology clinic at Duke); Murray, *Song in a Weary Throat*, 210–211; Doris Kearns Goodwin, *No Ordinary Time: Franklin and Eleanor Roosevelt: The Home Front* (New York: Simon & Schuster, 1994), 371.

40. Thurgood Marshall, "The Gestapo in Detroit," *Crisis*, August, 1943, pp. 232–233, 246–247; Murray, *Song in a Weary Throat*, 212; Pauli Murray to Lena [Caroline Ware], July 31, 1943, PM Papers, Schlesinger Library, Box 101, Folder 1816.

41. Pauline F. Dame, "Me and My Dogs," n.d., PM Papers, Schlesinger Library, Box 11, Folder 276 (a handwritten story, told in Pauli's voice, of the dogs Pauli began bringing home at the age of seven); Pauli to Lena, July 31, 1943, PM Papers, Schlesinger Library, Box 101, Folder 1816; John P. Lewis, "Pauli Murray," *PM* [magazine], June 14, 1944, PM Papers, Schlesinger Library, Box 73, Folder 1270; Pauli Murray, "Negroes Are Fed Up," *Common Sense*, August 1943, pp. 274–276.

42. Lenie to Mother, October 29, 1939, PM Papers, Schlesinger Library, Box 10, Folder 252; Murray, *Song in a Weary Throat*, 214; Pauli Murray, "Dark Testament," PM Papers, Schlesinger Library, Box 80, Folder 1401.

43. Murray, *Song in a Weary Throat*, 215.

44. Fitzpatrick, "Caroline Ware," 178.

45. Murray, *Song in a Weary Throat*, 215–177.

46. "16 Suffrage Women Sent to Serve 60 Days," *Atlanta Constitution*, July 18, 1917; Murray, *Song in a Weary Throat*, 216; Katherine H. Adams and Michael L. Keene, *After the Vote Was Won: The Later Achievements of Fifteen Suffragists* (Jefferson, NC: McFarland, 2010), 58–59; Murray, *Song in a Weary Throat*, 216.

47. Murray, *Song in a Weary Throat*, 217.

48. Pauli Murray to Leon Ransom, August 21, 1944, PM Papers, Schlesinger Library, Box 84, Folder 1467; Murray, *Song in a Weary Throat*, 221–222.

49. On the controversial nature of Murray's approach to the Thirteenth Amendment, and of its roots in her "unresolved crisis of identity," see Kenneth W. Mack, *Representing the Race: The Creation of the Civil Rights Lawyer* (Cambridge, MA: Harvard University Press, 2012), 227, 230–231. On civil rights lawyers' use of the Thirteenth Amendment to combat peonage, from the Progressive Era through World War II, see Michael J. Klarman, *From Jim Crow to Civil Rights: The Supreme Court and the Struggle for Racial Equality* (New York: Oxford University Press, 2004), 61, 71–76, 86–88, 95–96, 173, 233–235, 286–289, and on the Justice Department's use of the Thirteenth Amendment to combat forced labor during World War II, see Risa L. Goluboff, "The Thirteenth Amendment and the Lost Origins of Civil Rights,"

Duke Law Journal 50 (2001): 1609–1685. For the radical (dangerous to many) potential of the Thirteenth Amendment to protect not only those subject to forced labor but also those subject to other forms of oppression, including domestic violence, see Jack M. Balkin and Sanford Levinson, "The Dangerous Thirteenth Amendment," *Columbia Law Review* 112, no. 7 (November 2012): 1459–1499.

50. Pauli Murray to Caroline Ware, September 16, 1944, PM Papers, Schlesinger Library, Box 101, Folder 1816.

51. Farmer, *Lay Bare the Heart*, 155–157.

52. Pauli Murray, "Howard University Students Demonstrate New Technique in Securing Equal Rights," April 25, 1944, PM Papers, Box 18, Folder 402.

53. "Thompson Restaurant Settles Jim Crow Suit," *Chicago Defender*, January 12, 1935.

54. Murray, "Howard University Students Demonstrate New Technique."

55. Murray, "Howard University Students Demonstrate New Technique."

56. Murray, "Howard University Students Demonstrate New Technique"; Murray, *Song in a Weary Throat*, 223–224.

57. The Civil Rights Committee of the Howard Chapter, NAACP to Mordecai Johnson, (drafted by Pauli Murray), April 30, 1944, PM Papers, Schlesinger Library, Box 18, Folder 402.

58. "Seek to Oust Bilbo, 'Mayor' of Washington," *New Journal and Guide*, April 22, 1944.

59. Interview with Murray by Martin, 52–54, 65–66.

60. Interview with Murray by Martin, 67; Murray, *Song in a Weary Throat*, 230.

61. Murray, *Song in a Weary Throat*, 238; Pauli Murray, "Statement of Proposed Project: The Extension of Rights of Minority Groups under New Deal Legislation and Court Rulings," PM Papers, Schlesinger Library, Box 18, Folder 416; Jayne R. Beilke, "The Changing Emphasis of the Rosenwald Fellowship Program, 1928–1948," *Journal of Negro Education* 66, no. 1 (Winter 1997): 3–15 (women rose from 28 to 50 percent of the recipients).

62. Murray, *Song in a Weary Throat*, 238–239.

63. Mrs. William C. Haygood to Pauli Murray, April 20, 1944, PM Papers, Schlesinger Library, Box 18, Folder 416; "Rosenwald Fund's 1944 Awards Total $78,100," *Chicago Defender*, May 20, 1944.

64. Pauli Murray to Professor T. R. Powell and President James B, Conant, July 20, 1944, PM Papers, Schlesinger Library, Box 18, Folder 415; Murray, *Song in a Weary Throat*, 239. In her memoir, Murray reconstructed her early exchanges with Harvard from memory, since she had given the letters to Dean William Hastie in the hope that he might intervene on her behalf. He seems not to have kept the letters. The only correspondence with Harvard that remains is from mid-July to October 1944. See Pauli Murray, Note to File, July 2, 1981, Box 18, Folder 415.

65. Murray, *Song in a Weary Throat*, 241.

66. Resolution adopted by the Antislavery Society (January 27, 1843); referencing Isaiah 28:15: "We have made a covenant with death, and with hell are we at agreement"; *William Lloyd Garrison, 1805–1879: The Story of His Life Told by His Children* (1885) by Wendell Phillips Garrison and Francis Jackson Garrison—*Life*, vol. iii, page 390, as quoted in John Bartlett, *Familiar Quotations*, 10th ed., 1919; "Civil Rights Champion: Lloyd K. Garrison," *New York Times*, April 20, 1963; Lee A. Daniels, "Lloyd K. Garrison, Lawyer, Dies; Leader in Social Causes Was 92," *New York Times*, October 3, 1991; "Lloyd Garrison Dies: Was First NLRB Chief," *Washington Post*, October 3, 1991.

67. Murray, *Song in a Weary Throat*, 242.

68. Pauli Murray to the Faculty of Harvard School of Law, July 20, 1944, PM Papers, Schlesinger Library, Box 18, Folder 415.

69. Pauli Murray to Judge Sarah T. Hughes, July 20, 1944, PM Papers, Schlesinger Library, Box 18, Folder 415; Murray, *Song in a Weary Throat*, 243. Harvard Medical School admitted women the following year; the law school did not do so until 1950, at which point Murray applied once more. By that time she had earned a master's degree at Boalt Hall at Berkeley. Harvard told her that it admitted only students who had earned master's degrees at Harvard, something it had denied her the right to do in 1944.

70. List of grades at Howard, Box 1, Folder 4, also Box 15, Folder 385.

71. Interview with Murray by Martin, 43; Pauli Murray to Eleanor Roosevelt, June 4, 1944, PM Papers, Schlesinger Library, Box 99, Folder 1779; Harry McAlpin, "Mrs. F.D.R. Sends Posies

to Pauli for Commencement," *Afro-America*, June 10, 1944; Harry McAlpin, "Pauli Murray, Brilliant Howard Law School Graduate, Honored," n.d., and Grace Matthews, "Washington Notes," n.d., *Pittsburgh Courier*, PM Papers, Schlesinger Library, Box 4, Folder 70.

Chapter 7

1. Roger J. Traynor et al., "Barbara Nachtrieb Armstrong—In Memoriam," *California Law Review* 65, no. 5 (September 1977): 920–936; Pauli Murray, *Song in a Weary Throat: An American Pilgrimage* (New York: Harper & Row, 1987), 246.
2. "Graduates Urged to Go South by H.U. President," *Afro-American*, June 3, 1944. Johnson's advice became a staple of his public lectures; see Michael Carter, "Howard's Dr. Mordecai Johnson Advocates 'Go South' Formula," *Afro-American*, March 31, 1945.
3. Pauli Murray, "Shall I Go South? Asks H. U. Graduate," *Afro-American*, June 10, 1944; John P. Lewis, "Pauli Murray," *PM* [magazine], June 14, 1944, PM Papers, Schlesinger Library, Box 73, Folder 1270. See also "Go South, Commit Suicide," June 24, 1944, *Afro-American*, PM Papers, Schlesinger Library, Box 73, Folder 1270.
4. Isabel Wilkerson, *The Warmth of Other Suns: The Epic Story of America's Great Migration* (New York: Random House, 2010), 302–305; Thomas J. Sugrue, *Sweet Land of Liberty: The Forgotten Struggle for Civil Rights in the North* (New York: Random House, 2009), 87–90; Murray to Eleanor Roosevelt, July 22, 1944, PM Papers, Schlesinger Library, Box 99, Folder 1779.
5. Pauli Murray to William Hastie, August 3, 1944 [Murray mentioned that Mildred appeared to be the first black nurse ever to be hired at the Veterans hospital in Los Angeles], PM Papers, Schlesinger Library, Box 96, Folder 1698; John P. Lewis to Pauli Murray, June 21, 1944, PM Papers, Schlesinger Library, Box 73, Folder 1270; Murray, *Song in a Weary Throat*, 247. For Murray's use of "badges and incidents of slavery," see Pauli Murray, "Should the *Civil Rights Cases* and *Plessy v. Ferguson* Be Overruled?" pp. 14–15, 42, PM Papers, Schlesinger Library, Box 84, Folder 1467, and Murray, "Judicial Construction of the Thirteenth Amendment," (1944), 2, PM Papers, Schlesinger Library, Box 19, Folder 423.
6. Pauli Murray to William Hastie, August 23, 1944, PM Papers, Schlesinger Library, Box 96, Folder 1698; Pauli Murray, "Postwar Race Tensions Must Be Warded Off Now," *Sentinel*, September 14, 1944, PM Papers, Schlesinger Library, Box 1, Folder 12.
7. Pauli Murray to William Hastie, August 3, 1944, PM Papers, Schlesinger Library, Box 96, Folder 1698; Murray, *Song in a Weary Throat*, 252–253.
8. Pauli Murray, "An American Credo," *Common Ground* 5, no. 2 (December 1945): 22–24.
9. Pauli Murray to Caroline Ware, August 10, 1944, PM Papers, Schlesinger Library, Box 101, Folder 1816; Murray, "An American Credo," 22–24.
10. Pauli Murray, "An American Girl Works Out a Way of Life," *PM*, Sunday, August 20, 1944, PM Papers, Schlesinger Library, Box 4, Folder 70; Murray must have been embarrassed by the title chosen for her essay by the editors of *PM*, because she referred to it in other writings as "Footnote for Minority Americans," her title for it; Murray, *Song in a Weary Throat*, 255; Murray to Ware, August 10, 1944.
11. Pauli Murray, "Dark Testament," *The South Today* (Winter 1944); John Edgerton, *Speak Now against the Day: The Generation before the Civil Rights Movement in the South* (New York: Alfred A. Knopf, 1994), 265–266; Rose Gladney, "A Letter from Lillian Smith: 'Old Seeds Bearing a Heavy Crop,'" with an introduction by Rose Gladney, *Southern Changes* 12, no. 5 (1990): 4–5.
12. Pauli Murray, "Highlights of LARY Hearings," *Sentinel*, August 10, 1944; Murray, "Banks Not Ready to Drop Color Barriers, Reporter Finds," *Sentinel*, August 17, 1944, PM Papers, Schlesinger Library, Box 1, Folder 12; Pauli Murray to William Hastie, August 5, 1944, PM Papers, Schlesinger Library, Box 96, Folder 1698; Pauli Murray to Mother [Pauline Fitzgerald Dame], September 9, 1944, PM Papers, Schlesinger Library, Box 10, Folder 253.
13. Pauli Murray to Dr. Mazique [Edward C. Mazique], July 29, 1944, PM Papers, Schlesinger Library, Box 4, Folder 71; Florence Ridlon, *A Black Physician's Struggle for Civil Rights: Edward. Mazique, M.D.* (Albuquerque: University of New Mexico Press, 2005), 95–120.
14. Murray to Dr. Mazique.
15. Murray to Dr. Mazique [I have not been able to identify "Dave."]

16. Murray, *Song in a Weary Throat*, 254.

17. L-o-n-e-l-y L'le Lamb [Pauli Murray] to Skipper [Caroline F. Ware], September 16, 1944, PM Papers, Schlesinger Library, Box 101, Folder 1816; Walter A. Jackson, *Gunnar Myrdal and America's Conscience: Social Engineering and Racial Liberalism, 1938–1987* (Chapel Hill: University of North Carolina Press, 1990).

18. Jackson, *Gunnar Myrdal*, 68– 86.

19. Jackson, *Gunnar Myrdal*, 88–134.

20. Jackson, *Gunnar Myrdal*, 135–185.

21. Pauli Murray to George Stoney, December 6, 1939, PM Papers and Pauli Murray to Doxey A. Wilkerson, December 28, 1939, PM Papers, Schlesinger Library, Box 15, Folder 381; John Edgerton, *Speak Now against the Day*, 274; Jackson, *Gunnar Myrdal*, 102–122.

22. Pauli Murray, "Should the *Civil Rights Cases* and *Plessy v. Ferguson* Be Overruled?" May 1944 [submitted August 1944], Civil Rights Seminar, Howard University School of Law, pp. 1, 5–6, 29, 39–46, PM Papers, Schlesinger Library, Box 84, Folder 1467.

23. Murray, "Should the *Civil Rights Cases* and *Plessy v. Ferguson* Be Overruled?" 28, quoting Gunnar Myrdal, *An American Dilemma: The Negro Problem and American Democracy*, 2 vols. (New York: Harper & Bros., 1944), I: 577–578.

24. Linda Przybyszewski, *The Republic According to John Marshall Harlan* (Chapel Hill: University of North Carolina Press, 1999), 14–15, 81–85; Loren P. Beth, *John Marshall Harlan: The Last Whig Justice* (Louisville: University of Kentucky Press, 1992), 83, 92, 227–239.

25. Murray, "Should the *Civil Rights Cases* and *Plessy v. Ferguson* Be Overruled?" 15–22.

26. Murray, "Should the *Civil Rights Cases* and *Plessy v. Ferguson* Be Overruled?" appendix; Harlan's dissent in *Plessy v. Ferguson*.

27. Myrdal, *An American Dilemma*, I: 113–115.

28. Myrdal, *An American Dilemma*, 110–111, citing Ruth Benedict, *Race: Science and Politics* (1940), 237, and other work of scholars in anthropology at Columbia and in sociology at Chicago; Murray, "Should the *Civil Rights Cases* and *Plessy v. Ferguson* Be Overruled?" references this work in point 10 of her outline for the section on *Plessy*.

29. L-o-n-e-l-y L'le Lamb [Pauli Murray] to Skipper [Caroline F. Ware], September 16, 1944.

30. Myrdal, *An American Dilemma*, II, Appendix 5: "A Parallel to the Negro Problem," 1073–1077.

31. Alva Myrdal, "One Sex a Social Problem," *Nation and Family* (New York: Harper & Brothers, 1941), chapter 22, 398–426; Myrdal, *An American Dilemma*, II: Appendix 5, 1077; Yvonne Hirdman, *Alva Myrdal: The Passionate Mind* (Bloomington: University of Indiana Press, 2008), 246–251; Sissela Bok, *Alva Myrdal: A Daughter's Memoir* (Cambridge: Radcliffe Biography Series, 1991), 139–140.

32. Jackson, *Gunnar Myrdal*, 168.

33. Pauli Murray to Leon Ransom, August 21, 1944, PM Papers, Schlesinger Library, Box 84, Folder 1467; Pauli Murray to Ruth and Tom Emerson, June 30, 1970, PM Papers, Schlesinger Library, Box 45, Folder 802 (Murray mentions that she had conceived of "Jane Crow" before Myrdal's Appendix 5 came out).

34. Peter Panic [Pauli Murray], "Little Man from Mars," *Sentinel*, date written in ink is 7-14-44, but publication date was likely later, because she did not start writing for the *Sentinel* until August, PM Papers, Schlesinger Library, Box 1, Folder 12. This article seems to have been the first instance in which Murray referred to "Jane Crow" in print; Pauli Murray, "An American Credo," *Common Ground* 5, no. 2 (December 1945): 22.

35. Pauli Murray to William Hastie, August 23, 1944, PM Papers, Schlesinger Library, Box 96, Folder 1698; Pauli Murray, "Restriction Suit Asks Ouster of 12 Families," *Sentinel*, August 31, 1944, and Murray, "Pauli Murray Will Not Move," *Afro American*, September 2, 1944, PM Papers, Schlesinger Library, Box 1, Folder 12.

36. Pauli Murray to William Hastie, August 23, 1944, PM Papers, Schlesinger Library, Box 96, Folder 1698. On Loren Miller's legal campaign against restrictive covenants see Mark Brilliant, *The Color of America Has Changed: How Racial Diversity Shaped Civil Rights Reform in California, 1941–1978* (New York: Oxford University Press, 2010), 75, 76–87.

37. Pauli Murray, "Restriction Suit Asks Ouster of 12 Families," *Sentinel*, August 31, 1944.

38. Leon Washington (founder of the *Sentinel*) interview with Pauli Murray on the *Sentinel* radio station in Los Angeles, Sunday, September 3, 1944, typescript, p. 4, PM Papers,

Schlesinger Library, Box 1, Folder 12; *Buchanan v. Warley*, 245 U.S. 60 (1917); *Gandolfo v. Hartman* et al., Circuit Court S.D. California, 49 F. 181; 1892 U.S. App. LEXIS 1182; Pauli Murray to William Hastie, September 3, 1944, PM Papers, Schlesinger Library, Box 96, Folder 1698.

39. Your child [Pauli Murray], to Mother [Pauline Fitzgerald Dame], September 30, 1944, PM Papers, Schlesinger Library, Box 10, Folder 253; Pauli Murray to William Hastie, August 5, 1944, PM Papers, Schlesinger Library, Box 96, Folder 1698; Murray, *Song in a Weary Throat*, 258.

40. Murray, *Song in a Weary Throat*, 258-260; "Berkeley College Panel," October 1945, PM Papers, Schlesinger Library, Box 4, Folder 91; Pauli Murray to Caroline Ware, March 40, 1945, PM Papers, Schlesinger Library, Box 101, Folder 1816.

41. As of 1944, the law school's official name was the University of California, Berkeley, School of Jurisprudence, but it was commonly referred to as Boalt Hall, in memory of its early twentieth-century benefactor Elizabeth Josselyn Boalt.

42. Herma Hill Kay, "The Future of Women Law Professors," *Iowa Law Review* 77 (1991): 5-6; Roger J. Traynor et al., "Barbara Nachtrieb Armstrong—In Memoriam," *California Law Review* 65, no. 5 (September 1977): 920-936; Alice Kessler-Harris, *In Pursuit of Equity: Women, Men, and the Quest for Economic Citizenship* (New York: Oxford University Press, 2001), 75-78, 91, 117-118, 121-156.

43. Alexander Marsden Kidd et al., "In Memoriam—Dudley Odell McGovney, Jurisprudence: Berkeley (1877-1947)," (Berkeley: University of California Academic Senate, 1947): 1-4.

44. Pauli Murray to William Hastie, June 12, 1945, PM Papers, Schlesinger Library, Box 96, Folder 1696.

45. *Shelley v. Kraemer*, 334 U.S. 1 (1948); D. O. McGovney, "Racial Residential Segregation by State Court Enforcement of Restrictive Agreements, Covenants or Conditions in Deeds Is Unconstitutional," *California Law Review* 33, no. 1 (1945): 5-39.

46. On "frivolous," see McGovney, "Racial Residential Segregation by State Court Enforcement of Restrictive Agreements," 36; D. O. McGovney, notes on the back of page 31 of a draft of Pauli Murray, "Judicial Construction of the Thirteenth Amendment" (1944), PM Papers, Schlesinger Library, Box 19, Folder 423. This draft appears to precede the paper that Murray ultimately submitted to McGovney: Murray, "Congressional Debates on the Adoption of the Thirteenth Amendment," which begins with McGovney's suggested introduction, PM Papers, Schlesinger Library, Box 19, Folder 423.

47. Przybyszewski, *The Republic According to John Marshall*, xxiv. See also Edward F. Waite, "How Eccentric Was Mr. Justice Harlan?" *Minnesota Law Review* 37 (February 1953): 173-187.

48. D. O. McGovney, Memorandum for Miss Pauli Murray, October 11, 1944, PM Papers, Schlesinger Library, Box 19, Folder 423.

49. Murray to Hastie, June 12, 1945, PM Papers, Schlesinger Library, Box 96, Folder 1696.

50. Murray, "Congressional Debates on the Adoption of the Thirteenth Amendment," 36, PM Papers, Schlesinger Library, Box 19, Folder 423; Alexander Tsesis, *The Thirteenth Amendment and American Freedom: A Legal History* (New York: New York University Press, 2004), 53; Pauli Murray, "Judicial Construction of the Thirteenth Amendment" (1944), 2, PM Papers, Schlesinger Library, Box 19, Folder 423; Murray, *Song in a Weary Throat*, 262. For the history of the concept of slavery's "badges" and "incidents," see Jennifer Mason McAward, "Defining the Badges and Incidents of Slavery," *Journal of Constitutional Law* 14, no. 3 (February 2012): 561- 630, 561.

51. Murray, *Song in a Weary Throat*, 262.

52. Pauli Murray to William Hastie, June 12, 1945, PM Papers, Schlesinger Library, Box 96, Folder 1698.

53. Pauli Murray, "The Right to Equal Opportunity in Employment," *California Law Review* 33, no. 3 (1945): 388-433. Note that in footnote 8, Murray says that discrimination based on sex would be examined insofar as it is related to discrimination based on race or religion, but she defers to a later time a fuller discussion of this kind of discrimination. Note also footnote 42 (pp. 398-399) in which she mentions that the NLRB forbids discrimination on the basis of sex, when there is no difference in function to support it.

54. Murray, "Right to Equal Opportunity," 425–433.
55. Murray to Ware, March 30, 1945, PM Papers, Schlesinger Library, Box 96, Folder 1696.
56. Murray to Ware, March 30, 1945.
57. Pauli Murray, "For Franklin Delano Roosevelt," *Common Ground* (June 1945): 80–81, later published as "The Passing of F.D.R.," in Murray, *Dark Testament and Other Poems*, (Norwalk, CT: Silvermine, 1970), 36–37; Murray to Ware, March 30, 1945, PM Papers, Schlesinger Library, Box 96, Folder 1696.
58. Pauli Murray, "Notes on San Francisco Conference," Friday, April 27, 1945, PM Papers, Schlesinger Library, Box 73, Folder 1271. Murray laid out her educational and emotional woes in an "Excerpt from a letter from Pauli Murray to Betty Williams," March 15, 1947, PM Papers, Schlesinger Library, Box 19, folder 426. See also Pauli Murray to William L. Prosser, June 1, 1951, Box 19, Folder 426; Edwin D. Dickinson to Pauli Murray, May 16, 1947, PM Papers, Schlesinger Library, Box 19, folder 426.
59. Murray, *Song in a Weary Throat*, 262–263.
60. "Excerpt from a letter from Pauli Murray to Betty Williams," March 15, 1947; Edwin D. Dickinson to Pauli Murray, May 16, 1947, PM Papers, Schlesinger Library, Box 19, Folder 426.
61. Hastie to Murray, April 11, 1945, and Murray to Hastie, June 12, 1945, PM Papers, Schlesinger Library, Box 96, Folder 1698; Barbara N. Armstrong to Mr. Matthew Tobriner, December 10, 1945, PM Papers, Box 19, Folder 426.
62. Murray, *Song in a Weary Throat*, 263–264; Interview with Robert W. Kenny by Doyce Blackman, 1964, Oral History Program, University of California at Los Angeles, Bancroft Library, University of California at Berkeley, 169–173, 182–186, 250–255; "Pauli Murray Named to Deputy Attorney General Post," *Afro American*, January 14, 1946, clipping in PM Papers, Schlesinger Library, Box 28, Folder 545. See also, "Pauli Murray Gets High Law Position, First Negro Woman," *Amsterdam News*, January 19, 1946; "Named Deputy Attorney General of California," *Pittsburgh Courier*, January 19, 1946; "Woman Named State Deputy Attorney General," *New Journal and Guide*, January 19, 1946.
63. Pauli Murray to Robert W. Kenny, April 19, 1946, PM Papers, Schlesinger Library, Box 28, Folder 544.
64. Gene Roberts and Hank Klibanoff, *The Race Beat: The Press, the Civil Rights Struggle, and the Awakening of a Nation* (New York: Knopf, 2006), 5–11; Pauli Murray to Charles W. Johnson et al., Memo: Fontana Case, January 31, 1946, PM Papers, Schlesinger Library, Box 28, Folder 544; "Citizens Protest Failure to Probe Fontana Fire," *Sentinel*, January 31, 1946; Grace E. Simons, "R. W. Kenny Probing Fontana Deaths," *Sentinel*, February 7, 1946; Mike Davis, "Fontana: Junkyard of Dreams," in *Working People of California*, edited by Danial Conford (Berkeley: University of California Press, 1995), 453–455. In the end, the trail to the perpetrators proved too cold for Kenny to follow.
65. Pauli Murray, "On the Receiving End," *Afro-American*, March 9, 1946; Pauli Murray, "We Need a Blitzkrieg upon Segregation," *Afro-American*, March 16, 1946; "New Western Frontiers Must Be Opened," *Afro-American*, March 23, 1946; Pauli Murray, "Don't Get Mad; Get Smart," *Afro-American*, March 30, 1946.
66. "Women of the Year," *The Evening Star—Washington, D.C.*, March 16, 1946, PM Papers, Schlesinger Library, Box 4, Folder 92.
67. Murray, *Song in a Weary Throat*, 265.
68. Murray, *Song in a Weary Throat*, 265; Charles W. Johnson to Pauli Murray, June 18, 1946, PM Papers, Schlesinger Library, Box 28, Folder 544.

Chapter 8

1. Pauli Murray to Pauline Dame, May 14, 1947, PM Papers, Schlesinger Library, Radcliffe Institute, Harvard University, Box 10, Folder 254; Pauli Murray, *Song in a Weary Throat: An American Pilgrimage* (New York: Harper & Row, 1987), 268.
2. Ira Katznelson, *Fear Itself: The New Deal and the Origins of Our Time* (New York: Liveright, 2013), 328–333.

3. Pauli Murray to Eleanor Roosevelt, June 6, 1954, PM Papers, Schlesinger Library, Box 99, Folder 1780; David K. Johnson, *The Lavender Scare: The Cold War Persecution of Gays and Lesbians in the Federal Government* (Chicago: University of Chicago Press, 2004), 1–14.

4. "Friends, Ex-Students Testify Hastie Has No Red Leanings," *Washington Star*, April 2, 1946, and "Hastie Confirmed Governor," *New Journal and Guide* (Norfolk, Virginia), May 11, 1946, PM Papers, Schlesinger Library, Box 4, Folder 91; Murray, *Song in a Weary Throat*, 26.

5. Landon R. Y. Storrs, *The Second Red Scare and the Unmaking of the New Deal Left* (Princeton, NJ: Princeton University Press, 2013), 81–83.

6. Pauli Murray to Caroline Ware, June 3 and 5, 1946, PM Papers, Schlesinger Library, Box 101, Folder 1816; Cynthia Grant Brown, "Women in the Legal Profession from the 1920s to the 1970s," *Cornell Law Faculty Publications*, Paper 12 (2009): 5–8.

7. Murray, *Song in a Weary Throat*, 271, 312; Pauli Murray to Thurgood Marshall, November 4, 1945, PM Papers, Schlesinger Library, Box 73, Folder 1279; Thurgood Marshall to Pauli Murray, November 8, 1945, PM Papers, Schlesinger Library, Box 73, Folder 1279.

8. Pauli Murray to Mother [Pauline Dame], June 25, 1946, PM Papers, Schlesinger Library, Box 10, Folder 254; "Alexander Haim Pekelis," *Encyclopaedia Judaica* (Farmington Hills, MI: Gale Group, 2008); Mauro Grondona, "Alexander Pekelis: The Law, the State, and the Individual," working paper, Italian Academy at Columbia University, 2008.

9. Pauli Murray to Caroline Ware, July 3, 1946, PM Papers, Schlesinger Library, Box, 101, Folder 1816; Pauli Murray to Mother [Pauline Dame], June 25, 1946, PM Papers, Schlesinger Library, Box 10, Folder 254; Stuart Svonkin, *Jews against Prejudice: American Jews and the Fight for Civil Liberties* (New York: Columbia University Press, 1997), 84–100, and Max Ascoli, "Alexander Pekelis, 1902–1946," *Social Research*, 2 (March 1947): 1–2. For pay, see Pauli Murray, Tax Return for 1947, PM Papers, Schlesinger Library, Box 7, Folder 187.

10. *Mendez, et al. v. Westminster School District of Orange County, et al.*, 64 F.Supp. 544 (S.D. Cal. 1946), aff'd, 161 F.2d 774 (9th Cir. 1947) (en banc); Philippa Strum, Mendez v. Westminster: *School Desegregation and Mexican-American Rights* (Lawrence: University of Kansas Press, 2010), 2, 35–53. For the place of *Mendez* in the context of the broader legal campaign against racial discrimination in California in the 1940s, see Mark Brilliant, *The Color of America Has Changed: How Racial Diversity Shaped Civil Rights Reform in California, 1941–1978* (New York: Oxford University Press, 2010), 44–73.

11. *Westminster v. Mendez*, "Brief of the Attorney General of the State of California, No, 11,310; Thurgood Marshall, Robert L. Carter, and Loren Miller, "Brief for the National Association for the Advancement of Colored People as *amicus curiae* in *Westminster v Mendez*"; Shana Bernstein, *Bridges of Reform: Interracial Civil Rights Activism in Twentieth Century Los Angeles* (New York: Oxford University Press, 2011), 188–197.

12. Will Maslow, Pauli Murray, Carey McWilliams, and Alexander Pekelis (special adviser), "Brief for the American Jewish Congress as *Amicus Curiae*," in *Westminster School District of Orange Country, et al., v. Gonzalo Mendez*, pp. 3–4, 23, 31, 35, and *passim*, PM Papers, Schlesinger Library, Box 28, Folder 551; Application for extension of Rosenwald Fellowship, March 18, 1947, PM Papers, Schlesinger Library, Box 28, Folder 552; Pauli Murray to Caroline Ware, March 19, 1947, PM Papers, Schlesinger Library, Box 101, Folder 1816; Carey McWilliams, "Is Your Name Gonzales?" *Nation*, March 15, 1947, pp. 302–304.

13. Will Maslow et al., "Brief for the American Jewish Congress as *Amicus Curiae*," p. 23. On Gildersleeve and the United Nation's Charter, see Rosalind Rosenberg, *Changing the Subject: How the Women of Columbia Shaped the Way We Think about Sex and Politics* (New York: Columbia University Press, 2004), 186–188.

14. Will Maslow et al., "Brief for the American Jewish Congress as *Amicus Curiae*," p. 35.

15. For Pekelis on the stigmatizing possibilities in clothes, even if equal in quality, see Will Maslow et al., "Brief for the American Jewish Congress as *Amicus Curiae*," p. 6; for Murray, see Pauli Murray, "Pee Wee," 1939 (draft fragment of a short story), PM Papers, Schlesinger Library, Box 83, Folder 1451.

16. *Westminster v. Mendez* 161 F.2d 774 (April 14, 1947).

17. Strum, Mendez v. Westminster, 146–147; Bernstein, *Bridges of Reform*, 190–194. Frederick P. Aguirre, "*Mendez v. Westminster School District*: How It Affected *Brown v. Board of Education*,"

Journal of Hispanic Higher Education 4 (October 2005): 321–332; Murray, *Song in a Weary Throat*, 221–222, 255.

18. Application for extension of Rosenwald Fellowship, March 18, 1947, PM Papers, Schlesinger Library, Box 28, Folder 552; Pauli Murray, resume, n.d. (1947), PM Papers, Schlesinger Library, Box 73, Folder 1286; "FEPC Expires as Congress Refuses Funds," *Chicago Defender*, May 11, 1946.

19. "3 New Yorkers among 12 Dead in Eire Crash," *New York Herald Tribune*, December 29, 1946; "Pole in Plane Dies on Way to Refuge," *New York Times*, December 29, 1946.

20. Pauli Murray to Caroline Ware, March 19, 1947, PM Papers, Schlesinger Library, Box 101, Folder 1816; Pauli Murray to Mother [Pauline Dame], March 31, 1947, PM Papers, Schlesinger Library, Box 10, Folder 254; Pauli Murray to Will Maslow, Commission on Law & Social Action, March 12, 1947, PM Papers, Schlesinger Library, Box 73, Folder 1286.

21. Pauli Murray to Eleanor Roosevelt, April 19 and May 5, 1947, PM Papers, Schlesinger Library, Box 99, Folder 1780; Dr. Peter Marshall Murray to Pauli Murray, April 20, 1947 (report of appendectomy and pathological report), PM Papers, Schlesinger Library, Box 4, Folder 73; Murray spoke of "secreted male genitals" in Murray, Notes to herself, written at Long Island Rest Home, December 14–17, 1937, PM Papers, Schlesinger Library, Box 4, Folder 71.

22. Pauli to Mother [Pauline Dame], June 17, 1947, PM Papers, Schlesinger Library, Box 10, Folder 264; Pauli to Skipper (Caroline Ware), June 10, 1947, PM Papers, Schlesinger Library, Box 101, Folder 1816; Rider to No. 26(d) of Pauli Murray application for admission to the Bar of the State of New York, 1948, PM Papers, Schlesinger Library, Box 28, Folder 554.

23. Murray, *Song in a Weary Throat*, 271.

24. Kate Weigand and Daniel Horowitz, "Dorothy Kenyon: Feminist Organizing, 1919–1963," *Journal of Women's History* 14, no. 2 (Summer 2002): 126–131; Biographical Note on Dorothy Kenyon, Dorothy Kenyon Papers, Sophia Smith Collection, Smith College, Northampton, Massachusetts; Murray, *Song in a Weary Throat*, 271; Joseph Lash, *Eleanor and Franklin: The Story of Their Relationship Based on Eleanor Roosevelt's Private Papers* (New York: W. W. Norton, 1971), 13, 449.

25. Murray, *Song in a Weary Throat*, 271.

26. A newspaper clipping with a portrait of Murray in profile, in "The 'Life and Times' of an American called Pauli Murray," PM Papers, Box 1, Vertical Files, 21f. See also "Mlle Merit Awards," *Mademoiselle*, January 1947, pp. 166–167, PM Papers, Schlesinger Library, Box 4, Folder 89.

27. Pauli Murray, "Why Negro Girls Stay Single," *Negro Digest* 5, no. 9 (July 1947): 4–8.

28. Murray, "Why Negro Girls Stay Single," 6.

29. Murray, "Why Negro Girls Stay Single," 8; Johnson, *The Lavender Scare*, 2.

30. Pauli Murray to Mother [Pauline Dame], December 15, 1947, PM Papers, Schlesinger Library, Box 10, Folder 254.

31. David Ment and Mary S. Donovan, *The People of Brooklyn: A History of Two Neighborhoods* (Brooklyn: Brooklyn Educational & Cultural Alliance, 1980), 27–41.

32. Pauli Murray to Mother [Pauline Dame], December 15, 1947, PM Papers, Schlesinger Library, Box 10, Folder 254; Pauli Murray to Joshua Small, November 25, 1947, PM Papers, Schlesinger Library, Box 10, Folder 260.

33. Pauli Murray to Mother [Pauline Dame], December 15, 1947, PM Papers, Schlesinger Library, Box 10, Folder 254; Pauline Dame to Pauli Murray, April 12, 1948, PM Papers, Schlesinger Library, Box 10, Folder 262. For Aunt Pauline's pension see Notice of Retirement on Regular Allowance, for Mrs. Pauline F. Dame, July 25, 1946, PM Papers, Schlesinger Library, Box 11, Folder 270.

34. Pauli Murray to Mother [Pauline Dame], March 5, April 20, May 1, May 6, May 17, June 12 and 17, July 14, August 9 and 19, 1948, PM Papers, Schlesinger Library, Box 10, Folder 255; Mother [Pauline Dame] to Pauli Murray, December 11, 1947, PM Papers, Schlesinger Library, Box 10, Folder 260; Pauli Murray to Caroline Ware, October 17, 1948, PM Papers, Schlesinger Library, Box 101, Folder 1816; Murray, *Song in a Weary Throat*, 277–279.

35. Murray, *Song in a Weary Throat*, 272, 278. Pauli Murray to Mother [Pauline Dame], June 17, August 9, August 19, 1948, PM Papers, Schlesinger Library, Box 10, Folder 255;

Isabel Wilkerson, *The Warmth of Other Suns: The Epic Story of America's Great Migration* (New York: Random House, 2010), 181–431.

36. Mother [Pauline Dame] to Pauli Murray, June 4, July 14, 1948, PM Papers, Schlesinger Library, Box 10, Folder 255; Pauli Murray to [M. Hugh] Thompson, May 5, 1951, PM Papers, Schlesinger Library, Box 10, Folder 273 (the same letter reports that Marry Ruffin Smith gave $25,000 to the University of North Carolina at her death); Pauli Murray to Mother [Pauline Dame], December 15, 1947, PM Papers, Schlesinger Library, Box 10, Folder 254.

37. Pauli Murray to Caroline Ware, March 26, 1952, PM Papers, Schlesinger Library, Box 101, Folder 1818; Pauline Dame, "Me and My Dogs," a story, told in Pauli's voice, of the dogs she began bringing home at the age of seven, written during Mother [Pauline Dame]'s time in Brooklyn, PM Papers, Schlesinger Library, Box 10, Folder 276; Murray, *Song in a Weary Throat*, 278.

38. Pauli Murray to Mother [Pauline Dame], May 1, 1948, PM Papers, Schlesinger Library, Box 10, Folder 255; Yevette Richards, *Maida Springer: Pan-Africanist and International Labor Leader* (Pittsburgh: University of Pittsburgh Press, 2000), 47–48, 91–92; Murray, *Song in a Weary Throat*, 279.

39. Pauli Murray to Mother [Pauline Dame], May 1, 1948, PM Papers, Schlesinger Library, Box 10, Folder 255; "91 Year Old Transit Vet Retiring after 65 Years of Service," *MTA*, August 30, 2013 (African-American Thomas Merrick made 90 cents an hour when he started work at the New York Transit Service as a Railroad Clerk in 1948). Maida probably made about $50 a week as a business agent, extrapolating from data provided in Patrick Renshaw, "Why Shouldn't a Union Man Be a Union Man? The ILGWU and FOUR," *Journal of American Studies* 29, no. 2 (August, 1995): 185–198. See also Interview with Maida Springer Kemp by Betty Balanoff, Program on Women and Work, Institute of Labor and Industrial Relations, Walter P. Reuther Library, Wayne State, University of Michigan, January 4, 1977, pp. 39–46.

40. Interview with Dollie Lowther Robinson by Bette Craig, Program on Women and Work, Institute of Labor and Industrial Relations, Walter P. Reuther Library, Wayne State, University of Michigan, July 1976, p. 14; Richards, *Maida Springer*, 68.

41. Karen Pastorello, *A Power among Them: Bessie Abramowitz Hillman and the Making of the Amalgamated Clothing Workers of America* (Urbana-Champaign: University of Illinois Press, 2008), 112–113.

42. Murray, *Song in a Weary Throat*, 278–279; Pauli Murray to Caroline Ware, June 1, 1954, PM Papers, Schlesinger Library, Box 101, Folder 1819; Richards, *Maida Springer*, 33–34, 44, 48, and 99.

43. Pauli Murray to Mother [Pauline Dame], December 15, 1947, PM Papers, Schlesinger Library, Box 10, Folder 254; Murray, *Song in a Weary Throat*, 273; Pauli Murray to Caroline Ware, March 6, 1948, PM Papers, Schlesinger Library, Box 101, Folder 1816.

44. Question 18 of Pauli Murray's application for admission to the Bar of the State of New York: In the Matter of the Application of Pauli Murray for Admission to Practice as an Attorney and Counselor-at-Law, New York Supreme Court, Appellate Division, Second Department, June 11, 1948; Pauli Murray to Mother [Pauline Dame], March 5 and 10, 1948, PM Papers, Schlesinger Library, Box 10, Folder, 255; Pauli Murray to Skipper [Caroline Ware], March 6, 1948, Box 101, Folder 1816; Pauli Murray to Mother [Pauline Dame], May 1, 1948, PM Papers, Schlesinger Library, Box 10, Folder 255.

45. Interview with Marry Norris, by author, October 10, 2015 (after Murray's death, Maida Springer Kemp told Marry W. Norris, a mutual friend, that Pauli had told Maida about her struggles over her gender identity but that Maida had dismissed them, saying, "that's ridiculous"); Pauli Murray to Mother [Pauline Dame], June 2, 1943, PM Papers, Schlesinger Library, Box 10, Folder 253; Pauli Murray to Mother [Pauline Dame], May 1, 1948, PM Papers, Schlesinger Library, Box 10, Folder 255; Richard L. Baltimore, "Affidavit in the Matter of the Application of Pauli Murray to Practice as an Attorney and Counselor-at-Law," In the Matter of the Application of Pauli Murray for Admission to Practice as an Attorney and Counselor-at-Law, New York Supreme Court, Appellate Division, Second Department, June 11, 1948; for Harriet Baltimore, see also clipping on Hunter College graduates, mid-year 1933, PM Papers, Schlesinger Library, Box 4, scrapbook 83v.

46. Murray, *Song in a Weary Throat*, 273.
47. In the Matter of the Application of Pauli Murray for Admission to Practice as an Attorney and Counselor-at-Law, New York Supreme Court, Appellate Division, Second Department, June 11, 1948.
48. Murray's letters to her Aunt Pauline in the spring of 1948 testify to the stress she experienced in winning acceptance to the New York State Bar. See letters in PM Papers, Schlesinger Library, Box 10, Folder 255.
49. Murray, *Song in a Weary Throat*, 294–295.
50. Pauli Murray to Billy Wynn, May, 26, 1943; Pauli Murray to Lerner and Silberwitz, April 4, 1947; William Wynn to Pauli Murray, May 4, 1948; Pauli Murray to William Wynn, May, 6, 1948, all in PM Papers, Schlesinger Library, Box 3, Folder 70.
51. On Mildred's comments on Wynn see Pauli Murray to Mother, May 6, 1948, PM Papers, Schlesinger Library, Box 3, Folder 255.
52. Report of Examining Member of the Committee on Character and Fitness, June 11, 1948, In the Matter of the Application of Pauli Murray for Admission to Practice as an Attorney and Counselor-at-Law, New York Supreme Court, Appellate Division, Second Department. According to James E. Pelzer, Clerk of the Court for the Appellate Division, 2nd Department, the average application for admission to the bar ran to 25–30 pages (interview by author, April 16, 2008).
53. Pauli Murray to Mother [Pauline Dame], June 2, 1948, PM Papers, Schlesinger Library, Box 10, Folder 255; Murray, *Song in a Weary Throat*, 295; Pauli Murray, Legal Diary, June 23, 1948, PM Papers, Schlesinger Library, Box 34.
54. Pauli Murray, Rider to no. 25 (b), In the Matter of the Application of Pauli Murray for Admission to Practice as an Attorney and Counselor-at-Law, New York Supreme Court, Appellate Division, Second Department, June 11, 1948; "Carson Baker Gets Top Dem County Post," *New York Amsterdam News*, October 3, 1953; "Carson DeWitt Baker: Lawyer with a Purpose," *New York Times*, June 30, 1960; Pauli Murray to Mother [Pauline Dame], July 14, 1948, PM Papers, Schlesinger Library, Box 10, Folder 255; Pauli Murray to Caroline Ware, October 17, 1948, PM Papers, Schlesinger Library, Box 101, Folder 1816.
55. Ruth Whitehead Whaley, "Women Lawyers Must Balk Both Color and Sex Bias," *New York Age*, October 29, 1949, 27; Murray, *Song in a Weary Throat*, 283–284.
56. Pauli Murray, Legal Diary, 1948, PM Papers, Schlesinger Library, Box 34 (for evidence that Murray called Maida Springer every day and Ruth Whitehead Whaley frequently); Whaley, "Women Layers Must Balk Both Color and Sex Bias."
57. Pauli Murray to Mother [Pauline Dame], July 14, 1948, PM Papers, Schlesinger Library, Box 10, Folder 255. I have summarized the kinds of cases that Murray handled from the files found in PM Papers, Schlesinger Library, Boxes 29–35.
58. Pauli Murray to Mother [Pauline Dame], July 14, 1948, PM Papers, Box 10, Folder 255; Murray, *Song in a Weary Throat*, 274.
59. Urith Josiah case, PM Papers, Schlesinger Library, Box 31, Folder 591; Murray, *Song in a Weary Throat*, 274–275. Murray used the pseudonym of Judith Hinson when she wrote about her representation of the beleaguered attorney in her memoir, Murray, *Song in a Weary Throat*, 274. According to the Social Security Death Index, Josiah was born in 1907 in Richmond, Virginia. According to the 1940 Federal Census, she was married but living with her aunt on West 111th Street. On admission to the bar see "Successful Bar Candidates," *New York Herald Tribune*, December 3, 1943. On her position as teacher, see "Lincoln Debaters Humbled Second Time by Union University," *New Journal and Guide*, March 19, 1932.
60. Interview with Dollie Lowther Robinson by Craig, 1–3 58–59; Richards, *Maida Springer*, 67–68; "Wage Board Named in Laundry Trade," *New York Times*, December 6, 1937; "Wait Final Count in Laundry Vote," *New York Amsterdam News*, June 17, 1950. For personal data on Adelmond, see ancestry.com: social security record, ship manifest.
61. Interview with Dollie Lowther Robinson, by Craig, 3.
62. For Pauli Murray's representation of Adelmond, see PM Papers, Schlesinger Library, Box 29, Folder 559.

63. PM Papers, Schlesinger Library, Box 29, Folder 559. On suspensions see "Laundry Workers Charge Bias in Brooklyn Local," *New York Amsterdam News*, September 28, 1940, Carl Lawrence, "Laundry Workers Election Looms," *New York Amsterdam News*, June 10, 1950.

64. "Carson DeWitt Baker: Lawyer with a Purpose," *New York Times*, June 30, 1960; Murray, *Song in a Weary Throat*, 273.

65. Murray, *Song in a Weary Throat*, 283–284; Thelma Stevens to Pauli Murray, November 9, 1948, PM Papers, Schlesinger Library, Box 75, Folder 1322.

66. Murray, *Song in a Weary Throat*, 284–285; "Bureau of Educational Institutions to Committee on the Study of Racial Policies and Practices," June 14, 1948, PM Papers, Schlesinger Library, Box 75, Folder 1332; Thelma Stevens to Pauli Murray, November 9, 1948, PM Papers, Schlesinger Library, Box 75, Folder 1323.

67. Thelma Stevens to Pauli Murray, December 21, 1948, PM Papers, Schlesinger Library, Box 76, Folder 1323; Murray, *Song in a Weary Throat*, 286.

68. Murray, *Song in a Weary Throat*, 286–287.

69. "State Laws against Discrimination I. Places of Accommodation and Amusement," "State Laws against Discrimination, II. Fields Other Than Public Accommodation," "Segregation Authorized or Required by State Law," PM Papers, Schlesinger Library, Box 75, Folder 1337.

70. Pauli Murray to Caroline Ware, March 31, 1950, PM Papers, Schlesinger Library, Box 101, Folder 1817.

71. Pauli Murray, *State Laws on Race and Color* (Cincinnati, OH: Women's Division of Christian Service, Board of Missions and Church Extensions, Methodist Church, 1950), 343–348; "Valuable Addition to the New York Library," *New York Amsterdam News*, April 28, 1951; Murray, *Song in a Weary Throat*, 288; Pauli Murray to Mother [Pauline Dame], March 21, 1951, PM Papers, Schlesinger Library, Box 10, Folder 256; also see Pauli Murray to Department of Taxation and Finance, NYS, July 11, 1951, PM Papers, Schlesinger Library, Box 7, Folder 187; Pauli Murray to J. B., June 23, 1951, PM Papers, Schlesinger Library, Box 4, Folder 73.

72. Pauli Murray, "Know Your Civil Rights" (*Pittsburgh*) *Courier Magazine*, September 21 and 29, October 6 and 13, 1951, PM Papers, Schlesinger Library, Box 85, Folder 1475.

73. Skipper [Caroline Ware] to Pauli Murray, "Pixies in Politics," September 25, 1949, Pauli Murray to Caroline Ware, October 20, 1949, PM Papers, Schlesinger Library, Box 101, Folder 1816; Murray, *Song in a Weary Throat*, 281. For press endorsements see "Pauli Murray Receives Full Citizens Union Endorsement, *Bedford Press*, October 27, 1949; "Brooklyn Rallies to Support Pauli Murray," *New York Age*, October 29, 1949; "Pauli Murray Would Add Glamour, Brains to Council," October 29, 1949, PM Paper, Box 73, Folder 1273; Pauli Murray to Caroline Ware, October 27, 1949, PM Papers, Schlesinger Library, Box 101, Folder 1816.

74. Pauli Murray to "Voter," October 28, 1949, PM Papers, Schlesinger Library, Box 73, Folder 1273; Maida Springer to "Friend," December 1, 1949, PM Papers, Schlesinger Library, Box 73, Folder 1273.

75. Pauli Murray to Skipper [Caroline Ware], April 22 and June 13, 1950, PM Papers, Schlesinger Library, Box 101, Folder 1817.

76. Pauli Murray to Milton R. Konvitz, March 7, 1952, PM Papers, Schlesinger Library, Box 72, Folder 1282; Caroline Ware makes this point in her letter to "Pixie" [Murray], December 8, 1951, PM Papers, Schlesinger Library, Box 101, Folder, 1817; Murray, *Song in a Weary Throat*, 295–296.

77. Pauli Murray to Skipper [Caroline Ware], January 26, 1950, Box 101, Folder 1817; see also handwritten notes, PM Papers, Schlesinger Library, Box 73, Folder 1282.

78. Natalie Gordon, "Gracious Ladies," *Boston Traveler*, Wednesday, November 7, 1945—a partial clipping of this story is in PM Papers, Schlesinger Library, Box 96, Folder 1688; Pauli Murray to Peg [Margaret Holmes Gilbert], March 18, 1973, PM Papers, Schlesinger Library, Box, 96, Folder 1688; Herbert A. Philbrick, *I Led 3 Lives: Citizen, Communist, Counterspy* (New York: Grosset & Dunlap, 1952), 238; Sharon Hartman Strom, *Political Woman: Florence Luscomb and the Legacy of Radical Reform* (Philadelphia: Temple University Press, 2001), 227; *Commonwealth v. Gilbert* 334 Mass. 71 (1956); "Sedition Charge against Chicago Woman Quashed," *Chicago Daily Tribune*, May 11, 1956; Pauli to Mother [Pauline Dame], June 17,

1947, PM Papers, Schlesinger Library, Box 10, Folder 264; Pauli to Skipper [Caroline Ware], June 10, 1947, PM Papers, Schlesinger Library, Box 101, Folder 1816.

79. Pauli to Mother [Pauline Dame], June 17, 1947, PM Papers, Schlesinger Library, Box 10, Folder 264; Pauli to Skipper [Caroline Ware], June 10, 1947, PM Papers, Schlesinger Library, Box 101, Folder 1816; Caroline Ware to Pauli Murray, PM Papers, June 24, 1952, PM Papers, Schlesinger Library, Box 101, Folder 1818.

80. Ellen Shrecker, *Many Are the Crimes: McCarthyism in America* (Boston: Little, Brown, 1998), 203; Robert Justin Goldstein, *American Blacklist: The Attorney General's List of Subversive Organizations* (Lawrence: University of Kansas Press, 2008), 11; Paula Fuchsberg, "1950s: Cornell Battles Red Scare," *Cornell Sun*, December 8, 1978.

81. For a summary of Murray's effort to secure a position at Cornell, see Pauli Murray to Lloyd K. Garrison, Lester B. Granger, William H. Hastie, Elmer A. Carter, A. Philip Randolph, Morris Milgram, Thurgood Marshall, Will Maslow, Thelma Stevens, Caroline F. Ware, and Eleanor Roosevelt, Memorandum, May 6, 1952, PM Papers, Schlesinger Library, Box 73, Folder 1283; Box 73; Pauli Murray to Lloyd K. Garrison et al., Memorandum, May 6, 1952, PM Papers, Schlesinger Library, Box 73, Folder 1283; M. P. Catherwood to Pauli Murray, May 21, 1952, PM Papers, Schlesinger Library, Box 73, Folder 1284.

Chapter 9

1. M. P. Catherwood to Pauli Murray, May 21, 1952, PM Papers, Schlesinger Library, Box, 73, Folder 1284; Pauli Murray, Diary Notes, Saturday, January 31, 1953, PM Papers, Schlesinger, Box 1, Folder 27; for use of "queerness," see Pauli Murray to Helene Hanff, November 16, 1955, PM Papers, Schlesinger Library, Box 97, Folder 1732; Pauli Murray, undated notes made with same light blue pen on the same legal pad paper as note dated July 1952, PM Papers, Schlesinger Library, Box, 1, Folder 27; Dora Willson, *The Self to the Self*, Pendle Hill Pamphlet #35 (Wallingford, PA: Pendle Hill Publications, 1946).

2. Pauli Murray, New York Lawyer's Diary and Manual, 1952, PM Papers, Schlesinger Library, Box 35; Pauli Murray to Skipper [Caroline Ware], January 21, 1953, PM Papers, Schlesinger Library, Box 1010, Folder 1818; Pauli Murray, Lawyer's Diary, 1952, PM Papers, Schlesinger Library, Box 35; Pauli Murray, tax return for 1952, PM Papers, Schlesinger Library, Box 7, Folder 187; Sinclair Weeks of the US Department of Commerce and Robert W. Burgess of the Bureau of the Census, "Family Income in the United States," *Current Population Reports: Consumer Income*, April 27, 1954, Series P-60, No. 15, Washington, DC.

3. Pauli Murray, diary notes, January 13, 22, 23, 1953, PM Papers, Schlesinger Library, Box 1, Folder 27.

4. Pauli Murray to Skipper [Caroline Ware], January 21, 1953, PM Papers, Schlesinger Library, Box 101, Folder 1818.

5. "Lady Lawyers," cover of *Jet*, January 22, 1953, PM Papers, scrapbook 80v; Eleanor Roosevelt, "Some of My Best Friends Are Negro," *Ebony*, February 1953, 19; Pauli Murray to Eleanor Roosevelt, January 21, 1953, Eleanor Roosevelt Papers, Roosevelt Library, Hyde Park, quoted in Patricia Bell-Scott, *The Firebrand and the First Lady: Portrait of a Friendship: Pauli Murray, Eleanor Roosevelt, and the Struggle for Social Justice* (New York: Knopf, 2016), 212. Murray used "between" scores of times in Pauli Murray, *Proud Shoes: The Story of an America Family* (New York: Harper & Brothers, 1956), see, for example, 55, 66, 67, 158, 252, 257.

6. Murray, *Song in a Weary Throat: An American Pilgrimage* (New York: Harper & Row, 1987), 21.

7. Murray, *Song in a Weary Throat*, 299. Rodell would later represent Martin Luther King Jr., Rachel Carson, and Betty Friedan.

8. Murray, *Song in a Weary Throat*, 298; Pauli Murray to Mother [Pauline Dame], March 25, 1952, PM Papers, Schlesinger Library, Box 10, Folder 255. The title *Proud Shoes* came from a review by Stephen Vincent Benét, of Paul Engle's 1934 book of poetry, *American Song*: "Here is somebody walking in America in proud shoes," quoted by Murray in her introduction to the 1978 edition of *Proud Shoes*.

9. Pauli Murray, fourth draft of Prologue (never published) for *Proud Shoes*, no date but likely 1952 or 1953, PM Papers, Schlesinger Library, Box 77, Folder 1365.

10. Pauli Murray to Caroline Ware, May 21, 1951, PM Papers, Schlesinger Library, Box 101, Folder 1817; Caroline Ware to Pauli Murray, March 6, 1952, Box 101, Folder 1818; Pauli Murray to Caroline Ware, December 16, 1953, PM Papers, Schlesinger Library, Box 78, Folder 1373; Murray tax return for 1954; Murray, *Song in a Weary Throat*, 299.

11. Murray's research notes from these trips can be found in PM Papers, Schlesinger Library, Box 77, Folders 1357–1364.

12. Pauli Murray to Skipper [Caroline Ware], May 18, 1954, PM Papers, Schlesinger Library, Box 101, Folder 1818; Murray, *Song in a Weary Throat*, 255; note also the importance of *Mendez*, to which Murray contributed: Philippa Strum, *Mendez v. Westminster: School Desegregation and Mexican-American Rights* (Lawrence: University of Kansas Press, 2010), 146–147.

13. Pauli Murray to Skipper [Caroline Ware], June 17, 1952, PM Papers, Schlesinger Library, Box 101, Folder 1818.

14. "G. W. Students to Present Play," *Washington Post*, May 6, 1934. On the founding of the William Alanson White Institute in New York City, see Clara Thompson, "The History of the William Alanson White Institute," available from the institute's office; there is also a brief history on the Institute's web page.

15. Pauli Murray to Skipper [Caroline Ware], August 11, 1954, PM Papers, Schlesinger Library, Box 101, Folder 1819; Pauli Murray, "Acknowledgements," *Proud Shoes*, 277.

16. Joanne Meyerowitz, *How Sex Changed: A History of Transsexuality in the United States* (Cambridge, MA: Harvard University Press, 2002), 106–120.

17. Edmund Ziman, *Jealousy in Children: A Guide for Parents* (New York: A. A. Wyn, 1949), 119–125; Peter G. S. Becket et al., "The Significance of Exogenous Trauma in the Genesis of Schizophrenia," *Psychiatry*, 19, 2 (May 1, 1956): 137–142.

18. Dr. May Edward Chinn to Whom This May Concern, Re: Atty. Pauli Murray, June 12, 1954, PM Papers, Schlesinger Library, Box 4, Folder 73; Pauli Murray to B. H. Hauptman, September 15, 1954, PM Papers, Schlesinger Library, Box 4, Folder 73.

19. On the challenges of diagnosing hyperthyroidism see S. Melmed et al., *Textbook of Endocrinology*, 12th ed. (Philadelphia, PA: Elsevier Saunders, 2011), chap 12. The first reported use of radioiodine to diagnose hyperthyroidism was in 1951: J. F. Goodwin et al., "The Use of Radioactive Iodine in the Assessment of Thyroid Function," *Quarterly Journal of Medicine* 80 (October 1951): 353–387.

20. Pauli Murray to Mother [Pauline Dame], June 26, 1954, PM Papers, Schlesinger Library, Box 10, Folder 255; Pauli Murray to Eleanor Roosevelt, July 4, 1954, PM Papers, Schlesinger Library, Box 99, Folder 1780.

21. Pauli Murray to B. H. Hauptman [insurance adjuster], September 15, 1954, PM Papers, Schlesinger Library, Box 4, Folder 73; Pauli Murray to Joe Lash, undated memo in Letters to Eleanor Roosevelt Folder, June 19, 1954, PM Papers, Schlesinger Library, Box 99, Folder 1780.

22. Pauli Murray to J. B. Johnson, July 7, 1954, PM Papers, Schlesinger Library, Box 4, Folder 73 (the "second memo" seems to have disappeared); Pauli Murray to Eleanor Roosevelt, July 4, 1954, PM Papers, Schlesinger Library, Box 99, Folder 1780; Pauli Murray to Edmund Ziman, July 7, 1954, PM Papers, Schlesinger Library, Box 4, Folder 73.

23. For Ziman's tenure at St. Elizabeth's see Ziman, see *Jealousy in Children*, x.

24. Pauli Murray to Attorney General of Commonwealth of Maryland and Superintendent of Crownsville Sate Hospital, Re: William H. Murray and Grace Murray Gwynn, July 4, 1954, PM Papers, Schlesinger Library, Box 10, Folder 231; Dr. Ralph H. Meng to Pauli Murray, September 22, 1954, PM Papers, Schlesinger Library, Box 10, Folder 231.

25. Pauli Murray to Dr. Clark, Re: Rosetta Stevens, March 14, 1977, PM Papers, Schlesinger Library, Box 97, Folder 1728; use of lithium dates back to the mid-nineteenth century but came into common use for mania only after 1949; see E. Shorter, "The History of Lithium Therapy," *Bipolar Disorder*, June 11, 2009, Supplement 2:4–9.

26. Pauli Murray to J. B. Johnson, July 7, 1954, PM Papers, Schlesinger Library, Box 4, Folder 73.

27. Leah Cahan Schaeffer and Connie Christine Wheeler, "Harry Benjamin's First Ten Cases (1938–1953): A Clinical Historical Note," *Archives of Sexual Behavior* 24, no. 1 (1995): 79–80, and 73–93; Ethel Person, MD, "Harry Benjamin: Creative Maverick," *Journal of Gay & Lesbian Mental Health* 12, no. 3 (2008): 259–275.

28. Pauli Murray to Edmund Ziman, July 7, 1954, PM Papers, Schlesinger Library, Box 4, Folder 73; Pauli Murray to Skipper [Caroline Ware], July 21, 1954, PM Papers, Schlesinger Library, Box 101, Folder 1819.

29. Murray, *Song in a Weary Throat*, 299; Lewis Isaacs to Pauli Murray, May 7, 1954, PM Papers, Schlesinger Library, Box 97, Folder 1731; Pauli Murray to Maida Springer, August 3 and 22, 1954, PM Papers, Schlesinger Library, Box 97, Folder 1731; Carter Wiseman, ed., *A Place for the Arts: The MacDowell Colony, 1907–2007* (Hanover, NH: MacDowell Colony, 2006), 12.

30. Pauli Murray, "Murray's Thursday Afternoon Review," August 12, 1954, PM Papers, Schlesinger Library, Box 97, Folder 1731; Pauli Murray to Skipper [Caroline Ware], August 11, 1954, PM Papers, Schlesinger Library, Box 101, Folder 1819.

31. Joseph Berger, "A Literary Friendship in Black and White," *New York Times*, September 13, 2004.

32. Pauli Murray, "Murray's Thursday Afternoon Review," August 12, 1954, PM Papers, Schlesinger Library, Box 97, Folder 1731.

33. Pauli Murray to Maida Springer, August 22, 1954, PM Papers, Schlesinger Library, Box 97, Folder 1731; Pauli Murray, "A Legacy of the South," never published but later incorporated into Murray's autobiography, *Song in a Weary Throat*, PM Papers, Schlesinger Library, Box 84, Folder 1456; James Baldwin, "Stranger in the Village, *Harpers*, October 1, 1953, pp. 42–48 (this essay became the final chapter of Baldwin's *Notes of a Native Son*). Murray reflected on Baldwin's "devastating indictment" of whites, contrasted her own "conciliatory" tone in Pauli Murray to Helene Hanff, November 26, 1955, PM Papers, Schlesinger Library, Box 97, Folder 1732. Helene Hanff, who arrived in September 1954, criticized Murray for engaging in a non-stop racial "harangue" at MacDowell: Helene Hanff to Pauli Murray, November 29, 1955, PM Papers, Schlesinger, Box 97, Folder 1732.

34. Henrietta Buckmaster, *Let My People Go: The Story of the Underground Railroad and the Growth of the Abolition Movement* (New York: Harper & Brothers, 1941).

35. See correspondence between Helene Hanff and Pauli Murray, correspondence from October 4, 1955, to January 16, 1956, PM Papers, Schlesinger Library, Box 97, Folders 1731–1732; Margalit Fox, "Helene Hanff, Wry Epistler of '84 Charing,' Dies at 80," *New York Times*, April 11, 1997; Sandra Barwick, "Charing Cross Road Writer Dies," *Daily Telegraph*, April 11, 1997; Dennis Barker, "A Tale of Two Cities," *Guardian*, April 11, 1997; Pauli Murray to Helene Hanff, November 16, 1955, PM Papers, Schlesinger Library, Box 97, Folder 1732. For the masculine meaning of "queer" in the first half of the twentieth century, see George Chauncey, *Gay New York: Gender, Urban Culture, and the Making of the Gay Male World, 1890–1940* (New York: Basic Books, 1994), 99–127.

36. Pauli Murray to Butch [Helene Hanff], November 26, 1955, PM Papers, Schlesinger Library, Box 97, Folder 1732; Hanff to Sugar [Murray], November 29, 1955, (Cookie), December 9, 1955, PM Papers, Schlesinger Library, Box 97, Folder 1732; Pauli Murray to Helene Hanff, October 7, 1955, PM Papers, Schlesinger Library, Box 97, Folder 1731. On the history of the Daughters of Bilitis, see John D'Emilio, *Sexual Politics, Sexual Communities: The Making of Homosexual Minority in the United States, 1940–1970*, 2nd ed. (Chicago: University of Chicago Press, 1998), 101–125; Marcia M. Gallo, *Different Daughters: A History of the Daughters of Bilitis and the Rise of the Lesbian Rights Movements* (Emeryville, CA: Seal Press, 2007), 1–20.

37. Pauli Murray, fourth draft of Prologue, no date, PM Papers, Schlesinger Library, Box 77, Folder 1365; Caroline Ware to Pauli Murray, November 22, 1953, PM Papers, Schlesinger Library, Box 78, Folder 1373; Pauli Murray to Caroline Ware, December 16, 1953, PM Papers, Schlesinger Library, Box 78, Folder 1373; Pauli Murray to Helen Lockwood, December 16, 1953, PM Papers, Schlesinger Library, Box 78, Folder 1373; Helen Lockwood to Caroline Ware, December 6, 1953, PM Papers, Schlesinger Library, Box 78, Folder 1373.

38. Jacquelyn Dowd Hall, "The Long Civil Rights Movement and the Political Uses of the Past," *Journal of American History* 91, no. 4 (March 2005): 1233–1263.

39. Pauli Murray to Skipper [Caroline Ware], October 29, 1954, PM Papers, Schlesinger Library, Box 78, Folder 137.

40. Murray made $875 from typing in 1955. See Pauli Murray, tax return for 1955, PM Papers, Schlesinger Library, Box 7, Folder 187; Daniel Horowitz, *Betty Friedan and the*

Making of The Feminine Mystique: *The American Left, The Cold War, and Modern Feminism* (Amherst: University of Massachusetts Press, 1998), 180–184, 317, n. 31. I am grateful to Dan Horowitz for sharing with me an undated bill for typing from Murray in Friedan's papers.

41. Pauli Murray, *Proud Shoes: The Story of an America Family* (New York: Harper & Brothers, 1956), 1–23. For a particularly insightful reading see Saunders Redding, "Dramatic Chronicle of a Mixed Heritage," *New York Herald Tribune*, October 28, 1956.

42. Murray, *Proud Shoes*, 270–271.

43. Annette Gordon-Reed, *The Hemingses of Monticello: An American Family* (New York: W. W. Norton, 2008); Pauli Murray, *Proud Shoes*, p. 62.

44. Murray, *Proud Shoes*, 271; A. McBean to the editor of the *New York Amsterdam News*, November 9, 1939, PM Papers, Schlesinger Library, Box 4, Folder 71; Louis Wirth, "The Problem of Minority Groups," in *The Science of Man in the World Crisis*, edited by Ralph Linton (New York: Columbia University Press, 1945), 347–372; Helen Mayer Hacker, "Women as a Minority Group," *Social Forces* 30 (1951): 60–69.

45. Pauli Murray to Caroline Ware, August 21, 1955, PM Papers, Schlesinger Library, Box 97, Folder 1731; PM to Muriel Aylen, November 29, 1955, PM Papers, Schlesinger Library, Box 97, Folder 1732.

46. Henrietta Buckmaster, "Indomitable Family, *New York Times*, October 21, 1956; Ted Poston, "A Truly American Family," *New York Post*, October 21, 1956; Margaret Jackson, "A Negro Writes of Civil War, Slavery," *Akron Beacon Journal*, October 21, 1956; and Eleanor Roosevelt, "Mrs. Roosevelt: 'Proud Shoes' Will Bring Pride to Negro Citizens," *Washington Daily News*, October 24, 1956, all in PM Papers, Schlesinger Library, Box 79, Folder 1383v, saved in "Proud Shoes Scrapbook".

47. Roi Ottley, [a black journalist] "An Unknown Aspect of U.S.," *Chicago Daily Tribune*, November 18, 1956, PM Papers, Schlesinger Library, Box 79, Folder 1383v, saved in "Proud Shoes Scrapbook"; Edwin White to the editor of the *New York Times*, December 1, 1955; Pauli Murray to Helene Hanff (commenting on the White letter), December 10, 1955, PM Papers, Schlesinger Library, Box 97, Folder 1732.

48. Patricia Speights, "Only Half Picture Painted; Serves No Useful Purpose," *Clarion-Ledger & Jackson Daily News*, October 14 or 15, 1956, PM Papers, Schlesinger Library, Box 79, Folder 1383v, saved in "Proud Shoes Scrapbook" and marked "the only negative review."

49. See Murray's tax returns for these years, PM Papers, Schlesinger Library, Box 7, Folders 190–191.

50. Murray, *Song in a Weary Throat*, 306–307.

51. Pauli Murray to Eleanor Roosevelt, February 16, 1956, PM Papers, Schlesinger Library, Box 99, Folder 1780.

52. See Robert Halasz, "Paul, Weiss, Rifkind, Wharton, and Garrison," in the *International Directory of Company Histories*, edited by Jay P. Peterson (University Park: Pennsylvania State University Press, 2001, digitized in 2009). See also www.PaulWeiss.com for a history of the firm.

53. Louis Stark, "Lawyer of NLRB Changed Her Mind," *New York Times*, January 11, 1940; Landon R. Y. Storrs, *The Second Red Scare and the Unmaking of the New Deal Left* (Princeton, NJ: Princeton University Press, 2013), 6–10, 23–24, 47, 61–66.

54. Lloyd K. Garrison, Testimonial to Irene Barlow, read at the luncheon in her honor, on the occasion of her leaving Paul, Weiss, to take a job as personnel director, next door at the Rugoff Theaters, Inc., August 20, 1965, PM Papers, Schlesinger Library, Box 5, Folder 136.

55. Pauli Murray to Skipper [Caroline Ware], November 7, 1956; Skipper [Caroline Ware] to Pauli Murray, November 10, 1956, PM Papers, Schlesinger Library, Box 101, Folder 1820.

56. Pauli Murray to Skipper [Caroline Ware], November 7, 1956; Skipper [Caroline Ware] to Pauli Murray, November 10, 1956.

57. Pauli Murray to William Hastie, May 28, 1958, PM Papers, Schlesinger Library, Box 81, Folder 1424.

58. Jay Topkis, interview by author, February 21, 2008.

59. Topkis, interview by author; Anne Thacher Clarke Anderson, interview by author, May 17, 2008; Pauli Murray to William Hastie, May 28, 1958, PM Papers, Schlesinger Library, Box 81, Folder 1424.

60. Murray, *Song in a Weary Throat*, 312; Pauli Murray to William Hastie, May 28, 1958, PM Papers, Schlesinger Library, Box 81, Folder 1424. For a sampling of Murray's briefs see PM Papers, Schlesinger Library, Boxes 35–37.

61. Murray, *Song in a Weary Throat*, 312.

62. Pauli Murray to William Hastie, May 28, 1958, PM Papers, Schlesinger Library, Box 81, Folder 1424.

63. *Chambers v. Florida*, 309 U.S. 227 (1940); Pauli Murray to William Hastie, May 28, 1958, PM Papers, Schlesinger Library, Box 81, Folder 1424.

64. Debra Bruno, "Justice Ginsburg Remembers Her First Steps in the Law," *National Law Journal*, November 13, 2007; Murray, *Song in a Weary Throat*, 313.

65. Ann Thacher Clarke Anderson, interview by author, May 17, 2008.

66. On McIntosh, see Rosenberg, *Changing the Subject*, 215–216; for Ashbey, see "Miss Julia Lovett Becomes Engaged," *New York Times*, October 28, 1956; Julia E. S. Lovett Is Married Here," *New York Times*, March 3, 1957; "W. N. Ashbeys Have Child," *New York Times*, July 5, 1961; Mrs. Ashbey Has Daughter," *New York Times*, July 9, 1963; "Daughter to Mrs. Ashbey," *New York Times*, July 12, 1964; Norma Juliet Wikler and Lynn Hacht Schafran, "Learning from the New Jersey Supreme Court Task Force on Women in the Courts: Evaluation Recommendations and Implications for Other States," *Women's Rights Law Reporter* (Rutgers Law School) 12, no. 4 (Winter, 1991): 365, 371.

67. Debra Bruno, "Justice Ginsburg Remembers Her First Steps in the Law," *National Law Journal*, November 13, 2007; David Margolick, "Judge Ginsburg's Life: A Trial by Adversity," *New York Times*, June 25, 1993; Mitchel Ostrer, "A Profile of Ruth Bader Ginsburg," *Juris Doctor* (October 1977): 34.

68. Margolick, "Judge Ginsburg's Life: A Trial by Adversity."

69. Bruno, "Justice Ginsburg Remembers Her First Steps in the Law"; Ruth Bader Ginsburg to author, January 13, 1999 (by "two-fer" Ginsburg meant that the firm had both a black and a woman in Murray and saw no reason to hire another woman).

70. Ann Thacher Clarke Anderson, interview by author.

71. Ann Thacher Clarke Anderson, interview by author.

72. Ann Thacher Clarke Anderson, interview by author; Ruth Bader Ginsburg to author, October 20, 2015.

73. Murray, *Song in a Weary Throat*, 314–315.

74. Pauli Murray, "What I Learned from Irene Barlow," March 12, 1973, PM Papers, Schlesinger Library, Box 6, Folder 161.

75. Murray, "What I Learned from Irene Barlow," March 12, 1973; Irene Barlow, curriculum vitae, 1969, PM Papers, Schlesinger Library, Box 5, Folder 136.

76. Murray, *Song in a Weary Throat*, 315–316; Pauli Murray to William Hastie, May 28, 1958, PM Papers, Schlesinger Library, Box 81, Folder 1424.

77. Murray, *Song in a Weary Throat*, 316–317; Pauli Murray, "What I Learned from Irene Barlow," March 12, 1973, and Murray, To Those Who Loved Irene Barlow, March 7, 1973, PM Papers, Schlesinger Library, Box 6, Folder 167.

78. Murray, *Song in a Weary Throat*, 315, 363; Murray, To Those Who Loved Irene Barlow, March 7, 1973, PM Papers, Schlesinger Library, Box 6, Folder 161. Irene Barlow lived with her mother at 945 Second Avenue until they moved to Peter Cooper Village, for its elevator, light, and view of the East River.

79. Jay Topkis, interview by author; Caroline Ware to Pauli Murray, October 17, 1958, PM Papers, Schlesinger Library, Box 101, Folder 1821.

80. For her work handling small claims at Paul, Weiss, see PM Papers, Schlesinger Library, Box 35, Folder 650

81. Timothy B. Tyson, *Radio Free Dixie: Robert F. Williams and the Roots of Black Power* (Chapel Hill: University of North Carolina Press, 1999), 143; Pauli Murray, "Collect from Poplarville," and "For Mack C. Parker," in Murray, *Dark Testament* (Norwalk, CT: Silvermine Press, 1970), 38–39.

82. Tyson, *Radio Free Dixie*, 149, and 143–149.

83. Pauli Murray, notes on Robert F. Williams case, Box 127, Folders 2312; Tyson, *Radio Free Dixie*, 160, 164.

Chapter 10

1. Yevette Richards, *Maida Springer: Pan-Africanist and International Labor Leader* (Pittsburgh: University of Pittsburgh Press, 2000), 206. The potential impact of Murray's teaching is addressed in "Wide Wide World: Nigeria-Ghana," *New York Amsterdam News*, September 3, 1960. On the lure of Africa in 1960 for young Americans see Daniel Horowitz, *On the Cusp: The Yale College Class of 1960 and a World on the Verge of Change* (Amherst: University of Massachusetts Press, 2015), chapter 4.

2. Richards, *Maida Springer*, 95–102, 129, 206; James T. Campbell, *Middle Passages: African American Journeys to Africa, 1787–2005* (New York: Penguin Press, 2006), 315–319.

3. Richards, *Maida Springer*, 102.

4. Pauli Murray, *Song in a Weary Throat: An American Pilgrimage* (New York: Harper & Row, 1987), 318; Pauli Murray, diary, February 19, 1959, PM Papers, Schlesinger Library, Radcliffe Institute, Harvard University, Box 1, Folder 28.

5. Yevette Richards, *Conversations with Maida Springer: A Personal History of Labor, Race, and International Relations* (Pittsburgh: University of Pittsburgh Press, 2004), 227; Pauli Murray, "Dark Testament," *South Today* (Winter, 1944), 45.

6. J. A. H. Lang to Pauli Murray, June 3, 1959, and Pauli Murray to Ako Adjei, November 20, 1959, both in PM Papers, Schlesinger Library, Box 41, Folder 729; Arthur Sutherland to Pauli Murray, September 23, 1959, and Pauli Murray to Arthur Sutherland, October 2, 1959, both in PM Papers, Schlesinger Library, Box 41, Folder 729; William Blair [of Stevenson, Rifkind & Wirts in Chicago] to Pauli Murray, June 23, 1959; Adlai Stevenson to Robert Jackson, January 21, 1960; Pauli Murray to Lloyd K. Garrison, October 1, 1959; Geoffrey Bing to Pauli Murray, November 9, 1959; and Pauli Murray to Ako Adjei, November 20, 1959, all in PM Papers, Schlesinger Library, Box 41, Folder 729; Jayanth K. Krishnan, "Academic SAILERS: The Ford Foundation and the Efforts to Shape Legal Education in Africa, 1957–1977," *American Diary of Legal History* 52 (2012): 261–324.

7. J. H. A. Lang to PM, November 18, 1959, PM Papers, Schlesinger Library, Box 41, Folder 729; Pauli Murray, Tax Returns for 1959 and 1960, PM Papers, Schlesinger Library, Box 7, Folder 188–189. As of 1959, Murray's rent for her three-room flat at 388 Chauncey Street in Brooklyn was $600 a year. The proposed rent for a house in Accra was 150 pounds (or about $441): Pauli Murray, Budget, 1959, PM Papers, Schlesinger Library, Box 8, Folder 200. Murray revealed her distress at being underpaid in an undated fragment, PM Papers, Schlesinger Library, Box 41, Folder 723.

8. Pauli Murray, loose-leaf diary, February 7, 1960, and small bound diary, February 3 to February 23, 1960, PM Papers, Schlesinger Library, Box 41, Folder 710 (Murray recorded her crossing in both a small bound diary, given to her by a friend just before departure, and, at greater length, in loose-leaf pages); Murray to Family and Friends, May 15, 1960, PM Papers, Schlesinger Library, Box 41, Folder 723.

9. Harold Isaacs to Pauli Murray, December 7, 1959, PM Papers, Schlesinger Library, Box 97, Folder 1708; Murray, loose-leaf diary, February 7, 1960, PM Papers, Schlesinger Library, Box 41, Folder 710; Harold Isaacs to Pauli Murray, December 7 and 17, 1959, PM Papers, Schlesinger Library, Box 97, Folder 1708.

10. Murray to Family and Friends, May 15, 1960, PM Papers, Schlesinger Library, Box 41, Folder 723; "Negroes in South in Store Sit Down; Carolina College Students Fight Woolworth Ban on Lunch Service," *New York Times*, February 3, 1960; "N. C. Lunch Counter Bias Protest Spreads: Passive 'Sitdown' Protests Sweep Stores in Big Cities," *Atlanta Daily World*, February 10, 1960.

11. Pauli Murray to Family and Friends, May 15, 1960, PM Papers, Schlesinger Library, Box 41, Folder 723.

12. Pauli Murray to Family and Friends, May 15, 1960; Pauli Murray to Caroline Ware, March 14, 1960, PM Papers, Schlesinger Library, Box 101, Folder 1822; Murray wrote of her dissatisfaction in her diary, April 5, 1960, and June 3, 1960, Box 41, Folder 710.

13. Pauli Murray to Caroline Ware, March 14, 1960, PM Papers, Schlesinger Library, Box 101, Folder 1822; Murray, diary, April 5 and June 3, 1960, PM Papers, Schlesinger Library, Box 41, Folder 710. For a later reference to suffering malaria attacks, despite taking medication, see

Pauli Murray to Fowler and Miriam Harper, no date (but in context likely the spring of 1961), PM Papers, Schlesinger Library, Box 20, Folder 433.

14. Pauli Murray to Family and Friends, May 15, 1960, PM Papers, Schlesinger Library, Box 41, Folder 723.

15. Murray, diary, April 5 and August 21, 1960, PM Papers, Schlesinger Library, Box 41, Folder 710.

16. Murray, diary, June 4, 1960, PM Papers, Schlesinger Library, Box 41, Folder 710.

17. Murray, diary, March 1 and 8, April 5, and June 3, 1960, PM Papers, Schlesinger Library, Box 41, Folder 710; Campbell, *Middle Passages*, 333–334, 357.

18. Murray, diary, June 1 and 4, 1960, PM Papers, Schlesinger Library, Box 41, Folder 710; Skipper [Caroline Ware] to Pixie [Pauli Murray], December 27, 1960, PM Papers, Schlesinger Library, Box 101, Folder 1822; Pauli Murray to Irene Barlow, September 19, 1960, PM Papers, Box 5, Folder 138; Michael Scott, *A Time to Speak* (London: Faber and Faber, 1958), 177, 322.

19. Pauli Murray, Newsletter, February 29 and June 11, PM Papers, Schlesinger Library, Box 41, Folders 721–722; Murray to Irene Barlow, July 1, 1960, PM Papers, Schlesinger Library, Box 5, Folder 138.

20. Pauli Murray, "Newsletter: American in Ghana: Easter in Ghana," April 18, 1960, PM Papers, Schlesinger Library, Box 41, Folder 722.

21. Murray, "Newsletter: American in Ghana: Easter in Ghana."

22. Murray, "Newsletter: American in Ghana: Easter in Ghana."

23. Murray, "Newsletter: American in Ghana: Easter in Ghana."

24. Pauli Murray, "What Is Africa to Me? A Question of Identity," December 1960, draft essay, part II, p. 7, PM Papers, Schlesinger Library, Box 85, Folder 1479.

25. Murray, "What Is Africa to Me?" part II, p. 8.

26. "Wide Wide World: Nigeria-Ghana," *New York Amsterdam News*, September 3, 1960; Hazel La Marre, "Africa and the World," *Los Angeles Sentinel*, August 4, 1960; Harold Isaacs to Pauli Murray, May 11, 1960, PM Papers, Schlesinger Library, Box 41, Folder 713.

27. La Marre, "Africa and the World."

28. Campbell, *Middle Passages*, 316–317; Murray, diary, September 7, 1960, PM Papers, Schlesinger Library, Box 41, Folder 710; Leslie Rubin and Pauli Murray, *The Constitution and Government of Ghana* (London: Sweet & Maxwell, 1961), 59 footnote 15, 68–69; "Parliament of Ghana: A Historical Background of the Legislature of Ghana," African Elections Project, January 7, 2009.

29. Murray, diary, September 7, 1960, PM Papers, Schlesinger Library, Box 41, Folder 710.

30. Anna Arnold Hedgeman, *The Trumpet Sounds: A Memoir of Negro Leadership* (New York: Holt, Rinehart and Winston, 1964), 137–139; Hedgeman, "Women in Public Life," keynote address at the Conference on African Women and Women of African Descent, Accra, Ghana, July 18, 1960, PM Papers, Schlesinger Library, Box 129, Folder 2335.

31. Phil Bartle, "Modernisation and the Decline in Women's Status: Covert Gynocracy in an Akan Community," 2007, cec.vcn.bc.ca/cmp/; Christine Oppong and Katherine Abu, *Seven Roles of Women: Impact of Education, Migration, and Employment on Ghanaian Mother*, Women, Work, and Development, No.13 (Geneva: International Labour Office, 1987), 78; Murray, "American in Ghana: Easter in Ghana," Newsletter, April 18, 1960, PM Papers, Schlesinger Library, Box 41, Folder 722.

32. Pauli Murray, Newsletter, February 29, 1960, PM Papers, Schlesinger Library, Box 41, Folder 722; David Owusu-Ansah, "Society and Its Environment," in *A Country Study: Ghana*, edited by LaVerle Berry (Washington, DC: Federal Research Division, Library of Congress, 1995), ch. 2.

33. Pauli Murray, fragment of notes on the women's conference, July 22, 1960, PM Papers, Schlesinger Library, Box 41, Folder 723; Kevin Gaines, *American Africans in Ghana: Black Expatriates in the Civil Rights Era* (Chapel Hill: University of North Carolina Press, 2006), 123; Hedgeman, *The Trumpet Sounds*, 138–139; Murray, *Song in a Weary Throat*, 339.

34. Gaines, *American Africans in Ghana*, 120.

35. Murray, diary, June 22 and July 2, 1960, PM Papers, Schlesinger Library, Box 41, Folder 710; Murray, "American in Ghana," June 30, 1960, PM Papers, Schlesinger Library, Box 5, Folder 138; Pauli Murray to the editor of the *New York Times* (unpublished), August 28, 1960, PM

Papers, Schlesinger Library, Box 5, Folder 138, written in response to a series on Africa, by Dana Adams Schmidt, which culminated in "The United States in the Congo," August 21, 1960; Pauli Murray to Irene Barlow, 1960 (no day or month noted), and March 4, 1961, PM Papers, Schlesinger Library, Box 5, Folder 138.

36. Murray, diary, September 14, 1960, PM Papers, Schlesinger Library, Box 41, Folder 710; Harold Isaacs, "Reporter at Large: Back to Africa," *New Yorker*, May 13, 1961, 138.

37. Murray, diary, September 14, 1960, PM Papers, Schlesinger Library, Box 41, Folder 710.

38. Murray, diary, May 5 and September 3, 1960, PM Papers, Schlesinger Library, Box 41, Folder 710.

39. Pauli Murray, diary, September 18, 1960, PM Papers, Schlesinger Library, Box 4, Folder 710; Pauli Murray to Irene Barlow, undated fragment, marked 1960, PM Papers, Schlesinger Library, Box 5, Folder 138.

40. Richards, *Conversations with Maida Springer*, 227; Skipper [Caroline Ware] to Pixie [Pauli Murray], September 17, 1960, and November 13, 1960, PM Papers, Schlesinger Library, Box 101, Folder 1822; Pauli Murray to Irene Barlow, September 8, 1960, PM Papers, Schlesinger Library, Box 5, Folder 138.

41. Adlai Stevenson summarized what Murray expected to find in his letter to Robert Jackson, January 21, 1960, PM Papers, Schlesinger Library, Box 41, Folder 729; Murray, *Song in a Weary Throat*, 335–336.

42. Pauli Murray, "On Teaching Constitutional Law in Ghana," *Yale Law Report* 8, no. 1 (Fall 1961): 13, PM Papers, Schlesinger Library, Box 45, Folder 804; Murray, *Song in a Weary Throat*, 336.

43. Murray, *Song in a Weary Throat*, 339.

44. Thomas I. Emerson, "Fowler Vincent Harper," *Yale Law Diary*, 74 (1964–1965), 601; *Poe v. Ullman*, 367 U.S. 497 (1961); Murray, *Song in a Weary Throat*, 339; Murray, "Syllabus: Constitutional and Administrative Law, I, Ghana School of Law," Fall 1960 Term, PM Papers, Schlesinger Library, Box 42, Folder 732.

45. Pauli Murray to Fowler and Miriam Harper, no date (but in context likely the spring of 1961), PM Papers, Schlesinger Library, Box 20, Folder 433; Fowler Harper to Pauli Murray, May 25, 1961, PM Papers, Schlesinger Library, Box 20, Folder 432; Murray, *Song in a Weary Throat*, 340. For the approximate date of Harper's visit to Ghana School of Law see Murray, "On Teaching Constitutional Law in Ghana," 13. The second visitor was her friend William Hastie, by then a judge on the Third Circuit Court of Appeals, on his way back to the United States from the Logos conference in Nigeria in January 1961.

46. Leslie Rubin and Pauli Murray, *The Constitution and Government of Ghana* (London: Sweet & Maxwell, 1961), 59 footnote 15, 68–69.

47. Murray, *Song in a Weary Throat*, 340–342.

48. Murray, *Song in a Weary Throat*, 342; Robert Fay, "Joseph Kwame Kyeretwi Boakye Danquah," in *Encyclopedia of Africa*, vol. I, edited by Anthony Appiah and Louis Henry Gates (New York: Oxford University Press, 2010), 342; "Joseph Danquah, Foe of Nkrumah; Leader for Independence in Ghana Dies a Prisoner," *New York Times*, February 5, 1965.

49. Murray, *Song in a Weary Throat*, 342–343; George Goodman, "Africa and the World," *Los Angeles Sentinel*, February 18, 1965.

50. Murray, *Song in a Weary Throat*, 338, 346.

51. Pauli Murray to Irene Barlow, n.d (1960), PM Papers, Schlesinger Library, Box 5, Folder 138; Dana Adams Schmidt, "The United States in the Congo," *New York Times*, August 21, 1960.

52. Murray, diary, September 14, 1960, PM Papers, Schlesinger Library, Box 41, Folder 710.

53. Murray, diary, September 3, 1960, PM Papers, Schlesinger Library, Box 41, Folder 710.

54. Murray, diary, September 3, 1960.

55. Skipper [Caroline Ware] to Pixie [Pauli Murray], November 25, 1960; Pixie to Skipper, December 2 and 8, 1960; Skipper to Pixie, December 10, 1960, all in PM Papers, Schlesinger Library, Box 1010, Folder 1822; for a time, the article was really two in one: the first on the matter of identity, the second on the role of the American black in the Cold War. On West Africa, see Harold Isaacs, "Reporter at Large: Back to Africa," *New Yorker*, May 13, 1961, pp. 105–143; on East Africa, see Louis Lomax, *The Reluctant African* (New York: Harper & Brothers, 1960), 39–40, 48, 62–63.

56. Pauli Murray to Harold Isaacs, November 5, and 21, 1961, as well as January 2, 1961; and Isaacs to Murray, March 2, 1961, Isaacs Papers, MIT Archives, Box 37, quoted in Carol Polsgrove, *Divided Minds: Intellectuals and the Civil Rights Movement* (New York: W. W. Norton, 2001), 137–138. Murray mentioned trying to get published in the *Saturday Evening Post* in a letter to Caroline Ware, December 2, 1960, PM Papers, Schlesinger Library, Box 101.

57. Isaacs, "A Reporter at Large: Back to Africa," *New Yorker*, May 13, 1961, pp. 105–142; Isaacs to Murray, April 10, 1961, Isaacs Papers, quoted in Polsgrove, *Divided Minds*, 141.

58. Murray to Isaacs, May 28, 1961, Isaacs Papers, quoted in Polsgrove, *Divided Minds*, 141.

59. Ware to Isaacs, June 18, 1961; Isaacs to Ware, June 19, 1961, in Isaacs Papers, quoted in Polsgrove, *Divided Minds*, 142.

60. Harold Isaacs, "Reporter at Large: Back to Africa," *New Yorker*, May 13, 1961, pp. 116–119.

Chapter 11

1. Pauli Murray, *Song in a Weary Throat: An American Pilgrimage* (New York: Harper & Row, 1987), 340.

2. Murray, *Song in a Weary Throat*, 340.

3. Telegram from Eleanor Roosevelt to Pauli Murray, April 4, 1962, PM Papers, Schlesinger Library, Radcliffe Institute, Harvard University, Box 49, Folder 875; Pauli Murray to Mother [Pauline Fitzgerald Dame], June 18, 1946, PM Papers, Box 10, Folder 254.

4. Nancy Cott, *The Grounding of Modern Feminism* (New Haven, CT: Yale University Press, 1987); Alice Kessler-Harris, *In Pursuit of Equity: Women, Men, and the Quest for Economic Citizenship in 20th-Century America* (New York: Oxford University Press, 2001).

5. Murray, *Song in a Weary Throat*, 347; Eleanor Roosevelt, "Some of My Best Friends Are Negro," *Ebony*, February 1953, p. 19. For Roosevelt and Murray's influence on each other, see Patricia Bell-Scott, *The Firebrand and the First Lady: Portrait of a Friendship: Pauli Murray, Eleanor Roosevelt, and the Struggle for Social Justice* (New York: Knopf, 2016).

6. Pauli Murray, class notes for "Constitutional Litigation, Spring 1962" and "Political and Civil Rights, Spring 1962," PM Papers, Schlesinger Library, Box 20, Folder 437.

7. *Hoyt v. Florida* 368 U.S. 57 (1961); Linda K. Kerber, *No Constitutional Right to Be Ladies: Women and the Obligations of Citizenship* (New York: Hill and Wang, 1998), 177–185.

8. David Garrow, *Liberty and Sexuality: The Right to Privacy and the Making of Roe v. Wade* (New York: Macmillan, 1994), 170–171; Robert W. Gordon, "Professors and Policy Makers: Yale Law School Faculty in the New Deal and After," in *The History of Yale Law School: The Tercentennial Lectures*, edited by Anthony T. Kronman (New Haven, CT: Yale University Press, 2004), 75–137.

9. Joan Steinau Lester, *Fire in My Soul: Eleanor Holmes Norton* (New York: Atria Books, 2003), 106–107; Murray, *Song in a Weary Throat*, 345. Eleanor Holmes wrote the history paper for a master's degree in American Studies (in addition to her law degree).

10. Lester, *Fire in My Soul*, 106–107; see picture in Marylin Bender, "Black Women in Civil Rights: Is She a Second-Class Citizen?" *New York Times*, September 2, 1969. For Murray's use of lipstick, see Pauli Murray to Paul Goranson, PM Papers, Schlesinger Library, Box 22, Folder 463.

11. For ongoing psychotherapy, see Pauli Murray, names of Yale psychiatrists in address book for years at Yale, PM Papers, Schlesinger Library, Box 3, Folder 67.

12. Cynthia Harrison, *On Account of Sex: The Politics of Women's Issues, 1945–1968* (Berkeley: University of California Press, 1988), 109–110; Kessler-Harris, *In Pursuit of Equity*, 215–289.

13. Cynthia Harrison, *On Account of Sex*, 109–110; Dorothy Sue Cobble, *The Other Women's Movement: Workplace Justice and Social Rights in Modern America* (Princeton, NJ: Princeton University Press, 2004), 44, 52; "Mrs. Robinson Quits D.C. Post; Joins 144," *New York Amsterdam News*, June 1963.

14. Harrison, *On Account of Sex*, 113–115. Margaret Mead and Frances Balgley Kaplan, eds., *American Women: The Report of the President's Commission on the Status of Women and Other Publications of the Commission* (New York: Scribner, 1965), 264–265; Judith Hillman

Paterson, *Be Somebody: A Biography of Marguerite Rawalt* (Austin, TX: Eakin Press, 1986), 51, 56, 62.

15. Alvin Shuster, "President Names Panel on Women," *New York Times*, December 15, 1961; Murray, *Song in a Weary Throat*, 347.

16. Cobble, *Other Women's Movement*, 160–161.

17. Caroline Ware, "Background Memorandum on the Status of Women," Papers of the President's Commission on the Status of Women, John F. Kennedy Library, Boston, MA, available on microfilm, reel 3.

18. Bureau of the Census, United States, *The Statistical History of the United States, from Colonial Times to the Present* (New York: Basic Books, 1976), 131–133.

19. Susan Hartmann, "Women's Employment and the Domestic Ideal in the Early Postwar Years," in *Not June Cleaver: Women and Gender in Postwar America, 1945–1960*, edited by Joanne Meyerowitz (Philadelphia: Temple University Press, 1994), 86.

20. Harrison, *On Account of Sex*, 123–124.

21. Biography, Mary Eastwood Papers, Schlesinger Library; Harrison, *On Account of Sex*, 125–126.

22. Pauli Murray to Edith Green, August 19, 1962, PM Papers, Schlesinger Library, Box 49, Folder 875; "To Become Emeriti," *Barnard Bulletin*, May 3, 1967 (on Phoebe Morrison); Phoebe Morrison to Pauli Murray, September 10, 1962, PM Papers, Schlesinger Library, Box 49, Folder 879. See also notes on conversation with Phoebe Morrison: "Constitutional Approach to Discrimination against Women," September 20, 1962, PM Papers, Box 49, Folder 880.

23. Murray, *Song in a Weary Throat*, 350; Albert Lowenfels, "The Case of the Well-Known Woman with Unexplained Anemia," *Medscape*, September 9, 2010.

24. For an excellent analysis of Murray's use of race-gender analogies and its impact, see Serena Mayeri, "'A Common Fate of Discrimination': Race-Gender Analogies in Legal and Historical Perspective." *Yale Law Journal* 110, no. 6 (April 2001): 1045–1088, and Mayeri, *Reasoning from Race: Feminism, Law, and the Civil Rights Revolution* (Cambridge, MA: Harvard University Press, 2011).

25. Committee on Civil and Political Rights, "Report of the Meeting Held August 24, 1962," 3, PM Papers, Schlesinger Library, Box 49, Folder 880; Frank E. A. Sander to Pauli Murray, September 24, 1962, PM Papers, Box 49, Box 878; President's Commission on the Status of Women, Minutes of the Fourth Meeting, October 1–2, 1962, PM Papers, Schlesinger Library, Box 49, Folder 878, p. 7; Paterson, *Be Somebody*, 138; Edith Green to Pauli Murray, August 11, 1962, PM Papers, Schlesinger Library, Box 48, Folder 875. Rawalt later recalled that neither she nor Green had been notified in advance of the invitation to Murray, but Green's letter of August 11 and the minutes of the October session make clear that Green had invited Murray.

26. Murray, *Song in a Weary Throat*, 351; Skipper [Caroline Ware] to Pixie [Pauli Murray], October 12, 1962, PM Papers, Schlesinger Library, Box 49, Folder 878; President's Commission on the Status of Women, Minutes of the Fourth Meeting, October 1–2, 1962, p. 1.

27. President's Commission on the Status of Women, Transcript of the Fourth Meeting, October 1–2, 1962, PM Papers, Schlesinger Library, Box 49, Folder 885, p. 331, 337, 333.

28. President's Commission on the Status of Women, Transcript of the Fourth Meeting, 335–336.

29. President's Commission on the Status of Women, Transcript of the Fourth Meeting, 342–343.

30. President's Commission on the Status of Women, Transcript of the Fourth Meeting, 351–354.

31. President's Commission on the Status of Women, Transcript of the Fourth Meeting, 358.

32. President's Commission on the Status of Women, Transcript of the Fourth Meeting, 359; Paterson, *Be Somebody*, 138.

33. Katherine Ellickson to Pauli Murray, October 4, 1962, and Pauli Murray to Katherine Ellickson, October 13, 1962, PM Papers, Schlesinger Library, Box 49, Folder 878.

34. Skipper [Caroline Ware] to Pixie [Pauli Murray], October 12, 1962, PM Papers, Schlesinger Library, Box 49, Folder 878.

35. Murray, *Song in a Weary Throat*, 351; "Mrs. Roosevelt Seriously Ill," *Chicago Daily Tribune*, October 29, 1962; Henry Grossman, "Mrs. Roosevelt Dies at 78 after Illness of Six Weeks," *New York Times*, November 8, 1962; Laurence Burd, "FDR Widow Laid to Rest in Hyde Park," *Chicago Daily Tribune*, November 11, 1962; Sue Cronk, Chairman's Seat Remains Vacant,"

Washington Post, November 16, 1962; Nan Robertson, "Rare Bone Marrow TB Killed Mrs. Roosevelt," *New York Times*, November 22, 1962.

36. Pauli Murray, "A Proposal to Reexamine the Applicability of the Fourteenth Amendment to State Law and Practices which Discriminate on the Basis of Sex Per Se," December 1962, PM Papers, Schlesinger Library, Box 50, Folder 887, pp. 3, 15.

37. In *Gulf, Colorado and Santa Fe Railroad v. Ellis*, 165 U.S.150 (1897), 165–166, the Court ruled that Texas could not single out railroad companies for special penalties, imposed on no one else.

38. Murray, "A Proposal to Reexamine the Applicability of the Fourteenth Amendment," 12; Blanche Crozier, "Constitutionality of Discrimination Based on Sex," *Boston University Law Review* 15 (1935): 749.

39. Murray, "A Proposal to Reexamine the Applicability of the Fourteenth Amendment," 10–12.

40. Kerber, *No Constitutional Right to Be Ladies*, 185.

41. Murray, "A Proposal to Reexamine the Applicability of the Fourteenth Amendment," 13.

42. Murray, "A Proposal to Reexamine the Applicability of the Fourteenth Amendment," 13.

43. Murray, "A Proposal to Reexamine the Applicability of the Fourteenth Amendment," 7–9.

44. Murray, "A Proposal to Reexamine the Applicability of the Fourteenth Amendment," 10.

45. Ethel E. Murrell, "Full Citizenship for Women: An Equal Rights Amendment," *American Bar Association Journal* 38 (January 1952): 47–48.

46. Murray, "A Proposal to Reexamine the Applicability of the Fourteenth Amendment," 16–17.

47. Murray, "A Proposal to Reexamine the Applicability of the Fourteenth Amendment," 17–18.

48. For problems that Murray did not anticipate see Nancy Woloch, *In a Class by Herself: Protective Laws for Women Workers* (Princeton, NJ: Princeton University Press, 2015), 202–249.

49. Murray, "A Proposal to Reexamine the Applicability of the Fourteenth Amendment," 19–22.

50. Murray, "A Proposal to Reexamine the Applicability of the Fourteenth Amendment," 25; the case was *Shpritzer v. Lang*, 17 Appellate Division, 289 (1962); Pauli Murray to Felicia Shpritzer, October 2, 1963, and Felicia Shpritzer to Pauli Murray, November 10, 1963, PM Papers, Schlesinger Library, Box 94, Folder 1644. Shpritzer took and passed the exam, was promoted to sergeant, and retired as a lieutenant in 1976; William H. Honan, "Felicia Shpritzer Dies at 87; Broke Police Barrier," *New York Times*, December 31, 2000.

51. Murray, "A Proposal to Reexamine the Applicability of the Fourteenth Amendment," 27–34.

52. Esther Peterson to Pauli Murray, January 11, 1963, PM Papers, Schlesinger Library, Box 49, Folder 878; Katherine Ellickson to Pauli Murray, February 19, 1963, PM Papers, Schlesinger Library, Box 49, Folder 878.

53. Erwin N. Griswold to Pauli Murray, January 31, 1962, and Paul Freund to Esther Peterson, March 11, 1963, PM Papers, Schlesinger Library, Box 49, Folder 878.

54. Barbara Babcock to Pauli Murray, n.d., PM Papers, Schlesinger Library, Box 49, Folder 878.

55. Harrison, *On Account of Sex*, 128.

56. Harrison, *On Account of Sex*, 128–129; Miriam Y. Holden, "Argument in Favor of the Equal Rights Amendment, Made at the Request of the National Woman's Party," March 23, 1963, PM Papers, Schlesinger Library, Box 49, Folder 883; Miriam Holden to Anita Pollitzer, February 16, 1963, NWP Papers, available on microfilm, reel 108. On the competing constitutional strategies proposed by Murray, on the one hand, and members of the NWP, on the other, see Serena Mayeri, "Constitutional Choices: Legal Feminism and the Historical Dynamics of Change," *California Law Review* 92 (2004): 757–784.

57. Harrison, *On Account of Sex*, 129.

58. Frank E. A. Sander to the Members of the Equal Rights Subcommittee, Memorandum, March 14, 1963, PM Papers, Schlesinger Library, Box 49, Folder 876.

59. Dorothy Kenyon to Board of Directors of the ACLU, March 28, 1963, and John de J. Pemberton to Esther Peterson, April 1, 1963, PM Papers, Schlesinger Library, Box 49, Folder 876; Dorothy Kenyon to Pauli Murray, April 4, 1963, PM Papers, Schlesinger Library, Box 49, Folder 878.

60. Paterson, *Be Somebody*, 144.

61. Harrison, *On Account of Sex*, 128.

62. President's Commission on the Status of Women, "Transcript of Consultation on Minority Groups," April 19, 1963, in Papers of the President's Commission on the Status of Women,

John F. Kennedy Library, Boston, MA, available on microfilm, reel 3, p. 14. On the divergence in treatment of black and white mothers among psychologists and sociologists in the 1960s, see Ruth Feldstein, *Motherhood in Black and White: Race and Sex in American Liberalism, 1930–1965* (Ithaca, NY: Cornell University Press, 2000), 139–164.

63. Dorothy Height, "The Negro Woman," preliminary draft, February 1, 1963, in "Transcript of the Consultation on Minority Groups"; in her reference to "double jeopardy," Height may have been quoting Inabel Lindsay, another member of the Consultation, who was the dean of the Howard School of Social Work and a former classmate of E. Franklin Frazier, who is sometimes credited with coining the term. Three other consultations were arranged: "Private Employment Opportunities," "New Patterns in Volunteer Work," and "Portrayal of Women by the Mass Media."

64. Dorothy Height, *Open Wide the Freedom Gates: A Memoir* (New York: Public Affairs, 2003), 1–131. See also entries on "Dorothy Height" and "National Council of Negro Women," in *Black Women in American: An Historical Encyclopedia*, edited by Darlene Clark Hine (Brooklyn, NY: Carlson, 1993).

65. "Transcript of the Consultation on Minority Groups," list of participants.

66. Katherine Ellickson, "Women in Minority Groups," March 18, 1963, pp. 2–3, 6–10, and 19, Katherine Ellickson Papers, Box 94, Folder 31, Archives of Labor and Urban Affairs, Walter P. Reuther Library, Wayne State, University of Michigan. According to Ellickson, the median wage in 1960 for white men was $5,662, for black men the median was $3,789 (67 percent of white men's); for white women the median was $3,410 (60 percent of white men's, and 90 percent of black men's); and for black women the median was $2,372 (42 percent of white men's, 63 percent of black men's, and 70 percent of white women's).

67. Daniel Patrick Moynihan to Esther Peterson, March 26, 1963, Katherine Ellickson Papers, Box 95, Folder 1, Archives of Labor and Urban Affairs, Walter P. Reuther Library, provided by archivist William LeFevre.

68. Thomas Meehan, "Moynihan and the Moynihan Report," *New York Times,* July 31, 1966.

69. "Transcript of Consultation on Minority Groups," 18, 21–24, and *passim.*

70. "Transcript of Consultation on Minority Groups," 34–38, 62, 95, 105; Jennifer Mittelstadt, *From Welfare to Workfare: The Unintended Consequences of Liberal Reform, 1945–1965* (Chapel Hill: University of North Carolina Press, 2005), 137–139.

71. "Report to Commission on Consultation on Minority Groups," April 23, 1963 (a transcript of Caroline Ware's summary of the meeting of the Consultation on Minority Women on April 19, 1963, to her fellow PCSW commissioners), Esther Peterson Papers, Box 46, Folder 912, Schlesinger Library, Radcliffe Institute, Harvard University.

72. Dorothy Height, as quoted in "Transcript of Consultation on Minority Groups," 179–180; the "Report of Consultation on Problems of Negro Women," April 19, 1963, 3; Mead and Kaplan, eds., *American Women*, 220–221, 227; "Report of Consultation on Problems of Negro Women," April 19, 1963, 35.

73. Mittelstadt, *From Welfare to Workfare*, 178–180; but cf. Kessler-Harris, *In Pursuit of Equity*, 266–269, and Maria Chappell, *The War on Welfare: Family, Poverty, and Politics in Modern America* (Philadelphia: University of Pennsylvania Press, 2012), 47; both conclude that Height's contention that black women's "major underlying concern" was "the status of the Negro man" represented the consensus of the consultation participants.

74. Betty Friedan, *The Feminine Mystique* (New York: W. W. Norton, 1963); Pauli Murray, "The Negro Woman in the Quest for Equality," *Acorn*, June 1964, PM Papers, Box 86, Folder 1486.

Chapter 12

1. Pauli Murray, "Discrimination," in "Letters to the Editor," *Washington Post*, August 24, 1963.

2. Yevette Richards, *Maida Springer: Pan-Africanist and International Labor Leader* (Pittsburgh: University of Pittsburgh Press, 2000), 263.

3. Anna Arnold Hedgeman, *The Trumpet Sounds: A Memoir of Negro Leadership* (New York: Holt, Rinehart and Winston, 1964), 172–180. According to Hedgeman, Myrlie Evers, one of those invited to the platform, was allowed to say a few words but not to give a speech. Pauli Murray, *Song in a Weary Throat: An American Pilgrimage* (New York: Harper & Row, 1987), 353;

Lynne Olson, *Freedom's Daughters: The Unsung Heroines of the Civil Rights Movement from 1830 to 1970* (New York: Scribner, 2001), 13–17.

4. Pauli Murray, "Memorandum: The Role of the Negro Women in the Civil Rights Revolution," August 27, 1968, PM Papers, Schlesinger Library, Radcliffe Institute, Harvard University, Box 129, Folder 2338.

5. Dorothy I. Height, *Open Wide the Freedom Gates: A Memoir* (New York: Public Affairs, 2003), 145–146. Mahalia Jackson was invited to sing.

6. Height, *Open Wide the Freedom Gates*, 145–146; Murray, *Song in a Weary Throat*, 353. Marjorie Hunter, "Leaders of Civil Rights March to Meet Kennedy Tomorrow," *New York Times*, August 27, 1963, 23.

7. John D'Emilio, *Lost Prophet: The Life and Times of Bayard Rustin* (New York: Free Press, 2003), 327–328.

8. D'Emilio, *Lost Prophet*, 331–335; Taylor Branch, *Parting the Waters: America in the King Years, 1954–1963* (New York: Simon & Schuster, 1988), 77–78; Cynthia Levinson, *We've Got a Job: The 1963 Birmingham Children's March* (Atlanta: Peachtree, 2012).

9. Pauli Murray, "Roots of the Racial Crisis: Prologue to Policy," Ph.D. diss., Yale University, 1965, 2.

10. Murray, "Roots of the Racial Crisis," 8; Pauli Murray, "The Negro Woman in the Quest for Equality," *Acorn*, Official Publication of Lamba Kappa Mu Sorority, Inc. (1964), PM Papers, Schlesinger Library, Box 86, Folder 1486; James Baldwin, *The Fire Next Time* (New York: Dial Press, 1963).

11. The "Big Six" included Randolph, as director of the Negro American Labor Council (NALC); Roy Wilkins, as president of the National Association for the Advancement of Colored People (NAACP); Whitney Young, as president of the National Urban League (NUL); Martin Luther King Jr. as head of the Southern Christian Leadership Conference (SCLC); James Farmer, as head of the Congress of Racial Equality (CORE); and John Lewis, of the Student Nonviolent Coordinating Committee's (SNCC); D'Emilio, *Lost Prophet*, 343.

12. D'Emilio, *Lost Prophet*, 348–349. Murray's papers for the years 1961 to 1966 include address and date books, but no diaries. It is not clear whether they were discarded by a family member after her death or whether Murray was so preoccupied by her public activities that she did not have time for the kinds of personal reflections she had made earlier; nonetheless, it seems safe to say that she reacted to the public humiliation of her friend Bayard Rustin just as she had to earlier instances of exposure of friends charged with being Communists or "queer": with anxious fear that she might be next.

13. Murray, *Song in a Weary Throat*, 353–354. Martin Luther King Jr., "I Have a Dream," August 28, 1963, Lincoln Memorial, Washington, DC.

14. Dorothy Height to Pauli Murray, telegram, October 30, 1963, PM Papers, Schlesinger Library, Box 128, Folder 2373; Paula Cowan and Betty Barnes, "Reminiscences of Dorothy I. Height: Oral History, 1976," Black Women Oral History Project," Schlesinger Library, p. 146.

15. Sue Cronk, "Women Given a Back Seat," *Washington Post*, November 16, 1963; Jeanne Noble, *The Negro Woman's College Education* (New York: Teachers College, 1956), 39, 98; "Jeanne L. Noble, 76, Pioneer in Education," obituary, *New York Times*, November 2, 2002; Pauli Murray, "The Negro Woman in the Quest for Equality," *Acorn*, Official Publication of Lamba Kappa Mu Sorority, Inc. (June 1964): 1–4, plus Appendix.

16. Murray, "The Negro Woman in the Quest for Equality," 1–4, plus Appendix.

17. Murray, "The Negro Woman in the Quest for Equality," 1–4.

18. Murray, "The Negro Woman in the Quest for Equality," 4.

19. Murray, "The Negro Woman in the Quest for Equality," 1–2.

20. Murray, "The Negro Woman in the Quest for Equality," 4. On the demonizing of black mothers in the 1960s, see Ruth Feldstein, *Motherhood in Black and White: Race and Sex in American Liberalism, 1930–1965* (Ithaca, NY: Cornell University Press, 2000), 141–150, but note that Feldstein dates the black feminist reaction to this demonization to the years after 1966. Murray had already begun in 1963.

21. "Negro Men Cite Women," *New York Amsterdam News*, November 16, 1963.

22. Whitney M. Young Jr., to Pauli Murray, November 29, 1963, and James Farmer, to Pauli Murray, January 22, 1964, PM Papers, Schlesinger Library, Box 129, Folder 2337.

23. Phoebe Morrison to Pauli Murray, January 14, 1963, PM Papers, Schlesinger Library, Box 49, Folder 878.

24. Pauli Murray to Skipper [Caroline Ware], March 30, 1945, PM Papers, Schlesinger Library, Box 96, Folder 1696; Pauli Murray, "The Right to Equal Opportunity in Employment," *California Law Review* 33, no. 1 (1945): 398–399.

25. Thacher Clarke to Pauli Murray, August 8, 1960, PM Papers, Schlesinger Library, Box 41, Folder 713, and May 5, 1961, Box 41, Folder 716; Gardiner H. Shattuck Jr., *Episcopalians and Race: Civil War to Civil Rights* (Lexington: University Press of Kentucky, 2000), 87–108; Editors, "Comments and Notes: Sex Discrimination in Employment," *Duke Law Journal* (1968): 671; John W. Purdy, "Title VII: Relationship and Effect on State Action," *Boston College Law Review* 3, no. 3 (April 1966): 527; Ann Thacher Clarke Anderson, interview by author, May 17, 2008; unsigned [Ann Thacher Clarke Anderson] to Pauli Murray, January 21, 1963, PM Papers, Schlesinger Library, Box 49, Folder 878.

26. Resolution adopted by the National Woman's Party, December 16, 1963, NWP Papers, available on microfilm, reel, 108; Serna Mayeri, "Constitutional Choices: Legal Feminism and the Historical Dynamics of Change," *California Law Review* 92 (2004): 771; Carl Brauer, "Women Activists, Southern Conservatives, and the Prohibition of Sex Discrimination in Title VII of the 1964 Civil Rights Act, *Journal of Southern History* 49, no. 1 (February 1983): 41–43; Jo Freeman, "How 'Sex' Got into Title VII: Persistent Opportunism as a Maker of Public Policy," *Law & Inequality* 9 (1990–1991): 173; Clay Risen, *The Bill of the Century: The Epic Battle for the Civil Rights Act* (New York: Bloomsbury Press, 2014), 5.

27. Bruce J. Dierenfield, *Keeper of the Rules: Howard W. Smith of Virginia* (Charlottesville: University of Virginia Press, 1987), 194–195; Freeman, "How 'Sex' Got into Title VII" 170–171.

28. *Civil Rights: Hearings before the Committee on Rules, House of Representatives, Eighty-eighth Congress, Second Session* (Washington, 1964), 125; Brauer, "Women Activists, Southern Conservatives, and the Prohibition of Sex Discrimination in Title VII," 43–44; Hugh Davis Graham, *The Civil Rights Era: Origins and Development of National Policy, 1960–1972* (New York: Oxford University Press, 1990), 136–137; Dierenfield, *Keeper of the Rules*, 195.

29. Gary Orfield, *Congressional Power: Congress and Social Change* (New York: Houghton Mifflin Harcourt, 1975), 299; Charles Whalen and Barbara Whalen, *The Longest Debate: A Legislative History of the 1964 Civil Rights Act* (Newport Beach, CA: Seven Locks Press, 1984), 115–117, and 234; Brauer, "Women Activists, Southern Conservatives, and the Prohibition of Sex Discrimination in Title VII," 37–56; *Congressional Record—House*, February 8, 1964, pp. 2486, attached to Pauli Murray, "Memorandum Appendix II, "House Debate on 'Sex' Amendment," PM Papers, Schlesinger Library, Box 35, Folder 2456; Dierenfield, *Keeper of the Rules*, 195.

30. Freeman, "How 'Sex' Got into Title VII: Persistent Opportunism as a Maker of Public Policy," 175; Brauer, "Women Activists, Southern Conservatives and the Prohibition of Sex Discrimination in Title VII of the 1964," 37–56.

31. *Congressional Record—House*, February 8, 1964, pp. 2485, 2488–2489, attached to Pauli Murray, "Memorandum Appendix II, "House Debate on 'Sex' Amendment," PM Papers, Schlesinger Library, Box 35, Folder 2456.

32. *Congressional Record–House*, February 8, 1964, p. 2486.

33. *Congressional Record–House*, February 8, 1964, p. 2486; Graham, *The Civil Rights Era*, 138.

34. Robert Caro, *The Years of Lyndon Johnson*, Vol. 4, *The Passage of Power* (New York: Knopf, 2012), 565; Todd S. Purdum, *An Idea Whose Time Has Come: Two Presidents, Two Parties, and the Battle for the Civil Rights Act of 1964* (New York: Henry Holt, 2014), 95, 174, 194, 211; Joseph Hearst, "Dirksen Seeks Compromises on Rights Bill; Proposes 40 Changes to Civil Rights Bill," *Chicago Tribune*, April 8, 1964; 565.

35. Judith Paterson, *Be Somebody: A Biography of Marguerite Rawalt* (Austin, TX: Eakin Press, 1986), 153–154.

36. Pauli Murray, "Memorandum in Support of Retaining the Amendment to H. R. 7152, Title VII (Equal Employment Opportunity) to Prohibit Discrimination in Employment because of Sex," April 14, 1964, p. 18, PM Papers, Schlesinger Library, Box 85, Folder 1485.

37. Murray, "Memorandum in Support of Retaining the Amendment," 20–21.

38. Murray, "Memorandum in Support of Retaining the Amendment," 12; Serena Mayeri, "'A Common Fate of Discrimination': Race-Gender Analogies in Legal and Historical

Perspective," *Yale Law Journal* 110, no. 6 (April 2001): 1065–1067. Murray drew on the work of Eleanor Flexner, *A Century of Struggle: The Women's Rights Movement in the United States* (New York: Atheneum, 1959).

39. Mary Eastwood to Pauli Murray, April 21, 1964, PM Papers, Schlesinger Library, Box 135, Folder 2456; Pauli Murray [quoting Mary Eastwood], "Memorandum in Support of Retaining the Amendment to H. R. 7152, Title VII (Equal Employment Opportunity) to Prohibit Discrimination in Employment because of Sex," April 14, 1964, Appendix III, PM Papers, Schlesinger Library, Box 85, Folder 1485.

40. Mary Eastwood to Pauli Murray, April 21, 1964, PM Papers, Schlesinger Library, Box 135, Folder 2456; Murray [quoting Mary Eastwood], "Memorandum in Support of Retaining the Amendment to H. R. 7152. For a history of the Fair Labor Standards Act versus the "higher standard" in state law, see Nancy Woloch, *A Class by Herself: Protective Laws for Women Workers* (Princeton, NJ: Princeton University Press, 2015), 186, 264.

41. Pauli Murray to Marguerite Rawalt, April 14, 1964, and Pauli Murray to Lady Bird Johnson, April 14, 1964, PM Papers, Schlesinger Library, Box 135, Folder 2456.

42. Margaret Chase Smith to Pauli Murray, April 27, 1964, PM Papers, Schlesinger Library, Box 135, Folder 2456; Ward Wallace, *Politics of Conscience: A Biography of Margaret Chase Smith* (Westport, CT: Greenwood Press, 1995), 164; Paterson, *Be Somebody*, 154.

43. Bess Abell to Pauli Murray, April 29 1964, PM Papers, Schlesinger Library, Box 104, Folder 1872; Patricia G. Zelman, *Women, Work, and National Policy: The Kennedy-Johnson Years* (Ann Arbor: UMI Press, 1980), 71.

44. Caro, *The Years of Lyndon Johnson*, Vol. 4, *The Passage of Power*, 566.

45. James F. Findlay, *Church People in the Struggle: The National Council of Churches and the Black Freedom Movement, 1950–1970* (New York: Oxford University Press, 1997), 48–75. In 1975, the Senate reduced the number of votes required for cloture from two-thirds to three-fifths, or sixty of the current 100 senators.

46. Caro, *The Years of Lyndon Johnson*, Vol. 4, *The Passage of Power*, 369; Graham, *The Civil Rights Era*, 138–152.

47. Caroline Ware to Pauli Murray, July 11, 1965, PM Papers, Schlesinger Library, Box 20, Folder 445; Pauli Murray, "Roots of the Racial Crisis: Prologue to Policy," 3 vols., PM Papers, Schlesinger Library, Boxes 21 and 22.

48. Lee Rainwater and William L. Yancey, *The Moynihan Report and the Politics of Controversy* (Cambridge, MA: MIT Press, 1967), ch. 4; Daniel Patrick Moynihan, "The Negro Family: The Case for National Action," Office of Policy Planning and Research, US Department of Labor, March 1965. When the Department of Labor originally printed the Moynihan Report in March 1965, it labeled the report "For Official Use Only," but its contents became widely known in the summer of 1965. Murray had been following his argument since early 1963.

49. Pauli Murray, "Roots of the Racial Crisis: Prologue to Policy," 417–492, PM Papers, Schlesinger Library, Box 20.

50. Pauli Murray to Charles E. Silberman, May 23, 1964, PM Papers, Schlesinger Library, Box 20, Folder 445; Willie Less Rose to Pauli Murray, May 8, 1965, Schlesinger Library, Box 20, Folder 445.

51. Pauli Murray to Willie Lee Rose, June 4, 1965, PM Papers, Schlesinger Library, Box 20, Folder 445.

52. Murray, "Roots of the Racial Crisis: Prologue to Policy," 762.

53. On graduation day, see John C. Devlins, "Dr. Spock and Thant Honored by Yale," *New York Times*, June 15, 1965; Murray, *Song in a Weary Throat*, 359–361. For Murray's insistence on being known as "Dr." see, Pauli Murray, testimony before the New York City Commission on Human Rights, in Eleanor Holmes Norton, *Women's Role in Contemporary Society: The Report of the New York City Commission on Human Rights, September 21–25, 1970* (New York: Avon, 1972), 613.

54. Of the thirty-three students in Murray's entering graduate class at Yale Law School, seven remained for another year of study, twelve took law school faculty positions in the United States and abroad, "Yale Law School Graduate Students, 1961–62," PM Papers, Schlesinger Library, Box 20, Folder 432. On Murray's job search, see Pauli Murray to Caroline Ware, June 27, 1965, PM Papers, Schlesinger Library, Box 74, Folder 1313.

55. Pauli Murray to the editors, *Newsweek*, September 4, 1965. For later responses see, for example, William Ryan, "Savage Discovery: The Moynihan Report," *Nation*, November 22, 1965, pp. 380–384, and Benjamin Payton, "New Trends in Civil Rights," *Christianity and Crisis*, December 13, 1965, pp. 268–271. The emphasis in these articles was on what Ryan came to call "blaming the [male] victim."

56. Rainwater and Yancey, *The Moynihan Report and the Politics of Controversy*, 185–186; Jennifer Mittelstadt, *From Welfare to Workfare: The Unintended Consequences of Liberal Reform, 1945–1965* (Chapel Hill: University of North Carolina Press, 2005), 148; Marissa Chapman, *The War on Welfare: Family, Poverty, and Politics in Modern America* (Philadelphia: University of Pennsylvania Press, 2010).

Chapter 13

1. For the early history of the EEOC and the resistance of staff and commissioners to enforce the sex amendment of Title VII, see Alice Kessler-Harris, *In Pursuit of Equity: Women, Men, and the Quest for Economic Citizenship* (New York: Oxford University Press, 2001), 246–280.

2. *Wall Street Journal*, June 22, 1965, cited in Hugh Davis Graham, *The Civil Rights Era: Origins and Development of National Policy, 1960–1972* (New York: Oxford University Press, 1990), 211; Aubrey Graves, "Boat Hooks . . . : and Buggywrinkle CGs' Cutter, Vigilant, Hovering over Fleet, Was Big Morale Lifter," *Washington Times Herald*, June 27, 1965; "Roosevelt Finds Sex Discrimination in Jobs Is Big Problem; Appoints Seven Key Aides," *New York Times*, July 21, 1965.

3. On Hernandez, see Maggie Savoy, "NOW Leader Too Busy to Be Angry: Feminist Wants Alternatives," *Los Angeles Times*, June 3, 1970; Graham, *The Civil Rights Era*, 178.

4. Herman Edlesberg, *Not for Myself Alone: Memoir of a Lawyer Who Fought for Human Rights* (Berkeley: Interstellar Media, 1988), 173; Edelsberg's statement that the addition on "sex" was a "fluke" that was "conceived out of wedlock" was made at the New York University 18th Conference on Labor, and was cited in the *Labor Relations Reporter*, August 25, 1966, pp. 253–255; Mary Eastwood to Pauli Murray, February 2? [*sic*], 1965, PM Papers, Schlesinger Library, Box 95, Folder 1655; Richard K. Berg, "Equal Employment Opportunity under the Civil Rights Act of 1964," *Brooklyn Law Review* 31 (1964–1965): 79, 62–97; Murray, *Song in a Weary Throat*, 361.

5. Pauli Murray to Marguerite Rawalt, July 21, 1965, Mary Eastwood Papers, Schlesinger Library, Box 5, Folder 56; Pauli Murray to Mary Eastwood, August 9, 1963, PM Papers, Box 49, Folder 878; Murray, *Song in a Weary Throat*, 362–363; Pauli Murray to Mary Eastwood, August 9, 1963, PM Papers, Schlesinger Library, Box 49, Folder 878; Pauli Murray and Mary O. Eastwood, "Jane Crow and the Law: Sex Discrimination and Title VII," *George Washington Law Review* 34, no. 2 (December 1965): 232–256. Murray confirmed this division of responsibility in Pauli Murray to Larry Fuchs, July 15, 1970, PM Papers, Schlesinger Library, Box 45, Folder 803.

6. Murray and Eastwood, "Jane Crow and the Law," 242.

7. Murray and Eastwood, "Jane Crow and the Law," 244, 247; for "wet nurse" as BFOQ, see interview with Sonia Pressman, by Sylvia Danovitch, in *Women in Judaism: Contemporary Writings*, December 27, 1990.

8. Murray and Eastwood, "Jane Crow and the Law," 250.

9. Juliet Schor, *The Overworked American: The Unexpected Decline of Leisure* (New York: Basic Books, 2008), 43–82 and *passim*; Murray and Eastwood, "Jane Crow and the Law," 249–250; Margaret Mead and Frances B. Kaplan, eds., *American Women: The Report of the President's Commission on the Status of Women and Other Publications of the Commission* (New York: Charles Scribner's, 1965), 56.

10. Nancy Woloch, *In a Class by Herself: Protective Laws for Women Workers, 1890s–1990s* (Princeton, NJ: Princeton University Press, 2015), 194, 265, 268; Dorothy Sue Cobble, *The Other Women's Movement: Workplace Justice and Social Rights in Modern America* (Princeton, NJ: Princeton University Press, 2004): 177–178; Murray and Eastwood, "Jane Crow and the Law," 252–253.

11. Pauli Murray to Mary Eastwood, August 9, 1963, PM Papers, Schlesinger Library, Box 49, Folder 878. Pauli Murray to Ray Clevenger, June 19, 1965; Pauli Murray, Memorandum

Re: Conference with Ray Clevenger, articles co-editor of the *Yale Law Journal*, June 18, 1965, on "Jane Crow and the Law" draft article; and Pauli Murray to Mary Eastwood, June 19, 1965, PM Papers, Schlesinger Library, Box 95, Folder 1655. The most important citation was by Ruth Bader Ginsburg in her brief in *Reed v. Reed* (1971).

12. Louise Barnum Robbins, ed., *History and Minutes of the National Council of Women of the United States: Organized in Washington, D. C., March 31, 1888* (Boston: E. B. Stilling, 1898), 13, 18.

13. Pauli Murray, "The Legal Implication of Women-at-Work," 7,13, remarks delivered at the Women and Title VII Conference, National Council of Women of US, October 12, 1965, Catherine East Papers, Schlesinger Library, Carton 16, Folder 16; Edith Evans Asbury, "Protest Proposed on Women's Jobs: Yale Professor Says It May Be Needed to Obtain Rights," *New York Times*, October 13, 1965.

14. Margalit Fox, "Edith Evans Asbury, 98, Veteran Times Reporter, Is Dead," *New York Times*, October 30, 2008; Pauli Murray to Edith Evens Asbury, October 14, 1965, PM Papers, Schlesinger Library, Box 128, Folder 2325; Pauli Murray to Mary Eastwood, October 14, 1965, Mary Eastwood Papers, Box 3, Folder 28; Murray, diary entry, April 26, 1967, Box 2, Folder 30; Murray, *Song in a Weary Throat*, 365.

15. Miriam Holden to Alice Paul, October 16, 1965, NWP Papers, available on microfilm, reel 109. For an excellent analysis of Murray's success in bridging the gap between the warring factions of the women's movement over the course of the 1960s, see Serena Mayeri, "'A Common Fate of Discrimination': Race-Gender Analogies in Legal and Historical Perspective," *Yale Law Journal* 110, no. 6 (April 2001): 1045–1088; Mayeri, "Constitutional Choices: Legal Feminism and the Historical Dynamics of Change," *California Law Review* 92 (2004): 757–784, and Mayeri, *Reasoning from Race: Feminism, Law, and the Civil Rights Revolution* (Cambridge, MA: Harvard University Press, 2011).

16. Murray, *Song in a Weary Throat*, 216. Sonia Pressman Fuentes, interview by author, June 15, 2000; according to Fuentes, Murray began a tradition of giving the pin to other feminists. When she died in 1985, her friends donated the pin to the National Woman's Party, where it remains in the "Artifacts and Ephemera," in the National Woman's Party (NWP) collection housed at the Sewall-Belmont House and Museum, in Washington, DC.

17. Betty Friedan, *It Change My Life: Writings on the Women's Movement* (New York: Random House, 1976), 77–78; Dolores Alexander, "NOW May Use Sit-ins, Pickets to Get Equality," *Newsday*, November 25, 1966, 2B, PM Papers, Schlesinger Library, Box 52, Folder 913; Murray, diary entry, April 26, 1967, PM Papers, Schlesinger Library, Box 2, Folder 30; Murray, *Song in a Weary Throat*, 363.

18. Biographical Introduction to Inventory of Catherine East Papers, Schlesinger Library, Harvard University; Murray, *Song in a Weary Throat*, 362.

19. Cynthia Epstein, "Betty Friedan: An Appreciation," *Footnotes: Newsletter of the American Sociological Association* 34, no. 3 (March 2006), at asanet.org; Friedan, *It Change My Life*, 61; Murray, *Song in a Weary Throat*, 366.

20. Thacher Clarke Anderson, interview by author, May 17, 2008; for more on ESCRU, see PM Papers, Schlesinger Library, Box 122, Folders 2192–2194.

21. Murray, *Song in a Weary Throat*, 363.

22. John de J. Pemberton to Pauli Murray, November 18, 1965, PM Papers, Schlesinger Library, Box 59, Folder 1999.

23. Samuel Walker, *In Defense of American Liberties: A History of the ACLU* (New York: Oxford University Press, 1990), 83–85, 166–167; Susan M. Hartmann, *The Other Feminists: Activists in the Liberal Establishment* (New Haven, CT: Yale University Press, 1998), 56–57; *Hoyt v. Florida*, 368 U.S. 57 (1961); Linda Kerber, *No Constitutional Right to Be Ladies: Women and the Obligations of Citizenship* (New York: Hill & Wang, 1998), 170, and 124–183.

24. Dorothy Kenyon, chairman of the Equality Committee, to the Board of Directors of the ACLU, March 30, 1963, and John de J. Pemberton, executive director of the ACLU, to Esther Peterson, April 1, 1963, PM Papers, Schlesinger Library, Box 59, Folder 999; Hartmann, *The Other Feminists*, 61; "Black, Farmer On ACLU Board," *New York Amsterdam News*, April 6, 1963; Walker, *In Defense of American Liberties*, 267; Joan Steinau Lester, *Fire in My Soul: Eleanor Holmes Norton* (New York: Atria Books, 2003), 129–130.

25. Hartmann, *The Other Feminists*, 54; Dorothy Kenyon and Pauli Murray to the board of the ACLU, September 24, 1970, PM papers, Schlesinger Library, Box 55, Folder 956; John de J. Pemberton to Pauli Murray, December 2, 1965, PM Papers, Schlesinger Library, Box 59, Folder 999.

26. Howell Raines, "The Murderous Era of George C. Wallace," *New York Times*, April 26, 2000; Hasan Kwame Jeffries, *Bloody Lowndes: Civil Rights and Black Power in Alabama's Black Belt* (New York: New York University Press, 2009), 1–95.

27. Charles Eagles, *Outside Agitator: Jon Daniels and the Civil Rights Movement in Alabama* (Tuscaloosa: University of Alabama Press, 2000), 87, 119–144, 163–84; Jeffries, *Bloody Lowndes*, 58–61; Susan Youngblood Ashmore, *Carry It On: The War on Poverty and the Civil Rights Movement in Alabama, 1964–1972* (Athens: University of Georgia Press, 2008), 137–138; Charles Morgan Jr., interview by author, April 4, 1997; Charles Morgan Jr., *One Man, One Voice* (New York: Holt, Rinehart and Winston, 1979), 38.

28. Charles Morgan Jr., interview by author, April 4, 1997; Morgan, *One Man, One Voice*, 39; Wayne Greenhaw, *Fighting the Devil in Dixie: How Civil Rights Activists Took on the Ku Klux Klan in Alabama* (Chicago: Chicago Review Press, 2011), 183–184; Eagles, *Outside Agitator*, 199–200.

29. Greenhaw, *Fighting the Devil in Dixie*, 115–184; Charles Morgan, *A Time to Speak* (New York: Holt, Rinehart, and Winston, 1964), 10 and *passim*; Roy Reed, "Charles Morgan Jr., 78, Dies; Leading Civil Rights Lawyer," *New York Times*, January 9, 2009; Martin Arnold, "Alabama Lawyer Hits Moderates: In Speech, He Deplores Inaction on Racial Issue," *New York Times*, September 24, 1963; Morgan, *One Man, One Voice*, 4, 24; Walker, *In Defense of Civil Liberties*, 268–269; Morgan, interview by author. *White v. Crook*, brought as a class action on behalf of "male and female residents of Lowndes County" on August 25, 1965, initially sought a restraining order and stay of all proceedings in the Alabama Circuit Court pending determination of the suit; an amended complaint, calling for a three-judge court, was filed on September 23, 1965. The Justice Department intervened on October 27, 1965. For briefs, see ACLU Records, Box 3977, Folder "White v. Crook," Mudd Library, Princeton University.

30. Jeffries, *Bloody Lowndes*, 67; Morgan, interview by author; *White v. Crook*, 251F. Supp. 401, Civil Action No. 2263-N (1966). On federal rules see 28 U.S. Code § 2281, 2282.

31. Information on Gardenia White and the registration campaign comes from Hasam Kwame Jeffries to author, July 14, 2014, and Jeffries, *Bloody Lowndes*, 46–123; Eagles, *Outside Agitator*, 87, 119–144; Ashmore, *Carry It On*, 137–138; Morgan, interview by author; Taylor Branch, *At Canaan's Edge: America in the King Years, 1965–68* (New York: Simon & Schuster, 2006), 149, 312.

32. John de J. Pemberton Jr., to Pauli Murray, November 18, 1965, PM Papers, Schlesinger Library, Box 59, Folder 999; Mary Eastwood to the Honorable Hattie Belle Davis, December 4, 1965, PM Papers, Schlesinger Library, Box 38, Folder 672; Murray, *Song in a Weary Throat*, 363. In Murray's memoir, she says that she began work on the case after her election to the board, but in fact she completed work on the brief before.

33. Morgan, interview by author; Mayeri, *Reasoning from Race*, 27–29; Linda Kerber, *No Constitutional Right to Be Ladies*, 197–199; Dorothy Kenyon to Charles Morgan, November 29, 1965, and Dorothy Kenyon to Esther Peterson, February 28, 1966, Kenyon Papers, Smith College Archives.

34. Charles Morgan Jr., Orzell Billingsley Jr., Judge Dorothy Kenyon, Dr. Pauli Murray, Melvin L. Wulf, Plaintiffs' Brief in *Gardenia White v. Bruce Crook*, United States District Court for the Middle District of Alabama Northern Division, Civil Action no. 2263-N, [November 1965], 51, ACLU Records, Box 3954, Folder "White v. Crook: Plaintiffs' Brief," Mudd Library, Princeton University; Morgan, *One Man, One Voice*, 38–47.

35. Morgan et al., Plaintiffs' Brief in *Gardenia White v. Bruce Crook*, 61; "U.S. Asks Judges to Void Ban on Women Jurors in Alabama," *New York Times*, December 30, 1965.

36. Dorothy Kenyon to Melvin Wulf, January 10, 196[6], ACLU Records, Box 1832, Folder: *White, G. v. Jury Commission*, Mudd Library, Princeton University; *Gardenia White v. Bruce Crook*, Civ. A. No. 2263-N, United States District Court. M. D. Alabama, N.D., February 7, 1966.

37. Marguerite Rawalt to Mattie Belle [Davis], February 9, 1966, and Pauli Murray to Marguerite Rawalt, February 16, 1966, Marguerite Rawalt Papers, Schlesinger Library, Box 30, Folder 38; Mary Eastwood to Charles Morgan Jr., February 1966, Mary Eastwood Papers, Box 3, Folder 28, Schlesinger Library; Pauli Murray to Alma Lutz, December 9, 1965, PM Papers, Schlesinger Library, Box 97, Folder 1730. For Murray's relationship to members of the NWP, see Serena Mayeri, "Constitutional Choices: Legal Feminism and the Historical Dynamics of Change," *California Law Review* 92 (2004): 757–784.

38. Charles Morgan Jr., interview by author. Flowers lost the election to George Wallace's wife, Lurleen Wallace.

39. Pauli Murray to Charles Morgan Jr., April 20, 1966, PM Papers, Schlesinger Library, Box 59, Folder 1000. Another decade would pass before the Supreme Court took the final step of ruling unconstitutional any jury system that treated women differently from men in *Taylor v. Louisiana*, 419 U.S. 522 (1975); see Kerber, *No Constitutional Right to Be Ladies*, 276, and Holly J. McCammon, *The U.S. Women's Jury Movements and Strategic Adaptation: A More Just Verdict* (Cambridge: Cambridge University Press, 2012), 162–174.

40. Carolyn Lewis, "Dream Haunts Practical Poet," *Washington Post, Times Herald*, December 11, 1966; Graham, *The Civil Rights Era*, 211.

41. "Job Discrimination Ruling Bans the Firing of Brides: Ladies First," *Wall Street Journal*, September 17, 1965, cited in Graham, *The Civil Rights Era*, 215; Judith Hole and Ellen Levine, *Rebirth of Feminism* (New York: Quadrangle, 1971), 25–26.

42. Graham, *The Civil Rights Era*, 218–221; Hole and Levine, *Rebirth of Feminism*, 25–26.

43. Martha W. Griffiths, "Women Are Being Derived of Equal Rights by the Equal Employment Opportunity Commission," *Congressional Record*, June 20, 1966, in Pauli Murray, scrapbook, PM Papers, Schlesinger Library, 94v; Murray, *Song in a Weary Throat*, 367.

44. Graham, *The Civil Rights Era*, 212–213.

45. Murray, *Song in a Weary Throat*, 366.

46. Murray, *Song in a Weary Throat*, 367.

47. Murray, *Song in a Weary Throat*, 368; Betty Friedan, *It Changed My Life*, 104.

48. Daniel Horowitz, *Betty Friedan and the Making of the Feminine Mystique* (Amherst: University of Massachusetts Press, 2000), 227–228; Pauli Murray, conference draft #3 of "Now Statement of Purpose, 1966," October 29, 1966, with Murray's handwritten marginal notes, PM Papers, Schlesinger Library, Box 50, Folder 894; "Now Statement of Purpose," as voted on October 29, 1966, PM Papers, Schlesinger Library, Box 50, Folder 894; Pauli Murray to Kathryn (Kay) Clarenbach, August 9, 1966, and Kathryn Clarenbach to Pauli Murray, August 12, 1966, both in PM Papers, Schlesinger Library, Box 50, Folder 893; draft, "Targets of Action, 1966–1967," October 26, 1966, PM Papers, Schlesinger Library, Box 50, Folder 894.

49. Charles B. Markham to Pauli Murray, October 1, 1965, PM Papers, Schlesinger Library, Box 74, Folder 1313; Pauli Murray, Application for Federal Employment, General Counsel, Equal Employment Opportunity Commission, PM Papers, Schlesinger Library, Box 74, Folder 1299; Murray, draft of autobiography, pp. 13–14, PM Papers, Schlesinger Library, Box 81, Folder 1424.

50. Aileen Hernandez, "The Women's Movement, 1965–1975," for the Symposium on the Tenth Anniversary of the Equal Employment Opportunities Commission, Rutgers University Law School, November 28–29, 1975, PM Papers, Schlesinger Library, Box 96, Folder 1704; Graham, *The Civil Rights Era*, 190.

51. Murray, draft of autobiography, p, 13.

52. Murray, Application for Federal Employment, General Counsel, Equal Employment Opportunity Commission; Murray, draft of autobiography, pp. 13–14.

53. Cobble, *The Other Women's Movement*, 3; Woloch, *In a Class by Herself*, 204–205; Pauli Murray to Kay Clarenbach, August 9, 1966, PM Papers, Schlesinger Library, Box 50, Folder 893.

54. *Bowe et al. v. Colgate-Palmolive Co.*, 272 F. Supp. 332 (1967); *Weeks v. Southern Bell Telephone & Telegraph Company*, 277 F. Supp. 117 (S.D. Ga. 1967) District Court, S.D. Georgia; *Weeks v. Southern Bell Telephone & Telegraph Co.*, 408, F. 2nd 228 (1969); *Rosenfeld v. Southern Pacific Company*, 293 F. Supp 1219 (1968).

55. Sonia Pressman Fuentes, "Representing Women, *Frontiers: A Journal of Women's Studies* 18, no. 3 (1997): 101–102.

56. Velma L. Mengelkoch to Marguerite Rawalt, December 5, 1966, Box 50, Folder 896; Walt Murray, "Woman Fights Overtime Curb," *Press-Telegram* (Long Beach, CA), October 28, 1966, PM Papers, Schlesinger Library, Box 59, Folder 1000.

57. For the reluctance of the Court to take up cases for which there was not already broad public support, see Michael Klarman, *From Jim Crow to Civil Rights: The Supreme Court and the Struggle for Racial Equality* (New York: Oxford University Press, 2006).

58. Pauli Murray to Velma Mengelkoch, September 25, 1966; Velma Mengelkoch to Pauli Murray, September 26, 1966, PM Papers, Schlesinger Library, Box 39, Folder 685; NOW, "Minutes of the Organizing Conference of October 29–30, 1966, Washington Post Building, Washington, D.C.," January 20, 1967, PM Papers, Schlesinger Library, Box 5, Folder 898; Pauli Murray to A. L. Wirin and Fred Okrand, General Counsel, Southern California ACLU, September 25, 1966, PM Papers, Schlesinger Library, Box 39, Folder 685; Al Reitman to Dorothy Kenyon, September 29, 1966; Dorothy Kenyon to Pauli Murray, October 13, 1966, PM Papers, Schlesinger Library, Box 39, Folder 685; NOW, Late Bulletin, The Mengelkoch Case, NOW, January 13, 1967, Betty Friedan Papers, Carton 44, Folder 1551.

59. Pauli Murray, drafts for autobiography, n.d., PM Papers, Schlesinger Library, Box 81, Folder 1424.

60. Murray, Application for Federal Employment, General Counsel, Equal Employment Opportunity Commission.

61. Aaron Devor and Nicholas Matte, "Building a Better World for Transpeople: Reed Erickson and the Erickson Educational Foundation," *International Journal of Transgenderism* 10, no. 1 (2007): 47–68; Thomas Buckley, "A Changing of Sex by Surgery Begun at Johns Hopkins," *New York Times*, November 21, 1966; Harry Benjamin, *The Transsexual Phenomenon* (New York: Ace, 1966); Meyerowitz, *How Sex Changed*, 5.

62. FBI Report on Pauli Murray, April 4, 1967, secured through FOIA request; Bruce Webber, "Cartha D. Deloach, no 3 in F.B.I., Is Dead at 92," *New York Times*, March 15, 2013; Pauli Murray, drafts for autobiography, n.d., PM Papers, Schlesinger Library, Box 81, Folder 1424; Cathy Aldridge, "P.S." *New York Amsterdam News*, March 25, 1967.

63. FBI report; Glenda Elizabeth Gilmore, *Defying Dixie: The Radical Roots of Civil Rights, 1919–1950* (New York: Norton, 2009), 442, 565.

64. FBI report; Pauli Murray, diary, April 21, 1967, PM Papers, Schlesinger Library, Box 2, Folder 30; Sonia Pressman Fuentes, interview by author, June 15, 2000.

65. Murray, diary, April 18, 1967.

66. Pauli Murray, draft of autobiography, p. 15, PM Papers, Schlesinger Library, Box 81, Folder 1424; Pauli Murray, diary, April 22 and 18–28, 1967.

67. Murray, diary, May 16, 1967; "Benjamin F. Payton," in *Gale Contemporary Black Biography*; James F. Findlay, *Church People in the Struggle: The National Council of Churches and the Black Freedom Movement, 1950–1970* (New York: Oxford University Press, 1997), footnote 36, p. 193.

68. Pauli Murray, diary, May 21, 1967; Murray, *Song in a Weary Throat*,373.

69. Murray, *Song in a Weary Throat*, 373–375. Murray, diary, June 16, 1967.

70. Murray, diary, April 27, 1967.

71. Minutes of the Organizing Conference of NOW, October 29–30, 1966, Washington, D.C.," and January 30, 1967, PM Papers, Box 51, Folder 898; Minutes, NOW Board of Directors Meeting, February 22–23, 1967, Betty Friedan Papers, Box 44, Folder 1550; Minutes, NOW, Board of Directors, September, 16–17, 1967, PM Papers, Schlesinger Library, Box 51, Folder 899.

72. See letters between Lutz and Murray between October 1965 and April 1966 in PM Papers, Schlesinger Library, Box 97, Folder 1730.

73. Minutes, NOW, Board of Directors, September, 16–17, 1967, PM Papers, Schlesinger Library, Box 51, Folder 899; 1967 National Conference of N.O.W. Schedule, November 1, 1967, Betty Friedan Papers, Box 42, Folder 1491; Mary Eastwood to Pauli Murray, October 26, 1967, PM Papers, Schlesinger Library, Box 51, Folder 899; as recently as July 1966, Eastwood had wanted to defer consideration of the ERA: Unsigned [Eastwood] to Inka O'Hanrahan, July 25, 1966, PM Papers, Schlesinger Library, Box 50, Folder 893.

74. Dorothy Height, Anna Roosevelt Halstead, Margaret Mealey, and Caroline Ware, "To Fulfill the Rights of Negro Women in Disadvantaged Families," June 1–2, 1966, White House Conference, "To Fulfill These Rights," PM Papers, Schlesinger Library, Box 129, Folder 2338. For a fuller discussion of what the feminist anti-poverty coalition was up against at this moment, see Marissa Chappell, *The War on Welfare: Family, Poverty, and Politics in Modern America* (Philadelphia: University of Pennsylvania Press, 2010), 44–50.

75. Anna Arnold Hedgeman to Betty Friedan and Kay Clarenbach, September 13, 1967, PM Papers, Schlesinger Library,Box 51, Folder 899; Anna Arnold Hedgeman to Pauli Murray, sometime over the weekend of the second national conference, November 18–20, 1967, PM Papers, Schlesinger Library, Box 51, Folder 899.

76. Paterson, *Be Somebody*, 180; Minutes of the NOW Conference, November 18, 1967, Betty Friedan Papers, Schlesinger Library, Box 44, Folder 1553.

77. Pauli Murray to Katherine Clarenbach, November 21, 1967, PM Papers, Box 51, Folder 899; Leila Rupp and Verta Taylor, *Survival in the Doldrums: The American Women's Movement, 1945 to the 1960s* (New York: Oxford University Press, 1987), 181, based on an interview with Alice Paul: Amelia R. Fry, "Conversations with Alice Paul: Woman Suffrage and the Equal Rights Amendment," interviews conducted in 1972 and 1973, Regional Oral History Office, University of California.

78. Pauli Murray, "Memorandum in Support of the Amendment to H.R. 7152, Title VII (Equal Employment Opportunity) to Prohibit Discrimination in Employment because of Sex," April 14, 1964, p. 20, PM Papers, Schlesinger Library, Box 85, Folder 1485; Pauli Murray, "The Negro Woman in the Quest for Equality," *Acorn*. Official Publication of Lamba Kappa Mu Sorority, Inc. (June 1964), PM Papers, Schlesinger Library, Box 86, Folder 1486; Esther Peterson, "Negro Women in the Population and the Labor Force," US Department of Labor, December 1967, page 11; Lyndon B. Johnson, Commencement Address, Howard University, June 4, 1965: "Freedom is not enough. You do not wipe away the scars of centuries by saying: Now you are free." For a thorough analysis of Murray's use of both the parallels between black people in general and white women in particular and the interrelatedness between race and gender in the lives of black women alone, see Serena Mayeri, "'A Common Fate of Discrimination': Race-Gender Analogies in Legal and Historical Perspective," *Yale Law Journal* 110, no. 6 (April 2001): 1045–1088. On the limitation of formal freedom, see Nancy MacLean, *Freedom Is Not Enough: The Opening of the American Workplace* (Cambridge, MA: Harvard University Press, 2006).

Chapter 14

1. Pauli Murray to Irene Barlow, September 5, 1967, PM Papers, Schlesinger Library, Radcliffe Institute, Harvard University, Box 5, Folder 138; Pauli Murray, *Song in a Weary Throat: An American Pilgrimage* (New York: Harper & Row, 1987), 375–376.

2. Osagyefo means "victorious in battle" in the Akan language of Ghana; Pauli Murray to Laura [Bornholdt], draft of a letter, November 17, 1967, PM Papers, Schlesinger Library, Box 2, Folder 30.

3. Pauli Murray to Laura [Bornholdt]; Rip Van Winkle [Pauli Murray] to Ichabod Crane [Irene Barlow], November 14, 1967, PM Papers, Schlesinger Library, Schlesinger Library, Box 5, Folder 138. Murray and Barlow had a number of nicknames for each other: IB was Blanket, Ichabod Crane, Jane Bond, Chollie Brown, Julius, Renee; PM was Rip Van Winkle, Puddin' Head, Mushroom, Linus, Punkins, Luv, Seizer, and Pauli.

4. Pauli Murray to Laura [Bornholdt]; it is unclear whether Murray ever sent this letter. On Bornholdt's trip to Ghana, see www.archives.upenn.edu/history/ features/diversity/timeline; on her career more generally, see John Finn, "Trustee Emerita Laura Bornholdt Remembered as a Pioneer; College Salutes Advocate for Liberal Arts Colleges and Historically Black Educational Institutions," *College of Wooster*, July 20, 2012.

5. Mike Davis, "Pauli Murray Believes: Academic Community Must Reassert Leadership," *Afro American*, January 16, 1968, PM Papers, Schlesinger Library, Box 1, Folder 13; Murray, *Song in a Weary Throat*, 378–379. Hedgeman had been forced out of the National Council of Churches on account of age. With her husband, she had become an educational consultant;

Anna Arnold Hedgeman, *The Gift of Chaos: Decades of American Discontent* (New York: Oxford University Press, 1977), 168–171.

6. Murray, *Song in a Weary Throat*, 377.

7. Murray, *Song in a Weary Throat*, 377–378.

8. Pauli Murray, *Dark Testament and Other Poems* (Norwalk, CT: Silvermine, 1970); Pauli Murray, diary, May 31, June 4, 6, 1968, PM Papers, Schlesinger Library, Box 2, Folder 30.

9. Murray, diary, June 6 and 13, 1968; Murray, *Song in a Weary Throat*, 380.

10. *Gray v. Sanders*, 372 U.S. 368 (1963); Pauli Murray, diary, June 15, 1968; Murray, *Song in a Weary Throat*, 398; William Honan, Morris Abram Is Dead at 81; Rights Advocate Led Brandeis," *New York Times*, March 17, 2000.

11. Murray, *Song in a Weary Throat*, 387–388; Nancy Diamond, " 'The Host at Last': Abram Sachar and the Establishment of Brandeis University," *Perspectives on the History of Higher Education* 28 (2011): 223–252; Melvin Urofsky, *Louis D. Brandeis: A Life* (New York: Pantheon, 2009); "Mrs. Roosevelt Joins Board of Brandeis University," *New York Times*, June 18, 1949; Lawrence "Larry" Fuchs, interview by author, October 1, 1999; Murray, diary, June 27, 1968.

12. Fuchs, interview by author, October 1, 1999; Murray, *Song in a Weary Throat*, 387; Bryan Marquard, "Lawrence Fuchs; Professor Crafted Immigration Law Changes," *Boston Globe*, April 7, 2013; David E. Nathan, "Faculty, Alumni Remember Prof. Lawrence Fuchs," *BrandeisNOW*, March 21, 2013.

13. Murray, diary, June 15 and 17, 1968, PM Papers, Schlesinger Library, Box 2, Folder 30; Peter Diamandopoulos [dean of the faculty, Brandeis University] to Pauli Murray, July 12, 1968, Box 45, Folder 799; Murray, *Song in a Weary Throat*, 380–88.

14. Lenie [Caroline Ware] to Pixie [Pauli Murray], August 3, 1968, PM Papers, Schlesinger Library, Box 45, Folder 799; Murray, *Song in a Weary Throat*, 388.

15. See photograph of PM & IB's 1967 Volkswagen, 1969, PM Papers, Schlesinger Library, Box 8, Folder 218, filed in photographs; one day her personal papers would fill 135 boxes in the Schlesinger Library Archives at Harvard University; Murray, *Song in a Weary Throat*, 389.

16. Murray, diary, September 13, 1968. Marry Norris helped her find an apartment in Cambridge at 8 Maple Street: Murray, diary, September 15, 1968; Murray, *Song in a Weary Throat*, 389.

17. Peter Diamandopoulos [dean of the faculty, Brandeis University] to Pauli Murray, July 12, 1968, Box 45, Folder 799; Murray, diary, December 23, 1968 (Murray had learned from Abram that he had exceeded his authority in hiring her and had thereby alienated a number of senior faculty members). On action by the Department of Politics, see Roy C. Macridis to Pauli Murray, October 8 and 15, 1969, PM Papers, Schlesinger Library, Box 45, Folder 802.

18. Elaine Tyler May, "Radical Roots of American Studies," *American Quarterly* 48, no. 2 (1996): 179–200; Michael Holzman, "The Ideological Origins of American Studies at Yale," *American Studies* 40, no. 2 (Summer 1999): 71–99; Fuchs, interview by author, October 1, 1999.

19. Murray recalled her first use of "American Studies" at that time in a letter two years later: Pauli Murray to Larry Fuchs, July 15, 1970, PM Papers, Schlesinger Library, Box 45, Folder 802.

20. Dean Peter Diamandopoulos to Pauli Murray, July 12, 1968, PM Papers, Schlesinger Library, Box 45, Folder 799; Murray, diary, June 9, 1969, PM Papers, Schlesinger Library, Box 2, Folder 30; Murray, *Song in a Weary Throat*, 398.

21. Murray, *Song in a Weary Throat*, 398–399.

22. Murray, *Song in a Weary Throat*, 397–398.

23. Seizer [Pauli Murray] to Julius [Irene Barlow], November 1, 1968 ["All Saints Day"], PM Papers, Schlesinger Library, Box 5, Folder 139; for the names and descriptions of her courses, which she taught each year thereafter, adding two more after the first year, see –Brandeis University, *Bulletin—Arts and Sciences, 1969–1970*, p. 83, PM Papers, Schlesinger Library, Box 46, Folder 821; Murray, *Song in a Weary Throat*, 400.

24. Murray, *Song in a Weary Throat*, 397–408.

25. Murray, *Song in a Weary Throat*, 402–405; D. O. McGovney, Memorandum for Miss Pauli Murray, October 11, 1944, PM Papers, Schlesinger Library, Box 19, Folder 423, in which Murray crossed out every lowercase "n" in "negro" and inserted an uppercase "N" with her fountain pen.

26. R. Kent Newmyer, "Remembering Kitty," *Uncommon Sense: Omohumdro Institute of Early American History & Culture*, no. 121 (Fall 2005); Stanley Katz, "In Memoriam: Kathryn Preyer (1925–2005)," *Perspectives on History: The Newsletter of the American Historical Association* (March 2006). Kathryn Preyer was married to Robert O. Preyer of the Brandeis English Department.

27. Spark Plug [Pauli Murray] to Barney Google [Irene Barlow], October 22, 1968, PM Papers, Schlesinger Library, Box 5, Folder 139.

28. Pauli Murray to Chollie Brown [Irene Barlow], October 24, 1968, PM Papers, Schlesinger Library, Box 5, Folder 139; Murray, *Song in a Weary Throat*, 407.

29. Author's e-mail exchange with Stephen Deitsch, October 11, 2014. Marshall, by then on the Supreme Court, declined the interview; Pauli Murray to Chollie Brown [Irene Barlow], October 24, 1968, PM Papers, Schlesinger Library, Box 5, Folder 139.

30. Murray to Chollie Brown [Irene Barlow], October 24, 1968; Pauli Murray, Midterm Report, November 14, 1968, PM Papers, Schlesinger Library, Box 45, Folder 800.

31. Murray to Chollie Brown [Irene Barlow], October 24, 1968; office hours were listed on her syllabi.

32. Unsigned [Pauli Murray] to Skipper [Caroline Ware], November 2, 1968, PM Papers, Schlesinger Library, Box 101, Folder 1823.

33. Unsigned [Pauli Murray] to Skipper [Caroline Ware], November 2, 1968; Murray, *Song in a Weary Throat*, 406–407.

34. Seizer [Pauli Murray] to Julius [Irene Barlow], "All Saints Day" [November 1, 1968], PM Papers, Schlesinger Library, Box 5, Folder 139.

35. Unsigned [Murray] to Chollie Brown [Irene Barlow], October 24, 1968; Pauli Murray, handwritten draft of a letter, not clear to whom, November 1, 1968, PM Papers, Schlesinger Library, Box 2, Folder 30.

36. Pauli Murray, diary, January 8, 1968; author's e-mail exchange with Stephen Deitsch, October 11, 2014. As at most colleges in 1968, the fall term at Brandeis began in late September and ran through January.

37. John H. Fenton, "15 Negroes Seize Brandeis Center," *New York Times*, January 9, 1969; "Black Students Demands, 1969," Campus Unrest and Students Activism, 1968–2006, Division of Student Life, Box 6, Folder 4, Robert D. Farber University Archives and Special Collections, Brandeis University.

38. "Abram Answers Demands by Black Students," *Boston Globe*, January 10, 1969; "Black Advancement Stressed by Abram," *Boston Globe*, January 9, 1969; Earl Caldwell, "Brandeis Negroes Get Amnesty after They Relinquish Building," *New York Times*, January 19, 1969.

39. "Frisco State Strikers at Brandeis, Harvard," *Boston Globe*, January 9, 1969; "The Ten Demands"; "70 Seize Ford Hall at Brandeis," *Baltimore Sun*, January 9, 1969.

40. John H. Fenton, "Head of Brandeis Suspends Negroes," *New York Times*, January 12, 1969; "70 Seize Ford Hall at Brandeis," *Baltimore Sun*, January 9, 1969; Max Lerner, "Example at Brandeis U." *Los Angeles Times*, January 17, 1969.

41. James Reston, "Black Moderates vs. Black Militants," *New York Times*, January 15, 1969; "Black Power No Match for 'Mother Power,'" *Boston Globe*, January 15, 1969.

42. Murray, diary, January 16, 1969, PM Papers, Schlesinger Library, Box 2, Folder 30.

43. Caldwell, "Brandeis Negroes Get Amnesty," *New York Times*, January 19, 1969.

44. Unsigned [Pauli Murray] to Skipper [Caroline Ware], November 2, 1968, PM Papers, Schlesinger Library, Box 101, Folder 1823; Murray, diary, January 12, 1969, PM Papers, Schlesinger Library, Box 2, Folder 30; Murray, *Song in a Weary Throat*, 415–416. For the role of Mary Wyatt Norris in Murray's life, see Murray, diary, September 15, October 24, and November 11, 1968, PM Papers, Schlesinger Library, Box 2, Folder 30; Mary Wyatt Norris, interview by author, October 11, 2015. Murray referred to Barlow as her "partner" in her diary, on Christmas Eve, December 24, 1968.

45. Murray, diary, May 17 and June 2, 1969; R. [Irene Barlow] to Linus [Pauli Murray], September 29, 1969, PM Papers, Schlesinger Library, Box 5, Folder 139.

46. Murray, diary, June 2 and 18, 1969, PM Papers, Schlesinger Library, Box 2, Folder 30; Student Educational Policy Committee, Brandeis, May 3, 1971, PM Papers, Schlesinger Library, Box 45, Folder 800; Stephen Deitsch to author, October 11, 2014; Fuchs, interview by author,

October 1, 1999, Joyce Antler, "Pauli Murray: The Brandeis Years," *Journal of Women's History* 14, no. 2 (Summer 2002): 79.

47. Murray, diary, May 2, 1970, PM Papers, Schlesinger Library, Box 2, Folder 30.

48. Murray, diary, June 2 and 18, 1969; Lawrence Wien, chairman of the Board of Trustees, to Pauli Murray, April 1, 1969, PM Papers, Schlesinger Library, Box 45, Folder 800 (on the extension of a contract as visiting professor at a salary of $20,874.40); Pauli Murray to Morris Abram, November 14, 1968, PM Papers, Schlesinger Library, Box 45, Folder 800 (in which Murray demanded a permanent position from Morris Abram).

49. Syllabi for "Women in American Society," from fall 1969 forward are collected in PM Papers, Schlesinger Library, Box 45, Folder 845. Gerda Lerner offered a course in women's history at the New School in 1963 that included the black perspective; see Daniel Horowitz, "Feminism, Women's History, and American Social Thought at Midcentury," in *American Capitalism: Social Thought and Political Economy in the Twentieth Century*, edited by Nelsen Lichtenstein (Philadelphia: University of Pennsylvania Press, 2006), 191–212.

50. Syllabi for "Women in American Society"; Pauli Murray, "Liberation of Black Women," *Voices of the New Feminism*, edited by Mary Lou Thompson (Boston: Beacon Press, 1970), 89–90.

51. Evaluation of "Woman and American Society," n.d., PM Papers, Schlesinger Library, Box 45, Folder 800.

52. Murray, "Liberation of Black Women," 88, 89, 90–91, 100, 101–102, and *passim* 87–102; Murray, "The Liberation of Black Women," galleys of essay edited by Thompson, with Murray's handwritten corrections and notes to the editor, PM Papers, Schlesinger Library, Box 126, Folder 2282; Pauli Murray, "The Negro Woman in the Quest for Equality," *Acorn*, Official Publication of Lamba Kappa Mu Sorority, Inc. (June 1964); Pauli Murray to Gerda Lerner, May 10, 1971, PM Papers, Schlesinger Library, Box 99, Folder 1777, on "Liberation of Black Women" as a revision of "The Negro Woman in the Quest for Equality." Lerner published the original, 1964 essay as "Jim Crow and Jane Crow," in *Black Women in White America: A Documentary History*, ed. by Gerda Lerner (New York: Vintage Press, 1972), 592–599.

53. Frances Beal, "Double Jeopardy: To Be Black and Female," *Sisterhood Is Powerful: An Anthology of Writings from the Women's Liberation Movement*, edited by Robin Morgan (New York: Random House, 1970), 340–353 (a revision of a pamphlet of the same name published in 1969); Frances Beal, interview by Loretta J. Ross, Voices of Feminism Oral History Project, Sophia Smith Collection, Smith College, Northhampton, MA.

54. Murray, "Liberation of Black Women," 88, 95; Beal, "Double Jeopardy," 340–353. For other articles published in 1970 by younger black feminists, who aligned themselves with the black liberation movement, despite their critique of the idea of the "black matriarch" as a myth and their rejection of male domination, see Eleanor Holmes Norton, "For Sadie and Maud," in *Sisterhood Is Powerful: An Anthology of Writings from the Women's Liberation Movement*, edited by Robin Morgan (New York: Random House, 1970), 353–359; and Linda La Rue, "The Black Movement and Women's Liberation," *The Black Scholar* 1 (May 1970), 42.

Chapter 15

1. Murray used the terms "homosexuality," "bisexuality," and "transsexuality" in a draft letter she never sent to Johnny Walker, March 14, 1977, PM Papers, Schlesinger Library, Box 63, Folder 1078.

2. Louis Wirth, "The Problem of Minority Groups," in *The Science of Man in the World Crisis*, edited by Ralph Linton (New York: Columbia University Press, 1945), 347–372; Helen Mayer Hacker, "Women as a Minority Group," *Social Forces* 30 (1951): 60–69.

3. For accounts of the social, medical, and legal challenges transsexuals, especially female to males, faced from the mid-1960s to the early 1970s, and the growing news coverage of them, see Joanne Meyerowitz, *How Sex Changed*, 148–151, 226–248; Thomas Buckley, "A Changing of Sex by Surgery Begun at Johns Hopkins," November 21, 1966, *New York Times*; and Jane Brody, "500 in the U.S. Change Sex in Six Years with Surgery," *New York Times*, November 20, 1972. The ACLU had been an advocate for homosexuals since the mid-1960s. According to *ACLU History: Advocacy on Behalf of Transgendered People*, at www.aclu.org,

the ACLU represented "transgender and gender nonconforming people" as early as 1967, when ACLU lawyers "helped persuade the California Supreme Court to strike down a Los Angeles ordinance barring performers from 'impersonating' a person of the opposite sex." For more on the history of the ACLU's growing attention to the rights of those accused of "sexual deviance" in the 1950s and 1960s, see Leigh Ann Wheeler, *How Sex Became a Civil Liberty* (New York: Oxford University Press, 2012), 61–120.

4. The gender division on the board appears in "Resolution Proposed by the Ad Hoc Committee on Women's Rights," ACLU 1970 Biennial Conference, New York University, New York City, June 4, 1970, ACLU Papers, Seeley G. Mudd Manuscript Library, Princeton University; Pauli Murray, diary, August 8, 1968, PM Papers, Schlesinger Library, Box 2, Folder 30, bound diary.

5. Minutes, Equality Committee, ACLU, February 3, 1966, ACLU Papers, Mudd Manuscript Library.

6. Samuel Walker, *In Defense of American Liberties: A History of the ACLU* (New York: Oxford University Press, 1990), 294, 305.

7. Susan M. Hartmann, *The Other Feminists: Activists in the Liberal Establishment* (New Haven, CT: Yale University Press, 1998), 60; "Intended for All: 125 Years of Women at Texas A&M," Aggiewomen.org; Richard L. Lyons, "Texas A&M Ban on Women Upheld," *Washington Post and Times Herald*, April 7, 1959.

8. Margaret Rossiter, *Women Scientists in America: Before Affirmative Action, 1940–1972* (Baltimore: Johns Hopkins University Press, 1995), 374; Jo Freeman, *The Politics of Women's Liberation: A Case Study of an Emerging Social Movement and Its Relation to the Policy Process* (New York: McKay, 1975), 194–195, 374; Rosalind Rosenberg, *Changing the Subject: How the Women of Columbia Shaped the Way We Think about Sex and Politics* (New York: Columbia University Press, 2004), 245–246; Betsy Wade, "Women on the Campus Find a 'Weapon,'" *New York Times*, January 10,1972, PM Papers, Schlesinger Library, Box 45, Folder 807.

9. Rossiter, *Before Affirmative Action*, 375–377. Congress passed the Educational Amendments Act (which included Title IX) and the Equal Rights Amendment in 1972.

10. Statement of Dr. Pauli Murray before the Special Subcommittee on Education, in support of Section 805 of H. R. 16098, June 19, 1970, concerning discrimination against women in education, employment, and other areas, Chairman Honorable Edith Green, p. 5, PM Papers, Schlesinger Library, Box 89, Folder 1542v.

11. Susan Brownmiller, *In Our Time: Memoir of a Revolution* (New York: Dial Press, 1999), 82.

12. Murray came to the defense of Betty Friedan publicly after a profile on her in the *New York Times* had provoked another negative response from many feminists in 1973: Lauri Johnson, "Feminists Score Friedan Article Assailing Movement Disrupters," *New York Times*, March 8, 1973; Pauli Murray to the editor, *New York Times*, March 9, 1973, PM Papers, Schlesinger Library, Box 84, Folder 1473. Murray's letter appeared in the *Times* on March 25, 1973; Pauli Murray to Julie Lee [Daughters of Bilitis] April 3, 1973, PM Papers, Schlesinger Library, Box 95, Folder 1681.

13. Mary Norris, interview by author, October 11 and November 25, 2015.

14. Lawrence Fuchs, interview by author, October 1, 1999.

15. Statement of Dr. Pauli Murray before the Special Subcommittee on Education, in support of Section 805 of H. R. 16098, June 19, 1970, concerning discrimination against women in education, employment and other areas, Chairman Honorable Edith Green, pp. 12–14, PM Papers, Schlesinger Library, Box 89, Folder 1542v. On the phenomenon of southern whites segregating public schools by gender when no longer permitted to segregate by race, see Serena Mayeri, "The Strange Career of Jane Crow: Sex Segregation and the Transformation of Anti-Discrimination Discourse," *Yale Journal of Law & the Humanities* 18, no. 2 (2006): 287–272.

16. *Mengelkoch v. California Industrial Welfare Commission*, 393 U.S. 83 (1968), 284 F.Supp. 950, 956; *Mengelkoch v. California Industrial Welfare Commission*, 391 U.S. 352 (1968); Ronald J. Ostrow, "Crusade against Women's Work Law Kept Alive," *Los Angeles Times*, October 29, 1968; *Mengelkoch v. California Industrial Welfare Commission*, 442 F.2d 1119 (9th Cir. 1971).

17. *Bowe et al. v. Colgate-Palmolive Co.*, 272 F. Supp. 332 (1967); *Weeks v. Southern Bell Telephone & Telegraph Company*, 277 F. Supp. 117 (S.D. Ga. 1967); *Weeks v. Southern Bell Telephone &*

Telegraph Co., 408, F. 2nd 228 (1969); *Rosenfeld v. Southern Pacific Company*, 293 F. Supp 1219 (1968); *Rosenfeld v. Southern Pacific Company*, 444 F2D 1219 (1971). See also Nancy Woloch, *In a Class by Herself: Protective Laws for Women Workers* (Princeton, NJ: Princeton University Press, 2015), 212–224.

18. Barbara Babcock et al., *Sex Discrimination and the Law: Causes and Remedies* (Boston: Little, Brown, 1975), 262–263; Ronnie Steinberg, *Wages and Hours: Labor Reform in Mid-Twentieth Century America* (New Brunswick: Rutgers University Press, 1982), 157.

19. For evidence of why NOW attorneys did not follow through on the Ninth Circuit's decision that *Mengelkoch* did indeed present a "substantial constitutional issue," see comments on "dearth of funds and personal friction among the attorneys" in Mary Eastwood, Tully-Crenshaw Oral History Project, Schlesinger Library, Radcliffe Institute, Harvard University.

20. Pauli Murray to Aileen Hernandez and Wilma Heide, July 20, 1970, PM Papers, Schlesinger Library, Box 51, Folder 901 (on idea of drafting a uniform code of protective labor laws); Susan Deller Ross, "Sex Discrimination and 'Protective' Labor Legislation," May 1, 1970, PM Papers, Schlesinger Library, Box 131, Folder 2379.

21. Hartmann, *The Other Feminists*, 75, 80–81.

22. Statement of Pauli Murray on the Equal Rights Amendment (S.J. Res. 61) submitted to the Senate Judiciary Committee, September 16, 1970, p. 5, PM Papers, Schlesinger Library, Box 89, Folder 1542v. See also Pauli Murray, "Economic and Educational Inequality Based on Sex: An Overview," *Valparaiso Law Review*, Symposium Issue, 5, no. 2 (1971): 237–280.

23. Statement of Pauli Murray on the Equal Rights Amendment (S.J. Res. 61) submitted to the Senate Judiciary Committee, September 16, 1970, 12.

24. Statement of Pauli Murray on the Equal Rights Amendment, 16–17. The senate session on the ERA was cancelled the day she was scheduled to testify, so she submitted her testimony as prepared.

25. Suzanne Post to Pauli Murray, October 5, 1970, PM Papers, Schlesinger Library, Box 59, Folder 1004; Hartmann, *The Other Feminists*, 53, 77–81; Suzy Post, interview by author, May 4, 1997; Linda Kerber, *No Constitutional Right To Be Ladies: Women and the Obligations of Citizenship* (New York: Hill and Wang, 1998), 199–203; Fred Strebeigh, *Equal: Women Reshape American Law* (New York: Norton, 2009), 11–47; Serena Mayeri, *Reasoning from Race: Feminism, Law, and the Civil Rights Revolution* (Cambridge, MA: Harvard University Press, 2011), 61–72.

26. "Mary Maxine Reed [aka Sally Reed], Winner of Sex Discrimination Suit, Is Dead," *New York Times*, October 11, 2002; "1971 Landmark Case in Women's Rights Originated in Boise," *KBOI 2 News*, February 7, 2013; transcript of Ruth Bader Ginsburg's summary in "*Reed v. Reed* at 40: Equal Protection and Women's Rights," *Journal of Gender, Social Policy & the Law* 20, no. 2 (2012): 2–3; also, see "Fact Sheet: *Reed v. Reed* at 40: A Landmark Decision," National Women's Law Center, available at www.nwlc.org.

27. Linda Kerber, "Sally Reed Demands Equal Treatment: November 22, 1971," in *Days of Destiny: Crossroads in American History*, edited by James M. McPherson and Alan Brinkley (New York: DK Publishing, 2001), 441–451; Natalie Wexler, "Sally Reed," in Melvin Urofsky, *100 Americans Making Constitutional History: A Biographical History* (Washington, DC: CQ Press, 2004), 169–171; Ginsburg, "*Reed v. Reed* at 40," 2–3; Opinion of the Supreme Court of the State of Idaho in *Reed v. Reed*, no. 10417, Boise, November 1969 Term, p. 21a, as reprinted in an appendix to the ALCU brief in *Reed v. Reed*, 404 U.S. 71 U. S. Supreme Court Records & Briefs, no. 70–74, Appendix-2.

28. Strebeigh, *Equal*, 27; "High Court Suit Seeks Sex Bias Law Upset," *Philadelphia Inquirer*, July 28, 1970.

29. Debra Bruno, "Justice Ginsburg Remembers Her First Steps in the Law," *Legal Times*, November 13, 2007; Ari L. Goldman, "Gerald Gunther, Legal Scholar, Dies at 75," *New York Times*, August 1, 2002; Strebeigh, *Equal*, 11–14; Ruth Bader Ginsburg and Anders Bruzelius, *Civil Procedure in Sweden* (The Hague: M. Nijhoff, 1965); Wendy Webster Williams, "Justice Ruth Bader Ginsburg's Rutgers Years, 1963–1972," *Women's Rights Law Reporter* 31 (2009–2010): 229–257; Philip Galanes, "Ruth Bader Ginsburg and Gloria Steinem on the Unending Fight for Women's Rights," *New York Times*, November 14, 2015.

30. Ruth Bader Ginsburg, interview by author, August 1, 1985; Strebeigh, *Equal*, 13; Kerber, *No Constitutional Right to Be Ladies*, 202; "High Court Suits Seeks Sex Bias Law Upset," *Philadelphia Tribune*, July 28, 1970.

31. Strebeigh, *Equal*, 25–27.

32. Charles Morgan Jr., Orzell Billingsley Jr., Judge Dorothy Kenyon, Dr. Pauli Murray, Melvin L. Wulf, Plaintiffs' Brief in *Gardenia White v. Bruce Crook*, United States District Court for the Middle District of Alabama Northern Division, Civil Action no. 2263-N, [November 1965], 51, Dorothy Kenyon Papers, Smith College Archives; *Sail'er Inn, Inc. v. Kirby*, 5 Cal. 3d 1 [L.A. No. 29811. In Bank. May 27, 1971].

33. Melvin Wulf, Ruth Bader Ginsburg, Pauli Murray, Dorothy Kenyon, and Allen Derr, "Appellate Brief" in *Reed v. Reed*, p. 60.

34. *F. S. Royster Guano v. Virginia*, 253 U.S. 412 (1920). The year before Ginsburg wrote the brief in *Reed*, the editors of the *Harvard Law Review* had devoted one of its occasional essays on developments in the law to the question of "equal protection" under the Fourteenth Amendment. They included the *Royster* case as providing an articulation of the rational basis test: "Development in the Law: Equal Protection," *Harvard Law Review* 82 (1968–1969): 1076, as cited in the ACLU brief, 8 and 60–61.

35. Opinion of the Supreme Court of the State of Idaho in *Reed v. Reed*, no. 10417, Boise, November 1969 Term, p. 23a, as reprinted in an appendix to the ALCU brief in *Reed v. Reed*, 404 U.S. 71 U. S. Supreme Court Records & Briefs, no. 70–74, Appendix-2; Wulf-Ginsburg-Murray-Kenyon-Derr, Appellate Brief in *Reed v. Reed*, p. 13; Ruth Bader Ginsburg to author, January 13, 1999.

36. Strebeigh, *Equal*, 43–4.

37. *Reed v. Reed*, 404 U.S. 71 (1971).

38. Pauli Murray to Mary Keyserling, December 7, 1971, PM Papers, Schlesinger Library, Box 95, Folder 1657 (this letter was at some point misfiled in a folder of correspondence between Murray and Mary Eastwood).

39. Rosenberg, *Changing the Subject*, 261–262.

40. Hartmann, *The Other Feminists*, 85; Walker, *In Defense of American Liberties*, 294, 305.

41. Pauli Murray to Larry Fuchs, July 15, 1970, PM Papers, Schlesinger Library, Box 45, Folder 803.

42. Nancy Diamond, "The 'Host at Last': Abram Sachar and the Establishment of Brandeis University," *Perspectives in the History of Higher Education*, 28 (2011): 239–241. For financial reversals at two other universities that experienced similar challenges, see Robert A. McCaughey, *Stand Columbia: A History of Columbia University in the City of New York, 1754–2004* (New York: Columbia University Press, 2003), 496–500; and Morton Keller and Phyllis Keller, *Making Harvard Modern: The Rise of America's University* (New York: Oxford University Press, 2001), 307–329.

43. Roy C. Macridis to Pauli Murray, October 8 and 15, 1969; Pauli Murray to Dean Peter Diamandopoulos, October 21, 1969; Peter Diamandopoulos to Pauli Murray, October 27, 1969 and April 16, 1970, PM Papers, Schlesinger Library, Box 45, Folder 802.

44. Larry Fuchs to Pauli Murray, April 23, 1970; Thomas Emerson to Larry Fuchs, May 25, 1970; William Hastie to Larry Fuchs, May 25, 1970; Eugene Rostow to Larry Fuchs, May 28, 1970; Caroline Ware to Larry Fuchs, June 1, 1970; Peter Diamondopolous to Professors Shifrin, Aiken, Fuchs, Lipworth, Schwartz, June 4, 1970; Pauli Murray's notes on members of the ad hoc committee, June 4, 1970, PM Papers, Schlesinger Library, Box 45, Folder 802.

45. Pauli Murray to Ruth and Thomas Emerson, June 30, 1970, PM Papers, Schlesinger Library, Box 45, Folder 802.

46. Larry Fuchs to Peter Diamandopoulos, June 19, 1970, PM Papers, Schlesinger Library, Box 45, Folder 802.

47. Larry Fuchs to Peter Diamandopoulos, June 19, 1970.

48. Pauli Murray to Ruth and Thomas Emerson, June 30, 1970, PM Papers, Schlesinger Library, Box 45, Folder 802.

49. Pauli Murray to Ruth and Thomas Emerson, June 30, 1970.

50. Pauli Murray to Ruth and Thomas Emerson, June 30, 1970.

51. Pauli Murray to Ruth and Thomas Emerson, June 30, 1970.

52. Pauli Murray to Larry Fuchs, July 15, 1970, PM Papers, Schlesinger Library, Box 45, Folder 803.

53. Pauli Murray to Larry Fuchs, July 15, 1970; *Jones v. Alfred H. Mayer Co.*, 392 U.S. 409 (1968).

54. Pauli Murray to Larry Fuchs, July 15, 1970; Leo Kanowitz, *Women and the Law: The Unfinished Revolution* (Albuquerque: University of New Mexico Press, 1969), 155.

55. Pauli Murray to Larry Fuchs, July 15, 1970. Murray may have been influenced by Alfred North Whitehead, *Science and the Modern World: Lowell Lectures* (New York: Pelican Mentor Books, 1925), p. 5, in which Whitehead said, "It requires a very unusual mind to undertake the analysis of the obvious."

56. Pauli Murray to Larry Fuchs, July 15, 1970.

57. "Switch-hitter," in Robert L. Chapman, *Dictionary of American Slang*, 3rd ed. (New York: Harper Collins, 1995), 544: "**1 n** baseball by 1930s A player who bats both righthanded and lefthanded **2 n** by 1950s A versatile person **3 n** by 1956 A bisexual person . . . some people thought he was a switch-hitter But a nice guy—Elmore Leonard." By the turn of the twenty-first century at least some transgender/transsexual people gave "Switch Hitter" the same meaning that Murray did; see http://www.juliaserano.com/switchhitter; Lawrence Fuchs, interview by author, October 1, 1999. The classic statement of marginality as a source of innovation came from the early twentieth-century German sociologist Georg Simmel, whose idea Murray had first encountered in Myrdal's *American Dilemma*.

58. Pauli Murray to Ruth and Thomas Emerson, June 30, 1970, PM Papers, Schlesinger Library, Box 45, Folder 802; Pauli Murray to Family and Friends, July 5, 1970, PM Papers, Schlesinger Library, Box 45, Folder 803.

59. Larry Fuchs to Peter Diamandopoulos, July 23, 1970, PM Papers, Schlesinger Library, Box 45, Folder 802

60. Larry Fuchs to Pauli Murray, July 14, 1970, PM Papers, Schlesinger Library, Box 45, Folder 803.

61. Peter Diamandopoulos to Pauli Murray, February 16, 1971; Pauli Murray to Dean Eugene C. Black, September 16, 1971; Louis Stulberg to Pauli Murray, November 5, 1971, PM Papers, Schlesinger Library, Box 45, Folder 803.

62. Pauli Murray and Mordeca Jane Pollock to Peter Diamandopoulos, November 6, 1970; Peter Diamandopoulos to Pauli Murray and Mordeca Jane Pollock, November 16, 1970, PM Papers, Schlesinger Library, Box 45, Folder 808.

63. Mordeca Jane Pollack, secretary to the Women's Faculty Caucus to President Charles Schottland, March 3, 1971, PM Papers, Schlesinger Library, Box 45, Folder 808 (summarized agreement reached on women's grievances, January 10, 1972).

64. Pauli Murray and Mordeca Jane Pollock to Peter Diamandopoulos, November 6, 1970, PM Papers, Schlesinger Library, Box 45, Folder 808; Table 3, "Brandeis University, Men and Women Faculty of Arts and Sciences," PM Papers, Schlesinger Library, Box 45, Folder 803; Aileen Ward, "Committee on the Status of Women at Brandeis: Final Report," March 7, 1972, PM Papers, Schlesinger Library, Box 45, Folder 812.

65. Pauli Murray to Larry Fuchs, December 7, 1971, PM Papers, Schlesinger Library, Box 45, Folder 800.

66. Betsy Wade, "Women on the Campus Find a 'Weapon,'" *New York Times*, January 10, 1972; Frances Hagopian, "NOW Accuses University of Sexual Discrimination," *The Justice, Brandeis University*, February 27, 1973, Box 45, Folder 807. Pauli Murray to EEOC, PM Papers, April 3, 1973 (formal complaint against TIAA-CREF for sex discrimination in pension payments) and Ruth Bader Ginsburg to Pauli Murray, January 19, 1977 (reports EEOC determination that TIAA-CREF had violated Title VII in paying women less than men), PM Papers, Schlesinger Library, Box 45, Folder 806.

67. Pauli Murray, *Song in a Weary Throat: An American Pilgrimage* (New York: Harper & Row, 1987), 419–421. Murray lived at 504 Beacon St. in Boston from 1970 to 1973.

68. Murray, *Song in a Weary Throat*, 421–422.

69. Murray, *Song in a Weary Throat*, 422–425; "Lyndon Johnson, 36th President, Is Dead"; "High Court Rules Abortions Legal the First 3 Months," *New York Times*, January 23, 1973, p. 22.

70. Murray, *Song in a Weary Throat*, 425; "Irene Barlow, 1914–1973," Memorial Service, February 27, 1973, PM Papers, Schlesinger Library, Box 6, Folder 162; Pauli Murray to Those Who Loved Irene Barlow, March 7, 1973, PM Papers, Schlesinger Library, Box 6, Folder 167.

71. Pauli Murray to Those Who Loved Irene Barlow, March 7, 1973, PM Papers, Schlesinger Library, Box 6, Folder 167.

Chapter 16

1. Pauli Murray, "Diary of a Seminarian," September 1, 1973, PM Papers, Schlesinger Library, Radcliffe Institute, Harvard University, Box 2, Folder 31; Pauli Murray to Larry Fuchs, April 18, 1973, PM Papers, Schlesinger Library, Box 45, Folder 806.

2. Mary Wyatt Norris (who was living with Murray at the time), interview by author, October 11, 2015 (on friends' reaction); Pauli Murray to Peg Holmes, February 21, 1977, PM Papers, Schlesinger Library, Box 96, Folder 1688 (on mental health); Larry Fuchs to Pauli Murray, June 29, 1970, PM Papers, Schlesinger Library, Box 45, Folder 802 (on schedule at Brandeis).

3. Virginia Lieson Brereton and Christa Ressmeyer Klein, "American Women in Ministry: A History of Protestant Beginning Points," in *Women of Spirit: Female Leadership in the Jewish and Christian Traditions*, edited by Rosemary Ruether and Eleanor McLaughlin (New York: Simon & Schuster, 1979), 301–332; Paula S. Nadell, *Women Who Would Be Rabbis: A History of Women's Ordination, 1889–1985* (Boston: Beacon Press, 1998), 118–170.

4. Sarah Azaransky, *The Dream Is Freedom: Pauli Murray and American Democratic Faith* (New York: Oxford, 2011), 45.

5. Pauli Murray, *Song in a Weary Throat: An American Pilgrimage* (New York: Harper & Row, 1987), 48–49, 70; Pauli Murray, "In Unity of Spirit," sermon delivered at St. Philip's in Aquasco, Maryland, September 21, 1975, PM Papers, Schlesinger Library, Box 64, Folder 1090.

6. Pauli Murray, "Healing and Reconciliation," February 13, 1977, sermon delivered at the Church of the Cross, Chapel Hill, North Carolina, PM Papers, Schlesinger Library, Box 67, Folder 1148.

7. Gardiner H. Shattuck Jr., *Episcopalians and Race: Civil War to Civil Rights* (Lexington: University of Kentucky Press, 2000), 97; Robert Prichard, *A History of the Episcopal Church: Complete through the 78th General Convention*, 3rd rev. ed. (New York: Morehouse, 2014), 328–330.

8. Pauli Murray, "To the Members of the Vestry [of St. Marks in-the-Bowery]," March 27, 1966, PM Papers, Schlesinger Library, Box 63, Folder 1078; Prichard, *A History of the Episcopal Church*, 319–373. For a useful guide to terminology and key figures in the church, see Donald S. Armentrout and Robert B. Slocum, eds., *An Episcopal Dictionary of the Church* (New York: Church Publishing, 2000); on Murray and Barlow's move, see the program for Irene Barlow Memorial Service, held at Calvary Episcopal Church, February 27, 1973, PM Papers, Schlesinger Library, Box 6, Folder 162.

9. Prichard, *A History of the Episcopal Church*, 328–330; Murray, *Song in a Weary Throat*, 417–419.

10. Pauli Murray, "Who Do Men Say I Am?" sermon delivered on September 12, 1982, at the Church of the Holy Nativity in Baltimore, PM Papers, Schlesinger Library, Box 65, Folder 1106; Murray, *Song in a Weary Throat*, 427.

11. Thacher Clarke Anderson, interview by author, May 17, 2008; Susan Wrathall, "An Historical Tour of the Close: A History of the Building of the General Theological Seminary of the Protestant Episcopal Church," *Church History*, April 21, 2006, p. 15, www.library.gts.edu; Pauli Murray to Page Smith Bigelow, January 29, 1974, PM Papers, Schlesinger Library, Box 93, Folder 1623.

12. For tax returns for 1972 and 1973, see PM Papers, Schlesinger Library, Box 7, Folder 196; for plans to finance seminary and retirement see Murray, "Diary of a Seminarian," August 22 and 31, 1973; Pauli Murray, "Diary Notes," May 11, 1976, PM Papers, Schlesinger Library, Box 2, Folder 32; for Murray's budget while studying to be a priest see Pauli Murray, "VTS finances," 1975–1976, PM Papers, Schlesinger Library, Box 27, Folder 537; Murray, "Diary of a Seminarian," May 28, 1974. For inheritance see Malcolm E. Martin to Pauli Murray, August 1, 1973, PM Papers, Schlesinger Library, Box 6, Folder 158.

13. Pauli Murray to the General Theological Seminary (GTS) Community, Especially Women, February 16, 1974, PM Papers, Schlesinger Library, Box 22, Folder 462; Murray, "Diary of a Seminarian," August 22 and 31, and September 1, 1973.

14. Murray, *Song in a Weary Throat*, 427–428. For Murray's courses at GTS, see PM Papers, Schlesinger Library, Box 24: Fall 1973: "Junior Tutorial Seminar," "Primitive Christianity (taught by one of PM's favorite people, Pierson Parker—who specialized in the New Testament); Spring 1974 "Canon Law Seminar," "Systematic Theology," also a year-long course in "Church History"; Summer 1974: "Bellevue Clinical Pastoral Education" (CPE), which included an internship at Bellevue Hospital. Fall 1974: "Liturgies," "New Testament," "Philosophy of Religion," "Prayer Course"; Spring 1975: "Church in the Modern World," "Gospel of St. John," "Modern, Theological Systems." PM began as a special student, but after the first year shifted to regular status.

15. Prichard, *A History of the Episcopal Church*, 330.

16. Pauli Murray, "To the Board of Trustees," January 15, 1974, PM Papers, Schlesinger Library, Box 22, Folder 461. Other sources give slightly different numbers.

17. Pauli Murray to [the Right Reverend Morris F. Arnold], January 17, 1974, PM Papers, Schlesinger Library, Box 22, Folder 457. Murray calls herself an E-Pixi-Palian in a letter to two women friends: Pauli Murray to Page Bigelow and Sister Columba, March 5, 1974, PM Papers, Schlesinger Library, Box 22, Folder 463.

18. Pauli Murray to Paul Goranson [the class of 1974], March 11, 1974, and Paul Goranson to Pauli Murray, March 1974, PM Papers, Schlesinger Library, Box 22, Folder 463.

19. [James A.] Carpenter and [Richard W.] Corney, "Evaluation of Pauli Murray—Michaelmas [Fall] Term, 1973—Junior Tutorial-Seminar," PM Papers, Schlesinger Library, Box 22, Folder 463.

20. Pauli Murray, "Public Apology to the Members of Dr. Carpenter's Systematic Theology Preceptorial," February, 26, 1974; Richard Lincoln to Pauli Murray February 26, 1974 (doesn't want her to "shut up" but to experience the "dialectical" . . . "you must be patient with your fellow students"), PM Papers, Schlesinger Library, Box 22, Folder 462.

21. Pauli Murray to Earnest E. Pollack, March 24, 1974, PM Papers, Schlesinger Library, Box 23, Folder 466; Dean Roland Foster, Dean of GTS, to the Reverend John W. Burgess, Bishop of Massachusetts, May 17, 1974 (cover letter to report on Dr. Pauli Murray prepared by the Reverend Pierson Parker, PM's adviser, who comments on her hearing difficulty), PM Papers, Schlesinger Library, Box 26, Folder 516.

22. Pauli Murray to Alvin Kershaw, January 22, 1974, PM Papers, Schlesinger Library, Box 22, Folder 457 ("The attached Open Letter appeared on the Bulletin Board on January 15, affixed to the *New York Times* Op. Ed.").

23. Pauli Murray, "Open Letter to the Board of Trustees, General Theological Seminary" from Pauli Murray, January 15, 1974, PM Papers, Schlesinger Library, Box 22, Folder 461.

24. Pauli Murray, "Open Letter to the Board of Trustees, General Theological Seminary"; Dean Roland Foster to the GTS Community, January 14, 1974, urges all to introduce themselves to the trustees and to come to the Eucharist on Wednesday and pray for them; "help them see the life and mission that we have here." Pauli Murray to Page Bigelow and Sister Columba, March 5, 1974, PM Papers, Schlesinger Library, Box 22, Folder 463; see also Pauli Murray to Father Wright, January 4, 1974, PM Papers, Schlesinger Library, Box 22, Folder 46 (on the importance of hiring a woman to a faculty where there currently is none).

25. Pauli Murray to Alan Reitman, June 11, 1974 (nominating Ginsburg to replace her on the national board) and Pauli Murray to Equality Committee and Members of the National Board, re: ACLU Policy: Proposed Askin and Hopkins-Meyers Statements on Separatism, January 6, 1974, PM Papers, Schlesinger Library, Box 60, Folder 1011.

26. Pauli Murray to Thurgood Marshall, April 16, 1974, PM Papers, Schlesinger Library, Box 61, Folder 1037.

27. Archibald Cox, "Harvard College Amicus Curiae; DeFunis v. Odegaard," in *Reverse Discrimination*, edited by Barry R. Gross (New York: Prometheus, 1977), 185, and 184–197. The best article on the case, and the one that most influenced Murray, was Nina Totenberg, "Discrimination to End Discrimination: The Painful DeFunis Case Raises the Specters of Racism and Anti-Semitism," *New York Times*, April 14, 1974. Murray mentions being troubled by the issues raised in the article in her April 16 letter to Thurgood Marshall; Frederic

William Farrar, *The Early Days of Christianity* (London: Cassell, Petter, Galpin, 1882), 247. Farrar (1831–1903) was dean of Canterbury, a novelist, and a philologist. His comment is cited in the OED as an example of the use of "diversity."

28. Earnest E. Pollock to Pauli Murray, March 19, 1974, PM Papers, Schlesinger Library, Box 23, Folder 466.

29. Pauli Murray to Earnest "Ernie" Pollock, March 21, 21, 1974, PM Papers, Schlesinger Library, Box 23, Folder 466.

30. Pauli Murray to Dean Roland Foster, January 27, 1974, PM Papers, Schlesinger Library, Box 23, Folder 467; Pauli Murray to Barbara Schlachter, January 17, 1974, PM Papers, Schlesinger Library, Box 22, Folder 461.

31. Panic Panic!! [Pauli Murray] to Page [Bigelow], February 20, 1974, PM Papers, Schlesinger Library, Box 93, Folder 1623.

32. Panic Panic!! [Pauli Murray] to Page [Bigelow], February 20, 1974.

33. Pauli Murray to Barbara Ann Lucas and Helen M. Havens, January 19, 1977, PM Papers, Schlesinger Library, Box 63, Folder 1078 (urges them to take race as seriously as sex; quotes herself as having long said "Don't touch me; I'm full of slivers"). Larry Fuchs, interview by author, October 1, 1999 ("Eleanor Roosevelt was a hugger; Pauli was not"); Panic Panic!! [Pauli Murray] to Page [Bigelow], February 20, 1974.

34. Page [Smith Bigelow] to Beloved Pauli [Murray], February 21, and March 19, 1974, PM Papers, Schlesinger Library, Box 93, Folder 1623.

35. Murray, "Diary of a Seminarian," May 28, 1974.

36. Murray, "Diary of a Seminarian," June 1 and 9, 1974.

37. Murray, "Diary of a Seminarian," May 27, 1974. The funeral, sad though it was, provided the excuse for a rare family reunion. By that time the clan stood at twenty-seven: five siblings were left in Murray's generation; eight nieces and nephews in the next; and fourteen great nieces and nephews in the third.

38. Kenneth A. Briggs, "Ordination of Women: One Year After 11 Took Vows as Priests, the Issue Is Seen Headed for Civil Court," *New York Times*, August 6, 1975, PM Papers, Schlesinger Library, Box 67, Folder 1148; Prichard, *A History of the Episcopal Church*, 330; Pauli Murray, "Diary of a Seminarian," August 16–17 and 26, 1974.

39. Murray, "Diary of a Seminarian," September 10, 1974, December 20, 21, and 31, 1974, February 21, 1975, and May 16, 1975; see also Murray's reflections on her seminary career in Murray, "Diary Notes," May 12, 1976, PM Papers, Schlesinger Library, Box, 2, Folder 32.

40. Murray, "Diary of a Seminarian," April 5, 1975; E. Philip Davis, "Comparing Bear Markets— 1973 and 2000," *National Institute Economic Review* 183, no. 1 (January 2003): 78–89; Pauli Murray to Melissa, March 19, 1974, PM Papers, Schlesinger Library, Box 22, Folder 463; Prichard, *A History of the Episcopal Church*, 320–322.

41. Marianne Micks, "The Theological Case for Women's Ordination," in *The Ordination of Women: Pro and Con*, edited by Michael P. Hamilton and Nancy S. Montgomery (New York: Morehouse Barlow, 1975), 2–16; Murray, *Song in a Weary Throat*, 418–419; Murray, "Diary Notes," May 12 and 15, 1976, PM Papers, Schlesinger Library, Box, 2, Folder 32; Pauli Murray to Dean Roland Foster, June 12 (draft) and 13 (final), 1975, Box 27, Folder 525. I see no evidence that Murray was awarded this fellowship. She apparently made do with her savings and other earnings. See Pauli Murray, "VTS finances," 1975–1976, PM Papers, Schlesinger Library, Box 27, Folder 537.

42. Pauli Murray to Dean Roland Foster, May 30 and August 11, 1975, PM Papers, Schlesinger Library, Box 27, Folder 525; Roland Foster to Pauli Murray, September 16, 1975, Box 27, Folder 525; Pauli Murray to Bishop Burgess and Esther, June 6, 1973 [this should be 1975], PM Papers, Schlesinger Library, Box 63, Folder 1071; Pauli Murray to Ben [Bishop Morris Arnold], June 11, 1975, PM Papers, Schlesinger Library, Box 63, Folder 1071; Pauli Murray to Al [the Reverend Alvin Kershaw], June 14, 1975, PM Papers, Schlesinger Library, Box 63, Folder 1071; Pauli Murray to Vestry of Emmanuel Church, June 18, 1975, PM Papers, Schlesinger Library, Box 63, Folder 1071.

43. Pauli Murray to Dean [Roland] Foster, February 2, 1976, PM Papers, Schlesinger Library, Box 27, Folder 525; "Genesis," 5:2; and "Galatians," 3:28, *The Bible*, King James version; Mary Daly to Pauli Murray, August 26, 1976, PM Papers, Schlesinger Library, Box 107, Folder 1918;

Mary Daly, *Beyond God the Father: Toward a Philosophy of Women's Liberation* (Boston: Beacon Press, 1973), xxxiv (gives thanks to her friends, "especially to Pauli Murray"); Letty M. Russell, *Human Liberation in a Feminist Perspective—A Theology* (Philadelphia: Westminster Press, 1974), 188 (footnote 2); Pauli Murray, "The Liberation of Black Women," in Mary Lou Thompson, ed., *Voices of the New Feminism* (Boston: Beacon Press, 1970), 82–102; Rosemary Radford Ruether, *Liberation Theology: Human Hope Confronts Christian History and American Power* (New York: Paulist Press, 1972); Rosemary Radford Ruether, *New Woman, New Earth: Sexist Ideologies and Human Liberation* (New York: Seabury Press, 1975); Marianne H. Micks, "The Theological Case for Women's Ordination," in *The Ordination of Women: Pro and Con,* edited by Michael P. Hamilton and Nancy S. Montgomery (New York: Morehouse Barlow, 1975). On the origins of the phrase, "a useable past," see Henry Steele Commager, *A Search for a Usable Past and Other Essays in Historiography* (New York: Knopf, 1967), 3–27 (describes how the United States, as a new nation, created a history of its own).

44. Daly, *Beyond God the Father,* xvii, xxxiv.
45. Marianne H. Micks, "The Theological Case for Women's Ordination," 5, as quoted in Pauli Murray, "Law and Religion: Impact on the Relation between the Sexes," lecture delivered at the College of William and Mary in Williamsburg, Virginia, January 16, 1980, PM Papers, Schlesinger Library, Box 90, Folder 1569.
46. Pauli Murray, "Father's Day Sermon," sermon delivered at St. Philip's Church in Harlem, June 15, 1975, PM Papers, Schlesinger Library, Box 64, Folder 1090.
47. Pauli Murray, *Proud Shoes,* xix–xx; Azaransky, *The Dream Is Freedom,* 48; Pauli Murray, "Out of the Wilderness," sermon delivered at St. Luke's Presbyterian Church (location not given), July 21, 1974, PM Papers, Schlesinger Library, Box 64, Folder 1089.
48. "Luke," the *Bible,* 10:42, King James Version; Pauli Murray, "Mary Has Chosen the Best Part," sermon delivered at Good Shepherd Episcopal Church in Silver Spring, Maryland, July 14, 1977, PM Papers, Schlesinger Library, Box 64, Folder 1094; Bettye Collier-Thomas, *Daughters of Thunder: Black Women Preachers and Their Sermons, 1850–1979* (San Francisco: Jossey-Bass, 1998), 226–227.
49. Pauli Murray to Dean [Roland] Foster, February 2, 1976, PM Papers, Schlesinger Library, Box 27, Folder 525. The most extreme statement of Black Theology came from James H. Cone (of Union Theological Seminary); see Cone, *Black Theology and Black Power* (New York: Seabury Press, 1969) and *A Black Theology of Liberation* (New York: Lippincott, 1970). Murray preferred the work of J. Deotis Roberts (of the Howard School of Religion), who emphasized the need not only of black liberation but also black-white reconciliation; see Roberts, *Liberation and Reconciliation: A Black Theology* (New York: Lippincott, 1970), both cited in Pauli Murray, "Black Theology and Feminist Theology: A Comparative View," *Anglican Theological Review* 60, no. 1 (1978): 11, footnotes 25–29 and both faulted for failing to understand the value of female liberation within the black community.
50. See correspondence with Rosemary Radford Ruether (who spent 1965 to 1975 at Howard University and who was probably the most important theological influence on Murray) in PM Papers, speech and correspondence for Murray's speech, "Feminism and Nonviolence," at Garrett Theological Seminar (1983), PM Papers, Schlesinger Library, Box, 92, Folder 1595; and chronological correspondence, 1973, Box 107, Folder 1912. See also Ruether, *Liberation Theology;* preface to Ruether, *Religion and Sexism: Images of Women in the Jewish Christian Traditions* (New York: Simon & Schuster, 1974); Ruether, *New Woman, New Earth;* Paul K. Jewet, *Man as Male and Female: A Study of Sexual Relationships from a Theological Point of View* (Grand Rapids: Eerdmans, 1975). Mary Daly to Pauli Murray, August 26, 1973, PM Papers, Schlesinger Library, Box 107, Folder 1918, credits Murray as "godmother" of her new book, *Beyond God the Father,* for helping Daly to get the book "off the ground" during the year 1970–1971. Daly goes on to say, "though we seem to be moving in somewhat different ways, you were AND ARE (like it or not) the 'godmother' of the embryonic (no, not the beginning only) Beyond God the Father."
51. Pauli Murray, "Black Theology and Feminist Theology: A Comparative Study," Senior Thesis, Protestant Episcopal Theological Seminary of Virginia, Alexandria, Virginia, March 20, 1976, PM Papers, Schlesinger Library, Box 23, Folder 475, p. 52; Murray, "Diary Notes," March 20, 1976, PM Papers, Schlesinger Library, Box 2, Folder 32. On the recent use of diversity

in Anglican theology: Kathryn L. Reinhard, "Conscience, Interdependence, and Embodied Difference: What Paul's Ecclesial Principles Can Offer the Contemporary Church," *Anglican Theological Review* 94, no. 3 (Summer 2012): 403–428; John Kenneth Gibson, "A Pneumatological Theology of Diversity," *Anglican Theological Review* 94, no. 3 (Summer 2012): 429–449.

52. Pauli Murray, diary on loose-leafed pages, April 22–June 14, 1976, PM Papers, Schlesinger Library, Box 2, Folder 33.

53. See David E. Sumner, *The Episcopal Church's History: 1945–1985* (Wilton: Morehouse, 1987), 7–30; Denis Hevesi, "Constance E. Cook, 89: Wrote Abortion Law," January 24, 2009, *New York Times*; Editors, "Of Rites and Rights," *New York Times*, August 9, 1976, and Pauli Murray to editor, *New York Times*, August 29, 1975, PM Papers, Schlesinger Library, Box 67, Folder 1148; Eleanor Blau, "Ordination of Women as Priests Authorized by Episcopal Church; House of Deputies Decides to Concur with Resolution Passed by Bishops," *New York Times*, September 17, 1976, PM Papers, Schlesinger Library, Box 67, Folder 1148; Marjorie Hyer, "Episcopal Priests Ordained," *Washington Post*, Sunday, January 9, 1977, A3, PM Papers, Schlesinger Library, Box 63, Folder 1068.

54. "Page Bigelow Ordained Priest at St. George's," January 6, 1976, PM Papers, Schlesinger Library, Box 93, Folder 1624; Marjorie Hyer, "Episcopal Priests Ordained," *Washington Post*, Sunday, January 9, 1977, A3, PM Papers, Schlesinger Library, Box 63, Folder 1068; John Knoble, "Yale Law Grad First Black Woman Priest," *New Haven Register*, Sunday, June 26, 1977, A-15, PM Papers, Schlesinger Library, Box 63, Folder 1068. Marjorie Hyer, "Episcopal Priests Ordained," *Washington Post*, Sunday, January 9, 1977, A3, PM Papers, Schlesinger Library, Box 63, Folder 1068.

55. The Reverend James C. Wattley to the Right Reverend William F. Creighton, Episcopal Church House, Mt. St. Alban, Washington, DC, January 13, 1977, 1977, Pauli Murray to James C. Wattley, January 21–22, 1977, and Wattley to Murray, January 26, 1977, PM Papers, Schlesinger Library, Box 62, Folder 1050.

56. Pauli Murray, "Healing and Reconciliation," February 13, 1977, sermon delivered at Chapel of the Cross, Chapel Hill, North Carolina, PM Papers, Schlesinger Library, Box 67, Folder 1148.

57. Sandra G. Boodman, "The Poet as Lawyer and Priest," *Washington Post*, February 14, 1977, PM Papers, PM Papers, Schlesinger Library, Box 63, Folder 1068.

58. Pauli Murray, draft of a speech, possibly to be delivered at Hunter College, PM Papers, Schlesinger Library, Box 63, Folder 1078; Pauli Murray, "Memogram to Family and Friends," March 10, 1977, PM Papers, Schlesinger Library, Box 67, Folder 1148; J. Wynn Rousuck, "Pauli Murray," *Sun Magazine*, April 24, 1977, PM Papers, Schlesinger Library, Box 1, Folder 14; Pauli Murray to Peg Holmes Gilbert, February 8, 1977, PM Papers, Schlesinger Library, Box 96, Folder 1688; Doreen M. Drury, "Boy-Girl, Imp, Priest: Pauli Murray and the Limits of Identity," *Journal of Feminist Studies in Religion* 29, no. 1 (2013): 146.

59. Pauli Murray, "Memogram to Family and Friends," March 10, 1977, PM Papers, Schlesinger Library, Box 67, Folder 1148; Carolyn Lewis, "Dream Haunts Practical Poet," *Washington Post*, December 11, 1966, PM Papers, Schlesinger Library, Box 1, Folder 13.

60. Eleanor Blau, "Episcopal Bishops Call for Unity as Convention Ends," *New York Times*, September 24, 1976.

61. A. L. Kershaw, "Another View of Human Sexuality," January 25, 1976, Emmanuel Church, Boston, PM Papers, Schlesinger Library, Box 63, Folder 1073; The Right Reverend Hon B. Coburn, the Episcopal Diocese of Massachusetts, "To the Clergy of the Diocese," PM Papers, Schlesinger Library, Box 62, Folder 1050; Pauli Murray to John "Johnny" Walker, March 14, 1977 [Not Sent], PM Papers, Schlesinger Library, Box 63, Folder 1078.

62. "Episcopals to Ordain Black Woman, Lesbian," *News American*, January 8, 1977, 1 [Washington], PM Papers, Schlesinger Library, Box 63, Folder 1068; "A Clarification," *News American*, [front page], Saturday, January 15, 1977.

63. Pauli Murray to John "Johnny" Walker, March 14, 1977 [whole letter crossed out and NOT SENT written across it in red ink; specific sentences also crossed out, with lines through them, as indicated in quoted passage.] By "unisexuality" Murray probably meant "androgyny"; by "metabolic imbalance" she may have referred to the lingering effects of her thyroid condition;

and by "varieties of approach to mental health" she may have been thinking of the removal of homosexuality from the *DSM* as a mental illness.

64. D. O. Cauldwell, "Psychopathis Transexualis [note spelling]," *Sexology* 16 (December 1949): 274–280. Magnus Hirshfeld first to describe the phenomenon in the 1920s in Germany. Cauldwell, a psychiatrist and surgeon, retired from the War Department, was the first to name it. See Joanne Meyerowitz, *How Sex Changed: A History of Transsexuality in the United States* (Cambridge, MA: Harvard University Press, 2002), 10, 18–21, 281. For articles on transsexualism, search Proquest Historical Newspapers. In 1975, seventy stories on transsexualism appeared in major newspaper; in 1976, there were 239, and in 1977, 360 stories.

65. Rene Richards, *No Way Rene: The Second Half of My Notorious Life* (New York: Simon & Schuster, 2007), 23–24; Dave Anderson, " 'In a Glass Cage' with Rene," *New York Times*, September 2, 1977.

66. Pauli Murray to Margaret [Peg] Holmes Gilbert, February 8, 1977, PM Papers, Schlesinger Library, Box 96, Folder 1688.

67. Mary Wyatt Norris, interview by author, October 11, 2015; Marc Stein, *Encyclopedia of Lesbian, Gay, Bisexual, and Transgender History in America* (New York: Scribner's, 2004), 281; Susan Stryker, *Transgender History* (Berkeley, CA: Seal Press, 2008), 91–120.

68. Vermont Royster, "Thinking Things Over," *Wall Street Journal*, February 16, 1977, PM Papers, Schlesinger Library, Box 67, Folder 1148; the Reverend Peter James Lee, "Servant Children," February 13, 1977, PM Papers, Schlesinger Library, Box 67, Folder 1148.

69. "First Negro Woman Priest Holds Service in N.C." *Washington Post*, February 25, 1977, PM Papers, Scrapbook on Ordination of Women, Box 67, Folder 1148; the Reverend Peter James Lee, "Servant Children," February 13, 1977, PM Papers, Schlesinger Library, Box 67, Folder 1148; Sherry Shanklin, "Old Friends Turn Out to Hear Her Sermon," *Durham Morning Herald*, February 14, 1977, PM Papers, Schlesinger Library, Box 63, Folder 1068; Pauli Murray, "Healing and Reconciliation," February 13, 1977, Church of the Cross, Chapel Hill, North Carolina, PM Papers, Schlesinger Library, Box 67, Folder 1148.

70. Murray, "Healing and Reconciliation."

71. Pauli Murray to Jim [Reverend James A. Carpenter of GTS] and Mary [Mary Louise Dunbar Carpenter], February 4, 1977, PM Papers, Box 63, Folder 1078; Murray, "Healing and Reconciliation." For later references to homosexuality in Murray's sermons, see Anthony B. Pinn, *Pauli Murray: Selected Sermons and Writings* (Maryknoll, NY: Orbis Books, 2006), 33 (1978) and 157–158 (1981).

72. Murray, "Healing and Reconciliation."

73. Murray, "Healing and Reconciliation."

74. Murray, "Healing and Reconciliation."

Epilogue

1. Murray, diary, March 26, 1976, PM Papers, Schlesinger Library, Box 2, Folder 32.

2. Pauli Murray to the Very Reverend Roland Foster, dean of GTS, February 4, 1977, PM Papers, Schlesinger Library, Box 64, Folder 1078; Pauli Murray to Jim and Mary [Carpenter, from GTS], February 4, 1977, PM Papers, Schlesinger Library, Box 63, Folder 1078: mentions being approached by several seminaries for jobs—all non-Episcopalian—with retirement ages of sixty-five, sixty eight, and sixty-nine—which means that only the last would give her even a three-year chance of working.

3. Pauli Murray to the Right Reverend John B. Coburn, Office of the Diocesan Bishop, Massachusetts, April 8, 1977, PM Papers, Schlesinger Library, Box 62, Folder 1050; John Knoble, "Yale Law Grad First Black Woman Priest," *New Haven Register*, Sunday, June 26, 1977, PM Papers, Schlesinger Library, Box 63, Folder 1068.

4. Pauli Murray, Extra-Parochial Report, 1979 (reports presiding over twenty services, two marriages, one burial, forty-two Holy Eucharists), PM Papers, Schlesinger Library, Box 62, Folder 1051; Pauli Murray to the Right Reverent John B. Coburn, Office of the Diocesan Bishop, Massachusetts, April 8, 1977, PM Papers, Schlesinger Library, Box 62, Folder 1050; tape recording of Pauli Murray seminar in Dr. Micks's class "Adam & Eve" Virginia Theological

Seminary, April 5, 1978, 2623 audiotape. Request as T-245, reel 50; Pauli Murray, Virginia Theological Seminary, panelist, "Black Women, Racism, and the American Legal Process," at Black Women: An Historical Perspective, First National Scholarly Research Conference on Black Women, sponsored by the National Council of Negro Women, Inc., Washington DC, November 12–13, 1979, PM Papers, Schlesinger Library, Box 129, Folder 2338; Kasey Miller and Kate Swift, "Pauli Murray," *Ms*, March 1980, 64, 60–64, PM Papers, Schlesinger Library, Box 1, Folder 15.

5. Pauli Murray to Right Reverend John Coburn and Right Reverend Morris F. Arnold, January 30, 1978 [her annual letter, a little late], PM Papers, Schlesinger Library, Box 62, Folder 1051; Pauli Murray, Extra-Parochial Report, 1979 PM Papers, Schlesinger Library, Box 62, Folder 1051; Alan S. Binder, "The Anatomy of Double Digit Inflation in the 1970s," in *Inflation: Causes and Effects*, edited by Robert E. Hall (Chicago: University of Chicago Press, 2009), 261–282.

6. Pauli Murray to Right Reverend John Coburn and Right Reverend Morris F. Arnold, January 30, 1978; Pauli Murray, diary, January 13, 1980, PM Papers, Schlesinger Library, Box 2, Folder 33; Randi Henderson, "Co-founder of NOW Has Many Causes," *Baltimore Sun*, June 27, 1982, PM Papers, Schlesinger Library, Box 1, Folder.

7. For difficulty in persuading editors to publish new edition of *Proud Shoes*, see correspondence re: *Proud Shoes*, 1967 to 1977, PM Papers, Schlesinger Library, Box 78, Folder 1378.

8. For the papers relating to the sale and purchase of her automobiles, see PM Papers, Schlesinger Library, Box 8, Folders 217–221.

9. Murray, "Atonement," sermon given at a place unspecified, September 9, 1979, PM Papers, 64, Folder 1099; Murray, "What the Protestant Episcopal church of the USA Could Be Doing in the Next Century: 1975–2075," n.d., PM Papers, Box 67, Folder 1148; Pauli Murray, "Law and Religion: Impact on the Relation between the Sexes," lecture given at the College of William and Mary in Williamsburg, Virginia, January 16, 1980, PM Papers, Schlesinger Library, Box 90, Folder 1569; Pauli Murray, "Forgiveness without Limits," sermon given at the Church of the Atonement, Washington, DC, November 11, 1979, PM Papers, Schlesinger Library, Box 64, Folder 1100; Pauli Murray, Sermon, May 2, 1982, Church of the Holy Nativity, Baltimore, PM Papers, Schlesinger Library, Box 65, Folder 1106.

10. Pauli Murray to Page Bigelow, April 1, 1980, and June 2, 1982, PM Papers, Schlesinger Library, Box 93, Folder 1626.

11. Pauli Murray, diary, December 8, 1982, January 1 and 4, 1983, PM Papers, Schlesinger Library, Box 2, Folder 33.

12. Pauli Murray, diary, January 4 and March 10, 1984; Pauli Murray, Greetings! December 1984, PM Papers, Schlesinger Library, Box 223, Folder 2027.

13. Pauli Murray, Greetings! December 1984, PM Papers, Schlesinger Library, Box 223, Folder 2027.

14. Pauli Murray, diary, April 12, 1978, PM Papers, Schlesinger Library, Box 2, Folder 33; Pauli Murray to John B. Coburn, January 19, 1980, PM Papers, Schlesinger Library, Box 62, Folder 1052; Pauli Murray to Bishop John Coburn, December 31, 1982, PM Papers, Schlesinger Library, Box 62, Folder 1053 ("I retire as Priest-in-Charge of the Church of the Holy Nativity today"); Pauli Murray to Family and Friends, March 10, 1985, PM Papers, Schlesinger Library, Box 113, Folder 2027.

15. Pauli Murray to Family and Friends, March 10, 1985.

16. Hunter Commencement (1985), PM Papers, Schlesinger Library, Box 92, Folder 1602; "Dr. Pauli Murray, Episcopal Priest," *New York Times*, July 4, 1985.

17. Pauli Murray to Peg [Margaret Holmes Gilbert], March 18, 1973, PM Papers, Box 96, Folder 1688; Mary Norris, interview by author, November 25, 2015. For essays and books that brought Murray to a broader audience see, Cynthia Harrison, *On Account of Sex: The Politics of Women's Issues, 1945–1968* (Berkeley: University of California Press, 1988); Rosalind Rosenberg, "Pauli Murray and the Killing of Jane Crow," in *Forgotten Heroes*, edited by Susan Ware (New York: Free Press, 1998); Susan Hartmann, *The Other Feminists: Activists in the Liberal Establishment*. New Haven, CT: Yale University Press, 1998; Linda K. Kerber, *No Constitutional Right to Be Ladies: Women and the Obligations of Citizenship* (New York: Hill and Wang, 1998); Susan Ware, ed., "Dialogue: Pauli Murray's Notable Connections," *Journal*

of Women's History 14, no. 2 (Summer 2002): 54–57 (with introduction by Ware and essays by Patricia Bell-Scott, Glenda Elizabeth Gilmore, Rosalind Rosenberg, Susan M. Hartmann, Joyce Antler, Leila J. Rupp, and Verta Taylor); Glenda Elizabeth Gilmore, *Defying Dixie: The Radical Roots of Civil Rights, 1919–1950* (New York: W. W. Norton, 2008); Serena Mayeri, *Reasoning from Race: Feminism, Law, and the Civil Rights Revolution* (Cambridge, MA: Harvard University Press, 2011); Kenneth W. Mack, *Representing the Race: The Creation of the Civil Rights Lawyer* (Cambridge, MA: Harvard University Press, 2012); Patricia Bell-Scott, *The Firebrand and the First Lady: Portrait of a Friendship: Pauli Murray, Eleanor Roosevelt, and the Struggle for Social Justice* (New York: Knopf, 2016).

18. Pauli Murray, *Song in a Weary Throat: An American Pilgrimage* (New York: Harper Collins, 1987), 437.

19. Wendy Webster Williams, "Ruth Bader Ginsburg's Equal Protection Clause, 1970–1980," *Columbia Journal of Gender and Law* 25 (2013): 49, 41–49. As later scholars would point out, Ginsburg's strategy had serious limits, acting only on states and the federal government, and therefore failing to protect women where they sometimes needed protection most, within the family. For an alternative approach, see Reva B. Siegel, "She the People: The Nineteenth Amendment, Sex Equality, Federalism, and the Family," *Harvard Law Review* 115, no. 4 (February 2002): 948–1046. Moreover, many younger black feminists complained that white women too often used the "racist-sexist" analogy to compare discrimination against white women with discrimination against black men, excluding altogether black women; see, for instance, bell hooks, *Ain't I a Woman* (Boston: South End Press, 1981), 8, 140–141; and more broadly, Serena Mayeri, "'A Common Fate of Discrimination': Race-Gender Analogies in Legal and Historical Perspective," *Yale Law Journal* 110, no. 6 (April 2001): 1045–1088.

20. Pauli Murray, "Minority Women and Feminist Spirituality," 1983–1984, PM Papers, Schlesinger Library, Box 87, Folder 1508 (in which she discusses the Combahee River Collective's 1977 "Black Feminist Statement" on the multilayered oppression faced by black women), reprinted in Pinn, ed., *Pauli Murray: Selected Sermons and Writings*, 243; Pauli Murray to "Sisters," quoted in Bell-Scott, *The Firebrand and the First Lady*, 346–347, emphasis in the original. For essays and books that developed the idea of the interconnectedness of race and gender in the late 1970s and 1980s, see Combahee River Collective, "A Black Feminist Statement" (April 1977), in *Capitalist Patriarchy and the Case for Socialist Feminism*, edited by Zillah Eisenstadt (New York: Monthly Review Press, 1978); Cherrie Moraga and Gloria E. Anzaldua, eds., *This Bridge Called My Back: Writings of Radical Women of Color* (Watertown, MA: Persephone Press, 1981); Deborah King, "Multiple Jeopardy, Multiple Consciousness: The Context of a Black Feminist Ideology," *Signs: Journal of Women in Culture and Society* 14 (Fall 1988): 42–72 (King mentions Murray in passing without noting her contribution to the idea of the interconnectedness of race, gender, and economic oppression); Kimberlé Crenshaw, "Demarginalizing the Intersection of Race and Sex: A Black Feminist Critique of Antidiscrimination Doctrine, Feminist Theory, and Antiracist Politics," *University of Chicago Legal Forum* (1989): 139–167.

21. On diversity as a legal goal, see, for instance, Martha Minow, *Making All the Difference: Inclusion, Exclusion, and American Law* (Ithaca, NY: Cornell University Press, 1990), 19–78.

22. Pauli Murray to Patricia Bell-Scott, December 12, 1983, quoted in Bell-Scott, *The Firebrand and the First Lady*, xiii.

23. Cover of *Time*, June 9, 2014; Julie Hirschfeld Davis and Matt Apuzzo, "U.S. Directs Public Schools to Allow Transgender Access to Restrooms," *New York Times*, May 12, 2016.

24. Noah Remnick, "Yale Defies Calls to Rename Calhoun College," *New York Times*, April 27, 2016; Murray, *Song in Weary Throat*, 435; Murray, *Dark Testament and Other Poems* (Norwalk, CT: Silvermine, 1970), dedication page; Maida Springer Kemp served as her executor. Murray's remaining papers went to the Schlesinger Library at Radcliffe College, Harvard University.

BIBLIOGRAPHY

Archives

Archives of the Appellate Division, Supreme Court of the State of New York, Second Judicial Department, Brooklyn, New York

    Pauli Murray's application for admission to the Bar of the State of New York: In the Matter of the Application of Pauli Murray for Admission to Practice as an Attorney and Counselor-at-Law, New York Supreme Court, Appellate Division, Second Department, June 11, 1948

The Federal Bureau of Investigation [FBI]

    FBI Report on Pauli Murray

Schlesinger Library, Radcliffe Institute, Harvard University, Cambridge, MA

    Pauli Murray Papers

    Betty Friedan Papers

    Catherine East Papers

    Marguerite Rawalt Papers

    Mary Eastwood Papers

    NOW Papers

Manuscript Division, Moorland-Spingarn Research Collection, Howard University, Washington, DC

    Pauli Murray Papers

    Caroline Ware Papers

Walter P. Reuther Library, Wayne State, University of Michigan

    Esther Peterson Papers

    Katherine Ellickson Papers

Seeley G. Mudd Manuscript Library, Princeton University

    ACLU Papers

Sophia Smith Collection, Smith College

    Dorothy Kenyon Papers

Papers Available on Microfilm

    Records of the President's Commission on the Status of Women, Archival Collections, John F. Kennedy Presidential Library and Museum, Boston, MA

    Records of the National Woman's Party, Manuscript Division, Library of Congress, Washington, DC

Newspapers and Periodicals

Afro-American
Atlanta Constitution
Baltimore Sun
Chicago Defender
Crisis
Ebony
Negro Digest
New Journal and Guide
New York Herald Tribune
New York Times
New York Amsterdam News
Pittsburgh Courier
PM
Sentinel
The Survey
Washington Post

Published Sources, Dissertations, and Theses

Addams, Jane. "The College Woman and the Family Claim." *Commons* (September 1898): 3–7.

Aguirre, Frederick P. "Mendez v. Westminster School District: How It Affected *Brown v. Board of Education.*" *Journal of Hispanic Higher Education* 4 (October 2005): 321–332.

Anderson, James D. *The Education of Blacks in the South, 1860–1935.* Chapel Hill: University of North Carolina Press, 1988.

Antler, Joyce. "Pauli Murray: The Brandeis Years." *Journal of Women's History* 14, no. 2 (Summer 2002): 78–82.

Armentrout, Donald S. and Robert B. Slocum, eds. *An Episcopal Dictionary of the Church.* New York: Church Publishing, 2000.

Ascoli, Max. "Alexander Pekelis, 1902–1946." *Social Research* 2 (March 1947): 1–2.

Ashmore, Susan Youngblood. *Carry It On: The War on Poverty and the Civil Rights Movement in Alabama, 1964–1972.* Athens: University of Georgia Press, 2008.

Azransky, Sarah. "Jane Crow: Pauli Murray's Intersections and Antidiscrimination Law." *Journal of Feminist Studies of Religion* 11, no. 3 (2013): 155–160.

Babcock, Barbara et al. *Sex Discrimination and the Law: Causes and Remedies.* Boston: Little, Brown, 1975.

Baker, Ella and Marvel Cooke. "The Bronx Slave Market." *Crisis* 42 (November 1935): 330–331.

Baldwin, James. "Stranger in the Village. *Harpers,* October 1, 1953, pp. 42–48.

Baldwin, James. *Notes of a Native Son.* Boston: Beacon Press, 1955.

Baldwin, James. *The Fire Next Time.* New York: Dial Press, 1963.

Balkin, Jack M. and Sanford Levinson. "The Dangerous Thirteenth Amendment." *Columbia Law Review* 112, no. 7 (November 2012): 1459–1499.

Beilke, Jayne R. "The Changing Emphasis of the Rosenwald Fellowship Program, 1928–1948." *Journal of Negro Education* 66, no. 1 (Winter 1997): 3–15.

Bell-Scott, Patricia. "To Write Like Never Before: Pauli Murray's Enduring Yearning." *Journal of Women's History* 14, no. 2 (Summer 2002): 58–61.

Bell-Scott, Patricia. *The Firebrand and the First Lady: Portrait of a Friendship: Pauli Murray, Eleanor Roosevelt, and the Struggle for Social Justice.* New York: Knopf, 2016.

Bender, Marylin. "Black Women in Civil Rights: Is She a Second-Class Citizen?" *New York Times,* September 2, 1969.

Benedict, Ruth. *Patterns of Culture.* Boston: Houghton Mifflin, 1934.

Benjamin, Harry. *The Transsexual Phenomenon.* New York: Ace, 1966.

Berg, Richard K. "Equal Employment Opportunity under the Civil Rights Act of 1964." *Brooklyn Law Review* 31 (1964–1965): 62–97.

Bernstein, Shana. *Bridges of Reform: Interracial Civil Rights Activism in Twentieth Century Los Angeles.* New York: Oxford University Press, 2011.

Beth, Loren P. *John Marshall Harlan: The Last Whig Justice.* Louisville: University of Kentucky Press, 1992.

Binder, Alan S. "The Anatomy of Double Digit Inflation in the 1970s." In *Inflation: Causes and Effects,* edited by Robert E. Hall. Chicago: University of Chicago Press, 2009.

Black, Allida. *Casting Her Own Shadow: Eleanor Roosevelt and the Shaping of Postwar Liberalism.* New York: Columbia University Press, 1996.

Bloom, Jonathan D. "Brookwood Labor College." In *The Re-education of the American Working Class,* edited by Steven London, Elvira R. Tarr, and Joseph F. Wilson, Contributions in Economics and Economic History (Book 31). Westport, CT: Greenwood, 1990.

Bloom, Jonathan D. "Brookwood Labor College: The Final Years, 1933–1937." *Labor's Heritage* 2, no. 2 (April 1990): 24–43.

Boas, Franz. *The Mind of Primitive Man: A Course of Lectures Delivered before the Lowell Institute, Boston, Mass., and the National University of Mexico, 1910–1911.* New York: Macmillan, 1911.

Bok, Sissela. *Alva Myrdal: A Daughter's Memoir.* Cambridge: Radcliffe Biography Series, 1991.

Branch, Taylor. *Parting the Waters: America in the King Years, 1954–1963.* New York: Simon & Schuster, 1988.

Branch, Taylor. *At Canaan's Edge: America in the King Years, 1965–68.* New York: Simon & Schuster, 2006.

Brauer, Carl. "Women Activists, Southern Conservatives, and the Prohibition of Sex Discrimination in Title VII of the 1964 Civil Rights Act. *Journal of Southern History* 49, no. 1 (February 1983): 37–56.

Brereton, Virginia Lieson and Christa Ressmeyer Klein. "American Women in Ministry: A History of Protestant Beginning Points." In *Women of Spirit: Female Leadership in the Jewish and Christian Traditions,* edited by Rosemary Ruether and Eleanor McLaughlin. New York: Simon & Schuster, 1979.

Brilliant, Mark. *The Color of America Has Changed: How Racial Diversity Shaped Civil Rights Reform in California, 1941–1978.* New York: Oxford University Press, 2010.

Brodie, Janet Farrell. *Contraception and Abortion in Nineteenth-Century America.* Ithaca, NY: Cornell University Press, 1997.

Brooks, Cornell Williams. "Pauli Murray: A Great American Hero." Posted to MarriageEquality. org. February 2, 2015.

Brown, Cynthia Grant. "Women in the Legal Profession from the 1920s to the 1970s." *Cornell Law Faculty Publications,* Paper 12 (2009): 5–8

Brown, Elsa Barkley. "Womanist Consciousness: Maggie Lea Walker and the Independent Order of Saint Luke." *Signs,* 14 (Spring 1989): 610–633.

Brown, Leslie. *Upbuilding Black Durham: Gender, Class, and Black Community Development in the Jim Crow South.* Chapel Hill: University of North Carolina Press, 2008.

Brownmiller, Susan. *In Our Time: Memoir of a Revolution.* New York: Dial Press, 1999.

Bruno, Debra. "Justice Ginsburg Remembers Her First Steps in the Law." *National Law Journal,* November 13, 2007.

Buckmaster, Henrietta. *Let My People Go: The Story of the Underground Railroad and the Growth of the Abolition Movement.* New York: Harper & Brothers, 1941.

Campbell, James T. *Middle Passages: African American Journeys to Africa, 1787–2005.* New York: Penguin Press, 2006.

Caro, Robert. *The Years of Lyndon Johnson.* Vol. 4, *The Passage of Power.* New York: Knopf, 2012.

Cauldwell, D. O. "Psychopathis Transexualis [note spelling]." *Sexology* 16 (December 1949): 274–280.

Chappell, Marissa. *The War on Welfare: Family, Poverty, and Politics in Modern America.* Philadelphia: University of Pennsylvania Press, 2010.

Chauncey, George. *Gay New York: Gender, Urban Culture, and the Making of the Gay Male World, 1890–1940*. New York: Basic Books, 1994.

Cobble, Dorothy Sue. *The Other Women's Movement: Workplace Justice and Social Rights in Modern America*. Princeton, NJ: Princeton University Press, 2004.

Collier-Thomas, Bettye. *Daughters of Thunder: Black Women Preachers and Their Sermons, 1850–1979*. San Francisco: Jossey-Bass, 1998.

Combahee River Collective. "A Black Feminist Statement" (April 1977). In *Capitalist Patriarchy and the Case for Socialist Feminism*, edited by Zillah Eisenstadt. New York: Monthly Review Press, 1978.

Commager, Henry Steele. *A Search for a Usable Past and Other Essays in Historiography*. New York: Knopf, 1967.

Cone, James H. *Black Theology and Black Power*. New York: Seabury Press, 1969.

Cone, James. *A Black Theology of Liberation*. New York: Lippincott, 1970.

Cone, James. *My Soul Looks Back*. New York: Seabury, 1982.

Conford, Danial, ed. *Working People of California*. Berkeley: University of California Press, 1995.

Cooper, Britney. "Black, Queer, Feminist, Erased from History: Meet the Most Important Legal Scholar You've Likely Never Heard Of; Ruth Bader Ginsburg Is This Supreme Court's Liberal Hero, but Her Work Sits on the Shoulders of Dr. Pauli Murray." *Salon*, February 18, 2015.

Cott, Nancy. *The Grounding of Modern Feminism*. New Haven, CT: Yale University Press, 1987.

Cox, Archibald. "Harvard College Amicus Curiae; DeFunis v. Odegaard." In *Reverse Discrimination*, edited by Barry R. Gross. New York: Prometheus, 1977.

Cronk, Sue. "Women Given a Back Seat." *Washington Post*, November 16, 1963.

Crozier, Blanche. "Constitutionality of Discrimination Based on Sex." *Boston University Law Review* 15 (1935): 723–755.

Daly, Mary. *Beyond God the Father: Toward a Philosophy of Women's Liberation*. Boston: Beacon Press, 1973.

Davis, Anita Price. "Keeping the School Doors Open." *Tarheel Junior Historian*, Spring 2010.

Davis, E. Philip. "Comparing Bear Markets—1973 and 2000." *National Institute Economic Review* 183, no. 1 (January 2003): 78–89.

D'Emilio, John. *Sexual Politics, Sexual Communities: The Making of Homosexual Minority in the United States, 1940–1970*, 2nd ed. Chicago: University of Chicago Press, 1998.

D'Emilio, John. *Lost Prophet: The Life and Times of Bayard Rustin*. New York: Free Press, 2003.

Delany, Sarah and A. Elizabeth Delany, with Amy Hill Hearth. *Having Our Say: The Delany Sisters' First 100 Years*. New York: Kodansha America, 1993.

Devor, Aaron and Nicholas Matte. "Building a Better World for Transpeople: Reed Erickson and the Erickson Educational Foundation." *International Journal of Transgenderism* 10, no. 1 (2007): 47–68.

Diamond, Nancy. "'The Host at Last': Abram Sachar and the Establishment of Brandeis University." *Perspectives on the History of Higher Education* 28 (2011): 223–252.

Dierenfield, Bruce J. *Keeper of the Rules: Howard W. Smith of Virginia*. Charlotte: University of Virginia Press, 1987.

Douglas, Ann. *Terrible Honesty: Mongrel Manhattan in the 1920s*. New York: Farrar, Straus and Giroux, 1996.

Drachman, Virginia. *Sisters in Law: Women Lawyers in Modern American History*. Cambridge, MA: Harvard University Press, 2001.

Draper, Theodore. *American Communism and Soviet Russia*. New York: Viking Press, 1957; with new material, New Brunswick: Transaction, 2004.

Drescher, Jack and William Byne. "Gender Dysphoria/Gender Variant (GD/GV) Children and Adolescents: Summarizing What We Know and What We Have Yet to Learn." *Journal of Homosexuality* 59, no. 3 (March 2012): 501–510.

Drury, Doreen Marie. "'Experiment on the Male Side': Race, Class, Gender, and Sexuality in Pauli Murray's Quest for Love and Identity, 1910–1960." Ph.D. diss., Boston College, 2000.

Drury, Doreen Marie. "Love, Ambition, and 'Invisible Footnotes' in the Life and Writing of Pauli Murray." *Souls: A Critical Journal of Black Politics, Culture, and* Society 11, no. 3 (2009): 295–209.

Drury, Doreen Marie. "Boy-Girl, Imp Priest: Pauli Murray and the Limits of Identity." *Journal of Feminist Studies in Religion* 29, no. 1 (2013): 142–147.

Dublin, Thomas "Caroline Farrar Ware." In *Notable American Women: A Biographical Dictionary: Completing the Twentieth Century*, edited by Susan Ware. Cambridge: Belknap Press, 2004.

Eagles, Charles. *Outside Agitator: Jon Daniels and the Civil Rights Movement in Alabama*. Tuscaloosa: University of Alabama Press, 2000.

Edgerton, John. *Speak Now against the Day: The Generation before the Civil Rights Movement in the South*. New York: Alfred A. Knopf, 1994.

Edlesberg, Herman. *Not for Myself Alone: Memoir of a Lawyer Who Fought for Human Rights*. Berkeley: Interstellar Media, 1988.

Emerson, Thomas I. "Fowler Vincent Harper." *Yale Law Diary* 74 (1964–1965): 601.

Epstein, Cynthia Fuchs. *Women in Law*, 2nd ed. Champaign: University of Illinois Press, 1993.

Epstein, Cynthia Fuchs. "Betty Friedan: An Appreciation." *Footnotes: Newsletter of the American Sociological Association*, 34, no. 3 (March 2006), at asanet.org.

Erickson-Schroth, Laura, ed. *Trans Bodies, Trans Selves: A Resource for the Transgender Community*. New York: Oxford University Press, 2014.

Farmer, James. *Lay Bare the Heart: An Autobiography of the Civil Rights Movement*. New York: Arbor House, 1985.

Farrar, Frederic William. *The Early Days of Christianity*. London: Cassell, Petter, Galpin, 1882.

Fausto-Sterling, Anne. *Sexing the Body: Gender Politics and the Construction of Sexuality*. New York: Basic Books, 2000.

Fausto-Sterling, Anne. "The Dynamic Development of Gender Variability." *Journal of Homosexuality* 59, no. 3 (March 2012): 398–421.

Fay, Robert. "Joseph Kwame Kyeretwi Boakye Danquah." In *Encyclopedia of Africa*, vol. 1, edited by Anthony Appiah and Louis Henry Gates. New York: Oxford University Press, 2010.

Feinberg, Leslie. *Stone Butch Blues*. Ithaca, NY: Firebrand Books, 1993.

Feldstein, Ruth. *Motherhood in Black and White: Race and Sex in American Liberalism, 1930–1965*. Ithaca, NY: Cornell University Press, 2000.

Findlay, James F. *Church People in the Struggle: The National Council of Churches and the Black Freedom Movement, 1950–1970*. New York: Oxford University Press, 1997.

Fitzpatrick, Ellen. "Caroline F. Ware and the Cultural Approach to History." *American Quarterly* 43, no. 2 (June 1991): 173–187.

Flexner, Eleanor and Ellen Fitzpatrick. *A Century of Struggle: The Woman's Rights Movement in the United State*, enlarged ed. Cambridge, MA: Harvard University Press, 1996.

Frazier, E. Franklin. "Durham: Capital of the Black Middle Class." In *The New Negro*, edited by Alain Locke. New York: Albert & Charles Boni, 1925.

Freeman, Jo. "How 'Sex' Got into Title VII: Persistent Opportunism as a Maker of Public Policy." *Law & Inequality* 9 (1990–1991): 163–186.

Friedan, Betty. *It Changed My Life: Writings on the Women's Movement*. New York: Random House, 1976.

Fuentes, Sonia Pressman. "Representing Women." *Frontiers: A Journal of Women's Studies* 18, no. 3 (1997): 92–109.

Gacs, Ute. "Dorothy Louise Strouse Keur." In *Women Anthropologists: Selected Biographies*. New York: Greenwood, 1968.

Gaines, Kevin. *American Africans in Ghana: Black Expatriates in the Civil Rights Era*. Chapel Hill: University of North Carolina Press, 2006.

Gallo, Marcia M. *Different Daughters: A History of the Daughters of Bilitis and the Rise of the Lesbian Rights Movement*. Emeryville, CA: Seal Press, 2007.

Garfinkel, Harold. "Color Trouble." *Opportunity*, May 1940, pp. 144–152. Reprint in *The Best Short Stories of 1941*, edited by Edward J. O'Brien. Boston: Houghton Mifflin, 1941.

Garfinkel, Herbert. *When Negroes March: The March on Washington Movement in the Organizational Politics for FEPC.* New York: Macmillan, 1969.

Garrow, David. *Liberty and Sexuality: The Right to Privacy and the Making of Roe V. Wade.* New York: Macmillan, 1994.

Gatewood, Willard B. *Aristocrats of Color: The Black Elite, 1880–1920.* Bloomington: University of Indiana Press, 1990.

Genter, Alix Buchsbaum. "Risking Everything for That Touch: Butch-Femme Lesbian Culture in New York City from World War II to Women's Liberation." Ph.D. diss., Rutgers University, 2014.

Gibson, John Kenneth. "A Pneumatological Theology of Diversity." *Anglican Theological Review* 94, no. 3 (Summer 2012): 429–449.

Gilmore, Glenda Elizabeth. "Admitting Pauli Murray." *Journal of Women's History* 14, no. 2 (Summer 2002): 62–67.

Gilmore, Glenda Elizabeth. *Defying Dixie: The Radical Roots of Civil Rights, 1919–1950.* New York: W. W. Norton, 2008.

Gilmore, Glenda Elizabeth. "From Jim Crow to Jane Crow, or How Anne Scott and Pauli Murray Found Each Other." In *Writing Women's History: A Tribute to Anne Firor Scott*, edited by Elizabeth Anne Payne. Oxford: University Press of Mississippi, 2011.

Ginsburg, Ruth Bader and Anders Bruzelius. *Civil Procedure in Sweden.* The Hague: M. Nijhoff, 1965.

Gladney, Rose. "A Letter from Lillian Smith: 'Old Seeds Bearing a Heavy Crop,'" with an introduction by Rose Gladney. *Southern Changes* 12, no. 5 (1990): 4–5.

Goldstein, Robert Justin. *American Blacklist: The Attorney General's List of Subversive Organizations.* Lawrence: University of Kansas Press, 2008.

Goluboff, Risa L. "The Thirteenth Amendment and the Lost Origins of Civil Rights." *Duke Law Journal* 50 (2001): 1609–1685.

Goodman, James. *Stories of Scottsboro.* New York: Vintage, 1995.

Goodwin, Doris Kearns. *No Ordinary Time: Franklin and Eleanor Roosevelt: The Home Front.* New York: Simon & Schuster, 1994.

Gordon, Natalie. "Gracious Ladies." *Boston Traveler*, Wednesday, November 7, 1945.

Gordon-Reed, Annette. *The Hemingses of Monticello: An American Family.* New York: W. W. Norton, 2008.

Gordon, Robert W. "Professors and Policy Makers: Yale Law School Faculty in the New Deal and After." In *The History of Yale Law School: The Tercentennial Lectures*, edited by Anthony T. Kronman. New Haven, CT: Yale University Press, 2004.

Graham, Hugh Davis. *The Civil Rights Era: Origins and Development of National Policy, 1960–1972.* New York: Oxford University Press, 1990.

Greenberg, Cheryl Lynn. *Or Does It Explode: Black Harlem in the Great Depression.* New York: Oxford University Press, 1991.

Greenhaw, Wayne. *Fighting the Devil in Dixie: How Civil Rights Activists Took on the Ku Klux Klan in Alabama.* Chicago: Chicago Review Press, 2011.

Grondona, Mauro. "Alexander Pekelis: The Law, the State, and the Individual." Working Paper. The Italian Academy at Columbia University, New York, 2008.

Hacker, Helen Mayer. "Women as a Minority Group." *Social Forces* 30 (1951): 60–69.

Halberstam, Judith. *In a Queer Time and Place: Transgender Bodies, Subcultural Lives.* New York: NYU Press, 2005.

Hall, Jacquelyn Dowd. "The Long Civil Rights Movement and the Political Uses of the Past." *Journal of American History* 91, no. 4 (March 2005): 1233–1263.

Harrington, Michael. *The Other America: Poverty in America.* New York: Macmillan, 1962.

Harrison, Cynthia. *On Account of Sex: The Politics of Women's Issues, 1945–1968.* Berkeley: University of California Press, 1988.

Hartmann, Susan. "Women's Employment and the Domestic Ideal in the Early Postwar Years." In *Not June Cleaver: Women and Gender in Postwar America, 1945–1960*, edited by Joanne Meyerowitz (Philadelphia: Temple University Press, 1994).

Hartmann, Susan. *The Other Feminists: Activists in the Liberal Establishment*. New Haven, CT: Yale University Press, 1998.

Hartmann, Susan. "Pauli Murray and the 'Juncture of Women's Liberation and Black Liberation.'" *Journal of Women's History* 14, no. 2 (Summer 2002): 74–77.

Hauke, Kathleen A. *Ted Poston: Pioneer American Journalist*. Athens: University of Georgia Press, 1998.

Hedgeman, Anna Arnold. *The Trumpet Sounds: A Memoir of Negro Leadership*. New York: Holt, Rinehart and Winston, 1964.

Hedgeman, Anna Arnold. *The Gift of Chaos: Decades of American Discontent*. New York: Oxford University Press, 1977.

Height, Dorothy. *Open Wide the Freedom Gates: A Memoir*. New York: Public Affairs, 2003.

Hine, Darlene Clark. *Black Women in White: Racial Conflict and Cooperation in the Nursing Profession, 1890–1950*. Bloomington: Indiana University Press, 1989.

Hirdman, Yvonne. *Alva Myrdal: The Passionate Mind*. Bloomington: University of Indiana Press, 2008.

Hobbs, Allyson. *A Chosen Exile: A History of Racial Passing in American Life*. Cambridge, MA: Harvard University Press, 2014.

Holden, Charles J. *The New Southern University: Academic Freedom and Liberalism at UNC*. Lexington: University Press of Kentucky, 2012.

Hole, Judith and Ellen Levine. *Rebirth of Feminism*. New York: Quadrangle, 1971.

Holzman, Michael. "The Ideological Origins of American Studies at Yale." *American Studies* 40, no. 2 (Summer 1999): 71–99.

Horowitz, Daniel. *Betty Friedan and the Making of The Feminine Mystique: The American Left, the Cold War, and Modern Feminism*. Amherst: University of Massachusetts Press, 1998.

Horowitz, Daniel. "Feminism, Women's History, and American Social Thought at Midcentury." In *American Capitalism: Social Thought and Political Economy in the Twentieth Century*, edited by Nelsen Lichtenstein. Philadelphia: University of Pennsylvania Press, 2006.

Horowitz, Daniel. *On the Cusp: The Yale College Class of 1960 and a World on the Verge of Change*. Amherst: University of Massachusetts Press, 2015.

Hull, Gloria T., Patricia Bell Scott, and Barbara Smith, eds. *All the Women Are White, All the Blacks Are Men, but Some of Us Are Brave: Black Women's Studies*. New York: Feminist Press at City University of New York, 1982.

Hutchinson, Glenn. "They Call It Equal Opportunity." *Carolina Magazine*, February 1939, pp. 9–11.

Hutchinson, Glenn. "Jim Crow Challenged in Southern Universities." *Crisis*, April 1939, pp.103–105.

Isaacs, Harold. "Reporter at Large: Back to Africa." *New Yorker*, May 13, 1961, pp. 105–143.

Jackson, Kenneth T. *The Ku Klux Klan in the City, 1915–1930* (New York: Oxford University Press, 1967).

Jackson, Walter A. *Gunnar Myrdal and America's Conscience: Social Engineering and Racial Liberalism, 1938–1987*. Chapel Hill: University of North Carolina Press, 1990.

Jeffries, Hasan Kwame. *Bloody Lowndes: Civil Rights and Black Power in Alabama's Black Belt*. New York: New York University Press, 2009.

Jewet, Paul K. *Man as Male and Female: A Study of Sexual Relationships from a Theological Point of View*. Grand Rapids, MI: Eerdmans, 1975.

Johnson, David K. *The Lavender Scare: The Cold War Persecution of Gays and Lesbians in the Federal Government*. Chicago: University of Chicago Press, 2004.

Johnson, James Weldon. *Black Manhattan*. New York: Alfred A. Knopf, 1930.

Kahramanidis, Jane. "The She-She-She Camps of the Great Depression." *History Magazine*, February/March 2008, pp. 13–16.

Kanowitz, Leo. *Women and the Law: The Unfinished Revolution.* Albuquerque: University of New Mexico Press, 1969.

Katznelson, Ira. *Fear Itself: The New Deal and the Origins of Our Time.* New York: Liveright, 2013.

Kearney, James R. *Eleanor Roosevelt: The Evolution of a Performer.* Boston: Houghton Mifflin, 1968.

Keene, Michael L. *After the Vote Was Won: The Later Achievements of Fifteen Suffragists.* Jefferson, NC: McFarland, 2010.

Keller, Morton and Phyllis Keller. *Making Harvard Modern: The Rise of America's University.* New York: Oxford University Press, 2001.

Kerber, Linda K. *No Constitutional Right to Be Ladies: Women and the Obligations of Citizenship.* New York: Hill and Wang, 1998.

Kerber, Linda K. "Sally Reed Demands Equal Treatment: November 22, 1971." In *Days of Destiny: Crossroads in American History,* edited by James M. McPherson and Alan Brinkley. New York: DK Publishing, 2001.

Kessler-Harris, Alice. *In Pursuit of Equity: Women, Men, and the Quest for Economic Citizenship.* New York: Oxford University Press, 2001.

Kidd, Alexander Marsden et al., "In Memoriam–Dudley Odell McGovney, Jurisprudence: Berkeley (1877–1947)." Berkeley: University of California Academic Senate, 1947, 1–4.

King, Deborah. "Multiple Jeopardy, Multiple Consciousness: The Context of a Black Feminist Ideology." *Signs: Journal of Women in Culture and Society* 14 (Fall 1988): 42–72.

Kinsey, Alfred et al. *Sexual Behavior in the Human Female.* Philadelphia: W. B. Saunders, 1953.

Klarman, Michael J. *From Jim Crow to Civil Rights: The Supreme Court and the Struggle for Racial Equality.* New York: Oxford University Press, 2004.

Kosek, Joseph Kip. *Acts of Conscience: Christian Nonviolence and Modern American Democracy.* New York: Columbia University Press, 2009.

Kousser, J. Morgan. *The Shaping of Southern Politics: Suffrage Restriction and the Establishment of the One-Party South, 1880–1910.* New Haven, CT: Yale University Press, 1974.

Krishnan, Jayanth K. "Academic SAILERS: The Ford Foundation and the Efforts to Shape Legal Education in Africa, 1957–1977." *American Diary of Legal History* 52 (2012): 261–324.

La Marre, Hazel. "Africa and the World." *Los Angeles Sentinel,* August 4, 1960.

Lash, Joseph. *Eleanor and Franklin: The Story of Their Relationship Based on Eleanor Roosevelt's Private Papers.* New York: W. W. Norton, 1971.

Lester, Joan Steinau. *Fire in My Soul: Eleanor Holmes Norton.* New York: Atria Books, 2003.

Levinson, Cynthia. *We've Got a Job: The 1963 Birmingham Children's March.* Atlanta: Peachtree, 2012.

Logan, Rayford Whittingham. *Howard University: The First Hundred Years, 1867–1967.* New York: New York University Press, 1969.

Lomax, Louis. *The Reluctant African.* New York: Harper & Brothers, 1960.

Lovestone, Jay. "The Great Negro Migration." *Workers Monthly* 5 (February 1926): 182–184.

Lukoff, Kyle. "Taking Up Space." In *Gender Outlaws: The Next Generation,* edited by Kate Bornstein and S. Bear Bergman. Berkeley, CA: Seal Press, 2010.

Lukoff, Kyle. "How Do You Solve a Problem Like Barnard?" prettyqueer.com. June 27, 2011.

Mack, Kenneth W. *Representing the Race: The Creation of the Civil Rights Lawyer.* Cambridge, MA: Harvard University Press, 2012.

MacLean, Nancy. *Behind the Mask of Chivalry: The Making of the Second Ku Klux Klan.* New York: Oxford University Press, 1994.

MacLean, Nancy. *Freedom Is Not Enough: The Opening of the American Workplace.* Cambridge, MA: Harvard University Press, 2006.

Margo, Robert A. "Teacher Salaries in Black and White: Pay Discrimination in the Southern Classroom." In *Race and Schooling in the South,* edited by Robert A. Margo. Chicago: University of Chicago Press, 1990.

Margolick, David. "Judge Ginsburg's Life: A Trial by Adversity." *New York Times,* June 25, 1993.

Markowitz, Ruth Jacknow. "Subway Scholars at Concrete Campuses: Daughters of Jewish Immigrants Prepare for the Teaching Profession, New York City, 1920–1940." *History of Higher Education Annual* 10 (1990): 35.

May, Elaine Tyler. "Radical Roots of American Studies." *American Quarterly* 48, no. 2 (1996): 179–200.

Mayeri, Serena. "'A Common Fate of Discrimination': Race-Gender Analogies in Legal and Historical Perspective." *Yale Law Journal* 110, no. 6 (April 2001): 1045–1088.

Mayeri, Serena. "Constitutional Choices: Legal Feminism and the Historical Dynamics of Change." *California Law Review* 92 (2004): 757–784.

Mayeri, Serena. "The Strange Career of Jane Crow: Sex Segregation and the Transformation of Anti-Discrimination Discourse." *Yale Journal of Law & the Humanities* 18, no. 2 (2006): 187–272.

Mayeri, Serena. *Reasoning from Race: Feminism, Law, and the Civil Rights Revolution.* Cambridge, MA: Harvard University Press, 2011.

McCammon, Holly J. *The U.S. Women's Jury Movements and Strategic Adaptation: A More Just Verdict.* Cambridge: Cambridge University Press, 2012.

McCaughey, Robert A. *Stand Columbia: A History of Columbia University in the City of New York, 1754–2004.* New York: Columbia University Press, 2003.

McGovney, D. O. "Racial Residential Segregation by State Court Enforcement of Restrictive Agreements, Covenants or Conditions in Deeds Is Unconstitutional." *California Law Review* 33, no. 1 (1945): 5–39.

Mead, Margaret and Frances Balgley Kaplan, eds. *American Women: The Report of the President's Commission on the Status of Women and Other Publications of the Commission.* New York: Scribner, 1965.

Ment, David and Mary S. Donovan. *The People of Brooklyn: A History of Two Neighborhoods.* Brooklyn, NY: Brooklyn Educational & Cultural Alliance, 1980.

Meyerowitz, Joanne. *Women Adrift: Independent Wage Earners in Chicago, 1880–1930.* Chicago: University of Chicago, 1988.

Meyerowitz, Joanne. *How Sex Changed: A History of Transsexuality in the United States.* Cambridge, MA: Harvard University Press, 2002.

Micks, Marianne. "The Theological Case for Women's Ordination." In *The Ordination of Women: Pro and Con,* edited by Michael P. Hamilton and Nancy S. Montgomery. New York: Morehouse Barlow, 1975.

Miller, Kasey and Kate Swift. "Pauli Murray." *Ms,* March 1980, pp. 64, 60–64.

Minow, Martha. *Making All the Difference: Inclusion, Exclusion, and American Law.* Ithaca, NY: Cornell University Press, 1990.

Minow, Martha, "Breaking the Law: Lawyers and Clients in Struggles for Social Change." *University of Pittsburgh Law Review* 52 (1991): 723–751.

Mittelstadt, Jennifer. *From Welfare to Workfare: The Unintended Consequences of Liberal Reform, 1945–1965.* Chapel Hill: University of North Carolina Press, 2005.

Moraga, Cherrie and Gloria E. Anzaldua, eds. *This Bridge Called My Back: Writings of Radical Women of Color.* Watertown, MA: Persephone Press, 1981.

Morgan, Charles Jr. *A Time to Speak.* New York: Holt, Rinehart, and Winston, 1964.

Morgan, Charles Jr. *One Man, One Voice.* New York: Holt, Rinehart and Winston, 1979.

Morgan, Ted. *A Covert Life: Jay Lovestone: Communist, Anti-Communist, and Spymaster.* New York: Random House, 1999.

Murray, Pauli. "A Working Student." *Hunter College Echo,* Christmas 1932, pp. 42–44.

Murray, Pauli. "The Song of the Highway" and "Three Thousand Miles on a Dime in Ten Days." In *Negro: An Anthology,* edited by Nancy Cunard. New York: Continuum International, 1934.

Murray, Pauli and Murray Kempton. *"All for Mr. Davis": The Story of Sharecropper Odell Waller.* New York: Workers Defense League, 1940.

Murray, Pauli. "Negroes Are Fed Up." *Common Sense,* August 1943, pp. 274–276.

Murray, Pauli. "Dark Testament." *The South Today,* Winter 1944.

Murray, Pauli. "An American Girl Works Out a Way of Life." *PM,* Sunday, August 20, 1944.

Murray, Pauli. "The Right to Equal Opportunity in Employment." *California Law Review* 33, no. 3 (September 1945): 388–433.

Murray, Pauli. "An American Credo." *Common Ground* 5, no. 2 (December 1945): 22–24.

Murray, Pauli. "Why Negro Girls Stay Single." *Negro Digest* 5, no. 9 (July 1947): 4–8.

Murray, Pauli. *States' Laws on Race and Color.* Cincinnati: Women's Division of Christian Service, Board of Missions and Church Extensions, Methodist Church, 1950.

Murray, Pauli. "Know Your Civil Rights." *Courier Magazine.* September 22 and 29, October 6 and 13, 1951.

Murray, Pauli. *Proud Shoes: The Story of an American Family.* New York: Harper & Brothers, 1956; 2nd ed. with introduction, Harper & Row, 1978; reprint of 2nd ed. with foreword by Patricia Bell-Scott. Boston: Beacon Press, 1999.

Murray, Pauli and Leslie Rubin. *The Constitution and Government of Ghana.* London: Sweet & Maxwell, 1961.

Murray, Pauli. "On Teaching Constitutional Law in Ghana." *Yale Law Report* 8, no. 1 (Fall 1961): 10–14.

Murray, Pauli. "The Negro Woman in the Quest for Equality," *Acorn.* Official Publication of Lamba Kappa Mu Sorority, Inc., June 1964. Reprinted as "Jim Crow and Jane Crow." In *Black Women in White America: A Documentary History,* edited by Gerda Lerner. New York: Vintage Press, 1972.

Murray, Pauli. "Roots of the Racial Crisis: Prologue to Policy," 2 vol., JSD Thesis, Yale Law School, Yale University, New Haven, Connecticut, 1965.

Murray, Pauli and Mary O. Eastwood. "Jane Crow and the Law: Sex Discrimination and Title VII." *George Washington Law Review* 34, no. 2 (December 1965): 232–256.

Murray, Pauli. *Dark Testament and Other Poems.* Norwalk, CT: Silvermine, 1970.

Murray, Pauli. "The Liberation of Black Women." In *Voices of the New Feminism,* edited by Mary Lou Thompson. Boston: Beacon Press, 1970.

Murray, Pauli. "Economic and Educational Inequality Based on Sex: An Overview." *Valparaiso Law Review,* Symposium Issue, 5, no. 2 (1971): 237–280.

Murray, Pauli. "Black Theology and Feminist Theology: A Comparative View." *Anglican Theological Review* 60, no. 1 (1978): 3–24, a condensed version of Murray, "Black Theology and Feminist Theology: A Comparative Study," Senior Thesis, Protestant Episcopal Theological Seminary of Virginia, Alexandria, Virginia, March 20, 1976, PM Papers, Schlesinger Library, Box 23, Folder 475.

Murray, Pauli. *Song in a Weary Throat: An American Pilgrimage.* New York: Harper Collins, 1987; reprint, under the title, *Pauli Murray: The Autobiography of a Black Activist, Feminist, Lawyer, Priest, and Poet.* Knoxville: University of Tennessee Press, 1989.

Murrell, Ethel E. "Full Citizenship for Women: An Equal Rights Amendment." *American Bar Association Journal* 38 (January 1952): 47–49.

Myrdal, Alva. "One Sex a Social Problem." In *Nation and Family.* New York: Harper & Brothers, 1941.

Myrdal, Gunnar. *An American Dilemma: The Negro Problem and American Democracy,* 2 vols. New York: Harper & Bros., 1944.

Nadell, Paula S. *Women Who Would Be Rabbis: A History of Women's Ordination, 1889–1985.* Boston: Beacon Press, 1998.

Naison, Mark. *Communists in Harlem during the Depression.* New York: Grove Press, 1984.

Noble, Jeanne. *The Negro Woman's College Education.* New York: Teachers College, 1956.

Norton, Eleanor Holmes. "For Sadie and Maud." In *Sisterhood Is Powerful: An Anthology of Writings from the Women's Liberation Movement,* edited by Robin Morgan. New York: Random House, 1970.

Norton, Eleanor Holmes. *Women's Role in Contemporary Society: The Report of the New York City Commission on Human Rights, September 21–25, 1970.* New York: Avon, 1972.

Odum, Howard W. *Social and Mental Traits of the Negro.* New York: Columbia University Press, 1910.

Odum, Howard W. "What Is the Answer?" *Carolina Magazine,* February 1938, pp. 5–8.

Ogburn, William. "Howard Odum." *American Sociological Review* 20 (April 1955): 237.

Olson, Lynne. *Freedom's Daughters: The Unsung Heroines of the Civil Rights Movement from 1830 to 1970*. New York: Scribner, 2001.

Oppong, Christine and Katherine Abu. *Seven Roles of Women: Impact of Education, Migration, and Employment on Ghanaian Mothers*. Women, Work, and Development, No.13. Geneva: International Labour Office, 1987.

Orfield, Gary. *Congressional Power: Congress and Social Change*. New York: Houghton Mifflin Harcourt, 1975

Osofsky, Gilbert. *Harlem: The Making of Ghetto, 1890–1930*, 2nd ed. New York: Harper & Row, 1971.

Ostrer, Mitchel. "A Profile of Ruth Bader Ginsburg." *Juris Doctor* (October 1977): 34.

Owusu-Ansah, David. "Society and Its Environment." In *A Country Study: Ghana*, edited by LaVerle Berry. Washington, DC: Federal Research Division, Library of Congress, 1995.

Pastorello, Karen. *A Power among Them: Bessie Abramowitz Hillman and the Making of the Amalgamated Clothing Workers of America*. Urbana-Champaign: University of Illinois Press, 2008.

Paterson, Judith Hillman. *Be Somebody: A Biography of Marguerite Rawalt*. Austin, TX: Eakin Press, 1986.

Patton, Thomas W. " 'What of Her?' Eleanor Roosevelt and Camp Tera." *New York History* 87, no. 2 (Spring 2006): 229–247.

Person, Ethel, MD. "Harry Benjamin: Creative Maverick." *Journal of Gay & Lesbian Mental Health* 12, no. 3 (2008): 259–275.

Philbrick, Herbert A. *I Led 3 Lives: Citizen, Communist, Counterspy*. New York: Grosset & Dunlap, 1952.

Pinn, Anthony B. *Pauli Murray: Selected Sermons and Writings*. Maryknoll, NY: Orbis Books, 2006.

Polsgrove, Carol. *Divided Minds: Intellectuals and the Civil Rights Movement*. New York: W. W. Norton, 2001.

Prichard, Robert. *A History of the Episcopal Church: Complete through the 78th General Convention*, 3rd rev. ed. New York: Morehouse, 2014.

Przybyszewski, Linda. *The Republic According to John Marshall Harlan*. Chapel Hill: University of North Carolina Press, 1999.

Purdum, Todd S. *An Idea Whose Time Has Come: Two Presidents, Two Parties, and the Battle for the Civil Rights Act of 1964*. New York: Henry Holt, 2014.

Purdy, John W. "Title VII: Relationship and Effect on State Action." *Boston College Law Review* 3, no. 3 (April 1966): 525–533.

Rainwater, Lee and William L. Yancey. *The Moynihan Report and the Politics of Controversy*. Cambridge, MA: MIT Press, 1967.

Rampersand, Arnold. *The Life of Langston Hughes*. Vol. 1, *I, Too, Sing America, 1902–1941*. New York: Oxford University Press, 1986.

Ransby, Barbara. *Ella Baker and the Black Freedom Movement: A Radical Democratic Vision*. Chapel Hill: University of North Carolina Press, 2003.

Reinhard, Kathryn L. "Conscience, Interdependence, and Embodied Difference: What Paul's Ecclesial Principles Can Offer the Contemporary Church." *Anglican Theological Review* 94, no. 3 (Summer 2012): 403–428.

Reis, Elizabeth. *Bodies in Doubt: An American History of Intersex*. Baltimore: Johns Hopkins University Press, 2009.

Renshaw, Patrick. "Why Shouldn't a Union Man Be a Union Man? The ILGWU and FOUR." *Journal of American Studies* 29, no. 2 (August 1995): 185–198.

Richards, Renee. *No Way Renee: The Second Half of My Notorious Life*. New York: Simon & Schuster, 2007.

Richards, Yevette. *Maida Springer: Pan-Africanist and International Labor Leader*. Pittsburgh: University of Pittsburgh Press, 2000.

Richards, Yevette. *Conversations with Maida Springer: A Personal History of Labor, Race, and International Relations*. Pittsburgh: University of Pittsburgh Press, 2004.

Ridlon, Florence. *A Black Physician's Struggle for Civil Rights: Edward. Mazique, M.D.* Albuquerque: University of New Mexico, 2005.

Risen, Clay. *The Bill of the Century: The Epic Battle for the Civil Rights Act.* New York: Bloomsbury Press, 2014.

Robbins, Louise Barnum, ed. *History and Minutes of the National Council of Women of the United States: Organized in Washington, D. C., March 31, 1888.* Boston: E. B. Stillings, 1898.

Roberts, Gene and Hank Klibanoff. *The Race Beat: The Press, the Civil Rights Struggle, and the Awakening of a Nation.* New York: Knopf, 2006.

Roberts, J. Deotis. *Liberation and Reconciliation: A Black Theology.* New York: Lippincott, 1970.

Roosevelt, Eleanor. "Some of My Best Friends Are Negro." *Ebony,* February 1953, pp. 16–20, 22, 24–26.

Rosenberg, Rosalind. "Pauli Murray and the Killing of Jane Crow." In *Forgotten Heroes: Inspiring Portraits from Our Leading Historians,* edited by Susan Ware. New York: Free Press, 1998.

Rosenberg, Rosalind. "The Conjunction of Race and Gender." *Journal of Women's History* 14, no. 2 (Summer 2002): 68–73.

Rosenberg, Rosalind. *Changing the Subject: How the Women of Columbia Shaped the Way We Think about Sex and Politics.* New York: Columbia University Press, 2004.

Rossiter, Margaret. *Women Scientists in America: Before Affirmative Action, 1940–1972.* Baltimore: Johns Hopkins University Press, 1995.

Ruether, Rosemary Radford. *Liberation Theology: Human Hope Confronts Christian History and American Power.* New York: Paulist Press, 1972.

Ruether, Rosemary Radford. *Religion and Sexism: Images of Women in the Jewish Christian Traditions.* New York: Simon & Schuster, 1974.

Ruether, Rosemary Radford. *New Woman, New Earth: Sexist Ideologies and Human Liberation.* New York: Seabury Press, 1975.

Rupp, Leila and Verta Taylor. *Survival in the Doldrums: The American Women's Movement, 1945 to the 1960s.* New York: Oxford University Press, 1987.

Rupp, Leila. "Pauli Murray: The Unasked Question." *Journal of Women's History* 14, no. 2 (Summer 2002): 83–87.

Russell, Letty M. *Human Liberation in a Feminist Perspective—A Theology.* Philadelphia: Westminster Press, 1974.

Schaeffer, Leah Cahan and Connie Christine Wheeler. "Harry Benjamin's First Ten Cases (1938–1953): A Clinical Historical Note." *Archives of Sexual Behavior* 24, no. 1 (1995): 73–93.

Schor, Juliet. *The Overworked American: The Unexpected Decline of Leisure.* New York: Basic Books, 2008.

Schrecker, Ellen. *Many Are the Crimes: McCarthyism in America.* Boston: Little, Brown, 1998.

Scott, Anne Firor. *Unheard Voices: The First Historians of Southern Women.* Charlottesville: University Press of Virginia, 1993.

Scott, Anne Firor, ed. *Pauli Murray and Caroline Ware: Forty Years of Letters in Black and White.* Chapel Hill: University of North Carolina Press, 2006.

Scott, Michael. *A Time to Speak.* London: Faber and Faber, 1958.

Sharfstein, Daniel J. *The Invisible Line: A Secret History of Race in America.* New York: Penguin Books, 2012.

Shattuck, Gardiner H. Jr. *Episcopalians and Race: Civil War to Civil Rights.* Lexington: University Press of Kentucky, 2000.

Sherman, Richard B. *The Case of Odell Waller and Virginia Justice, 1940–1942.* Knoxville: University of Tennessee Press, 1992.

Shridharani, Krishnalal. *War without Violence: A Study of Gandhi's Method and Its Accomplishments.* New York: Harcourt Brace, 1939.

Siegel, Reva B. "She the People: The Nineteenth Amendment, Sex Equality, Federalism, and the Family." *Harvard Law Review* 115, no. 4 (February 2002): 948–1046.

Simon, Gabrielle. *From Swastika to Jim Crow: Refugee Scholars at Black Colleges.* Malabar, FL: Krieger, 1993.

Slate, Nico. *Colored Cosmopolitanism: The Shared Struggle for Freedom in the United States and India.* Cambridge, MA: Harvard University Press, 2012.

Smith, Barbara, ed. *Home Girls: A Black Feminist Anthology.* New York: Kitchen Table: Women of Color Press, 1983.

Stein, Marc. *Encyclopedia of Lesbian, Gay, Bisexual, and Transgender History in America.* New York: Scribner's, 2004.

Steinberg, Ronnie. *Wages and Hours: Labor Reform in Mid-Twentieth Century America.* New Brunswick, NJ: Rutgers University Press, 1982.

Stocking, George. "Basic Assumptions of Boasian Anthropology." In *The Shaping of American Anthropology, 1883–1911: A Franz Boas Reader.* New York: Basic Books, 1974.

Storrs, Landon R. Y. *The Second Red Scare and the Unmaking of the New Deal Left.* Princeton, NJ: Princeton University Press, 2013.

Strebeigh, Fred. *Equal: Women Reshape American Law.* New York: W. W. Norton, 2009.

Strom, Sharon Hartman. *Political Woman: Florence Luscomb and the Legacy of Radical Reform.* Philadelphia: Temple University Press, 2001.

Strum, Philippa. *Mendez v. Westminster: School Desegregation and Mexican-American Rights.* Lawrence: University of Kansas Press, 2010.

Stryker, Susan. *Transgender History.* Berkeley, CA: Seal Press, 2008.

Sugrue, Thomas J. *Sweet Land of Liberty: The Forgotten Struggle for Civil Rights in the North.* New York: Random House, 2009.

Sumner, David E. *The Episcopal Church's History: 1945–1985.* Wilton: Morehouse, 1987.

Svonkin, Stuart. *Jews against Prejudice: American Jews and the Fight for Civil Liberties.* New York: Columbia University Press, 1997.

Tannen, Deborah. "The Power of Talk: Who Gets Heard and Why." *Harvard Business Review* (September–October 1995): 139–148.

Taylor, James T. "Higher Education for Negroes." *Carolina Magazine,* February 1938, pp. 2–4.

Thomas, William B. "Howard W. Odum's Social Theories in Transition, 1910–1930," *American Sociologist* 16 (February 1981): 25–34.

Traynor, Roger J. et al. "Barbara Nachtrieb Armstrong–In Memoriam." *California Law Review* 65, no. 5 (September 1977): 920–936.

Tsesis, Alexander. *The Thirteenth Amendment and American Freedom: A Legal History.* New York: New York University Press, 2004.

Tyson, Timothy B. *Radio Free Dixie: Robert F. Williams and the Roots of Black Power.* Chapel Hill: University of North Carolina Press, 1999.

Urofsky, Melvin. *Louis D. Brandeis: A Life.* New York: Pantheon, 2009.

Walker, Samuel. *In Defense of American Liberties: A History of the ACLU.* New York: Oxford University Press, 1990.

Wallace, Ward. *Politics of Conscience: A Biography of Margaret Chase Smith.* Westport, CT: Greenwood Press, 1995.

Ware, Caroline F. *The Early New England Cotton Manufacture: A Study in Industrial Beginnings.* Boston: Houghton Mifflin, 1931.

Ware, Susan. Introduction to "Dialogue: Pauli Murray's Notable Connections." *Journal of Women's History* 14, no. 2 (Summer 2002): 54–57.

Waters, Mary C. *Black Identities: West Indian Immigrant Dreams and American Realities.* Cambridge, MA: Harvard University Press, 2001.

Weigand, Kate. *Red Feminism: American Communism and the Making of Women's Liberation.* Baltimore: Johns Hopkins University Press, 2001.

Weigand, Kate and Daniel Horowitz. "Dorothy Kenyon: Feminist Organizing, 1919–1963." *Journal of Women's History* 14, no. 2 (Summer 2002): 126–131.

Weisenfeld, Judith. *African American Women and Christian Activism: New York's Black YWCA, 1905–1945.* Cambridge, MA: Harvard University Press, 1997.

Whalen, Charles and Barbara Whalen. *The Longest Debate: A Legislative History of the 1964 Civil Rights Act.* Newport Beach, CA: Seven Locks Press, 1984.

Whaley, Ruth Whitehead. "Women Lawyers Must Balk Both Color and Sex Bias." *New York Age*, October 29, 1949.

Wheeler, Leigh Ann. *How Sex Became a Civil Liberty*. New York: Oxford University Press, 2012.

White, Deborah Gray. *Too Heavy a Load: Black Women in Defense of Themselves, 1894–1994*. New York: W. W. Norton, 1999.

Whitehead, Alfred North. *Science and the Modern World: Lowell Lectures*. New York: Pelican Mentor Books, 1925.

Wilkerson, Isabel. *The Warmth of Other Suns: The Epic Story of America's Great Migration*. New York: Random House, 2010.

Williams, Wendy Webster. "Justice Ruth Bader Ginsburg's Rutgers Years, 1963–1972." *Women's Rights Law Reporter* 31 (2009–2010): 229–257.

Williams, Wendy Webster. "Ruth Bader Ginsburg's Equal Protection Clause, 1970–1980." *Columbia Journal of Gender and Law* 25 (2013): 41–49.

Williamson, Joel. *New People: Miscegenation and Mulattoes in the United States*. New York: Free Press, 1980.

Willson, Dora. *The Self on the Self*. Pendle Hill Pamphlet #35. Wallingford, PA: Pendle Hill Publications, 1946.

Winslow, Anne, ed, *Women, Politics and the United Nations*. Westport, CT: Greenwood Press, 1995.

Wirth, Louis. "The Problem of Minority Groups." In *The Science of Man in the World Crisis*, edited by Ralph Linton. New York: Columbia University Press, 1945.

Woloch, Nancy. *A Class by Herself: Protective Laws for Women Workers*. Princeton, NJ: Princeton University Press, 2015.

Yellin, Eric S. *Racism in the Nation's Service: Government Workers and the Color Line in Woodrow Wilson's America*. Chapel Hill: University of North Carolina Press, 2013.

Zelman, Patricia G. *Women, Work, and National Policy: The Kennedy-Johnson Years*. Ann Arbor: University of Michigan Press, 1980.

Ziman, Edmund. *Jealousy in Children: A Guide for Parents*. New York: A. A. Wyn, 1949.

INDEX